The Case for Christian Nationalism

The Case for
CHRISTIAN
NATIONALISM

STEPHEN WOLFE

CANON  PRESS

MOSCOW, IDAHO

Published by Canon Press
P.O. Box 8729, Moscow, Idaho 83843
800.488.2034 | www.canonpress.com

Stephen Wolfe, *The Case for Christian Nationalism*
Copyright ©2022 by Stephen Wolfe.

Cover design by James Engerbretson
Interior design by Valerie Anne Bost

Printed in the United States of America.

22 23 24 25 26 27 28 29 30 31   10 9 8 7 6 5 4 3 2

Dedicated to my children

Contents

Introduction:
The Great Renewal

I. The Storm

The indignant crowd, waving flags and gripping their weapons, gathered around the barriers and gates, pushing and shouting amidst smoke and furor. The guards of the building—a towering symbol of civil authority and sanctity—struggled to decide what to do, as an insurrection or worse seemed imminent. Suddenly, the mob rushed a courtyard, and some protestors began climbing onto buildings. A gate was opened, and the most fanatical of the crowd surged to enter, as if it were a planned assault. The guards shouted at them to leave, but in all the excitement many interpreted the guards' gestures to be welcoming them in. Gunfire broke out and several were killed, including officers. An observer might have heard cries of "liberty" from one side, "equality" from the other, then also "fraternity."

But another sinister sound could be heard: "or death." The fighting continued and calls for ceasefire were rejected. The building was taken, and the victors declared, "Thus we take revenge on traitors." This day changed everything, and we live in its consequences.

One famous writer later called it a "turning-point of modern times." This day—that is, July 14, 1789, the storming of the Bastille in Paris, France—marked the "secularization of our history and the disincarnation of the Christian God," as Albert Camus wrote in *The Rebel*. This day sparked the French Revolution, the instigators of which sought to "overthrow the principle of divine right." Camus continues:

> God played a part in history through the medium of kings. But His representative in history has been killed, for there is no longer a king. Therefore, there is nothing but a semblance of God, relegated to the heaven of principles. The revolutionaries may well refer to the Gospel, but in fact, they dealt a terrible blow to Christianity from which it has not yet recovered.[1]

The regicide (or tyrannicide) of Louis XVI was a sort of deicide—not that God was killed, of course, but that in the king's execution the revolutionaries sought to establish political atheism. The *seculum* was secularized, and the recognition of God and his will for man—both the principles and purpose of life—were set aside, relegated to heaven or to religious institutions. The children of the French Revolution, both Christian and non-Christian, are still with us and continue the revolution.

1. Albert Camus, *The Rebel: An Essay on Man in Revolt*, trans. Anthony Bower (1956; New York: Vintage Books, 1991), 120.

The explicit absence of God in public life is now normal, and this new normal hardly needs official enforcement. With weakness of will and self-abnegation, Western Christians gaze at the ravishment of their Western heritage, either blaming themselves or, even worse, reveling in their humiliation. Christians today live in and fully embrace the conditions of deicide. We have not simply tied our own hands; we've handed over, without much fuss, the divine powers ordained for our good. The people of God have become accustomed to a life without them, even learning to love abuse from God-granted authorities that he ordained for their good.

The chief philosopher of the French Revolution, Jean-Jacques Rousseau, was wrong in his understanding of Christianity, but he did accurately capture the tendency of Christians to take pleasure in their oppression. His comments are so remarkably recognizable that they are worth quoting in full. He writes,

> Christianity as a religion is entirely spiritual, occupied solely with heavenly things; the country of the Christian is not of this world. He does his duty, indeed, but does it with profound indifference to the good or ill success of his cares. Provided he has nothing to reproach himself with, it matters little to him whether things go well or ill here on earth. If the State is prosperous, he hardly dares to share in the public happiness, for fear he may grow proud of his country's glory; if the State is languishing, he blesses the hand of God that is hard upon His people. . . . If the power is abused by him who wields it, it is the scourge wherewith God punishes His children. There would be scruples about driving out the usurper: public tranquility would have to be disturbed, violence would have to be employed, and blood spilt; all this accords ill with

Christian meekness; and after all, in this vale of sorrows, what does it matter whether we are free men or serfs? The essential thing is to get to heaven, and resignation is only an additional means of doing so. . . . Christianity preaches only servitude and dependence. Its spirit is so favourable to tyranny that it always profits by such a régime. True Christians are made to be slaves, and they know it and do not much mind: this short life counts for too little in their eyes.[2]

Sound familiar? You see it daily in Christian think-pieces. Rousseau is indeed right, in a way. Christianity is often used as a coping device for inaction, even when under tyranny and slavery. It is a theological means to psychologically endure one's gnostic unwillingness to struggle against earthly abuse. At its worst, theology is wielded to find pleasure in one's humiliation. Many Christian leaders today are children of Rousseau in this regard, actively undermining Christian political action that opposes political atheism. They advance a sort of Stockholm syndrome theology.

Such Christians—who separate God from public institutions—have even adopted Rousseau's "civil religion," though likely unwittingly. Instead of establishing Christianity, Rousseau called for a "civil profession of faith," consisting of "social sentiments without which a man cannot be a good citizen." Violators are declared to be "anti-social." These "dogmas" must be "few, simple, and exactly worded, without explanation of commentary."[3] After the January 6, 2021 riot, Christians leaders expressed dismay that our "democracy,"

2. Jean-Jacques Rousseau, *Social Contract and Discourses*, trans. G.D.H. Cole (New York: E.P. Dutton, 1950), 136.

3. Ibid., 139.

which affirms universal "tolerance" and "pluralism," was attacked by a mob that rampaged through the "sacred halls" of Congress. Their commitment to these modern norms should not surprise us. For decades, theologians have developed theologies that exclude Christianity from public institutions but require Christians to affirm the language of universal dignity, tolerance, human rights, anti-nationalism, anti-nativism, multiculturalism, social justice, and equality, and they ostracize from their own ranks any Christian who deviates from these social dogmas. They've effectively Christianized the modern West's social creed. The Christian leaders most immersed in the modern West's civil religion are those who loudly denounce the "civil religion" of "Christian nationalism."

This book challenges the social dogmas of our time—the secularist civil religion—by offering a positive account of Christian nationalism. In addition to justifying the institutionalization of Christianity, I offer reasons and exhortations for Christians to act in confidence for that institutionalization. The problem we face today is not simply the absence of arguments but the lack of *will* for our political objectives. I hope to enliven in the hearts of Christians a sense of home and hearth and a love of people and country out of which springs action for their good.

II. Definition

Past Usage

The term *Christian nationalism* is in our time a word of derision used against groups of white evangelicals and Pentecostals in America. Few agree on what it means, though all agree that whatever it means, it is most certainly bad. Indeed, "it is bad" is ultimately all that matters for those who use it. It is a "plastic word," to use Uwe Poerksen's expression: "The precise meaning of plastic words cannot be discerned. . . . But, through context, an author can be precise about which *connotation* of the word is being used."[4] Since anti-nationalism is a social dogma, connecting "Christian" and "nationalism" is effective for wielding social power or the public ire against dissident Christian groups—whether these groups are real or imagined. It is no surprise that "Christian nationalism" is used in the context of the 2021 riot at the Capitol Building in Washington, DC. Associating the term with a widely condemned event gives the accusation of Christian nationalism tremendous weight in rhetoric. The term has socio-rhetorical power. The connotation is far more useful than its possible denotations.

But this negative connotation and lack of denotation is new to the term. Well back into the 19th century, *Christian nationalism* was used almost exclusively in a positive sense. Indeed, there were self-described Christian nationalists. For example, William Henry Fremantle, a well-respected and accomplished Anglican priest, published a lecture in 1885 on Christian nationalism. He affirmed the belief in the "divine character of political rule, and in the unity of the sacred and the secular in the Christian nation."[5] Opposing those who wanted "the system of public worship [to] be held apart from the general life," he argued that

---

4. Emphasis added. He continues, "In contrast, authors have no powers of definition over plastic words; they are general, autonomous, vague and toneless." Uwe Poerksen, *Plastic Words: The Tyranny of Modular Language*, trans. Jutta Mason and David Cayley (University Park, PA: Pennsylvania State University Press, 1995), 8.

5. W.H. Fremantle, *The World as the Subject of Redemption* (1885; New York: Longmans, Green, 1901), 209.

> the whole life of man is essentially religious; and politics, the
> sphere of just relations between men, especially become re-
> ligious when conducted in a Christian spirit. Nothing can be
> more fatal to mankind or to religion itself than to call one set
> of things or persons religious and another secular, when Christ
> has redeemed the whole.[6]

Thus, for Fremantle, we should not compartmentalize the "Christian religion" to an instituted church and clergy. All of life, including
public life, ought to be Christian. The institutional church simply fulfills "one function of the great community [or nation] which itself,
and as a whole, possesses this divine sanction."[7] In other words, the
institutionalized ministry that ministers to a Christian people springs
from the people, which itself originally possesses this ministry.

A few decades later the Chinese theologian, T.C. Chao (1888–
1979), wrote in 1927 about Chinese Christians "wanting a Christian nationalism." He reasons this way:

> Chinese Christians are Christians; but they are also citizens of
> China. According to them, nationalism and Christianity must
> agree in many things; for if there are no common points between
> the two, then how can Chinese citizens become Christians and
> how can Chinese Christians perform the duties of citizens?[8]

6. Ibid., 222–23.

7. Ibid., 220. Being Anglican, Fremantle held to the view that "the principle of Royal
Supremacy . . . that the Christian community as a whole, represented by its Sovereign, is
to be supreme over all its parts." His view is consistent with the "national church" ecclesiology in classical Anglican theology.

8. Quoted in Jun Xing Chun Hsing, *Baptized in the Fire of Revolution: The American
Social Gospel and the YMCA in China, 1919–1937* (Bethlehem, PA: Lehigh University
Press, 1996), 132.

In 1972, Albert Cleage published *Black Christian Nationalism* in which he calls for a redefinition of salvation along black Christian nationalist lines: "Black Christian nationalism . . . calls men to a rejection of individualism, and offers a process of transformation by which the individual may divest himself of individualism and submerge himself in the community life of the group."[9]

The most recent discourse around Christian nationalism is both negative and almost always ascribed to white Americans. Indeed, it is often called "white Christian nationalism." Philip Gorski and Samuel Perry recently published *The Flag and the Cross: White Christian Nationalism and the Threat to American Democracy*. Their definition is a "constellation of beliefs,"[10] which is technically not a definition, and the unstated point of the book is certainly to secure the term's negative connotations by associating it with heretical social views. Since it is largely a work of (activist) sociology, its content is mostly irrelevant to the content of this book. They disregard and dismiss the reasons for Christian nationalist beliefs and instead rely on racial explanations, such as "whiteness," to account for Christian nationalism. My intent here is neither to defend nor reject what they consider Christian nationalism, nor to denounce or distance myself from its alleged connotations. This is a work of Christian political theory, not sociology. If the social scientists wish to critique my book, they must step out of social science, suspend their belief in social dogma, and enter rational inquiry.

9. Albert Cleage, *Black Christian Nationalism: New Directions for the Black Church* (New York: William Morrow, 1972), 73.

10. *The Flag and the Cross: White Christian Nationalism and the Threat to American Democracy* (New York: Oxford University Press, 2022), 14.

Definition for This Book

One of the oddest aspects of Christian nationalism discourse is that, despite its "great threat to democracy," few people in recent years have self-identified as Christian nationalists. Thus, very few have explicitly argued for it in recent years.[11] Recent attempts to define the term begin with some idea of the people they want to capture with it. Hence, they define it by their desired *extension*, that is, based on the things or people they want the term to refer to.

My definition, however, begins not with the term's extension but with the *intension* of the words. That is, I proceed from the meaning or denotation of the words involved, particularly *nation* and *nationalism*, and I then consider nationalism modified by the term *Christian*. Here is my definition:

> *Christian nationalism is a totality of national action, consisting of civil laws and social customs, conducted by a Christian nation as a Christian nation, in order to procure for itself both earthly and heavenly good in Christ.*

The purpose of this book is to show that Christian nationalism (as defined) is just, the ideal arrangement for Christians, and something worth pursuing with determination and resolve.[12]

---

11. While I was in the later stages of editing this book, Andrew Torba and Andrew Isker published *Christian Nationalism: A Biblical Guide for Taking Dominion and Discipling Nations* (Clarks Summit, PA: Gab AI, 2022).

12. Not all examples of Christian nationalism that meet the definition are desirable, just, or perfect. The central conclusion of this work justifies Christian nationalism in principle. Moreover, my account in the following chapters advances a more Presbyterian form of Christian nationalism, but the definition above has its Anglican and Lutheran forms (and others). I would disagree with features of those forms but still affirm that they are equally Christian nationalist with regard to the definition.

The reader likely had a different definition in mind, but this may not indicate substantive disagreement. Maybe (like Gorski and Perry) you list a set of beliefs—perhaps something about "national obligations to God." I agree that nations have obligations to God. My intent is to define Christian nationalism according to the denotation of the two words in relation to each other. Whether you like my definition or not is largely irrelevant to the arguments that follow, since I likely affirm at some point what you include in your definition.

Since parts of my definition may be unclear or unexpected, I devote some space in this introduction to explicating the definition. I break this down carefully and in detail because the discussion on Christian nationalism today lacks the sort of precision and care that early generations of Reformed writers brought to Christian political thought. What I say below and in the following chapters might be difficult and complex, but my intent is to continue in (or perhaps help resurrect) the Reformed political tradition's commitment to complete, analytical, and demonstrative argumentation.

III. Explicating the Definition

Christian nationalism is nationalism modified by Christianity. My definition of Christian nationalism is a Christianized form of nationalism or, put differently, a species of nationalism. Thus, I treat nationalism as a genus, meaning that all that is essential to generic nationalism is true of Christian nationalism. Whatever I ascribe to nationalism in this work is *ipso facto* ascribed to Christian nationalism. My definition of *nationalism* is similar to that of Christian nationalism, though with less content:

> *Nationalism refers to a totality of national action, consisting of civil*
> *laws and social customs, conducted by a nation as a nation, in order*
> *to procure for itself both earthly and heavenly good.*

Absent from this definition is Christianity—the Christian nation
and the sole, post-fall means of obtaining heavenly good, namely, in
Christ. As we'll see in the following chapters, the addition of these
words *in Christ* matters a great deal. Nevertheless, the Gospel does
not supersede, abrogate, eliminate, or fundamentally alter generic
nationalism; it assumes and completes it.

Modern Christian political theorists often call nationalism an
ideology, usually assuming that all ideologies are bad and idolatrous. I see no use in disputing whether it is an ideology. "Ideology"
is usually either loosely defined or defined according to its abuse
rather than according to what it is. Whether my conclusions clas-
sify Christian nationalism under "ideology" has no relevance as to
whether those arguments are sound. The reader will also have to
keep in mind that I am not necessarily affirming any supposed connotations of nationalism, whatever those might be, and thus they
cannot be ascribed to my definition or positions *prima facie*. In other words, the reader should not assume that I'm trying to justify or
explain away any historical example of nationalism, or any of the
various moral qualities often attributed to nationalism.

"a totality of national action"

A totality of action is not as difficult to comprehend as it might
first appear. I'll begin with an example. Though a soccer team
wins its match by individual players scoring goals, we say that the
team won the match, not the individuals who scored the goals.

This is because, although the individual action of scoring is the key to winning, these actions were supported and made possible by the actions of the other team members, including the defensive players. So we say that the *team* won and that winning is a "team effort" because each player has his role with regard to winning. Thus, *a totality of action* can be defined as a set of actions that are interrelated such that their effect (e.g., winning the match) is a product of the whole (e.g., both defensive and offensive actions), not any particular part of the whole.

A totality of *national* action, being the formal cause of Christian nationalism, refers to all the actions that a nation expects of its members for their overall, national good. These range from great acts of sacrifice to mundane, everyday things, like caring for one's children. It is a "totality" because although each action has a good unique to it, together each strengthens, supports, or makes possible other actions to form an organic whole. A mother nursing her child has the child's immediate good in mind, but that action—as part of a totality of action in the nation—is also for the national good, for well-nursed children grow up to be healthy, productive, and sacrificial participants in the nation. In this way, the nursing of children is a national action, and the good of nursing is not only the child's good directly but also the nation's good. In other words, the good of the mother in nursing her child transcends the immediate good of child nourishment. National action, therefore, is not merely extraordinary or heroic action but also includes the ordinary and mundane. One can hardly expect anything extraordinary in a nation where the ordinary is absent.

These actions are interrelated such that each depends on the others to do them well. One cannot expect mothers to care well for

their children when they exist in poor conditions, where fatherly affection, productive activity, good civil governance, social discipline,
manners, and religion are absent. Thus, national actions compose a
totality of action—each relying on the others for its possibility, support, and perfection; and together those actions procure for the nation its national good. Or, to put things simply, you typically cannot
do anything well unless conditions are set for you to do it well, and
those conditions are established by other actions conducted both
by you and others. Subsequently, by this mutual support, a nation
achieves its national good.

"... consisting of civil laws and social customs ..."

Civil laws and social customs are the material cause, or content,
of Christian nationalism. These are rules of action that determine
what you ought to do and ought not to do. Civil law commands
action explicitly, while social customs implicitly predispose people
to action. These rules are often very general, allowing people the
freedom to choose among different options (e.g., choosing one's
vocation). Now, since the end of Christian nationalism is the nation's good (which I discuss in more detail below), rules of action
are proper only if they conduce to the nation's good. Thus, civil law
and social customs, when proper, order the Christian nation to
their earthly and heavenly good. Being a totality of action, law and
custom form an interrelated and oftentimes redundant web of obligation that orders everything ultimately to the national good. For
example, tossing trash from cars is illegal in the United States, but
it is clear that social opprobrium must assist those laws to keep the
streets clean. Furthermore, there are many desired rules of action
covered by custom that civil law cannot effectively command.

"... conducted by a Christian nation as a Christian nation ..."
In Christian nationalism, the nation is conscious of itself as a Christian nation and acts for itself as a Christian nation. Christian national consciousness is the ground and animating principle of its action. This is the efficient cause of nationalism, for it speaks of who is acting and also of the impetus of action. It is analogous to a man with faith in Christ who, understanding himself to be a Christian man, acts as a Christian man for the good of body and soul. Or it is like a family of Christians who, seeing themselves as a Christian family, act as such for their earthly and heavenly good (e.g., family worship). Christian nationalism is a Christian people acting for their own good in light of their Christian nationhood.

Viewed as a whole, the Christian nation acts for itself by a three-step process: (1) It achieves a national will for itself; (2) that will is mediated through authorities that the people institute; and (3) the people act according to the dictates of that mediation. That is, the national will for its good establishes civil authority and constructs a social world—both of which prescribe concrete duties and norms—which the people then act on. Thus, the entity that causes Christian nationalism is chiefly the people, not Christian magistrates, though magistrates are necessary to direct the will of the people into concrete action.

"... to procure for itself both earthly and heavenly good in Christ."
The purpose or final cause of Christian nationalism is to establish the best possible conditions for the procurement of what I call the "complete good"—the goods of this life and of the life to come.

In my generic definition of nationalism, I delineated earthly good and heavenly good. I did this because, as I argue in the next chapter, ordering people to heavenly life is a natural end for even the generic nation; that is, it is neither a new command nor something introduced by the Gospel. Had Adam not fallen, the nations of his progeny would have ordered themselves to heavenly life. Thus, heavenly good is an end of the nation. Since the Gospel is now the sole means to heavenly life, nations ought to order themselves to the Gospel in the interest of their heavenly good. "In Christ" modifies "earthly good" as well. The Gospel adds no new principles of earthy life, but earthly life is restored because of sanctification, which is the infusion of Christ's holiness in us. Furthermore, all earthly goods ought to be ordered to Christ. Thus, the totality of Christian national action orders the nation to procure the complete good in Christ. The specific difference between generic nationalism and Christian nationalism is that, for the latter, Christ is essential to obtaining the complete good. Pagan and secularist nations are true nations but they are incomplete nations. Only the Christian nation is a complete nation.

I am not saying that a nation *as a nation* can receive eternal life, strictly speaking. Rather, a nation as a nation can act for itself (by social and civil power) so that, *externally*, heavenly goods are made apparent and available to all and so that each person is prepared and encouraged to take them for eternal life. Hence, a Christian nation would, for example, support the spiritual administration of Word and Sacrament. A nation has no power in itself to bring anyone internally to true faith—to realize heavenly good in individuals. But nations have the power to ensure that outwardly the things of salvation—the preaching of the Word and the administration of the Sacraments—are available to all and that people are encouraged, even culturally expected, to partake and be saved unto eternal life.

As a concise summary, we can think of Christian nationalism as a Christian nation acting as such and for itself in the interest of the nation's complete good.

IV. Method

This is a work of Christian political theory. It is not, overall, a work of political theology. I say this both to manage expectations and to explain my method. There are two main reasons why I consider this a work of political theory.

Assuming the Reformed Tradition

The first is that I assume the Reformed theological tradition, and so I make little effort to exegete biblical text. Some readers will complain that I rarely appeal to Scripture to argue for my positions. I understand the frustration, but allow me to explain: I am neither a theologian nor a biblical scholar. I have no training in moving from scriptural interpretation to theological articulation. Francis Turretin, the great 17th-century Reformed theologian, spoke of "supernatural theology" as "the system of saving doctrine concerning God and divine things *drawn from the Scriptures*."[13] In this sense, "theology" can be understood *systematically*, that is, as a systematic articulation of revealed truth taken *from* Scripture (e.g., the doctrine of the Trinity). Instead of drawing from Scripture to prove the Reformed system of doctrine, I've chosen to assume this system and work from it. I am unable to exegete better than the Reformed exegetical tradition anyway, and I frequently cite theologians whose work, to my mind,

13. Francis Turretin, *Institutes of Elenctic Theology* (*IET*), ed. James T. Dennison and trans. George M. Griger (Phillipsburg, NJ: P&R Publishing, 1994), 1:1.2.7.

demonstrates the soundness of the Reformed system. All arguments have to begin somewhere. To my knowledge, my theological premises throughout this work are consistent with, if not mostly taken directly from, the common affirmations and denials of the Reformed tradition. To be sure, some of my *conclusions* are expressed differently than this tradition. After all, *Christian nationalism* was not used in the 16th through the 18th centuries. But none of my conclusions are, in substance, outside or inconsistent with the broad Reformed tradition. And, of course, I would certainly welcome any work of political theology in favor of Christian nationalism that can stand side-by-side with this work of Christian political theory.[14]

If the reader does not have Reformed theological commitments, then I cannot guarantee that you share many of my theological assumptions. This is a work of Reformed Christian political theory, to be more precise. My desire for systematic argumentation led me to pull from a robust tradition within the Christian tradition. But since I pull mainly from the 16th and 17th centuries, in which Reformed theology was very Thomistic and catholic,[15] many of my theological

14. The reader is free to cite Scripture against my arguments. This is, of course, a valid method of refutation. In citing Scripture against me, you're seeking to support some proposition that opposes one of my propositions. Again, this is fine. But keep in mind that your theological propositions must fit into a coherent system of doctrine. In affirming any proposition, one affirms also what is logically antecedent and consequent to it: propositions come from and lead logically to other statements. Too often, Christians use Scripture to support theological statements and ethical claims without considering their logical implications in a systematical way (e.g., whether it leads to absurdity or heresy, or contradicts other beliefs). I am not claiming that anyone who disagrees with me is theologically, ethically, or politically incoherent, but I do think that much disagreement could be avoided and the discourse improved if we thought more logically and systematically and with a view to coherence. Even in theology, one cannot affirm a contradiction.

15. By "Thomistic," I mean that Reformed theologians in these centuries were heavily influenced by Thomas Aquinas. This is less evident in Calvin's work, though clear in the

premises are widely shared among Christians.[16] Furthermore, when I cite non-Protestants (e.g., Francisco Suárez) or pre-Reformation theologians (e.g., Thomas Aquinas), I am not opposing or correcting Reformed Protestantism but recognizing and pulling directly from the catholic sources in the Reformed tradition.[17]

Proceeding from Natural Principles

The primary reason that this work is political theory is that I proceed from a foundation of natural principles. While Christian theology assumes natural theology as an ancillary component, Christian political theory treats natural principles as the foundation, origin, and source of political life, even *Christian* political life. The nation, for example, is not merely a necessary component of Christian nationalism; it fuels that nationalism; it enlivens a Christian people for Christian nationalism. Whereas Christian theology considers the Christian mainly in relation to supernatural grace and eternal life, Christian political theory treats man as an earthly being (though bound to a heavenly state) whose political life is fundamentally natural.

I call this a work of *Christian* political theory because I rely on both natural and supernatural propositions—i.e., from what is true from nature and from revelation—and I integrate them in my arguments. My method seeks not to prove the same proposition

---

work of Peter Martyr Vermigli in the 16th century and many in the 17th century (e.g., Franciscus Junius and Francis Turretin). I use "catholic" as the Reformers used it—referring to the fundamental articles of faith taught by and since the Church Fathers. See, for example, *A Reformed Catholic* (1597) by William Perkins.

16. One important resource is Thomas Achord and Darrell Dow's *Who is My Neighbor? An Anthology in Natural Religions* (n.p.: Thomas Achord, 2021).

17. Francisco Suárez, for example, despite being anti-Protestant, was often cited by Protestant thinkers (themselves critical of Roman Catholicism), particularly for his work on law and politics.

from reason and revelation separately but to integrate natural and supernatural truth into a systematic political theory. So throughout this work I use *mixed syllogisms*, referring to syllogisms in which one premise is known by reason and the other known only by faith. For example, assuming that *civil leaders ought to order the people to the true God* (a natural principle), we can conclude that *civil leaders ought to order the people to the Triune God*. Why? Because *the Triune God is the true God* (a supernatural truth). I integrate natural principles and supernatural truths such that nature is applied and fulfilled by means of supernatural truth.[18] In this way, revealed theology serves to complete politics, but it is not the foundation of politics.

Complexity

Academically, my world is that of the early modern period (the 16th through the 18th centuries). What I love about this period is that authors made serious attempts to persuade using rational demonstration, and they were deeply conscious of the systemic nature of truth and the necessity of internal coherence. Unfortunately, the expectation for demonstration and coherence is largely absent in the Christian world today, especially in books and articles on politics. Instead, Christians resort to rhetorical devices, tweetable shibboleths, and credibility development to assert disparate principles and applications.[19] I've decid-

18. This method is in stark contrast with much political theology today, since political theologians typically treat Christian political life as if it were, fundamentally speaking, a matter of grace and of supernatural truth. This misunderstands the role of grace and supernatural truth in politics, which I explain thoroughly in the next chapter.

19. By "credibility development," I mean that they do not rationally demonstrate their conclusions, but develop their credibility to assert things. They might give their professional credentials (or another's), provide their socio-political identity, personally attack those who would disagree, praise the sort of people who would hold such a position, appeal to common prejudice or sentiment, or create a nice, genuine, and "good faith" persona.

ed to return, as best I can, to an older style, though I am an infant in comparison to their learning and abilities. As a result, my arguments are often not simple. I try to prove my most important conclusions such that if you accept the premises, you would have to accept the conclusion by the force of logic. Whether I succeed in that is up to the reader's determination. In any event, that was my intent. To be sure, at obvious times, I grant myself some liberty to speak freely.

My account of Christian nationalism is a Presbyterian Christian nationalism. It contains all the essential features of Christian nationalism, so it shares much with other forms of it. Thus, even if I cannot convince my readers of Presbyterianism, much of my argument remains applicable to their own tradition. And one might come to agree with the justness of Christian nationalism but not follow me in my Presbyterianism. Given the state of our world today, I will consider that a success.

V. Summary of Argument

General Summary

In this section, I summarize the arguments of the book. The reader should consult the chapters to see my complete arguments, but I want to explain their general structures first. Chapters 1 and 2 show the theological possibility of Christian nationalism through a discussion of theological anthropology (i.e., the study of man in theology) and how it shapes social and political life. The several chapters that follow (chapters 3–7) explicate the definition of Christian nationalism, working through the concepts and its elements. These chapters complete my defense of Christian nationalism. I include chapters on two important related matters (revolution and liberty of conscience) and one chapter that provides sources for a resurgent American Christian nationalism. The conclusion is a series of thoughts on our current situation and how Christian nationalists can begin thinking about and acting for national renewal.

What follows is a slightly expanded summary of this structure.

What is Man?

In chapters 1 and 2, I discuss man in his three states: the state of integrity, the state of sin, and the state of redemption (or restoration). These follow the familiar Reformed schema of creation, fall, and redemption. (The state of glory is crucial to my argument, but it does not get its own section.) I describe man in each state and how the events of creation, fall, and redemption affect and change man. The purpose is to establish the continuity and discontinuity between the three states. I first argue that man has always had two ends— earthly and heavenly. Adam's original task, his dominion mandate, was to bring the earth to maturity, which served as the condition for eternal life. His work did not itself bring heaven to earth but rather was the divinely prescribed condition for God to bestow eternal life on him and his progeny. Adam was equipped with *all* the skills and natural drive to accomplish this task. Indeed, fulfilling the dominion mandate was natural to him, as his *telos* or natural end. The rule to this end was the natural law, and obedience to the natural law is manifested in dominion.

If Adam had not fallen, he and his progeny would have multiplied on the earth. They would have formed communities, for no man can live well when alone and when not in combination with others. These communities would have been distinct, or separate nations, because even unfallen man would have had natural limitations and been bounded by geography, arability, and other factors.

Furthermore, each community would have been culturally distinct, since they would have been at least somewhat separated from others and would have developed their own way of life and culture, though without any sin. Though the principles of culture are natural and universal, the particular expressions of culture are not in themselves natural. For this reason, although all cultures distinguish men and women with differences in clothing, the manner of distinction varies from culture to culture. Thus, cultural diversity does not necessarily reflect differences in natural principle. It follows that Adam's progeny would have formed many nations on earth, and thus the formation of nations is part of God's design and intention for man.

The fall of man placed man in a state of sin. The state of sin, or total depravity, is misunderstood, even in Reformed circles. The fall's principal effect concerned man's relationship to God and the promised heavenly life, for it removed man's highest gifts (those that drew him to heavenly life). Man retains his earthly gifts, those that lead him to the fundamental things of earthly life, such as family formation and civil society. Thus, man still has his original instincts and still knows the principles of right action, which incline him to what is good. But the loss of his heavenly orientation affects his whole being such that he sins not only in relation to God but also toward his fellow man. The question is, what is the extent of discontinuity from prelapsarian (or pre-fall) Adam? I argue that postlapsarian social organization—viz., as human society has manifested in post-fall history—reflects true and good *principles*, but in every time and place there is some degree of abuse of those principles. Thus, the formation of nations is not a product of the fall; it is natural to man as man. But the evil in nations and caused by nations is the *abuse* of what is intended for man's good. Neither is civil government introduced by the fall, for civil government would have been necessary for unfallen people to coordinate action for the common good. The fall required civil government to be *augmented* to restrain sin, though it still retained its same original principles and end.

The redemption of man brings him into a state of grace. This takes us to chapter 2. It is crucial to affirm that grace does not destroy, abrogate, supersede, or undermine nature but rather affirms and completes it. The instinct to live within one's "tribe" or one's own people is neither a product of the fall nor extinguished by grace; rather, it is natural and good. In the state of redemption, grace secures for man both a title to eternal life—the same life promised originally to Adam—and the restoration of his gifts. That is, salvation grants eternal life in Christ and a sanctified life in Christ. Having the same gifts as Adam, man is able to do (at least in form) what Adam could have accomplished in his work, which is to form nations under the true God. The people of God on earth are a restored humanity. Restored man ought to be naturally drawn to dominion, for dominion is the natural end or purpose of these gifts.

Pursuing Christian dominion is not seeking to bring heaven to earth, nor is it seeking to earn heaven by works. One does not place himself back under the covenant of works by seeking to establish Christian civil communities on earth. As I said, even prelapsarian Adam could not bring heaven to earth through his labor; he could only order earthly life to the promised heavenly life. That is precisely what restored humanity does in his labor—order earthly life to heavenly life. The difference is that since Christ is the sole means to heavenly life, earthly life is ordered to Christ, mainly by supporting his visible church.

Nation and Nationalism

Having established the theological possibility and some background theology for the project overall, I move on to directly discuss Christian nationalism. Chapter 3 is on the nation and nationalism. Everything I affirm of the nation and nationalism I can also affirm of Christian nationalism, as I stated earlier. My approach to the nation is different from that of others. Instead of relying on a bird's-eye view of the concept, I mainly appeal to the reader's own experience with people and place to reveal to them their own belonging to a people and place. That is, I appeal to what I hope is common experience. I can do this because the previous chapters demonstrated that neither the fall nor grace eliminated the natural instinct for an attachment to people and place. Grace does not destroy natural affection, and our basic experience with regard to people and place reflects the way God created us. I show that we operate in our everyday lives according to a background sense of familiarity, allowing us to relate to others with common understanding and mutual expectations. These are based in *particulars*, as opposed to universal things, being unique to *us* as a people. With these, we can complete civic projects and other collective ends. Shared norms, customs, and meanings of places make possible the highest acts of earthly life. Language, for example, is a particularity (for there is no universal language), and sharing language is necessary for most meaningful civic activities. Since those who share a culture are similar people, and since cultural similarity is necessary for the common good, I argue that the natural inclination to dwell among similar people is good and necessary. Grace does not destroy or "critique" it. Choosing similar people over dissimilar people is not a result of fallenness, but is natural to man as man. Why? Because we are drawn by deep instinct to our good. Indeed, one *ought* to prefer and to love more those who are more similar to him, and much good would result in the world if we all preferred our own and minded our own business. Furthermore, since shared culture is necessary for living well, nations have a right of exclusion in the interest of cultural preservation.

The Christian tradition recognized three types of love: benevolence, beneficence, and complacence. The first can be universal and equal, since one wishes the good of all. Beneficence, however, can only be directed practically at some, because one can help only so many people. The Christian tradition has recognized that one cannot love all people equally, and indeed one should not. Each of us ought to prioritize those who are closest and most bound to us. But beneficence, to my mind, does not fully explain why we actively labor for the good of those closest to us—for the good of our children, for example. It is too rationalist of an explanation; something pre-rational is at work. The Christian tradition has only hinted at this underlying motivation—which I call "complacent love." *Complacent* was once used positively as a sort of delightful love for something. In my usage, it refers to the pre-rational preference we have for our own children, family, community, and nation. We have complacent love for our own children because they are most similar to us and most intimately come from us. We also have complacent love for our parents, extended family, and, as Johann Herder would say, the "family writ large"—the nation. In this way, the background impulse to love some over others is a sort of complacent *self*-love, for the ground for the preference is similarity. Calling it "complacent self-love" won't preach, to be sure, but it is an accurate label for the position I'm advancing. Anyone concerned about "self-love" will find an extensive Christian tradition that affirms it.

As for nationalism, the reader might expect that I follow the trend in treating it as a historical phenomenon. But I offer a more conceptual defense. Nationalism is the nation acting as a nation for its good. This is the *ism* of nationalism, in my account. I do not appeal to historical examples of nationalism, nor do I waste time repudiating "fascist nationalism." Indeed, in chapter 3, I do not spend much time on nationalism at all, except to argue that nations can exclude others in the interest of cultural particularity. Since Christian nationalism is a species of nationalism, much of my discussion of the former applies to nationalism considered generically and vice versa.

Christian Nation and Christian Nationalism

In chapter 4, I discuss the Christian nation and I address one major feature of Christian nationalism—the civil support for true religion. The Christian nation is a nation of Christians in which their everyday life is infused or adorned with Christian practices and Christian things. Christianity has not replaced their particularity, nor does Christianity undermine it. Though Christianity is a universal religion—a religion for *all* nations—it does not eliminate nations, nor does it create one global alternative nation, nor does it provide a universal "gospel culture." Rather, Christianity assumes nations (as previously described) and completes them. Thus, we can speak of Christian nations. The Christian nation is a *perfected* nation in form, though no Christian nation is materially the same as another. Each one's shared and unique culture makes possible the nation's collective pursuit of the highest good.[20]

---

20. We can speak of two men as being the same *in form* (since both are men), but they are still different in a variety of ways (e.g., personality and skills), even if they are equally virtuous.

The second half of this chapter begins my discussion on the things that Christian nations do for their good, which continues for two more chapters. These are the actions of Christian nationalism. A major component of Christian nationalist action is the civil government ordering the people to true religion. This is a natural duty of civil government, for civil government was *always* intended to order man to his complete good, which includes heavenly life. I offer several arguments, each of which concludes that *civil government ought to direct its people to true religion*. This is a natural principle of civil government. Throughout the book I rely on this important point of logic: A supernatural conclusion can follow from a natural principle when it interacts with supernatural truths. Thus, given this supernatural truth that *Christianity is the true religion*, it follows from the above principle that *civil government ought to direct people to the Christian religion*. So civil government fulfills a natural principle when it directs its people to revealed religion, and thus the secular and sacred are not confounded but properly ordered—the lower serving the higher.

As we shall see, an important question is whether a Christian nation can refuse to allow the immigration of fellow Christians from foreign lands. I argue that they can. The argument is that a spiritual relation—something that Christians share regardless of nationality—is different in kind from a civil relation and therefore cannot serve as the ground for flourishing civil society. Sharing the highest good—a title to eternal life—does not mean that all Christians share what can provide the complete good, and indeed the journey to eternal life in this world requires cultural particulars for that journey. A common language, for example, is necessary for the highest form of encouragement in one's spiritual life. Imagine Christian and Faithful in *Pilgrim's Progress* being unable to communicate; how far would they get? So a unity in at least some particular things is a necessary condition for pursuing the highest good together. Thus, relying on conclusions from chapter 3, I argue that a Christian nation may exclude foreign Christians from immigrating when immigration would harm their ability to pursue their good. Nations ought to be hospitable, but they are not obligated to be hospitable to their detriment, just as a household ought to practice hospitality but not to such an extent that it harms it or leads to its destruction.

Cultural Christianity

In chapter 5, I defend cultural Christianity. Instead of defining it by its abuse, I define it as a supplemental mode of religion, which means that it supplements the work of spiritual ministry. It implicitly orders people to the Christian faith, though it cannot bring anyone to faith. Though not a spiritual force, it does remove hindrances to faith by making Christianity plausible, and it socializes people into religious practices in which one hears the Gospel. I use the term *social fact* in this chapter as a way of describing how cultural Christianity operates in a community. It refers to social norms that are not centrally enforced but still act as a sort of authority over the community and upon individuals in that community. It delineates what is normal and abnormal, and people proceed into these norms and expect others to do the same. All societies have these, and we too are thoroughly socialized into the norms of our society. My argument is that cultural Christianity, as the normalization of Christianity in civil society, sets social conditions that aid in the reception of the Gospel and people coming to faith. It is akin to the Christian norms of the Christian family, which requires certain practices and forbids others in the interest of spiritual formation.

Many are concerned with the hypocrisy that arises from cultural Christianity. I offer several reasons against this concern, though I fully admit that cultural Christianity *by itself* cannot produce anything but hypocrites. But it is not meant to stand alone. It ought to be one part of an organic whole that orders man to true religion (viz., family, civil government, and the instituted church). Furthermore, cultural Christianity is not limited to explicitly Christian things, for what perfects something is not a mere addition but affects the whole of it. It shapes the totality of action for a nation's good. I argue that since cultural Christianity permits people in society to relate to each other as Christians, they are able to achieve a commodious (or just) earthly life together that exceeds what would otherwise be possible.

In this chapter, I discuss the Christian nation's Christian self-conception. A people can say *we* are Christian and call themselves a Christian nation. Out of this self-conception comes the national will for both earthly and heavenly life in Christ. This national will for itself is channeled through implicit and explicit authorities and results in a particular way of life. One role of this Christian way of life is socializing or discipling its people, especially younger ones, in the faith.

Civil Law

Though civil law can seem like a topic for lawyers, its philosophical and theological foundations are important for a range of questions and issues in Christian nationalism, from civil justice and civil power to justifying civil resistance and revolution. Civil law is an explicit ordering of communities, and every civil law reflects a particular judgment of civil rulers for public action. This is the emphasis of chapter 6.

Only God can bind the conscience; fellow man cannot, except by divine sanction, command you to do this or that particular thing. Man, as a moral being, is bound only by the natural law (or God's moral law) as the rule for his action. But the natural law in itself does not prescribe specific action—it must be applied. Applications are necessary in every sphere of life: the civil sphere, the family, and the individual. For the civil sphere, God ordained civil power as a *mediator* of divine civil rule, authorizing civil rulers to determine applications of natural law for the public good. This was necessary because individuals cannot always determine appropriate public action for the common good. Civil leaders, having the whole in view, determine suitable public action. Being mediators of God's civil rule, civil rulers issue civil commands—expressed and promulgated as civil law—that are ordinances of God and bind the conscience, though only when they are just (viz., follow rationally from natural law). Thus, the true power of civil rulers is limited by justice, and any commanded injustice is not an ordinance of God and therefore does not bind the conscience. This becomes more relevant when I get to the chapter on revolution.

Civil law is the chief means by which civil rulers order their people to their good. The emphasis in chapter 6 is on civil law as a determination of the civil lawgivers and on how their determinations must reflect what is righteous and what conduces to good. A civil law is righteous if it flows rationally from the natural law, but this does not necessarily make it a good law. Each law must be *suitable*, given the circumstances and characteristics of the community. Thus, deliberation about civil law requires two things: a consideration of what is just in itself and a consideration of whether the law in question would conduce concretely to the good of a community. So civil law is not mere philosophical reflection, nor should it be the rubberstamped Mosaic civil code.

Civil law can direct men only outwardly; it cannot command the soul. The conscience is free from coercion. Still, civil law can outwardly order people to that which is good for the soul. Thus, Sabbath laws are just, because they remove distractions for holy worship. Laws can also penalize open blasphemy and irreverence in the interest of public peace and Christian peoplehood. The justification for such laws is not simply that God forbids these things in the First Table of the Ten Commandments, but that they cause public harm, both to the body and the soul.

The Christian Prince

Chapter 7 investigates the chief agent of Christian nationalism, the Christian magistrate. I chose to use "Christian prince" because *prince* connotes a great man, not a bureaucrat or policy wonk. Our time calls for a man who can wield formal civil power to great effect and shape the public imagination by means of charisma, gravitas, and personality.

The civil power of the prince comes immediately from God as the root of civil power, but the people, by their consent, are the instrument or mode by which God confers it on him. The people need civil authority because the national will for its good is insufficient to order the nation; it needs some intermediating authority between the national will and national action. The prince has his authority precisely because of this national will, and thus he is charged by the people to order them concretely to the end of that will, namely, to their national good.

The second half of chapter 7 concerns the prince's relationship to the visible church, which I frame with a Presbyterian view of two-kingdoms theology. I will not go into specific details here, but I will offer some principles and conclusions. In my view, the visible church in itself—referring to things that materially conduce to a supernatural end (pastorship, profession of faith, preaching, Sacraments, exercising keys of the kingdom, etc.)—are outward manifestations of the spiritual kingdom of God. As such, these things are outside the prince's (civil) jurisdiction. For example, while the pastor as man is under civil jurisdiction, he is not under it *as pastor* but immediately under Christ, the only Head of the Church. The Christian prince can, in principle, remove error and reform the visible church, because no error is actually in the visible church in itself, for no error can exist in the kingdom of God. Error has only the appearance of proceeding from the visible church, and thus it is not (properly speaking) *of* God's visible kingdom. As such, it is subject to the jurisdiction of the civil magistrates. Furthermore, the prince can also approve of ministers as an expression of finding no fault with them. I also argue that the prince can institute religious days that, though not holy in themselves or necessary for the true worship of God, become relatively holy on account of their relationship to holy things. These are national celebrations or lamentations that conduce to national solidarity, a national Christian self-conception, and spiritual good unto heavenly life. Thus, even though the prince cannot institute sacred ceremonies, he can institute national events that facilitate and support these ceremonies, which also strengthen the nation as a nation.

The end of chapter 7 marks the end of my direct discussion of Christian nationalism itself. The next few chapters concern important related issues.

Revolution

Whether Christians may violently resist tyrannical authority was once debated among Christians. Hoping to reignite this debate, in chapter 8 I argue that Christians are morally permitted to violently remove tyrants. The right to revolution follows from the civil ruler's mediatorial role and the fact that his power was ordained by God for the *good* of

civil communities. It is not ordained for evil. Thus, any civil command
to do evil or abstain from what is good is not a command of God, nor is
it backed by divine power; it is a command of *men*, and no man by his
own power can bind another man's conscience to action. To resist such
power is not to resist God but to resist tyrannical men.

When refusing to obey an unjust command of a civil ruler, one
can still recognize him as the true and legitimate civil ruler, having a
right to command what is just by the power ordained of God. Thus,
Nero was certainly a tyrant and ought to have been resisted when
he commanded what was unjust, but his tyranny did not itself dethrone him. Christians ought to have obeyed him, for he could and
did in many cases command what was just, even though he was a
tyrant. Just disobedience is directed at the civil ruler as a *man* or as a
person, not at the civil ruler as civil ruler. One can honor the man in
his formal capacity but disobey him as man, for any civil ruler commanding what is unjust commands as a mere man, not as civil ruler.

There is a difference between resistance to specific commands
and resistance by means of revolution to dethrone and replace an
existing ruler. A tyrant is one whose habit of tyrannical actions
strikes at a fundamental good of human society; his actions are akin
to an unprovoked war against the people. Thus, he is a man warring
against the nation, and since any nation can defend itself against
national threats, the nation can conduct war against him. A just, violent revolution is a type of defensive war.

Revolution itself is the forcible reclamation of civil power by the
people in order to devolve that power on just and more suitable political arrangements. I offer several arguments that justify deposing
civil rulers. Generally, they rely on the conditional nature of rule—
that the people installed or consented to his rule, and they can

withhold their consent, if he acts to their detriment. Remember, the civil ruler mediates the nation's will for its good by determining concrete national action. If his commands harm them, they can depose or remove him and enact better arrangements. National harm can include oppression against true religion, and thus the people can conduct revolution in order to restore true religion. I also argue that the people can forcibly remove rulers who act to the detriment of their particularity (viz., when he undermines their way of life), for particularity is necessary for a people's good.

Liberty of Conscience

Since my argument seeks to justify the political and social privileging or exclusivity of Christianity, questions naturally arise about the liberty of conscience, religious liberty, and religious toleration. These are legitimate and serious questions, for I affirm that the conscience is sacred and free and that no civil ruler has jurisdiction over the conscience. But there are many misunderstandings today concerning what Protestants once believed about the role of civil government with regard to false religion. Chapter 8 seeks to address those issues and misunderstandings.

Much of the chapter involves a process of determining precisely what is at issue between modern religious liberty advocates and the classical Protestant position. Everyone agrees (1) that the civil magistrate cannot compel things that are properly internal, such as belief or feelings; (2) that he must not punish one for simply holding a false belief; (3) that he must not punish in order to reform an errant mind; and (4) that he must not punish someone whose false religion causes no outward harm. The classical Protestant position is that the civil magistrate can punish external religion—e.g., heretical teaching, false rites, blasphemy, and Sabbath-breaking—because such actions can *cause public harm*, both harm to the soul and harm to the body politic. Thus, the civil restraint of false external religion is not punishment for offending God but the prevention of public harm. The role of civil government is to act upon society to remove what outwardly prevents or hinders man from achieving his ends, including his supernatural end.

But even if civil rulers may in principle act against false religion, can they determine what is true and what is false? I provide several arguments demonstrating that they can know both the general duties of natural religion and the truths of Christianity. Here is one argument: We generally agree that civil magistrates know, at least in principle, the natural duties captured in the Second Table of the Decalogue (the fifth through tenth commandments). Knowing these commands *as law*, the magistrate can conclude that there is a divine Lawgiver. But if he knows of the Lawgiver, he can know (at least logically and in principle) the First Table commands, since those follow logically from God as God. Thus, there is no principled barrier to him knowing the duties of natural religion. In addition, the magistrate can know *revealed* truth, because a Christian civil ruler is installed *from* and *by* the people of God, who originally possess the Scriptures. So in principle he can know both natural religion and revealed religion, and therefore he may act against false religion and can in principle distinguish it from true religion.

But will he in fact do that? What about the prudential questions? Can we trust that civil rulers will not attack true religion? Doesn't history prove otherwise? And what about sectarian conflict? These questions are difficult to answer, for there is precedent in Protestantism of bloody conflict, especially in the first two centuries after the Reformation. One might ask, "Haven't we learned from experience to leave government out of religion?" I agree that we've learned much, but we should also learn from our own time that governmental and societal "neutrality" are impossible and that secularism is pervasive and relentless. It has evolved into a sort of pagan nationalism, in which bizarre moralities and rites are imposed upon all areas of life. Let us learn from *all* our experience. It seems to me that experience teaches us that established Christianity is better than its secularist alternative.

Anglo-Protestant Experience

Recognizing the importance of experience, I include a chapter on Protestant experience in early America. The purpose of this chapter is to show, first, that the political thought between the Puritan settlements and the American founding is coherent, at least with regard to the government role in religion, and second, that the apparent discontinuities between those eras are products of experience, not indicative of changes in principles. Thus, chapter 9 shows that the religious toleration in the founding era was rooted, not in Enlightenment thought or liberalism, but in good Protestant principles applied in light of Anglo-Protestant experience. Early America is a Protestant resource for an American return to Christian nationalism.

At least in their own telling, the New England Puritans applied the same principles of conscience that I outlined above. In every famous incident, they claimed that their action to suppress dissenting religion was in the interest of the community, often to quell suspected sedition and civil disruption (e.g., Roger Williams, the Antinomians, and the Quakers) or to maintain the unique and particular characteristics of the community (e.g., Baptists). One 17th-century minister, Increase Mather, affirmed that it is not wrong in itself to extend toleration to Baptists (to erect their own churches), and it would be appropriate in England. But he denied that New England ought to do it, given their unique composition, fledgling status, and the original intention for settling. By the early 18th century, things had changed, and Increase's son, Cotton Mather, was preaching an ordination sermon for a Baptist in Boston. Increase was likely in the audience, and he approved of his son's actions. What changed was not principles or the injection of the Enlightenment. Rather, experience demonstrated the possibility of a pan-Protestant civil order in which brothers in the Lord, though not sharing any formal institutional alignment, could live together in peace and even cooperate in a civil project.

Jump to the founding era and we see continued discussion on religious liberty and institutional changes. I argue that the two opposing positions on religious liberty in that era assume explicitly Protestant principles and that the majority position is the same as that of the New England Puritans and virtually indistinguishable from Cotton Mather's. Experience taught them that suppressing false religion is counterproductive—that it both encourages false religion and causes cycles of war and conflict. Contrary to what many scholars have concluded, the founding era assumed Protestantism as the background condition for religious liberty.

Thus, American religious liberty in the early American Republic was a people-specific development. Though its foundation was something universal—Protestant principles—the application of these principles was Anglo-Protestant. As such, religious liberty in the founding era was a cultural product from the self-reflection of a particular people. American Christian nationalists can pull from this part of the American political tradition, and so they do not need to reject the American founding or the entire American political tradition. In other words, *American Christian nationalist* is not a contradiction in terms but rather an appropriate label for those who identify with the old American Republic.

VI. Foreword

Christian nationalists seek the *instauratio magna*—the Great Renewal. We struggle for the instauration of our homeland and the revitalization of our people. We are not "conservative," nor are we "traditionalist." We do not merely look to the past or to some past golden age. This is not an ideology of nostalgia. Still, we do not repudiate the past, nor do we desire to progress from some "checkered" ancestry. Rather, we look forward: we strive to take the future because we love our past; we love our homeland and its people.

The desire of the nations must be a national desire, and the hope of the nations must be a national hope. The work of the Christian nationalist is convincing his Christian nation to be a nation *for itself*. A Christian nation ought to seek its good, both earthly and heavenly. This book justifies the Christian national will for its good, and it shows how that will properly manifests in natural, social, and civic relations and authorities. I pray that it also cultivates in the reader a love of home and a will for its renewal.

Instaurabunt civitates desertas dissipatas
in generationem et generationem. (Isaiah 61:4)

1

Nations Before the Fall:
What Is Man? Part I: Creation

"'Tribal behavior' is what makes human beings human. Take it away from 'man' or 'humankind' and what you get is not 'pure man' or 'liberated man' but dehumanization, and from that, tyranny." —Samuel Francis[1]

I. A Rational Animal

The great political theorists in the Western political tradition often began their political thought with an account of human nature. They first asked, "What is man?" and they asked this with good reason.

1. "Christmas And the National Question (2): Thumbs Down on Dionne," VDARE.com, December 23, 2004, available at https://vdare.com/articles/christmas-and-the-national-question-2-thumbs-down-on-dionne. This article concerns, as Francis said, "[W]hether Christians can celebrate or even observe in public their own religious holidays in a country (or even local community) that is overwhelmingly Christian and has been so throughout its history."

How we understand the nature of man determines how we understand human social organization. We observe that some animals are solitary creatures; others are social and communal. Among the latter, we find a variety of hierarchal arrangements and instinctive rules of cooperation that ensure survival and flourishing. But what works for ants does not work for apes. Each species has its peculiar behaviors that constitute its social relations and its use of space. The human animal is a *rational* animal—the only earthbound creature with a reasonable soul and capable of acting in accordance with a moral law. But rationality, despite being what distinguishes man in essence from beasts, does not capture all the constitutive characteristics of the human being. Man is a rational *animal* after all, and hence the question "What is man?" is not answered fully with a description of his rationality or highest faculties.

What can we say of man's animality? It seems possible that a rational animal could also be a solitary animal. But the human animal is not solitary; we are social creatures. And what sort of social creatures are we? It is not enough to say that we are social. What are the distinctively *human* principles of our social nature that enable us to live well? To answer the question "What is man?" requires us to inquire not only about man's rationality but also about his distinct social nature. It requires us to ask, "What is this rational animal in its totality?"

Inherent in human nature (and all creatures) is an end or purpose toward which his nature leads him, and in this end he finds his happiness and completion. Now, any end requires some *means* to attain the end. A painter completes his portrait by means of skill, materials, instruments, etc. Any inquiry into man's ends must include an account of the means to those ends. Since man cannot achieve his earthly and heavenly ends when solitary, man congregates (by instinct and reason) into familial, social, and political groups for mutual support, cooperation, and protection. This is not controversial.[2] But acknowledging this alone does not tell us which particular social arrangements are most suitable given his nature.

The Christian narrative of man's creation, fall, redemption, and glorification complicates this question. When we say that *by nature* man is social, are we assuming a state of integrity, a state of sin, a state of pre-glory redemption, or a state of glorification? And how does each state affect our nature, our manner of living, and how we arrange our communities? These four different states raise important questions concerning the continuity and discontinuity of social life as one passes from one to the next. How does fallen social life differ from unfallen social life, and what is the role of grace, the Gospel, and redemption? Surprisingly, no Christian writer (of which I'm aware) has sought to provide a systematic treatment of human sociality that shows continuity and discontinuity between these states. The result has been significant confusion and incoherence in Christian political theologies. One purpose of this chapter is to provide clarity along these lines.

Since this book is not intended to be a complete work of political theory, my account of man in each state is not exhaustive. I include only what grounds my defense of Christian nationalism, though I chose some of the content specifically to challenge modern-day prejudices that hinder the reception of it. I offer a classical Protestant understanding of man and his relations, and I rely

---

2. Religious hermits, even if one recognizes their legitimacy (which I do not), are exceptions, not counterexamples to this claim. Even social contractarians, such as Hugo Grotius and John Locke, affirm that man is fundamentally social.

heavily on the classical Protestant tradition. Despite some Protestant distinctives, however, my account is largely catholic: I rely on a broad Christian theological and political tradition. Admittedly, I assume much from this tradition, as a complex argument involving theology, philosophy, and politics must start somewhere. For those who reject this tradition or understand it differently, I trust that my argument at least shows that distinctive theological systems matter to these debates. "Evangelical" or "Christian" political theology (though certainly broad in market appeal) is far too vague and imprecise to reach actionable conclusions and to produce a systematic political theory or theology.

My presentation in this chapter and the next uses a familiar schema: creation, fall, and redemption. I describe the pertinent features of man in each of his corresponding states—integrity, sin, and redemption—highlighting the continuity and discontinuity of features between these states. Along the way, I provide much of the relevant theology that grounds the rest of the book. I do not discuss the state of glory in detail, but its qualitative difference with the state of integrity is crucial for the logic of this work. In this chapter, I focus on creation.

II. The Ends and Dignity of Man

The Two Ends of Man

For our purposes, the most important distinction in Reformed theological anthropology is the distinction between the two ends of man. God created Adam with both earthly and heavenly ends. The latter refers to eternal, heavenly life, which God would grant to Adam and his progeny upon their meeting a divinely instituted condition. The condition was obedience in man's earthly duties, which involved fulfilling the "dominion mandate"—multiplying, filling, and subduing creation as the vice-regents of God on earth. Fulfilling this mandate is not a process of progressively bringing heavenly life to earth by human effort. Man cannot bring ultimate rest by the work of his hands; he cannot transform the state of integrity into the state of glory. The state of glory—the promised heavenly life—is a *gift* of God's grace; man can neither merit it (as if it were a wage due to him) nor bring it about in his work. Adam's task was indeed to work, even to build, mature, and perfect the earth to God's glory and man's good. But the best he could achieve was a complete life according to the standards of the state of integrity—a sort of lower perfection. A matured earth by the hands of man remains below that of glory; it is qualitatively less excellent. As Herman Bavinck said, "The state of integrity is not yet the state of glory. . . . [It] is a preparation for eternal glory, when God will be all in all."[3] The maturing of earthly life is the *condition* for the divine bestowing of heavenly life, which requires a divine act.[4] Adam and his progeny's work on earth was always

---

3. Herman Bavinck, *Reformed Dogmatics,* ed. John Bolt and trans. John Vriend, vol. 2, *God and Creation* (1895–1901; Grand Rapids: Baker Academic, 2004), 563. "The state of integrity cannot be equated with the state of glory." Later he writes, "We may not draw conclusions from the former [state of integrity] for the conditions of the latter [state of glory]." Ibid., 2:576.

4. This is not to say that completing Adam's task would *merit* him eternal life, as if eternal life is a mere wage for work performed. It remains a gift by the grace of God, who would stoop to reward Adam's feeble work. As Bavinck wrote, "There is no such thing as merit in the existence of a creature before God. . . . [The Reformed] firmly asserted that a higher state of blessedness than that which prevailed in paradise on earth could never, in the nature of the case, be merited but could only be granted by a free dispensation of God." Ibid., 2:570, 572. This also entails that Adam, in his state of integrity, "did not possess the

penultimate;[5] it was subordinate to a higher end obtained *only* by a divine act of grace.

This two-ends theological anthropology, though questioned in some Neo-Calvinist circles today, was held almost universally by classical Protestants and the Christian tradition. Francis Turretin states that "[t]he *received opinion* among the orthodox is that the promise given to Adam was not only of a happy life to be continued in [earthly] paradise, but of a heavenly and eternal life."[6] Martin Luther wrote,

> [M]an was created to another and a higher end than any of the other living creatures. . . . Adam was created by an immortal and spiritual life to which he would assuredly have been translated and conveyed without death after he had lived in Eden and the other parts of the earth to his full satiety of life, yet without trouble or distress.[7]

highest kind of life. The highest kind of life is the material freedom consisting of not being able to err, sin, or die." Ibid., 2:573.

5. *Penultimate* means "next or second to ultimate."

6. Turretin, *IET*, 1:5.12.3, emphasis added. Petrus van Mastricht writes that "in addition to all the life which he possessed from creation, from constant obedience there would have come another degree of life and blessedness." *Theoretical-Practical Theology*, trans. Todd M. Rester and ed. Joel R. Beek, vol. 3, *The Works of God and the Fall of Man* (1698; Grand Rapids: Reformation Heritage Books, 2021), 381. Thomas Goodwin disagreed with this view, taking what I estimate to be the minority view that Adam, if he remained obedient, would have remained in earthly life, and that "Christ was the first and only author of that heavenly life which the saints in heaven do enjoy." "Of the Creatures, and the Condition of Their State by Creation," in *The Works of Thomas Goodwin* (1682; Grand Rapids: Soli Deo Gloria Publications, 2021), 7:49–53. This seems to cohere well with Goodwin's supra-lapsarianism, which he expounds in book 2 of his "Discourse on Election," in *Works*, vol. 9.

7. Martin Luther, *Commentary on Genesis*, trans. and ed. John Nicholas Lenker (Minneapolis: Lutherans in All Lands, 1904), 1:173 [on Gen. 2:16, 17].

Scottish theologian John Brown of Haddington states that "Reason itself suggests that God would promise to Adam and his seed something better than that happiness which he enjoyed;—and that after his state of service, there would probably happen one of reward."[8] By reason, one discovers that he cannot "obtain on earth his full felicity, but must be gifted with it at length in heaven where he can enjoy the fullest and most perfect communion with God," argues Turretin.[9] Adam's life on earth was but a foretaste of heaven, as he looked forward (through the eyes of faith) to a future heavenly bliss.[10] Indeed, the maturation of earthly life would likely intensify

8. Here is the quote in full: "Reason itself suggests that God would promise to Adam and his seed something better than that happiness which he enjoyed;—and that after his state of service, there would probably happen one of reward; and that, as the garden of Eden was chiefly calculated to promote the temporal felicity of his body, there would be a future state of happiness, chiefly correspondent with the noble nature of his soul. . . . The law was originally ordained to be the instrument of conferring eternal life in heaven, as well as temporal and spiritual life on earth." John Brown of Haddington, *Systematic Theology: A Compendious View of Natural and Revealed Religion* (1817; Grand Rapids: Reformation Heritage Books, 2002), 201.

9. Turretin states, "Since his noblest part is spirit (even of heavenly origin) touched with a vehement desire of heavenly goods (by which alone its infinite appetite for the highest good can be satisfied), he could not obtain on earth his full felicity, but must be gifted with it at length in heaven where he can enjoy the fullest and most perfect communion with God, in whom his highest good resides. For although on earth he could in some measure give himself to be enjoyed, it is certain that the immediate and absolute fruition of God is not to be sought apart from the beatific vision which can be looked for only in heaven." *IET*, 1:8.6.8. Calvin said that Adam's "earthly life truly would have been temporal; yet he would have passed into heaven without death, and without injury." John Calvin, *Commentary on the First Book of Moses Called Genesis*, trans. John King, vol. 1 of *Calvin's Commentaries* (Grand Rapids: Baker Books, 2005), 1:127 [on Gen. 2:16].

10. Many Reformed theologians claim that Adam was under a probationary period, which is often described as a test of his obedience with regard to protecting the Garden of Eden from foreign, malicious creatures. Upon passing the test (viz., killing the serpent), he would be blessed and elevated. But this position is imposed on the text of Genesis and is theologically unsound. If the heavenly blessing promised to Adam is the same in

one's desire for something higher, as earthly life is disclosed as lower, even uncanny, and unable to fully satisfy. People would increasingly feel like strangers and aliens in this world.

To complete his task, Adam required two distinguishable and complementary sets of gifts (or abilities), each suitable for one of the two ends of man. Reformed theologians often identified these as natural and supernatural gifts, though both were native to and "concreated" in Adam at creation. The natural gifts are constitutive to man *as man* and include knowledge of what is good, free will with regard to natural things, the faculties of reason and

---

substance as that blessing promised to believers in Christ (which is standard Reformed theology), then Adam would be elevated to a state without marriage or childbirth, for there is no marriage and childbirth in eternal life (Luke 20:34–36). Adam would then be unable to propagate and thus, be incapable of fulfilling the dominion mandate (Gen. 1:28). Coherence demands that the probationary period would end during or after the filling of the earth. G.K. Beale in *A New Testament Biblical Theology* (Grand Rapids: Baker Academic, 2011) rightly argues that Adam's "commission" included both "ruling over and subduing creation" and "guard[ing] the sanctuary from threats." These served as "several indications of escalated eschatological blessings that Adam would enjoy if he faithfully obeyed and carried out his commission" (p. 916). But in his rightful emphasis on Adam as a representative head, he errs in making Adam's subduing of the serpent during its work of temptation the "climactic" event that would trigger the eschatological blessing. Filling and multiplying must be a necessary condition to meet the covenant. If the eschatological blessing includes the elimination of marriage and natural propagation (which is widely affirmed in the Reformed tradition; see Turretin, *IET*, 2:12.2.8), then the blessing must come *after* the human race fills and multiplies on the earth. We can affirm that Adam, as the covenantal representative of his posterity, would have to perform special covenantal acts (e.g., killing the serpent) perhaps as the ground of the eschatological blessings. But filling and subduing must, nevertheless, be a condition for that blessing. Moreover, it is best to follow Petrus van Mastricht in affirming that what passes on from Adam to his posterity is the covenant, not his obedience to the covenant. Van Mastricht addressed the question "How would the [covenant of nature] have been accomplished?" He states that "it is entirely more probable that from the pact of divine promise their [Adam's and Eve's] posterity would have each merited [eternal life] for themselves by their own obedience." *Theoretical-Practical Theology*, 3:395.

understanding, and natural sociability (among other gifts). They are essential to man, meaning that without any one of them, the thing ceases to be a human being. Calvin says that these gifts pertain to "earthly" things, enabling man in "matters of policy and economy, all mechanical arts, and liberal studies."[11] In other words, they chiefly concern the principles, means, and ends that guide life in this world and the substance or essence of *outward* action. These gifts, however, concern man not merely as an animal but also as a rational animal. Reason elevates the dignity of man above beasts in the order of being. But while these gifts are sufficient for life as an earth-oriented rational being, they do not supply what might properly orient man in knowledge, desire, and action to anything higher than earthly life. For this reason, as Reformed theologian Franciscus Junius writes, "It is necessary that other principles above nature be inspired and infused by God so that we may know that end beyond nature to which we have been ordered, and the truth that would certainly lead to that end."[12]

Supernatural (or spiritual) gifts, which Calvin identifies as knowledge of "true righteousness and future blessedness," pertain to "heavenly" things. Many theologians have called this "original righteousness"[13] and also the image of God.[14] Though these gifts

11. John Calvin, *Institutes of the Christian Religion*, trans. Henry Beveridge (Grand Rapids: Eerdmans, 1989), 2.2.12.

12. Franciscus Junius, *Mosaic Polity*, trans. Todd M. Rester (1593; Grand Rapids: CLP Academic, 2015), 52.

13. Turretin writes, "Although the body of Adam was in origin earthly (and as composed, so also resolvable, through the indisposition of matter), yet it could have been immortal through the dignity of original righteousness [*originalis justitiae dignitatem*] and the power of God's special grace" *IET*, 1:5.12.9.

14. Peter Martyr Vermigli states, "The image of God is the new man, who understands the truth of God and desires its righteousness. . . . Our mind truly expresses God when it pos-

are relevant to outward life on earth, man exercises them primarily *internally*—as acts of the mind and heart in orientation to God and eschatological life. With these gifts, man can set his mind on the things above and fix his mind on his heavenly end. In ordering the soul, they ensure that one follows the proper internal principle, mode, and end of action: as to principle, proceeding from a pure heart; as to mode, performed with internal obedience to the spiritual demands of God's law; and as to end, performed to God's glory as the ultimate end. Original righteousness is, therefore, not that which enables one to perform right outward action or to do what is good in substance. Rather, original righteousness *perfects* works that are good in substance with theological good—ensuring that they are performed well before God with the eyes of faith fixed on heaven.[15] In other words, the higher gifts are necessary to perform good works well, for with them one performs with a good conscience inwardly before God and to his glory, but such gifts are

---

sesses the knowledge of God and is adorned with righteousness. For righteousness and the knowledge of divine things are nothing else than a sort of influx of the divine nature into our minds." "Image of God: Commentary on Genesis," in *Philosophical Works: On the Relation of Philosophy to Theology*, trans. Joseph C. McLelland (Kirksville, MO: Sixteenth Century Journal, 1996), 43.

15. Although these natural and supernatural gifts are distinguishable by their principal ends (one for earthly life and the other for heavenly life), each needs the other to meet its proper end. That is, both sets of gifts are required to properly meet both earthly and heavenly ends. The faculty of reason is, for example, a natural endowment—something essential to man as man—but it is still necessary for the contemplation of the heavenly kingdom and the worship of God. Original righteousness, though perfective and of heavenly origin, is necessary for the proper ordering of man's soul and life in the world. Nevertheless, each set is merely ancillary to (or a necessary support or condition for) the proper functioning of the other. The removal of original righteousness leads to wickedness, but it does not obliterate the basic structures of man as man, or his ability to perform the substance (or outward form) of right action, or his knowledge of the natural principles for a commodious civil life.

unnecessary to perform good works outwardly. This distinction becomes very important in the section on fallen man.

The Moral Law

The divinely instituted condition for heavenly life is often called the "covenant of works." It is variously described by Reformed theologians, but it is simplified as the following: *If you do this, you will live; if you fail to do this, you will die.* "This" refers to the moral law as a rule or standard of action. It is also called the natural law or the law of nature. Simply put, this law in itself states, *Do this; don't do that,* but more specifically it is a rule by which man fulfills his nature. The moral law can be viewed separately as a rule or as a covenant of works—as a rule for man's happiness, according to his nature, or as the divinely prescribed condition for eternal life. These are interrelated in that obeying the moral law as a rule is the condition of the covenant. In other words, if you obey the moral law as the rule of life, you meet the condition for eternal life. Nevertheless, it is important to maintain the distinction between the moral law as a rule and the moral law as a covenant. If one fulfills the moral law as a covenant on your behalf, the moral law does *not* thereby cease to be the only rule of righteousness. That is to say, even if the covenant is fulfilled for you by another, the law remains binding to you as the only rule of life.[16] This distinction is very important for the section on man in a state of redemption. The key takeaway here is that man is bound to obey the moral law regardless of his covenantal status

16. Samuel Willard writes, "The law is to be considered, either as it is a covenant, or only a rule. This distinction must be allowed or else we shall not be able to reconcile many texts in Scripture." *A Complete Body of Divinity in Two Hundred and Fifty Expository Lectures,* ed. Mike Christian (1727; n.p.: MC Design, 2015), Kindle loc. 30729.

before God, for obeying the moral law is the sole means to his happiness and the fulfillment of his nature as man.

Let's examine the moral law in more detail. Samuel Willard, a second-generation New England Puritan minister, defines the moral law as "a divine unchangeable rule given to man, and accommodated to his nature, as he was created by God, obliging him to serve to God's glory as his last end."[17] God gave to Adam this "law of nature" immediately at this creation in order to "regulate life and action."[18] Since it binds rational creatures—i.e., those who know their duty and must choose to obey it—it is a *moral* law. Humans are moral beings only because they exist under moral duty, which requires that they obey the natural law consciously, by choice, and above mere instinct. Willard goes on to explicate his definition. It is *divine*, because God himself "imprinted on the heart of man in his creation, and [man] was able to read [these laws] by the light of nature."[19] It is *unchangeable*, for it is the immutable standard of righteousness. Reformed theologians universally agreed that the natural law was not eliminated at the fall of man, nor was it abolished, superseded, added to, or modified by the Gospel. Willard states that Christ "came not to abolish the moral law, or law of nature . . . but confirmed it." He continues:

> the moral law took place as soon as man was made, and continues to the end, without any alteration. The same that it was,

17. Ibid., loc. 30635.

18. In recent years, scholars have shown definitively what should have been obvious to generations preceding them, namely, that the affirmation of natural law is ubiquitous in the Reformed tradition and no less among Puritans. I will assume this throughout without further comment. See Stephen Grabill's *Rediscovering the Natural Law in Reformed Theological Ethics* (Grand Rapids: Eerdmans, 2006).

19. Willard, *Body of Divinity*, loc. 12433.

when given to Adam in integrity, the same it was when renewed
on Mount Sinai, and is still the same in the days of the gospel.[20]

Willard then states that the moral law is a *rule*, for it "direct[s] us
in our action by showing what is right and what is wrong."[21] And it
is a rule of *man*, being the universal and exclusive means to human
happiness and way for life.

Next, Willard says that the moral law is *accommodated* to human
nature, being "adapted to his powers" as a "suitable medium to his
great end"[22] and is "fitted for the regulating of man in all the actions
of his will."[23] It is important to emphasize that the powers, desires,
and order required for Adam and his race to meet the demands of
the moral law were innate to him. The moral law is not arbitrary; it
is not a system of morality distinct from, opposed to, or indifferent to man's nature. As Willard states, "The law of nature, or those
rules imprinted on the natures of things, was most harmonious and
agreeable to their natures."[24] Their natures were "put into the things
themselves by the God of nature." In other words, God as creator
put his will for man in man's very design. Therefore, God cannot
rescind any requirement of the moral law (including dominion), for
to do so would pit God against God; viz., he would command us to
go against our nature in which the divine will already inheres.

Lastly, Willard says that this law obliges man to act to *God's glory as
his last* [ultimate] *end*. This refers to internal obedience, as I described.

20. Ibid., loc. 30685.
21. Ibid., loc. 30650.
22. Ibid., loc. 30711.
23. Ibid., loc. 30714.
24. Ibid., loc. 9207.

Perfect obedience to the natural law is not merely a matter of outward action but requires the best part—a pure heart before God.

Image of God and Human Dignity

The ways that 16th- and 17th-century Reformed theologians discussed the "image of God" are largely foreign to us today. Calvin and generations of Reformed theologians after him distinguished between the "chief part" of the image and what is ancillary to it, which respectively correspond to the supernatural gifts (i.e., original righteousness) and the natural gifts discussed above. Calvin states, for example, that "the chief seat of the Divine image was in [Adam's] mind and heart."[25] Similarly, Willard writes, "Man had God's image on him at first, which was necessary, not so much to enable him to do the matter of duty, as to do it graciously; there must be holiness attending it."[26] The divine image "shines forth" from every part of man, including from his body," says Calvin, but this indicates a "suitable correspondence with . . . internal order." So the image of God chiefly concerns our inward faculties that orient us to heavenly things. But in perfecting our being, the image of God puts the whole in order. As Calvin writes, the divine image ensured the "perfection of our whole nature" and that Adam "had right judgment, had affections in harmony with reason, had all his

---

25. Calvin, *Commentary on the First Book of Moses Called Genesis*, 1:95 [on Gen. 1:26]. As Turretin states, "By the divine image, we do not understand generally whatever gifts upright man received from God (spoken of in Gen. 1:26, 27) or specially certain remains of it existing in the mind and heart of man after the fall (in which sense we understand Gen. 9:6 and Jam. 3:9). Rather we understand it strictly of the principal part of that image which consisted of holiness and wisdom (usually termed original righteousness)." *IET*, 1:9.8.7. Willard writes, "By the image of God, we are to understand those habits of sanctification which were infused into man at the first." *Body of Divinity*, loc. 12253.

26. Willard, *Body of Divinity*, loc. 12253.

senses sound and well-regulated, and truly excelled in everything good."[27] It also, in consequence, elevates us in dignity above the rest of creation. Zacharias Ursinus writes that the "dignity and majesty of man" elevates him above the rest of creation, and from this position he "excels and rules over all other creatures."[28] Put differently, *in form* the "image of God" ensures rectitude, integrity, purity, and order of body and soul, but *in consequence* to this dignity, man can exercise dominion well. In other words, while dominion is one purpose of the divine image, in itself the divine image concerns rectitude, integrity, and order.

This might seem to be an unimportant distinction, but it allows us to conclude that the right to rule over creation follows from human excellence. The dominion mandate *cannot* be a bare divine command that is disconnected from human nature and the sort of gifts God gave us. Taking dominion is not an adventitious duty or a divine positive command.[29] It proceeds from the very nature of man, and so it cannot be rescinded, even by God, without violating the fundamental nature of man. The right to rule creation as vice-regents is derived naturally and necessarily from divinely-granted majesty. And since grace assumes nature (as we see in the next chapter), it does not rescind or abrogate the dominion mandate, and taking dominion well is one result of sanctification.

---

27. Calvin, *Commentary on the First Book of Moses Called Genesis*, 1:95 [on Gen. 1:26].

28. The full quote: ". . . the spiritual and immortal nature of the soul, and the purity and integrity of the whole man; a perfect blessedness and joy, together with the dignity and majesty of man, in which he excels and rules over all other creatures." Zacharias Ursinus, *Commentary on the Heidelberg Catechism*, 4th ed., trans. G.W. Williard (Cincinnati: Elm Street, 1888), 54.

29. That is, the command to take dominion is not some extraneous and non-natural duty added to man's natural duties; it flows from his nature.

Human dignity is grounded in the image of God. But having dignity is not uniquely human, for (contrary to the modern notion) dignity refers to something's station within a hierarchy. Indeed, without hierarchy, dignity is meaningless. Plants have higher dignity than stones due to their possession of life.[30] In human social relations, dignity is ascribed to magistrates, nobles, or anyone with eminence in the social order. Indeed, until perhaps the influence of Immanuel Kant, dignity was typically used to denote elevation in a social hierarchy.[31] When dignity was ascribed to all mankind, it referred to the distinctive gifts and qualities that elevate us above the rest of creation. We share materiality with rocks, life with plants, and animality with beasts, but only humans have rationality, moral duty, choice, and the ability to acknowledge and worship God. The image of God, and therefore human dignity, is not some fiat stamp of value, but refers to the possession of distinctive faculties the completion of which is found in noble action.[32] To be a complete human—to fully express human dignity—one must exercise those gifts for their penultimate and ultimate ends; it is a matter of faculty *and* action. In short, human dignity refers to divinely inscribed properties that elevate man above all other earthly creatures and have inherent ends

30. See Richard Hooker, *Divine Law and Human Nature: Book I of Hooker's Laws; A Modernization*, ed. W. Bradford Littlejohn, Brian Marr, and Bradley Belschner (Lincoln, NE: Davenant Press, 2017), 26.

31. Calvin writes, for example, "Nevertheless forasmuch as it has pleased God to set certain degrees: we must hold us thereunto, and keep that order, so as the party which has any preeminence and dignity, may be acknowledged for such a one as is to be honored." John Calvin, "Sermon 37," in *The Sermons of Master John Calvin upon the first book of Moses called Deuteronomy*, Monergism.com, accessed September 24, 2022, https://www.monergism.com/sermons-deuteronomy-ebook.

32. Turretin writes, "We cannot conform ourselves to the image of God . . . except by regulating our lives in accordance with the precepts of this [natural] law." *IET*, 2:11.2.11.

that require noble action.[33] Moreover, when lacking any of these properties, or when possessing them and failing to exercise them, a human being remains distinct from beasts (for he retains bare rationality), but he is lower in dignity compared with those who possess and exercise them.[34] Human dignity is far more than a status we can enjoy passively; it is a call for the dignified to *act* in ways that are worthy of his elevated station in the cosmic order.

III. Civil Fellowship

Prelapsarian Social Relations

How would Adam's progeny have arranged themselves had Adam not sinned? Would nations have existed in a pre-fall world? Though answering this question requires many counterfactuals and could lead to vain speculation, most notable Christian thinkers have

33. This relationship of faculty, *telos*, and dignity is found in Calvin's understanding of worship. A good example is in the following: "Since the chief object of life is to acknowledge and worship God, (which alone is our principal distinction from the brutes) we ought to prefer it to all things, even to the most valuable, so as to direct to him all our prayers, and, in a word, all the thoughts of our heart." *Commentary on the Prophet Isaiah*, trans. William Pringle, vol. 8 of *Calvin's Commentaries* (Grand Rapids: Baker Books, 2005), 3:368–69 [on Isa. 44:9]. Since our ability to acknowledge and worship God distinguishes man from the rest of creation, exercising this ability is our "chief object of life," and so we ought to consider it our highest end and our chief desire. As such, it is a natural right, meaning that no one may interfere with or hinder one's ability to worship God. Since worship is the chief end, the worst violation of another's dignity is hindering one's ability to worship.

34. For this reason, people who failed to act humanly were often called "animals." Calvin writes, for example, "For since God will punish all the wicked, how can they escape who abandon themselves like brute beasts to every kind of iniquity? To walk after the flesh, is to be given up to the flesh, like brute animals, who are not led by reason and judgment, but have the natural desire of their flesh as their chief guide." *Commentaries on the Catholic Epistles*, trans. John Owen, vol. 22 of *Calvin's Commentaries* (Grand Rapids: Baker Books, 2005), 2:400 [on 2 Pet. 2:10].

ventured to theorize about the social life and civil organization of an unfallen world. Thomas Aquinas, for example, repeatedly discusses social arrangements in the state of integrity, as we see below. Many people indirectly and perhaps unintentionally describe prelapsarian life. For example, affirming that some institution exists only because of the fall (e.g., slavery) entails that it would not exist in a sinless world. Similarly, when one states that some action or relation is good in itself (e.g., friendship, parental love, and worship), he must by logical consequence affirm that this good would exist in a sinless world.

Also, in asking whether this or that good thing would be in the state of integrity, we have to reflect on how we relate to that thing—whether tragically (i.e., that it is good relative only to our fallen state) or inherently (i.e., that it is good in itself). So, for example, is the effort required in mastering some craft or trade a tragic good or an inherent good? We (typically) relate to it as an inherent good—that the struggle to master something is itself a human good. Therefore, we might conclude (as I do below) that in the state of integrity specific craftsmanship skills are *acquired*, not innate.

Since we can affirm or deny whether something would exist in the prelapsarian state (or at least conclude things above mere speculation), we might be able to construct some robust theory about prelapsarian social life. But even if we can, what purpose does it serve? I contend that providing an account of human society in the state of integrity is essential to Christian political theory. Only then can we determine continuity and discontinuity between the four states of man. For example, if the formation of distinct nations is natural to prelapsarian man and grace affirms and restores nature, then the nation in principle is not a consequence of the fall and grace does not undermine it. The same is true of the natural and civil relations that exist in nations and the relations between them. Below, I demonstrate that prelapsarian people would form geographically and culturally distinct nations.

The Natural Family

Men and women were created for monogamous and perpetual heterosexual union. We call this the natural family, which forms the "domestic society" (from the Latin for house—*domus*). This society consists of man and wife with children or the anticipation of children, and it is maximally communal; that is, its relations are non-transactional and characterized by sharing, common possession, and sacrifice. Each person's chief duty, as it concerns earthly relations, is the communal good of the household. Genesis 2:18 tells us that the wife is the "help meet" for the husband, which (whatever else that relation entails) logically implies that the monogamous man-woman union is the basic unit of human society; the basic unit is not individuals but *teams* of husband and wife. Herman Bavinck writes, "[T]he manner in which the woman received her existence serves to place her in the kind relationship to the man such that she is inseparably bound to him."[35] She assists him in his divinely ordained work, as one "who does not stand above him to dominate him, nor beneath him as one degraded to the status of a tool for pleasure, but one who stands alongside him, stationed at his side and therefore formed from his side."[36] The man does not exist to empower the female, as if his role is merely to bring resources home. Rather, the man governs the

35. Herman Bavinck, *The Christian Family*, trans. Nelson D. Kloosterman (Grand Rapids: Christian's Library Press, 2012 [1912]), 4.

36. Ibid., 6.

household, orienting it to the divine mission *he* received from God, which *he* is responsible to see fulfilled. The wife is a necessary support for the man as he meets his obligations to the civil community and the broader mission of humanity. Hence, the divine task given to Adam and his race is reducible not to the efforts of individuals but of domestic teams—of husband and wife. The household is the basic unit composing civil society; it is a society of households.[37] We speak more properly, therefore, of households filling the earth rather than individuals filling the earth.

Households combine to form distinct civil societies for these main reasons: man is by nature a gregarious being, and he is naturally limited. I discuss each in the following sections.

Gregariousness

That man is a gregarious (or social) animal is affirmed universally in the Christian tradition. Man cannot live well by "living alone as wild beasts do, nor wandering about as birds . . . [nor as] stateless hermits, living without fixed hearth or home," writes Johannes Althusius.[38] He continues, "[M]an by nature is a gregarious animal born for cultivating society with other men."[39] Many have spoken of an "instinct" that draws people to society,[40] which points to a phil-

---

37. By *civil* society, I refer to a self-consciously combined collection of households. This is the basic criterion for a civil society, though a more complex one will include vocational associations (*collegia*) and civil government. The Directory for Worship for the Presbyterian Church in America (PCA) states that "the family, as ordained by God, is the basic institution in society."

38. Johannes Althusius, *Politica*, ed. and trans. Frederick S. Carney (1625; Indianapolis: Liberty Fund, 1995), 22 [1.24–25].

39. Ibid.

40. Bartholomäus Keckermann writes, "The origin of political society derives from God and the nature of man, to which man is driven by the law of nature and instinct." *Systema*

anthropic (as opposed to misanthropic) drive to be with and for others. This is a feature of human animality, a sort of pre-rational or pre-reflective passion that we share with other animals. But humans form civil societies to satisfy distinctively human desires and needs as well. As Willard writes,

> He is πολιτικον; man was made a sociable creature, and has a natural disposition to hold converse with his own kind. Nor does this inclination arise merely from the necessity of his lapsed estate for mutual support and defense, though that has augmented the necessity of it; but it was put into the constitution of man, and he sought it, not only by instinct, as brutes so with their kind; but the exercise of reason, and the consideration of the relations which God at first constituted between mankind, and the affection put into them towards their correlates therein. It is therefore a brutish opinion of those, who would have men, if their integrity had remained, to have lived in the fields and woods after the manner of wild beasts, whereas it is evident that men do seek familiarity with such whom they have the least necessity for. [41]

We form societies to provide what I will call "civil fellowship." This fellowship extends not only to what serves bodily, material, and security needs, but to what serves higher needs as well. In civil fellowship, man can exercise his distinctively human faculties to

---

disciplinae politicae (Hanover: Guilielmus Antonius, 1608), 9. Calvin states, "Since man is by nature a social animal, he is disposed, from natural instinct, to cherish and preserve society." *Institutes*, 2.2.13.

41. Willard, *Body of Divinity*, loc. 37662.

love his neighbor as himself. He can converse with and serve moral beings as a moral being.

By reason and experience, man knows that the set of earthly goods necessary to live well in this world are available only in civil society. Concerning material goods, no man or household has the skills necessary to produce the full range of material goods. As Althusius writes,

> God distributed his gifts unevenly among men. He did not give all things to one person, but some to one and some to others, so that you have need for my gifts, and I for yours. And so was born, as it were, the need for communicating necessary and useful things, which communication was not possible except in social and political life. God therefore willed that each need the service and aid of others in order that friendship would bind all together, and no one would consider another to be value-less. . . . Every one therefore needs the experience and contributions of others, and no one lives to himself alone.[42]

A prelapsarian world is a world of diverse vocations, each vocation being distinct in its art and end-product, and excellence in any vocation is made possible only by that diversity. One can achieve excellence in some productive art only if he is among others pursuing excellence in other productive arts. Althusius calls this relations of production a "symbiosis"—a living-together of "co-workers who, by the bond of an associating and uniting agreement, communicate among themselves whatever is appropriate for a comfortable life of soul and body. In other words, they are participants or partners

---

42. Althusius, *Politica*, 23 [1.26–27].

in a common life."[43] This symbiosis is an interdependent relation of whole and parts. That is, each part depends on the whole for its existence, for no carpenter (for example) can achieve mastery without living with and depending on the service of farmers (and vice versa). Thus, for mastery one is dependent on a particular whole— on a particular group of people.

Regardless of man's state, excellence in any given vocation is not a trait of birth or something innate. Practical knowledge is acquired. If it were innate, then vocation would be an innate calling, not one by choice, circumstances, or family relations. But one's vocation, though a providential calling, is not a purely natural calling. It is similar to choice in marriage: while one should seek a naturally fitting spouse, one is not bound by his or her nature to marry a specific person. Likewise, one's vocation should be naturally fitting given his endowments, but his vocation is not, on that account, innately natural to him, as if doing any other trade or craft is fundamentally contrary to his nature. Furthermore, it is hard to separate excellence in some art from the time one gave to acquire it. Time spent mastering something creates a sort of intimacy with the material involved. As an early 20th–century author on craftsmanship said about wheelwrights, they "were friends, as only a craftsman can be, with timber and iron. The grain of wood told secrets to them."[44] Knowledge of

---

43. Ibid., 19 [1.6]. Calvin recognizes this in his commentary on Isaiah: "Were [men] alone, they could not plough, or reap, or perform other offices indispensable to their subsistence, or supply themselves with the necessaries of life. For God has linked men so closely together, that they need the assistance and labor of each other; and none but a madman would disdain other men as hurtful or useless to him." *Commentary on the Prophet Isaiah*, vol. 7 of *Calvin's Commentaries*, 1:172 [on Isaiah 5:8].

44. George Stuart, *Wheelwright's Shop* (Cambridge: Cambridge University Press, 1923), 54–55.

the material assumes time spent with it. Mastery assumes that one underwent a process of mastering, and this is a large part of why we celebrate such people. If mastery were innate, then we would have to see the process of acquiring mastery as a necessary evil, and thus our efforts to improve in some skill is a product of the curse. Since this conclusion violates our basic instincts about self-improvement and the experience of mastering, we can safely affirm that vocational skill, even in the state of integrity, is acquired by instruction, time, experience, and practice.[45] This means that maturing in skill would have been a feature of life and also that people-groups would pass on these skills to new generations—no doubt inflected with each group's particular way or style of exercising this skill.

This system of mechanical arts takes on a higher, more distinctively human quality than mere material interdependence. After all, even non-rational animals group together in a sort of symbiosis, each member having its role for a well-functioning whole. For civil societies, the "communication of gifts" (as Althusius put it) involves consciously working for the common good. One aims at the common good through his productive activity. This act is above mere instinct and animality; it is self- and others-conscious and falls under a moral relation. The products of our labor embody our will for another's good—the sort of communication that non-moral animals cannot perform. In receiving these products for use (either through exchange or gift), one can recognize the producer's good will by means of the product. For example, when you make something with your own hands and give it to another, you want her not only to enjoy that gift but also to recognize that *you* made it for *her*

---

45. Immaturity in practical skills does not entail immorality, for then a toddler's struggle to walk would be a moral failure.

enjoyment. There is a sort of reciprocation at work here: the good of your productive activity is completed in another's recognition of your excellence in it *for them*.

A similar reciprocation can occur in civil society. Since all aim at the common good in their work and all receive these products in recognition of that collective good will, all work for and receive from all. The combined products of labor manifest a common will for the common good. Hence, the production and enjoyment of products are thought in terms of the first-person plural—*we* made this for all, and *we* recognize it as our will for our good. In this sort of bounded, particular community, one most intensely loves his neighbor as himself.

Civil fellowship extends beyond a relation of production. It includes place-making, aesthetic judgment, conversations on contemplative things, expression of wonder, and ordered liberty (some of which I discuss in subsequent chapters). We desire to do all these things with others. Sacred fellowship, which is another type of fellowship, is an otherworldly, heaven-oriented fellowship for worship and the good of the soul, and it also draws people together. Hence, we come together not only to secure bodily protection and needs, as many animals do, but for reasons distinctive to man, which are suitable for our higher dignity. The satisfaction of these needs requires a certain boundedness that constitutes a particular people and place.

Natural Limitedness

Man by nature, even when having full command of his faculties, is not only an earth-bound being but a place-bound being. He dwells in a particular place and can move long distances only with great trouble. Everyday interactions with others are limited by a locale, and he is ignorant of events and individuals in faraway places and even in the next town over. The fall did not cause this. The fall did not eliminate some faculty through which man receives knowledge of all happenings and individuals on earth. We are limited beings by design. One's presence is delimited by the body and sense-experience, being the only means for immediate knowledge of our surroundings. All other knowledge of the world outside this experience is *mediated* knowledge, communicated by another in some way. All this is commonsense, of course, but it is not trivial. Our natural limitedness entails that individuals mature within a delimited space of interaction, and communities develop from these interactions and are themselves partly independent from other communities. Individuals and communities mature and develop in a localized space.

Once a group leaves a developed community and establishes a community elsewhere, it begins to take on its own unique characteristics, largely through spontaneous coordination, deliberation, and collective judgment. In many if not most cases, the community would be relatively independent from others, since not all places on earth are suitable for human dwelling. There would be geographic separation and uninhabited space between them. Thus, the culture and institutions that develop in these new places would be distinct vis-à-vis other communities. Would each community produce the same style of dance, music, dress, stories, food, manners, games, and productive specialties? Would the language remain exactly the same? Likely not. The particularities of culture, language, and literary arts are not innate to man. They flow from common principles, but localized interaction shapes their application and generation.

Thus, an unfallen world would host diverse ways of life. But diversity is not merely a consequence of geography interacting with epistemic limitedness. Man's limitedness is also expressed in the natural need for a sort of directed gregariousness. That is, he is close at heart with a particular, bounded people, who ground and confirm his way of life in the world and who provide for him his most cherished goods. Unfallen man is benevolent to all but can only be beneficent (i.e., act for the good of) to some, and this limitation is based not merely in geographic closeness but in shared understanding, expectations, and culture. I describe boundedness in greater detail in chapter 3.

Cultural diversity is, therefore, a necessary consequence of human nature, and so it is *good* for us. It is good that particular practices are made habitual by localized socialization and are "owned" in a sense by a particular place and people. It is good that the particularity of each community distinguishes it from the others. Even the in-group/out-group distinction is good, since it establishes who "we" are in relation to "them"—effectively bounding particular expectations and preserving cultural distinctives. Man's limitedness was not a divine mistake; neither is cultural diversity, separated geographically, an error. It was God's design for man and thus a necessary feature of his good.

Human gregariousness and limitedness lead us to constitute civil governments for our good. I demonstrate this in the next section. But in this section we should note that civil governance drives cultural diversity. Since civil rulers are men, they have natural human limitedness, restricting the extent of their governance in terms of geographic space. They can only govern so much and only so many people. This consideration led Samuel Willard to conclude that

as the world had began to be peopled, there would of necessity have been a multiplying of civil societies, and these distinct, for the upholding of civil commerce and amity. They are
therefore in a great error who tell us that so many kingdoms
or commonwealths as there are in the world, so many testi-
monies of divine displeasure.[46]

Thus, civil governments, having necessarily bounded jurisdictions, will promote cultural distinctives, not only through official
promotion of these distinctives but by binding people to one another under a particular set of laws in a particular place.

I have more to say about nations, ethnicity, and cultural diversity in the next few chapters, including the argument that man, by
his nature, requires particularity and must dwell among similar
people to live well. But my account here at least prepares us for
the following chapters.

IV. Civil Order and Civil Virtue

Hierarchy, Civil Subjection, and Inequality

The egalitarian spirit of our age leads us to imagine that the state of
integrity would be one of perfect equality. But this is fairly novel in
the Christian tradition. Indeed, inegalitarian principles are so common and foundational in the Christian political tradition that one
might call inegalitarianism a catholic political doctrine. Inequality
in bodily stature, beauty, knowledge, virtue, domestic authority,
and civil authority were regularly affirmed as good and not due to
the fall. Aquinas states, for example, that "some would have made

46. Willard, *Body of Divinity*, loc. 37666.

a greater advance in virtue and knowledge than others." On bodily disparities, he states that differences in food sources, climate, and other factors would make some "more robust . . . and also greater, and more beautiful, and all ways better disposed."[47] Here, he has in mind not only individual difference but also differences between groups. Of course, the inferior are not ascribed some natural defect; good things of the same class can differ in excellence.[48] As Calvin states, "[T]here would have been, I allow, a difference of endowments had nature remained perfect," though all "would be alike in their integrity."[49] Herman Bavinck also speaks of "disparities" in the state of integrity:

> The history of the human race did not begin atomistically, with a group of isolated individuals, but organically, with a marriage and a family. . . . The disparity, which we presently observe everywhere in human society, is in principle and in essence not a result of sin, as many people thought in earlier and later times, but it existed from the beginning, even before sin entered the world.[50]

47. Thomas Aquinas, *Summa Theologica of St. Thomas Aquinas* (*ST*), trans. Father of the English Dominican Province (New York: Benzinger Brothers, 1920), I.96.3.

48. Aquinas writes, "The perfection of the universe is obtained essentially through a diversification of natures, which natures, so diversified, fill the various ranks of goodness; it is not obtained through the purification of the individuals in any of these given natures." *Commentary on the Sentences,* I.44.2.6, quoted in *The Political Ideas of St. Thomas Aquinas,* trans. Dino Bigongiari (New York: Free Press, 1953), xi.

49. Calvin, *Commentaries on the Twelve Minor Prophets,* trans. John Owen, vol. 15 of *Calvin's Commentaries* (Grand Rapids: Baker Books, 2005), 5:477 [on Mal. 1:2–6]. Willard states, "Had man abode in his primitive state, there would have been always some naturally superior to others." *Body of Divinity,* loc. 37675.

50. Bavinck, *Christian Family,* 109.

Now, those who are subject to superiors are (theoretically speaking) either slaves or free subjects. Slaves are not only instruments of a master, but are also instruments whose "good" is nothing but the good of the master. As Aquinas states, "[E]very man's proper good is desirable to himself, and consequently it is a grievous matter to anyone to yield to another what ought to be one's own." Thus, slavery violates a principle of human nature and so is forbidden in the state of integrity. Free subjects, however, submit to an authority that, as Aquinas says, directs him "towards his proper welfare, or to the common good."[51] The wife is subject to her husband, children to their parents, and citizens to their civil rulers. Instead of speaking of superior or inferior gifts (or skills, talents, etc.), it is more precise to say that the possession of certain gifts makes one suitable for a position of superiority and others suitable for obedience.

Hierarchy is, therefore, not some postlapsarian necessity. But neither is it morally neutral. It is good in itself, even of higher worth than egalitarian arrangements. Many in the Christian tradition would speak of the divine wisdom emanating from a diverse, hierarchical whole. For example, John Winthrop, in his famous sermon "A Model of Christian Charity," said,

> God Almighty in his most holy and wise providence, hath so
> disposed of the condition of mankind, as in all times some
> must be rich, some poor, some high and eminent in power
> and dignity; others mean and in submission . . . [in which he
> was] delighted to show forth the glory of his wisdom in the
> variety and difference of the creatures, and the glory of his

51. Aquinas, *ST*, I.96.4.

power in ordering all these differences for the preservation
and good of the whole.[52]

In his *City of God*, Augustine (borrowing from Cicero) used an
analogy of musical harmony, which Christian political theorists repeated for centuries up through the Reformation. Petrus Gregorius
(quoted by Althusius) stated it succinctly:

> Just as from lyres of diverse tones, if properly tuned, a sweet
> sound and pleasant harmony arise when low, medium, and high
> notes are united, so also the social unity of rulers and subjects
> in the state produces a sweet and pleasant harmony out of the
> rich, the poor, the workers, the farmers, and other kinds of per-
> sons. If agreement is thus achieved in society, a praiseworthy,
> happy, most durable, and almost divine concord is produced.[53]

The goodness of creation is not found in each part obtaining
equality with every other part, nor is the completeness of humanity

---

52. "A Modell of Christian Charitie," in *The Sacred Rights of Conscience: Selected Readings on Religious Liberty and Church-State Relations in the American Founding*, ed. Daniel Dreisbach and Mark David Hall (Indianapolis: Liberty Fund, 2009), 123, spelling modernized.

53. Gregorius, *De republica*, IV.1.5. Quoted in Althusius, *Politica*, 26 [1.38]. Echoing this tradition, Calvin writes, "For the system of proportional right in the Church is this—that while they communicate to each other mutually according to the measure of gifts and of necessity, this mutual contribution produces a befitting symmetry, though some have more, and some less, and gifts are distributed unequally." *Commentary on the Epistles of Paul the Apostle to the Corinthians*, trans. John Pringle, vol. 20 of *Calvin's Commentaries* (Grand Rapids: Baker Books, 2005), 2:296 [on 2. Cor. 8:14]. Calvin approvingly cites Aristotle. The editors of Calvin's translation cite the Reformed theologian J.H. Heidegger (1633–1698): "Equality must by all means be aimed at, but *proportional*, such as subsists among the members of the human body, according to which they are not, indeed, all held in same estimation or dignity, but all of them notwithstanding, that require ornament or clothing, are adorned and clothed." Ibid., 2:295n6.

achieved by eliminating superior/inferior relations. The diversity of ranks in human society, each performing its function for the whole, is society's perfection. Hence, by nature the perfection of human societies assumes an inegalitarian principle.

Civil Government

Civil governments would have existed in the state of integrity. I am aware that important figures in the Christian tradition, such as Augustine and Martin Luther,[54] explicitly denied the necessity of civil government for an unfallen world. Others affirmed the necessity, and I am with this latter camp for the reasons I offer below.

Since each community has a diverse set of members—each member contributing his gifts to the whole—it would contain a multiplicity of interests, pursuits, and ends. All would share in ultimate ends, such as the good of the whole (i.e., the common good) and the glory of God, but *pen*ultimate ends would vary. Vocational diversity and complexity produce potentially clashing interests, which (absent some organizing agent) would destroy liberty and the health of the community itself. Clashing interests occur not from ill-will or from the neglect of neighbor, but from natural epistemic limitations: we cannot know in every case how our actions might hinder or frustrate others in pursuit of their ends. We can mutually affirm collective ends (viz., the end of the whole), but we lack access to knowledge of all individual ends. Clashing interests include externalities in production or in community development. For example, the construction of a

54. Martin Luther, likely following Augustine, states that "as to civil government (*politia*); before sin there was none; nor was it needed. For civil government is a necessary remedy for corrupt nature." *Commentary on Genesis*, 1:172 [on Gen. 2:16, 17]. This is, in my view, clearly false, since man must, by his nature, cooperate with others to live well, and cooperation requires some positive set of rules to coordinate collective action.

dam might harm those living downstream. Conflicts in land-use and materials might occur as well. The interest of one trade might conflict with another's. In such cases, the absence of rules hinders liberty. Shared rules coordinate diverse activities and provide order and a well-functioning symbiosis.[55]

Not all rules require a rule-maker; rule-making is often spontaneous and decentralized. People interact with others and observe which actions have worked for mutual benefit. Subsequently, they self-sort, form hierarchies, and adopt effective practices and mutually understood rules with little deliberation and centralized decision-making. But not all problems are easily resolved in a decentralized way, especially in complex communities; and many inconveniences arise when there is no authority that guides the whole. Civil communities, therefore, require governors—those who direct, guide, and coordinate the many to their common end. As Althusius writes, "It pertains to the office of a governor not only to preserve something unharmed, but also to lead it to its end."[56] And as Willard writes, "Mankind cannot live like men, unless they

---

55. Aquinas argued for the necessity of civil government as well. He writes, "If, then, it is natural for man to live in society of many, it is necessary that there exists among men some means by which the group may be governed. For where there are many men together and each one is looking after his own interest, the multitude would be broken up and scattered unless there were also an agency to take care of what pertains to the commonweal.... [T]here must exist something which impels towards the common good of the many, over and above that which impels towards the particular good of each individual." *On Kingship: To the King of Cyprus*, trans. Gerald B. Phelan (Toronto: Aeterna Press, 1949), §8, 9.

56. Althusius, *Politica*, 21 [1.13]. Aquinas writes, "[B]ecause man is naturally a social being, and so in the state of innocence he would have led a social life. Now a social life cannot exist among a number of people unless under the presidency of one to look after the common good; for many, as such, seek many things, whereas one attends only to one. Wherefore the Philosopher says, in the beginning of the Politics, that wherever many things are directed to one, we shall always find one at the head directing them." *ST*, I.96.4.

combine in societies, who must mutually support each other. Civil societies cannot uphold this combination comfortably without government, but must become a mere rout and either disband or be a continual plague one to another."[57]

The ordering agent of civil society, even in a prelapsarian world, is civil government. Its original function is not to restrain sin, since it orders an unfallen people. Its purpose is positive: it reconciles the diverse interests of families and vocations in order to establish and maintain civil peace. Civil government accomplishes its end with deliberation, and by enacting and promulgating civil law. Unfallen subjects would willingly submit to these laws, trusting that the laws are for their good and will assist them in loving their neighbors. As I'll argue in chapter 6, laws do not require civil penalties by definition, but such penalties are effective in a fallen world to shore up societal law-keeping. What motivates individuals to obey the law is the end of the law: one's good and that of one's neighbor, toward which the laws order.

The necessity of civil government also follows from the inequality of gifts. Aquinas argues that it would not be "fitting" for one to possess great gifts if not for the "benefit of others."[58] That is, egalitarian social arrangements leave no means for those suited for command to govern others, and therefore nature would be in contradiction, if egalitarianism were natural. Thus, the necessity of civil hierarchy, and the denial of egalitarianism, follows from the existence of unequal civil virtue by nature. We can also conclude that a natural aristocracy would arise in each community to rule, establishing a rule by the best. And while these leaders would possess

57. Willard, *Body of Divinity*, loc. 38495.
58. Aquinas, *ST*, 1.96.4.

humility and magnanimity, they would nevertheless assume their rank with proper dignity and self-respect. This would be naturally fitting, for as Althusius says, "[I]t is inborn to the more powerful and prudent to dominate and rule weaker men, just as it is also considered inborn for inferiors to submit."[59] Still, all civil rule is by consent of the ruled, as I show in chapter 7. Consent remains the efficient cause of civil society and is expressed when one pledges his service to the whole by participating in and benefiting from the symbiosis under the direction of government.

Since civil society is a composition of households and men are the head of households, the public signaling of political interest (whether through voting or other mechanisms) would be conducted by men, for they represent their households and everyone in it. Vocational associations (or *collegia*) would likely be male-dominated as well, because households as productive operations would participate in them, and men would represent their households in them. This would be ubiquitous around the world, as it follows logically from the divinely ordained (and hence universal), hierarchical arrangement of the household.[60]

---

59. Althusius, *Politica*, 26 [1.38]. There is a sort of natural equality between all men, which I discuss in chapter 7.

60. One might try to deny this conclusion by insisting on an individualist basis for civil society. But if one affirms male-headship in households *and* individualism, then household representation is an empty title (lacking a distinct outward-facing end), for the woman (the non-head) would have just as much access to political participation. It is contradictory or at least creates an empty title. One could affirm non-gender-specific household headship and a corporatist foundation for civil society. In this case, women could be the head of households. But this, (1) is still exclusionary (of those not deemed head) and (2) contradicts both the creation narrative and the Christian tradition. Whether or not unmarried people (both men and women) and widows (in a fallen world) can participate in politics is a matter of prudence and subject to the determination of each community.

Lastly, I'll briefly address the relationship of Adam to civil leaders in a state of integrity. Adam is the head of the human race, but not in a civil sense. He is the *covenantal* head, meaning that he represents his progeny in all that pertains to the covenant, and the covenant is binding through him to all his progeny. Whatever special acts are required in the covenant, I suspect he would have to perform them (e.g., killing the serpent). He is also owed supreme paternal reverence by all his progeny, though he doesn't rule over all in a civil sense. Adamic civil rule would not be possible or practicable anyway. Whether I'm right or wrong about Adam's right to rule, local civil authority would in either case be far more consequential in everyday life, since these authorities would intimately know the circumstances, characteristics, and needs of their communities.

Self-Preservation and Martial Virtue

The Reformed tradition broadly affirms that the duty of self-preservation is inherent to human nature. It is a property natural to all animals, including rational animals, though in addition to his body, man must preserve his soul. Self-preservation might seem to be postlapsarian, since we speak of it typically when countering violence with violence. But self-preservation would have been essential to the state of integrity. For one thing, man was to preserve his integrity through obedience. But another type of self-preserving is required, one that takes into consideration a world where sinful man is *possible* and adversaries roam (e.g., the serpent and fallen angels). Indeed, many theologians believe that one of Adam's covenantal tasks was protecting the garden and killing the serpent (and other creatures) that threatened its peace. This would seem to demand also that households and civil societies identify, resist, and defeat threats to both soul and body.

Threats from one's fellow man must be kept in consideration, for all were capable of sinning in ways other than eating from the tree of the knowledge of good and evil.[61] Thus, physical violence was always a possibility, both from sinful individuals and groups. Countering such violence with violence is the ordinary means to preserve one's life and the lives of those under your care. All life is a gift of God, and so self-defense protects a divine gift. The duty to conduct violence to preserve the good was not divinely authorized after the fall. It is a duty for man in all possible states, except the state of glory.[62] Since the ability to repel violence with violence requires martial virtues, martial virtue and training in martial excellence would have been a feature of life in the state of integrity.

But we should not limit martial virtue to repelling violence. It refers more generally to skills by which one subdues an opponent, and so it extends to subduing untamed beasts in the wilderness (viz., lands outside the Garden of Eden)[63] and perhaps to hunt-

61. Being under the natural law, Adam (and so his progeny) was bound to more commands than the prohibition on eating from this tree. Adam and his descendants could have violated any of these commands and brought sin into the world. Since any individual could sin, it follows from the principle of self-preservation that communities would prepare for the possible encounter with sinful individuals and even sinful groups.

62. This is not intended as a proof against Christian pacifism but rather is intended to argue that the duty of self-preservation is natural and hence extends into the prelapsarian state.

63. Thomas Aquinas denies that all beasts would be tame in the state of integrity. He writes, "In the opinion of some, those animals which now are fierce and kill others, would, in that state, have been tame, not only in regard to man, but also in regard to other animals. But this is quite unreasonable. For the nature of animals was not changed by man's sin, as if those whose nature now it is to devour the flesh of others, would then have lived on herbs, as the lion and falcon. . . . They would not, however, on this account have been excepted

ing game, especially megafauna.[64] It might surprise people but, as Bavinck states, "most Reformed theologians were of the opinion that eating meat was permitted to humans even before the flood and the fall."[65] Martial virtue was not, therefore, a sort of virtue in reserve in the case that sin might enter the world. It was an essential and active element of dominion and living well.

Since martial virtues involve physical strength, men would typically have this duty, and some degree of martial skill would be required of all men, as a necessary feature of their masculinity.[66] This is the case not because all would hunt or necessarily take part in military drills, but because each would need to protect his household. Martial virtue is, therefore, a necessary feature of masculine excellence, and effeminacy is no less a vice in a state of integrity than in a postlapsarian world.[67]

---

from the mastership of man: as neither at present are they for that reason excepted from the mastership of God, Whose Providence has ordained all this." *ST*, I.96.1.

64. Aquinas affirms that man has a "natural right" to hunt wild beasts. He writes, "Therefore it is in keeping with the order of nature, that man should be master over animals. Hence the Philosopher says (Polit. i, 5) that the hunting of wild animals is just and natural, because man thereby exercises a natural right." Ibid.

65. Bavinck, *RD*, 2:575. Bavinck directly addresses the objections to this position, including those that reference Genesis 9:3 [*RD*, 2:575–76]. He cites Calvin, Heidegger, Voetius, Coccejus, and others for support.

66. Militaries today have women service-members partly from egalitarian ideology; partly due to the bureaucratic, technical, service-based, and clerical nature of modern warfare; and partly due to an abundance of resources that permit inefficient allocation. Since man in a state of integrity would not have such resources—and would exist under conditions of scarcity and of necessity—I doubt that women (ordinarily) would take an active role in conducting the sorts of tasks for which martial skills are employed.

67. Heinrich Bullinger writes, "Dainty fools and effeminate hearts will not hazard the loss of a limb for their religion, magistrates, wives, children, and all their possessions." *The Decades of Henry Bullinger*, ed. Thomas Harding and trans. H.I. (1587; Grand Rapids: Reformation Heritage Books, 2004), 1:277 [Second Decade, Sermon v].

Civil Magistracy and Spiritual Ministry

In the state of integrity, the same people in civil fellowship are also in sacred fellowship. Membership in these fellowships is co-extensive, for each person is properly ordered toward both earthly and heavenly ends, and each fellowship aids in meeting one or the other end. But despite being co-extensive, we must not conflate the two fellowships. They are different species of fellowship, each serving directly only one aspect of man. They are different, because the two ends (as discussed above) are different in kind—one being otherworldly and seen by the eyes of faith (trusting in the promises of God for heavenly life), and the other being earthly and a matter of external works. Just as the body and soul of man are immutably distinct, so too are the fellowships that serve man, regardless of his state.

Civil fellowship exists under civil magistracy (or secular authority), which can touch only the external forum or body. By nature, the magistracy has no jurisdiction over the conscience, the inward part of man. Magistrates direct the public by means of civil command (promulgated as law), obligating people to particular outward actions. They cannot make laws concerning inward action, and hence they cannot command people to act according to the proper inward principles, such as exercising faith.[68] God alone is Lord of the conscience; nature supplies no mediator between man and God. Civil authority, for this reason, lacks the power to direct conscience, for civil law is in essence human command, and only God commands the conscience.

Spiritual fellowship, however, falls under spiritual ministry, which serves spiritual things to the soul, the inward being, in

68. See chapter 6 for a discussion on how civil law and civil command relate to the conscience.

which one acts to the glory of God and is oriented to the promised heavenly life. The definite form of this ministry in the state of integrity is not clear to me—whether it would be institutional or not, with official ministers or not—but, for our purposes, determining the definite form is irrelevant. Spiritual ministry, under natural religion, would have been the same in principle and end as we see in the instituted church in the state of grace: by this ministry, God is worshipped and man is exhorted to keep God as his ultimate end, to remember the covenant and God's promise of heavenly life, and to keep his law.[69] The means of administration would be similar as well, being primarily exhortation and remembrance, for fellow man (by nature) can address the soul only aurally. Perhaps, (as many have suggested) there would have been instituted prelapsarian Sacraments as well. Spiritual ministry was not created when God instituted the Church in the postlapsarian world; rather, upon instituting that church he deposited and entrusted that pre-existing ministry in it and to it.

What is most important is that, by the nature of man, civil magistracy and spiritual ministry are separate but complementary, and they are independent with regard to office but not opposed.[70] These two species of administration are distinguishable by their means (secular law and sacred things), their direct objects (body and

69. This sameness does not diminish the "in Christ" nature of the New Covenant but simply recognizes that natural religion—both its principles and chief end—remains fully operative and assumed by New Covenant ministry.

70. I see no reason why (in the state of integrity only) the same person could not rightly exercise both magistracy and ministry, though he would do this through two separate offices. He could not exercise both functions through the same office, for each has its own office. Nor does one office arise or receive its power from the other; they are independent, separate, and equal.

soul), and their immediate ends (civil peace and right conscience before God), but they have the same ultimate end—eternal life. Hence, both are ultimately oriented and subordinated to this higher end, and both are necessary for man to achieve his ends. Spiritual ministry is, in a sense, the soul of the community, not because it dominates secular magistracy, but because it serves the soul, which reigns over the body. Well-ordered individuals make well-ordered households and civil communities. Magistracy, for its part, serves the body, that it might in part facilitate the operations of the soul. Therefore, the two fellowships or relations, which fall under magistracy and ministry, are mutually supporting and serve to guide man to his earthly and heavenly ends.

The fact that civil government does not wield a spiritual sword or administer spiritual things for eternal life does not preclude it from erecting public religious displays (e.g., monuments), incorporating religious elements into civil events (e.g., evocations), or publicly supporting spiritual ministry. These functions fall under its outward jurisdiction that serve to encourage man in his inward worship and his outward work of dominion. Civil government cannot command people to contemplate heavenly things, but it can create the best outward conditions for such contemplation, which serve as visible reminders of the highest purposes for which man was created.

V. Conclusion

More could be said about the state of integrity, but this suffices to describe the nature of prelapsarian man and his potential social life. Adam's race, as it spread across the earth, would have formed distinct civil communities—each being culturally particular. The nation, therefore, is natural to man as man, and the matured earth would be a multiplicity of nations. I now turn to discuss how the fall and redeeming grace affect the nature of man and his social relations.

2

Redeemed Nations:
What Is Man? Part II: Fall and Redemption

"The Adamic human race perverts the cosmos; the Christian human race renews it." —Albert Wolters[1]

I. State of Sin

Having discussed man in his state of innocence, we now turn to the states of sin and grace. The intent is to identify the theological basis for continuity and discontinuity in social relations between the three states. In other words, what changed and what stayed the same in human society before and after the fall?

1. Albert Wolters, *Creation Regained: Biblical Basics for a Reformation Worldview,* 2nd ed. (Grand Rapids: Eerdmans, 2005), 69–73.

Total Depravity

The fall of man led to total depravity. In the 20th century especially, there has been considerable confusion, even in the Reformed world, over what this means. *Total* is not to be conflated with *utter* depravity, as if sinful man sins in every respect. Rather, sin affects every aspect of man's being—his intellect, will, desires, heart, etc. Corruption is thorough. But the Reformed doctrine of sin, as classically stated, did not assert the doctrine of *natura deleta*, as several Roman Catholic authors have alleged about Reformed doctrine.[2] That is, no Reformed theologian claimed that the fall of man separated man entirely from knowledge of the natural law and the ability to perform it. Nor did man lose the faculty of reason or even civil virtue. Indeed, the Reformed doctrine of sin as articulated by post-Reformation Reformed theologians is not unlike that of Roman Catholic Thomists.[3]

Recall that we distinguished the two species of gifts that God gave to man—natural and supernatural—or, perhaps better put, constitutive and perfective gifts. I said that the former (e.g., reason, body, understanding) are essential to man as man and principally concern earthly things. The perfective gifts are non-essential to man as such, but necessary for his perfection and his knowledge of, desire for, and ability to strive after eternal life and to worship God rightly in the heart. These latter gifts are primarily *inward*, since they provide the ability to perform theological good—a good conscience before God in all one's works. These are the highest gifts

2. Etienne Gilson, for example, writes that "the popular idea of a Christin universe corrupted in its very nature by sin owes much of it favour to the influence of Luther, Calvin, and Jansenius." *The Spirit of Medieval Philosophy* (Notre Dame: University of Notre Dame, 1936), 122. It seems more likely that this popular myth owes its favor to the influence of people like Gilson.

3. Turretin quotes Aquinas on the nature of the fall *against* Bellarmine. *IET*, 1:9.11.13.

and the principal part of the divine image. The two sets of gifts were necessary for man to be righteousness, in both his being and his actions. Hence, the loss of the perfective gifts alone makes man unrighteous in being and worthy of condemnation.

It might be surprising to discover that Reformed theologians, including Calvin, affirmed that man lost only the supernatural gifts at the fall. The natural gifts were corrupted but not lost. Calvin writes, for example, that man's natural gifts were corrupted by sin, and his supernatural gifts withdrawn; meaning by supernatural gifts the light of faith and righteousness, which would have been sufficient for the attainment of heavenly life and everlasting felicity.[4] The devastation of the fall is found in man's inability to worship God in heart to attain his ultimate heavenly end. Man can no longer choose spiritual things or achieve theological good. He can no longer perfect outward action with proper inward spiritual obedience.[5] Man lost his chief good—the divine image that ensured his righteousness and holiness. As Jonathan Edwards wrote, "For immediately his image, his holy spirit, and original righteousness, which was the highest and best life of our first parents, were lost; and they were immediately in a doleful state of spiritual death."[6]

4. Calvin, *Institutes*, 2.2.12.

5. Peter Martyr Vermigli writes, "But once [Adam] had sinned, immediately crookedness ensued. He no longer regards God and heavenly things any more but is continually bent toward earthly and carnal things and is bound to the constraints of concupiscence. That is what it means to lack original righteousness, since actions have not been taken away from human beings, but the power of acting well is removed." *On Original Sin*, ed. Kirk Summers (Lincoln, NE: Davenant Press, 2019), 31.

6. Jonathan Edwards, "Sermon XI: The Eternity of Hell Torments," in vol. 6 of *The Works of President Edwards* (New York: Carvill, 1830), 118. Turretin likewise wrote, "We maintain that the loss of the divine image (or of original righteousness) followed the fall of Adam doubly—both meritoriously and morally (on account of the divine ordination) and efficiently and really (on account of the heaviness of that sin)." *IET*, 1:9.8.5.

Thus, the chief effect of the fall concerned what is invisible to man and visible only to God. The natural or constitutive gifts remain, though "corrupted," because such gifts could not be "polluted in themselves," states Calvin. Indeed, "reason, by which man discerns good and evil, and by which he understands and judges, is a natural gift, [so] it could not be entirely destroyed [by the fall]."[7] Turretin argues that in losing original righteousness "nature indeed remains mutilated and depraved (since it has lost what perfected it) but is not destroyed as to essence."[8] The absence of original righteousness, however, introduces an active and efficacious inclination toward evil.

Civil Virtue

Since the fall did not eliminate the natural gifts, it follows that man did not lose the knowledge of the principles and the faculties that most concerned his outward, earthly life.[9] He retained his basic instincts for social relations. Reformed writers, for this reason, have used remarkably positive language when describing man's

---

7. Calvin, *Institutes*, 2.2.16, 12.

8. Turretin, *IET*, 1:5.11.11.

9. Herman Bavinck writes, "Since after the fall people have remained human and continue to share in the blessings of God's common grace, they can inwardly possess many virtues and outwardly do many good deeds that, viewed through human eyes and measured by human standards, are greatly to be appreciated and of great value for human life. But this is not to say that they are good in the eyes of God and correspond to the full spiritual sense of his holy law." *Reformed Dogmatics*, ed. John Bolt and trans. John Vriend, vol. 4, *Holy Spirit, Church, and New Creation* (Grand Rapids: Baker Academic, 2008), 256–57. Willard writes, "Though sin has depraved man's whole nature, so that there remains no theological goodness in him naturally; yet there are few sinners, if any in this world, that are utterly debauched, but that they have some principles of morality abiding and active in them; what are a civil ornament to them, and so far commend them to the liking of men." *Body of Divinity*, loc. 13787.

capabilities and actions with regard to civil virtue.[10] Althusius wrote, for example, that "in political life even an infidel may be called just, innocent, and upright."[11] Calvin states that "all men have impressions of civil order and honesty." They "comprehend the principles" of civil law and have "universal agreement in regard to such subjects, both among nations and individuals" and "their ideas of equity agree in substance."[12] The "consent of all nations" on "principles of equity and justice" is the "voice of nature."[13] Turretin states that "the consent of the nations . . . [shows that] even without a teacher they [pagan nations] have learned that God should be worshipped, parents honored, a virtuous life be led and from which as a fountain

---

10. Willard writes, for example, that "[t]here is a great deal which a man may do in morality, by the improvement of his natural powers, with the common assistance of the Spirit of God. We are here warily to distinguish between the Moral Powers which belong to the nature of man, and the Moral Image which was connatural to him in his state of integrity: this latter indeed is lost by the Apostasy, but the former abides, as belonging essentially to humanity, though this is very much crazed, and hath lost a great deal of its vigour. And, although the power of lust be so strong in natural men, that they cannot of themselves alone withstand the impetuosity of it, yet the Moral Powers which remain in the man, may be so far improved by the common influences of the Spirit of God, which he affords to some, on whom he doth not bestow his Sanctifying Grace, as to make a natural man to proceed far in compliance with the Law." *Morality not to be relied on for life* (Boston: B. Green and J. Allen, 1700), 8–9.

11. Althusius, *Politica*, 147 [21.41].

12. Calvin, *Institutes*, 2.2.13. Elsewhere, Calvin writes, "But as some principles of equity and justice remain in the hearts of men, the consent of all nations is as it were the voice of nature, or the testimony of that equity which is engraven on the hearts of men, and which they can never obliterate." *Commentaries on the Twelve Minor Prophets*, trans. John Owen, vol. 14 of *Calvin's Commentaries* (Grand Rapids: Baker Books, 2005), 4:92–93 [on Hab. 2:6].

13. Herman Bavinck, *Reformed Dogmatics*, ed. John Bolt and trans. John Vriend, vol. 3, *Sin and Salvation in Christ* (Grand Rapids: Baker Academic, 2006), 134. Bavinck goes on: "With respect to the moral commandments of the second table of the law there is always much agreement among the nations, inasmuch as the work of the law continues to be written on their hearts." The Second Helvetic Confession states, "In regard to earthly things, fallen man is not entirely lacking in understanding" (ch. 9).

have flowed so many laws concerning equity and virtue enacted by heathen legislatures, drawn from nature itself."[14] Fallen man cannot please God in his works, but his actions can be good as to outward duty, and, generally speaking, fallen man's actions reflect knowledge of natural principles (even when he errs in applying them).[15]

It follows that the fallen world, though very different from what could have been, is not radically different from the state of integrity with regard to the *principles* of social relations. Bavinck writes,

> All the essential components existing today were present also
> before the fall. The distinctions and dissimilarities between men
> and women, parents and children, brothers and sisters, relatives

---

14. Turretin continues: "And if certain laws are found among some repugnant to these principles, they were even with reluctance received and observed by a few, at length abrogated by contrary laws, and have fallen into desuetude." *IET*, 2:11.1.13.

15. Calvin writes, "When they speak of works morally good, they refer only to the outward deeds; they regard not the fountain or motive, nor even the end. When the heart of man is impure, unquestionably the work which thence flows is also ever impure, and is an abomination before God." *Commentaries on the Twelve Minor Prophets*, 3:67 [on Jonah 1:16]. Ursinus writes, "The difference which exists between the works of the righteous and the wicked, goes to prove that the moral works of the wicked are sins, but yet not such sins as those which are in their own nature opposed to the law of God: for these are sins in themselves, and according to their very nature, while the moral works of the wicked are sins merely by an accident; viz., on account of some defect, either because they do not proceed from a true faith, or are not done to the glory of God." *Commentary on Heidelberg Catechism*, 849. Althusius wrote, "If the external and civil life of words, deeds and works is accompanied by faith—together with holiness of thought and desire, and with right purpose, namely, the glory of God—then it becomes theological. So therefore, when the works of the Decalogue are performed by the Christian to the glory of God because of true faith, they are pleasing to God." *Politica*, 147 [21.41]. Turretin writes, "Although various practical notions have been obscured after sin and for a time even obliterated, it does not follow either that they were entirely extinguished or that they never existed at all. For the commonest principle (that good should be done and evil avoided) is unshaken in all, although in the particular conclusions and in the determination of it good men may often err because vice deceives us under the appearance and shadow of virtue." *IET*, 2:11.1.20.

and friends; the numerous institutions and relations in the life of society such as marriage, family, child rearing, and so forth; the alternation of day and night, workdays and the day of rest, labor and leisure, months and years; man's dominion over the earth through science and art, and so forth—while all these things have undoubtedly been modified by sin and changed in appearance, they nevertheless have their active principle and foundation in creation, in the ordinances of God, and not in sin.[16]

Certainly, the effects of sin are all around us: Man rebels against God and commits varieties of moral offenses against his fellow man. Polygamy was prevalent; domestic and civil tyranny is common; people defraud their fellow man; nations unjustly dominate others. But these are *abuses* of these relations. The fundamental relations of man—domestic, kin, national, international, civil, and spiritual— are ubiquitous among fallen man, because natural law, reason, and instinct remain operative. As Charles Hodge wrote, commenting on Romans 9:3, "The Bible recognizes the validity and rightness of all the constitutional principles and impulses of our nature. It therefore approves of parental and filial affection, and, as is plain from this and other passages, of peculiar love for the people of own race and country."[17] Thus, the basic, near-universal structures of our fallen world—and the instincts we have for these structures—help us to imagine what an unfallen world would be like. Our fundamental

16. Bavinck, *RD*, 2:576.

17. Charles Hodge, *Commentary on the Epistle to the Romans* (1835; Grand Rapids: Eerdmans, 1993), 298. In Romans 9:3, the apostle Paul wishes that he could be "accursed from Christ for my brethren." By "race" Hodges has in mind (as he states) those of "natural descent from the same parent" (ibid.). See the next chapter for my view of the role of natural descent in nationhood.

instincts—say, a mother's preference for her own children—are reliable; they say something about our nature *as created*. The same is true of our instincts or "biases" for our own people and country. These are natural to us by design. We can further conclude that the diversity of nations throughout history is not a product of the fall but of human nature.

Augmentation of Institutions

In the state of integrity, civil government is necessary to direct well-intentioned, though inherently uncoordinated, individuals to the common good. However, the introduction of sin causes social disharmony. To achieve its purpose, civil government now must be *augmented* with the power to suppress sin "else all would certainly run into confusion and end in ruin," writes Willard.[18] Augmentation is not the same as modification. An augmentation extends the functions of what is augmented to new objects with expanded means in order to enable or strengthen the original whole for its original end. Thus, even after augmentation, civil government continues to apply the same principles (natural law), use the same fundamental means (civil law), and retain the same end (civil peace), but now (by divine authorization) it uses coercion and targets public vice. The end of civil government has not changed, because its end is subordinate to the ends of human nature, and human nature *in itself* has not changed. Civil government is not, in origin, a postfall *ad hoc* institution intended only to preserve sinful mankind. It is necessary by the nature of man and serves man for his good. Hence, even after the fall, civil government must enact the best possible

18. Willard, *Body of Divinity*, loc. 37646.

outward conditions for man to pursue his proper ends. Indeed, this is precisely why civil government must be augmented—to shore up its ability to achieve its original role in relation to man. If something is natural to man, then civil government must provide conditions for people to freely and harmoniously pursue it. This includes suppressing the things that hinder man in achieving his full humanity.

The nature and degree of augmentation of civil government must be sufficient for civil government to shore up its role in ordering civil society. The *means* must always be suitable for its *ends*. Thus, if politics is the art of establishing and cultivating necessary conditions for social life for the good of man, then post-fall political order must have what is necessary to enact and enforce those ends. Civil rulers must have sufficient license to fulfill their calling. I am not saying that the ends justify the means, but that any justified means must be suitable for its end. A set of political principles that are ineffective for governance and inadequate to shore up civil order for man's complete good is not from God, no matter how lofty or "moral" those principles might appear to be.

Nevertheless, civil government in a postlapsarian world is limited on *how well* it can establish and sustain conditions for good. It must prioritize its objectives. The first objective is the preservation of civil society, and so civil government is rightly called a "kingdom of preservation." But this does not imply a modification or fundamental change of purpose, for preservation was *always* essential to its end. Nor is a bare preservation its *only* objective. Again, civil government was necessary, from the beginning, to establish and preserve social relations for our good. Civil government in a postlapsarian world must implement and preserve the *best possible* conditions for man to pursue his good. In other words, the fall of man did not rescind functions of civil government in principle, but it practically limits the degree to which civil government can achieve its original purposes. Furthermore, given the sinful state of mankind, civil magistrates must make difficult decisions between options that have competing goods. Choosing for some good x means losing some good y. Though this type of choice is itself not due to the fall, for it is based in natural scarcity, the fall introduced choices between greater and lesser goods that might cause or result in harm. Hence, crafting policy (and ethics generally) in a fallen world requires us to consider unpleasant trade-offs, and magistrates must have the fortitude to enact and enforce the greatest good, despite unfortunate costs involved, and Christians should recognize the *necessity* of such choices and shun the moralism that limits action.

Lastly, we should recognize that, on account of the fall, natural hierarchical power is now abused. Checks on authority are therefore required to ensure good behavior, and these typically inject a degree of egalitarianism into the socio-political system. This might include free, frequent, and regular elections and other egalitarian institutions and norms, such as universal suffrage, civil rights, and anti-discrimination labor laws. These are, however, all postlapsarian institutions and norms, intended only to prevent the abuse of power, and they are not purely natural to humankind.[19] The right to vote or hold office, for

---

19. Anglo-American civil rights, though we relate to them as natural, were developed over centuries in response to abuse (e.g., the Magna Carta and English Bill of Rights). In the American founding era and prior to the Declaration of Independence, American patriots claimed that the English Crown had violated their "English liberty" and their rights as "natural-born subjects within the realm of England." "Declaration and Resolves of the First Continental Congress," October 14, 1774, accessed September 26, 2022, https://avalon.law.yale.edu/18th_century/resolves.asp. I affirm the existence of natural rights, but most rights are civil and particular (e.g., habeas corpus, ex post facto, and jury trial)—products of civilizational development—intended to secure natural rights and ensure a commodious and just civil society.

example, are not natural or human rights. Indeed, many such institutions, norms, and rights, which today we consider essential to civil justice, are merely checks on abuse and would be unnecessary if abuses were absent. Thus, they are *positive* rights, not strictly natural, and are a particularity of a people—an inheritance from ancestors—not things owed by "inviolable dignity." It follows that the more righteous the community, the fewer required egalitarian institutions.

Conclusion

Since the principal effect of the fall was the loss of man's perfective gifts, which oriented him to heaven, man's outward sins with regard to earthly life are largely *abuses* of natural principles of social relations. We see these underlying natural principles manifesting almost universally in human society. Civil government, which would have been a necessary feature of unfallen life, is augmented (not modified) to shore up its role in human relations, though it retains the same principles and end. The question for us becomes, "What is the role of grace in relation to nature?"

II. State of Grace

The Moral Law as Covenant and as Rule

Civil life, indeed nature itself, cannot remedy man's sinful state. God as the creator did not include in creation an inherent means to reconcile sinful man and a holy God. Salvation required a gracious act of God as redeemer. By trusting in the person and finished work of Christ, one is reconciled to God (i.e., justified) and enters the covenant of grace. Obtaining a title to eternal life is no longer conditioned on working; rather, one possesses a title to eternal life by faith in Christ. The substance of this eternal life was not introduced in the Gospel: it is the same life promised to Adam. As Bavinck states, "The covenant of grace differs from the covenant of works in method, not in its ultimate goal. It is the same treasure that was promised in the covenant of works that is granted in the covenant of grace."[20] Redeemed man is not only restored to Adam's state of integrity; he is given a full deposit of the glory promised to Adam.

It is crucial to recognize that though having a title to eternal life rescinds our relationship to the moral law as a *condition of works* for eternal life, the moral law still remains our only *rule* for duty and happiness in this life. Or, as New England theologian Cotton Mather states,

> We are not under the law as a *covenant of works*: our own exactness in performing good is not now the condition of entering into life; (wo be to us if it were) but still, the *covenant of grace* holds us to it as our *duty*: and if we are in the covenant of grace, we shall make it our study to perform those good works which were once the condition of entering into life.[21]

20. Bavinck, *RD*, 3:577–78. Elsewhere, he writes, "religion, the moral law, and man's final destiny are essentially the same in both the covenant of works and the covenant of grace. In both the goal and end is a kingdom of God, a holy humanity, in which God is all in all." *RD*, 2:577–58. John Brown of Haddington writes, "[Adam's] eternal life would have been the same in substance with that which believers enjoy there, through Christ." *Systematic Theology*, 201. Turretin writes, "For as [Christ] rendered to God the Father no other obedience than what the law demanded, so by fulfilling the law, he acquired no other life than what was promised by the law. . . . Christ died that through him we might recover what we lost in Adam and merited for us eternal life." *IET*, 1:8.6.5. Later he states, "The promises of the new covenant are said to be 'better' than those of the old (Heb. 8:6), not as to substance (because the same heavenly and eternal life is promised in both), but as to mode (because . . . they were acquired in a far nobler manner through Christ. . . .)" (ibid., 8.6.13).
21. Cotton Mather, *Essays to do Good addressed to all Christians, whether in public or private* (1710; Boston: Lincoln and Edmands, 1807), 35–36.

Thus, whatever was required of the covenant *in terms of its moral content* remains required of the Christian. The content of duty has not changed. Working is no longer about obtaining eternal life; good works—which accord with the moral law—are "the way appointed to eternal life," says John Davenant.[22] This is more evident in the Reformed view of sanctification.

Definitive Sanctification

The state of grace in Reformed theology involves both the pardoning of guilt (i.e., justification) and the sanctification of moral pollution. Sanctification most concerns us here. Recall that total depravity means that the fall affects every aspect of man's being, though not to the same degree (some gifts being entirely lost). Now, just as depravity was total, sanctification is total as well. It affects the whole being. Theologians have called this "definitive sanctification." The sanctified on earth are not perfect, but all the gifts that were either eliminated or corrupted by the fall are restored. *Grace restores nature* and thereby completes man with the full complement of prelapsarian gifts. As Bavinck states, "Regeneration . . . restores to us what we, in keeping with the design of our being, should have but lost as a result of sin. In principle it restores us to the likeness and image of God."[23]

Just as the principal effect of the fall was the utter loss of supernatural gifts, redemption is principally the restoration of these gifts. In particular, total sanctification restores the divine image. Calvin states, for example, that "spiritual regeneration is nothing else than

---

22. For example, John Davenant writes, "Good works are necessary to the salvation of the justified . . . as the way appointed to eternal life, not as the meritorious cause of eternal life." *A Treatise on Justification*, trans. Josiah Allport (London: Hamilton, Adams, 1844), 1:302.

23. Bavinck, *RD*, 4:93.

the restoration of the same image [given to and lost by Adam]."[24]
Turretin writes that the "renewed" image of God is "the spiritual image (as to supernatural gifts)" (*IET*, 1:5.10.2). The restored image is
the same in substance as that which Adam possessed before his fall,
which oriented his heart to heavenly life.[25] Again, Bavinck clarifies:

> Hence, though these are new qualities that regeneration implants
> in a person, they are nevertheless no other than those that belong
> to human nature, just as health is the normal state of the body.
> They are "habits," dispositions, or inclinations that were original-
> ly included in the image of God and agreed with the law of God.[26]

Thus, definitive sanctification principally restores one to *true dignity* by re-infusing the perfective features of prelapsarian man: the
knowledge of and desire for eschatological life; the proper internal
principle, mode, and end of action; and the true worship of God.
These renewed gifts are not fictive; they are a *real* possession. The
believer is a complete human being, restored to integrity. The state
of grace is a state of restored integrity. Reformed theologians of
the 17th century were not scared of the term *inherent righteousness*.
Turretin writes, for example, that "we are renewed because we derive the Spirit from our head, Christ, who renews us after the image

---

24. Calvin, *Commentary on the First Book of Moses Called Genesis*, 1:94 [on Gen. 1:26].

25. As William Farel writes, "Righteousness is the true image of God, shining by the regeneration which is effected by the Word of God received by faith (1 Peter 1:3–5), and inscribed
on the hearts of the sons of God (Jer. 31:33). By it, men dead to themselves, renounce themselves and all things, love God solely having the heart for His holy law, draw away from all
terrestrial things, [and] burn for the celestial things." "William Farel's Summary (1529),"
in James T Dennison, comp., *Reformed Confessions of the 16th and 17th Centuries in English
Translations*, vol. 1, *1523–1552* (Grand Rapids: Reformation Heritage Books, 2008), 59.

26. Bavinck, *RD*, 4:94.

of Christ and bestows upon us inherent righteousness."[27] Willard states that we have "holiness in us":

> Christ is not our sanctification by way of imputation, as he is our righteousness, but as he is the author of our holiness in us, and the subject in whom all those graces are laid up which are requisite for our sanctification, as in a treasury, from whom they are to derive unto us, that so we may be sanctified by them; so that virtue proceeds from him to us for this end. And what is this communicated unto us for, but that we may hereby be enabled again to perform true obedience to the law or command of God, which we were before altogether incapable of doing? And this is by restoring of the Image of God again to us.[28]

Since man is restored to integrity, rectitude, and purity as to his faculties, he is capable of pleasing God in soul and body. Definitive sanctification, therefore, restores us to true obedience to the law of God, and progress in sanctification is not a process of transcending the law of God or of escaping it or fulfilling a new law.[29]

---

27. Turretin, *IET*, 2:16.3.6.

28. Samuel Willard, *The law established by the Gospel* (Boston, MA: Bartholomew Green, 1694), 28–29.

29. Grace does not abrogate, supersede, replace, correct, or add to the natural law as the standard of righteousness. Calvin affirms this in his exposition of the Sermon on the Mount: "We must not imagine Christ to be a new legislator, who adds any thing to the eternal righteousness of his Father." *Commentary on a Harmony of the Evangelists, Matthew, Mark, and Luke*, trans. William Pringle, vol. 16 of *Calvin's Commentaries* (Grand Rapids: Baker Books, 2003), 1:283 [on Matt. 5:21]. Turretin writes, "Is the moral law so perfect a rule of life and morals that nothing can be added to it or ought to be corrected in it for the true worship of God? Or did Christ fulfill it not only as imperfect, but also correct it as contrary to his doctrines? The former we affirm; the latter we deny against the Socinians, Anabaptists, Remonstrants, and papists." *IET*, 2:11.3, heading. This follows from the na-

Rather, we progress in conformity to the original and immutable law of God.[30]

Therefore, since grace restores to us the *same* gifts that Adam possessed, we are equipped for the *same* sort of works. Whatever tasks Adam had, Christians too have those tasks, for those tasks are the only *telos* of those gifts by their nature. Adam's original tasks were not simply a matter of divine command; these tasks are the ends of human nature as restored by grace. The tasks are inherent to the gifts as their natural ends.

Adam's Original Task
A brief critique of David VanDrunen will help clarify my argument. He writes,

> Christians will attain the original destiny of life in the world-to-come, but we do so not by picking up the task where Adam left off but by resting entirely on the work of Jesus Christ, the last Adam who accomplished the task perfectly.... *This is absolutely essential for issues of Christianity and culture!* If Christ is the *last Adam*, then we are not new Adams. To understand our own cultural work as picking up and finishing Adam's original task is, however, to compromise the sufficiency of Christ's work....

ture of sanctification. If grace restores to man what was native to Adam, then the moral law remains the only suitable rule for man to happiness and righteousness. As a matter of duty, both to God and himself, the Christian ought to exercise the fullness of his gifts toward their proper ends. Thereby, he obeys God, fulfills his nature, achieves his good, and attains happiness.

30. Ursinus writes, "The law alone, without the gospel, is the letter [that kills]. . . . But when it is joined with the gospel, which is the Spirit, it also commences to become the Spirit, which is effectual in the godly, inasmuch as those who are regenerated commence willingly and cheerfully to yield obedience to the law." *Commentary*, 617.

[Christ] achieved the new creation through his flawless obedience in this world. He has left nothing yet to be accomplished.[31]

VanDrunen's main target is neo-Calvinist transformationalism.
I reject transformationalism too, since I reject the idea that human
work can—whether by Adam or restored humanity—bring the
"new creation" to earth. As I stressed in chapter 1, human work
can *mature* the earth, but that work, apart from a divine act, will
remain below the state of glory. VanDrunen is correct in this sense:
if Adam's original task was to bring the world-to-come to earth by
human effort, then Christians "picking up and finishing" this work
would seem to deny Christ's sufficient work. That task—achieving
the condition for eternal life—was accomplished by Christ. But, as
I argued in the previous chapter, the premise is false: Adam's task—
as to the *content* of his task—was not to immanentize ultimate rest
on earth, or to build the heavenly kingdom of God on earth, or to
transform earth into heaven. The world-to-come was *always* a divine gift, not a work of man. The work of dominion for Adam would
not itself immanentize the state of glory, nor would it be sufficient
to merit eternal life. The *natural* end of his work was not eternal life.
Rather, *by grace*, God declared that Adam's obedience would meet
the condition for bestowing blessed life upon him.

Christ's work is sufficient to provide his people a title to eternal
life *and* to sanctify them, even in this world. No one "compromise[s]
the sufficiency of Christ's work" by taking up Adam's "original task"
with regard to his moral requirements. One can rest from trying to
merit eternal life and still labor according to the restored gifts that

---

31. David VanDrunen, *Living in God's Two Kingdoms: A Biblical Vision for Christianity and
Culture* (Wheaton, IL: Crossway, 2010), 50–51.

Adam originally possessed but lost. That is, one can and ought to mature earthly life for the good of oneself and one's fellow man. Indeed, in having these gifts restored to man, man ought to use them according to their inherent purpose. In doing so, Christians order earthly life according to natural principles to support their journey to heaven. Christians cannot bring heaven to earth, for Adam never had that ability in the first place, and Christians are not given any gifts beyond what was given to Adam. He could only *order* earthly life to the promised heavenly life.

VanDrunen falsely assumes that Adam's "original cultural responsibilities" were entirely bound up in the covenant of works.[32] He fails to recognize that heavenly life was the *gracious* end of Adam's obedience, not the *natural* end of it. Maturing the earth by his labor was natural to him, according to his nature,[33] and this was natural to him even when considering Adam apart from the covenant of works. The natural end of his gifts was dominion under God, earthly maturity, and an ordering of this world to the next. Again, heavenly life was a gift of grace, not a natural consequence of Adam fulfilling his work, and thus the direct end or purpose of these gifts remains the same when one is no longer under the covenant of works. Thus, VanDrunen is simply wrong when he entirely couples Adam's task with the attainment of a state of glory. Being in Christ *restores* us to Adam's moral responsibilities, including taking

---

32. Ibid., 80.

33. Turretin writes that the covenant of nature "is called 'natural' . . . because it is founded on the nature of man (as it was at first created by God) and on his integrity or powers. It is also called 'legal' because the condition on man's part was the observation of the law of nature engraved within him; and of 'works' because it depended upon works or his proper obedience." *IET*, 1:8.3.5.

dominion under God, not as a matter of achieving eternal life, but as a matter of sanctification and of exercising the gifts restored to us.

To state things differently for clarity: Since a Christian—having restored integrity—possesses the same gifts as Adam, he is equipped and drawn, by his nature, to exercise the same sort of dominion—to mature earthly life according to its principles and to order this world to the next. Christians are empowered and obligated to act according to Adam's original task, though not to meet any gracious condition for eternal life. The intent of the work is *not* to obtain a title to eternal life or to transform earthly life into the kingdom of God, but to order this life to the next. The Christian work of dominion in this world, like the task given to Adam, matures the earth such that it *points to* that heavenly rest to come and *supports* the goods of that heavenly rest offered primarily through spiritual administration (viz., the instituted church).

Moreover, Christian dominion relies on natural principles, which were the same for Adam, but the Christian applies them in light of revelation. As I've said, the heavenly end promised to Christians is the same heavenly kingdom that was promised to Adam. But in the state of grace, that heavenly kingdom is known to be Christ's kingdom, and thus all of life, including the institutions that serve human life, ought to be ordered to Christ and his kingdom. So Christian dominion does not bring the heavenly New Jerusalem to earth but rather orders life to it.

To avoid problems, VanDrunen would have to adopt either a neonomian or antinomian view of righteousness in a state of restored integrity: either Christians follow a new or modified law of God or obedience is obsolete in the state of grace. Neither, of course, is a Reformed position. The only consistent Reformed position is this:

Restored integrity entails that Adam's task in terms of moral content is part of Christian obedience. That is, Christians take up the task of true and complete humanity. Thus, ordering this world to the next is not only justified but part of Christian duty. VanDrunen might deny that fulfilling Adam's original task flowed from his nature. He might say that it as an adventitious duty—an addition to natural duty. But it is widely held in the Reformed tradition, as I demonstrated in the previous chapter, that dominion follows necessarily from man's nature, particularly in his having the divine image.

Another problem in VanDrunen's work is that he arbitrarily rescinds certain elements of man's original duty, presenting a dubious view of the Noahic covenant that limits Christians to "ordinary cultural activities," or those they can share with non-believers.[34] His position is simply incoherent. Logically, the Noahic covenant *cannot* rescind what was natural to prelapsarian man. It would mean that God commands against the very things that man's nature calls for him to do. God is then opposed to God, who gave man his nature. To be sure, there is important commonality between the redeemed and unredeemed, both being human. But restorative grace sets the redeemed apart on earth—constituting a restored humanity on earth—and, on that basis, Christians can and ought to exercise dominion in the name of God.

It is evident that VanDrunen's positions logically lead to a form of antinomianism. In his most recent work, he replaces "grace perfects nature" with "(common) grace preserves nature, and (saving) grace consummates nature."[35] So, it would seem, for VanDrunen,

---

34. VanDrunen, *God's Two Kingdoms*, 79.

35. David VanDrunen, *Politics after Christendom: Political Theology in a Fractured World* (Grand Rapids: Zondervan Academic, 2020), 76.

saving grace only provides eternal life. But does not saving grace also sanctify man and restore him to God's law? Does the believer in his outward duty operate only by common grace, the same sort of grace as his unredeemed neighbor, and by the same grace that he himself had before conversion? Wouldn't this mean that salvation in Christ has *no* effect on one's obedience to God's law and that no one is restored to obey it? "Grace perfects nature" is preferable because it allows one to acknowledge both the primary and secondary (or subsequent) effects of grace: one is perfected for heavenly life but also restored in their perfection for obedience in earthly life. VanDrunen's view is not consistent with the Reformed doctrine of sanctification, and I do not see how he avoids antinomianism. Thus, rejecting antinomianism (following Reformed doctrine) entails rejecting VanDrunen's view of grace and indeed much of what is distinctive to his political theology. Grace both redeems *and* restores, making man fit once again for man's work on earth under God.

The Gospel and Natural Relations

Since grace restores nature and natural law contains all the moral principles concerning social relations, the Gospel does not alter the priority and inequality of loves amongst those relations. A Christian should love his children over other children, his parents over other parents, his kin over other kin, his nation over other nations. The instincts that lead one to these unequal loves are reliable. Grace did not, despite what is popularly suggested, introduce equal love for all, or an overriding duty to the abstract "marginalized" or to the abstract "outcast" or to "identify with the weak." There are no "Gospel duties" that undermine duties to those who are closely bound to you. Grace affirms these natural hierarchies of love. Matthew Henry rightly said that "the highest degrees of divine affection must not divest us of natural affection."[36]

The influence of neo-Calvinism has led many Reformed churches to assume that the Gospel ushered in a social and political revolution and is the basis of a full-scale "critique" of the fundamental structures of our world. Philosopher Nicholas Wolterstorff, for example, argues for a "world-formative Christianity" in which the Christian "struggle" for social reform is "among the very motions of Christian spirituality." He rejects the idea that the social world is an "order of nature," arguing instead that it is a matter of "human decision." What medieval Christians considered the natural order is actually a "fallen structure."[37] The Gospel inaugurated a social program that strikes at the fundamental constitution of all pre-Gospel social relations.

Is the Gospel world-formative? I distinguish. First, the Gospel is primarily about eternal life, and eternal life is obtained not by works but by faith. This is why Luther states, for example, that "the Gospel does not trouble itself with these matters [of civil affairs]. It teaches about the right relation of the heart to God."[38] His fellow reformer, Philip Melanchthon, wrote, "For Christ did not come into the world to teach precepts about (civic) morals, which man already knew by reason, but to forgive sins, in order that he may give the Holy Spirit to those who believe in him."[39] Willard states, "Christ did not come

---

36. See Matthew Henry, *Commentary on the Whole Bible*, ed. Leslie F. Church (Grand Rapids: Zondervan, 1961), 43 [on Gen. 24:29–53].

37. Nicholas Wolterstorff, *Until Justice and Peace Embrace* (Grand Rapids: Eerdmans, 1983), 3.

38. Martin Luther, "The Sermon on the Mount," in *Luther's Works*, ed. Jaroslav Pelikan, vol. 21, *The Sermon on the Mount and the Magnificat* (Saint Louis: Concordia, 1956), 108.

39. Philip Melanchthon, *In Aristoteles ethica commentarii* (Argentoratum, 1535). Quoted in Eric Parker, trans. "On the Difference between Philosophy and Theology from Philip

to procure for us earthly favors only, which had been little things in comparison, but a crown and a kingdom, a title to life eternal, and inheritance among those that are sanctified."[40] The Gospel did not inaugurate a social program that rejects the basic structure of pre-Gospel

---

Melanchthon's Commentary on Aristotle's Ethics," *Epistolé* (blog), June 20, 2009, accessed May 27, 2020, https://epistole.wordpress.com/2009/06/20/on-the-difference-between -philosophy-and-theology-from-philip-melanchthons-commentary-on-aristotles-ethics. In his preface to Cicero's *On Duties*, Melanchthon writes the following: "Nor here am I speaking about religion, which must be sought from the sacred books. The customary manner of civic life is described by Cicero, with which religion does not conflict at all. Divine Ambrose also wrote an On Duties, I believe in order to inculcate religion in children, [a subject] about which he saw that there was no instruction in Cicero's treatise. But I think that religion ought to be drawn from divine literature. Concerning civic morals I would prefer to listen to Cicero, who, acquainted with the greatest affairs in the chief commonwealth in all the world, learned of very many things by experience, [and] he translated very many things from the writings of the Greeks, who governed the greatest cities." Philip Melanchthon, preface to Cicero, *On Duties* (1525), quoted in Eric J. Hutchison, trans., "The Protestant Heritage of Classical Humanism: Melanchthon and Cicero," *VoegelinView*, August 7, 2019, accessed September 27, 2022, https://voegelinview.com/the-protestant-heritage-of-classical-humanism-melanchthon -cicero/. Martin Luther similarly said that the Word of God "is not here to teach a maid or a servant how to . . . earn his bread. . . . [I]t neither gives nor shows temporal goods for the preservation of this life, for reason has already taught all this to everyone. But it is intended to teach us how we are to come to that other life." *Works*, 21:9.

40. Willard, *Body of Divinity*, loc. 31876. Melanchthon denies that the Gospel establishes an alternative political order: "Neither does the Gospel bring new laws concerning the civil state, but commands that we obey present laws, whether they have been framed by heathen or by others, and that in this obedience we should exercise love. . . . They were in the error that the Gospel is an external, new, and monastic form of government, and did not see that the Gospel brings eternal righteousness to hearts [teaches how a person is redeemed, before God and in his conscience, from sin, hell, and the devil], while it outwardly approves the civil state." "Of Political Order," Augsburg Confession, art. 14. Practically speaking, the Gospel has little to say to civil law and government, for as Willard writes, "There have been governments among mere pagans, which have had many excellent laws in respect of righteousness toward men, under which they have greatly flourished and been a shame to such as had the word of God. And whence had they this but from the relics of the law of God in them and the common gifts of the Spirit enabling men to improve the remaining light in them to high measures." Willard, *Body of Divinity*, loc. 30850.

social life. But the Gospel *did* inaugurate a new means to eternal life; and thus all social structures, which were originally designed to support man in his pursuit of eternal life, should point to and be formed to support this new means to it. This is world-formative, but more in the sense of direction and adornment than replacing structures. It is world-formative with regard to applications of principles, not with regard to principles themselves. Thus, Christians are not required to conduct a thorough critique of the "order of nature" reflected across time and nations but rather to consider that order as indicative of man's natural needs in social organization. Reflecting the broad Christian consensus, Richard Hooker writes,

> The most certain mark of goodness is the general conviction of all humanity. . . . The general and perpetual voice of mankind is as the judgment of God Himself, since what all men at all times have come to believe must have been taught to them by Nature, and since God is nature's author, her voice is merely His instrument.[41]

Second, Christian spirituality and worship are, properly speaking, about eternal life, not political struggle. Religion should be mainly about the Gospel, that is, about the means to eternal life. And so corporate worship ought primarily (though not exclusively) to address souls and administer sacred things for heavenly life. Thus, pastors should not, in their official capacities at least, be social activists or political coordinators, especially from the pulpit. Althusius rightly said, "Sacred and secular duties are distinct, and ought not to be confused. For each demands the whole man."[42] Classical Protestantism, and by extension

41. Hooker, *Divine Law*, 35.
42. Althusius, *Politica*, 59 [8.32].

Christian nationalism, affirms this sacred/secular distinction. The *sacred* is always in reference to the things of God that address or relate to man's highest gifts—those that make possible the knowledge of and desire for heavenly life. These are things that materially conduce to a supernatural end. The *secular* are temporal things pertaining to the life of this world. Pastors should concern themselves mainly with sacred things. But Christians in general, as restored human beings, have obligations to sacred *and* secular things. The sacred, being higher, ought to be sought above all lesser things, but the lesser things are essential to our complete good and ought to be ordered to the sacred. Thus, Christians ought to correct, direct, and adorn social life with Christianity not only as a matter of obedience but also to order mankind to sacred things and his highest good. Indeed, the chief aim of Christian nationalism is ordering the nation to the things of God—subordinating the secular to the sacred in order to orient it to the sacred.[43]

The claim that the Gospel is mainly about eternal life does not preclude the Christianization of civil institutions and laws or the improvement and correction of civil life by appealing to Scripture. Nor does it preclude the civil support and protection of true religion. It means, rather, that the Gospel does not eliminate, undermine, or "critique" the basic principles that have structured societies and relations of all ages and peoples. Indeed, the fact that the Gospel is mainly about eternal life makes it possible to direct and adorn the "order of nature" to Christian ends without conflating nature and grace, earth and heaven, and the secular and the sacred.

---

43. I clarify the relationship of the sacred and secular in chapter 7. It is worth saying here that I do *not* mean that the state ought to submit formally to the instituted church, as if the church can command the state. Rather, the state serves the kingdom of God by ordering outward things for the good of the kingdom's outward spiritual administration.

Nation and Grace

Since the nation and the affections of nationhood are natural to man as man, grace does not undermine, subvert, or destroy them. Augustine, in his commentary on Galatians (3:28–29), states that "The difference of nations [*gentium*] or condition or sex is indeed taken away by the unity of faith, but it remains embedded in mortal relations, and this order is to be preserved in the journey of this life."[44] Here Augustine makes a fundamental distinction between spiritual unity in Christ—a unity that takes no account of gender, class, nationality, or other earthly difference—and the inequality and differences necessitated by earthly life in accordance with natural principles.

Calvin followed this Augustinian tradition quite closely. In a sermon on 1 Corinthians 11:2–3, he writes,

> [R]egarding our eternal salvation it is true that one must not distinguish between man and woman, or between king and shepherd, or between German and Frenchman. Regarding policy however, we have what St. Paul declares here; for our Lord Jesus Christ did not come to mix up nature, or to abolish what belongs to the preservation of decency and peace among us.[45]

44. My translation of "*Differentia ista vel Gentium vel conditionis vel sexus iam quidem ablata est ab unitate fidei, sed manet in conversatione mortali eiusque ordinem in huius vitae itinere servandum esse.*" Augustine, *Expositio epistolae ad galatas*, accessed September 27, 2022, https://la.wikisource.org/wiki/Expositio_epistolae_ad_Galatas.

45. John Calvin, *Men, Women, and Order in the Church*, trans. Seth Skolnitsky (Dallas: Presbyterian Heritage, 1992), 19. Calvin continues: "Regarding the kingdom of God (which is spiritual) there is no distinction or difference between man and woman, servant and master, poor and rich, great and small. Nevertheless, there does have to be some order among us, and Jesus Christ did not mean to eliminate it, as some flighty and scatterbrained dreamers believe" (20).

The Reformed tradition affirms that all who have true faith in Christ—who are thereby members of the invisible church—are equally justified; their social station, sex, and nationality have no relevance. But, at the same time, their obligations in earthly life are based on outward earthly qualities and circumstances. Here we see two-kingdoms theology at work. As Calvin said, "[T]he spiritual kingdom of Christ and civil government are things very widely separated. . . . [The civil] government is distinct from the spiritual and internal kingdom of Christ, [which] begins the heavenly kingdom in us."[46] The two are "widely separated" in the sense that the spiritual leveling and unifying consequences of the Gospel have their own place and are kept from mixing up nature and thereby subverting the natural order. The state of glory, in other words, has begun in the hearts of believers, but believers still must outwardly act in accordance with the principles of this world.[47]

Calvin criticized those who balk at this separation, saying that they want to subject the "whole world" to a "new form"—a world with "neither courts, nor laws, nor magistrates."[48] It is quite common today for Christians to speak of "gospel politics," but the application of the Gospel to their politics is entirely *ad hoc*, lacking a clear and coherent principle. By what principle do they permit the realization of some aspects of glory and not others? Is marriage now rescinded because there is no marriage in the state of glory? Two-kingdoms theology—keeping the spiritual kingdom of Christ

46. Calvin, *Institutes*, 4.20.1, 2.

47. Calvin summarizes the position: "[I]n the government of the world distinctions of rank are admitted, but in the spiritual kingdom of Christ they can have no place." *Commentaries on the Epistles of Paul to the Galatians and Ephesians*, trans. William Pringle, vol. 21 of *Calvin's Commentaries* (Grand Rapids: Baker Books, 2005), 54 [on Gal. 2:6].

48. Calvin, *Institutes*, 4.20.1.

and the outward socio-political order separate—follows logically from Reformed theological anthropology and is necessary for theological coherence.

It follows that the grace of salvation, which brings one into the spiritual kingdom of Christ, does not sever one from his distinct, national way of life—far from it. Indeed, the glory and honor of nations was destined to be in the state of glory. As Bavinck writes,

> In that community, which Christ has purchased and gathered from all nations, languages, and tongues (Rev. 5:9; etc.), all nations, Israel included, maintain their place and calling (Matt. 8:11; Rom. 11:25; Rev. 21:24; 22:2). And all those nations— each in accordance with its own distinct national character— bring into the new Jerusalem all they have received from God in the way of glory and honor (Rev. 21:24, 26).[49]

The Gospel gives us a title to the state of glory *and* reconciles us to the principles of the state of integrity, and so we ought to act in the world according to those principles and not "critique" them by appealing to the state of glory. Christians should affirm the nation and nationality and even seek to order their nations to heavenly life.

The Church and the People of God

The failure to distinguish the various meanings of "church," and the frequent conflation of them, has resulted in a number of errors and problems in Protestant political commentary. In Protestant theology, "church" can refer to the "invisible church," which is a mystical communion of all true believers (i.e., the elect). The invisible

49. Bavinck, *RD*, 4:720.

church is known only to God, for true faith is an active, inward trust of conscience. This is the spiritual kingdom of Christ in essence.[50]

"Church" also refers to the "visible catholic church," which is well-defined by the Savoy Declaration (chap. 26):

> The whole body of men throughout the world, professing the faith of the gospel and obedience unto God by Christ according to it, not destroying their own profession by any errors everting the foundation, or unholiness of conversation, are, and may be called the visible catholic church of Christ; although as such it is not entrusted with the administration of any ordinances, or have any officers to rule or govern in, or over the whole body.

The Westminster Confession of Faith states that the "visible church" is "catholic or universal under the gospel (not confined to one nation, as before under the law) . . . and is the kingdom of the Lord Jesus Christ."[51] The visible church, therefore, is composed of men who profess Christ, considered apart from (or prior to) any ecclesiastical and civil institution. Outward unity in the visible church is not based on any institutional alignment or in a common subordination to an earthly ecclesiastical or civil head. Nor does the visible church, as a whole, share common cultural and national similarities. The visible church is an outward thing but refers to the outward

50. Turretin states, "Now although the word 'church' popularly speaking denotes an external and visible assembly, it does not on that account follow (speaking accurately of the church of Christ) that its proper and natural signification implies simply a visible assembly or a simple external profession: for a spiritual and internal communion constitutes its essence." *IET*, 3:18.6.4.

51. See chapter 25 of the Westminster Confession of Faith.

manifestation of a spiritual relation—a common orientation to its heavenly life. I discuss this with more precision in chapter 7.

We should distinguish between the visible church and the "people of God." The distinction here is subtle but important. Both refer to the same people, but "people of God" refers to Christians as restored humans—not only to their common profession of faith in Christ for heavenly life but also to their earthly life in Christ. The visible church, in my use of the term, refers *only* to the spiritual, heavenward aspect of those who profess Christ. It refers to the sharing in and common pursuit of the *highest* good. But "people of God" refers to restored men in their completeness, pursuing not merely the highest good but the *complete* good. The people of God are like what Adam's race would have been, only they are under the Final Adam—Jesus Christ. They remain human and, by grace, are *fully* human, having been sanctified and having received the divine image. They constitute a restored humanity on earth. "When men betake themselves to God, the world, which was formerly disordered, is restored to its proper order," says Calvin.[52] They are what Adam and his race could have been and as such are equipped to form and constitute commonwealths for their complete good. In sum, the term *people of God* recognizes that Christians are not simply heaven-oriented but are also restored to the principles of earthly life and thus can order earthly life to heavenly life in pursuit of the complete good.

This distinction helps us avoid the claim that the church that Christ founded, which is one church both visible and invisible, has in and from itself a worldly mission and focus; it was, after all, founded in grace principally for heavenly life. While all members

---

52. Calvin, *Commentary on the Prophet Isaiah*, 2:25 [on Isa. 17:7].

of the visible church are also the people of God (with regard to the extension of these terms), these people have their mission of dominion not from the visible church but on account of their status as restored humanity. The church is a kingdom of grace for eternal life, but in consequence of grace, man is restored to nature and thus is restored to the original mission of Adam with regard to dominion. This is the mission of the people of God.

Civil and Ecclesiastical Administrations

"Church" also refers to the instituted church. The instituted church is a divine order designed for the particular local administration of sacred things to a particular assembly of the faithful. The *ministerium* or spiritual ministry, which I described in the previous chapter, is deposited in the instituted church. Since civil magistracy and spiritual ministry are different and separate, the instituted church, having spiritual ministry only, principally administers to the soul for salvation and eternal life. The instituted church, therefore, does not replace, undermine, or create necessary tension with civil order. It does not form an alternative *polis* or civil community. It complements civil administration by ministering to the soul.

The civil and ecclesiastical orders are two species of order. Franciscus Junius defines and juxtaposes the two: "[T]he ecclesiastical administration is nothing but a divine order of the faithful for sacred fellowship around sacred things. . . . But we define the political administration as a human order of men for human fellowship around civil things."[53] Since each principally serves one

---

53. Franciscus Junius, *Ecclesiastici sive de natura et administrationibus ecclesiae Dei: libri tres* (Frankfurt: Andream Wechelum, 1581), 186 (my translation). As Bartholomäus Keckermann writes, "Civil politics is an order by which human society is administered

aspect of man—the body or the soul—the same people can belong to both with perfect harmony. New England Puritan John Davenport put this best:

> [Christians] are considerable under a twofold respect answerable to the twofold man . . . the inward and the outward man. Whereunto the only wise God has fitted and appointed two sorts of administrations, ecclesiastical and civil. Hence they are capable of a twofold relation, and of action and power suitable to them both; viz. civil and spiritual, and accordingly must be exercised about both in their seasons, without confounding those two different states, or destroying either of them, while what they transact in civil affairs, is done by virtue of their civil relation, their church-state only fitting them to do it according to God.[54]

Membership in the instituted church does not itself negate, undermine, or even alter what is fundamental to one's natural and civil relations. And how could it? Having the role of spiritual ministry, its principal role is administering what concerns heavenly life, the kingdom of God, and performing deeds with a pure conscience. The instituted church is not a nation in a nation or a heavenly embassy for an alternative political order. It is not even the primary place in which Christians learn about citizenship. It is an institution that serves the spiritual, heavenward needs of the people of God.

and directed to honesty. Ecclesiastical politics is [an order] by which the society of the church is directed to the worship of God and the salvation of souls." *Systema disciplinae politicae*, 5 (my translation).

54. Davenport, *A Discourse About Civil Government* (Cambridge: Samuel Green and Marmaduke Johnson, 1663), 5.

Given this ecclesiology, the people of God on earth, being both an earthly- and a heaven-bound people, are capable of a complementary civil and spiritual relation; and thus the same people, in appropriately sized groups of similar people, can constitute and submit to twin institutions—civil and ecclesiastical—for their earthly and heavenly good.

III. Dominion and the Divine Image

Before moving to discuss the nation in detail, we should consider the role of the restored divine image in dominion. As I've said, Adam's right of dominion was originally based in his possession of the divine image. Willard calls this a "spiritual right," for God "first put man in possession of these things [i.e., the earth and its outward benefits] as his tenant."[55] It is *spiritual* because one's claim for what he subdues is recognized by God (by grace)—that is, God has bound himself not to override anyone's claim. But at the fall, all men broke the terms and were subject, by divine right, to ejectment. This is evident when God commanded Israel to dispossess the nations of Canaan. However, God forbade Israel from dispossessing any nation outside of Canaan. These nations possessed the land by God's forbearance and by a *civil* right granted to them. Willard repudiates the "error" of those who "pretend [that] dominion is founded in grace" and who thereby "usurp the possession of his ungodly neighbor." He writes that "so long as they [the ungodly] keep within the bounds of civil righteousness, their claim *ad hominem* is as good as that of the godly. And God may, yet men may not, lawfully make a seizure of their estates on the score of their being

55. Willard, *Body of Divinity*, loc. 41884.

pagans, idolaters, or strangers to the gospel covenant."[56] Turretin writes that "the usurpation of another's possession cannot but be a grievous sin, repugnant to natural right."[57]

The re-possession of supernatural virtues has two effects in relation to dominion. First, the redeemed are able to exercise dominion *well*—to build truly just households and civil communities that practice civil righteousness *and* worship the true God. Second, we should follow Calvin in affirming the following:

> God has appointed to his children alone the whole world and all that is in the world. For this reason, they are also called the heirs of the world; for at the beginning Adam was appointed to be lord of all, on this condition, that he should continue in obedience to God. Accordingly, his rebellion against God deprived of the right, which had been bestowed on him, not only himself but his posterity. And since all things are subject to Christ, we are fully restored by His mediation, and that through faith; and therefore all that unbelievers enjoy may be regarded as the property of others, which they rob or steal.[58]

Now, this may seem to contradict Turretin and Willard, but Calvin elsewhere distinguishes the "use" of good things and the "right to them." Unbelievers, by the mercy and providence of God, can use the good things of this world. As for believers, Calvin writes, "Christ, by whom we are admitted into this family, at the same time admits us into a participation of this right, so that we may enjoy the

56. Ibid.

57. Turretin, *IET*, 2:11.9.2.

58. Calvin, *Commentaries on the Epistles to Timothy, Titus, and Philemon*, vol. 21 of Calvin's Commentaries (Grand Rapids: Baker Books, 2005), 104 [on 1 Tim. 4:5].

whole world, together with the favor of God."[59] We can enjoy the things of this world with a true and good conscience, for they are truly ours in Christ. Also, our disposition toward all good things, even those possessed by unbelievers, should be informed by the fact that they are ours in Christ. To be sure, we have no license to seize these things for ourselves, but by this disposition we can stand over the world as the true heirs of the world, even *this* world, for (as Bavinck states) "substantially nothing is lost" in the final reformation of all things.[60] This world is not eradicated in substance but made more excellent.

Finally, Christian nations should regard themselves as nations of true dignity, being a people of the true God on earth. This status should give them confidence and even boldness in their national and international affairs. They can and ought to use their resources and influence to spread the Gospel in non-Christian nations and to support fellows Christians in establishing and maintaining Christian political orders. This dignity also places domestic obligations on them to uphold national holiness and righteousness; they ought to act in a way befitting their dignity. What this entails fills much of this book.

IV. Conclusion

This and the previous chapter established the background anthropology and theology for the rest of the book. We can now move safely into a description of the *nation*, knowing that any true description of its fundamental features is true in all three states of

---

59. Calvin, *Commentaries on the Epistle of Paul the Apostle to the Hebrews*, trans. John Owen, vol. 22 of *Calvin's Commentaries* (Grand Rapids: Baker Books, 2005), 1:57 [on Heb. 2:5].
60. Bavinck, *RD*, 4:720.

man. Neither grace nor the unity of faith, nor the spiritual kingdom of God, nor the instituted church undermines or subverts the nation. Grace does not destroy what is natural but *restores* it. Grace also *perfects* nature, and thus nations can be Christian nations and commonwealths can be Christian commonwealths.

3

Loving Your Nation: The Nation and Nationalism

"I think love for one's country means chiefly love for people who have a good deal in common with oneself (language, clothes, institutions) and is in that way like love of one's family or school: or like love (in a strange place) for anyone who once lived in one's home town." —C.S. Lewis[1]

I. Method

One of the conclusions from the previous chapter is that neither the fall nor grace destroyed or abrogated human natural relations. The

---

1. C.S. Lewis, *The Collected Letters of C.S. Lewis,* ed. Walter Hooper, vol. 3, *Narnia, Cambridge, and Joy 1950–1963* (New York: HarperCollins, 2007), 119.

fall did not introduce the natural instinct to love one's own, and grace does not "critique" or subvert our natural inclinations to love and prefer those nearest and most bound to us. The fall introduced the *abuse* of social relations and *malice* towards ethnic difference. Grace corrects this abuse and malice, but it does not introduce new principles of human relations. The instinct to love the familiar more than the foreign is good and remains operative in all spiritual states of man.

Having established these conclusions, this chapter explains how human social relations make and sustain nations. My method of approach is different from most. Instead of unfolding the nation as a concept or analyzing it with historical examples, I use a phenomenological method to uncover and reveal the nation as we exist and dwell in it.[2] I attempt to bring to consciousness the fundamental relations of people and place—relations so familiar to us that we are largely unaware of them. For many, this unfolding will help to clarify one's people-group. For all, it explains and justifies our preference for some people (family, kin, countrymen) over others. Additionally, this chapter shows (1) that each of us has a people-group (i.e., an ethnicity), (2) that each people-group can be conscious *of* itself, and (3) that each people-group has the right to be *for* itself. These last two elements are essential to *nationalism*, which I discuss briefly at the end.

One might accuse me of assuming and norming the "Western European male" experience in this chapter. I am not worried about this, since I am male, and am rooted ancestrally in Western

2. This approach certainly has limitations. I am trying to disclose for people the background of our experience. So I'm assuming that there is some commonality in our experience, which risks asserting what another does not share or recognize. I doubt, however, that what I uncover will strike people as foreign to them, though some may disagree with the conclusions I pull from experiences.

Europe, and am speaking largely to a Western European male audience. I fully acknowledge that my goal is to reinvigorate Christendom in the West—that is my chief aim. The question for most
of my audience is, "Which way, Western Man—the suicide of the
West or its revitalization?"[3]

The intimate connection of people and place as described here
undermines the so-called creedal nation concept, which is popular
in the United States among neo-conservatives, mainstream Republicans, and left-liberals. The creedal nation is a nation united around
a set of propositions that creedalists consider universally true or at
least practically advantageous for all and so readily acceptable by all.
Creedal statements usually include egalitarian themes and rights-
talk: human and civil rights, equal protection under the law, equal
opportunity, etc. These propositions sufficiently transcend cultural
particularities, so creedalists contend, making possible and preferable a multicultural social project. The most striking creedal statement is found in Justice Anthony Kennedy's opinion in *Planned
Parenthood v. Casey* (1992): "At the heart of liberty is the right to
define one's own concept of existence, of meaning, of the universe,
and of the mystery of human life." This statement is the inevitable
conclusion of a liberal creedalist project. But, as I hope to show in
this chapter, neutrality between contrary conceptions of existence
in the same space is impossible. There is always a norm by which all
others judge themselves.

3. Given my friendships and associations with people of different ancestry, I can say that
being "white" is unnecessary both to recognize themselves in what I describe and to cooperate with someone like me in a common national project. This is not a "white nationalist"
argument, for in my view the designation "white," as it is used today, hinders and distracts
people from recognizing and acting for their people-groups, many of which (to be sure)
are majority "white" but are so not on the basis of a modern racialist principle.

To be sure, my argument in this book does not preclude political or social creeds that serve to unite a people. The statement "Jesus is Lord," which is a universally true statement, certainly serves to unite the people of a Christian nation. However, propositions do not and cannot serve as the *foundation* for nations, even Christian propositions.[4] Our sense of familiarity with a particular place and the people in it—the sense of *we*—is rooted not in abstractions or judicial norms (e.g., equal protection) or truth-statements. Rather, the nation is rooted in a pre-reflective, pre-propositional love for one's own, generated from intergenerational affections, daily life, and productive activity that link a society of the dead, living, and unborn. Concrete *action*—past, present, and future—which enlivens space to the benefit of generations, is what grounds the nation. Political creeds are ancillary or supplemental, but not fundamental.

II. People, Place, and Things

Space and Place

The key to uncovering the nation in lived experience is the notion of "place." I'll begin with some foundational thoughts about place and then move to higher-order considerations.[5]

4. Of course, unity around the statement "Jesus is Lord" is *essential* for a nation to be Christian. By "foundation," I mean the principles of our nature, which the things of grace—such as the truth-statement "Jesus is Lord"—assume and perfect. This should be clearer as I proceed through my argument.

5. I am not attempting to provide a complete phenomenology of place or a systematic presentation on metaphysics. One hoping to find either will be disappointed and perhaps frustrated. Certainly, my argument below is open to critique from both phenomenologists and metaphysicians, but not because it is incomplete or lacking in some areas. My attempt is to provide an accessible account of the experience of place and people that serves my overall argument for Christian nationalism.

Place is a spatial term, though it is not synonymous with *site* or generic *space*. In my usage, place is *meaning-invested* space, generated by human activity, whose meaning is entirely dependent on a human relation to it. For example, we designate some space to be a "house" because we relate to it as a place for human dwelling. The meaning for that space depends on the particular demands of human dwelling, and hence its meaning exists entirely in the human relation to it. Viewed apart from our relation to it, that space lacks inherent meaning; it is bare space. Likewise, we designate some spaces as "marketplace" and "school" and "church" due to particular relations we have with the structures and activities of these spaces. Place is a sort of adorned space, having invested meaning based in a human/space connection. In this way, the meaning of some space is not merely a projection of meaning by man, nor merely something inherent to the object independent of man. The meaning is irreducible to subject or object; it is inherent to the *relation* of man to the object.

It is challenging to imagine space as bare and meaningless. An example will help to clarify. If a time-traveling Celt happened upon a 21st-century empty parking lot, he would be bewildered by the painted lines on the surface. He would have no background context or experience to understand their order and purpose. The readily accessible meaning that we (unconsciously) ascribe to them would be, at least at first, utterly incomprehensible to him. After all, the lines themselves do not manifest the meaning that we give to them; their role in our daily lives relies entirely on a meaning we bring to them. We might also imagine non-human, sentient beings with no concept of permanent dwelling who, upon seeing houses, become utterly bewildered.

My point is that the space we inhabit is invested with meaning that depends on the nature of the human being (e.g., the need for dwelling) and on cultural particularity (e.g., parking lots). This is true for everything in our social world, from parking lots to houses to ballparks to civic monuments. Thus, our world in experience is thoroughly placial; our world is one of places, each place having meaning that exists only in our human or cultural relation to these spaces. In this sense, our world is a sort of life-world, having been enlivened for and by us in a subject/object relation.

It would be a mistake, however, to limit the meaning of places to their basic functionality or their universal meaning. All can recognize a house as a house, but only some can call it *home*. Of course, as a concept, "home" is universally understood. But, for any given house, only some can relate to this house as home—only you have this higher *particular* relation to it. This distinction—between house and home—is crucial for our purposes here, and I discuss it further below. We should not demote these particular meanings in comparison with universal ones. Relating to a house as *home* (a particular relation) certainly matters more for our well-being in this world than simply our relation to a house as house (a universal relation).

Socialization and Meaning

Much of the meaning of our world was handed down to us, and we adopted it through socialization. Parenting consists largely of socializing children into the meaning already invested in spaces. Take the "street," for example. When our children are very young and newly mobile, we command them not to enter or even get near the street. In this simple act, we are distinguishing places for them: the "street," as opposed to say the "driveway," is a no-go space. This no-go rule is not inherent to the space we call "street" itself or even to the material used to make it. "Street" designates a certain human activity or meaning for that space, one that comes with particular rules for both drivers and pedestrians. Like innumerable other designations, street refers to a space brought into the human social world and, in this case, for a particular human function.

But places such as streets embody more than rules for us. We take on dispositions in relation to them. Knowing that our children are not machines or computers but creatures of habit, we train them to have a cautious disposition toward the street. We want them to feel something in relation to it, to have a sort of habitual, pre-rational response of caution. The tone of our voice in denying them access to a street communicates the seriousness of that place. In effect, we create a subject/object relation such that the street discloses itself as a place of danger to the child. That is to say, we are not just attempting to develop an emotional or psychological response or trigger; rather, we are building the child's world—a subject/object relation—in which that space is a place of danger.

Another example of the dispositional nature of place is our relation to libraries. Most of us at a young age were quieted by our parents or teachers when in a library. In adulthood, whispering in a library is second nature to us, and it is a rule most fitting for a library. But the rule is the conscious articulation of a pre-reflective disposition we have to the space. In adopting quietness, we make ourselves fitting to the place; we are conforming ourselves to it, as if it commands us to act properly. The place embodies the commands of our parents and teachers, and hence it serves as an authority over us. Their commands have become lodged in these places. It informs us as to our proper disposition towards it. And we feel these commands the moment we enter the place. Places are means through which duty is communicated and embodied. These place-lodged commands make possible confident action, for by them we know the ways of being, or the manners, dispositions, and rules of these spaces. Put simply, we know what to do; we know the expectations of ourselves and of others. Without them, we are lost, disoriented, and clash with others. Places prevent collective-action problems; they not only facilitate collective action but also provide the anticipation that people will sufficiently comply with the rules and not hinder others. The stability of community requires that the people have a common relation to the space they inhabit.

Sacred spaces are good examples of both communicated duty and lodged sentiment as well. Grave sites are treated as sacred places, embodying an array of sentiment and memory, typically for individuals and families. Civic memorials embody the same, though they embody the sentiment of communities. These places are unique in that one can disrespect and desecrate them. While on a bike ride with my young children, we came upon a small firefighters' memorial. We stopped to look, and after a few minutes one of my children decided to climb on one of the displays. I stopped her and in that moment was able to explain the meaning of this place: that it is a place of remembrance and reverence for past sacrifice. I created in her world a new sort of place and began socializing her into the appropriate posture and rules for such places.

Innumerable examples could be provided, and certainly the reader can supply with his or her own experiences what might be lacking here. By aid of our parents and others, we were socialized into a social world—a world of places, each with its rules, appropriate disposition, and lodged sentiments. According to a naturalistic stance, we could explain this with neuroscience or psychology, but those explanations do not describe lived experience, and, despite the naturalistic biases that prevail in our time, it is by the everyday mode of life that we dwell in this world.

Memory and Sentiment

Memory is an essential element of place, creating sentiment between people and place. Sentiment here is a sort of affectivity that is generated by time and activity and intergenerational love. To understand the relationship of memory, sentiment, and place, let us return to house and home. The house of one's youth is not merely another house among houses; it is your childhood home. As the place of your time and activity, it is set apart from the other houses. Even after moving out, that house remains unique; it is distinct *to you* from the rest of the houses on the row. And this is not your choice, as if one can freely ascribe this unique relation to any dwelling. It is an unavoidable product of *your* activity in that space—an activity that generated familiarity and lodged memory. If one's childhood was generally positive, he relates to that space with positive affection.[6] It is elevated with an affective value—a value that is neither transferable nor exchangeable, nor marketable; and yet this value is real for you and for others who were with you.

6. Sentiment can, however, be negative, depending on one's experience. For example, in the movie *Forrest Gump*, the character Jenny, who was sexually abused as a child by her father, returns to her childhood home in adulthood and hurls rocks at it, as if trying to eradicate the memories still present there. In her encounter with it, the house reveals itself to her and only to her as the embodiment of these painful memories. Forrest, her friend and later husband, bulldozes it. She goes on to live and die in Forrest's house, which he inherited from his loving mother.

I recently heard one man speak fondly of his grandparents' front porch, where they and he would sit, talk, and eat. The grandparents are gone now, and a stranger owns the house, but when he drives by and gazes at the porch, he thinks of them and reflects on his memories. That house has captured these memories for him and his love for his grandparents. We all have lodged memories like this, which speaks not merely of a common emotion but of the power of place to enliven our world.

Other places besides houses are spaces of memory. Indeed, any space, even those outside the built environment, can bear these features. My father and I backpacked into the backcountry of Yosemite and camped at a site by ourselves several miles from the nearest road. We were standing around a campfire talking about my future (I was a teenager) when a black bear behind us crashed to the ground, taking with it our food, which we (stupidly) suspended from a tree. The bear proceeded to eat our food as I threw rocks and my father wildly banged pans to scare it. The bear ran off, after finishing all our food. Neither of us has returned to that site, though it lives on as a setting for our "bear stories" (we encountered others) that we tell my children. That site, which I will return to with my children (God willing), is a place with deep, significant memory for me, though it is nothing but dirt, grass, and trees (and maybe a bear).

We all have unique places like this. But I should emphasize that spaces of memory are typically mundane places for common everyday activities. The town square, high school, local park, shopping mall, and Little League ballparks are such places. Indeed, one's hometown or even a wider region (e.g., county) is a place—a space of memory.

Time and Intergenerational Love

Memory temporalizes place. That is, embodied memory in places generates a connection between the past, present, and future. Our activity with loved ones elevates sites to places of intergenerational love such that through them we experience these places as deposits of familial affection. A trace of love remains. Cicero once said that "[w]e are somehow moved by the places in which the signs of those we love or admire are present."[7] Our love for others is re-presented in places and things, effectively linking the past with the present. The result is that the world is enlivened as a *gift* for us. It is not a mere representation of love but a *medium* of love that endures after a loved one's death. And our response to that gift is something more than gratitude; we conserve and improve upon it for future generations as *our* gift to them. Dante was right when he said in *De Monarchia* that "[a]ll men on whom the Higher Nature has stamped the love of truth should especially concern themselves in laboring for posterity, in order that future generations may be enriched by their efforts, as they themselves were made rich by the efforts of generations past."[8]

This connection between the dead, living, and unborn once animated the ideals of aristocracy. As historian Ellis Wasson wrote, "It was not unusual for a landed proprietor [i.e., aristocrat] to plant trees in his park that would not mature for more than a century. He was laying down pleasure for the eye and money in the bank for his great-great-grandson."[9] The trees are gifts to future generations, as

7. Marcus Tullius Cicero, *On the Commonwealth and on the Laws*, ed. and trans. James E.G. Zetzel (Cambridge: Cambridge University Press, 1999), 2.4.

8. Dante Alighieri, *The De Monarchia of Dante Alighieri*, trans. Aurelia Henry (Boston: Houghton, Mifflin, 1904), 3.

9. Ellis Wasson, *Aristocracy and the Modern World* (New York: Palgrave Macmillan, 2006), 10.

enduring conduits of love; and they communicate his duty to give something to his progeny. His enjoyment of these trees is based in the future enjoyment they will provide, which affectively unites him with those whom he will not meet in this present life. The trees are mediums of affection for the unborn. The man experiences these trees as if he were (and will be) the dead ancestor channeling his love for the living. Thus, the dead-living-unborn connection refers not to any given snapshot in time but to a sort of timeless linkage or, what Edmund Burke calls the "eternal society."[10] Each individual, in relation to intergenerational love, is simultaneously the dead, living, and unborn. Place, as spaces of memory, makes this possible.

Since many people today lack this intergenerational experience of inherited land, I'll focus for a moment on *things*. Family heirlooms are, by their nature, objects with high affective value, though they often have little market value. For example, people value their grandfather's military discharge documents from WWII. The value of such documents is confined to the affective, since their abundance in society and familial relevance make them worthless in the market. Still, they serve a vital function in uniting the past, present, and future. The love for the dead is embodied in the document, a love that is then shared with the next generation. It also connects a family to the past, documenting a loved one's participation in great national events. Other heirlooms include pocket watches, jewelry, and cars. Furniture, in particular, can embody the affections from and for those who have passed away. My wife and I have a chair that once belonged to her grandfather, and on it we read bedtime stories to our children.

10. Burke, *Reflections on the Revolution in France* (London: J. Dodsley, 1790), 144.

The things that people make and/or maintain are the conduits for intergenerational love as well. Such objects owe their existence to human labor and come to communicate intention, care, craft, and time. They embody the expenditure of life and the imbuing of personality. Upon completion, the product manifests for others the life of the producer. But this manifestation appears only if others have knowledge of and affection for the producer. That is, this higher, particular meaning manifests not from the material of the object considered objectively; it manifests only on account of familial affection, which adorns it. Our cheval mirror, made by the hands of my wife's father (a labor that my wife remembers), is an enduring means of affection between generations. It manifests the will of its creator—a will for her good and that of future generations. Products of our natural relations adorn our world and enliven our dwelling place; they are potential means by which the dead, living, and unborn are connected. Lord willing, this mirror, with its full array of meaning, will continue to manifest affection in one of my children's homes.[11]

Returning to place as a conduit of intergenerational love, consider Cicero's insightful exchange in his work *On the Laws*, in which he includes a discussion on affection for one's "native land." It perfectly captures what I'm trying to describe. Cicero asks his friend Marcus whether he would prefer to continue their

11. Gaston Bachelard speaks of furniture that has received an abundance of care: "Objects [in a house] that are cherished [by care] really are born of an intimate light, and they attain to a higher degree of reality than indifferent objects, or those that are defined by geometric reality. For they produce a new reality of being and they take their place not only in an order but in a community of order. From one object in a room to another, care weaves the ties that unite a very ancient past to the new epoch." *The Poetics of Space*, trans. Marisa Jolas (New York: Penguin Books, 1964), 88.

discussion on an island formed by a river. He says that the place is a "delicious retreat . . . delightfully ornamented by all the decorations of art." Marcus agrees, saying that he often goes there "on account of the beauty of the scenery." So far the two have spoken only of what both can recognize about the place—the beauty of it and its suitability as "a place for undisturbed meditation, or uninterrupted reading or writing." But Marcus adds something exclusive to his relation to the place: "There is one reason, however, why I am so fond of this Arpinum, which does not apply to you . . . ."[12] Marcus explains:

> Because, to confess the truth, it is my fatherland. Here is the most ancient origin of our stock; here are our family rituals and our family; here there are many traces of our ancestors. In brief: you see this house? It was made larger and fancier by our father, who spent most of his life here in study, because of his poor health; but on this very spot, while my grandfather was still alive and it was a small house of the old style . . . I was born. And so something abides deep in my mind and feelings which makes me take all the more pleasure in this place. . . .[13]

Marcus explicitly attributes his deep love for this place to the imprint left behind by his natural relations, whom he loves. It is not merely a place of residence but also, and more importantly, a place of his loved-ones' activity. They left behind "traces" of themselves.

12. Marcus Tullius Cicero, *The Political Works of Marcus Tullius Cicero*, trans. Francis Foster Barham (London: Edmund Spettigue, 1841), 75–76.
13. Cicero, *On the Commonwealth and On the Laws*, 130–31.

His relation to this place is unique to him because they are *his* relations. This place is his familial home.

Cicero calls this an "excellent reason . . . for loving this place" and
adds that he is now "more fond of that house and this whole land
in which you were born and raised." What was once to Cicero only
a beautiful place is now, as result of his friend's brief story, elevated
in affection through his friend's relation to it. Cicero experiences
this fondness *through* his friend. "I cannot tell you how this affection arises," says Cicero, "but certainly we cannot behold, without
emotion, the spots where we find traces of those who possess our
esteem or admiration."[14] In this brief exchange, we see that places
can take on a highly particular kind of affection, one based exclusively in our relation with others. These places are means by which
we re-encounter loved ones—places enlivened in experience by the
traces of the dead.

Given its particularity, the affections embodied and communicated via places are fragile. They depend on a particular human
relation, and so the adornment of meaning is lost when that relation ceases. That is not to say that such meaning is ephemeral; it can
endure across generations. But, as we saw with the parking lot and
the cheval-mirror examples, meaning is not imprinted such that
anyone at any time will comprehend it. If there is significant good
and necessity in having a world adorned with affection, developed
across generations, then this fragile adornment must be an object
of conservation and protection. The stories of people, places, and
things—whether of familial or national importance—must be told
to future generations.

14. Cicero, *The Political Works of Marcus Tullius Cicero*, 77.

Familiarity

More needs to be said before we can talk directly of the nation. Most of the examples above involve a conscious articulation of one's relations to things and places. But in everyday life, in a pre-reflective mode, place is experienced as *familiarity*. Familiarity is the background condition of our ease of activity and confidence of action, and our sense of home and self-fittingness in a place. The house/home distinction is again a helpful example. Your house is a home because your activity in it has made it a sort of extension of yourself. You are "at home" when home because in a sense you are at home with yourself when in it. Entering a friend's house reveals the stark difference between types of familiarity. Though you might be familiar with his house and with houses generally, his home does not have the higher-order familiarity of your home. What distinguishes the home from the house is not the comfort and security provided by it but the higher-order reality imbued in it through care and activity with loved ones.

Familiarity is not limited to the private sphere, however. One's neighborhood and town, the marketplace, playgrounds, a landscape, and many other places are places of familiarity. At the most basic level, familiarity is the background condition for action—you know what to do, how to do it, what the proper disposition and posture when doing it are, whom to do it with, etc. For this reason, familiarity of place is essential for living well because it coordinates action with others and permits predictability of success in our daily endeavors. But higher-order familiarity makes possible a public home to which we belong with others. The familiarity of place as a *public home* transcends utility; it is our *home*land, a place worthy of our sacrifice.

But since we are regularly enmeshed in familiarity, we dwell in it almost fully asleep to its significance. We fall back into our everyday-ness, carrying out our business, failing to see consciously our-*selves* in, on, and around it. While there is a peaceful aloofness in this, it is also tragic: people are too late to become fully conscious of their homeland, and it disappears from neglect. A people's will to live comes too late. Like coming to appreciate a loved one only when he or she is gone, we don't feel the love of home until that home is distant from us or has changed. Victor Hugo, in *Les Misérables*, captures this beautifully when speaking of the Paris of his youth, and it is worth quoting in full:

> So long as you go and come in your native land, you imagine that those streets are a matter of indifference to you; that those windows, those roofs, and those doors are nothing to you; that those walls are strangers to you; that those trees are merely the first encountered haphazard; that those houses, which you do not enter, are useless to you; that the pavements which you tread are merely stones. Later on, when you are no longer there, you perceive that the streets are dear to you; that you miss those roofs, those doors; and that those walls are necessary to you, those trees are well beloved by you; that you entered those houses which you never entered, every day, and that you have left a part of your heart, of your blood, of your soul, in those pavements. All those places which you no longer behold, which you may never behold again, perchance, and whose memory you have cherished, take on a melancholy charm, recur to your mind with the melancholy of an apparition, make the holy land visible to you, and are, so to speak, the very form of France, and

you love them; and you call them up as they are, as they were,
and you persist in this, and you will submit to no change: for
you are attached to the figure of your fatherland as to the face
of your mother.[15]

The lesson for us today, being in a time of radical and hostile
change, is that we must become consciously aware of home, of those
latent affections that we naturally leave in the background of life.
These affections now need to be articulated, affirmed, and protected.

III. Nation

The idea of nation is notoriously difficult to define, and identifying true nations is equally challenging. This is especially true in an
age of the nation-state, which tends to conceal difference under a
homogenizing state project. My interest, however, is not to discuss
and identify nations and nationhood as if trying to sketch a map
of cultural geography from a bird's-eye view. My goal is to provide
reflections on lived experience such that one's own people-group
is brought to conscious articulation (i.e., we become consciously
aware of it). Here, I assume what I've shown above, namely, that
what is most meaningful to our lives and what is required to live
well are *particularity* and sharing that particularity with others.
Particularity is distinctive to a people not only with regard to the
people but also to a people *in place*. The place of a people is not necessarily co-terminus with state jurisdiction, as should be clear by
this point. It refers more to a sort of phenomenological topography

15. Victor Hugo, *Les Misérables*, trans. Isabel Florence Hapgood, vol. 2 (New York: T.Y. Crowell, 1887), 5.1.

in which one dwells with others in shared meaning, which could in principle extend across political boundaries.

In the West, people-groups have become either concealed and suppressed or celebrated and purified by an ideology of universality, partly through the homogenizing forces of state capitalism and capitalist statecraft and through the ethnic privileging of woke capitalism—all in the interest of a cosmopolitan, super-rich elite of "nowheres." This chapter critiques that ideology of universality by showing that each person has an ethnicity with a delimited people-group and by insisting that each people-group ought to self-affirm and act for itself. This for-itself posture is necessary to combat globalism, homogenization, sanctified ethno-narcissism, and the weak collective will that prevails in our time. More importantly, it provides an important premise for my justification of Christian nationalism: a Christian people, whose good is found both in cultural particularity and in a universal religion, can and must be for itself as a *distinct people* in the interest of earthly and heavenly good, for itself and its posterity.

I do not argue here for the sort of 19th-century nationalism that homogenized the socio-economic classes of peoples. My principal interest is a reinvigoration of a collective will that asserts and stands up for itself. Prerequisite to such self-regard, at least today, is a conscious articulation or sense of one's people as distinguished from others.

I use the terms *ethnicity* and *nation* almost synonymously, though I use the former to emphasize the particular features that distinguish one people-group from another. Since every people-group has internal differences (e.g., class-based differences), *nation* is used to emphasize the unity of the whole, though no nation (properly speaking) is composed of two or more ethnicities.

Ethnicity

When most white Americans assign themselves an ethnicity, they typically point to some distant European ancestry. I might say that I'm Italian, German, and English. Ancestry tests give us the mixed origins present in our DNA. But while these origins are not entirely irrelevant, they say little about who you are, at least with regard to your everyday life. They make your ethnicity some distant relation who is practically foreign to you and usually serves as some mildly interesting fact you use in small-talk.

Ethnicity, as something *experienced*, is familiarity with others based in common language, manners, customs, stories, taboos, rituals, calendars, social expectations, duties, loves, and religion. These permit the ease of action and communication, the efficient completion of common projects, clarity of mutual understanding, and the ability to achieve the highest ideals and works of civil life. Put differently, the members of a people-group have the same world—sharing the same or very similar topography of experience—which makes possible the full range of human cooperation, activities, and achievements, and a collective sense of homeland.

Reflecting on familiarity and foreignness helps us to see our true ethnicity and who belongs to it. Think of the people with whom you feel at ease conducting your daily life; with whom you share similar expectations of conduct, aesthetic judgments (viz., beauty, taste, decorum), and recreational activities; whom you can effectively rebuke or offer sufficient justification for your actions to; and with whom you can join in a common life that achieves the highest ends of man. Think of those people. With such people, you can cooperate in things above mere material exchange and consumption and common defense—above a mere alliance of households or individuals. There is mutual trust, not based in some procedural, social contract, but in a shared sense of *we*, centered around particularities that elevate the people in, as Edmund Burke said, "a partnership not only between those who are living, but between those who are living, those who are dead, and those who are to be born."[16] These are the people to whom you are naturally drawn, bearing similarities by which you can complete activities and care for your common dwelling place.

In our everyday mode of life, familiarity is very much left in the background. But the experience of foreignness typically discloses the familiar to us. A foreign place is not necessarily frightening; indeed, it is often thrilling and fascinating, even life-changing. Nevertheless, a foreign place is strange and exotic; it is not home. Such places are enjoyable only because you can leave them and return to what is familiar. Even when you're in a foreign land, the familiar remains operative as the background condition for the experience of foreignness. This is why your thrill of foreignness would quickly change to anxiety, or worse, if you were suddenly forced to stay past your expectation. You can enjoy foreignness because you have a plan to leave it and return to what is familiar. More importantly, the experience of foreignness discloses the familiar and its importance to us. In Homer's *Odyssey*, Odysseus says,

> So nothing is as sweet as a man's own country,
> his own parents, even though he's settled down
> in some luxurious house, off in a foreign land
> and far from those who bore him.[17]

16. Edmund Burke, *Reflections on the Revolution*, 144.

17. Homer, *Homer: The Odyssey*, trans. Robert Fagles (New York: Penguin Books, 1996), 212 [9.38–41].

Language barriers, spatial disorientation, and confusions over laws, manners, and how to complete basic activities reveal to us the importance of familiarity for life and that each of us belongs to a bounded "we," a people, who do things differently. Reflecting on this should demonstrate that *everyone* has a people, an ethnicity. Everyone has "ethnic" distinctives.

Blood relations refers to natural relations that originate several generations back, often emphasizing ancestry known in story and myth among one's kin. In the Old Testament, Moab has blood ties with the Israelites, because Abraham and Lot were uncle and nephew. It was once widely accepted that old blood relations generate special duties. For example, God chastised the Moabites in Jeremiah 48 because they, as Calvin comments, disregarded their connection "by blood with the Israelites." He continues: "They ought then to have retained the recollection of their brotherhood, and to have dealt kindly with them. . . . [N]ature itself ought to have taught them to acknowledge the Israelites as their brethren, and to cultivate mutual kindness."[18]

---

18. Calvin, *Commentaries on the Prophet Jeremiah and the Lamentations*, trans. John Owen, vol. 11 of *Calvin's Commentaries* (Grand Rapids: Baker Books, 2005), 5:5, 6 [on Jer. 48:1, 6]. In his commentary on Genesis 29:13, Calvin writes, "[T]he sense of nature dictates that they who are united by ties of blood should endeavor to assist each other; but though the bond between relatives is closer, yet our kindness ought to extend more widely, so that it may diffuse itself through the whole human race." *Commentary on the First Book of Moses Called Genesis*, 2:128–29. Commenting on Amos 1:11–12, he states that the Idumeans "deserved a much heavier punishment. . . . Since nearness of blood, and that sacred union, could not make them gentle to the Jews, we hence perceive how brutal was their inhumanity." They displayed "barbarity . . . in forgetting their kindred, and in venting their rage against their own blood. . . . It was a monstrous thing past endurance, when a regard for their own blood did not reconcile those who were, by sacred bonds, connected together." *Commentary on the Twelve Minor Prophets*, 2.128–29.

Nations today are not built around bloodlines stretching back to arch-patriarchs. But blood relations remain relevant to nations, when referring to one's ancestral connection to a people and place back to time immemorial. The originating source for one's affection of people and place is his natural relations—those of his kin.[19] But the ties of blood do not directly establish the boundaries of one's ethnicity. Rather, one has ethnic ties of affection because one's kin conducted life with other kin in the same place. Christian philosopher Johann Herder was correct in saying that the *volk* is a "family writ large." This is an apt description not because everyone is a cousin by blood but because one's kin lived here with the extended families of others for generations, leaving behind a trace of themselves and their cooperation and their great works and sacrifices. Blood relations matter for your ethnicity, because your kin have belonged to *this people* on *this land*—to this nation in this place—and so they bind you to that people and place, creating a common *volksgeist*.

We should not, however, disregard the work of intermarriage over time in creating bonds of affection, as Aristotle argues. Out of marriage form various brotherhoods and tribes and shared or public pastimes. "This sort of thing is," writes Aristotle, "the work of affection," making possible the highest civic virtues.[20] The same people living in the same place for many generations can see each other as cousins of a sort, since all are connected to a *core* ancestry.

19. Aquinas writes, "Friendship of kindred is more stable, since it is more natural and preponderates over others in matters touching nature: consequently we are more beholden to them in the providing of necessaries." *ST*, II-II.26.8. In article 7, he writes, "[S]ome neighbors are connected with us by their natural origin, a connection which cannot be severed, since that origin makes them to be what they are."
20. Aristotle, *Politics*, trans. Carnes Lord (1984; Chicago: The University of Chicago Press, 2013), 3.10.

My intent here is not to discount or dismiss the importance of blood ties in ethno-genesis—a dismissal that is fashionable, politically correct, and could save me some trouble. It simply is the case that a "community in blood" is crucial to ethnicity. But this should not lead us to conclude that blood ties are the sole determinate of ethnicity, as if all we need are DNA tests. Ernest Renan says it well:

> A nation is a soul, a spiritual principle. Two things that, in truth, are but one constitute this soul, this spiritual principle. One is in the past, the other in the present. One is the possession in common of a rich legacy of memories; the other is present consent, the desire to live together, the will to perpetuate the value of the heritage that one has received in an undivided form. Gentlemen, man cannot be improvised. The nation, like the individual, is the culmination of a long past of efforts, sacrifices, and devotion. The cult of ancestors is the most legitimate of all; our ancestors have made us who we are. A heroic past, great men, glory (I mean the genuine kind), this is the capital stock upon which one bases a national idea. To have common glories in the past, a common will in the present; to have performed great deeds together, to wish to perform still more, these are the essential preconditions for being a people. One loves in proportion to the sacrifices to which one has consented, and to the ills that one has suffered. One loves the house that one has built and passes down. The song of the Spartiates—"We are what you were; we will be what you are"—is in its simplicity the abridged hymn of every fatherland.[21]

21. Ernest Renan, *What is a Nation? And Other Political Writings*, trans. M.F.N. Giglioli (1882; New York: Columbia University Press, 2018), 260–61.

Principle of Similarity

Members of ethnic groups share similarities that are distinct to them. They possess similarities not only with regard to their common humanity but also in particulars. By "particulars," I refer to what one cannot ascribe to all mankind; or, to put it positively, it refers to features (e.g., culture) that can be ascribed only to *some* people. The classical world and the Christian tradition prior to the modern era widely recognized similarity as essential for the highest fellow feelings. Aquinas, for example, argued that "likeness causes love of friendship or well-being. For the very fact that two men are alike, having, as it were, one form, makes them to be, in a manner, one in that form." For Aquinas, similarity in animal species is, for man, a cause for universal love, but he takes the principle of similarity further. Similarities in particulars is the ground of greater love for some over others. He reasons this way: "Since the intensity of an act results from the principle of action, and the principle of action is union and similarity, we ought to love in a higher degree and more intensely those who are more like us and more closely united to us."[22] Bishop Lancelot Andrewes said that "nearness of nature, or kindred" is one of three "motives to loves."[23] David Hume, with his usual eloquence, argues in effect for the principle of similarity:

> Nature has preserv'd a great resemblance among all human creatures, and that we never remark any passion or principle in others, of which, in some degree or other, we may not find a parallel

22. Aquinas, *Commentary on the Letters of Saint Paul to the Galatians and Ephesians,* trans. Fabian R. Larcher and Matthew L. Lamb (Lander, WY: Aquinas Institute, 2012), 364.

23. Lancelot Andrewes, *The Pattern of Catechistical Doctrine at Large,* 3rd ed. (1650; London, 1675), 75.

in ourselves. . . . There is a very remarkable resemblance, which preserves itself amidst all their variety; and this resemblance must very much contribute to make us enter into the sentiments of others, and embrace them with facility and pleasure. Accordingly we find, that where, beside the general resemblance of our natures, there is any peculiar similarity in our manners, or character, or country, or language, it facilitates the sympathy. The stronger the relation is betwixt ourselves and any object, the more easily does the imagination make the transition, and convey to the related idea the vivacity of conception, with which we always form the idea of our own person.[24]

Particulars make possible the highest form of social life, for through them one knows another as he knows himself. One is able to love another as himself.

The human instinct to socialize and dwell with similar people is universal, though for many today, especially Westerners, this instinct is understood as evil or pathological. Of course, such people typically denounce this "evil" when found among Westerners, while celebrating the ethno-centrism of others. But this instinct in itself is good actually, even universally good. Your instinct to conduct everyday life among similar people is natural, and being natural, it is for your good. To use a Thomistic framing of the good, since man is drawn to the goods made possible in social life, he is naturally drawn to the necessary conditions for that good, which includes in-grouping according to a principle of similarity. That is, by nature (which grace does not destroy) people are led to create and maintain societies of similar people, for only in societies of similar

24. David Hume, *A Treatise of Human Nature* (London: John Noon, 1739), 2:1.11.

people can people achieve the complete good. Hence, the preference for those who are similar is natural and arises not necessarily from maliciousness toward those who are dissimilar. Similarity
enables you to exercise the highest love to your fellow man and to
receive the highest love in return.

The clearest example of this enablement is having a common
language. How can two people who lack any verbal means of communication cooperate in a productive, common life or even share
deeply and widely in affection? Calvin writes that "by language, we
know, not only words, but also feelings are communicated. Language is the expression of the mind, as it is commonly said, and
it is therefore the bond of society."[25] This echoes Plato, who wrote,
"When a single people speaks the same language and observes the
same laws you get a certain feeling of community."[26] Augustine argues that the absence of a common language leads not only to frustrated collective action but to conflict:

> if two men, each ignorant of the other's language, meet, and are
> not compelled to pass, but, on the contrary, to remain in com-
> pany, dumb animals, though of different species, would more
> easily hold intercourse than they, human beings though they
> be. For their common nature is no help to friendliness when
> they are prevented by diversity of language from conveying

25. Calvin, *Commentaries on the Prophet Jeremiah and the Lamentations*, vol. 9 of *Calvin's
Commentaries*, 1:286 [on Jer. 5:15]. He continues: "Had there been no language, in what
would men differ from brute beasts? One would barbarously treat another; there would
indeed be no humanity among them."

26. Plato, *Laws* 708c. As Althusius said, "The use of speech is truly necessary for men in
social life, for without it no society can endure." *Politica*, 85 [11.16]. He also states that the
civil government ought to regulate language for this same end.

their sentiments to one another; so that a man would more readily hold intercourse with his dog than with a foreigner.[27]

Several ethnicities can share the same language, of course. But since language is a particular and is necessary for civil fellowship, it follows that a least *some* particularity is a prerequisite for civil fellowship. Hence, sharing only what is universal—viz., common humanity—is wholly inadequate for a complete social bond. And even a cursory reflection on one's daily habits and everyday life reveals that more extensive unity in particulars is necessary for living well.

Since the familiarity of everyday life operates in the background of life, we often fail to see the work of particulars in our daily lives—the little rules, expectations, manners, and meanings of things, actions, expressions, etc. That these are all comfortably in the background means that familiarity is working. Only when one violates or acts contrary to our expectations does our expectation for them come to consciousness. But if we take a deliberately reflective stance towards our collective particularity, we can see firstly how much of our everyday life is necessarily taken up in particularities, and secondly how these things make possible a mutually beneficial and loving relationship with others. We do not, and indeed *cannot*, live (let alone live well) according to universal rules. Nor can we live well among contrary particulars; there must be a *normal* to which all conform or assimilate, at least in order for people to live well together. Thus, an instinct for a suitable normal is a *good* instinct; so too is the moral expectation that people conform to that normal or else face some degree of social separation.

27. Augustine, *The City of God*, trans. Marcus Dods (Buffalo, NY: Christian Literature, 1887), 19.7.

The Principle of Difference

If some set of goods are made possible only in conditions of similarity, then a similar, multi-kin people—i.e., an ethnic-group—must be a self-conscious in-group. Only then are they able to conserve the conditions of similarity when confronted with encroaching difference. An in-group, by definition, has out-groups—a distinction of *us* and *them* that excludes others. Exclusion follows not necessarily from maliciousness or from the absence of universal benevolence, but from a natural principle of difference that recognizes for oneself and for others the goods provided by similarity and solidarity in that similarity. To exclude an out-group is to recognize a universal good for man—a good made possible only by respecting and conserving difference. Since it is a universal good, you and your people are entitled by nature to a *right* of difference. This is a *natural* right, because particularity is necessary to live well according to the nature of man.

One expression of this principle of difference is the citizen/alien distinction—a distinction once widely held by Christians. For example, Althusius writes,

> The rights (*jura*) of the city, its privileges, statutes, and benefits, which make a city great and celebrated, are also communicated by the citizens. They are shared with the people in the suburbs, outposts, and surrounding villages, but not with travellers and foreigners. For citizens enjoy the same laws (*leges*), the same religion, and the same language, speech, judgment under the law, discipline, customs, money, measures, weights, and so forth. They enjoy these not in such manner that each is like himself alone, but that all are like each other.[28]

28. Althusius, *Politica*, 48 [6.39].

The civic designation of "foreigner" is not necessarily arbitrary, prejudicial, or based in suspicion. Rather, it recognizes that particularity is necessary for civic fellowship and living well. Dissimilar people have trouble forming and sustaining a political community. When foreigners enter in mass, they undermine and disrupt the host people's civil fellowship and symbiosis, generating hostility and antipathy. The idea that "diversity destroys unity," as Althusius wrote,[29] was well recognized in the Christian tradition. Indeed, Althusius explicitly affirms that cultural diversity produces conflict:

> [A]s the customs of regions often express diverse interests and discernments, so persons born in these regions hold diverse patterns in their customs. Accordingly, they are unable to come together at the same time without some antipathy toward each other, which when once aroused tends to stir up sedition, subversion, and damage to the life of the commonwealth.[30]

Antipathy between ethnic groups is a consequence of sin, but conflict between such groups is itself a natural consequence of contrary customs. Even good customs can prescribe opposing expectations of conduct, duties, and manners, which lead to frustration in collective action and to misunderstanding, hesitance in relations, and avoidance due to the inefficiency of interaction. Aquinas even asserts that regular interaction with foreigners is harmful to civil life:

> A city which must engage in much trade in order to supply its needs also has to put up with the continuous presence of foreigners. But association with foreigners, according to Aristotle's

29. Ibid., 78 [9.45].
30. Ibid., 150 [23.14].

Politics, is particularly harmful to civic customs. For it is inevitable that strangers, brought up under other laws and customs, will in many cases act as citizens are not wont to act and thus, since the citizens are drawn by their example to act likewise, their own civic life is upset.[31]

In his poem "The Stranger," Rudyard Kipling captures the difficulties and limitations when interacting with a foreigner.

> The Stranger within my gate,
>   He may be true or kind,
> But he does not talk my talk—
>   I cannot feel his mind.
> I see the face and the eyes and the mouth,
>   But not the soul behind.
>
> The men of my own stock,
>   They may do ill or well,
> But they tell the lies I am wonted to,
>   They are used to the lies I tell;
> And we do not need interpreters
>   When we go to buy or sell.
>
> The Stranger within my gates,
>   He may be evil or good,
> But I cannot tell what powers control—
>   What reasons sway his mood;
> Nor when the Gods of his far-off land
>   Shall repossess his blood.

31. Aquinas, *On Kingship: To the King of Cyprus*, trans. Gerald B. Phelan (Toronto: Pontifical Institute of Mediaeval Studies, 1949), §138.

The men of my own stock,

   Bitter bad they may be,

But, at least, they hear the things I hear,

   And see the things I see;

And whatever I think of them and their likes

   They think of the likes of me.

This was my father's belief

   And this is also mine:

Let the corn be all one sheaf—

   And the grapes be all one vine,

Ere our children's teeth are set on edge

   By bitter bread and wine.[32]

People of different ethnic groups can exercise respect for difference, conduct some routine business with each other, join in inter-ethnic alliances for mutual good, and exercise common humanity (e.g., the good Samaritan), but they cannot have a life together that goes beyond mutual alliance. As Aristotle said, "[A] city [*polis*] is not a community sharing a location and for the sake of not committing injustice against each other and conducting trade. . . . [T]he city is the community [κοινωνία] in living well both of households and families for the sake of a complete and self-sufficient life." Community is not "for the sake of living together" but "for the sake of noble action," he states. And, as Aristotle makes clear, noble action is possible only when "affection" binds the people.[33]

32. Rudyard Kipling, "The Stranger," in *Rudyard Kipling's Verse: 1885–1918*, inclusive ed. (Garden City, NY: Doubleday, Page, 1922), 616.

33. Aristotle, *Aristotle's Politics*, 3.9.

To be sure, I am not saying that ethnic majorities today should work to rescind citizenship from ethnic minorities, though perhaps in some cases amicable ethnic separation along political lines is mutually desired. What I am saying is that in-group solidarity and right of difference along ethnic lines are necessary for the complete good for each and all; and, therefore, even in multinational civil arrangements (e.g., the United Kingdom), national distinctions must be prudently upheld, and each person ought to (in normal circumstances) prefer their own people over others.

IV. Loving the Neighbor

Degrees of Love

The in-group/out-group distinction, which prioritizes concern for one's own people and native soil, troubles many in the West, at least when Western ethnic-groups begin to distinguish themselves in this way. Christians will ask, "Aren't we called to love all equally?" assuming the affirmative answer is obvious. But despite modern Christian sentiment, a quick glance at the Christian tradition (and mild reflection on one's own relationships) reveals the almost ubiquity of the opposite view—that the intensity of love varies by degree according to similarity and the extent that another is bound to you. Augustine writes, for example, that "[s]ince one cannot help everyone, one has to be concerned with those who by reason of place, time, and circumstances, are by some chance more tightly bound to you."[34] Of course, Christians are to

---

34. Augustine, *De Doctrina Christiana*, 1.28. Calvin likewise states, "[A]mong men, in proportion to the closeness of the tie that mutually binds us, some have stronger claims than others." *Commentary on a Harmony of the Evangelists*, 1:471 [on Matt. 10:37].

love their neighbor, which includes all people, but the Christian moral tradition has distinguished near and far neighbors. Samuel Willard writes, for example, that though the "word neighbor comprehends in it all mankind. . . . [I]t [also] involves all the several relations, natural, civil and religious that men may bear to each other." We are not, therefore, "to love all equally alike," an idea that "flows from the ignorance of the relations which God has fixed among men; unto which he has annexed those special duties, which are to be discharged by a special love one to another. . . . There are some whom we ought to be more concerned for than others."[35] There is a difference between a basic love for all and greater love for those nearer to you. As Cicero states, "There is a nearer relation of race [*gens*], nation, and language, which brings men into very close community of feeling."[36]

No one questions that we ought to love our own children over other children and our own family over other families and our own church over churches. Thus, the equal-love doctrine is false, at least with regard to those relations.[37] We do not question this, because we *feel* natural affection for these people (and not for others) and we clearly see the good of preferring them over others. That is to say, we know by *instinct* and *reason* that we ought to prefer some over others. It is also evident, from both instinct and reason, that we ought to prefer our own nation and countrymen over others. This instinct is not from the fall or due to sin; it is natural and, therefore,

---

35. Willard, *Body of Divinity,* loc. 31641.

36. Cicero, *On Duties,* trans. Andrew P. Peabody (Boston: Little, Brown, 1887), 1.17.

37. Those who exhibit a preference for foreigners have disordered loves—a condition we can call xenophilia, or the love of foreignness. Its conjoined condition is what Roger Scruton called "oikophobia," or the fear of home and familiarity.

good. We are naturally drawn to what, in principle, is necessary for our complete good. If the reader lacks this instinct, consider the good in it. Aquinas states that "we love more those who are more nearly connected with us, since we love them in more ways."[38] As I argued above, a community of similar people provides the best social conditions for the communication of gifts and achieving collective goals. Dissimilar people together can achieve the basic goods of humanity, but not the complete good. Similarity is a necessary prerequisite to well-functioning symbiosis in and by which a people come to live well. The common good is a *bounded* common good, and the whole is best served by individuals preferring the common good to which they are bound. One ought to give his people priority in his heart and action. As Aquinas said, "In matters pertaining to . . . relations between citizens, we should prefer our fellow-citizens."[39]

Types of Love

The Christian tradition recognized three types of love: benevolence, beneficence, and complacence. Benevolence, or wishing and desiring the good of another, is love for all people simply on account of shared humanity.[40] Beneficence is the actual doing of good, which

38. Aquinas, *ST*, II–II.26.7.

39. Aquinas, *ST*, II–II.26.8. Jonathan Edwards wrote, "The law of nature and the law of divine revelation teach us to be united with those that we dwell with in the same country, to have a special affection for them, and makes us, in many respects, one body with them." *The Works of Jonathan Edwards*, ed. Amy Plantinga Pauw, vol. 20, *The "Miscellanies" 833–1152* (1740; New Haven, CT: Yale University Press, 2002), no. 928.

40. Jonathan Edwards defines the "love of benevolence" as "that affection or propensity of the heart to any being, which causes it to incline to its well-being, or disposes it to desire and take pleasure in its happiness." *The Nature of True Virtue* (1765; Eugene, OR: Wipf and Stock, 2003), 6.

is universal in principle (viz., all people ought to be *potential* objects of love) but is practically delimited by means and opportunity.[41] Generosity with resources, for example, requires that you have resources and a suitable means of transferring those resources. The absence of either resources or means precludes the act of beneficence toward another. Similar people have more opportunities for acts of beneficence for several reasons, including (most importantly) that similar people share a commitment to certain particular or cultural goods. Thus, there are more ways to love similar people in concrete action.

Beneficence would seem to fully explain the degrees of love described above; similarity effectively expands the opportunity for beneficence. But beneficence leaves out an important feature of experience. A parent is generous toward his child not simply because the parent-child relation offers an easy means of generosity. Rather, a parent is generous because the child is *his* child. Furthermore, the love that a man owes to any female non-spouse and the love he owes to his wife are certainly different, not only as to the kinds of love but also as to the disposition in his love. The sort of delight one has in loving his wife, if directed to any other woman, would violate the seventh commandment. Similarly, we wish not merely for the good of our friends or simply for our delight in seeing their good; we delight in the *presence* of our friends, as an end in itself. In all of these examples, love is not merely a matter of opportunity or ease of doing good, but something about the person in relation to you. Thus, there must be something higher than the practical opportunity for beneficence that explains such love.

41. As Aquinas said, "As regard beneficence, we are bound to observe this inequality [of love], because we cannot do good to all." *ST*, II-II.26.6.

Perhaps, counterintuitively, the missing element is self-love. Though not itself a type of love, self-love was for centuries and across theological traditions regarded as the ground of love for neighbor. After all, Christ said, "Love your neighbor *as yourself*" (Matt. 22:39, NIV). Augustine ranks self-love as the second of the four necessary loves (second to loving God) and considered it so obvious that "there is no need of a command that every man should love himself and his own body."[42] Aquinas states that "a man ought, out of charity, to love himself more than he loves any other person."[43] Willard reflects the classical Protestant view, saying, "Self-love is the rule of our loving our neighbor."[44] English Puritan Stephen Charnock writes that self-love is "a rule to measure that duty we owe to our neighbor, whom we cannot love as ourselves, if we do not first love ourselves."[45] Thus, as Willard writes, "[E]very man owes the first and principal of this love [of neighbor] to himself. Every man is his own next neighbor."[46]

Self-love, with regard to beneficence, is the fulfillment of duties to oneself, which are the same duties one owes to others. Since one has the duty of beneficence toward others, that they might live well, one has a duty of beneficence toward himself, that he might live well. Now, living well requires shared cultural particularity. Thus, cultural particularity is an object of self-love—one ought to have both a positive regard for his cultural distinctives and ought to act

42. Augustine, *De Doctrina Christiana*, 1.26.

43. Aquinas, *ST*, II-II.26.4.

44. Willard, *Body of Divinity*, loc. 31632.

45. Stephen Charnock, *Discourses upon the Existence and Attributes of God*, 2 vols. (New York: Robert Carter, 1874), 1:136. As Willard writes, "I may not suffer myself to starve, to keep another alive." *Body of Divinity*, loc. 31647.

46. Ibid.

to secure them in the interest of his own good.[47] But since cultural particularity is necessarily something shared with others, the duty of self-love with regard to cultural particularity requires the conservation of the common life of which one is a part. We can conclude, then, that the object of this duty is not merely a matter of private good but also a matter of the common good. Securing particularity is simultaneously an act of self-love and an act of love for others. The good of one cannot be separated from the good of all. Though again this would seem to explain the particular love we have for some, it doesn't fully explain something deeper in our relation to others. There must be something more pre-reflective and instinctive, something that operates in the background.

Complacent Self-Love

I want to propose that what explains the degrees of love is the third type of love: complacent love. The love of complacency is rarely mentioned today, though it was a common term in discussions of love and in theology in the medieval and early modern periods. Far from referring to indifference or smugness, complacent love refers to "pleasing assent" or "delighting" in some person or thing on account of something in or about the person or thing. In theology, it refers to God the Father's love for his Son, through whom he loves the Church; and Protestant theologians once argued that the church deserves our love of complacency on account of God's love for it. I want to develop this love of complacency to explain and justify the sort of love for people and place that is irreducible either to well-wishing or doing good. Indeed, complacent love, in my view,

47. This assumes that his cultural distinctives are good. Calvin affirms "just customs" in *Men, Women, and Order in the Church*, 55–59.

is necessary to direct our priorities of beneficence and is the natural mechanism that leads us to the complete good.

Complacent love is difficult to describe in terms of experience because it operates in our familiarity. To give a preliminary definition: complacent love (with regard to human relations) is a delight in dwelling among your people on your native soil. Calvin captures this love when he writes, "Delightful to everyone is his native soil, and it is also delightful to dwell among one's own people."[48] Complacent love for one's country is not simply delighting in its virtues, for all countries have virtues. Complacent love is a bounded love by principle, reserved for one's own people and place. In view is not simply delighting in good, but a delight bound up with one*self* in relation to his country and countrymen—a sort of union of affection.

Here is a more refined definition: complacent love with regard to one's nation is *a kind of self-love in which one delights in the totality of himself—a totality that extends to people and place.* One might appropriately call it "complacent self-love." In other words, among these people and in this place, one encounters him*self*, for a part of himself (phenomenologically speaking) is invested here. The delight in people and place is simultaneously a self-delight. This definition is, admittedly, difficult and novel, so I'll take some time for clarification.

Recall Marcus's delight in his familial home and how through it he encounters himself, his father, and his grandfather. They left a "trace" through their activity on the place. We can see traces of past activity anywhere in the world. A European can visit the Great Wall of China, for example, and see what these distant and (to him) very foreign people built, and anyone can marvel at the achievement. But

48. In the "Prefatory Address" of his *Institutes*, Calvin states, "I cherish towards it [my native land] the feelings which become me as a man" (p. 5).

Marcus's case is different. Since Marcus has a sort of natural union with his natural relations, what manifests from his ancestral land is not simply a generic trace of human activity but Marcus himself. His delight in the place, therefore, is self-delight on account of his natural, affective union with his family.

The "self" is not some abstract or purely inward thing. It is not reducible to the mind or soul or even the body and soul together. In saying "I exist," the "I" for you is not some vacuous or arbitrary identifier, but rather it assumes a concrete reality. You *are* your relations. Thus, the self has an extension beyond the inward. Your unique concerns and love for certain people, places, and things are self-concern and self-love. The parent-child relation, for example, is part of the extended self—a union of persons based in natural generation—such that the parent feels intense delight in *that* child to the exclusion of the others.[49] Thomist scholar David Gallagher states that for Aquinas, "the basis for the extension of one's self to the other is *similitude* or *likeness* (*similitudo*)." This is a "unity of affection" (*unitas affectus*)—"a unity at the level of affections or will by which one person affectively takes the other to be part of himself."[50] Complacent self-love, therefore, is not an inward delight only but delight in and arising from the relation itself—from the unity of affection.

As I've argued, ethnicity is largely a product of sharing particulars—the sharing of customs, pastimes, and traditions; and the

49. Many will be tempted to interpret this parent-child union in psychological terms, as reducible to some bodily or brain response to one's own children. Whatever value there is in this sort of analysis, it doesn't describe *actual experience*, and it devalues the experience by reducing it to brain activity.

50. David M. Gallagher, "Thomas Aquinas on Self-Love as the Basis for Love of Others," in *Acta Philosophica* 8, no. 1 (1999), 32–33.

union of someone in relation to his fellow countrymen is based in those particulars.[51] Thus, to encounter a countryman is to encounter oneself—to be, in a sense, with one's self. As Hume said, with similar people we can "always form the idea of our own person."[52] Hence, one's self is extended to others, according to the degree that they are similar to you, bringing some people into a unique sphere of concern and extending self-love to a particular people.

One might say that this is too romantic. Who goes about his daily life consciously delighting in those around him? My answer is that although the conscious delight in one's people typically occurs only on special occasions, these occasions simply disclose what operates in the background of experience. Experiences of foreignness and patriotic celebrations, for example, do not generate delight but *reveal* it to consciousness. Familiarity is, in this way, *pre-reflective delight*—something concealed in everyday life. Your delight in your wife or children is not sporadic and occasional; rather, your delight in them is constant, but it surfaces on special occasions. The same is true with regard to one's countrymen.

Though complacent self-love is not in itself an act for the good of others (which is the love of beneficence), it operates as the background impulse that orients action for good. It directs you to love your children more than others and to love your people more than all other peoples. Being in the background, it doesn't require reflection for its operation; it is implicit in action and often revealed in action in retrospect. It is a reliable and essential instinct for human good. A parent does not first reflect on his complacent love for his

51. The degree of union varies based on the union of particulars.

52. David Hume, *A Treatise of Human Nature*, ed. David Fate Norton and Mary J. Norton, (Oxford: Clarendon Press, 2007), 1:207.

child to prefer his child over others and act in love for her. The same is true of one's countrymen.

Action and Extending the Self

The role of action in extending the self is rarely acknowledged today, though it is embedded in much of Western thought. John Locke was onto something when he argued that mixing one's labor into the earth generates a claim of ownership.[53] One can deny his account of property rights and still see the principle at work: that such activity creates a relation between the actor and the thing acted upon such that the subject and object are united and the self of the former is extended into the latter, even into inanimate objects.

John Steinbeck's *Grapes of Wrath* contains several insightful accounts of this connection of self and land. Here is one:

> The tenant [farmer] pondered. "Funny thing how it is. If a man owns a little property, that property is him, it's part of him, and it's like him. If he owns property only so he can walk on it and handle it and be sad when it isn't doing well, and feel fine when the rain falls on it, that property is him, and some way he's bigger because he owns it. Even if he isn't successful he's big with his property. That is so."[54]

The property is not merely his; it *is* him—an extension of himself. He feels with it; he is well when it is well. He is bound to and in it. He is bigger with it, because it concretizes his self into the world.

---

53. John Locke, *Second Treatise of Government*, ed. C.B. McPherson (1690; Indianapolis: Hackett, 1980), 5.27.
54. John Steinbeck, *The Grapes of Wrath* (New York: Viking, 2014), 38–39.

This is not simply an "emotional" connection; it is the actualization of the self into the world through our activity in it.

We have intense connections with the land on which we and our natural relations have labored. We encounter it as *mastered* land— land that has come under one's dominion through self-mastery. Self-mastery is not merely the control of our faculties and desires; it extends to things and places, as an extension of our dominion. Just as we master our minds and bodies with care and love, so too do we master the world with care and love.[55] Out of this activity, we come to a sense of ownership—of owned space—and come to see the objects of our activity as images of ourselves, and we include them in our sphere of concern.

Steinbeck includes this sense of ownership later in his narrative. He writes of farmers who were illegally cultivating "secret gardens" on uncultivated land:

> A sheriff comes along and says to them, "I had my eye on you. This ain't your land. You're trespassing." The man responds to the sheriff, "The land ain't plowed, an' I ain't hurtin' it none." The sheriff replies, "You goddamned squatters. Pretty soon you'd think you owned it. You'd be sore as hell. Think you owned it. Get off now." ... The little green carrot tops were kicked off and the turnip greens trampled. And then the Jimson weed moved back in. But the cop was right. A crop raised—why, that makes ownership. Land hoed and the carrots eaten—a man might

---

55. Indeed, the excesses of dominion—the ravishing and exploitation of creation—results from the absence of self from the land. Such men in relation to land are "small," says Steinbeck. The highest ideals of self-mastery, when self is extended to places, results in harmonious cultivation, conservation, and sustainability.

fight for land he's taken food from. Get him off quick! He'll think he owns it. He might even die fighting for the little plot among the Jimson weeds. Did ya see his face when we kicked them turnips out? Why, he'd kill a fella soon's he'd look at him.[56]

The land that comes under one's mastery is worth dying for. An offense against it is an offense against the man, for he and it are united on account of his activity on it. The offense is based not merely in the loss of food or in the wasted labor, but in the sheriff's flagrant attack on something that the farmer himself, by his own activity, mastered and thereby brought into a relation of delight.

The labor of your ancestors is also brought into your relation of delight. Your kin acted on *this* ground, leaving traces of their activity; and being united affectively, their activity is your activity. The son of a construction worker will point to a building in his hometown and say, "My father built that." In saying this, he expresses far more than the indicative and even more than pride in his father's accomplishments; he's expressing delight in the building. It is not just one building among others. His loved one expended life for its creation. Likewise, one delights in his hometown, because this is where his natural relations conducted their daily lives, completing their mundane tasks here and there. One is delighted by this place, for it has traces of those in whom he delights.

Broadening this analysis to nations, we can see that through a people's dominion-taking and dominion-sustaining activity, the people as a corporate entity has owned space. This owned space is not simply a combination of individual legal ownership. It is a whole that transcends its parts. The people have a sense of collective

56. Steinbeck, *Grapes of Wrath*, 247–48.

ownership—that this is *ours*—because they and their natural relations have mastered it (i.e., brought it under dominion) and thereby
have affectively united a people and place. "The sweetness of [one's]
native soil holds nearly all men bound to itself," said Calvin.[57] The
people's homeland is both an object of delight for the people and a
basis for self-delight as a people. As Johann Herder said,

> Everyone loves his country, his manners, his language, his wife,
> his children; not because they are the best in the World, but
> because they are absolutely his own, and he loves himself and
> his own labors in them.[58]

Idolatry

One expected objection to this understanding of complacent self-
love is that it constitutes idolatry or ethno-narcissism. It is difficult to
respond to an accusation of idolatry today because the term is lazily
deployed against those who love something "too much." I will simply
say that complacent love explains one's deep, instinctual preference
for his own children, his kin, and his countrymen. Such preferences
are not the result of a bare divine command or purely from human
choice, but arise from God's design of man. By nature, we have an
instinct to prefer some over others, and we are rarely conscious of it.
This instinct is not arbitrary, nor is it a product of the fall, nor is it a
holdover from millions of years of evolution; rather, it is fundamental
to our natural constitution, drawing us to form and sustain the necessary social organization in which man can achieve his complete good,

57. Calvin, *Commentary on the First Book of Moses Called Genesis*, 1:343 [on Gen. 12:1].

58. Johann Herder, *Outlines of a Philosophy of the History of Man* (New York: Bergman
Publishers, 1800), 10.

according to his nature. Benevolence and beneficence—though essential to fully understand human love—are not enough; there must be something else. The delight in complacent self-love provides an explanation for our instinct for belonging. Each person is not some independent agent of beneficence to undifferentiated others. One's belonging, as a background union of affection, directs one's preferences in order to achieve the complete good. Nothing that is natural to man, according to his design, can in itself be idolatrous.

Complacent self-love is not so much a delight in your child's or your county's virtues. Nor is it some means of excusing bad behavior or blaming it on others, or for propagating fantasies and self-destructive myths about one's people. You still love your child even when he or she is being disobedient; indeed, your great disappointment in their disobedience is *because* of your love and preference for your child. The same is true for you and your people. This explains why the apostle Paul had "great heaviness and continual sorrow in [his] heart" for his "kinsmen," who had rejected Christ (Rom. 9:2–3).

Conclusion

The nation is not a people united around propositions alone; no nation can be so disembodied and dis-embedded from concrete things. In ancient times, people-groups often explained their origins by claiming to have sprung from the ground they lived on. This says something about the human relation to place—people enliven it with their activity; their culture is a sort of cultivation of space. The people and place are one, for the adorned meaning of space depends on the people, and the people, taken as a whole, *are* the place. This people-place symbiosis is held together by ties of affection, based fundamentally on natural affection toward kin. One loves a particular people in a particular place because his family did so too, and through his connection with his family and their activity with others, he has a *home*-land and a people. This love, though it motivates the love of beneficence, operates in the background of experience, as pre-reflective familiarity with people and place, drawing us (by instinct) to prefer particular people. The instinct for distinct nationality is good and reliable.

V. Nationalism

Nationalism is typically treated as a historical phenomenon, even in normative accounts that praise or denounce it. Given its 20th-century manifestations, theorists in favor of nationalism have an uphill battle, often having to repeatedly and tiresomely disclaim and denounce any hint of "xenophobia" and "racism." Despite its past, however, people on both the right and the left have favored forms of nationalism. From the right, Yoram Hazony, who expounds its virtues in his much-discussed *Virtue of Nationalism*, points to Protestantism as a crucial source for the rise of the nation-state in late 16th century. From the left, Yael Tamir argues in *Why Nationalism* that nationalism's roots in the French Revolution and 19th-century liberalism show that nationalism is useful for the popular support of center-left causes and policies (e.g., egalitarianism and redistributive policies). Both of these accounts assume the modern nation-state model of the nation, which requires each nation to be geographically bounded, separated, and equal—that is, each is under its own national government.[59]

59. A nation can be arranged as a nation-state or as a semi-autonomous, regional entity in a broader empire or as part of a confederation of nations. Each nation ideally has enough

Though I favor Hazony's account over others, nationalism in this book follows conceptually from my account of the nation, and so I do not describe nationalism by appealing to historical examples or historical development. Thus, I have no need to celebrate or defend or denounce past "fascist" regimes or "populism" and other socio-political phenomena. Nor do I call for ethno-states in the modern sense, though I *do* affirm that each nation ought to seek and have sufficient political and social autonomy to order and secure themselves according to their particularities. In a postlapsarian world, existing under an empire of nations can provide better conditions for national life than being a wholly independent nation contending with anarchic international conditions. Still, nations must have and ought to fight to secure law-making authority, even if that authority is subordinate to a higher imperial law.

I defined *nationalism* in the introduction in this way:

> *Nationalism refers to a totality of national action, consisting of civil laws and social customs (e.g., culture), conducted by a nation as a nation, in order to procure for itself both earthly and heavenly good.*

Put simply, nationalism refers to a nation acting as a nation for its national good. Considered apart from specific accounts of the nation, this definition captures something fairly uncontroversial and trivially true. We expect nations (however one defines it) to seek their national good, and most would affirm that this is good and right, in principle. Shouldn't the people of the United States

---

power in civil affairs so that each can act for its conservation and maturation as a people. The particular arrangements necessary for a people's flourishing depends on several variables, and even if there is a "best regime" for all nations, that subject goes beyond the scope of this work.

seek their national good? Even the Americans who denounce the "America First" slogan will generally affirm the primacy of American interests, at least publicly. Thus, despite the -*ism* of nationalism, it is not itself an ideology. It certainly can carry an ideology, but nationalism itself is simply the nation acting for its national good.

What makes my view of nationalism controversial is my account of the nation and, more specifically, the Christian nation: the nation, properly understood, is a particular people with ties of affection that bind them to each other and their place of dwelling; and thus nationalism is the nation acting for its national good, which includes conservation of those ties of affection. That, I suspect, is controversial at least to liberal and left-wing nationalisms.

My discussion of nationalism in this chapter is fairly brief, mainly because the content of the definition is the subject of the next few chapters, which cover Christian nationalism directly. Christian nationalism is a species of nationalism, and thus it assumes and relies on everything essential to nationalism. Furthermore, I already discussed each part of the definition in the introduction. Still, I will address a few things here.

Though the nation is essential to nationalism, a nation can be incompletely nationalist. The essential conditions for complete nationalism are (1) a national self-conception, and (2) a national will to act for itself. A nation can exist *implicitly*. In this situation, the people implicitly act as a nation—being drawn to each other by natural instinct and similarly—but the people lack explicit consciousness of their nationhood. Hence, a nation can exist even if the people are not fully cognizant of their nationhood, and that nation can be implicitly nationalist, for the nation unconsciously acts for its good. A nation with *explicit* awareness of itself has a national self-conception (i.e., a collective recognition of nationhood) and can openly deliberate about its national good, and it wills that good explicitly. This is complete nationalism—a nation *in itself* has become a nation *for itself*. Thus, the steps to perfect nationalism begin with a nation moving from implicit to explicit knowledge of itself and then, on the basis of that self-conception, acting for itself by willing its national good. The national will is deposited in civil and social institutions as mediums for national good, which determine concrete actions.

The national will presupposes a positive and protective national disposition toward the nation and the place in which the nation dwells. The people affirm that *this place is ours*. They have a collective sense of owned space. It follows that the principle of exclusion is a necessary object of the national will. A nation for itself (when rational) is actively exclusionary, for it recognizes its own concrete and fragile particularity, based in intergenerational customs, material culture, and adorned meaning. Since particularity is universally necessary for human good, the nation's particularity is necessary for its own human good.

As a matter of moral principle, nations by means of civil law would deny the universal reception of foreigners. For as theologian Alastair Roberts affirmed,

> Mass immigration [from culturally alien nations], in the form it
> is practiced in the liberal West, is a profoundly socially destruc-
> tive force, antagonistic to historic modes of life. It fractures the
> foundations of society upon which liberal institutions and free-
> doms are built. . . . It is less a matter of welcoming the stranger
> into our society as a guest and much more typically a matter

of a host people being steadily dispossessed of their land by a liberal polity to which all are slowly subjected as an ever more atomized and amorphous mass of people.[60]

The principle of exclusion does not preclude the reception of foreigners absolutely. Nations ought to be hospitable. At the individual and familial levels, hospitality demands generosity to strangers, especially to those in need. A nation, as a sort of corporate person, can and ought to be hospitable as well. But hospitality is subordinate to higher duties: no individual, family, or nation is duty-bound to welcome strangers to the detriment of the good of those most near and bound it. Furthermore, guests have duties toward their hosts. Foreigners who are granted residence thus have unique duties. As Althusius writes,

> Differing from citizens, however, are foreigners, outsiders, aliens, and strangers whose duty it is to mind their own business, make no strange inquiries, not even to be curious in a foreign commonwealth, but to adapt themselves, as far as good conscience permits, to the customs of the place and city where they live in order that they may not be a scandal to others.[61]

The foreigner's fundamental principle is *conformity*, to the greatest extent possible; they are not at home but guests in another's home. Their posture or disposition to the place must be respect,

60. "President Trump's Executive Order and the Moral Confusion of the Immigration Debate," Alastair's Adversaria, January 30, 2017, accessed October 7, 2022, https://alastairadversaria.com/2017/01/30/president-trumps-executive-order-and-the -moral-confusion-of-the-immigration-debate/.
61. Althusius, *Politica*, 40 [5.10].

humility, deference, and gratitude. They must have no attitude of "mine" in relation to space except to what is allotted to them. Nor may they subvert or exploit the commonwealth for their own gain. The foreigner should mute his own customary ways. His ways are not necessarily bad, evil, barbarous, or inferior in any way. Indeed, his customs might be superior and more refined than the host country's. But the foreigner has a duty not to disrupt the host people's way of life, and the hosts have every right to hold such people to these duties, even to the point of deportation.

Moreover, nations have every right to make strict conditions for receiving people into civil fellowship (e.g., conferring citizenship). Aquinas, following Aristotle, suggested that newcomers should not receive citizenship until the second or third generation of residence.[62] This ensures that those granted civil fellowship have an intimate, natal connection to people and place.

VI: Conclusion

The talk of ethnicity as something fundamental to everyday life makes many in the West, especially in America, very uncomfortable. But the modern West is weird. Its strangeness is most acute in its dogmatic commitment to an ideology of universality. The modern West sees its values of openness, tolerance, and liberty not as products of the Western experience and thus its particular inheritance, but as *universal* values and easily accessible to all. For this reason, its habitation is, in its mind, a place of this universality—a space fit for *all* people. A universal space has a place for universal humanity. This explains in part why Western peoples are so willing

62. Aquinas, *ST*, I-II.105.3.

to receive masses of non-western immigrants. It should come as no shock to outside observers that these newcomers, far from assimilating to this ideology of universality, often end up transforming neighborhoods into their own particular cultural image.

Western man is enamored of his ideology of universality; it is the chief and only ground of his self-regard. His in-group is *all* people—it is a universal in-group. Everyone is an object of his beneficence. But in perverse fashion he is his own in-group's out-group. The object of his regard is the non-Westerner at the Westerner's expense—a bizarre self-denigration rooted in guilt and malaise. Loss and humiliation is the point, however. It is euphoric to him; his own degradation is thrilling. This is his psycho-sexual ethno-masochism, the most pernicious illness of the Western mind.

Ultimately, the modern Westerner resides in another's land. This is true not because he stole it centuries earlier but because he keeps and maintains it for the taking of outsiders, whom he invites and who ultimately dispossess him. Indeed, his own dispossession has become the Westerner's only good. Thus, Western man, whose birthrates have plummeted, creates well-ordered spaces and civil institutions not for himself and his natural progeny but for his replacements.

Repeatedly, in the face of ethnic identity politics, we see Western man retreating to this universality—to the universal values of the Declaration of Independence, for example—not realizing that these values come from the collective experience of a cluster of European nations. In this retreat, he perpetuates the conditions for ethnic identity politics. The promise of universality, and its accompanying "inclusive" space, includes a guarantee for equal group outcomes. But since Western values lack universality *in reality*, equality is never achievable. Most immigrants know this; they experience the non-universality of the West; they know the foolishness of Western claims of universality. Hence, identity politics has become a group strategy—an exploitation of the *promise* of Western values in order to secure group advantage in the face of unequal background conditions. This is why the rhetoric of "equity" requires institutions to actively discriminate against the "privileged." Most left-wing social movements exploit Western universality and Western guilt, leveraging the bizarre tendency of Western man to out-group himself.

You would think that Western man would come to his senses. But universality is so ingrained in him and is so strongly enforced that he psychologically cannot reject it, even in the face of its absurdity. Thus, he gets caught in a feedback loop: universality promises equality; it fails; Western man blames himself; he reaffirms the promise; he offers restitution or reparation at his own expense; he receives more immigration; equality fails again; there is further balkanization and dispossession; and it repeats over and over. It ends with his dispossession. Western man is trapped in a cycle of universality, unable to wake up into and embrace his own particularity.

The Western mind needs to be critiqued in order to free it from exploitation and self-disparagement. The key is having the moral and psychological fortitude to endure the psychological discomfort that arises from affirming the truth and denying the false and absurd. Indeed, you must critique and deliberately decline to act on certain mental habits designed to extinguish this discomfort, such as accusations (whether against oneself or others) like "racist" or "fascist" or "xenophobe"; appeals to universality; and ascribing altruism. This last one—altruism—refers to the Western assumption that all non-Western peoples in the West have universalistic aims, not ethno-centric ones. That is, we tend to impute Western altruism to all people, concluding that their first love is humanity, not their ethnicity.[63] But this is obviously false and foolish. We must train the mind to resist the psychological inclination to affirm error. This is not the tug of conscience but a product of psycho-social conditioning, triggering discomfort and then a mental habit that returns us to the euphoria of fantasy and absurdity.

I say all this because, in my estimation, the primary obstacle for the embrace of nationalism is modern Western psychology. If you do not eradicate or suppress the habits of the mind that (at best) suppress natural aspirations for national greatness or (at worst) project your aspirations on the other (to whom you toss your national birthright), then you'll never fully embrace nationalism; and ultimately your people will self-immolate in national suicide.

---

63. In ascribing altruism to all, Western man denies his own altruism, effectively out-grouping himself from his own in-group (viz., all people).

4

Perfecting Your Nation:
The Christian Nation

"The Christian religion was only ever able and meant to
permeate everything." —Johann Herder[1]

We move now from the nation and nationalism to the Christian nation and Christian nationalism. The Christian nation is a species of nation, meaning that the "Christian" qualification does not destroy, eliminate, or preclude the features of the nation described in the previous chapter. Christian nationalism, likewise, is a species of

---

1. *Another Philosophy of History and Selected Political Writings,* trans. Ioannis D. Evrigenis and Daniel Pellerin (Indianapolis: Hacket Publishing, 2004), 37.

nationalism, denoting a Christian nation acting for itself to secure both earthly good and heavenly good. I begin with a discussion of the Christian nation.

I. The Christian Nation

The Nation Christianized

A Christian nation is a nation whose particular earthly way of life has been ordered to heavenly life in Christ, having been perfected by Christian revelation as grace perfects nature, without undermining that particularity but rather strengthening it so that the people might achieve the complete good.

The people of God on earth are a renewed people—definitively sanctified and restored to integrity—and now possess all the native gifts once given to Adam. So, as to form, they can achieve all that Adam was commanded to do with those gifts, though materially their achievements will be imperfect. Being complete in dignity, they are capable of civil fellowship before God, and thus they can relate to each other as fellow human beings *and* as God's children, or simply as Christian human beings. The Christian nation is a nation in accord with nature and grace—nature supplying the principles (e.g., the principle of similarity) and ends (e.g., earthly and heavenly good), and grace supplying the only means to man's ultimate end (viz., the Gospel). The Christian nation, therefore, is the nation perfected, for Christianity makes possible the national ordering of all things to the complete good, thereby fulfilling the ends of the nation. Just as grace clarifies for sinful man his true end and supplies the means to attain it, Christianity completes the nation by ordering the law, customs, and social expectations to heavenly life.

Nations have always, even for prelapsarian Adam, had the duty to acknowledge God and orient themselves collectively to his heavenly kingdom; indeed, this is the chief end of nations. The Christian nation, therefore, has not transcended the nation according to nature but has fulfilled it; it is complete in form.

Now, the Christianity of a nation is not something superadded to it, as if it were merely a new set of distinct and higher practices. Rather, the Christianity of a nation is best understood as an adornment or infusion of Christianity into the national way of life such that Christianity and national particularity are inseparable. Nations express Christianity like they express gender through dress—a universal is expressed in a particular way. Of course, there will be universal features of all Christian nations, such as the priority of worship and resting on the Sabbath. But my point is that the national way of life as a whole is both Christian and particular. For this reason, if we were to assume that America is a Christian nation, then to say "Christian American" is redundant; Christianity is assumed in "American,"[2] and the American flag implicitly symbolizes the Christian flag. Christianity perfects the whole but not by eliminating earthly particularity, just as any man who comes to Christ does not lose his personality and other unique characteristics. The Christian nation is still a nation as described in the previous chapter, having intergenerational memory and love, the degrees and types of loves, and a delight in people and place. Grace sanctifies sinners, but it does not homogenize personality; likewise, Christianity sanctifies nations but not does not eliminate national distinctness.

2. In this case, any non-Christian American would have to hyphenate their Americanness, symbolizing their separation from the core of American religious life.

The Christian nation is analogous to the Christian family. The Christian family is the natural family Christianized. That is, it is fundamentally natural as to its principles, being a society of a man and a woman with (or expecting) children, all bound to each other with familial relations. But it is Christianized, for it conducts family worship in Christ, forgives one another in Christ, and has a collective vision for itself that is oriented to heavenly life in Christ. These Christian features are universal in a way, for all Christian families ought to have them. But this universality does not eradicate the particularity of each family. Grace does not make us all the same; it does not eradicate difference. Each family has its own personality and particular activities, pastimes, traditions, and place. No Christian child could seamlessly join another Christian family without discomfort and disorientation. The same is true of Christian nations. Their members are not seamlessly interchangeable. The universal truths of Christianity do not nullify national particularity. Each Christian nation has a distinct way of life.

A Holy Nation

A Christian nation is not a holy nation in the sense that Israel was holy when under the Mosaic Covenant. No nation today is God's nation by some special divine command or by exclusive divine favor. The Christian nation acknowledges God as the author of nations in general and as the providential author of their particular nation. Such nations are indeed set apart or holy in relation to non-Christian nations, though not by divine national election or new principles but because the nation has brought itself, by grace, *under God* as nations ought to do by nature. Becoming or maintaining itself as a Christian nation, in an explicit sense, is an act of *national will*.

An *implicit* Christian nation is an unfaithful nation, one that lacks the will to explicitly place itself under God, to conceive of itself as a Christian nation, and to will for its Christian good. Thus, the complete Christian nation comes into being *synergistically*—by the grace of God *and* the will of man.

Being a holy nation and under God, the Christian nation may look upon national prosperity as a divine blessing and national troubles as divine displeasure. They may attribute prosperity to their national obedience and troubles to their national disobedience. Nations as such, like individuals, may learn humility, righteousness, and discipline in times of divine displeasure. They can also celebrate their national good as a providential gift of God. Nations are analogous to individuals in this way because nations are real entities, not *ad hoc* creations of man. They exist by nature to be under God and thus are subject to the blessing and disciplining of God. As Vermigli wrote, "Where outward discipline is kept [in civil polities], God often grants many blessings, not for the merit of the deeds but in the order he established in nature. For God wants to preserve the good order of things, so that certain consequences should follow from others."[3] I'll leave the criteria for discerning divine pleasure and displeasure to the theologians (for we should not say that *all* national troubles are due to national disobedience or that national flourishing is always a divine blessing for national obedience), but we should affirm that we may in principle attribute national flourishing and national troubles to God's directed countenance and discountenance.

3. Peter Martyr Vermigli, "Locus on Justification," part 2 in *Predestination and Justification: Two Theological Loci,* trans. and ed. Frank A. James III, vol. 8 (Kirksville, MO: Sixteenth Century Essays and Studies, 2003), prop. 1, point 29. Matthew Pearson pointed me to this quote.

Moreover, Christian nations may consider their governing documents or established laws as products of God's good providence. These are neither holy writ nor divine law; but since they are monumentally important for their good, the people can see them as unique blessings of providence and special expressions of his loving-kindness. Likewise, the people may look upon the architects of these laws as great men, inspired by God as instruments of God's will for his people's good.[4]

Christianity, People, and Place

In a Christian nation, the people relate to each other and their place of dwelling as Christians. In the previous chapter, I spoke of a man who encounters his love for his grandparents when looking at their old porch. Since they taught him about Christ on that porch, it is not only a place of natural intergenerational love but a place of eternal significance for him. There he learned earthly and heavenly wisdom for the good of both body and soul. That place has both natural and supernatural significance for him. In a way, it is a place of grace, a sort of sacramentalized site that, upon encountering it, works for his spiritual good. A guitarist friend of mine plays hymns on his porch with his cello-playing son, no doubt generating lifelong Christian and familial meaning in that place for his children. All sorts of activities can generate Christian significance in places, serving as conduits for spiritual communication for future generations. I'm not justifying superstition (though it does make some pagan superstitions understandable) but simply describing what

4. Girolamo Zanchi states that "the laws of Solon, Lycurgus, Romulus, and Numa" were "divinely inspired." If this is true of pagans, why exclude Christian civil leaders? *On the Law in General*, trans. Jeffrey J. Veenstra (Grand Rapids: CLP Academic, 2012), 6, 7.

lodged memory does in our social world. We encounter the Gospel
when we experience the places made spiritually significant by our
Christian loved ones.

The place of a Christian people is a Christian land—a homeland preparing them for a better home. Being a place of their activity and of their ancestors, this land is *their* Christian country, their
Christian homeland. Their Christian ancestry speaks through it, as
a mode of discipleship in Christian faith and life, and only they can
hear it. Their Christian homeland is not suitable for all Christians,
let alone all mankind. The land itself is a means of intergenerational
national love for both earthly and heavenly good.

The Christian indeed has a hierarchy of loyalties—a lesser loyalty to his earthly home and a higher loyalty to his heavenly home.
But these are not "dual loyalties" in the sense of being separate from
each other. No Christian homeland is itself the heavenly kingdom
of God, but one's loyalty to his Christian homeland is loyalty to the
work of the kingdom of God. Christian homeland is a mode of true
religion; it directs you to your ultimate home. Thus, serving one's
Christian homeland is serving the kingdom of God.

Objection

Many today reject the possibility of the Christian nation, claiming that only individuals and churches can be qualified as "Christian." *God redeemed individuals and established the church to serve
Christians*, they might claim. But don't we have Christian colleges,
Christian seminaries, Christian publishers, Christian businesses,
Christian charities, Christian coffee shops, and more? *Yes, but these
are voluntary associations*, I suspect they would say. But what then
about the family? Can the family be Christian? It would seem that

if nations cannot be Christian, then the family cannot be Christian. After all, the family, as an entity, is not redeemed by the work of Christ, nor is it an institution of grace.[5]

But of course there *is* such a thing as the Christian family—the natural family Christianized. Its natural principles are fulfilled in light of grace. The family worships God in Christ, exhorts and forgives one another in Christ, and adorns their collective lives with Christianity. In short, the entity as a whole is oriented to eternal life. And in doing so, it does not become a micro-eschaton. It is not "redeemed" as individuals are redeemed. Rather, the Christian family is a complete family, according to nature and grace. It is the natural family of restored integrity.

Now, if the family can be Christian, then so too can the nation, for the Christian nation is similar in form: it is a complete nation according to nature and grace. It is not the New Jerusalem on earth. It is a nation Christianized, and, like the family, it has not immanentized eternal life but has ordered itself *to* eternal life.

II. Christian Nationalism

The concept of Christian nationalism contains the concepts of the nation, nationalism, and the Christian nation, as described above. What is distinctive to Christian nationalism in relation to generic nationalism is that it expresses a Christian nation's will for heavenly good in Christ and that all lesser goods are oriented to this higher good. Thus, Christian nationalism is a Christian nation acting to secure and protect itself as a distinct Christian people and to direct itself (via Christian leaders) to procure the

5. I address the issue of hypocrisy in Christian societies in chapter 5.

complete good, including heavenly life in Christ. Or, as I defined it in the introduction,

> *Christian nationalism is a totality of national action, consisting of civil laws and social customs, conducted by a Christian nation as a Christian nation, in order to procure for itself both earthly and heavenly good in Christ.*

Much of the discussion so far in this book has pertained to the nation and the Christian nation. As we can see from the definition, there is much more to discuss. In this section, I give arguments for why the nation can act for its heavenly good through civil government. This is the chief act of a Christian civil government. Any Christian nation that is capable of self-government or has sufficient political autonomy will establish civil laws for its good.[6] Thus, this section justifies one essential part of Christian national action, namely, civil direction in true religion.

Civil Power and Spiritual Things

First, I will briefly outline the limits of civil power in relation to spiritual things. I speak to this issue in detail in chapter 7, but addressing it here will clarify my positions below and in the next few chapters. Civil power cannot directly bring about spiritual good.

---

6. Using civil power to aid the instituted church requires the possession of civil power. It is increasingly rare today for a Christian people to possess such power explicitly, though in many places this is a problem of will rather than numbers (e.g., the United States). Christians who cannot act through civil institutions for their good ought to do the best with what they have. I will not discuss this further because this book is tailored for Christian peoples who at least can dominate the public square, socially and politically, if they exercise the will for it.

No civil magistrate can command or exercise dominion over the conscience. Civil power cannot legislate or coerce people into belief; it can only command outward things—to outwardly do this or not do that. No classical Protestant has *ever* claimed that civil action can itself bring about assent to, let alone true faith in, the Gospel. Though the ultimate purpose of civil action can be the spiritual good of the people, the direct object cannot be the conscience. Spiritual good is a matter of the heart before God in Christ. Thus, civil action for the advancement of the Gospel only *indirectly* operates to that end.

The classical Protestant position is that civil authorities ought to order outward goods to this highest good or, put differently, to establish and maintain the best possible outward conditions for people to acquire spiritual good. Their objects of action are things *circa sacra*—around sacred things. This can include the funding of church construction; ministerial and seminary financial support; the suppression of public blasphemy, heresy, and impious profanation; obligating Sabbath observance; and other things. The extent and nature of such policies will vary with circumstances.[7] In accepting these limitations, civil authorities recognize a distinction or separation of church and state. The instituted church is the God-ordained order that administers spiritual things for the good of the soul; it offers the highest good. Having the office of the Word, it wields the spiritual sword to change hearts for eternal life. Civil authorities do not have this sword. Nevertheless, civil authorities can serve the body politic by making it outwardly fit for receiving what is good for the soul.

---

7. I offer my account of American Christian nationalism in chapter 10.

Religio est summus politicae finis[8]

One important principle of this work is that a supernatural application can follow from a natural principle, or put differently, that
a natural principle can be fulfilled by a thing of grace. Many today
assume the opposite. They claim something like the following:

> Civil action to protect the instituted church violates the limits
> of civil authority. If civil authority is natural, then how can it act,
> even indirectly, for supernatural good? Its objects are natural and
> earthly, pertaining to the body, not the soul. Civil power was es-
> tablished by God the Creator, not God the Redeemer. Since the
> means to heavenly life are *super*natural, not natural, heavenly life
> is outside the purview of the state and civil society. Civil power
> cannot act properly to secure supernatural, heavenly ends.

So, at least, they might claim. I recognize the force of this objection. But it fails to recognize that natural principles can have supernatural conclusions.[9] Consider the following syllogism:

> (1) Civil government ought to direct its people to the true religion.
>
> (2) The Christian religion is the true religion.
>
> Therefore, (3) civil government ought to direct its people to
> the Christian religion.   .

The major premise is, in my view, a principle of nature, meaning
that its truth is creational. I provide several arguments below for this

---

8. "Religion is the highest end of politics." Johann Heinrich Alsted, "Politicae," in
Encyclopaediae (Herborne, 1630), 1389.

9. Turretin, *IET*, 1:1.8.14.

major premise. The minor premise is supernatural (viz., known from Scripture by faith), and all Christians affirm this statement. The syllogism is valid.[10] Since one premise is natural and the other supernatural, it is a "mixed" syllogism. This fact has no effect on the regular operations of logic, but it does make the conclusion supernatural (or theological), for the subject "Christianity" is of revelation. Thus, we see a supernatural conclusion from a natural principle.[11]

One might prefer a less controversial syllogism:

(1) You ought to obey all that God commands.

(2) God commands, "But of the fruit . . . ye shall not eat of it."

Therefore, (3) you ought to obey, "But of the fruit . . . ye shall not eat of it."[12]

As in the first syllogism, the major premise is a principle of nature (based on the Creator-creation relation), and the second is supernatural (or adventitious to nature). The conclusion that follows is not disputed. Thus, we see that a supernatural truth can interact with a natural principle and soundly produce a supernatural

10. In proper form, the syllogism is:
(1) The true religion is something to which civil government ought to direct its people.
(2) The Christian religion is true religion.
Therefore, (3) The Christian religion is something to which civil government ought to direct its people.
This is a first-figure syllogism, the most common categorical syllogism in classical logic.
11. We can call it a "supernatural conclusion" because its truth was not accessible prior to revelation, and it is not a truth found in the book of nature.
12. In proper form:
(1) Everything that God commands is something you ought to obey.
(2) "Do not eat of the fruit" is something that God commands.
Therefore, (3) "Do not eat of the fruit" is something you ought to obey.

conclusion. And, more importantly, this supernatural conclusion, flowing from a practical syllogism, is *actionable*; and thus in obeying this supernatural conclusion, one obeys the *natural* principle from which it is derived. This is precisely how nature and grace interact in Christian politics and Christian ethics.

One might object to the first syllogism, claiming that "true religion" is equivocal—one refers to natural religion at creation, and the other to revealed religion in Scripture. But this concerns only the *referents* (or extension) of true religion, not to its sense (or comprehension). The national park ranger who must protect the wildlife in the park from poachers is not obligated to protect only the animals present in the park at the time of his commissioning. The referents of *wildlife* change over time. That is, the park ranger's commission was to protect anything within the park that would fall under the term *wildlife*. The same is the case with true religion. And in this case, every truth of natural religion (expressed in the First Table) remains fully operative and binding in the Christian religion. Thus, if civil government ought to direct its people to true religion, then it ought to direct them to the Christian religion, for that is the true religion.[13]

The fact that natural principles can have supernatural conclusions is crucial for my argument throughout this book. It permits me to claim that natural principles ground the Christian nation and Christian nationalism, and so I am not confounding nature and

13. Prior to revealed religion, civil government ought to have directed people in natural religion, for that was true religion. Now, Christianity is the true religion and natural religion (considered alone) is no longer true religion, even though natural religion is not rescinded and its truths are assumed in the Christian religion. "True religion," by its comprehension, concerns the truth of the whole. Thus, natural religion alone today is false religion, because by itself it is incomplete religion. Only the Christian religion is true religion, for it contains both natural and revealed religion, making it complete and therefore true.

grace, the two kingdoms, earth and heaven, the secular and the sacred, and temporal life and eternal life. The Christian nation is not the spiritual kingdom of Christ or the immanentized eschaton; it is not founded in principles of grace or the Gospel. Propositions of faith (e.g., "Christianity is the true religion") are essential to Christian nationalism but are not the ground of it. Affirming both the principles of nature and the truths of grace necessarily leads to Christian nationalism or, if you prefer different terms, to the traditional claims of Christendom. The universality of natural law does not lead necessarily to a purely "common" kingdom, as some have recently claimed.[14] Nor do truths that are exclusive to Christianity—viz., truths contained *only* in Scripture—ground Christian political order. Rather, the things of God as creator (natural principles) and the things of God as redeemer (supernatural truths) interact such that a Christian political order is grounded in natural principles that are fulfilled by the truths of grace.

Let us turn now to a set of arguments for the first premise, namely, that civil government ought to direct its people to the true religion. If this premise is true, then the syllogism is sound and so the conclusion is true—that civil government ought to direct its people to the *Christian* religion. These arguments do not depend on each other. They are independent, each separately demonstrating the same conclusion.[15]

---

14. VanDrunen, *Politics after Christendom*, 73–78; Andrew Walker, *Liberty for All: Defending Everyone's Religious Freedom in a Pluralistic Age* (Grand Rapids: Brazos Press, 2021). Walker writes, "Christianity is not a political program. The gospel does not create a new political agenda actionable with government qua government. Christianity, with its belief in common grace and natural law, is meant to shape consciences and help the world be the best version of itself as justice is recognized" (67).

15. The use of a set of independent and concise arguments is an early modern method, exemplified in Samuel Rutherford's *Lex, Rex*. I have followed his example, though I am unaware whether any argument here resembles one of his own.

1. Since the people of God are prior to civil government[16] and
    since any particular group of them may institute a civil govern-
    ment that is of and for the people, they can establish one that
    (a) is cognizant of true religion (since this institution is *of* them
    and they possess knowledge of true religion), and (b) is for
    their spiritual good (since the establishment is *for* their good).
    Hence, they can enact civil policies through civil government
    that direct them to true religion and its principal site for the ad-
    ministration of spiritual good (viz., the instituted church). And
    since they can, they *ought* to do this, for a people ought always
    to act for the highest good to the fullest extent of their power.

2. (a) Since civil government is entrusted with directly securing
    and ordering goods that are subordinate to the highest good
    (viz., outward goods), it must be cognizant of these goods *as*
    subordinate (or inferior) so that it can order them properly. If
    civil government were to lack cognizance of this, it must act as
    if earthly goods are the highest goods and constitute the com-
    plete good. Therefore, in the eyes of any civil government that
    lacks in principle any knowledge of the highest good, earthly
    goods must be the *chief* and highest good of man.

    (b) But since earthly goods by themselves do *not* constitute the
    complete, chief, or highest good, any such government would
    necessarily order its people to their earthly detriment; its or-
    dering must necessarily be disordering. Why? They would en-
    courage feverishness for earthly things. Civil government could

16. Man is "prior" to civil government in the sense that man institutes government and
it exists for man.

do nothing else in principle, for earthly good is the *only* good of man in its eyes. But inferior goods, when not ordered to their highest good, must necessarily take on corruption and so corrupt man. The good we ought to pursue for its own sake—heavenly good—orders lesser goods, assigning them their proper place.[17] It follows that civil government in this situation cannot even serve man for his earthly good; it fails to meet its natural end or *telos*. This leads to a contradiction: Though the natural end of civil government is serving the people with regard to earthly good, it can only harm the people by encouraging feverishness for earthly things. In other words, its design contradicts its end, for its design precludes it from meeting its end. But since God does not make mistakes, civil government must, by its design, be capable of knowing man's higher end so that it can order man properly to earthly good. Only then can it fulfill its natural end. Therefore, civil government has principled cognizance of man's highest end (viz., heavenly life).

(c) Now, since the people best attain earthly good only when they are ordered to heavenly good, civil government ought also to direct its people to the highest good within the limits of its power. Thus, even if one were to assume falsely that civil government's chief end is earthy good, it may still in principle (and ought to in practice) direct man to his heavenly good in the interest of his earthly good.

17. Samuel Willard writes, "We pursue all other inferior ends for the sake of the last, but the last for its own sake. Religion does not disallow those, but only regulates them. It gives them their place, and, if we do so too, we do well. And this is done when we endeavor so to follow them, as to help and encourage us in following that, and not to hinder us." *Body of Divinity*, loc. 1163.

3. Civil government ought to regulate outward things for the complete good of the people. Heavenly good is one part of the people's
    complete good. Therefore, civil government ought to regulate outward things for the people's heavenly good. Since some outward
    things directly promote man's heavenly good (e.g., Sabbath observance), civil government ought to direct the people in them.[18]

4. Civil government, as a prelapsarian institution,[19] was necessary
    to order man to all his original ends. The principles and ends of
    civil government arise from and are subordinate to the nature
    of man,[20] for civil government is an instrument for man's good
    according to his nature. It is not an arbitrary or *ad hoc* institution but is necessary by nature to meet man's natural needs;
    its design flows from the nature of man. Since the fall did not
    change the good or fundamental nature of man, the fall did not
    alter the design of civil government; and hence, civil government in a postlapsarian world can and ought to order man to all
    his original ends. It should, therefore, direct its people to true
    religion, for true religion is an original end of man.

5. Human civil society, conceived apart from civil government, is
    a community of mutual cooperation, arising naturally by man,

---

18. Turretin similarly argued, "Because he [the civil magistrate] ought to procure all the
good of the subjects for whose sake he has been constituted and to render an account of
it to God; now religion and things pertaining to it are without controversy the principal
good of these." *IET*, 3:18.34.6.

19. See chapter 1 for a defense of civil government as a prelapsarian institution.

20. This nature includes his full complement of gifts, both earthly and heavenly, as discussed in chapter 1. Civil government ought to act upon civil society to maximize the
ability for Christians to exercise their gifts.

for procuring things earthly and heavenly. That is, the natural *telos* of civil society—with regard to its function for man—is both earthly and heavenly, and its ultimate end is directing people to eternal life. Why, after all, would man come together to form society if not for mutual support in procuring *all* good things? Now, civil government is subordinate to society in the sense that it acts upon it (as a means) to order society to these good things. As a means to society's ends, it can act for those ends, including for things heavenly, within the limits of its power, which includes directing the people to true religion.

6. Civil government has an interest in directing the people to anything that contributes to the safety of the people and its administration of law, justice, and good order and discipline. A citizenry of well-ordered souls contributes to this administration. Therefore, civil government has an interest in directing people such that they have well-ordered souls. Well-ordered souls are made possible only by true religion. Thus, civil government has an interest in directing people in true religion.

7. In his *Law of Nations*, Emer de Vattel writes, "In order to conduct [the nation] to happiness, it is still more necessary to inspire the people with the love of virtue, and the abhorrence of vice." Since "nothing is so proper as piety to strengthen virtue and give it its due extent . . . a nation ought then to be pious."[21] Since civil government must encourage the civic virtue of its people, it must

---

21. Emer de Vattel, *The Law of Nations* (1757; Philadelphia: T. and J.W. Johnson, 1883), 122, 127, [§115, §125], quoted in Bradford Littlejohn, "Honoring God as a Nation?," in *American Reformer*, March 2022, https://americanreformer.org/honoring-god-as-a-nation.

be able in principle to direct the people in true piety (i.e., true religion), for piety is necessary for civic virtue. Since civil government is able, it ought to direct people to true piety.[22]

8. (a) Since the principles of natural law were not eliminated in the fall of man but remain operative (though poorly applied) in fallen man, the patterns of civilization throughout the ages manifest the principles of nature. Now, since most civilizations instituted some means of support for religion (though usually erring in practice), this indicates that such support is, as to its principle, permissible in natural law and part of the *telos* of civil communities.

(b) This argument is an appeal to the "consent of the nations," an appeal that is ubiquitous in classical Protestantism. Christian theologians, political theorists, and jurists regularly appealed to pagan sources to support their position that civil authority ought to direct man to true religion.[23] They cited Plato, Aristotle, Cicero, Plutarch, and others. All of these philosophers believed that civil support for religion was necessary for civil

22. Althusius writes, "[T]he magistrate before anything else, and immediately from the beginning of his administration, should plant and nourish the Christian religion as the foundation of his imperium. If he does this, all the virtues will flourish among his subjects, and he will be prospered in his actions." *Politica*, 162 [28.10].

23. For example, Calvin wrote, "That [the duty of the magistrate] extends to both tables [of the Decalogue], did Scripture not teach, we might learn from profane writers; for no man has discoursed of the duty of magistrates, the enacting of laws, and the common weal, without beginning with religion and divine worship. Thus all have confessed that no polity can be successfully established unless piety be its first care, and that those laws are absurd which disregard the rights of God and consult only for men. Seeing then that among philosophers religion holds first place, and that the same thing has always been observed with the universal consent of nations, Christian princes and magistrate may be ashamed of their heartlessness if they make it not their care." *Institutes*, 4.20.9. See also Turretin, *IET*, 2:18.34.6.

solidarity, law-keeping, and order.[24] Since these pagan authors reasoned apart from special revelation, their conclusions concerned natural principles. Thus, the classical Protestant appeal to these authors was used to support natural principles. Civil support for true religion is a principle of *nature*, not of grace. And thus neither grace, nor the Gospel, nor the New Testament, nor anything subsequent to creation could destroy or abrogate this principle. Pagan support is not decisive proof, to be sure, but most early modern authors considered it good evidence for their position.[25] And despite recent Western trends,

---

24. Aristotle writes about what is "essential" to the state, including "service of religion, termed a priesthood," which he considered "a primary need." . . . δὲ καὶ πρῶτον τὴν περὶ τὸ θεῖον ἐπιμέλειαν, ἣν καλοῦσιν ἱερατείαν. *Politics*, trans. H. Rackham (Cambridge: Harvard University Press, 1944), 1328b. Plutarch said, "[I]f you will take the pains to travel through the world, you may find towns and cities without walls, without letters, without kings, without houses, without wealth, without money, without theatres and places of exercise; but there was never seen nor shall be seen by man any city without temples and Gods, or without making use of prayers, oaths, divinations, and sacrifices for the obtaining of blessings and benefits, and the averting of curses and calamities. Nay, I am of opinion, that a city might sooner be built without any ground to fix it on, than a commonweal be constituted altogether void of any religion and opinion of the Gods,—or being constituted, be preserved. But this . . . is the foundation and ground of all laws." Plutarch, *Adversus colotem*, ed. William Goodwin (Boston: Little, Brown, 1874), §31. Cicero wrote, if "holiness and religious obligation should also disappear . . . a great confusion and disturbance of life ensues; indeed, when piety towards the gods is removed, I am not so sure that good faith, and human fraternity [*societas generis humani*], and justice, the chief of all the virtues, are not also removed." *On the Nature of the Gods*, trans. Francis Brooks (London: Methuen, 1896), 1.2. Silius Italicus wrote, "Alas! Their ignorance of the divine nature is the chief cause that leads wretched mortals into crime." *Punica*, trans. A.S. Kline, (n.p.: Poetry in Translation, 2018), 4.792–93 at https://www.poetryintranslation.com/PITBR/Latin/ItalicusPunicahome.php.

25. See, for example, Hugo Grotius, *The Rights of War and Peace*, trans. A.C. Campbell (1625; Washington: M. Walter Dunne, 1901), 2.20 [On Punishments], §XLIV-XLVI. He writes, "The belief in a supreme being, and in the controul of his providence over human affairs, is one of those universal tenets to be found in all religions, whether true or false. And in reality to deny the being of a God, and to deny the interposal of his providence in human affairs, amounts in

instigated by those whose social dogma has replaced traditional religion, the pagan testimony remains a good indicator of natural principles.

Having supported the major premise above, it follows that civil government can and ought to direct the people to the Christian religion.

III. Objections

Redemptive Kingdom

One common objection to civil government supporting true religion (and to Christian nationalism in general) comes from those who hold the modern version of two-kingdoms theology. They stress that the instituted church is the redemptive kingdom, and so it alone is the site of redeeming grace. Hence, the Christian's duty (so they say) is not to "redeem" or transform creation (including human institutions), for it is not an object of redemption in the Gospel.[26] Limiting the redemptive sphere to the visible church and its administration is an old position in the Protestant tradition, which I consider to be the classical Presbyterian view. I affirm it in

its moral consequences to the same thing. And it is for this reason these two opinions have been inseparably united in all ages, and among every civilized people. Consequently we find, that in all well governed states, wholesome laws have been enacted to restrain those, who disturb those opinions, which have always been regarded as the chief support of social order; and all contempt, shewn to those opinions, has always been considered as contempt shewn to society itself, and which it consequently has a right to punish" (2.20, §XLVI).

26. Other versions of two-kingdoms theology extend the redemptive sphere beyond the instituted church, and we can call this the classical Anglican view. I distinguish my view from this view in chapter 7. Also see W. Bradford Littlejohn, *The Two Kingdoms: A Guide for the Perplexed* (Lincoln, NE: Davenant Press, 2017) for a presentation of what I consider the Anglican view.

this work. That is, I affirm with the modern two-kingdoms advocates that the principal scope and purpose of the redemptive kingdom concern eternal life, not temporal life, and that the instituted church administers the sacred things of that kingdom. But limiting the scope of redemption in this way does not preclude the thorough and comprehensive *restoration* of earthly life. In chapter 2, I distinguished between redemption and restoration, the latter concerning the goods of earthly life and their orientation to heaven. Thus, the question between me and the modern two-kingdoms advocates concerns this conception of restoration, viz., whether Christians ought to seek the Christianization of the family, civil society, and civil government.

In chapters 1 and 2, I distinguished the two ends of man: earthly and heavenly. Heavenly life was always the ultimate end of man, but Adam's task was not to bring heaven to earth by his labor. His work was one of obedience in earthly life in light of heavenly life. He was required to order earthly life to the promised heavenly life and thereby fulfill the *natural* principles of earthly life. Now, the Gospel supersedes the original condition and grants all believers a title to heavenly life by faith. Thus, because obtaining a title to eternal life is by faith, working is no longer (for the believer) the *condition* for eternal life. But this does not rescind the work itself; ordering this world to the next remains natural to man, especially to restored man. It is something that neither grace nor the Gospel, nor a title to eternal life can abrogate, supersede, or undermine.

Most importantly, this work of ordering does not *redeem* earthly life, properly speaking, for redemption concerns man's original ultimate end, namely, heavenly life. Instead of being a work of redemption, the Christian's work in the non-redemptive realm is a work of *renewal.* It restores this realm according to its nature and ours. To use two-kingdoms language, we do not redeem the civil kingdom; we order the civil kingdom to the redemptive kingdom. New England minister John Cotton said it best:

> When the Kingdoms of the earth become the kingdoms of the Lord (Revelation 11:15) it is not by making Christ a temporal king, but by making temporal kingdoms nursing fathers to his church.... The church and the commonwealth are still distinct kingdoms, the one of this world, the other of heaven, and yet both of them from Christ; unto whom the father hath committed all judgment (Job 5:22).[27]

An earthly kingdom is a *Christian* kingdom when it orders the people to the kingdom of heaven. Limiting the redemptive kingdom to eternal life does not preclude the Christianization of the civil kingdom.

Distinguishing "redemption" and "restoration" is not a distinction without a difference, nor are they unrelated.[28] The work of restoration is not akin to that of a church minister, whose work is sacred and involves sacred things directly for a world-to-come. The redemption of souls principally concerns eternal life, and the instituted church administers the things of that redemption. But the *effect* of that redemption is the restoration of earthly life, for the believer is definitively sanctified. Since the Christian possesses

27. John Cotton, *Bloudy Tenent Washed and Made White in the Blood of the Lamb* (1647; Shropshire, UK: Quinta Press, 2009), 1.92, spelling modernized.

28. Wolters also distinguishes "redemption" and "restoration" in *Creation Regained*, 69–73.

restored integrity, his work follows the same principles that directed Adam. It is the work of true and complete humanity. And although redemption is monergistic, restoration is synergistic. The former is the principal end of salvific grace; the latter is an outgrowth or sec-ondary effect of salvific grace. It follows that restoration is a work of human *will*. It is a matter of striving; man cooperates with grace to restore the natural world for his good.

Relatedly, people will claim that *the principal mission of the (insti-tuted) church is not to transform the world*. I agree. But must every-thing "Christian" flow from or out of the instituted church and its leadership? Should a Christian father not order his household to Christ? If he should, why shouldn't civil ruler order the civil realm to Christ and his kingdom? The fact that the instituted church serves the soul does not preclude Christians from ordering the things of the body to the soul.

Exile, Sojourner, Stranger

Another objection is the exile argument. Appealing to 1 Peter 1:17, some claim that, due to their heavenly citizenship, Chris-tians are exiles in this world; heaven is our home, not earth. They conclude that Christians should not Christianize civil and social institutions. Christians can and should participate in politics, they claim, but only for a basic civil peace—one rooted in mod-ern notions of tolerance and legal conceptions of freedom (e.g., freedoms of religion, expression, assembly, and speech).[29] On its face, this objection appears to be highly historically conditioned,

---

29. VanDrunen says that "political communities and authority structures . . . should be of common rather than holy character. That is, they should be open and just toward human beings of whatever religious and ethnic identity." *Politics after Christendom*, 97.

for the Reformed tradition prior to the 20th-century would not recognize it, and to my mind, it reflects the post–World War II consensus of values.[30]

In substance, however, the exile argument strikes me as deeply confused, particularly in its anthropology. As I've said, the Gospel not only grants a title to eternal life apart from works, but it also restores humanity for works. The restored man is reconciled to nature, and as such he is set apart not from earthly life or from natural principles, but from the *fallenness* of the world. He is a stranger to this world because he is reconciled to nature, not because grace has elevated him above nature. He is restored to the true way, which runs contrary to the false way; and the principles of the true way are nothing but those original to Adam. A Christian is a foreigner in relation to fallenness—to a world in "bondage to decay" (Rom. 8:21)—but fallenness itself is foreign to nature.

Furthermore, the Christian feeling of foreignness is natural to restored man. Even Adam in the state of integrity, as he grew in maturity, would have felt as if he were a stranger in this world, not because of any defect in creation, but because his ultimate end was always heaven—where he would find his *true* rest. Thus, we can imagine Adam and his progeny feeling out of place on earth, ready and eager for heavenly life, though without sin and apart from any fallenness. Adam before the fall was a sort of pilgrim, passing through to a higher life. Since a Christian already has a title to eternal life, wouldn't we expect this world to feel foreign

30. See R.R. Reno, *Return of the Strong Gods: Nationalism, Populism, and the Future of the West* (Washington, DC: Regnery Gateway, 2019) for a discussion of the post–World War II anti-nationalist consensus. It is difficult to explain, at least sociologically, the emergence of the modern two-kingdoms theology—which affirms multiculturalism, anti-nationalism, and a "common" kingdom—apart from the postwar consensus of values.

to him? Both our possession of eternal life and the fallenness of the world intensify this *natural* feeling that this world is not our ultimate home. But that feeling does not undermine our work in this world.

Triumphalism

I suspect that people will label my position a "triumphalist" theology or a "theology of glory" as opposed to a "theology of the cross." I'll simply say that I've laid out my premises and my argument, and I welcome anyone to refute them or demonstrate my argument's invalidity. Simply labeling my view a "theology of glory" proves nothing. If you want to claim that the cross and the resurrection revealed new universal and binding principles of outward human action, then explain their place theologically. Explain how these principles of grace cohere with those of nature. Explain how adventitious heavenly duties conduce to natural earthly goods. That is to say, do more than assert disparate ethical principles; provide a coherent system.

The Christianization of the civil realm is a necessary consequence of natural principles. If civil societies ought to be under the true God by nature, then they ought to be under the Triune God, for the Triune God is the true God. Just as Adam was to acknowledge God in all his works, so too must Christians acknowledge God *as further revealed* in all their works. In doing so, Christian human beings are not following some positive divine command (i.e., a supernatural duty above nature); they are following the law of nature and nature's God. The Gospel neither rescinds man's nature nor suppresses it; it restores and strengthens it. The relationship of nature and grace necessarily entails Christian nationalism.

IV. Excluding Fellow Christians

Since the Christian nation is not merely a nation of Christians, we have to address the issue of foreign Christian immigration. On what grounds can a Christian nation exclude fellow Christians from their land?

As I've stressed, nationalism is firstly concerned with a nation's good, and the good of any nation is in part found in its particular features. The particularities of a people are those things that could be otherwise; they are not in themselves natural, and so they are not universal. Nor can you separate particularity from the place in which that particularity occurs; the culture is part of the place, as a territorial cultivation. The necessity of particularity leads to the principle of difference, by which peoples derive a right to difference. From this right comes the necessity of exclusion in civil policy. My view is that the principle of exclusion, which is necessary for a people's complete good, morally permits a Christian nation to deny immigration to Christian foreigners. Christian nations are not required to exclude them, but they can in principle.

To demonstrate this, we should first recognize that fellow Christians, regardless of nationality, are united *spiritually,* as fellow members of the kingdom of God. This is chiefly a heavenly or eschatological relation, made possible by grace, not nature. The spiritual kingdom, after all, is in essence invisible or yet-to-be-revealed. Thus, all Christians share in the highest good—all being spiritually united to Christ—and thus have a spiritual brotherhood. But this brotherhood—being fit for a *heavenly* kingdom—is wholly inadequate as to its kind for cooperating to procure the full range of goods necessary for living well in this world. Spiritual brotherhood is a common salvation in Christ, an orientation to heaven, a common interest in the sacred things for eternal life, and spiritual unity in the worship of God. But something as basic as a common language, by which we could cooperate and belong together in the same place, is absent from spiritual brotherhood. Unity in Christ does not entail or provide unity in earthly particulars, which are necessary for living well in this world. Though the people of God share the highest good, that does not make any random selection of them mutually suitable for civil fellowship. Thus, it is a categorical error to make unity in Christ the sole basis of civil fellowship. We cannot ground civic brotherhood on spiritual brotherhood. It simply doesn't work, no matter how much modern sentiment you place on spiritual unity.

Indeed, civil fellowship is what makes strong church fellowship possible, because people do not lose their particularity when they pass through the doors of a church building. Spiritual unity is inadequate for formal ecclesial unity. People do not suddenly speak some Gospel language and then assume a Gospel culture. The people's way of life permeates the visible church, and it serves as an ancillary feature that makes possible the administration of sacred things (e.g., preaching in the vernacular). The administration of the Word and Sacraments require, at a bare minimum, a common language; and church fellowship requires at least a core culture serving as the cultural norm for social relations.

Culturally distinct groups of Christians could, of course, start their own churches, and this would solve one problem. But it remains the case that cultural diversity harms civil unity, for it undermines the ability for a community to act with unity for its good. The community will have trouble ordering themselves through law and especially through culture. The consequence of multiculturalism is secularization (i.e., "neutrality"), open conflict, or civil action that suppresses the activity and status of the newcomers. One key factor is the limitation of social power among a diverse population: an individual from one culture cannot easily correct one from another, nor can one people-group offer clear reasons for its behaviors to the others. Most likely the injection of diversity, if on a mass scale, will result in a community of strife, distrust, discord, apprehension, and misunderstanding. A disordered body politic is not conducive to a well-ordered soul. As I've argued, the most suitable condition for a group of people to successfully pursue the complete good is one of cultural similarity. This is a natural principle of civil communities. Thus, receiving masses of people who are similar with regard to faith and dissimilar in other ways is generally bad policy. This is evident in the fact that the chief practical argument against Christian nationalism in Western countries, especially in the United States, is that cultural diversity renders it politically impossible.

Of course, the issue of restricting Christian immigration is neither simple nor outside the realm of prudence and generosity. Christians ought to help fellow Christians, including those who are culturally dissimilar. Christian nations in the Reformation era received Christian refugees—the Marian exiles to Geneva, Strasbourg, and Frankfurt; the French Huguenots to England; and other refugees, such as the Italians who settled in Basle. Though Christians typically praise these receptions of refugees and point to the good that came out them, these cases offer important insights and examples of how mass migration causes civil disruption and strife between Christian natives and Christian foreigners. The city of Basle, for example, after receiving numerous Italian Protestants, had to deny entry to refugees in 1555, in part due to overcrowding and the unavailability of housing.[31] Historian Christina Garrett states that the English refugees, not knowing the native tongues of their host countries, became "isolated and segregated" and unable to become an "integral part" of their host societies.[32] She continues:

> Thus the peculiar segregation of the English, due in part to a native distaste for foreigners . . . was in even greater part the result of sheer inability to hold speech with their neighbours, or their neighbours with them.[33]

In most places, with the exception of Aarau and (possibly) Geneva, English craftsmen were not allowed to practice their craft, since native artisans disliked the competition and accused Englishmen of unethical and unlawful commercial practices.[34] Concerning Frankfurt, historian Maximilian Miguel Scholz has argued that the refugees "transformed the society they entered" and "destabilized the power structures in Frankfurt."[35] He writes, "[T]he encounter between refugees and native Frankfurters ruptured Protestantism in the city and led to the construction of two distinct confessional camps, Lutheran natives and Reformed foreigners . . . [which] fractured Protestant fraternity."[36] Refugees in Frankfurt also served as a wedge between the city's nobility (who

31. Christina Hallowell Garrett, *The Marian Exiles: A Study in the Origins of Elizabethan Puritanism* (Cambridge: Cambridge Univeristy Press, 2010), 19.

32. Ibid.

33. Ibid., 21.

34. Ibid., 21, 51.

35. Maximilian Miguel Scholz, *Strange Brethren: Refugees, Religious Bonds, and Reformation in Frankfurt, 1554–1608* (Charlottesville, VA: University of Virginia Press, 2022), 165.

36. Ibid., 161.

generally supported the refugees) and the native clergy and native artisans.[37] Reformation history is replete with examples of Christian refugees in foreign Christian countries causing public disturbance, civil strife, and social segregation; and in most cases, these conditions led to official action to secure civil peace and stability, such as shutting the city gates to foreigners, suppressing commercial activity, and restricting voting rights.

A self-confident Christian nation will be hospitable to its spiritual brothers and sisters, but they will not be self-destructive or easily manipulated. No Christian nation is obligated to do what will destroy itself or undermine its long-term ability to provide the complete good to its people. New England Puritan statesman John Winthrop rightly said,

> If we are bound to keep off whatsoever appears to tend to our ruin or damage, then we may lawfully refuse to receive such whose dispositions suit not with ours and whose society (we know) will be harmful to us, and therefore it is lawful to take knowledge of all men before we receive them. . . . A family is a little commonwealth, and a commonwealth is a great family. Now as a family is not bound to entertain all [new]comers, no not every good man (otherwise than by way of hospitality) no more is a commonwealth.[38]

37. Ibid., 75–76.

38. John Winthrop, "A Declaration in Defense of an Order of Court Made in May, 1637." He continues, "If strangers have right to our houses or lands etc., then it is either of justice or of mercy; if of justice let them plead it, and we shall know what to answer: but if it be only in way of mercy, or by the rule of hospitality etc., then I answer 1st a man is not a fit object of mercy except he be in misery. 2d. We are not bound to exercise mercy to others to the ruin of ourselves. . . . As for hospitality, that rule doth not bind further than for some present occasion, not for continual residence."

The nation's first duty is to its *own* people, including its future generations—a duty that is grounded in the nature of man. It is the nation's right to factor in cultural suitability and the potential for successful assimilation when determining immigration policies.

Let us remember that universal benevolence does not permit universal beneficence. The good in this world is not achieved by will alone but in concrete conditions; and those conditions for good are based in the nature of man as created. It is not due to sin that dissimilar people cannot (ordinarily) achieve together what similar people can achieve. It is not sin's fault that "diversity destroys unity," as Althusius said.[39] There are trade-offs in this world, and those who want to be radically selfless should return to their instincts lest they harm people for generations. Sentimentality and untethered empathy are the modern killers of nations. Grace does not destroy what God created, and thus to adopt a "radical" principle of inclusion is to oppose God, as the creator of man.

The best way a Christian nation can help another Christian nation is by aiding it in flourishing as a people in their own place. It is not by importing that people. Just as families help families while maintaining healthy separation, nations ought to help other nations while maintaining separation.

V. Conclusion

This chapter demonstrated the possibility of a Christian nation and that Christian nations can act through civil government for their heavenly good. The next three chapters complete the discussion of the definition. The next chapter on cultural Christianity discusses

39. Althusius, *Politica*, 78 [9.45].

both the national action of culture as a means of directing people to eternal life and the Christian self-conception as the original ground of national action. The following chapter is on civil law, focusing largely on its divine source and character. Lastly, I discuss the civil magistrate—the one entrusted by the people to act concretely and resolutely on their behalf for their good.

5

The Good of Cultural Christianity

"Religion is a way of life, involving customs and ceremonies that validate what matters to us, and which reinforce the attachments by which we live. It is both a faith and a form of membership, in which the destiny of the individual is bound up with that of a community." —Roger Scruton[1]

I. Mode of Religion

The primary mode of religion is found in the instituted church—where the Word and Sacraments are administered by means of a spiritual power to the faithful for eternal life. But in a Christian nation there are two *supplemental* modes of religion: the *civil power* of

1. Roger Scruton, *Our Church: A Personal History of the Church of England* (London: Atlanta Books, 2012), 20.

civil magistrates and the *social power* of cultural Christianity. Neither is a spiritual power and so cannot of itself produce a spiritual effect. Each is an indirect mode for spiritual things.[2]

Social power is natural to man in community, serving as the principal, *implicit* director in social behavior and thought-patterns, though there is no seat of power or centralized decision-maker. It shapes a wide range of action, both outward and inward, even ordering people to ultimate things, like religion. In a Christian nation, social power is placed in the service of the Christian religion. I call this use of social power "cultural Christianity," a term that has become an object of derision. But the errors identified under that term are, in my view, *abuses* of something vitally important for Christians. The Christian religion as delivered through culture prepares people to receive the Gospel and encourages them to stay on the path to eternal life. It is even necessary for a just, commodious civil society.

II. Definition and Explication

I begin with a definition of cultural Christianity and proceed with an explication of the definition:

> *Cultural Christianity is a mode of religion wherein social facts*
> *normalize Christian cultural practices (i.e., social customs) and a*
> *Christian self-conception of a nation in order (1) to prepare people*

---

2. The family is a mode of religion as well and should be classified separately from the instituted church, civil power, and cultural Christianity. The family is a society of intimate, personal interaction, making the Christian family an ordinarily means of spiritual good, albeit still subordinate to the institutional church in that regard. With face-to-face interaction, parents instruct their children to believe and obey, and the Lord uses this often to bring young ones to faith.

to receive the Christian faith and keep them on the path to eternal
life, (2) to establish and maintain a commodious social life, and
(3) to make the earthly city an analog of the heavenly city.

Cultural Christianity is a "mode of religion" because it orders people to eternal life in Christ. It joins civil administration, paterfamilial authority, and ecclesiastical administration as a distinct mode for this end.

This mode uses a certain species of ordering—an ordering of *prejudice.*[3] Though the modern connotation of prejudice treats it with suspicion, this is an example of defining something according to its abuse. Prejudice is simply habituated thought and action in which one feels, by cultivated instinct or second nature, that some thought or action is true, good, necessary, or proper. As Edmund Burke wrote, prejudice complements reason:

[P]rejudice, with its reason, has a motive to give action to that reason, and an affection which will give it permanence. Prejudice is of ready application in the emergency; it previously engages the mind in a steady course of wisdom and virtue, and does not leave the man hesitating in the moment of decision, skeptical, puzzled, and unresolved. Prejudice renders a man's virtue his habit, and not a series of unconnected acts. Through just prejudice, his duty becomes a part of his nature.[4]

Prejudice is an instinctive, pre-reflective judgment on particular thoughts and actions. It is not in principle opposed to reason but

3. Civil law, as we will see in the next chapter, is an ordering of reason.
4. Burke, *Reflections on the Revolution,* 130.

perfects it, for in prejudice the heart owns what the mind can decide upon. Cultural Christianity, as a mode of Christian religion,
is pre-reflective, prejudicial judgment on the rightness of Christian
belief and practice.

While Christian magistracy as a mode of religion relies on law, cultural Christianity relies on societal prejudices or what I'll call "social
facts." As Émile Durkheim put it, a social fact "is capable of exercising
an external constraint on the individual; or, which is general throughout a given society, whilst having an existence of its own, independent
of its individual manifestations."[5] Put simply, social facts are the norms
or customs into which members of a people-group are socialized, such
as what is decorous, suitable, appropriate, and right. Social facts set the
cultural parameters of the cultural in-group; the deviant is a misfit and
outsider. Durkheim stressed that social facts are external authorities
over individuals. Their existence does not rely on any individual or an
identifiable and centralized enforcer of these norms. They are not rules
issued by some "ministry of culture." Yet, like civil authority, social facts
are both from the people and above the people. That is to say, they are
simultaneously theirs and something over them.

The term *social fact* captures a general social phenomenon that is
natural and universal to human society. All societies, even non-con-
formist ones, are thoroughly normed with social facts. Indeed,
chapter 3 was in part an examination of social facts, though I did
not use the term. Social facts exist because they supply something
vital to human social life: we are designed to receive and adopt as
second nature a "habitual practice of ethical living . . . [in which]
the soul of custom permeat[es] through and through" as Hegel

5. Émile Durkheim, *The Rules of Sociological Method*, trans. W.D. Halls (New York: Free
Press, 1982), 59.

wrote.[6] Social facts ground social customs and expectation, permit ease of interaction, and provide confidence that one's actions and judgments are suitable, fitting, and appropriate. Our everyday life requires a certain *common* sense, a common judgment. If the social facts are good, then they lead us to the common good.

Inherent to social facts is a certain force—*social power*. Unlike civil power, which operates *explicitly* via law (viz., law is officially promulgated and overtly enforced), social power operates *implicitly*. It is an authority *felt* more than beheld and embodied in the people, not in an official. Social power is to social facts what the civil magistrate is to civil laws: social power enlivens these social facts with force and life. It is a sort of collective social pressure to conform to a common way of life and a common self-conception. This power, however, is not necessarily coercive. It operates most effectively through socialization and a learned sense of expectation, informing a felt sense of what is right and proper. It is fundamentally a formative power. It habituates the will, provides incentives to act a certain way, and even shapes structures of thought that make some ideas more plausible than others. In short, social power normalizes the concrete content of social facts. Still, social facts in a postlapsarian world are backed by threats of punishment, exacting social costs for deviancy.

Social power works both behind and alongside civil power. It encourages law-keeping and shapes the people in areas of life that civil law cannot touch (e.g., manners). Both social power and civil power, therefore, are necessary for a complete ordering of society. Social power is not evil in itself or a result of the fall. It arises naturally and necessarily in human relations, and it directs people to act in ways

6. Georg Wilhelm Friedrich Hegel, *The Philosophy of Right*, trans. T.M. Knox (1820; London: Oxford University Press, 1952), 108.

that are necessary for living well but that nature does not directly supply. Its *abuse* can direct one to sin, of course, but the force itself is good, for it serves a necessary function in human society.

Cultural Christianity is social facticity in the service of the Christian religion. A Christian nation as a nation has social power and as a *Christian* nation, this power is directed to Christian ends. Thus, Christian nations have a social force that prejudices the people for Christian belief and practice.[7]

Christian Culture

To help clarity what I mean by cultural Christianity, we should distinguish it from *Christian culture*. Christian culture refers to concrete Christian practices, or the normalized Christian content of social facts. Here is a definition:

> *Christian culture is a public culture in which a people presume a Christian relation between themselves and adorn their collective, everyday life with Christian symbols, customs, and social expectations in order to mutually orient one another to worship God and love one's neighbor in Christ.*

Cultural Christianity, in contrast, refers to the force that normalizes Christian culture. It warms the people's heart to Christianity, making them receptive to Christian belief and practice. Hence, Christian culture is a necessary element of cultural Christianity. It refers to the concrete set of beliefs and practices by which cultural Christianity, as

---

7. By "belief" I do not mean faith, but assent to Christian truths. So cultural Christianity can set conditions that lead to assent to Christianity but *not* to saving faith. I discuss this later in the chapter.

a mode of religion, achieves its ends. To put it plainly, cultural Christianity produces the *felt* rightness of one's Christian culture.

This distinction between cultural Christianity and Christian culture allows us to emphasize that cultural Christianity cannot itself bring about anyone's salvation. It is a *preparative* mode. Like civil power, it lacks the means to save, for social power is not spiritual power. Cultural Christianity internalizes the felt duty to perform Christian practices; it engenders a heightened sense of one's sin and need for salvation; and it forms structures of plausibility that lead people to assent to Christian belief. But neither conforming to its direction nor existing in or under it can save someone.

Christian culture, however, is both preparative *and* persuasive, for the content of Christian culture communicates the Gospel. The prayer before a Little League baseball game, for example, can communicate the Gospel. Festivals, feast days, and civic observances—though not in themselves holy or administered by spiritual authority—are occasions for spiritual good. They can be means of faith, sanctification, repentance, and spiritual reconciliation. These can be means of grace because they speak truth, and faith comes by hearing. All believers are priests, in a way, and we can communicate truth to one another for eternal life and to mutually strengthen our journey to the Celestial City. We can say, therefore, that while cultural Christianity itself, as a social power, cannot bring about spiritual good, it directs people *to* activities wherein they can procure the things of eternal life, both inside and outside the instituted church.

Consider the Dutch Reformed cultural practice of family Bible reading after dinner. Every day, upon finishing dinner, the father reads from the Bible. This simple practice was once widespread in Dutch Protestant culture. It is cultural, and the felt appropriateness to conduct it after dinner is an instance of cultural Christianity. The father has internalized a duty to provide informal spiritual ministry to his family. So, while the social force that led to its widespread practice cannot generate true faith or sanctification, the activity itself creates an occasion for it, for the Word of God is read.[8]

We see in this example that cultural Christianity provides what no ecclesial institution can fully provide—social direction to perform Christian practices in every area of life. Church ministers often assume that they can effectively exhort church members to adopt such practices, and perhaps they can persuade some people to do them. But, as Burke said, reason is typically not enough, and it is no surprise that ministers have largely failed to engender longevity in such practices. In our day, with the erosion of cultural Christianity, family worship and family Bible reading—all of which were once common Protestant practices—have almost vanished. Catechizing children has likewise disappeared. Such practices are no longer parts of the rhythm of life, nor are they felt to be part of parental duty. The blame should not be entirely placed on ministers, however. They lack the means to accomplish what only society can achieve. We expect far too much of pastors and the pastoral office. The church can and should admonish you to conduct certain extra-ecclesial practices and explain why you should do them, but society is, by its nature, most effective at ensuring that the people's *heart owns it.* Neglecting culture and the cultural mode of religion upsets the natural order of things and increases the challenges and burden of spiritual ministry (and the family). The combined efforts of ecclesiastical, civil, familial, and social forces—each having a

8. A Dutch Christian who conforms to Dutch Christian cultural norms is being simultaneously a good Christian outwardly (performing spiritual practices) and a good Dutchman (conforming to cultural norms).

unique species of power—provide the complete conditions that order Christians to perform good Christian practices and encourage them to embrace the Gospel unto eternal life.

Christian Self-Conception

Cultural Christianity arises out of the people's Christian self-conception. Having a Christian self-conception, the nation is aware of itself as a Christian nation, and from this awareness flows the ordering of social and civil powers for the nation's earthly and heavenly good in Christ. Christian peoplehood does not refer simply to a people who are submitted to both the church and the state. In a fundamental sense, the people are *prior* to both, as those who established these public administrations for their good. The instituted church is a divine order, of course, and its power and elements of worship come immediately from God; they are not devolved from the people to ministers. But the formation of this or that local assembly and the installation or designation of this or that man as minister are actions of the people in the interest of their good.[9] Likewise, civil government, though arising from the instinct of man, is established voluntarily, since no man is king over another by reason of pure nature.[10] These administrations in their local establishment

9. Turretin writes, "For as in a society, we first conceive that God made men; second congregated them into one; finally, from that union (which cannot be conserved without order) the magistrate took his rise; so in the church, grace in the first place makes believers, then unites them together by the bond of mutual fellowship and because fellowship cannot exist without order and government, then the necessity for the ministry arises. And thus the ministry is posterior to the church; nor does it make the church true, for it has this from the truth of faith, but the true church makes the ministry legitimate because on the truth of the church depends the righteousness of the ministry. . . . [T]he church precedes the ministry and produces it and not the ministry the church." *IET*, 3:18.24.10.

10. I discuss this further in chapter 7.

are made "Christian" by the will of the people constituting them. Hence, the designation of "Christian civil government" originates from a nation that is conscious of itself as a Christian nation and acting for its Christian good. In order to have a totality of national action to procure earthly and heavenly good *in Christ*, the national will for action must be a *Christian* national will for action. There must be an antecedent Christian national will for action that conduces to the national good.

A Christian self-conception unites a people and the Christian religion, making the Christian religion fundamental to who they are as a nation. It is a normalized social fact. To be a good member of the people, one must be a Christian (at least outwardly), and anyone who denies Christ in word or deed is subject to social separation or other social costs. The unity of peoplehood and Christianity will also produce civil religion as expressions of civil piety. This follows the reasoning of Aquinas:

> The principles of our being and government are our parents and our country, that have given us birth and nourishment. Consequently man is debtor chiefly to his parents and his country, after God. Wherefore just as it belongs to religion to give worship to God, so does it belong to piety, in the second place, to give worship to one's parents and one's country.[11]

One pays homage to his country out of gratitude for the various modes of religion that have directed him in what is good. This is expressed with national celebrations, loyalty oaths, pledges, and other acts of national solidarity.

11. Aquinas, *ST*, II-II.101.1.

Moreover, a Christian self-conception permits national self-reflection without disempowerment. Days of fasting, national days of prayer, and special services in response to national calamity or national sins neither stifle action nor resign the people to dissolution, nor pacify the spirit of action, nor allow any exploitation for material gain, nor turn "men of action" into managers of national decline, as we see prevalent today. Rather, a Christian self-conception permits a confident Christian people to seek God's blessing through special and temporary acts of humiliation and then, subsequently, to carry on in their duty with self-regard. They do not suffer the indignity of perpetual humiliation.

Baptism

Many readers may by now be frustrated that I have not mentioned the issue of baptism. My hope is that my arguments so far have appealed to a pan-Protestant audience. But I should say here that paedobaptism (i.e., infant baptism) is the position most natural to Christian nationalism, for baptizing infants brings them outwardly (at least) into the people of God. When the body politic is baptized, all are people of God. All religious expectations are then social expectations, and the socialization of children is the socialization of young Christians. Baptism is both a social and spiritual event, for society treats that child as a full member of their Christian peoplehood. But credobaptism likely creates problems for Christian nationalism. It is no accident that Baptists tend to be advocates for near absolute religious liberty, and this is not only due to their tradition of dissent. Their theology of baptism restricts Christian obligation to the credobaptized, and thus the mass of society, at least in people's formative years, do not (in principle) have Christian obligations. It is difficult to see how cultural Christianity, as I've described it, could operate effectively with that theology. Paedobaptism is consistent with Christian nationalism because it makes possible a society that is baptized in infancy and thus is subject to Christian demands for all of life.

Since I am not credobaptist myself, I don't have any great personal interest in reconciling Baptist doctrine and Christian nationalism. Such reconciliation might be possible, and I *hope* that it is. But I'll leave that to Baptist thinkers. In any event, Baptists can join with non-Baptists in a Christian nationalist project as equal members, though I suspect that paedobaptists would be the most stabilizing force in a pan-Protestant political community.

III. The End of Cultural Christianity

The end of cultural Christianity is threefold: eternal life, commodious earthly life, and imaging heavenly life. I discuss each below.

Eternal Life

Eternal life is the ultimate end of cultural Christianity. As I've emphasized, social force cannot directly achieve this end, but this end determines its direct objects—concrete Christian practices and beliefs. Its chief object is church attendance, where the ordinary means of grace are administered for eternal life.

Commodious Life

The next end is a commodious life together. I might have used "happy" or "just" instead of "commodious." But happiness is a consequence of commodious living, and justice is a precondition of it.

A commodious life is a fitting life, one in which people are in their proper places, according to their gifts, and each receives the full measure that providence allots him. There is mutual respect and mutual expectations of conduct among one's fellows, and each is granted space and encouragement to perfect his gifts through his household for the good of himself and his community. In this way, the individual does not collapse into the collective, nor does the collective erode on account of excessive self-interest.

Cultural Christianity does not import abstract theories of justice to critique the "systems" that govern our world. Rather, it is a force for the perfection of organic communities, not subverting the foundation of them, but strengthening the natural ties that bind people together in a common life. It does this in three ways. First, it strengthens the nation by ordering people to eternal life, which sets the soul in order and thereby orders one's concerns for earthly things. Stated negatively, it undermines the disordered, feverish desires for material things. Second, presuming a spiritual relation, the people consider one another special objects of love and service, as fellow members of the household of faith (Gal. 6:10). Each could be expected to fulfill his or her duties and not to exploit another's beneficence. Third, social discipline is strengthened, for people can confront bad behavior in the name of Christian faith and practice. Together, these generate a high degree of social trust.

The recent interest in Christian social ethics, particularly welfare for the poor and the "marginalized," shows a curious lack of interest in the unique social-spiritual relations in which poverty relief was conducted in the medieval and early modern periods. These were Christian communities, regulated closely by both church and state. Today, people mistakenly assume that the degree of generosity that is made possible by a Christian society is viable in modern, secularist, and diverse societies. To see this mistake, let us consider the virtue of generosity. Generosity is giving a proper gift to a proper receiver when it is proper to do so. The virtue itself does not prescribe the appropriate amount or type of gift, nor who is worthy of the gift. These are matters of prudence, requiring one to discern his circumstances. A generous gift in one set of circumstances might be wasteful or destructive or exploited in another. Without networks of trust and authorities, many will take advantage of people's beneficence. A Christian community with high social trust and overlapping authorities permits greater generosity, for people can expect that generosity is put to good use and not exploited or wasted.

But today Christians presume a "radical" command of poverty relief, following a principle divorced from prudence and context. The object of Christian beneficence in modern Christian thought is simply the abstract other. The other has no relation to you beyond common humanity and bare proximity. You do not share a particular context or a particular culture, nor do you belong to overlapping authorities. You are nothing but two image-bearers, two abstract humans with human needs. Your "radical" duty is a placeless duty, fit for a placeless, contextless (pseudo)love—a love springing from an otherworldly and flattened benevolence operating on bare geographic space. It is a Christian ethic flowing from "exile" theology, telling us that Christians are not to belong, or fit in, or have robust earthly loyalties. Modern Christian ethics tends to reject the idea that love springs from an organic unity, from similarity, out of a shared and particular civil project. We are left with a mechanical ethics without heart, without a people and place. Every person is a Very Special abstract human. Thus, "radical" Christian ethics today is a prodigal ethics, harming both the giver and the receiver, and failing to prudently exercise virtue for the common good. What are Christians for? They are to love, but not according to abstraction or outside of context and particularity, and not without reference to social relations, shared authorities, and shared particular loves.

Christian social ethics is captured beautifully by John Winthrop, the great statesmen of Puritan New England. He spoke these words to those who landed with him at Massachusetts Bay in 1630:

> We must be knit together, in this work, as one man. We must entertain each other in brotherly affection. We must be willing to abridge ourselves of our superfluities, for the supply of others' necessities. We must uphold a familiar commerce together in all meekness, gentleness, patience and liberality. We must delight in each other; make others' conditions our own; rejoice together, mourn together, labor and suffer together, always having before our eyes our commission and community in the work, as members of the same body. So shall we keep the unity of the spirit in the bond of peace. The Lord will be our God, and delight to dwell among us, as His own people, and will command a blessing upon us in all our ways, so that we shall see much more of His wisdom, power, goodness and truth, than formerly we have been acquainted with.[12]

Few people know that the entirety of the sermon was about the relations of rich and poor. Fewer know that the pinnacle of Christian ethics for Winthrop was not aiding the poor or the "marginalized." Rather, it was an ethics for an organic whole, a hierarchical

---

12. "Modell of Christian Charitie," 130, spelling modernized.

community with a variety of stations, duties, and gifts. Such communities do not follow an abstract morality or one singularly focused on the lowest members of society. As a community of "regenerates," God "exercise[es] His graces in them, as in the great ones, their love, mercy, gentleness, temperance etc., and in the poor and inferior sort, their faith, patience, obedience etc."[13] The ethics of mutual aid requires a collective, symbiotic life—the powerful showing an abundance of love while the lowly show an abundance of trust and service. In a community of grace—one where *all* parts are perfected in form by grace—the virtue of generosity is perfected, allowing what many would call "radical" generosity today, though without violating the natural principles of generosity.[14]

Imaging the Heavenly City

"*Respublica est documentum & imago vitae aeternae,*" wrote Johann Alsted.[15] Alsted points to the people's subjection to magistrates, which images the people of God's submission to Christ, but Christian culture also images heavenly life. Christian culture expresses the people's spiritual relation; it is a foretaste of life in the world to come. And indeed the glory and honor of the nations—that is, "whatever is excellent and valuable in this world," said Matthew Henry—will enter into the New Jerusalem.[16]

Many today want to call the instituted church a "colony" or an "outpost" of heaven, but this conflates the principal image of

13. Ibid., spelling modernized.

14. It is worth noting that a more removed generosity is often in order, especially in the form of special gifts to fellow Christians in foreign lands (e.g., 1 Cor. 16:1–4).

15. "The republic is an example and image of eternal life." Johann Alsted, *Theologia Naturalis* (1615), 731.

16. Matthew Henry, *Commentary on the Whole Bible*, 1985 [on Rev. 21:26].

heavenly life (viz., public worship) with the complete image of
heavenly life. The Christian nation is the complete image of eternal life on earth. For in addition to being a worshipping people,
the Christian nation has submitted to magistrates and constitutes a
people whose cultural practices and self-conception provide a foretaste of heaven.

IV. Celebrating Decline

I am often bewildered by the wholesale rejection of cultural
Christianity among evangelicals. Concerns about hypocrisy are
legitimate, and I address this below. But wouldn't you prefer to
live in a community where you can trust your neighbors, having
mutual expectations of conduct, speech, and beliefs according to
Christian standards? Wouldn't you prefer to have neighbors with
Christian standards of decency, respect, and admonishment, *even
if* it is merely cultural? Wouldn't you prefer some common and
good standard of living by which one neighbor can confront and
correct another?

Perhaps *you*, being a strong, independent adult, can withstand
the moral degeneracy of our time. But try raising kids in today's
social environment. Or perhaps *you* are exceptional at protecting
your children; you can afford to send them to a Christian school,
effectively paying an ideological security service. But most people
are not exceptional; most people are average; and most cannot pay
to secure their kids from society's ideology. Oh, if only they bought
your parenting book or sat through your church seminar or sermon
series or listened to all your ideas. If only they put their kids in all
your church programs . . .

Regardless of wealth, all Christian parents today have to stay wearingly vigilant to protect their children from some "authority," or television show (or commercials), or even neighbor kids from pushing the latest progressive moral agenda. Conscientious parents are exhausted from the embattlement, and increasingly they must separate their children from basic programs, services, and events. Think of all the well-meaning, though ill-equipped, parents who still trust the nightly news and are unaware of what their kids face everyday. What is the fate of these kids? Left-wing ideology is now the norm; it is the social fact of our society, impressed upon the minds of us all. What is most worrisome is not the moral anarchy but the moral ideology. We're not entirely in a state of moral free-for-all. Our problem is not moral relativism, as we were told for decades. Our problem is a regime-enforced moral ideology as the standard of moral respectability.

Why would one desire our current situation? How could one thank God for secularism and celebrate the decline of Christian culture? How could the demise of cultural Christianity in America be good?

Remarkably, some have celebrated its downfall. Russell Moore, the former president of the Ethics and Religious Liberty Commission (ERLC) and now a "public theologian" and editor-in-chief at *Christianity Today*, published an article on his blog in 2015 titled "Is Christianity Dying?"[17] He writes,

> Bible Belt near-Christianity is teetering. I say let it fall. For
> much of the twentieth century, especially in the South and

17. Russell Moore, "Is Christianity Dying?" accessed at https://www.russellmoore.com /2015/05/12/is-christianity-dying.

parts of the Midwest, one had to at least claim to be a Christian to be "normal." During the Cold War, that meant distinguishing oneself from atheistic Communism. At other times, it has meant seeing churchgoing as a way to be seen as a good parent, a good neighbor, and a regular person. It took courage to be an atheist, because explicit unbelief meant social marginalization. Rising rates of secularization, along with individualism, means that those days are over—and good riddance to them.[18]

I was dumbstruck when I first read this. The Southern Baptist Convention's leading ethicist *prefers* a society in which hostility to Christianity is normal and acceptable. Moore celebrates the loss of those mild social norms that led to safe and commodious neighborhoods and engendered social trust and that brought people to gospel preaching on Sundays. "Good riddance," he says. He continues,

In the Bible Belt of, say, the 1940s, there were people who didn't, for example, divorce, even though they wanted out of their marriages. In many of these cases, the motive wasn't obedience to Jesus' command on marriage but instead because they knew that a divorce would marginalize them from their communities. In that sense, their "traditional family values" were motivated by the same thing that motivated the religious leaders who rejected Jesus—fear of being "put out of the synagogue." Now, to be sure, that kept some children in intact families. But that's hardly revival.

18. *Russell Moore* (blog), May 12, 2015, accessed September 30, 2022.

Moore acknowledges the social benefits of cultural Christianity, but then, with remarkable callousness, shrugs his shoulders: "[T]hat's hardly revival." As an outsider to the SBC, I often marveled at Moore's ability to maintain his good standing as an official in his denomination; he explicitly rejoices in social atomization, deracination, and the elimination of American Southern culture. It gets worse. After calling it "good news" to "have more honest atheists," he tells us

> We don't have Mayberry anymore, if we ever did. Good. Mayberry leads to hell just as surely as Gomorrah does. But Christianity didn't come from Mayberry in the first place, but from a Roman Empire hostile to the core to the idea of a crucified and resurrected Messiah. We've been on the wrong side of history since Rome, and it was enough to turn the world upside down.

Mayberry is the fictional North Carolinian town of *The Andy Griffith Show*. That show depicts a Southern form of commodious life: a community of few and small concerns, high social trust, and an ease of life. The residents had common songs and customs, often singing them together on porches, at times for consolation. They all went to church on Sundays. The children, known by all, ran around town perfectly safe, being protected and watched by the community. Any American who watches that lighthearted, heartwarming show cannot but feel nostalgia for an America lost by negligence and malevolence. But as Moore says, it was "hardly revival." He prefers "a Roman Empire hostile to the core to" Christianity. In other words, Moore wants a society and government that actively destroy communities like Mayberry and use every means to manipulate your children to reject Christ. He doesn't want mere liberal neutral-ity, but active hostility.

Moore's influence is considerable in evangelicalism. Few evan-gelical elites today will defend cultural Christianity, even if they (si-lently) cringe at Moore's comments. But I must ask: How is the loss of cultural Christianity going for you? How much effort and time do you and your Christian friends devote to protecting yourselves and your children and grandchildren? How much space in your church bookshop is taken up with resources to resist the evil in modern secularist life? The absence of cultural Christianity has brought hostility, not religious neutrality. The social power that might have helped convert your parents or grandparents is now actively wield-ed against orthodox Christianity, against your children. Christians have abandoned this God-ordained power to the enemies of Christ.

Consider the strange incongruity at work in the rejection of cul-tural Christianity. In Moore's view, the Gospel flourishes when the enemies of God have social power, and it flounders when Christians have this social power. Thus, a God-ordained natural power—a means of ensuring social solidarity—aids the church when this power is hostile to Christ. The God of the Gospel turned something that he ordained, as the God of nature, against the Gospel so that it would advance. Bizarrely, social power remains a means to faith, but only when that power is abused. This is patently absurd. What is the basis for this nature/grace disharmony? Why is God the creator opposed to God the redeemer? How can the proper use of a natural power harm the Gospel but its abuse support it? We should affirm what is most obvious: the ordinary operations of nature and grace ought to cooperate for eternal life, and therefore social power ought to be put in the service of true religion.

V. Preparation and Hypocrisy

The most common objection against cultural Christianity, and one Moore has used repeatedly, is that it makes "fake Christians" or hypocrites. Indeed, cultural Christianity is usually defined precisely along these lines, making it bad by definition.[19] But this is a bad definition. It identifies not cultural Christianity itself but one of its possible effects, condemning it according to what it cannot do, namely, save souls. I readily admit that cultural Christianity cannot save souls and that it often produces hypocrisy. As I said above, it is not a means of salvific grace. It is a supplemental mode of religion.

Statement of the Question

Having defined cultural Christianity, I can state what is at issue between those who affirm and reject it. The question concerning cultural Christianity is not whether it can lead to religious hypocrisy, for I affirm that it can. Nor is the question whether it contributes positively to a commodious and peaceful life and would be preferred in the absence of any concerns about religious hypocrisy. This is affirmed explicitly by Moore and seemingly by most critics of cultural Christianity. Nor is the question whether social power is a means to faith, for Moore and others affirm that social power *as a hostile force* is a necessary condition for Christianity to thrive. I agree that it is a means to faith, though I affirm that it ought to be a *positive* force to this end.

The question is whether the normalization of Christianity in society prepares people for the reception of the Gospel such that (ordinarily) more come to true faith than in the absence of

19. That is, it is like the definition of *murder*—"an *unjust* taking of life." A moral valuation is inherent to the definition.

cultural Christianity. That question is, on one level, an empirical question. But since true faith is invisible, we cannot add up numbers of salvations. Still, there are several reasons to answer the question in the affirmative.

Preparation

Preparation, or what has been called the *praeparatio evangelica*, has been widely acknowledged in the Christian theological tradition. Originally, it referred to the function of Greek philosophy in preparing one to receive the Gospel. The principle behind it, however, equally applies in a culturally Christian context: the plausibility of the Gospel eases one into the reception of it. Background conditions that positively point to Christianity prepare people for receiving the Gospel. Human relations form people into the faith. Timothy had his mother and grandmother, and Augustine had his mother Monica, demonstrating the work of natural relations in spiritual formation. Why exclude one's relationship to a magistrate or his neighbors? Neither a neighbor, nor a mother, nor a magistrate can bring one to faith, but they can prepare one for faith. We can think of faith itself as an individual thing, but its preparation and formation are relational and even social.

Many Christians today think that a belief is authentic only if coming to it required one to resist their prejudices against that belief. There is something commendable in resisting one's prejudices for error, but this speaks to character, not to the quality of one's belief. Some, if not most, of our strongest beliefs are those that we are disposed to hold. My strong (and true) belief that my mother is a kind and generous woman, which is well supported by evidence and held by all who know her, is not inauthentic or weakened by my predisposition (being her son) to think well of my mother or by the commonality of the belief. The preparation to believe something does not make the resulting belief inauthentic; indeed, it would seem to make the belief *more* authentic, for you feel its truth. Prejudice completes reason. At the very least, being against the world on some issue is not a necessary condition for authentic belief.

Moore's main problem with cultural Christianity is that it conceals hypocrisy, thereby leaving people safe and comfortable in their unconverted state. A hostile society reveals who is and is not converted. He writes, "Christianity thrives when it is, as Kierkegaard put it, a sign of contradiction. . . . It is easier to speak a gospel to the lost than it is to speak a gospel to the kind-of-saved."[20] In other words, hostile social conditions lead fake Christians to abandon the faith, thereby making it easy to recognize who needs to hear encouragement in the faith and who needs conversion to the faith. Society is an instrument in visibly separating sheep and goats.

But living amidst hostility, social disintegration, and deracination, and subjecting Christian families to relentless, hostile social forces constitute a high price to pay for a clear distinction between saved and lost; and a clear distinction is entirely unnecessary. First, the presumption that all or most in a community share the Christian faith, at least in terms of assent, does not prevent anyone from denouncing faithless assent and hypocrisy of heart. Indeed, pastors regularly admonish such people from the pulpit, and Christians as members of civil society can do the same. And in conditions of cultural Christianity, in which people participate in Christian things, pastors and Christians will have *more* opportunities to call people to faithfulness.

---

20. Moore, "Is Christianity Dying?"

Second, a clear distinction is quite irrelevant to the operations of grace. There is power in the Word of God; and the reading of Scripture, whether private or public, is backed with that power. The Word is "the sword of the Spirit," (Eph. 6:17) striking at the soul for salvation. There is a unique, divinely ordained power in preaching, as the Second Helvetic Confession states: "The preaching of the Word of God is the Word of God."[21] The power of the Word does not increase or decrease based on the speaker's knowledge of who is and is not truly converted.

Third, it is rather foolish, especially in our time, to think that hostility to orthodoxy will create a clear distinction between saved and unsaved. We are no longer in the late 90s and early 2000s, when the New Atheists contended against the faith. Today, the American regime, though hostile to historic Christianity, is supportive of certain modern versions of Christianity that are either supportive of or harmless to that regime. Priestesses now have regular columns in national newspapers, and "religion reporters" generate buzz around regime-friendly churches and leaders and disparage those deemed hostile. Some genuine believers (though in serious error, in my view) will gain a certain *ad hoc* respectability from the regime for their passivity or willingness to punch right, and others will straddle between orthodoxy and heterodoxy in order to actively support the regime while also serving as examples of "moderation" or a "third way." The regime simply will not permit a clear line distinguishing regenerate and non-regenerate. Why? Because the American regime realized after the 2016 election that making Christian orthodoxy a sworn enemy is dangerous. The evangelical voting bloc is the most effective bloc

---

21. Second Helvetic Confession, "Of the Holy Scripture Being the True Word of God," chap. 1.

against them, and so the regime needs seemingly orthodox leaders as insiders to dismantle the bloc. It is no surprise that people like Moore in the past decade have widened orthodoxy into the political left and have "critiqued" the political right, accusing their theology of reflecting and justifying "white militant masculinity."

Thus, a clear distinction between regenerate and unregenerate is unnecessary, and in our time, the line between the two is increasingly blurred and utilized in the interest of the secular American regime.

Faith and Assent

While the costliness of faith in times of persecution can reveal the authenticity of *faith*, it does not clearly reveal the authenticity of *belief*, as in the inward assent to propositions. Persecution challenges one's faith, not his assent to propositions, for one can outwardly deny what he inwardly assents to. Persecution, if directed at those who affirm orthodox beliefs, will reveal true and false faith. I acknowledge this. But this speaks only to the direct effects of the less frequent *overt* form of persecution. More often, persecution arises out of a more general and implicit social hostility against the Christian faith. That hostility conditions society against not merely faith itself but *assent* to the Gospel. It portrays the Gospel as ridiculous, implausible, immoral, dangerous, or subversive. Now, since direct assent to the Gospel is a precondition for faith in the Gospel (according to Protestantism), social hostility eliminates a necessary condition for faith. In consequence, society seeks to inject into each person's sentiments an anti-Christian prejudice.

Conversely, cultural Christianity does the work of directing people to the preconditions for faith: knowledge of and assent to the Gospel. Though cultural Christianity cannot save, it prepares people for salvation by supplying the plausibility of Christian truth. Hence, in such conditions, the work of ministry is not convincing people of the truth of Christianity but of the need for true *faith* in those truths—that people move from *assensus* to *fiducia*. Ministry is less apologetical and more a call to faithfulness.

The most legitimate concern is that cultural Christianity might actually undermine the calls for faithfulness—that the people will ridicule the work of ministry because it calls them out of their passivity and indifference to heavenly things. This is indeed a legitimate concern, but it constitutes an *abuse* of cultural Christianity. And correcting this abuse is the role of magistrates, church ministers, and any serious member of society.[22] Cultural Christianity is only one mode of religion among others, and each relies on the others for its health. And since social power is unwielded by a central figure, it often requires correction by magistrates and churches. Still, even in its abuse, cultural Christianity prepares people to receive Christ and provides conditions for a commodious life, and people are better off living in its abuse than in its absence.

There is good reason, therefore, to affirm that cultural Christianity is a net positive for civil society, since it effectively prepares people for faith, results (in the ordinary course of providence) in more believers, and supports civil and social institutions for the common good.

VI. Final Considerations

The Family and the Church

All Christians today agree that the family is a vital source for transmitting the faith to the younger generation. It is not clear, however,

---

22. See chapter 9, where I address concerns about religious liberty.

why the family can play this role but not civil society. Being a member of a Christian family does not save any of its members. No one accuses Christian families of being hypocrite-factories, sending their kids straight to hell. So why is preparation permitted in the home but not in civil society? It seems that the typical reasons to reject cultural Christianity strike just as hard against Christian families.

One might argue that while the family and the church call people to faith, civil society plays the role of testing that faith. But what a strange interaction of forces! Was God's plan really to subject the little family and local churches to such powerful hostile forces and give them this narrow window of time (perhaps a dozen or so years) to prepare children for faith before tossing them to the world for testing? It is absurd to think that this arrangement is part of God's prescriptive will.

By its design, the family is naturally permeable; it is not buffered or shielded from outside forces. It was not designed to be a bulwark against a godless social world. Living well in this world requires a combination of spheres that form a whole: the family, civil society (including civil government), and churches. We can distinguish them, but each nevertheless permeates the other. The critics of cultural Christianity recognize this permeability and wholeness, but they think that the institutional church is able to permeate the family to aid them in resisting any negative influence from hostile civil society. Ray Ortlund, a Baptist minister in Tennessee, in celebrating "the decline of Bible Belt Religion," calls for churches to "stand out" with "the beauty of gospel culture."[23] As with most critics of cultural Christianity, Ortlund assumes a sort of ecclesio-centrism in which the institutional church has become a quasi-alternative civil society,

23. Ray Ortlund, *The Gospel: How the Church Portrays the Beauty of Christ* (Wheaton, IL: Crossway, 2014), 68, backcopy.

taking on a distinct Christian culture. Hence, he does not deny that Christians need a Christian culture, only he makes the church the sphere of that culture. The church is thus more than an administration of sacred things for eternal life; it is a site for "gospel culture," which supplies Christians the sort of relationships and goods that they might get in civil society, if it were Christian.[24]

At least intuitively, everyone seems to recognize that when you reject the idea of Christian civil society, some essential element of life is left unaccounted for, and so you must expand the church's functions and roles in the life of a believer. As a result, you get a church full of programs, ministry teams, and on-site outlets for Christian resources for most areas of life. You effectively get an ecclesial-civil association—a conflation of two species of association that effectively confounds both.

I am no longer surprised by the regularity of Christian opinion pieces claiming that "the church must do more" for this or that group or to solve this or that problem among Christians. There is an ever-expanding mission creep and an expanding market of resources to cope with social hostility. It is popular to attack the programs mindset of megachurches, but what should we expect from churches? If Christians must live in a hostile society, they will naturally begin demanding the sorts of goods and services that civil society is supposed to provide. Can we blame the average Christian for desiring a church that provides her a range of trusted services? This is why churches have created extensive programs and large signs to advertise them. Churches have children's ministries, schools, sports programs, family counseling, and an array of special-interest

24. Ibid.

support groups and clubs—all accented with Christianity, each labeled a "ministry." In consequence, Sunday morning is oriented around advertising spiritual resources for seekers or "ways to serve" rather than the worship of God. This is a natural consequence of giving up civil society to godlessness.

The institutional church, however, was not designed to be a replacement for civil society, nor is the pastoral office a civil office or a business CEO or a mental health administrator. We're fools if we think that a "Gospel culture" that is limited to the ecclesial sphere is sufficient. The church's concern—per its divine design—is with the worship of God, administering sacred things for the good of the soul and eternal life. Churches can certainly take on additional services and roles, but these are accidental to its purpose. The rejection of cultural Christianity necessarily leads to an erroneous and confused ecclesiology in which the ecclesial sphere takes on duties suitable for civil society. As a result, it performs these duties poorly and distracts the church from its principal role, and families remain ill-equipped to resist the world.

Motivations

Some reject cultural Christianity because it leads people to conform to Christian practices for incomplete or bad reasons. Let's evaluate this claim by considering the nature of motivation.

Having only social power, cultural Christianity cannot, by itself, lead anyone to act internally according to the proper spiritual motivation. The best cultural Christianity can do is inculcate in someone a deep, internalized sense of duty to participate in Christian practices, viz., to perform the *substance* of Christian duty. Performing only the substance of duty is still sinful, for the subject of action must flow from, as Turretin says, an "internal rectitude of heart and intention of the end." There must be a "spiritual obedience" in accordance with the "spiritual law of God."[25] This limitation of cultural Christianity is no strike against it, unless we want to attack every institution of moral formation. We can raise our children to act in virtue, habitually forming in them a sense a duty, and we can call for them to do all things to the glory of God. But only they, by grace, can choose spiritual obedience; only they can adorn their virtuous habits with true piety.

It should be obvious that an internalized sense of duty is good for us and others. Should a father decline to minister to his family because he has no motivation but a sense of duty? What about a preacher on Sunday morning who doesn't feel like preaching? What if you wake up on Sunday and feel compelled to sleep in and miss church? You ought to do all things to God's glory, but our sense of duty is what makes society function and creates the conditions for good outward action and internal piety. A father may on occasion catechize his kids with no motivation but duty, but the children nevertheless are catechized.

To be sure, cultural Christianity does lead some people to conform in order to keep up appearances. In these cases, cultural Christianity has partly failed, because these people have not internalized Christian duty. But their conformity is still good as to the outward action, for (1) it has led them to regularly hear the Gospel; (2) their conformity helps to sustain the cultural practices in the community, leading others to hear the Gospel; and (3) it helps to sustain civil honesty, social institutions (e.g., marriages), and civil manners that work for the common good.

25. Turretin, *IET*, 1:10.5.3, 4.

But doesn't cultural Christianity lead the unregenerate to sin? After all, they (lacking grace) are unable to act internally to God's glory. In response, one can easily point out that virtually no one would consistently apply the principle behind this question. Would you exclude a known unbeliever from attending a church service because he might join in congregational singing or perform other elements of the liturgy? No. You would rejoice that he witnessed the service and hears the Gospel. Would you leave your unbelieving child at home, fearing that he might sin grievously in hypocrisy? No. Will you reject evangelism because non-Christians sin when they reject the Gospel? No. The fact that cultural Christianity leads unregenerate people to sin is no reason in itself to repudiate it.

Moral Witness

One often hears that cultural Christianity harms "Christian moral witness." Rarely, if ever, is moral witness defined or theologically grounded, but it is often used to denounce the pursuit of worldly power (both social power and civil power). Since the language of "witness" implies an audience, we ought to ask, "Who is the audience?" It cannot be most of humanity, since most would recognize that a people's culture ought to reflect their spiritual commitments. Take Islamic civilization, for example. Nations of Muslims are Islamic nations, for they affirm the principle that true religion ought to comprehensively shape human society. To them, Christian nations are not violating a principle but rather have a false religion. Even in the United States, a sizable portion of the population, including the majorities in midwestern and southern states (I suspect), would support some degree of Christian culture.

The audience most likely in mind for "Christian moral witness" are American coastal elites. Ironically, coastal elites also believe that one's spiritual commitments should shape culture via social power, though their spiritual commitments are social dogmas like egalitarianism, human rights, and gender fluidity. In the service of their dogmas, they destroy lives for using the wrong pronouns; they create "professional ethics" that effectively exclude orthodox Christians; they scour old tweets for ways to cancel people. These people love the sort of "moral witness" that renders evangelicalism unthreatening to the American regime. Moral witness, in other words, is a way to reconcile evangelicalism and the current American regime.

It is bizarre that, in the interest of Christian moral witness, we must celebrate our people and place being overrun with moral chaos; offer little or no resistance to the anti-Christian ideology driving children from the faith; cower behind "religious exemptions" to affirm and practice truth; welcome marginalization, persecution, and embattlement of Christian families; and even accelerate into a social epistemology that renders Christian truth implausible. Why shouldn't Christian witness include a confident socio-cultural assertion of its truth? In what way is resigning to malaise and indignity appealing to the world? This appeals only to those whose socio-economic class makes them largely immune to the social consequences of losing cultural Christianity. Cultural Christianity may have kept homes intact, but as Russell Moore said, it is "hardly revival."

Patriotism in Worship

There is no avoiding the presence of cultural particulars in church worship. Sermons, for example, are in the vernacular language. Congregational prayer will contain prayers for the people's civil leaders and thanks to God for good governance, for ancestral witness to the faith, and for national blessings.

But the instituted church was not instituted to organize patriotic song-singing or national flag-waving or to host campaign speeches. It administers Word and Sacraments to a sacred assembly for heavenly life; its main orientation is to heaven. I'm ambivalent about national flags located inside or outside churches, but national flags should not be displayed in a sanctuary and especially not within sight during worship. The worshipper should see pulpit, table, and font.

I say this not to denigrate Christian patriotism; certainly the reader could not accuse me of that. My concern is that God is given his due in worship and that worship remains a heavenly assembly oriented to heavenly life. As I've made clear, you do not need the instituted church or church ministers to certify political action as Christian action. Nor must Christian politics be some extension of formal Christian ministry, organized by the instituted church. There is no need, therefore, to incorporate national symbols or patriotic elements in formal worship, except as fitting our heaven-oriented worship of God.

VII. Conclusion

Christians need to recover an assertive will for their good and have the spirit and resolve to exclude what is bad. We should use social power to oppose those who threaten them and who attempt to subvert our faith or exploit its moral demands. That means opposing, suppressing, and excluding the very sort of people who run the American regime. A Christian society that is for itself will distrust atheists, decry blasphemy, correct any dishonoring of Christ, orient life around the Sabbath, frown on and suppress moral deviancy, and repudiate neo-Anabaptist attempts to subvert a durable Christian social order. A Christian nation that is true to itself will unashamedly and confidently assert Christian supremacy over the land.

Since cultural Christianity is simultaneously both Christian and cultural, its conservation depends essentially on continuity of peoplehood through generations. Christian culture, being particular, is an inheritance of a people; only they can conserve it. For this reason, you cannot separate this chapter from the analysis in chapter 3. The enduring connection of people and place conserves culture, including cultural Christianity. There is no universal "Gospel culture." Christianity as expressed culturally is *always* particular and transmitted through natural generations.

However, the vestiges of cultural Christianity are disappearing in the West today. I offer my ideas for recovering it in the conclusion of this volume. Here, I'll simply say that it requires a fiercely resolute will. A people must have spirit, self-affirmation, self-regard, and confidence in themselves. They must, in other words, become the opposite of what Western Christianity has become. The spirit to live says, "This is ours for our good," and it drives a people to endure the sacrifices to keep it.

6

What Laws Can and Cannot Do: Civil Law

"For when the authority is of God and that in way of an ordinance (Rom. 13:1) and when the administration of it is according to deductions and rules gathered from the word of God and the clear light of nature in civil nations, surely there is no human law that tendeth to [the]common good (according to those principles) but [but what] is mediately a law of God, and that in way of an Ordinance which all are to submit unto and that for conscience sake (Rom. 13:5)." —*The Laws and Liberties of Massachusetts* (1647)

I. Law in General

This chapter completes what I've identified as the material cause of Christian nationalism, or the content of Christian national action.

In the previous chapter, we discussed social custom; here we discuss civil law. Social custom, as I argued, *implicitly* orders us to earthly and heavenly ends by the force of social power. But this prejudicial ordering has limitations: it is neither centralized nor possessed and exercised by a decisional authority, nor does it permit the use of outward force to achieve compliance. In its nature, prejudice is unwieldly; difficult to direct, shift, and change; and lacks flexibility. It is insufficient for a complete ordering of civil society for a postlapsarian world and even a world of innocence. All civil societies, for this reason, need an *explicit* ordering, that is, something public and promulgated and decided upon through deliberation, wisdom, prudence, and authority. Societies need, in other words, an ordering of *reason*—reason expressed as civil law.

God made man a reasonable creature. Man's possession of reason is what most distinguishes him from beasts. Being reasonable, man is placed under a moral (or natural) law. Recall that the moral law is a *rule* to life, for by it man achieves his natural end. Reason is that faculty by which man discerns this law and thereby judges what must be done and must not be done. Cicero famously wrote that "law is the highest reason, rooted in nature, which commands things that must be done and prohibits the opposite."[1] Non-rational creations are under types of ordering (appetitive, vegetative, etc.), but these are not under *laws* properly speaking, for such creatures have neither the faculty to discern nor a free will to conform to the principles of their natures. The reason of man allows him to discern and understand both the laws of his nature and why those laws are good for him.

We can proceed with a definition of law in general:

---

1. Cicero, *On the Commonwealth and On the Laws*, 1.18.

> *Law is an ordering of reason by an appropriate lawgiver for the*
> *good of the community.*

This definition of law is true of all types of law: eternal, natural, and human (or civil). The "ordering of reason" includes, as Reformed theologian Franciscus Junius writes, "(1) the reason of the one who orders, (2) the reason of those who are governed by the ordering, and (3) that very reason of ordering intervening between both. If one of these is lacking, it is not properly called a law."[2] Ordering is a relation between one who orders and those who are ordered. But an ordering *of reason* is a public dictation of judgment for others by an authority who judges for the common good.

The natural law is an ordering of reason, consisting of moral principles that are innate in rational creatures, given by God, who is the author of nature. Put differently, God has ordered man with a rule by which he discerns what he must do and must avoid in order to achieve his ends. This natural law applies to every sphere of life, not merely civil life; it is comprehensive. But being a set of universal principles, it requires particular applications according to the sphere in which one is acting and according to the circumstances of that sphere. The natural law orders family life, for example, providing its form, structure, and end, but natural principles require application by the familial authority to direct it to its end. No two families are exactly the same as to the specific judgments on what conduces to their good, yet both can, despite their varying judgments, achieve the end of family life.

Natural law prescribes universal principles and universal conclusions from those principles. As Junius writes,

2. Junius, *Mosaic Polity*, 46.

We call principles those that are known in themselves, are immovable, and (as the scholastic call them) are indemonstrable . . .
just as, for example, "God exists," and in life is "preserving our existence, our species, and justice." We call common conclusions,
however, those things that natural reason, with the light of nature
leading the way, constructs from the principles, such as, for example, that God must be worshipped, and our life, our species,
and the supports of justice must be cared for.[3]

These conclusions are universal (viz., true for all situations) and
are the ground for action, but they are not prescriptive of action
in themselves. They require a reasoning subject to make particular
determinations (or applications) concerning concrete action, given
the circumstances. Determinations are practical decisions on what
to do or not do, given the circumstances; and these can be individual, familial, civil, and ecclesiastical determinations. Junius, for example, discusses Deuteronomy 22:8, which requires one to "make
a railing for your roof." This is a determination (given by God) that
follows from a principle and its subsequent conclusion, namely, "no
one must be injured" and "nothing that could injure anyone may
be built," respectively.[4] The determination that roofs ought to have
railings is suitable only if roofs in the community are designed such
that they might be hazardous. Most single-family homes today do
not require railings, for ordinarily roofs are not hazardous. Though
this determination is no longer relevant, the principle and conclusion remain valid, and building codes (which are determinations)
recognize the same principle and conclusion.

3. Ibid.
4. Ibid., 77.

Since every sphere of life is under natural law and that natural law requires particular applications, it follows that every sphere of life requires a suitable authority, with a suitable power, to make determinations. For this reason, God has granted specific types of power by which the authorities of each sphere make judgments. The family has the *pater familias* with *patria potestas* ("fatherly power"); civil life has the civil magistrate with civil power; the instituted church has the minister with spiritual power; and the individual has a power unto himself. The nature of each sphere dictates the species of power required. These powers and their differences are not arbitrary but arise from the nature of each sphere.

II. Civil Law

Ordering of Reason

Civil determinations are *civil laws*. Now, civil laws are necessary for civil society because households in combination create problems of collective action that individuals and households cannot effectively resolve on their own. Put differently, social life apart from civil law creates gaps in judgment of what to do and what not to do. We have natural epistemic limitations, and so civil society requires rules of action for proper coordination. Absent these rules, we would unintendedly frustrate each other's activities and ends. Imagine, for example, a community with cars that also lacks traffic laws. Without common rules, we would be unable to effectively coordinate our actions, even with the best intentions. This is why the Western political tradition has called civil law, as Plutarch famously said, the "life of cities." Agreeing with him, Cicero wrote the following:

> For law is the bond which secures these our privileges in
> the commonwealth, the foundation of our liberty, the foun-
> tain-head of justice. Within the law are reposed the mind and
> heart, the judgement and the conviction of the state. The state
> [*civitas*] without law would be like the human body without
> mind—unable to employ the parts which are to it as sinews,
> blood, and limbs.[5]

Following Cicero, Bullinger wrote that "laws undoubtedly are
the strongest sinews of the commonweal."[6] Civil laws coordinate
our activities, making possible a collective, symbiotic life.

Since civil law is a species of law in general, we can define *civil
law* as

> *an ordering of reason, enacted and promulgated by a legitimate civ-*
> *il authority, that commands public action for the common good of*
> *civil communities.*

Civil law is the outward and official expression of *public judgment*. Public judgment is simply the conclusion of the civil authority's reasoning about suitable public action for the common good.
Civil law is the enacted and promulgated form of public judgment,
and so civil law is the outward and official expression of the civil
authority's reasoning about suitable action for the common good.

Civil law has command over the outward man but not from an
authority in and of itself. Its authority, as Junius states, "proceed[s]

5. Cicero, *Pro Cluentio*, Loeb Classical Library 98 (Cambridge, MA: Harvard University
Press, 1927), 379.
6. Bullinger, *Decades*, 1:338–39 [Second Decade, Sermon vii].

by reason from those other preceding laws," namely, the natural law.[7] Hence, it is a derived authority, and so laws are just *only if* they command what proceeds from the natural law. This derivative character is precisely why such laws bind our conscience to them. As Aquinas said, "[Human] laws ... have the power of binding conscience, from the eternal law whence they are derived [via natural law]."[8] However, a purported law that does *not* order according to reason is no law at all. That is to say, unjust laws are not laws, properly speaking, and so they do not bind the conscience to obedience. This position—expressed famously in Latin as *lex iniusta non est lex* [an unjust law is not a law]—was affirmed from Cicero to Augustine through Aquinas to classical Protestantism. Zacharias Ursinus said, for example, that law "commands that which is upright and just, otherwise it is no law."[9] Though this raises questions of tyranny and civil disobedience, the important point here is that civil law, when true and just, is neither arbitrary nor has its force from the will of the magistrate alone; rather, it orders civil life in accordance with a higher law and has its force from that higher law, namely, the natural law. In this way, the magistrate *mediates* divine civil rule, as the one who determines appropriate action from natural law principles.

7. Junius, *Mosaic Polity*, 55. Junius also mentioned "divine law," which I discuss later.

8. Aquinas, *ST*, I-II.96.4. Calvin argues practically the same thing, though he says that we are not bound by particular human laws in themselves, but by the power of God and the general end of law. *Institutes*, 4.10.5.

9. Ursinus, *Corpus doctrinae christinae* (Heidelberg, 1616), 583. Zanchi, likewise, states that "[i]f natural law is indeed the measure for human laws, then it is also the rule for human actions. Therefore just as every action that does not agree with natural law is sinful, so, too, is every human law. ... For this reason, Augustine rightly, in his *On Free Will*, claimed that a law that is not just should not be called so, and it is not just if it does not agree with natural law." *On the Law in General*, 30–31.

An important principle of civil law is that its reach is limited to things that the other spheres of life cannot effectively regulate to the common good. Thus, the individual, family, society, civil associations, and churches have primacy in ordering the things of life. When the other spheres can effectively determine suitable action, civil authorities should not interfere. They should not take from families, churches, and individuals what each sphere can best determine for itself. For example, the state might forbid cruelty in the parental discipline of children, but it should still leave disciplining itself to parents. Nevertheless, despite the extensive powers of these non-civil spheres, much is left for civil law to order in our lives.

This principle permitted the augmentation of government after the fall of man, which I discussed in chapter 2. Civil law now contends with the disordering effects of sin. Much of what the other spheres of life could once determine is now subject to the reach of civil law. The husband's abuse of his power, for example, is restrained by the state. With this augmentation of civil power, civil authority is able to order civil society toward its original end, according to the same natural principles.

Civil Command

Civil power and social power are two species of power. They differ on an essential point: social power is implicit and civil power is explicit, as I've said. Civil power is explicit power because it is externalized and personalized as *command*. Implicit power is analogous to command in that it directs people to "do this" and "don't do that." But it operates as a sort of self-admonishment, even though at the same time it is an authority outside oneself. Explicit power has a more pronounced subject-object relation—command and obedience. It directs as a force outside oneself. Civil command, being the command of magistrates, is what gives civil laws their life and force; it supplies the imperative to the judgment.

Though civil command is backed by penalties for non-compliance, it is not inherently a coercive power. Reformed theologian Herman Witsius correctly wrote,

> It is not the rigour of coercion that properly constitutes a law, but the obligatory virtue of what is enjoined, proceeding both from the lawgiver, and from the equity of the thing commanded, which is here founded on the holiness of the divine nature, so far as imitable by man.[10]

Civil law is, after all, an ordering of reason; it is right practical reason. Since you should always follow right reason, you should always follow (just) civil law. Also, since man's private judgment concerning suitable civil action is naturally limited, public judgment is both necessary for living well and natural for him to obey. Thus, civil command is not inherently coercive, for man is naturally willing to be directed in life by a civil authority.

Coercion has become a crucial feature of civil command in the postlapsarian augmentation of civil power. Backing civil command with sanctions is necessary, given the state of things, for civil government adequately achieve its original end. It brings sinful man

---

10. Herman Witsius, *The Economy of the Covenants between God and Man* (New York: Thomas Kirk, 1804), 1.3.6. As Bullinger says, "The law is not troublesome to the just man, because it is agreeable to the mind and thoughts of upright livers, who do embrace it with all their hearts." *Decades*, 1:337 [Second Decade, Sermon vii].

into compliance with the conditions for commodious civil life. Civil command becomes coercive for someone when he fails or refuses to comply or when he obeys the law simply out of fear of the sanction.

The correlate of civil command is civil *obedience*. The basis for obedience is not persuasion as to the specific reasons of any law, but one of *deference* to the lawgiver. Deference is necessary because private persons cannot determine many of the actions necessary for the common good, and most people are unable to sufficiently judge the reasons for every action required of them. Thus, the motivating basis for obedience is deference to the lawgiver, who occupies a civil office charging him to make judgments for the whole. The ultimate grounds of obedience are the reasons for the action, but the act of deference presumes that sufficient reasons formed the lawgiver's judgment. Obeying civil commands, therefore, is acting according to reason (when the commands are just), even though one may not know the reasons for the action.

It follows that civil power is a power to command, not to persuade, and that the duties of civil subjection includes the duty of deference. This is clarified when we recognize that commands are not propositions—they are not statements to affirm or deny. Rather, commands are statements to be *obeyed* or *disobeyed*. A child cannot affirm "Go clean your room"; he can only obey or disobey. He may affirm or deny the reason for the command, that "rooms need to be tidy." But the command itself can only be obeyed or disobeyed.[11] Thus, while all good commands are backed by good rea-

11. When children ask, "Why must I clean my room?" many parents say, "Because I told you to," which is not justifying the reason behind the command but asserting the nature of parental command itself—that children ought to obey their parents deferentially, trusting that their commands are for the child's good. This is one reason why civil magistrates are often called "fathers" by their people.

sons for the commanded action, commands themselves are matters of obedience. The citizen or subject is not required to affirm a law or the reason for the law but simply to obey the law; and though one may affirm the reasons behind the law, the law itself remains a command and so only requires obedience. In military command, for example, subordinate commanders defer to the judgment of superiors, assuming that their superior commander (who commands more than one subordinate unit) is in a better position to make judgments that concern the whole.

To be sure, deference does not require absolute obedience or eliminate the possibility of just disobedience. The command is not itself the ultimate ground of action. Deference is simply the *presumption* that the lawgiver has good reasons for his judgments— the presumption that you are being ordered according to reason. But the absence of good reasons can become apparent to many in the community, either by examining the substance of the required action or its consequences. Our first impulse should be deference, but we are not helpless, amoral, non-rational beings, unable ever to judge the substance and consequences of our actions. Hence, just disobedience is still possible; deference can and ought (at times) to be suspended. I discuss civil disobedience later in the chapter and in the chapter on revolution.

As for power over the conscience, implicit power can influence beliefs, such as assent to Christian truth, but civil law cannot command belief. It can only direct bodies. It orders outward action. Civil power cannot touch the conscience. Why? Because the conscience is a forum of persuasion and civil power is a power of command. The civil command "believe in Christ" violates a necessary condition of belief, namely, that belief is a matter of persuasion—something that one affirms.[12] You cannot affirm commands, as I've said. Therefore, since inward faith is essentially a matter of persuasion (or motivated in part by reasons for faith), exercising faith cannot be an object of civil command, even for the baptized.

But if civil law cannot touch the inward man, how is it an ordering of reason? After all, we "reason" in the mind. Here is my answer: Civil order is an ordering of *practical* reason, and thus the ordering of reason in civil life is reason *outwardly manifested in action*. Civil law orders civil society according to the reason of the lawgiver—a reasoning that is presumed in the act of deference. The outward actions of the people disclose or manifest an ordering of reason, though the people may not know the specific reasoning for the actions.[13]

Civil Authority

Civil law is promulgated and enforced by a legitimate civil authority. I will discuss the civil magistrate in the next chapter. But we must say something here to complete our explication of the definition. Civil laws in themselves have no force; they are, as Cicero said, a *mutus magistratus* or a "dumb magistrate."[14] Civil law has

---

12. "Believe in Christ" when said by an evangelist should be understood as an *admonishment*. It prompts one to *affirm* the reasons given for belief or to complete the reasoning concerning oneself given the truths communicated to them. That is, it directs one back to the reasons for believing in Christ. A true command is one in which the immediate reason for obedience is nothing but the authority of the one commanding.

13. My discussion may sound as if civil life is a sort of simulation engineered by great overlords whose ways and reasons are distant from the people. But I'm simply laying out principles for authority in civil life. When this discussion is integrated with the other chapters in this work, it becomes evident that my political philosophy has much room for disobedience (even revolution), individual self-regard, and critical thinking about the demands of our leaders.

14. Cicero, *On the Laws*, 3.2.

command only when enlivened by the magistrate, for *magistratus lex est loquens* ("The magistrate is the living law"), as Cicero said. As Bullinger writes, only through magistrates do laws "shew forth their strength and lively force."[15] Furthermore, since magistrates make judgments with a view to the common good, magistrates must be prudent. They must be capable not only of discerning the public good (viz., going beyond personal interest), but have that public's good at heart. "[T]he king is constituted over affairs that belong to another, namely, over the affairs of the people," writes Althusius.[16]

Righteous and Good Laws

Though natural law is a universal law, you cannot derive from it a universally suitable body of civil law. Bodies of law will vary in content based on peculiarities of geography, commerce, the people's character, religious diversity, and numerous other types of circumstances. Some laws will be present in all or most civil societies, such as prohibitions of murder. These are universal because they are so close to human nature that they will not alter with changes in circumstances. But many laws are indeed based in circumstances and thus particular and mutable.

To understand why they are mutable, we should think of civil law in terms of principle, means, and end. The principle is *ordering civil life in accordance with natural law principles and circumstances*, and the end is *a commodious, quiet, and godly life*. The principle and end are immutable, for they are rooted in human nature and hence universally true for all civil orders, regardless of circumstance and moral integrity. The means, however, are mutable and vary, for their

---

15. Bullinger, *Decades*, 1:339 [Second Decade, Sermon vii].
16. Althusius, *Politica*, 111 [18.93].

suitability is contingent on circumstances. The means are *civil judgments concerning outward action.* Civil law must order the community to its end in light of circumstances and in accordance with natural law. But since circumstances can change, so too can laws. Zanchi writes that civil laws that "are enacted for circumstances of place, time, and personality, cannot be eternal and unchangeable because their circumstances can change."[17] Over time, some existing laws become ineffective and unnecessary; the reasons for them cease. Gratian famously said that "when the reason for the law ceases, the law itself ceases." They become laws in name only.

All just laws are both righteous *and* good. They are righteous when they inherently accord with the natural law; the commanded action is good in its substance. But being inherently righteous says nothing about their suitability for any given people. As Junius writes, "[T]hings that are absolutely and intrinsically good sometimes become evil in certain circumstances."[18] Laws that oppose libel and slander are righteous, according to the ninth commandment, as a means to protect reputations and to encourage honesty. But if these laws permit the adjudication of any perceived slight, the law itself would likely promote a litigious society and do harm. Consider also a law that permits unlicensed fishing on government land. It is intrinsically righteous, and it may be good as well, if the fisherman are few and do not exploit the lack of regulation. But if the number of fishermen increase, or abuses arise, this law can result in harm. Junius said that "there is a place in which a good or indifferent thing is rendered evil because it is out of place."[19] Thus,

17. Zanchi, *On the Law in General*, 38.
18. Junius, *Mosaic Polity*, 135.
19. Ibid.

all righteous laws are only *potentially* just. They must also be *good* laws. That is, they must suit the circumstances and conduce concretely to the common good. It follows, then, that all good laws are righteous laws, for nothing inherently opposed to the natural law could be good for man, but also that righteous laws are good laws only when suitable to the circumstances. This is why the magistrate cannot rubberstamp a ready-made divine civil code; he must apply discernment and prudence to determine appropriate public action. This also explains why civil law will differ from place to place—it must be suitable to the habits, characteristics, heritage, geography, and other particular features of each people.

Though good laws require human determination, they are nevertheless from God, not only providentially but also in root and mode: They follow from God's natural law (the root) and are promulgated and enlivened by God's servant, the civil magistrate (the mode). Therefore, we can say with Demosthenes that "all law is a gift of God."[20] A just body of civil law is from God. It is, in this sense, theonomic.

The End of Civil Law

The end of civil law is the common good of the civil community. The common good is *common* in that it refers to good conditions of the whole. Civil law aims at the common good by seeking to establish and cultivate social conditions in which each part of the whole is afforded the opportunity to seek for himself and his household the complete good. I emphasize the individual here to correct an overemphasis today on the collective in discourse around the "common good." The

---

20. πᾶς ἐστι νόμος εὕρημα μὲν καὶ δῶρον θεῶν. "All law is an invention and gift of the gods." Demosthenes, *Against Aristogiton I*, 1.16. See also Bullinger, *Decades*, 1:338 [Second Decade, Sermon vii].

completeness of the individual is not in a zero-sum competition with the completeness of the community. That is, the individual is not subsumed in the collective; rather, complete individuals are the parts to the complete whole. The whole is a symbiosis—each member contributing his gifts and each depending on the various gifts of others. The whole makes possible the completeness of the individual, and complete individuals (or the individual pursuit of completeness) make possible the completeness of the whole.

This might seem overly abstract, but my interest is ensuring the preservation of individual agency and vitality. The venerated Thomist view that "law is to make men good" is true; I affirm it. But it is more precise to say that the law *facilitates* the pursuit of goodness—the will for right action and a will for life. Civil law is not a substitute for individual action, as if law itself procures for man the complete good. Of course, civil law's first role, as I've argued, is to provide judgments on matters indeterminate or inaccessible to private judgment, which order the civil community in accord with reason. They are made good to the extent that civil law directs them in the good. But civil law is limited to public judgments and its postlapsarian augmentation. There remains ecclesiastical, domestic, and individual authority—each being a part of man's complete good, and all are mutually complementary. To get to the point, civil law should make space for civic virtue, for self-willed individual action, for free association, and for natural hierarchy formation. Indeed, these spaces are necessary for the common good.

The Objects and Scope of Law

The objects of law are things that, in principle, the law can touch, direct, or order. It refers to the things of civil jurisdiction. The scope of

objects includes *all* outward things, except spiritual ceremonies and
the ecclesiastical order (which are matters of divine law). Though
the scope of objects is extensive in principle, the scope is limited
in application. This reiterates the principle I identified earlier: Civil
authority should leave alone what the other spheres of life can effectively govern themselves. And there must be great awareness of
this principle so that the citizens or subjects who must claim and assert their own governability can resist encroachments from modern
busybodies and schoolmarms. Of course, communities that lack
self-governability will require more law and more law enforcement.

Though often disparaged today, natural rights simply follow
from natural law. A natural right is a claim for oneself with regard to
some good that is essential by nature for him to achieve his natural
ends. An obvious example is the right to worship God: one has a
claim against others to conduct free, unhindered, and undistracted
worship. One has a natural right to life and a right to liberty to the
extent of his self-governability. I also affirm a natural right to one's
property,[21] though I will not argue for it here. Civil law, in facilitat-
ing one's pursuit of his good, must secure natural rights, for natural
rights are essential to the good of men. I am not claiming that the
only object of civil law is securing rights but that natural rights are
essential and the principal objects of civil law.[22] Nor am I claiming
that these rights are absolute and utterly inalienable; natural rights
are means to man's good, not ends in themselves. Hence, they can

---

21. Samuel Rutherford said, "Men are just owners of their own goods, by all good order,
both of nature and time, before there be any such thing as a king or magistrate." *Lex, Rex,
or The Law and the Prince* (London: John Field, 1644), 67 [Q. 16].

22. Civil rights, however, are positive rights, not natural or universal rights, and they arise
from within societies as promises to each other and as a particular inheritance. The codifi-
cation of natural rights can be part of an inheritance along with civil rights.

be suspended but only in extraordinary times and only with extreme caution and wisdom.

III. Civil Law in a Christian Commonwealth

A Christian commonwealth is the civil regime of Christian nationalism. Christian nationalism, as I've argued, is a Christian nation acting for itself to secure (across generations) both its earthly and heavenly good. Achieving these goods requires civil government—an entity that explicitly and effectively acts upon society via civil law. Civil government is Christian not because it declares itself Christian (whether through pomp, titles, or constitutional preambles) but because it actually orders a Christian people to their complete good. This includes acting for the peace and good order of the instituted church, which administers the chief good. Thus, *action*, not declaration, makes a commonwealth Christian.

Not every particular civil law of a Christian civil government is distinctively Christian. Indeed, most are simply human; they concern human things. After all, the foundational principles of all civil societies, even Christian ones, are universal human principles, and Christians are fully human. As Junius rightly states,

> For to the extent that we may be Christians, we do not cease being humans, but we are Christian human beings [*homines Christiani*]. So also we must state that therefore we are bound by Christian laws, not that we are consequently released from human ones.[23]

---

23. Junius, *Mosaic Polity*, 38.

A Christian commonwealth, therefore, enacts many laws that (considered separately) pertain in object and end to man as man, not as a Christian. But these laws are Christian as parts to a Christian whole. That is, they belong to a totality of law that is Christian, for a Christian body of law orders to the complete good, including that which is heavenly. We can say, then, that every law that pertains to man as man is a Christian law, albeit indirectly, when it belongs to a body of law that is Christian as to the whole. This is precisely why I've used the word *totality* in my definition of Christian nationalism; it allows us to say that *all* national actions—whether directed by custom or law—are *Christian* customs and laws, even if in themselves they are not distinctly Christian or religious and are merely human and mundane. Such actions are Christian actions because they contribute what is necessary to the whole (e.g., nursing mothers, commercial activity, military service)—a whole that is Christian because it orders to both earthly and heavenly good.

Junius continues:

> For grace perfects nature; grace does not, however, abolish it. And therefore with respect to the laws by which nature itself is sustained and renewed, grace restores [*restituit*] those that have been lost, renews [*instaurat*] those that have been corrupted, and teaches [*tradit*] those that are unknown.[24]

Grace has three functions vis-à-vis nature: (1) it restores what was lost at the fall; (2) it renews what the fall corrupted; and (3) it teaches what is above nature. These functions constitute the general

24. Ibid.

operations of grace in the world, and restored humanity is a product of these functions of grace.

By the grace of God, Scripture contains both natural truths and supernatural truths—the latter consisting mainly of the adventitious and exclusive means to eternal life. Since Scripture contains the natural law (in scripturated form), Scripture can and ought to inform our understanding of the natural law, the common good, proper determinations for civil law, and the means to heavenly life.

No civil law can be fundamentally derived from a supernatural principle (i.e., a principle of grace). Civil society is fundamentally a human order and is ordered according to principles of human nature. Nevertheless, as I argued in chapter 4, the basis for a civil law can be a supernatural *conclusion* from natural principles that have interacted with supernatural truth. For example, if civil government ought to support the spiritual administration of true religion (a natural principle), then civil government ought to support the spiritual administration of the Christian religion (supernatural conclusion). Why? Because the Christian religion is the true religion (a supernatural truth). This syllogism demonstrates that civil laws can be distinctively Christian and yet grounded in a natural principle. Commonwealths can enact distinctively Christian laws that serve Christian ends. Enacting Sabbath laws, for example, follows not from a principle of grace but from a principle of nature—that civil government ought to order outward conditions for the good of man, including the highest good. Civil law cannot command inward worship or belief, but it can suppress public blasphemy, heresy, and flagrant disregard for public worship among the baptized.[25]

---

25. For a more thorough justification of restraining religious error and for a refutation of objections, see chapter 9.

A Christian body of law remains an ordering of reason, despite the fact that some of the laws are distinctively Christian, because the end or *telos* of natural reason is Christian truth. To worship the true God, which is the preeminent command of reason, means worshipping the Triune God—a truth known only by faith. To be rightly ordered in reason is to be ordered to what is above reason. Since we have Scripture, sound reason no longer terminates at natural religion. Special revelation is above reason, but it is not contrary to reason; and reason is fulfilled in it as that which supplies reason's highest object and its perfection. Therefore, a Christian body of law, which contains laws that are distinctively Christian, order the community in reason, indeed to the highest reason and its fulfillment. A Christian body of law is the only *complete* and *true* body of law.

It is tempting to list a set of laws that the typical Christian commonwealth would have, and certainly the practically minded reader would prefer this. But the suitability of this or that law is highly dependent on circumstances, the character of the people, and religious demographics. As Aquinas said, "General principles of the natural law cannot be applied to all men in the same way on account of the great variety of human affairs: and hence arises the diversity of positive laws among various people."[26] A Christian people may want to censure atheism and blasphemy through civil law, but another people may find social power sufficient to that end. No doubt all would have Sabbath laws, but these will vary in degree and type. Church establishment will certainly look different in different places, and perhaps official church establishment is unnecessary. A Christian commonwealth would enact

26. Aquinas, *ST*, I-II.95.2.

distinctive laws that secure and support the people's particular-ity, encourage their pride of place, and reinforce one's duties to this country. Supplying a set of laws, in my judgment, only feeds into the tendency of Westerners to retreat to universality, where-by people look for something outside themselves to order them-selves concretely. A people need the strength, resolve, and spirit to enact their own laws, and they should not seek some universal "blueprint" they can rubber-stamp into law. The 19th-century German jurist Friedrich Stahl said it best:

> God's world order is the archetype of all positive legal con-struction, but it is not itself a legal construction. Its concepts and commandments, the purpose inhering in life relations, are the principles and the guideline for the laws; but they are not themselves laws by which men in accordance therewith maintain ordered human relations and are able to decide cases of conflict. . . . The people themselves, in accordance with the particularity of spirit and their conditions and with their own creative power, are to give definitive shape to them, to particu-larize them and thus also to individualize them; and only then do they become applicable norms, or law.[27]

27. Friedrich Stahl, *Principles of Law*, trans. Ruben Alvarado (Aalten, Netherlands: Wordbridge, 2007), 34. Bullinger gives a more conventional answer: "Therefore every country has free liberty to use those laws which are best suited and most requisite for the es-tate and necessity of every place, and of every time and persons. Yet this is to be done in such a way, that the substance of God's laws is not rejected, trodden down, and utterly neglected. For the things which are agreeable to the law of nature and the Ten Commandments, and whatever else God has commanded to be punished, must not in any case be either clean forgotten, or lightly regarded. Now the end to which all these laws tend, is that honesty may be nourished, peace and public tranquility be firmly maintained, and judgment and justice be rightly executed." *Decades*, 1:280 [Third Decade, Sermon viii].

The Law of Moses

Questions around the Mosaic law are typically more theological in nature and best left for the theologians. But some comments touching on principles of law will help us understand how Christian nations should view and use the law of Moses. The Mosaic law is, as Junius states, a "perfect example" of law, for it is divinely prescribed law, and God prescribes for man only what is good and true. For this reason, "it is necessary to praise the law of Moses above other human laws because it proceeds from that legislator whose reason is most perfect," says Junius.[28] But although the Mosaic law is of divine origin, the law in itself, in substance, shares the same classification as other examples of civil law—it is one possible body of law that "proceed[s] from the immovable principles and general conclusion" of the natural law.[29] The Mosaic law is not *above* natural law; it is a perfect application of it.

Put differently, although the Mosaic law is specifically different from all other bodies of law with regard to types of content,[30] it still belongs to the same genus as all bodies of civil law. Essential to that genus is that *all laws ought to be both righteous and good.* The Mosaic law was a perfect body of law for the Jewish people not simply because God declared it to be perfect but because it was actually perfect. It was, according to God's natural law, both righteous and good, and it was *good* because it perfectly conduced to the common

28. Junius, *Mosaic Polity*, 95.

29. Ibid.

30. But the Mosaic law is a different *species* of civil law. This is true not simply because it is divinely ordained law (i.e., divine law) but because it contains laws that only God could immediately bind upon man. Purity codes and cultic ceremonies, for example, are the sort of commands only God can bind on man. These constitute the specific difference between the Mosaic law and other bodies of civil law.

good of the Jewish people in their circumstances, if obeyed. But it is not thereby a suitable body of law for *all* nations. For this reason, as the Reformed tradition has almost universally affirmed, Mosaic law, taken as a whole, is not binding on all nations, even Christian nations. Yet because the Mosaic law perfectly follows from the natural law (albeit suited for a certain people), it *can* serve as a guide or source of law for all nations. The Mosaic law, therefore, remains relevant to all civil polities.

The "ancient" division (as Calvin called it) of the Mosaic law divides it into moral, ceremonial, and civil (or political) law. The moral law refers to "nothing else than the testimony of natural law, and of that conscience which God has engraven on the minds of men." This law is itself divided under two heads: we are to "worship God with pure faith and piety [and] to embrace men with sincere affection."[31] Calvin has in mind the two tables of the Decalogue. The moral law is immutable and universal and serves as the ground for the other two types of law, which are mutable and particular. As Junius writes,

> For the civil or political law serves the moral law with respect to human society in the way established by each republic, which is particular, but the ecclesiastical law, which is commonly called ceremonial, serves the moral law as it pertains to the worship of God and to piety.... And indeed it is the nature of the moral law that in and of itself it should be constant and immutable, but regarding those laws that have been enacted on account of that moral law, and look to it as if to their own end, it is

31. Calvin, *Institutes*, 4.20.15.

demonstrated that these laws are mutable even in themselves, because they exist on account of something else.[32]

The ceremonial laws were, as Calvin said, a "tutelage" for the people of God until the Lord "was fully to manifest his wisdom to the world, and exhibit the reality of those things which were then adumbrated by figures."[33] For this reason, they are "deadly," as Augustine said, for they foreshadowed what was to come, and in their practice one denies Christ.[34]

The civil law of the Mosaic law did not in itself foreshadow Christ and so did not undergo a change as to their righteousness—they are, in other words, not *deadly*. But they are *dead*; they are "no longer living in such a way as to obligate," says Junius. He continues, speaking of civil law in general: "In circumstances it undergoes as many changes as possible, and varies according to time, place, person, deeds, modes, causes, and supports—in the past, the present, or the future—as well as in public and private matters."[35] In other words, whether any civil law is *good* depends on circumstances, which requires the discernment and prudence of man. Calvin writes, "[E]ach nation has been left at liberty to enact the laws which it judges as beneficial."[36] Nothing about this disparages the

32. Junius, *Mosaic Policy*, 126.

33. Calvin, *Institutes*, 4.20.15.

34. Augustine, "Letter 75," in *Letters 1-99*, ed. John E. Rotelle and trans. Roland Teske, series 2, vol. 1 of *The Works of St. Augustine: A Translation for the 21st Century* (Hyde Park, NY: New City Press, 2001), 289. "The ceremonial part . . . at this time has generally passed away and no longer obligates human beings." Junius, *Mosaic Polity*, 141.

35. Ibid., 140–41.

36. Calvin, *Institutes*, 4.20.15. Junius writes, "In every human administration, those who do not temper their own counsels in such a way that they may accommodate the variety of judgments to the variety of things, will be least helpful to the republic. Or rather, they

Mosaic law—a law of God. It is a perfect example of law. But it is not a universal body of law.

Some civil laws in the Mosaic law *are* universal in a way. But they are universal because they are necessary for any just and commodious human society. Indeed, such laws are a part of the Mosaic law precisely because their absence would make the law imperfect; and God, being good, could not create anything but perfect law. These laws include punishing "reprehensible" crimes, requiring capital punishment.[37] One might also consider Deuteronomy 19:15—"One witness shall not rise up against a man for any iniquity, or for any sin, in any sin that he sinneth"—to be a universally wise law.

Though not universally suitable, the civil laws of Scripture provide certainty as to their inherent righteousness. They are, therefore, morally *permissible* in civil law, and the closeness of circumstances aid in determining whether any of them is suitable. Permissibility does not necessarily mean suitability, of course, but I remind the modern reader that his modern discomfort at some of the prescribed punishments is an unreliable measure of their suitability.

destroy it entirely by the inflexibility of their judgments because they strive for constancy or stubbornness more than understanding and discernment, without which a republic cannot stand." *Mosaic Polity*, 141.

37. Junius, *Mosaic Polity*, 117. He writes, "If capital punishment is not established in this way the most offensive injury is done to right reason, the common law, and the civil order, which themselves—in accordance with that eternal reason and the natural and divine law—most carefully protect human life, liberty and the honor of parents from all injury, and which declare to be unworthy of life anyone who has deprived either his neighbors of life or liberty." Ibid., 119. The Massachusetts Body of Liberties (1641), a New England Puritan legal code that systematized the laws enacted in Massachusetts, includes laws derived from both the English common law and the Mosaic law. Laws from the latter all concern the death penalty, e.g., for worshipping other gods, witchcraft, blasphemy, murder, adultery, and several others. Each is followed by references to Scripture.

The fear of "human autonomy" in determining suitable law, which some corners of Protestantism today voice, is misplaced. Although civil law is a sort of self-given human law—for the civil magistrate deliberates and determines it—the law still must be in accord with God's immutable law, and every civil law is binding only if it is derived from God's law and conduces to the end of that law. Hence, just civil law, even when determined by man, is both theonomic and, in a sense, autonomic. The magistrate enacts and enforces laws of his own design, though only as a mediator, a sort of vicar of divine civil rule.

IV. Modern Theonomy

The previous section, though theonomic in my view, opposes most versions of modern theonomy. Instead of belaboring my critique, it will be helpful for us to briefly discuss the sociological origins of modern theonomy. Modern theonomist movements arose in the late 20th century, a time of great conflict between competing universal visions—between liberalism and communism. At the same time, the West underwent rapid changes that eroded the social forces and institutions that maintained a seemingly Christian morality or at least a Christian self-conception. Modern theonomy provided both a universalist alternative to the prevailing visions and promised to reverse moral decay. It had an easily identifiable and communicable political program based in biblical law.

One can understand why American Christians, bewildered at the pace of change and befuddled as to what to do about it, would find this appealing. It is a simple way to be on God's side. I say this not to dismiss theonomy, though I do disagree with it. The theonomists had the right spirit; they knew that civil order, liberty, and justice require bold action, confidence in truth, and resolve to succeed. They saw what was coming, and they were largely correct about many of their critics: that their critics, wittingly or not, were designing political theologies of defeat and surrender. The modern version of two-kingdoms theology, advanced by theologians such as Michael Horton (a long critic of theonomy of all sorts), sets forth an endless series of compromises and defeats. It is time to recognize that the theonomists were right about the direction of Reformed political theology as it manifested in the late 20th century up to today.

Though I have trouble discerning the popularity of theonomy today, it seems to be in decline. This concerns me, because I suspect that it represents a decline in spirit. The pull towards quasi-Anabaptist political theology, which requires a pacifist spirit, is thriving today, even in Reformed and Lutheran contexts. That it was once cool to be anti-theonomist was a mistake.

My disagreement with the theonomists is different from that of their typical critics. Christian nationalism is a coherent alternative to modern theonomy that achieves the same or at least similar ends, though to my mind Christian nationalism, as I've presented it, flows directly out of classical Protestantism, and modern theonomy does not. Furthermore, I affirm a form of theonomy: civil law ought to be in accordance with God's law, and civil law ought to order man to both earthly and heavenly ends. I deny, however, that the civil laws in the Mosaic law are immutable and universally applicable. Also, in their emphasis on law, theonomists seem to have neglected social power, social cohesion, and culture particularity. Indeed, in my experience, sometimes they are downright hostile to nationalism, the principle of similarity, and cultural preservation. Still, I hope that modern theonomy's spirit finds a home in Christian nationalism—a spirit that is not afraid to apply God's law to civil life; is willing to use God-ordained civil power to order man to righteousness and to suppress the enemies of civilization and the church; and desires to elevate God's people to the first rank in civil society and to declare the eternal good as the highest good.

But ordering ourselves to God must spring in large part from self-affirmation, from an instinct of peoplehood, and from the felt need to act for our good. We do not fight for Christian civilization in the abstract or according to a ready-made, universal set of civil laws. We do not fight according to a bare divine law but according to a law of God that inheres and enlivens our whole being.

V. Disobeying the Law

The ancient maxim that "an unjust law is no law" is justified on the grounds that laws are civil commands to act according to reason in accordance with the natural law. Civil law, as we've said, is an ordering of reason for civil society. Deference to the civil magistrate's reason is necessary, since civil law orders the whole, and the lawgiver has in view not merely his own interest (as a private person) but that of the community. He has what one might call public reason, as opposed to private reason. But laws that fail to order the whole according to natural law—being either unrighteous or righteous but ill-suited (i.e., bad)—are unjust laws; they are, for this reason, laws in name only, and God does not bind one's conscience to them.[38]

38. Zanchi writes, "[U]njust laws do not obligate our consciences, because God does not bind our conscience to unjust laws." *On the Laws in General*, 32.

There are two types of unjust laws, each corresponding roughly to the righteousness/goodness requirements discussed above. The first type are unjust in themselves or in substance; they directly oppose God's law. Civil law must not demand what God's law opposes or forbid what God's law demands. Man must "obey God rather than men" (Acts 5:29). The second type of unjust laws are those that in themselves conform to God's law or are indifferent to it but are unjust in accident. This type divides into at least four sub-types: (1) Illegitimate authorities or non-authorities cannot obligate anyone to some civil action, even if the action is good; only legitimate authorities can enact law; (2) nor can legitimate authorities demand what is beyond another's ability, for an ought always implies ability; (3) when the magistrate's personal good is the reason for some law, then that law is unjust, for the reason for any law is the ground of its legitimacy; (4) lastly, any law that does not conduce to the common good is unjust, for essential to any just law is the suitability to achieve the end of law. In each of these cases, the purported law does not formally obligate subjects or citizens, and, therefore, God does not bind their consciences to it.

However, one can choose to obey laws that are accidentally unjust, *if* obeying such laws is harmless to others and does not violate just laws. Christ said that "whosoever shall compel thee to go a mile, go with him twain" (Matt. 5:41). His command here does not obligate us to be naive and freely and knowingly subject ourselves to exploitation. As Calvin comments, Christ demands ultimately that each man "bear[s] patiently the injuries which he receives."[39] Commenting on Matthew 5:40 ("... let him that thy cloak also"), Calvin writes,

---

39. Calvin, *Commentary on a Harmony of the Evangelists*, 1:297 [on Matt. 5:38].

> None but a fool will stand upon the words, so as to maintain, that
> we must yield to our opponents what they demand, before com-
> ing into a court of law: for such compliance would more strongly
> inflame the minds of wicked men to robbery and extortion.[40]

What Christ demands is ultimately that we exercise patience
when we have no just recourse to avoid such injustice. Concerning
"turn the other cheek," Augustine says that "this does not lay down
a rule for outward actions."[41] Thus, Christ's instructions in Matthew
5:39–42 establish an absolute rule with regard to patiently bearing
injustice but not with regard to suffering exploitation and injustice.

However, he clearly denies that we have an absolute duty to resist
all injustice. It is a personal decision according to our situation. Perhaps the injustice is too insignificant to fuss over, or perhaps resistance
would cause greater harm overall. Or perhaps complying demonstrates
Christian patience or a reverence for authority in that concrete situation. These decisions require wise deliberation and consideration of
the potential harm to others in the act of compliance and defiance.
After all, harm against you can easily become harm to those who are
dependent on you, and failing to counter injustice often leads to and
encourages further injustice towards others. But obedience to injustice
is not absolutely required, and Christians ought to practice forbearance
with fellow Christians who choose one way or the other, though the
choice still ought to be subject to charitable discussion and substantive
disagreement on the prudence of this or that action.

A Christian has a right to confront injustice and exploitation
in order "to protect himself and his property from injury," states

40. Ibid., 1:299 [on Matt. 5:40].
41. Quoted in ibid.

Calvin.[42] In everyday life this permits self-defense and other actions,[43] but in terms of civil law it permits a Christian to use the full, legitimate powers of law to secure his person and property. That is, Christians can use the power of the civil government to correct any financial, physical, or reputational wrongs done to them.

Epistemic Limitations

Though we can in principle disobey unjust laws, we should recognize the inherent difficulty in determining whether a law is unjust. It is one thing for law to be unjust and another for you to *know* that it is unjust. Civil magistrates are necessary, as I've said, because of natural epistemic limitations in individuals to determine expedient actions for the common good. How then can a private person reliably determine whether a law is unjust? First, we can say with confidence that some laws are clearly unjust, such as forbidding the public worship of God, demanding that one worship false gods or renounce Christ, arbitrary taking of life, manstealing, and many others. Individuals know that such laws are unjust and that they ought to disobey them. Thus, exercising private judgment in determining the injustice of laws is not itself forbidden.

But many or perhaps most laws evade a simple evaluation, mainly because civil authorities are typically in a better position than private persons to make judgments about what serves the common good. One critical factor here is the credibility of the lawgiver. A

42. Ibid., 1:299 [on Matt. 5:39].

43. On self-defense, Althusius says, "The protection of one's body and life is how nature makes a body free. This is within his power and character. For this reason, the law allows any man the protection, defense, and preservation of his body and life from harm. Thus he is allowed to carry weapons." Quoted in John Witte's introduction to Althusius, *On Law and Power*, trans. Jeffrey J. Veenstra (Grand Rapids: CLP Academic, 2013), lxxi.

law is just if it has the common good in view. But if civil authorities repeatedly demonstrate that they serve only one segment of the people or serve all except one segment, or if they openly express contempt for you or affirm moral absurdities and a degenerate conception of the common good, then motivations for deference are undermined, and it would be wise to question their judgments. If the body of law *as a whole* is corrupt and significantly harmful or repeatedly applied in corrupt and harmful ways, then it may justify revolution, which I demonstrate in chapter 9.

In all situations, whether the injustice of some law is obvious or suspected, the entity most responsible to resist the law or mitigate its effects is a lesser magistrate. The lesser magistrate, or a lower civil authority, is in a better position than private persons to determine whether a law enacted from a higher civil authority is just or unjust. He is already charged with the common good and therefore can in principle determine its effects on his jurisdiction. Our first appeal, after judging that some law is unjust, should be to the lesser magistrate, who is charged with securing the common good for his civil community.

Pastors can admonish erring magistrates to correct injustice in the law, but pastors must not mistake their theological training or scriptural knowledge for expertise in jurisprudence. Pastors as pastors are no more competent to analyze or make civil law than any other private person. Now, a pastor can admonish his congregants to disobey a clearly unjust law, and he can exercise spiritual discipline over one who commits injustice in obeying that law. But his primary concern is not civil justice but souls. If civil laws forbid what is good and prescribe what is evil, they threaten the souls of his flock, and for that reason, he has a duty to admonish disobedience.

VI. Conclusion

Civil law by itself, however, is dead. The civil magistrate enlivens it by his authority and person. The civil magistrate, or what I'll call the "Christian prince," mediates the people's national will for their good, providing them the necessary and specific civil actions for that end. More than that, however, the magistrate is also the head of the people—the one to whom they look to see greatness, a love of country, and the best of men. He is their spirit. Civil law is the life of the commonwealth in relation to its activities and operations, but the magistrate is the heart and spirit of the people. He is, or ought to be, the quintessential great man, and we turn to him next.

7

The Christian Prince

"There is more true virtue in one politic man, who governeth the commonweal and doth his duty truly, than in many thousands of monks and hermits." —Henry Bullinger[1]

I. Introduction

Having discussed the things (or material cause) of Christian nationalism—social customs and civil law, which compose the totality of national action for the complete good—we now come to the chief agent of Christian nationalism. The national will alone cannot terminate *immediately* into national action. It must terminate upon a *mediator*—upon one who translates that national general will into specific commands of action that lead the nation to its good. In

1. Bullinger, *Decades*, 1:280 [Second Decade, Sermon v], spelling modernized.

large part, Christian nationalism, as a totality of national action, is an orchestration of civil leadership.

This chapter is a discussion of the *efficient cause* of Christian nationalism; that is, I discuss the agents that bring about the things of Christian nationalism. The efficient cause begins and ends with the people—their will and their concrete actions. But their will is mediated through civil leadership wielding the power to command action. Thus, Christian nationalism exists when the Christian national will for itself is mediated through Christian civil leaders who command and inspire concrete actions performed by the people.

II. The Prince

Civil leadership is difficult to describe with specificity, since there are several types of civil leaders. In the 16th and 17th centuries, Protestant writers would speak of kings, princes, civil magistrates, governors, etc. Today, we have presidents, congressmen, prime ministers, members of parliament, and others. And unlike many traditional civil polities, many countries today have an institutionalized separation of powers, such that (for example) the legislative, executive, and judicative powers of civil government are located in different branches of government. I might have devoted this chapter to the role of *civil government*—a term that captures most of the civil roles and functions necessary for Christian nationalism. But this term is impersonal and emphasizes the administration of civil affairs, even connoting the work of bureaucracy and management.

I cannot conceive of a true renewal of Christian commonwealths without *great men* leading their people to it. Nor can we expect the national will to find its end through an administration led by wonks and regulators. So I will primarily use "prince" as the mediator of the nation's will for itself. This title denotes both an executive power (viz., one who administers the laws) and personal eminence in relation to the people. The prince is the first of his people—one whom the people can look upon as father or protectorate of the country. I am not calling for a monarchical regime over every civil polity, and certainly not an autocracy, though I envision a measured and theocratic Caesarism—the prince as a world-shaker for our time, who brings a Christian people to self-consciousness and who, in his rise, restores their will for their good.[2] "Prince" is a fitting title for a man of dignity and greatness of soul who will lead a people to liberty, virtue, and godliness—to greatness.

III. The Origin of Civil Power

As a collective entity, a nation has a collective will for its collective good. It must have a collective will, because the nation is a moral person, responsible for itself before God. A collective will is expressed in the first-person plural—*we* desire the good of the whole, the good of *us* as a people.[3] This is national self-love. Political

---

2. Contrary to the calumnies of G.K. Chesterton against "Caesarism" (see *Heretics*, chap. 19), men trust a great man not because they distrust themselves but because social conditions deny their self-trust an outlet for noble action, and the great man offers a path to noble action. viz., a path out of ideological mediocrity, slavishness, and indignity. Caesarism is often described as "authoritarian" and "autocratic" by those who see politics dualistically: regimes are either "democratic" or "authoritarian" (or dictatorial). I reject the framing and would point out that modern democracy is often more oppressive than its alternatives. I prefer Caesarism in our time because it emphasizes *personality* in civil rulers.

3. John Winthrop uses this language: "Thus stands the cause between God and us. We are entered into covenant with Him for this work. We have taken out a commission. The Lord hath given us leave to draw our own articles. We have professed to enterprise these and those

theorists have long argued that a people's collective will is the means of consent to be under civil government, and I agree. But the nation can will only for its *general* good. Nations in themselves, viewed simply as a people, lack an ordering agent and so cannot effectively act for their own good in any *immediate* sense. Put differently, while each member of the nation might have perfect benevolence for the common good, there is no inherent or purely natural organization to the nation that permits people to realize their benevolence in action. The people lack coordination, and disorder (though unintended) will frustrate acts of good. The nation can act for its good but only *mediately*: They must establish an ordering agent, namely, a civil government. They must install a prince. The prince is the one through whom the people act for their own good.

The will of the people is not a set of policies, as if the prince were a mere delegate to enact their will concerning particulars. Rather, the people's collective will expresses consent to be ordered according to both the general conception of the common good and their own particularities. They place trust in the prince as an intermediary to actualize their good. Hence, a prince is not bound to any specific dictates of the people (though certainly these should be taken seriously when expressed clearly); he is bound to what is good, namely, the moral law of God.

Now, since the nature of man necessitates civil society and since the nature of that society requires an ordering agent, the power of that ordering agent must be natural as well. This is a consequence of natural reason: Would God create something that lacks what is necessary for that thing to achieve its purpose? Would God create

accounts, upon these and those ends. We have hereupon besought Him of favor and blessing." "A Modell of Christian Charitie," in *The Sacred Rights of Conscience*, 130, spelling modernized.

human society with an inherent need for an ordering agent and not provide the power for ordering? No. God's designs are always coherent. It follows that the power of magistracy—civil power—is part of the created order. As Samuel Rutherford writes, "God and nature intendeth the policy and peace of mankind, then must God and nature have given to mankind a power to compass this end; and this must be a power of government."[4]

But what is the origin of this power? Perhaps the right to rule is inherent to the nature of certain individuals; they are born, in other words, with magisterial power. But as the Western tradition has long affirmed, men are by nature free and equal in relation to each other. Thus, as Francisco Suárez stated, "no person has political jurisdiction over another person, even as no person has dominion over another."[5] Put differently, no one possesses an inherent, natural superiority in relation to other men such that, by pure nature alone, natural inferiors are bound by their nature to submit to them.[6]

But perhaps civil powers (e.g., to punish evil doers or to exact restitution for injuries) are original to each individual and are transferred from individuals to civil rulers. This is the view of John Locke, who wrote that the "*execution* of the law of nature is in that state [of nature], put into every man's hands, whereby every one has a right to punish the transgressors of that law to such a degree, as may hinder

4. Rutherford, *Lex, Rex*, 1 [Q. 1].

5. Francisco Suárez, "On the Laws and God the Lawgiver," in *Selections from Three Works of Francisco Suárez*, trans. Gwladys L. Williams, Ammi Brown, and John Waldron (Oxford: Clarendon Press, 1944), II.373.

6. For example, children are bound by pure nature to submit to parents, given the nature of the parent-child relation. A child is not born free and equal in relation to parents, and thus consent is unnecessary for that relation. But in civil relations, no man is required, by his very nature, to submit to another; civil subjection is a matter of consent.

its violation." His reason for this view is similar to Rutherford's, quoted above. Locke writes, "[T]he *law of nature* would . . . be in vain, if there were no body that in the state of nature, had a *power to execute* that law."[7] That is, nature demands that this power exists. Locke, however, locates this power in each and every individual, not in the community—a position he admits is a "strange doctrine."[8]

It is worthwhile to reconcile these views, for it permits us to recognize both collective and individual powers. By pure nature, every man has certain powers of his own. Rutherford rightly says, for example, "that we defend ourselves from violence by violence is a consequent of unbroken and sinless nature."[9] The duty of self-preservation entails a right to self-defense. And I contend, with Locke, that individuals, when outside the jurisdiction of civil government, are permitted to punish transgressors of the natural law, and I agree that individuals transfer these powers to civil rulers in trust for their execution. Nevertheless, civil power, as to its principal part, cannot have its origin in individuals, for no man has an inherent power to bind another man's conscience to *particular* applications of natural law for the common good. That is, no man, by right of his nature, can order the whole; he cannot command his neighbor to obey his positive judgments on particular actions that conduce to the common good. Only the Lord of the conscience has this power, namely, God. Thus, as Rutherford states, "All civil power is immediately from God in its root."[10] The power to order the whole must come from God; it does not inhere in or originate from any man or men in aggregate.

7. Locke, *Second Treatise of Government*, 2.7.

8. Ibid., 2.9.

9. Rutherford, *Lex, Rex*, 2 [Q. 2].

10. Ibid., 1 [Q. 1].

Yet we should say with Suárez that "God does not give this power by a special act or grant distinct from creation."[11] This would require him to "manifest [it] through revelation."[12] Civil power is neither inherent nor adventitious to man. God does not (ordinarily) declare by special revelation that this or that person has civil power.

Rather, it is "a characteristic property resulting from nature," writes Suárez. He continues:

> This [civil power] does not emerge in human nature until men gather in one perfect community and untie politically. . . . Once constituted, this body is at once, and by force of natural reason, the site of this [civil] power. The power is correctly understood then, only as a property entailed by such a mystical body so constituted.[13]

The people possess civil power as a necessary and natural consequence of their combination.

One important corollary is that recognizing the true God (or Christ) is unnecessary to possess this power, for having this power is simply a natural consequence of the people's combination into human society. And they can likewise devolve this power upon those who do not recognize the true God. Hence, true civil authority does not depend on true religion, though certainly in failing to acknowledge the divine source of civil authority, the people and civil ruler are in a perilous situation. It doesn't bode well for them, but being godless or idolatrous does not itself preclude true

11. Suárez, "On the Laws," II.379.

12. Rutherford cites Suárez. God does not confer civil power by a "special action or grant." *Lex, Rex*, 2 [Q. 2].

13. Suárez, "On the Laws," II.380.

political order. Hence, Peter instructs his recipients to "honor the [Roman] emperor" (1 Pet. 2:17, NIV).

Now, although combining into civil society is instinctive to man, the combination itself is voluntary.[14] It is similar to marriage in this regard. By natural instinct, men and women are drawn toward marriage, but the union of any particular man and woman is a matter of choice.[15] Likewise, the instinctive act of forming a civil society is voluntary.[16] But unlike the family, in which domestic power is immediately granted to the man,[17] "[civil] power is (so to speak) a natural attribute of a perfect human community, viewed as such," writes Suárez, and it "may be taken from that community—by its own consent or through some other means—and transferred to another."[18] The community possesses that power in indefinite form, and they must devolve it into a definite form, viz., into a particular civil arrangement.[19] Thus, as Rutherford writes, "this or that power

14. Suárez writes that "community is welded together by means of the consent and volition of its individual members." "On the Laws," II.377.

15. That is, while any particular marital union is natural according to the kind of union, the particular union of this man and this woman is not prescribed in nature such that the man marrying another woman would violate nature. Any particular marital union is not purely natural in itself but natural in kind and grounded originally by consent.

16. Rutherford writes, "As domestic society is by nature's instinct, so is civil society natural *in radice*, in the root, and voluntary *in modo*, in the manner of coalescing." *Lex, Rex*, 1 [Q. 2].

17. That is, the power of *pater-familias* is neither original to the woman (and transferred to the man upon marriage) nor possessed by the domestic society as a whole (and then resigned to the man). Rather, God, at the act of union of man and woman, confers upon the man his power immediately, though this power is natural to the man in the same way that civil power is natural to civil society.

18. Suárez, "On the Laws," II.380–81.

19. Suárez says that "although the power in question is in an absolute sense an effect of the natural law, its specific application as a certain form of power and government is dependent upon human choice." Ibid., II.382. The civil arrangement could be, at least theoretically, a pure democracy in which the whole people take part in ordering them-

is mediately from God, proceeding from God by the mediation of the consent of a community, which resigneth their power to one or more rulers."[20] Consent is the mechanism by which divine civil power is bestowed upon the prince.

We should emphasize that bestowing civil power upon civil leaders—though natural and necessary—is not perfunctory or performed carelessly or without caution and watchfulness. As Junius Brutus, author of *Vindiciae contra tyrannos*, said,

> Everyone consents that men by nature loving liberty and hating servitude, born rather to command than obey, have not willingly admitted to be governed by another, and renounced as it were the privilege of nature by submitting themselves to the command of others, but for some special and great profit that they expected from it.[21]

The proper motivation to submit arises not from viewing domination as a good in itself or from a psychological need to *feel* dominated; these are effeminate motivations. The proper motivation is quite the opposite. Submission is motivated by the *rational* need for ordered liberty wherein one finds opportunity to act with his neighbor for his own and his neighbor's good. Submission is good only insofar that it conduces to living well. Being a means, it is not

selves. But setting aside whether this is feasible, it is still an *arrangement*—a definite form of government.

20. Rutherford, *Lex, Rex*, 5 [Q. 3]. Suárez states, "[S]uch power, in the nature of things, resides immediately in the community; and therefore, in order that it may justly come to reside in a given individual, as in a sovereign prince, it must necessarily be bestowed upon him by the consent of the community." Ibid., II.384.

21. Stephen Junius Brutus, *Vindiciae contra tyrannos: A Defense of Liberty against Tyrants*, trans. William Walker (1579/1648; Moscow, ID: Canon Press, 2020), 91.

an end in itself. The people transfer this power in trust, and so civil leaders hold a fiduciary power. We should never forget that although the power of civil leaders is rooted in God, they possess this power mediately and conditionally—by an act of the people and in trust for their good. And we should never suppress that natural love of liberty and the manly desire to command ourselves.

IV. A Divine Office

The prince, as a civil leader, holds an office on behalf of God, the creator. "The principle and supreme end of the civil magistrate as such," writes Turretin, "is the glory of God, the Creator, conservator of the human race, and the ruler of the world."[22] It is a natural office, required by the nature of man, whose function is ordering civil society for commodious and pious living. Civil power being original to God, the prince mediates God's divine civil rule. He is not a steward or a simple administrator, as if he simply promulgates a divinely prescribed civil code. Rather, he makes public judgments in application of God's natural law, effectively creating law (though derivative of natural law), and he has the power to bring about what he commands. Thus, the prince holds the most excellent office, exceeding even that of the church minister, for it is most like God. The prince, unlike the church minister,[23] is a mediator—"a vicar of God"—in outward, civil affairs.[24] As Calvin said, civil rulers "represent the person of God, as whose substitutes they in a manner act."[25]

---

22. Turretin, *IET*, 3:18.29.15.

23. With regard to spiritual good, Christ is the sole mediator between God and man (1 Tim. 2:5), and thus church ministers are instruments of spiritual good but not mediators of it.

24. Turretin, *IET*, 3:18.34.5.

25. Calvin, *Institutes*, 4.20.4.

For this reason, the prince is called a "god" in Scripture (Ps. 82:6). He has, as Calvin said, a "sacred character and title."[26] In a sense, we see God in the magistrate. Rutherford says, for example, that the king "hath a politic resemblance of the King of heavens, being a little god, and so is above any one man."[27] Calvin likewise states that "when good magistrates rule, we see God, as it were, near us, and governing us by means of those whom he hath appointed."[28] Elsewhere he writes that "the image of God shines forth in them when they execute judgment and justice."[29] The dignity of civil rulers is so great in Calvin's view that even the "palaces of princes ought to resemble a sanctuary: for they occupy the dwelling-place of God, which ought to be sacred to all."[30] This comment is fascinating, especially in light of Calvin's efforts to lock church buildings to suppress superstitions. Calvin demonstrates the divine magnitude of the princely office, especially in terms of *presence* in relation to the people. Having the highest office on earth, the good prince resembles God to the people. Indeed, he is the closest image of God on earth.

This divine presence in the prince speaks to his role beyond civil administration. Through him, as the mediator of divine rule, the prince brings God near to the people. The prince is a sort of *national god*, not in the sense of being divine himself, or in materially transcending common humanity, or as an object of prayer or spiritual worship, or as a means of salvific grace, but as the mediator of divine

26. Calvin, *Commentary on the Book of the Psalms*, trans. James Anderson, vol. 5 of *Calvin's Commentaries* (Grand Rapids: Baker Books, 2005), 3:334 [on Ps. 82:6].

27. Rutherford, *Lex, Rex*, 77 [Q. 19].

28. Calvin, *Commentaries on the Twelve Minor Prophets*, 5:396 [on Zech. 13:7].

29. Calvin, *Commentaries on the Prophet Jeremiah and the Lamentations*, 3:103 [on Jer. 22:15].

30. Calvin, *Commentaries on the Prophet Isaiah*, 1:142 [on Isa. 3:14].

rule for *this* nation and as one with divinely granted power to direct them in their national completeness. He embodies the people as one who, by divine power, executes their will for themselves. He is a master in the Master's universe. The prince personifies their national spirit, unifies them under a mission, and inspires an intergenerational will to live. He directs men in fulfilling the dominion mandate—to fulfill man's nature.[31] He inspires noble action, sacrifice, and common affection, and he casts a vision for national greatness. "We all love great men," said Thomas Carlyle. "Ah, does not every true man feel that he is himself made higher by doing reverence to what is really above him?"[32] The prince promotes national self-love and a manly, moral liberty. He recognizes national sins but swiftly resolves them, leaving no license for exploitation or room for lingering self-doubt and the lack of national confidence. He encourages and channels the boldness and spirit of youth, while elevating the old and venerating the dead. He silences the social mammies and countenances the spartan bootstrapper. He loves and enacts justice. He worships God and calls his people to do the same. As an embodiment of the people, he is the best of the people—a man reflecting both their image and God's image, signifying that they are God's and that they live in and for him. With martial virtue, resolve, and *thumos* he fights foreign aggressors, sacrificing himself for his people's good, and he establishes peace with other nations. In a word, he ought to be a great man—the hero of the people. As such, his death only solidifies the nation, creating a "heroic past," as Ernest

31. See my discussion on the relationship between the covenant of works and the moral law in chapters 1 and 2.

32. Thomas Carlyle, *On Heroes, Hero-Worship, and the Heroic in History* (1841; n.p.: Compass Circle, 2019), 8.

Renan said. "Great men, glory (I mean the genuine kind), this is the capital stock upon which one bases a national idea."[33]

It goes without saying that though the prince is a national god, he does not, and indeed cannot, mediate salvific grace. No earthly office has such power, and Christ alone is the mediator of grace unto eternal life.[34] Nevertheless, the prince, even as a mediator of divine civil rule, is an instrument for eternal life. The prince administers things for the complete good—for both earthly and heavenly good, and he orders the former to the latter. He ensures both outward peace and the sort of civic dynamism that conduces to spirited, commodious, and pious living. Thus, one looks more to the prince for his good than even church ministers.[35] Though pastors are essential, of course, the prince establishes the conditions for a peaceful and quiet life in all godliness.[36] This has always been his duty, whether man were in a state of integrity or a state of sin, to

33. Renan, *What is a Nation?*, 261.

34. Even the church minister, despite administering the sacred things of God, is no mediator but rather an instrument of Christ, who is the sole mediator of grace.

35. We expect far too much from church ministers today. Though pastors often have great wisdom and insight in earthly things (including in politics and ethics), their role *as ministers* in the life of Christians is administering the sacred means for the good of the soul. Ministers should redirect us from the things of this world and fix our eyes on Christ in heaven, not lead social programs or drive our hearts downward. Their office is holy because they offer us holy things for a higher life to come.

36. Elizur Goodrich, a Congregationalist pastor ministering in Connecticut in the American founding era, said the following: "The immediate ends of the magistracy and ministry are different, but not opposite: They mutually assist each other, and ultimately center in the same point. The one has for its object the promotion of religion and the cause of Christ; the other immediately aims at the peace and order of mankind in this world: Without which, there could be no fixed means of religion; nor the church have a continuance on earth, but through the interposition of a miraculous providence, constantly displayed for its preservation. Hence the church of Christ will have no fixed residence, where there is no civil government, until he, whose right it is, shall take to himself his great power, and reign

direct outward man to his complete good. Indeed, nothing changed at the fall with regard to the principles or ends of his office; only the *means* changed.[37]

The prince mediates divine rule both by a sort of divine presence or *gravitas* and in civil judgment. For the latter, the prince is the instrument by which natural law becomes human law.[38] The prince enlivens laws not as an agent of coercion but as the divinely sanctioned vicar of God who binds conscience to just applications of natural law, as one who directs public reason.

Great Men and Egalitarianism

Our age suffers from a dearth of great men. This is largely because acquiring power and influence requires one to debase himself with egalitarian appeal. We live under a *de facto* gynocracy where masculinity is pathologized in the name of "fairness" and "equity." To achieve acceptance or relevance today, men must become female-adjacent; that is, to adjust to toxic-feminine conditions of empowerment: sameness, credentialism, risk-aversion, victimology, and passive-aggression. Mediocrity today is barely concealed by institution-dependent accolades. Therapy and self-care are praised as an achievement; struggle and self-willed action are deemed toxic. Competition, agonistic assertion, and the pursuit of concrete achievement threaten

---

king of nations, even as he is king of saints." Quoted in Ellis Sandoz, ed., *Political Sermons of the American Founding Era*, vol. 1, *1730–1805* (Indianapolis: Liberty Fund, 1991), 933–34.

37. As I discussed in chapters 2 and 6, the means changed in two respects: (1) civil power is augmented to deal with the social ills of sin, and (2) since God, as redeemer, has disclosed the only means by which man can reach his original, eternal end, namely, by faith in the person and work of Jesus Christ, the prince points his people to Christ as the sole means of attaining their original, eternal end.

38. Of course, a variety of institutions can create law, such as an elected assembly.

the egalitarian regime. Instead of analytical thought, viewpoints are backed by institutionally conferred credibility and by threats of managerial-bureaucratic reprisal for disagreement. Everything must be rigged for "equitable" outcomes, which suppresses spontaneous hierarchy formation. Masculinity is enlisted as a means to empower the female objects of empathy (the abstract "marginalized")—at the man's expense. As a result, Western nations are leading themselves into decline (especially demographically) as feminine empathy, which is suitable for the domestic sphere, enacts gynocratic contradictions and self-destructive inclusivist civil policies.[39] We should not ascribe greatness to most of the powerful men of our time; great men lead other men and together direct their nation to its destiny. Great men show that heroic masculinity is not simply about protecting the weak but is also about leading the whole to greatness. In civil affairs today, men should go their own way.

Our moment requires of us to stand against that feminine egalitarian impulse, ingrained within us from early age, that views the arc of providence as bending towards equality. Certainly, there is a sort of fundamental equality between men that makes each one his own. But we must not delude ourselves to think that civilizational maturity is measured by its acceleration towards social, political, economic, and expressive equality and towards the bad fruit of equality, namely, inclusivity and universality, as discussed in chapter 3. The prince must be committed to natural hierarchy (wherein

39. Gynocratic practical contradictions, which result from overzealous empathy, include forbidding active policing (the absence of which leaves women more vulnerable), support for trans athletes (who have a clear advantage over biological females in most sporting competitions), lax immigration controls (which has led to a rise in sexual assault in places like Germany and Sweden and other European countries), and restrictive COVID policies (which has exacerbated women's already fragile mental health).

individuality is harmonized with hierarchy), exclusivity (which respects difference but keeps it away), and particularism (the conservation of the people's unique cultural features); and he should return us to a masculine society, which alone can remedy the gynocratic contradictions that plague our society.

V. The Christian Prince

When we designate any prince as a *Christian* prince, we are not simply referring to his religion. Nor are we saying that his office is fundamentally of grace, as if "Christian prince" is entirely a creation of the Gospel. The Christian prince occupies the natural office of civil ruler; it is not fundamentally a new office, though the office is Christianized by his service to Christ. The Christian prince retains everything pertaining to the office of civil ruler, considered generically. We can then come to this definition:

> *The Christian prince is a civil ruler (as divinely ordained in nature)*
> *who possesses and uses powers (both civil and interpersonal) to order*
> *his people to commodious temporal life and to eternal life* in Christ.

The phrase "in Christ" (which modifies "temporal life" as well) is the sole addition of grace to the definition, without which the definition simply reflects the natural office or simply "prince." The phrases "commodious temporal life and . . . eternal life" is the end of the princely rule. Thus, ordering one's people *in Christ* is what distinguishes the generic prince from the Christian prince. Furthermore, this definition reflects the relationship of nature and grace: If the prince must order his people to eternal life (by natural duty) and eternal life is attained only in Christ (as revealed by grace), then the prince ought to order his people to eternal life in Christ.[40]

A prince is a Christian prince only if he wields his power so that the totality of national action is Christian. Indeed, as the executive and head of the nation, he is responsible for national action. Having civil power, he can directly command actions as civil law, as I've said. But he also can shape the people's cultural Christianity. Civil law and social customs are separate and different means of order, but each can support the other; and the prince can enact laws that both correct ungodly and unrighteous features of national culture and support good features of culture. Punishing blasphemy would certainly solidify a culture of pious speech. He can also use his personality—as the first man of the people, an image of their ideal—to persuade, admonish, and encourage righteousness and piety. In this way, he acts as a pious father to the people, wielding a non-spiritual and non-coercive power of admonishment and exhortation. His personal example of piety and faith can shape that of his people. He *can* touch the heart—as a father touches the hearts of his children.

The Christian prince ought to do everything in his power to advance the kingdom of Christ. Calvin was being neither pragmatic nor unprincipled when he addressed the king of France in the preface of his *Institutes*:

> Your duty, most serene Prince, is not to shut either your ears or
> mind against a cause involving such mighty interests as these:

40. Prelapsarian civil leaders were duty-bound to order their people to fulfill the covenant of works, but this duty applied to them only as a *consequence* of a more fundamental principle, namely, that civil rulers ought to order their people to eternal life *according to the proper condition for eternal life*. Since that condition is now the covenant of grace, they ought to order people in accordance with that covenant.

> how the glory of God is to be maintained on the earth inviolate,
> how the truth of God is to preserve its dignity, how the king-
> dom of Christ is to continue amongst us compact and secure.
> The cause is worthy of your ear, worthy of your investigation,
> worthy of your throne. The characteristic of a true sovereign, is
> to acknowledge that, in the administration of his kingdom, he
> is a minister of God.[41]

In the ordinary course of God's providence, civil rulers are necessary for the renewal, health, and advancement of the people of
God and the administration of the church.

The prince ought to keep the church "compact and secure," for
(1) the civil sphere is "the lodging of the church [*ecclesiae hospitium*]
and defends it with the secular sword," said Johann Alsted;[42] (2) the
highest good, which is the highest end of the princely office, is found
only in the kingdom of Christ; (3) the prince's civil kingdom is the
lower kingdom, and the lower must order itself to its higher; and (4)
the prince ought to serve Christ as Christ is king of the church, for
the prince is bound by his office to obey the divine institutor of the
means to eternal life. I discuss this last point in detail later in the chapter. The precise nature of the kingdom of Christ is complicated and
deserves more attention, but we can say here that the prince's service
to this kingdom extends both to its institutional aspects (the ecclesiastical order and administration) and to the prince's people in that
kingdom. Indeed, the prince serves the former because it is the ordinary means for the spiritual good of the latter.

41. Prefatory Address to Francis I, 1536, in Calvin, *Institutes*, 5.

42. Johann Alsted, *Scientiarum omnium enclyclopaediae tomus tertius: pars quarta, quinta,
et sexta* (1649), 163. "*Politia est hospitium ecclesiae et illam defendit gladio seculari.*"

Lacking dominion over conscience, the prince can reach only temporal goods, not the soul. A prince must not, as John Cotton writes, "draw his sword to compel all his subjects to the obedience of the faith of Christ, and to the profession of it." But a prince can "draw his sword, though not in matters spiritual, yet about matters spiritual to protect them in peace, and to stave off the disturbers, and destroyers of them."[43]

Adorning the Temporal

The Christian prince should use civil power to ensure that the culture of his people reflects true religion. A Christian people will naturally produce this themselves, if they have the proper will for their good. But the Christian prince orders, approves, and supplements it. Christian civil culture is an adornment of the temporal with the eternal. What I have in mind here are things and events that originate from life in this world but are adorned with something higher. In the domestic sphere, for example, the Christian family has not simply added Christian elements or replaced what is natural to the family, but has infused (or invested or adorned) natural family life with the Christian religion. Likewise, in the civil sphere, the Christian prince can Christianize civil life, not by replacing what is fundamentally particular and earthly in civil life, but by adorning and perfecting it with true religion.[44] This adornment does not sacramentalize earthly life (strictly speaking). It serves as support,

43. Cotton continues: "It were improper and unfitting, for carpenters to bring their axes and hammers to build up the spiritual kingdom and church of Christ. But yet their tools are fitting to build up scaffolds, that the people may draw near to hear the word and by hearing be brought to faith and salvation." *Bloudy Tenent Washed*, 1.94–95, spelling modernized.

44. In this way, the universal (true religion) neither destroys nor supersedes the particular (civil culture) but rather assumes, strengthens, and perfects it.

means, and occasions for the Christian to contemplate heavenly life in earthly life. Petrus van Mastricht said it well:

> Our mind, even in earthly things, should be heavenly, that is, it should perceive, in earthly things, heavenly things, and mediate upon them: for example, in the natural sun, the Sun of Righteousness; in earthly food, spiritual food; in the clothing of the body, the clothing of the soul. Through earthly things it should allow itself to be led to heavenly things; its earthly things, its riches, its honors, it should devote to a heavenly use, to the kingdom of God, to the lifting up of the poor.[45]

Consider the Christian harvest festival. Fundamentally this event concerns earthly things: material procurement, rest from labor, sharing, civil fellowship, and thanksgiving to fellow man. At another level, it involves thanksgiving to God for his merciful providence: that he provides what they need to live and live well. But at the highest level, this harvest festival is a means to thank God for providing Christ, who is the bread of life and the one through whom people are given eternal life. Hence, the Christian harvest festival, though fundamentally about something earthly, is also heavenly in orientation—it is adorned with the heavenly. The whole of civil life can and ought to be adorned and perfected in this way.

The prince can erect monuments that recall deeds of civic virtue but that point the people heavenward—praising one of their own for his deeds in the community and, at the same time, thanking God for securing their commodious life and free worship. The prince can adorn himself and his residence with Christian symbols,

45. Van Mastricht, *Theoretical-Practical Theology*, 3:156.

as crosses were once painted on royal armor and portraits of monarchs with scepters and crosses. His military or militia, which defends a Christian people and their church, can be designated "soldiers of Christ." Many other examples could be given. The point is that the Christian prince should exercise his power to secure and supplement Christian civil and material culture and do everything in this power to make his people's culture, as a whole, Christian.

Along related lines, the prince should devote himself to public aesthetics. Public works endure across generations, connecting them through gift and affection. They bring that "eternal society" of the dead, living, and unborn to memory; as fixed and venerable points of reference, they make intergenerational national love possible. The great architect Christopher Wren famously said that "architecture has its political use; public buildings being the ornament of a county; it establishes a nation, draws people and commerce; makes the people love their native country, which passion is the original of all great actions in a commonwealth."[46] The prince, therefore, must not underprioritize public aesthetics or sacrifice form for function, or permit narcissistic architects to ruin a cityscape, or chase after the cosmopolitan trend. Public works should be designed and arranged for the good and affections of the nation, built with confidence that one's people will endure and that God will continue to bless it with true religion. This may be false in fact, but it will never be *true* unless the present generation projects that truth upon the future. The future is secured by hope *in action*—in civilizational confidence. If the national will for itself endures, then by God's grace future generations will say, "*We* built this," referring

46. Christopher Wren, "Tract I on Architecture," reprinted in Lydia M. Soo, *Wren's 'Tracts on Architecture' and Other Writings* (Cambridge: Cambridge University Press, 1998), 153.

to their people across generations manifesting from place. Serving this function, architecture "aims at eternity," as Wren said.[47] The built environment inspires a people's will to live in this world and, on that account, strengthens their will for the life to come.

We were made to live on earth amidst penultimate glory, much of which would be products of our labor, and through that glory to yearn for the highest glory in the next life. Suffering too can and ought to send our minds upward, but the middling deadness, instrumentality, and impermanence of our modern built environment inspires nothing but nihilism, consumption, and presentism; it suppresses our sense of future things, throwing us into the present and fleeting pleasures. The Christian prince greatly serves his people when he erects a built environment that inspires them to live and live well—for this life and for the next. Contrary to deadened, modern sentiment, penultimate glory is the best medium to see and desire the ultimate glory.

To reiterate a point from a previous chapter, the Christian commonwealth—wherein a Christian prince rules over a Christian people who dwell in a Christian land—is an earthly image of heavenly life. As an *image*, the life of the commonwealth remains fundamentally and visibly earthly. But it is a public foretaste of the heavenly commonwealth to come—a life submitted to Christ as king who reigns over all things. Indeed, the Christian commonwealth's heavenly adornment points to the commonwealth's own obsolescence, though the people will remain and their glory and honor will be brought into it (Rev. 21:26). On that day, the Christian prince, tossing his crown before Christ, will yield to Christ

47. Ibid.

what has always been his, and he will join his people as a spiritual co-equal in Christ.

VI. The King and Kingdom of God

It is crucial to emphasize that the duty of the Christian prince is not to replace earthly life with heavenly life; he must not conflate his earthly kingdom with the kingdom of God. This was uncontroversial among Reformed Protestants until recently. John Cotton, for example, explains it well:

> Christ hath enjoyed (even as mediator) an everlasting kingdom, not only in the church, but in the government of all the kingdoms of the earth, by his glorious power and righteousness. But the kingdoms of the earth are then said to be the kingdoms of our Lord, when they submit their laws to the laws of this word. But that neither maketh him a temporal king, nor his kingdom in the church to be a kingdom of this world. The church and the commonwealth are still distinct kingdoms, the one of this world, the other of heaven, and yet both of them from Christ.[48]

I quoted part of this passage in chapter 4. In the extended quote, we see the doctrine of the two kingdoms, a standard doctrine of the Reformed theological tradition. I briefly discussed this doctrine earlier in the book, and I return to it now to discuss the prince's relationship to the instituted church and sacred things.

Specifically, I discuss the limits on civil rulers with regard to ecclesiastical order and administration. It highlights my distinctive

---

48. Cotton, *Bloudy Tenent Washed*, 1.92, spelling modernized.

Presbyterianism. In this work thus far, I have tried to be as pan-Prot-estant as possible, or at least as widely Reformed Protestant as I could, without sacrificing vital points of theology. Here, I depart from that. I am neither an absolutist nor a theological royalist (in the traditional sense), and I think that a strictly indirect role for civil leaders in intra-ecclesial affairs is both preferable and most consis-tent with Protestant principles. My position might be surprising, since talk of a "Christian prince" would seem to be a royalist posi-tion on civil authority of ecclesiastical matters. There is, I admit, a natural fittingness to Christian nationalism and the prince as the "head of the Church." But granting the prince this title would be, in my view, an abuse of power and constitute the usurpation of Christ's kingship over the church. I offer my reasoning below.

The Two Kingdoms

The two-kingdoms doctrine refers to the two ways that Christ ex-ercises kingship over men. The two are often distinguished with language such as civil/spiritual, natural/gracious, earthly/heav-enly, power/grace, or outward/inward. Each set of terms has its strengths and limitations, each referring to the differences in pow-ers, essential locations, and the forums of operation. I'll use the *civil* kingdom and *spiritual* kingdom because these terms highlight (in my view) the specific differences between the two, namely, a differ-ence in species of power.

Christ's civil kingship is universal, extending to all mankind (re-gardless of one's spiritual state), and directly concerns the outward man and temporal goods. Christ's civil rule is mediated through earthly civil rule, as I stated above, and civil leaders exercise civil power only. Christ's spiritual kingship, however, extends over the church and directly concerns the inward man and eternal good. Christ reigns over the soul immediately—he alone is the mediator between man and God (1 Tim. 2:5)—though he has instituted church ministry as an instrument to administer the sacred things for the ends of the kingdom. Since Christ is the sole mediator or vicar of salvific grace and is in heaven, there is no earthly mediator of grace unto eternal life.

Calvin distinguishes the two kingdoms as follows:

> [T]here is a twofold government in man, . . . the one which, placed in the soul or inward man, relates to eternal life, . . . the other, which pertains only to civil institutions and the external regulation of manners. . . . [The civil] government is distinct from the spiritual and internal kingdom of Christ, [which] begins the heavenly kingdom in us.[49]

The spiritual kingdom of Christ is in essence a heavenly, inward, and spiritual government, exercised internally over the elect alone, who submit to Christ in their hearts. These elect constitute the church in its essence, and so the church in itself is an *invisible* church, for true membership is a matter of internal faith and piety, not an external profession of faith. As Turretin states, the church is a "mystical union of believers with Christ and with each other, [for] the external union alone with him does not make anyone a member of the church."[50] Though there are external signs of true faith, the

---

49. Calvin, *Institutes*, 4.20.1, 2

50. Or the "kingdom of God." Turretin, *IET*, 3:18.6.4. As Turretin writes, "Now although the word 'church' popularly speaking denotes an external and visible assembly, it does not on that account follow (speaking accurately of the church of Christ) that its proper and

ground of membership in Christ's church is internal faith and piety, which God alone can see. The invisible church is the spiritual kingdom of Christ.

It is a mistake, however, to limit the boundaries of Christ's spiritual kingdom to the inner man. The visible church is not another church, as if the visible and invisible differ in species; we cannot speak of *two* churches, for Christ founded only one church. Rather, the visible church and invisible church are the *same* church of Christ, just as any man is both visible and invisible.[51] Turretin is helpful on this distinction:

> The visibility and the invisibility of the church is drawn from the twofold call directed to it—the external by the word, the internal by the Spirit; and from the twofold form thence emerging—the one internal and essential, the other external and accidental. For by reason of the external call and form (to wit, the preaching of the word and professing of faith), it strikes altogether the sense and is called visible; but the same is invisible by reason of the internal call and mystical communion with Christ by faith.[52]

The visibility of the church, or the visibility of Christ's kingdom, refers to the external things of that kingdom, all of which have a

---

natural signification implies simply a visible assembly or a simple external profession: for a spiritual and internal communion constitutes its essence." Ibid.

51. Turretin writes, "Hence it is evident that the distinction of visible and invisible [church] is not a division of genus into species, as if we formed two churches in species opposed to each other (as our opponents slander us); but is only a limitation of the subject according to its various relations. As the same man numerically can be said to be invisible and visible in different respects. Thus the same church is rightly said to be visible as to external form and invisible as to internal." *IET*, 3:18.7.4.

52. Turretin, *IET*, 1:8.7.4.

fundamental relation and orientation to the essence of the kingdom, which is heavenly, internal, and spiritual. [53]

When Christ said that his kingdom is not of this world, he meant that the *power* of his spiritual kingdom is not like the power of earthly kingdoms. As Samuel Rutherford said, "Christ opposeth his Kingdom to a fighting Kingdom." Christ is contrasting civil power and spiritual power: "The one power is coactive by the Sword, the other free, voluntary by the Word," states Rutherford.[54] Hence, the spiritual kingdom of Christ manifested on earth refers to Christ's external and particular reign over his people, for whom he institutes an ecclesiastical order, the ministry of the Word, and sacred ceremonies—by which the spiritual power of that kingdom is made effective for his kingdom's advancement. Put differently, Christ's external reign as Head of the church extends to those external things that *materially conduce to a supernatural end*. The visible church, or the people of God on earth considered with respect to their heavenly orientation, is subject to Christ's spiritual reign, receiving from him "the ministry, oracles, and ordinances of God, for the gathering and perfecting of the saints, in this life, to the end of the world," as the Westminster Confession of Faith (WCF) states.[55] Therefore, the instituted church, though itself temporal, is the principal part of the external kingdom of Christ, for it administers the sacred things of that kingdom.

53. The Erastian claim that Christ's kingdom is only internal entails that the visible church is essentially another church. For if the invisible church is Christ's kingdom and the visible church is not Christ's kingdom, then the invisible church is not the visible church.

54. Samuel Rutherford, *The Divine Right of Church-Government and Excommunication* (London: John Field, 1646), 510–11, spelling modernized.

55. The Westminster Confession of Faith, 25.3. In this sense, the "visible church, which is also catholic or universal under the gospel... is the kingdom of the Lord Jesus Christ" (25.2).

The instituted church, to be clear, is not a supranational soci-ety or institution, as we see in the Roman church. The instituted church is a divine order that is instantiated in local assemblies (or perhaps regional or national churches, depending on your view), not requiring (or permitting) an earthly ecclesiastical head over a global organization. The King of the church is in heaven, and he has no singular, centralized representative on earth. His kingdom manifests wherever the Word is preached and the Sacraments are rightly administered.

Furthermore, no ecclesiastical institution wields civil-like power over itself or over its members. Church ministers as men are subject to regular civil jurisdiction not simply for pragmatic reasons but due to principle. Church ministers are instruments of the spiritual kingdom in their formal capacity as ministers of Christ, and so in this capacity and in the proper exercise thereof, they are outside civil jurisdiction,[56] but *as men* they are subject to civil authorities as any other man. The local (or particular) church, as a public associa-tion, is subject to civil jurisdiction as well. It has special privileges as a divine species of association (the civil realm being the *hospitium* of the church), but the local church remains subject to regulations in all things pertaining to its genus (viz., public association). Today, this subjects churches to building safety codes and even emergen-cy orders in the case of extraordinary circumstances (e.g., natural disasters, plagues, etc.). But anything that pertains exclusively to its species of association is outside direct civil jurisdiction. That is,

56. A pastor *as pastor* holds, in a sense, a supranational office, permitting him to admin-ister Word and Sacrament anywhere and to any group of Christians, though his first duty is to his own flock, for whom he will give an account to God (Heb. 13:17). But a pastor *as man* is bound to his civil obligations as is any other man.

because it is a *divine* order, those things in it that are divine (e.g., the preaching of the Word, the administration of the Sacraments, exercising the keys, etc.) are outside civil jurisdiction.

The visible kingdom of Christ, though extending to things external and temporal, does not destroy or abrogate what is earthly. Men and women are members of the spiritual kingdom as co-equal objects of spiritual administration, each having full and equal rights to the Word and Sacrament. But they remain men and women according to the standards of nature, even when in the walls of a local church, and they continue to be under the civil kingdom and the natural order when in the pews. Civil rulers do not lose their titles when passing through the doors of a church, nor does a man cease to be a husband to his wife. Christ did not come, as Calvin said, to "mix up nature" in this life.[57] But superiority and inferiority of rank in the civil and domestic spheres are irrelevant to one's right to receive the things of the kingdom of Christ, for in Christ "there is neither bond nor free, there is neither male nor female: for ye are all one in Christ Jesus" (Gal. 3:28).[58] Christ reigns firstly over souls—the essence of the kingdom being invisible—and he institutes external means (e.g., sacred ceremonies and the pastoral office) for the good of their souls. The spiritual kingdom strikes the senses in hearing the profession of faith and the Word preached, by seeing and participating in the Sacraments administered, and in witnessing the laying on of hands for Gospel ministry. As Calvin

57. Calvin, *Men, Women, and Order in the Church,* 19. Also quoted in chapter 2.
58. The pastor still addresses his flock with regard to their earthly relations (as husbands, fathers, mothers, etc.), but (1) with admonishment and exhortation, not with civil power and coercion; (2) as part of their sanctification; and (3) to address their inward disposition when performing the duties of these relations (that they do these things to the glory of God).

said concerning preaching, for example, "When a man preaches, although we may perceive him to be as we are, and of no great repute or refinement, nevertheless Jesus Christ is present and has His royal throne there."[59] The external things of Christ's spiritual kingdom are both the instituted things that supernaturally conduce to heavenly life and the people *as spiritually united to Christ*. This kingdom does *not* extend to earthly relations or to external things that are ancillary to or supportive of the instituted church, such as church buildings.

Although Christ as God does indeed reign over the nations, Christ's spiritual reign does not extend directly into matters suitable to civil power. Thus, his heavenly kingdom, though it manifests on earth, is not an earthly kingdom. Indeed, it cannot be an earthly kingdom, because spiritual power is insufficient to order outward life. Spiritual power is neither intended nor able to directly order this life; it orders our souls for the next life. Christ's mediatorial reign *does* extend to all things in a way, in that all things ought to be ordered to the spiritual kingdom. The civil kingdom, by its nature, is obligated to order the people to the things of eternal life, and the things of eternal life are found only in Christ's spiritual kingdom. Thus, *indirectly* Christ's spiritual reign extends to the civil kingdom, for Christ as spiritual Head of his church has instituted what the civil kingdom ought to order itself to. It is best, however, to view the two kingdoms as separate but complementary, like the way an ordered soul complements and supports the body and vice versa.

The people of God as a people united in Christ (i.e., as members of the visible church) can be said to "use" the civil kingdom for

---

59. Calvin, *Men, Women, and Order in the Church*, 41–42.

their spiritual purposes, as the soul uses the body for its contemplative activity. This is accurate if by visible church we are referring specifically to a Christian people's life around sacred things. The visible church as such requires earthly means for undistracted worship. But according to the fullness of life and the complete set of goods possible for man, the civil realm is not merely useful; it is not only ancillary to the highest end but also *essential* for man's complete good. The Christian is sanctified and reconciled to God the creator and prepared for good earthly works and restoration according to their nature. As I argued in chapter 2, the visible church and the people of God are co-extensive—both are predicated of the same people—but "people of God" refers to Christians as they are redeemed and sanctified for a complete life, and the "visible church" refers to the same people as under Christ the mediator pursuing the highest good of that complete life. A Christian *as a Christian* is oriented not merely around the highest good manifested in the visible church but also, being a man of God, around the goods of this life.

Since the spiritual kingdom does not possess civil power, the civil kingdom cannot arise out of the spiritual kingdom. The spiritual cannot devolve civil power. Nor does the civil kingdom arise out of the visible church (strictly speaking), for the visible church is the externalized spiritual kingdom. Civil power is indeed divine in origin but still natural to man as man. It is an instrument of human institutions. It originates in God, the creator, and is devolved through human consent. Hence, a Christian people can erect a civil kingdom, though not as the visible church but as the people of God. It is worth citing Franciscus Junius again: "For to the extent that we may be Christians, we do not cease being humans, but we are Christian human beings."[60] A civil kingdom, instituted by a group of the people of God, is fundamentally human, follows natural principles, and possesses the same kind of civil power as all civil kingdoms. Yet, as I've repeatedly stressed, the fact that it is fundamentally human does not (like the family) preclude it from being Christian.

We can say, then, that the people of God on earth are under two kingdoms and outwardly under the twin administrations of those kingdoms. This sounds strange until we realize that these kingdoms have the same King, have essentially different though complementary powers, do not overlap in jurisdiction, and refer to the twofold way that Christians admonish or encourage each other towards the complete good. We know that only the Word—the spiritual sword—will correct a fellow Christian in heart, and so we (both ministers and laypeople) admonish an erring brother audibly with the Word, trusting that God will work in his heart. Our spiritual admonishment manifests Christ's spiritual reign, for his Word is outwardly proclaimed to the soul. At the same time, we would expect the civil power to correct the man as well, if his error is worthy of civil action. This manifests Christ's civil reign, which touches the outward order. Thus, we relate to this erring man in a twofold respect, even outwardly, knowing that we are in both kingdoms, each with its distinct power, and both powers are exercised (in some respect) outwardly.[61]

The two kingdoms are different in this important respect: Christ's spiritual kingdom is the sole redemptive kingdom. In it alone are we redeemed by grace for eternal life. Still, the civil kingdom, though not itself redemptive, is renewed as an effect of sanctification and,

---

60. Junius, *Mosaic Polity*, 38.

61. Of course, though both are exercised outwardly, one is for an outward end, while the other is for an inward end.

hence, is a secondary object of redemption through the work of re-stored humanity, who Christianize civil life for the complete good. In this respect, the civil kingdom is indirectly redemptive, having become ordered by the sanctifying effects of the redemptive king-dom for the advancement of redemption. This relationship is clari-fied when we consider Christ as mediator.

Christ as Mediator

Earlier, I identified the prince as the mediator of civil rule, and I described him in god-like terms, following Scripture. His elevated status does not steal glory from Christ. Everything the prince has is from Christ. As John Davenport wrote, "Christ, as the Essen-tial Word and Wisdom of God creating and governing the World, is the Efficient and Fountain of Civil Order & Administration."[62] The prince is, as George Gillespie said, "Christ's deputy, as Christ is God."[63] The prince is an image of Christ to his people.

To be more precise, the prince images Christ not as Christ is mediator of salvific grace (not as the God-man) but as Christ is the Son of God.[64] This position was once controversial, especially

62. Davenport, *A Discourse About Civil Government*, 6.

63. George Gillespie, *Aaron's Rod Blossoming, or The Divine Ordinance of Church Government Vindicated* (Edinburgh: Robert Ogle and Oliver & Boyd, 1844), 97.

64. On the distinction between Christ as God and as Mediator, Turretin states, "Again the actions of Christ can be viewed in a threefold order as Christ can be regarded under a threefold relation (*schesei*)—either as God, or as man, or as God-man (*theanthrōpos*). Some are merely divine, which he effects only as God (such as creation and conserva-tion). Others are merely human (such as eating, walking and sleeping). Others are mixed, which are called theandric (*theandrikai*) (such as redemption, to accomplish which both his divine and human natures concurred)." *IET*, 2:14.2.4. And "Although God the Son (or Logos) does not differ from Christ the Mediator (or person) or his nature considered in it-self and absolutely, still he does differ by economy and in relation to the mediatorial office. Since it is one thing for God to be the Son; another for him to be a Mediator; one thing

in England and Scotland in the 16th and 17th centuries. Though
this dispute might seem trivial to political theology, it is in fact vital
for determining whether the prince can be the so-called "head of
the church." One might expect a Christian nationalist like myself to
support royalist authority over ecclesiastical affairs (as the English
monarchy claims for itself), but I deny that any civil leader can be
the head of the church, for the following reason: Since the prince
wields civil power only—a power of this world—he cannot be
under Christ as mediator, for Christ as mediator acts according to
his mediatorial office, which concerns the mediation of grace unto
heavenly life, and he acts in this capacity with a power *not of this
world* (viz., spiritual power).[65] Christ as mediator, as he relates to his
mediatorial office, lacks civil power. Thus, the prince as a civil leader, having only civil power, cannot be directly subordinate to Christ
as mediator.[66] Put differently, if the Christian prince is over the people as one under Christ as mediator, then the civil magistrate would

to be offended as God, another as God-man (*theanthrōpōn*) to act as Mediator." Ibid;,
14.2.14. Calvin seems to support this position in his commentary on Psalm 2:9.

65. Turretin writes, "That dominion [kingdom of nature] is called natural and essential to distinguish it from the economical [kingdom of grace] which belongs to Christ (Phil. 2:9) and
differs from it in many respects.... With regard to the objects—the kingdom of nature is universal, embracing all creatures; the kingdom of grace is especially terminated on the church,
whence by a peculiar reason he may be called the King and Lord of the church.... With regard
to administration; that is, exercised by Christ as God together with the Father and the Holy
Spirit—whence it is called essential because common to the whole divine essence; but this
is exercised by him as Mediator and God-man (*theanthrōpō*)—whence it is called personal
because it pertains to the person of the Son and is appointed to his economy." *IET*, 1:3.22.3.

66. Rutherford makes a similar argument: "The power that beareth the [civil] sword,
which is the very essence of the magistrate's office as a magistrate, is not a part of [Christ's]
kingdom, for his kingdom is of another world, and spiritual; but the magistrate's power is
of this world, and useth worldly weapons, as the sword. Then it is evident that the magistrate as the magistrate, 1. Is not subordinate to Christ as mediator and head of the church."
Samuel Rutherford, *Divine Right of Church-Government*, 511, spelling modernized.

have a spiritual power. However, since he doesn't have this sort of power but rather has only a power of this world, he is not under Christ as mediator. It follows, then, that the prince cannot rule over the church as a sort of intermediary or "head."[67] Furthermore, since Christ is the sole ruler of the invisible church, and since the invisible church and the visible church are the same church, Christ is the sole ruler of the visible church. We can conclude from these arguments that the prince's reign does not extend directly to the visible kingdom of Christ.

I will concede that the Christian prince can direct the church to a great extent, if that direction relies on an "extrinsic, objective or defensive power about ecclesiastical matters," as Turretin says.[68] The Christian prince cannot exercise civil power *in* the mediatorial kingdom (though as a Christian man, he is in this kingdom). But he exercises his power *for* the kingdom—on things extrinsic but necessary and supplemental to the advancement of that kingdom.[69]

67. Gillespie writes, "[A] twofold kingdom of Jesus Christ: one, as he is the eternal Son of God, reigning together with the Father and the Holy Ghost over all things; and so the magistrate is his vicegerent, and holds his office of and under him; another, as Mediator and Head of the church, and so the magistrate doth not hold his office of and under Christ as his vicegerent." *Aaron's Rod Blossoming,* 90. And Calvin states, "They who at first extolled Henry, King of England, were certainly inconsiderate men; they gave him the supreme power in all things: and this always vexed me grievously; for they were guilty of blasphemy when they called him the chief Head of the Church under Christ. This was certainly too much: but it ought however to remain buried, as they sinned through inconsiderate zeal." *Commentary on the Twelve Minor Prophets,* 2:349 [on Amos 7:10–13].

68. Turretin, *IET,* 3:18.34.20.

69. Rutherford asks, "[D]oes not the Mediator Christ, as Mediator, promote his Mediatory Kingdom in, and through the Christian prince, as his instrument, subordinate to him as Mediator? Answer: Not at all, for Christ uses the Christian magistrate as his servant to beat the wolves from the flock, but not as King, Mediator as God-man, Head of the Church, for Christ Mediator as Mediator, works not by external violence, or, by the sword, in his mediatory Kingdom (John 16:36), 'If my Kingdom were of this world, mine

Princely Power and the Church

Now, there is a difference between the power to act for the procurement and disposition of sacred things and the power to exercise or administer sacred things themselves. The former power belongs to the prince, while the latter only to pastors. The power for procurement and disposition is common in other earthly spheres and relations. A husband does not ordinarily fulfill the duties of his wife, but he procures what is necessary for her to perform those duties, establishes the conditions for her to perform them well, approves her good performance, and corrects her when she performs her duty poorly. In doing these things, he has not performed the duties of a wife. Similarly, a restaurant owner (who is not the chef) procures what is necessary for the chef to cook and sets the restaurant in good order. The owner does not himself cook, nor does he tell the chef how to cook. Yet he does cast judgment on the quality of the food, and if the chef fails to perform his duties, the owner corrects or fires him. In doing these things, the owner has not become a chef or overstepped his bounds as an owner.

The Christian prince has a similar relationship with the instituted church. He should procure what is necessary for the pure worship of God but not lead worship or institute new articles of faith or sacred ceremonies. If the ministry degrades, he should reform it. He should correct the lazy and erring pastor but not perform the duties of pastor. He should protect the church from heretics and disturbers of ecclesiastical peace, ensuring tranquil spiritual administration. But in dealing with such people, he must let the ministry of the Word go before him, for the sword of the

---

own would fight for me.'" Samuel Rutherford, *A Free Disputation against Pretended Liberty of Conscience* (London: R.I., 1649), 224.

Spirit alone can reform the errant heart. The prince should also fund the ministry of the Word and provide schools for theological education. Lastly, he has the power to call synods in order to resolve doctrinal conflicts and to moderate the proceedings. Following the proceedings, he can confirm or deny their theological judgments; and in confirming them, they become the settled doctrine of the land. But he considers the pastors' doctrinal articulations as a father might look to his medically trained son for medical advice. He still retains his superiority.[70]

Indeed, the prince is not subordinate to pastors in any respect with regard to his civil reign. Though pastors as pastors are ministers of Christ's kingdom—the higher kingdom—and they preach the things of God found in Scripture (much of which is applicable to civil affairs), the prince is not to submit to ministers as he would to Christ, for pastors are neither mediators nor vicars of Christ; they are ambassadors of Christ and only when speaking truth. The prince *as prince* is not subordinated to pastors, even if he ought to affirm the divine teachings communicated through them.[71] They are special heralds of Christ, and no prince submits to the heralds of a higher king, only to the true *message* delivered through them. The prince executes the judgments of church ministers (e.g., concerning

70. Experience over centuries might make the Christian students of history wary of this civil power. I share that concern. But I state it here not to insist that all civil rulers everywhere exercise it but to simply affirm that civil rulers have this power and, at appropriate times, can exercise it. See chapter 9 for further discussion.

71. Bullinger writes, "The politic magistrate is commanded to give ear to the ecclesiastical ruler, and the ecclesiastical minister must obey the politic governor in all things which the law commandeth. So then the magistrate is not made subject by God to the priests as to lords, but as to the ministers of the Lord: the subjection and duty which they owe is to the Lord himself and to his law, to which the priests themselves also ought to be obedient, as well as the princes." *Decades*, 1:329 [Second Decade, Sermon vii].

heretics, doctrinal standards, moral teaching) not as a blind follow-
er of ministerial judgment and not with implicit faith in their rightness, but with discretion and with his own judgment as the agent
of civil order. He is in the best position to judge appropriate action,
and pastors ought to have a spirit of deference to civil leaders with
regard to civil action. As I discussed in the previous chapter, a policy that is righteous in itself may not be good in its effect, and civil
leaders must enact good policies. Pastors are in a good position to
determine what is righteous, but they are (ordinarily) not in the
best position to determine what would conduce to the common
good with regard to policy.

Being ministers of a spiritual kingdom, pastors cannot depose
the prince (i.e., strip him of formal civil authority), nor can ministers absolve the people of their oath to the prince, nor as ministers
can they lead or command a revolt against him, even if the prince
errs in his judgment concerning morals and ecclesiastical things.
Ministers as ministers simply lack the authority to do these things.
They can cast spiritual judgment, admonish, and even excommuni-
cate him from the visible church, but their spiritual authority can
neither remove his authority nor command the prince's subject to
disregard his authority. They neither gave him his civil power (and
so cannot take it away) nor do they represent the kingdom of civil power. Even in his excommunication, the prince retains his civil
station, for being in a state of grace is not a necessary condition to
possess civil power.[72] Still, the prince as a *Christian man* submits

72. Rutherford writes, "Nor do we deny the king, and the minister of God, whose person
for his royal office, and his royal office, are both to be honoured, reverenced, and obeyed.
God forbid that we should do so as the sons of Belial, imputing to us the doctrine of the
anabaptists, and the doctrine falsely imputed to Wicliffe [sic],—that dominion is founded

to ministers on matters concerning his own soul. He is not exempt from pastoral authority with regard to the keys of the kingdom.

The prince as prince, therefore, protects the church as a servant of Christ, not as a servant of pastors. More specifically, the prince is a servant of Christ as mediator, though not as one formally under Christ as mediator (viz., as if the prince is the head of the church)— but as one obligated by nature (as one under Christ, the Word and Wisdom of God) to order the civil realm according to the fullness of revealed religion. Thus, he ought to order the civil realm to the divine precepts of Christ, the king of the church. The actions of the prince, in advancing Christ's spiritual kingdom, bring Christ's two modes of reign—as God and as Mediator—into explicit unity. Put another way, albeit less precisely, God the creator has obligated civil rulers to enforce the First Table of the moral law, and so they must concern themselves with religion, even revealed religion. The second commandment permits the prince both to suppress false religion and to establish true religion according to divine precepts of ceremonial worship. These precepts come from Christ *via* his Word and are expounded by the ministers of his spiritual kingdom. The prince "kisses the son" (Ps. 2:12) by establishing and maintaining these laws of Christ in order to advance Christ's spiritual kingdom.

The Prince and Sacred Ceremonies

National uniformity in sacred ceremonies will certainly contribute to national solidarity. What better way for a people to imagine their Christian community than for all to worship the same way? The question, however, is not whether uniformity is possible, desirable,

---

upon supernatural grace, and that a magistrate being in a state of mortal sin, cannot be a lawful magistrate,—we teach no such thing." *Lex, Rex*, 114 [Q 15].

and ideal. I affirm that it is, and the magistrate ought to strive within the limits of his power to achieve uniformity. The question here is whether the prince has the power in principle to institute sacred ceremonies not prescribed in Scripture. I deny this, since Scripture sufficiently prescribes the sacred acts that God requires for his worship.[73] Turretin is correct when he says that magistrates cannot "institute or enjoin new worship because it is will-worship."[74] That is, it presumes that man can *will* some act or thing into sacredness. Neither pastors nor civil leaders have the power to will something into sacred use—as something that conduces to a supernatural end. God alone has that power. While the people ought to obey their civil leaders "for conscience sake" (Rom. 13:5) in things concerning the civil kingdom, it doesn't follow that civil leaders can bind their people's conscience to participate in sacred ceremonies not commanded in Scripture. Sacred ceremonies are material to the visible kingdom of Christ, which is outside the prince's jurisdiction. The prince has civil authority in principle over all outward things *negatively*, viz., he can eliminate error, even error that purports to belong in Christ's kingdom, for error is not actually in Christ's kingdom.[75]

73. "We ought not to bring any thing of our own when we worship God, but we ought to depend always on the word of his mouth, and to obey what he has commanded. All our actions then in the worship of God ought to be, so to speak, passive; for they ought to be referred to his command, lest we attempt any thing but what he approves." Calvin, *Commentary on the Twelve Minor Prophets*, 2:298 [on Amos 5:25, 26].

74. Turretin, *IET*, 3:18.34.12.

75. Since the church as a divine order cannot itself have an element of error; it is of God. Rather, when error has "crept" into the church, the church itself has the appearance of error. For example, the pastor proclaims the kingdom when he preaches the truth—the preached word *is* the word of God. But if he were to speak error, he speaks not the word of God, nor does he proclaim the kingdom. In speaking error, he has the *appearance* of being a herald of Christ; i.e., he appears to be a pastor of Christ, but in speaking error he is a minister of Christ only in appearance.

Denying the prince any jurisdiction over the institutional church pertains only to what Christ actually instituted, not to the creations of man that purport to be part of that church. Hence, he can eliminate error in the church, for it exists in the church in appearance only. As for the prince's positive authority, it is limited—it does not extend to all outward things because he cannot institute sacred things, which is a prerogative of God alone. Nor can he, as Turretin writes, "prescribe to ministers the form of preaching or of administering the sacraments, because the pastor has that authority immediately from Christ, not from the magistrate."[76]

However, ordering the church according to standards of natural decency *around* sacred things is not will-worship, even when the ordering has spiritual signification. A prince may require the elevation of the pulpit above the Lord's Table in church construction, for example. This follows a natural principle of order, signifying that the dependent element is beneath the thing upon which it depends (viz., the preaching of the Word goes before the administration of the Lord's Supper). This policy directs churches in suitable arrangements of church furniture and does not lend itself to superstition.

The requirement to kneel to receive the Lord's Supper is an important case-study on the limits of the prince's power in ecclesiastical matters. Kneeling for the Lord's Supper is nowhere commanded in Scripture, and so it is unnecessary for receiving the Sacrament rightly, and one's outward posture counts for nothing in itself. There is a certain fittingness to it, for one is spiritually receiving the body and blood of Christ, and so the posture is not in itself an improper posture to receive it, and certainly one ought to kneel in his heart.

76. Turretin, *IET*, 3:18.34.13.

However, the practice goes beyond the demands of Christ, who did not require a posture of obeisance when he instituted the Supper but permitted an everyday posture (viz., reclining). Neither the king nor the ministers should demand from their people more than what Christ demanded, and that goes for any ecclesiastical practice. Furthermore, there is the real danger of superstition. Christ's body and blood are not locally present—the bread and wine are not transubstantiated—and yet physically kneeling might easily lead one to think that Christ *is* locally present. This seems to be implied in the orientation of the kneeling. It is unwise, for this reason, to require it, because it is unnecessary for all and can lead to superstition for some. To put the principle directly, the prince can enact certain practices that conform to natural principles of order, decency, and posture, even those that have a spiritual signification, but he must beware of practices that lead to superstition.

Religious Observances

Despite these limitations, the prince can greatly contribute to national solidarity by instituting distinctions in days, even days set aside for religious purposes. Commenting on Galatians 4:10, Calvin rightly says that

> [t]he civil observation of days contributes not only to agriculture and to matters of politics, and ordinary life, but is even extended to the government of the church. Of what nature, then, was the observation which Paul reproves? It was that which would bind the conscience, by religious considerations, as if it were necessary to the worship of God, and which, as he expresses it in the Epistle to the Romans, would make a distinction between one

day and another. . . . When we, in the present age, intake a distinction of days, we do not represent them as necessary, and thus lay a snare for the conscience; we do not reckon one day to be more holy than another; we do not make days to be the same thing with religion and the worship of God; but merely attend to the preservation of order and harmony. The observance of days among us is a free service, and void of all superstition.[77]

A Protestant Christian nationalism has the benefit of national independency, by which a Christian nation can have, in addition to civic observances, its own religious observances. A Protestant nation does not recognize some universal, supranational, and earthly authority that decides what it observes and when it observes it. Hence, all its religious observances are either peculiar to the nation or, if common among Christian peoples in all places, still self-instituted. By "observance," I do not mean new ceremonies but both civil-religious practices (e.g., Christmas traditions) and the circumstantial content to divinely instituted ceremonies (e.g., Easter sermons). Far from demanding a dry and flat calendar, the classical Protestant view of civil-religious observances permits an organic civil-religious life in which the people can claim these special days collectively as theirs, since they've arisen from them.

I do not have in mind the sort of heaven-adorned civic practices outlined earlier in the chapter. These fundamentally concern earthly life. Rather, I'm thinking of more distinctively religious observances, emphasizing features or elements of religion or great religious acts. Of course, the boundaries between these types of observances are vague

77. Calvin, *Commentaries on the Epistles of Paul to the Galatians and Ephesians*, 124 [on Gal. 4:10].

(e.g., a celebration of the nation's conversion to Christianity). Still, there is a fairly clear difference between, say, a week set aside for remembering Christ's resurrection and the civic celebration for victory in war. The difference between the two is evident in several ways, including in their origination. An Easter service originates from the direction of church ministers, and the prince approves and supplements them and regulates their extra-ecclesiastical cultural observance.

Assigning a particular day for religious remembrance, which provides the content of that day's thoughts, prayers, and activities, is not the same as elevating the day to holiness in an absolute sense. It is holy in a relative sense—relative to its religious content.[78] This distinction should not be controversial, for we commonly assume it in our Christian daily life. Christians today often praise God on the anniversary of their salvation, making it an occasion to reflect on God's work in their life. In doing so, one is certainly ascribing significance to that day, but he is not instituting a sacred or holy day, as if the observance is necessary for holiness and the true worship of God. Similarly, the anniversary of a relative's death, when she went to be with the Lord, might occasion a family to praise God for her life and her Christian witness. Perhaps on the following Lord's Day, this family reflects on their communion with the saints, both living and dead. Thus, just as individuals can set aside days for some religious end, so too can nations.

Sabbath Laws

The fourth commandment, instructing us to keep the Sabbath holy, is a moral (or natural) command to set aside a day in seven

78. Turretin writes, "A thing can be called 'holy' either absolutely (with regard to some inherent sanctity) or relatively (with regard to its destination to a sacred use)." *IET*, 2:11.15.11.

for special holy use—to minimize the concerns of this world and worship and contemplate God. As John Owen said,

> [N]one will deny but that it is required of us, in and by the law of nature that some time be set apart and dedicated unto God, for the observation of his solemn worship in the world. [This is] indispensably required of [man] and his posterity, in all their societies and communion with one another.[79]

Whether or not Sunday is now a holy day by divine positive command is irrelevant here; the fourth commandment, like all the other commandments, is perpetually binding as to its underlying moral principle. All ought to set aside a day for undistracted worship and divine contemplation. Hence, there must be some positive institution of the Christian Sabbath, and the most fitting day (given apostolic practice and by long tradition) is each Sunday.

The prince's duty in relation to the fourth commandment is not to enforce the command in itself, for the command does not fundamentally concern a bare outward observance but a matter of the heart, and the prince cannot command anything of the heart. Still, he ought to make the outward observance of the Sabbath one of his chief concerns. That day, more than any other, is the day of the Lord—the day in which Christ's kingdom is most made manifest:

---

79. He continues, "This cannot be denied, unless we shall say that God making man to be a sociable creature, and capable of sundry relations, did not require of him to honour him in the societies and relations whereof he was capable; which would certainly overthrow the whole law of his creation with respect unto the end for which he was made, and render all societies sinful and rebellious against God. Hereunto the Sabbatical rest was absolutely necessary." John Owen, *An Exposition of the Epistle to the Hebrews* (Edinburgh: J. Ritchie, 1812), 2:344. I thank Timon Cline for pointing me to this passage.

God's people hear the Word preached and receive the Sacraments. It is the day of the ordinary means of grace. Since even the most godly of men are easily drawn to earthly concerns on the Sabbath, the prince must, to the furthest extent possible, remove the earthly temptations and distractions of this world so that his people's attention is on God and the heavenly kingdom. Sabbath laws train people in virtue; they are pedagogical. The imposed earthly constraints declare the day holy and thereby instruct the heart and remind people of their duty, and they witness to outsiders both that the land is Christian and that they are committed to God's worship. Furthermore, the establishment of the Christian Sabbath contributes to Christian national solidarity. It is the most regular outward display of Christian peoplehood in their Christian homeland, affecting one's relation to the place itself and declaring to all outsiders that this is a Christian country.

VII. Conclusion

The probability of a great Christian prince arising in the near future seems slim, given the forces at work both in the West and in Christian churches. But things change quickly, and the prospects of continued domestic peace in the future is becoming unlikely. An explosion of energy might disclose to us the possibilities of Christian civil order. We need to be prepared, having some blueprint for Christian civil and moral leadership. This chapter contributes to that preparation. And I trust that although my conclusions will not be shared by all Christian nationalists, the reader will discern here a spirit of pan-Protestantism and will have the patience and forbearance for cooperation when our time comes.

Though in the meantime we may need to settle for civil leaders who fail to live up to the standards of a Christian prince, we should pray that God would raise up such a leader from among us: one who would suppress the enemies of God and elevate his people; recover a worshipping people; restore masculine prominence in the land and a spirit for dominion; affirm and conserve his people and place, not permitting their dissolution or capture; and inspire a love of one's Christian country. In a word, pray that God would bring about, through a Christian prince, a great renewal.

8

The Right to Revolution

"Let us take this affliction from our people, and let us fight for our nation and our religion." —1 Maccabees 3:43[1]

The dire situation of Christianity in the West calls for action. But what kind of action? If the general thrust of this work has been true, then the spheres and powers outside the instituted church and family are important, if not vital, for the Christian life. That is, each of the natural orders of life—civil, familial, ecclesiastical—has its distinct powers for our good, and together they constitute a holistic ordering of man to the complete good. Today, the civil sphere is given a subordinate status in Christian thought, shut off from cognizance of eternal things, and we are conditioned to believe this is normal and

---

1. Quoted in Bullinger, *Decades*, 1:277 [Second Decade, Sermon v].

good. But the result is a deadening of our sense towards impropriety and impiety. Open blasphemy in our public square is shrugged off as "to be expected" or part of the world's "brokenness." We have settled into a posture of passive defense, bunkered behind the artificial walls of churches and the porous borders separating the family from society. A hostile and secularist ruling class roams free, and few Christians are willing to take the struggle to a higher level.

But we do not have to live like this. And no matter how insistent our evangelical leaders are to the contrary, the Christian religion does not suppress or "critique" that fighting human spirit calling Christians to "hazard the loss of a limb for their religion, magistrates, wives, children, and all their possessions," as Bullinger said.[2] Here I will justify violent revolution.

I. Definition and Explication

I will begin with a definition of *revolution*. My definition is idiosyncratic because I'm assuming conclusions from previous chapters.

> *Revolution is the forcible reclamation of civil power by the people*
> *in order to transfer that power on just and more suitable political*
> *arrangements.*

As a "forcible reclamation of civil power," revolution uses force as the instrument to unseat civil rulers. At the most basic level, forcible reclamation reclaims civil power outside of established procedures or ordinary transfer of power, and the people unseat civil rulers against the will (at least initially) of those rulers. The unseating

---

2. Bullinger, *Decades*, 1:277 [Second Decade, Sermon v].

is, therefore, forced. The manner of unseating can be the ruler's acquiescence or flight, effectively unseating himself, or by direct physical capture. Both modes of unseating could be "bloodless" or non-violent, though that is less likely in the latter case.

The act of unseating, whether voluntary or not, effectively reclaims civil authority from the ruler. The people reclaim it not as the new wielders of civil power, for (as I said in the previous chapter) the people cannot themselves wield civil power; civil power must be deposited in definite political form for its exercise. But the people can possess it in an indefinite form. Having reclaimed this authority, they can "transfer that power on just and more suitable political arrangements." The purpose or end of revolution is not violence, nor is it to vanquish enemies of God or humanity, but to establish just and suitable arrangements for a peaceful and godly life.

The agents of force must be "the people," for the act of revolution rescinds the people's consent and aims to reclaim civil power for their good. If existing rulers are overthrown without the people's consent, then the actors are invaders or insurrectionists and the new rulers are usurpers, having no right to civil authority, nor the power to make law.

Revolutions can be either just or unjust. The justness of any revolution, in terms of the justification to revolt, depends on whether conditions are actually tyrannical. A just revolution is instigated in response to *real* tyranny. But the people might err in judgment and conduct an unjust but still successful revolution. In this case, the revolution was illicit but still valid. That is, civil power is actually reclaimed and transferred elsewhere.

There are different types of revolutions with regard to geography. People can seek either to (1) separate geographically from their civil rulers, leaving them with power but not power over them and their land (e.g., the American revolution); or (2) remove and replace civil leaders without separation (e.g., the French Revolution). The former is a revolution because the act of independence by the people effectively declares the old civil order null over a particular geographic space. That is, it unseats not the ruler himself but the ruler in relation to their homeland.

II. Statement of the Question

The question concerning Christians and violent revolution is not whether people can conduct revolution to establish a Christian nation, for force cannot generate a Christian nation. A Christian people share particular norms, customs, blood, etc., which are not easily forced upon them. Nor is the question whether a group of Christians, dwelling in a non-Christian nation under *non*-tyrannical conditions, may revolt to establish a Christian commonwealth. Establishing a Christian commonwealth is a worthy goal, but non-Christian rulers still have true civil power, and resisting them is resisting God.[3] Similarly, the question is not whether a Christian nation can revolt against rulers on account of their heresy or infidelity or excommunication, for possession of legitimate civil power does not depend on theological orthodoxy or on one's proper standing in the visible church.

The question is whether a Christian people, being under tyrannical conditions, may conduct revolution to establish a Christian commonwealth in order to arrange themselves for their temporal and eternal good. Given the arguments of this book, one can

---

3. A Christian people, however, can request separation and independence.

affirm that nations can be Christian nations and that these nations can seek their temporal and eternal good through their own civil arrangements. The dispute is whether they can conduct revolutions against tyrants to that end. Below I argue that such revolutions can be just.

III. Just Revolution

Grounds for Resistance

As we've seen, civil power is natural to man, not in root (for God is the root of civil power), but as something necessary for living well according to man's social nature. Being natural to man, it is *for* man, meaning that it serves a purpose for him—ordering him to temporal and eternal good. The agent who wields that power is entrusted with it by the people and only for their good. That power specifically authorizes civil rulers to enact suitable civil law that is derived from God's natural law. God's law is thereby mediated through the judgment and promulgation of appointed human magistrates, effectively making these judgments ordinances of God. For this reason alone, they bind the conscience: they are derivative of God and hence (mediately speaking) God's judgments. When a legitimate ruler uses civil power to command what is just and the people disobey this command, they are disobeying God himself, not only because God requires obedience to civil rulers, but also, and more importantly, because the law itself, though human, is an ordinance of God.

God bestows civil power on men that they might act in his name for the good of their fellow man; they are God's ministers for our good, not for evil. Thus, civil authority extends only to what is for our good. God does not bestow civil authority to command what is unjust, for civil authority mediates God's civil rule, and God's ordinances for man are always just. Since no unjust command is an ordinance of God, no unjust command binds man's conscience; only ordinances of God bind the conscience. Unjust commands are commands of men, backed by nothing but the power of man, and no power of man can bind the conscience. As Rutherford said, "[A] man commanding unjustly, and ruling tyrannically, hath, in that, no power from God."[4]

Now, there is a distinction between the civil ruler as ruler and the civil ruler as a man—i.e., between his power and office in the abstract and the person himself. This refers to the difference between, as Rutherford states, "the king *in concreto*, the man who is king, and the king *in abstracto*, the royal office of the king."[5] Obedience is due to civil rulers when his office in the abstract is one with his person, viz., when he commands what is just. In commanding what is just, the two become one (so to speak), because the person is the necessary agent of the office.

When he commands what is unjust, the civil ruler still retains his office in the abstract, but he acts not by means of that office; he acts by a power of man, and so he acts as a fellow man, not as civil ruler. Such commands are neither backed by a power of God nor do they cohere with the duties of his office. Thus, as Rutherford said, "[A]bused powers are not of God, but of men, and not ordinances of God; they are a terror to good works, not to evil; they are not God's ministers for our good."[6] In commanding injustice, they

4. Rutherford, *Lex, Rex*, 144 [Q. 19].

5. Ibid., 265 [Q. 29].

6. Ibid., 261 [Q. 28].

neither act as God's vicar nor command with his power. The power he wields is of men and only accidentally from his civil office. Rutherford said it well:

> Tyranny being a work of Satan, is not from God, because sin, either habitual or actual, is not from God: the power that is, must be from God; the magistrate, as magistrate, is good in nature of office, and the intrinsic end of his office (Rom. xii. 4) for he is a minister of God for thy good; and, therefore, a power ethical, politic, or moral, to oppress, is not from God, and is not a power; and is no more from God, but from sinful nature and the old serpent, than a license to sin.[7]

The implications of this distinction between ruler as such and ruler as a man are common in all superior-subordinate relations. Consider the father-child relation. The child ought to obey his father within the scope of fatherly order. But if the father were to lose his mind and seek to murder his son, the son is free to resist, seize, and incapacitate his father. In this case, a son indeed resists his father, but the father is subject to resistance not as a father but as a fellow man, and the son resists him but not as a son. In other words, in assaulting his son, the father is not acting fatherly (viz., not acting within the scope of fatherly authority) but as a deranged man, and all deranged men can be resisted. The same is true with the husband-wife relation and with other relations.[8] In each case, the principle is that when some superior acts in ways ill-fitting his

---

7. Ibid., 34 [Q. 6].

8. Rutherford writes, "If the pilot should willfully run the ship on a rock to destroy himself and his passengers, they might violently thrust him from the helm." Ibid., 142 [Q. 28].

office, he acts not as a superior but as a fellow man and, thus, as an equal, albeit under the pretense of superiority and authority. For this reason, the authority can be resisted as an aggressor, though he retains his title as father, military officer, ship captain, or civil leader.

Consider another example. The US military gives officers the power to give "lawful orders," and those lawful orders are backed ultimately by the power of the state. Yet the military also insists that service members have the moral obligation to disobey any *un*lawful order. The officer who commands an unlawful order is acting "outside his authority"—an authority granted by the state—and, thus, he commands not as an officer of the state but as a man to other men. The power he wields *appears* to be his officership, but this is accidental, and his subordinates are entitled to disobey. Yet, despite his unlawful command, he still retains his authority and rank in the abstract, until the entity that gave him that authority, namely, the state, rescinds his commission. Civil rulers are under the same principle, though the entity that gave them power is the people. Thus, in resisting an unjust command, the people are simply resisting a fellow man. He remains God's deputy *formally* and is due reverence as such, but he is resisted as a man, not as God's deputy.

Types of Resistance

The term *resistance* is ambiguous and typically calls to mind civil disobedience. But resistance has three types: (1) civil disobedience towards unjust civil commands, which largely occurs on the individual level; (2) forcible and organized resistance to tyranny without the intention to reclaim power but to force the tyrant to enact reforms; and (3) forcible confrontation of a tyrant to reclaim civil power (i.e., revolution). This last one most concerns us here, for the first was justified in the chapter on civil law, and the second is permissible if the third is permissible.

The Tyrant

One or two tyrannical acts do not make one a tyrant, just as one act of vice does not make one vicious.[9] A tyrant is, as Althusius says, "one who, violating both word and oath, begins to shake the foundations and unloosen the bonds of the associated body of the commonwealth."[10] This is an acceptable definition, but a more expansive one is in order, since modern political technique can tightly bind a body politic and still be thoroughly unjust.

> *A tyrant is any civil ruler whose actions significantly undermine the conditions in which man achieves his true humanity or, as I've called it, the complete good.*

Tyrannical conditions strike at the fundamental and necessary features of human society that conduce to our good.[11]

All tyrants act for their "private good," as many theorists have claimed. But we should bear in mind that the greatest tyrants may be those who think or give the appearance that they are here to help—whose smiling, smothering, mammish, and credentialed

9. Althusius writes, "When a ruler failed only in some part of his office or government, however, he is not immediately to be called a tyrant." *Politica*, 191 [38.3].

10. Ibid.

11. Indeed, the tyrant can even be subject to execution, since he is liable for actions he conducts *as a man*, not as civil ruler. Thus, while regicide as such is forbidden, for the civil ruler as God's deputy cannot commit actions worthy of execution, the civil ruler acting with a power of man to commit capital offenses is subject to just execution.

love infantilizes the people. A tyrant is not necessarily one with bad motivations or one who acts in "bad faith"; and the tyrant might even appear to be self-sacrificing or self-disregarding.[12] Such tyrants ultimately serve their own psychological pathologies, and in this way serve their private good. But our principal focus should not be on motivations or pseudo-benevolent appearances but on the actions of tyrants—a body of actions that strikes at the core of civil society.

A tyrant in effect is one who, though having the appearance of civil authority, is but a man ordering fellow men to great evil. His injustice is worthy of a higher type of resistance, for it concerns the whole of civil life; it is not merely an injustice here or there. He is a private man waging an unjust war against the people. With force, the people can pressure him to act justly, remove him from office, or declare separation and independence (when possible). Since the people resist an aggressor, revolution is a type of defensive war.

Forcible and Violent Resistance

Christians are justified in dissolving their formal relationship with tyrannical civil leaders for the following reasons:

---

12. C.S. Lewis wrote of such tyrants, "Of all tyrannies, a tyranny sincerely exercised for the good of its victims may be the most oppressive. It would be better to live under robber barons than under omnipotent moral busybodies. The robber baron's cruelty may sometimes sleep, his cupidity may at some point be satiated; but those who torment us for our own good will torment us without end for they do so with the approval of their own conscience. They may be more likely to go to Heaven yet at the same time likelier to make a Hell of earth. This very kindness stings with intolerable insult. To be 'cured' against one's will and cured of states which we may not regard as disease is to be put on a level of those who have not yet reached the age of reason or those who never will; to be classed with infants, imbeciles, and domestic animals." *God in the Dock: Essays on Theology* (Grand Rapids: Eerdmans, 1972), 292.

1. The people devolved civil power on civil rulers *conditionally*, and hence their power is a fiduciary power, possessed on the condition of just governance. The tyrant, having violated his oath to govern justly, is subjected to dispossession of civil power by those who gave him that power.

2. Aquinas similarly argued that a people can depose or restrict the power of a civil ruler who abuses his power:

    > If to provide itself with a king belongs to the right of a given multitude, it is not unjust that the king be deposed or have his power restricted by that same multitude if, becoming a tyrant, he abuses the royal power. It must not be thought that such a multitude is acting unfaithfully in deposing the tyrant, even though it had previously subject itself to him in perpetuity, because he himself has deserved that the covenant with his subjects should not be kept, since, in ruling the multitude, he did not act faithfully as the office of a king demands.[13]

3. Althusius argues that if some conditions permit marital divorce—a union that God declared "indissoluble"—then certainly there are conditions that permit a nation to separate from their magistrates:

    > [T]he superiority and power the husband has over his wife he derives from the marriage. And this is only for a time and with a condition, namely, that it lasts as long as the marriage endures, that is, as long as the marriage is not dissolved by adultery,

13. Aquinas, *On Kingship*, §49.

desertion, or death. When the marriage is dissolved, every marital power he exercises over his wife is ended. Of equal seriousness with desertion is the intolerable cruelty of a husband that makes it impossible to live with him. Because of incurable cruelty, and its hazard to life and health, theologians concede a dissolution of marriage, and defend divorce by the authority of sacred scripture. Is there not equal reason for conceding divorce between a king and a commonwealth because of the intolerable and incurable tyranny of a king by which all honest cohabitation and association with him are destroyed? No bond is considered to be stricter than that of matrimony, which is ordained by divine authority to be indissoluble. However, for the previously mentioned causes it is dissolved. Cannot the bond between magistrate and subjects likewise be dissolved for equally serious reasons?[14]

4. A Christian is not less human on account of his possession of grace than a man who is without grace; he is a Christian human being. Erecting civil government is fundamentally a *human* act, even for Christians; and thus a Christian people's institution of civil government involves a human transfer of power, which rulers hold conditionally—on their good and proper use of it. In other words, the possession of grace does not fundamentally alter or replace the fundamental principles of civil life; and thus if man as man can reclaim civil power from tyrants, then so too can Christians. For this reason, grace does not eliminate or impede the right for a Christian people to dissolve their formal relationship with tyrannical civil rulers.

14. Althusius, *Politica*, 115 [18.105].

Now, the previous arguments justify the most basic feature of forcible reclamation, namely, the national act of dissolving formal civil relations with rulers. But what about using *violent* means to that end? The following justify violent reclamation of civil power:

1. The nation as a nation is not an *ad hoc* collection of individuals but an entity in itself, a body politic. Just as individuals have the right and duty of self-preservation and self-defense in the interest of their life and goods, so too does the nation, for both are moral entities. The nation as such—its national life being a gift of God—is responsible to God for its self-preservation. Thus, if the individual can use force to protect, defend, and secure his person and property, why can't the nation? Now, the tyrant as such is not a civil ruler but a sort of domestic enemy, an aggressor against the people. Therefore, having a right to self-preservation and the right to defend what is theirs, the people can use violence, when necessary, to end the unjust aggression of this man and subsequently depose him.

2. Since national self-preservation is a command of God and since the injustice of tyrants harms the nation, violent resistance is morally permissible, for God sufficiently augmented earthly powers to shore up earthly good in response to the fall (as I argued in chapter 2), and violence is necessary at times to eliminate tyranny and preserve the nation.

3. If a man aggresses against a nation, doing it harm, then the nation can respond as a nation to end the aggression. This is true in ordinary international relations, when one nation unjustly

attacks another. When the aggressor is the civil ruler, he aggresses *as a man*, not as civil ruler or as God's deputy; and thus the nation can treat him as a domestic enemy and subject him to a violent response, just as they would any other aggressor against the nation. Upon capture, he can be unseated for the reasons argued above.

IV. Conditions for Revolution

Revolution for True Religion

Are Christians permitted to conduct revolution against a tyrant whose actions are significantly detrimental to true religion? I affirm this. We should first acknowledge that any action that is directly detrimental to the highest good is unrighteous in itself and so is evil absolutely and universally. In other words, no set of circumstances would permit a civil ruler justly to destroy true religion, whether by secularization or by replacing it with heresy, infidelity, or paganism. Such actions, in themselves, make the civil ruler a tyrant, for he has attacked the principal object of human life, namely, the acknowledgment and worship of God, which is the also the ultimate end of civil society. In doing this, he has denied man the space to exercise his highest gift and tyrannized over the soul. Indeed, he denies his people the greatest right by nature, namely, the right to worship God. What's worse is that he has attacked King Jesus himself, whose visible kingdom—both the people and the institution—is under outward assault. The civil ruler who attacks true religion is not acting as a minister of God. He is an enemy of his people's good, an enemy of the human race, and an enemy of God.

Having assaulted the natural right to worship the true God, which is essential to complete humanity, the civil ruler is justly subjected to revolt and removal. If a people may revolt over temporal things, why not *a fortiori* over eternal things? As Junius Brutus, the author of *Vindiciae contra tyrannos*, writes,

> Now, if to bear arms and to make war are lawful things, can there possibly be found any war more just than that which is, by the command of the superior, for the defense of the church, and the preservation of the faithful? Is there any greater tyranny than that which is exercised over the soul? Can there be imagined a war more commendable than that which suppresses such a tyranny?[15]

Violence cannot itself advance Christ's kingdom. Indeed, this is the very reason why his kingdom is not of this world. But violence can be used to secure it indirectly and outwardly. As Brutus said, "Although then the church be not increased by arms, notwithstanding it may be justly preserved by means of arms."[16] That is, the church in itself does not increase by any earthly force—for its power is spiritual and operates in the forum of conscience—but earthly forces can preserve and indirectly advance that kingdom by confronting and eliminating outward threats to it.

Religion in the Modern West

If only the enemies of true religion were so bold to openly attack the church. In the Western world, such direct and outward assaults on religion from authorities are rare. Today, we contend with the soft

15. Brutus, *Vindiciae contra tyrannos*, 59.
16. Ibid., 60.

power of liberalism—a power that has been remarkably effective at destroying religiosity in the West without firing a shot and without significantly undermining "religious liberty."[17] Ryszard Legutko, a Polish philosopher who lived under both communism and liberalism, states this well:

> If the old communists lived long enough to see the world of today, they would be devastated by the contrast between how little they themselves had managed to achieve in their antireligious war and how successful the liberal democrats have been. All the objectives the communists set for themselves, and which they pursued with savage brutality, were achieved by the liberal democrats who, almost without any effort and simply by allowing people to drift along with the flow of modernity, succeeded in converting churches into museums, restaurants, and public buildings, secularizing entire societies, making secularism the militant ideology, pushing religion to the sidelines, pressing the clergy into docility, and inspiring powerful mass culture with a strong antireligious bias in which a priest must be either a liberal challenging the Church or a disgusting villain. Is not—one may wonder—this nonreligious and antireligious reality of today's Western world very close to the vision of the future without religion that the communists were so excited about, and which despite the millions of human lives sacrificed on the alter of progress, failed to materialize?[18]

17. I'm referring to the freedom of worship in a traditional sense, viz., the right to one's own ceremonies, ecclesiastical order, etc. There have been significant violations of religious liberty in a broad sense, as understood in American constitutional law.
18. Ryszard Legutko, *The Demon in Democracy: Totalitarian Temptations in Free Societies*, trans. Teresa Adelson (New York: Encounter Books, 2016), 167–68.

The decline of religion in the West is remarkably complex, and I will not attempt to do justice to the topic.[19] But we can safely affirm that it has occurred both without the use of explicit power and under the guise of "freedom" and "toleration." There was no explosive event of anti-religious tyranny. A thousand nudges seemingly led Christians, largely willingly or at best begrudgingly, to confine their religion to churches, privatize religion, and surrender the public to hostile secularization. The uniqueness of our time is that modern liberal power seemingly protects religious liberty while simultaneously undermining religion with implicit social power. Secularism dominates the institutions and has normalized a "neutral" value system that conflicts with Christian moral teaching. "Neutrality" and "diversity" provide the perfect cover for the pervasive use of implicit power to undermine and control religion.

Christians were not ready for this. We are ever-vigilant for that explicit, outward, open, physical, declared, and official persecution. We received this expectation from the Christian tradition—a tradition formed in times very different from our own. But we don't live in the same world as our spiritual forefathers, in the world of *Foxe's Book of Martyrs*. The powers of our modern world—the ones that undermined true religion in the West—are more implicit and psychological; they operate in the *normalization* of secularism. Its normalization is evident in the fact that "normal" people affirm it, live it, and expect it. Our secularized minds are shaped for it, and thus theological traditions that are clearly opposed to secularism had to be recast as its greatest adherents (e.g., modern two-kingdoms

19. Joseph Minich, in *Enduring Divine Absence: The Challenge of Modern Atheism* (Lincoln, NE: Davenant Press, 2018), discusses the ways that modernity can hide God's presence.

theology).[20] With our minds enmeshed in the secularist norm, we confidently think that pleading for religious exemptions before secularist overlords is the timeless politics of Jesus. How convenient for us that we happen to live in secularist times.

The idea of Christian dominion of public space makes even your typical Christian uncomfortable. When confronted with the accusation of "Christian nationalism," for example, we retreat to universality. That is, we claim that we want "freedom for all" and that Christian values "benefit everyone equally," and we point to hospitals, charities, adoptions, and a love for the "outcast." But this is a mental habit that our spiritual forefathers *did not have*; they were not habitually trained to retreat to universality, to justify all their claims of public life by making *the other* the chief beneficiary or to make the object of policy *all* people without discrimination. Nor did they need or seek the approval of the godless to order their communities to God. The retreat to universality is an expression not of Christianity but of normalized modern liberalism, operating as a background assumption for Christian ethics, exegesis, and theology. It ought to be deconstructed.

Christians in the West are enmeshed in totalizing liberal regimes. Though seemingly limited in explicit power, liberal regimes have universal reach: Every square inch is secularist, unless granted an exception by the state. Christians in civil life must adopt either a secularist or a non-threatening religious posture. Contrary to what is promised and assured, there is no neutrality or contestability in

20. VanDrunen, for example, resolves the "contradictions" of traditional two-kingdoms theology with a theological system that affirms post–World War II norms of secularism, multiculturalism, and anti-nationalism. His political theology might rightly be called "post–WWII consensus theology," and I suspect that historians, looking back at it, will conclude that his theology is highly historically conditioned. *Politics after Christendom*, 97, 379.

the public square. As Lugutko said, "In defense of pluralism, we give people the right to choose any available philosophy, provided that they choose liberalism."[21] And, of course, churches are not exempt from the "ism" of secularism. The ideas pervades the mind and now even theology, and any dissidents in churches who threaten secularist norms are denounced from pulpits, in seminaries, and by the eager Christian twitterati—all of whom serve as the Christian in-group enforcers of the secularist norm.

The regime's chief objective is suppressing an *activist* Christian religion that seeks Christian normalization and anti-secularism. The American regime does not want to eradicate religion. Thinking so was the error of prior generations of concerned Christians and perhaps also the error in strategy of the New Atheists twenty years ago. Rather, modern liberalism, at least in the post-Trump era, requires that the distinctives of the religion are either rendered harmless to the regime or the regime harnesses it for its own ends. Harmless religion is a quirk, an expressive identity among other identities, or some harmless way to LARP a medieval fantasy or transcendent rites. Threatening religion is browbeaten by other Christians who find psychological comfort in being subservient to those who despise them. Religion thereby is neutralized as a public threat to the regime, and the resulting Christian ethos is a perverse euphoria in being dispossessed of one's Christian heritage and celebrating the decline of the Bible belt or cultural Christianity or the ideals of Mayberry. It is a bizarre and inhumane inversion and distortion of true religion—our brave new religion does not give hope in the midst of decay and loss but obligates you to celebrate the

21. Legutko, *Demon in Democracy*, 79.

destruction of the very people and place that nourished you, even led you to the faith.

The regime also works to channel religion to support it. This is evident in the rise of what I call the "regime evangelical"—the evangelical arm of the ruling class that Christianizes regime narratives and talking points, feigning as insiders in the evangelical camp in order to shape Christian godliness and "witness" from within. One of their products—regime theology—retains a semblance of orthodoxy and yet has a "social teaching" that effectively advances the regime. Such theology undermines efforts of Christianization while calling for Christians to serve the "marginalized," which happen to be the same sacralized identities of the regime.

Christian Americans should see themselves as under a sort of occupation. Forces largely from outside your communities suppress that natural drive, confirmed by grace, for public religion. The ruling class is hostile to your Christian town, to your Christian people, and to your Christian heritage. The occupation universalizes their ideology, forcing your Christianity to exist only in the walls of churches, denying any civil and social ordering to God and Christ's kingdom. The top-down and foreign imposition of secularism is evident in Supreme Court decisions, though these are only the tip of the iceberg and most visible to us. In 1962, the Supreme Court denied any public school in the United States the right to require students to recite a prayer (*Engel v. Vitale*); it denied any school the right to open the day with Bible reading (*Abington School District v. Schempp*, 1963); and it even denied high school students the right to elect a student to pray before high school football games (*Santa Fe Independent School District v. Doe*, 2000). The universalized culture in the US, generated largely by those on the coasts, has created conditions—foreign to much of Western history and theology—that preclude Christian culture and a Christian self-conception at the state, county, and town levels.

Much more could be said, but I'll simply get to the point: When Christians are under a universalizing and totalizing non-Christian regime that wields implicit powers against true religion, how is this not tyranny? Is this not an assault on the people of God, who are forced to live in a public square that wars against Christ's kingdom and against the nature of true humanity? The natural spheres of life, each with its own God-ordained power, are ordered against God and his people. This certainly *is* tyranny, though there isn't, at first glance, a clear tyrant. We see a modern regime made up of politicians, bureaucrats, media, Hollywood, public intellectuals, academics, corporations, HR directors, public health officials, foundations, medical associations, etc. The *regime* is the tyrant.

In deciding upon forcible reclamation in any situation, we should consider the justice of and in war: the feasibility of success, the acceptability of the consequences, and the suitability of return, given the circumstances. Many revolutions are militarily successful but politically disastrous in the aftermath. I mention these considerations not to inject doubt into the discourse, as many Christians try to do after they say something "edgy," as if to signal that they are unserious and that their ideas are harmless and meant only to ground an identity in our liberal order. I am not seeking to suppress the spirit of action. I'm simply pointing out that resisting tyranny does not necessitate revolution, and other options ought to be considered. Nevertheless, revolution is morally permissible in these conditions, even when the church is "free," according to the modern liberal conception of religious freedom.

Christians in the Minority

Another question is whether a Christian people, constituting a *minority* of the population under a civil government, can revolt against a tyranny directed at them and, after successfully revolting, establish over *all* of the population a Christian commonwealth. The issue here centers on whether a Christian minority can establish a political state over the whole without the positive consent of the whole. I affirm that they can. The reason is that although civil administration is fundamentally natural, human, and universal, it was always for the people of God. Civil administration was created to serve Adam's race in a state of integrity, as an outward ordering to God. Today, those who are restored in Christ are the people of God. Thus, civil order and administration is for them.

But what about consent? Would not Christians have to disregard the non-Christian withholding of consent? They likely would. But no one and no group can withhold consent such that they effectively deny the establishment of a properly constituted commonwealth. None can withhold consent in order to prevent the establishment of true justice. Can a group of people withhold consent to prevent laws against murder? We would find this unacceptable and disregard their lack of consent. But if we would disregard them in the case of murder, why not for a group's disregard for the highest good and the things of God? If we can disregard in the name of lesser goods, then certainly we can disregard in the name of the highest good. Therefore, if a Christian minority can constitute a secure commonwealth for true justice and the complete good, then they can disregard the withholding of consent by non-Christians. Non-Christians living among us are entitled to justice, peace, and safety, but they are not entitled to political equality, nor do they have a right to deny the people of God their right to order civil institutions to God and to their complete good.

We lack the spirit for this sort of dominion today—a once-uncontroversial spirit that animated the magisterial Protestant reformers and Christians prior to the Reformation. We must revitalize and return to it. The Christian's posture towards the earth ought to be that it is *ours*, not theirs, for we are co-heirs in Christ.

Temporal Goods

As for temporal goods, it should follow from the discussion so far that civil rulers who commit actions that are absolutely and universally wrong and concern fundamental features of temporal life can be subjected to violent revolt. This might include, for example, mass murder, prevention of marriage, manstealing, consorting with invading armies, etc. Nothing more needs to be said to justify a revolution in response to these acts.

But what about civil commands that are not wrong in themselves but evil in effect? It is not evil in itself to receive immigrants into one's country, for example. But it can produce certain evils. In chapter 2, I quoted Althusius, who wrote that "persons born in [different] regions hold diverse patterns in their customs . . . [and] are unable to come together at the same time without some antipathy toward each other."[22] As I've argued throughout this book, the particularity of people and place is a necessary good for living well, for it is the ground of robust civil fellowship. Being a necessary good, it is worthy of conservation, and civil authority ought to conserve it. It also creates conditions for true religion to flourish, serving as the ethno-cultural substructure

22. Althusius, *Politica*, 150 [23.14].

for cultural Christianity, Christian civil law, and strong Christian civil rulers. Thus, the Christian religion, though itself universal, flourishes in particularity. Christianity flourishes in nations. It would seem, then, that too much immigration and bad immigration policies damage the people, even striking at fundamental goods. Therefore, such policies, though not absolutely and universally unjust, can be tyrannical and can create tyrannical conditions.

There many other ways besides open immigration policies that civil rulers can damage cultural particularity (e.g., tax incentives to multinational corporations), and immigration itself (if done properly) can benefit a nation. But instead of listing more examples of culture-destroying policies, we can get straight to the question: Is revolution permissible in defense of particularity? Since particularity is a fundamental condition of living well, undermining that good is tyrannical and so it is a just cause for revolution.[23]

V. Lesser Magistrate

The lesser-magistrate doctrine states that violent resistance against tyranny is permitted, but only by means of a lesser magistrate

---

23. Cultural degradation through tyrannical policy is often incremental, however. When the effects of policy are finally felt and seen, it is usually too late. Revolution is typically, for this reason, not an effective means to secure cultural particularity. Rather, a vehement insistence on good policy is necessary, combined with prescience on how policies will be applied over time. The people must have a long-term view of policy to see and predict the effects. For example, any given year of high immigration is not in itself culturally damaging, but multiple years of the same levels of immigration is damaging. Those Americans who denounced the Immigration and Nationality Act of 1965 were right about its consequences, as was British politician Enoch Powell with regard to British immigration policies; but they were ignored or dismissed as "racists." My hope is that the recovery of intergenerational love—based in affections for one's progeny decades and centuries into the future—will supply the firm resolve to prevent such policies and to suppress the modern presentism that views policy-effects merely year-by-year.

interposing himself between a tyrannical higher magistrate and the people. I affirm this view, though perhaps with some differences. The first is that it should not be called a "doctrine." Protestants should not speak of "social doctrine." This is a minor quibble, but I insist on it only to emphasize that our political thought is not determined by a *collegia* of clerics. We're speaking of a natural principle, not a doctrine of grace. Indeed, I'd prefer to call it the "authority principle of resistance."

The entity that interposes between the tyrant and people is necessary not so that the people can act against tyranny. People can justly act apart from a lesser magistrate or an established interposing body.[24] That is, they can act for themselves outside any higher earthly authority. But their actions are limited and cannot properly be called acts of the people. Remember, the people require an agent of order. A mediating authority is necessary as that by which the people can act collectively. Thus, the people can truly revolt, or conduct revolution, only by the express declaration and direction of an interposing entity. The Declaration of Independence, for example, was a collective act of the American colonies, because the Continental Congress was an interposing authority—albeit in a more confederate form—between the British Crown and the American people. The interposing authority does not necessarily reclaim the people's power for itself, but rather it is an instrument in reclaiming that power to the people, and it can be the interim agent by which that power is subsequently devolved.

To get more technical, the authority principle clarifies the efficient cause of revolution. Complete agency in revolution is *antecedently* the people's will for revolution, *formally* the interposing

---

24. I have the Battles of Lexington and Concord in mind here.

authority as mediator of that will, and *consequently* the people's concrete actions of force, directed as a whole by the interposing authority. These three must be present for a true and just revolution.

VI. Romans 13

For reasons that I provided in the introduction, I have not addressed scriptural arguments for and against my positions in this work. However, it is worth briefly discussing Romans 13.

Paul instructs us to "be subject unto the higher powers." These powers are "ordained of God . . . for good" (vv. 1, 4). The scope of power permits civil rulers to be "not a terror to good works, but to the evil" (v. 3). Subjection to this power is "for conscience sake" (v. 5), meaning that God binds the conscience through the command of civil rulers. It follows from the text that since the powers ordained of God are only for good, no power ordained of God can command what is evil, and thus no evil command is conscience-binding, for only God can bind the conscience, whether immediately or mediately. A magistrate that is a terror to good works acts outside his authority. With regard to those specific unjust commands, he ought to be resisted. This is not controversial, for we should "obey God rather than men" (Acts 5:29).

The most important question is whether Romans 13 denies the right of the people to forcibly reclaim civil power from their civil rulers. The question boils down to whether these two statements are contrary to each other: *you shall not resist powers ordained of God* and *you may conduct revolution against tyrannical civil rulers*. The common assumption today is that revolution necessarily resists the powers ordained of God, and thus the two statements cannot both be true. But I affirm both and deny that they are contraries. In conducting just revolution, a people are fighting a defensive war against the *person* holding civil office, not against the office itself, i.e., not against the civil ruler *as ruler*. In resisting a tyrant, a people are not resisting the powers ordained of God, for a power for tyranny is not ordained of God. Thus, a people can conduct revolution against tyrannical civil rulers and, in so doing, *not* resist the powers ordained of God.

Many point to the tyrannical character of the Roman emperors around the time that Paul wrote Romans. Paul instructs us to obey rulers like Nero, a ruler who was clearly a tyrant. But my argument has made clear that a tyrant, even one as degenerate as Nero, has not lost his office; he still wields *true* civil power of God; he is still at least *formally* God's deputy for our good. A civil ruler who becomes tyrannical has not thereby lost his office. Now, even tyrants can command what is just, for while his commands considered as a *whole* are tyrannical, not every part or every specific command is tyrannical. Though Nero was indeed a tyrant, worthy of violent removal, he still had true authority to command what is just, and many civil commands of the Roman empire were indeed just. Paul instructs us to obey these commands, for they are ordinances of God commanded mediately through God's deputy. Therefore, Paul's instruction to obey civil rulers (even those who are tyrants) does not entail that the people lack the right to forcibly reclaim civil power from tyrants.

Paul's silence with regard to revolution is easily explained by the fact that commanding it at the time would have been absurd. Christians were in no position to revolt. His silence on revolution cannot be construed as a denial of its permissibility. When revolution is unfeasible, Christians must patiently wait on God for deliverance—disobeying what is unjust and obeying what is just.[25]

VII. Conclusion

Many want me to end with a word of caution, perhaps to reassure everyone that these are academic conclusions, that they are not serious. Instead, I'll say this: It is to our shame that we sheepishly tolerate assaults against our Christian heritage, merely sighing or tweeting performative outrage over public blasphemy, impiety, irreverence, and perversity. We are dead inside, lacking the spirit to drive away the open mockery of God and to claim what is ours in Christ. We are gripped by a slavish devotion to our secularist captors. But we do not have to be like this. We have the power and right to act. Let us train the will and cultivate our resolve.

25. Aquinas writes, "Should not human aid whatsoever against a tyrant be forthcoming, recourse must be had to God, the King of All, Who is a helper in due time in tribulation. For it lies in this power to turn the cruel heart of the tyrant to mildness." *On Kingship*, §51.

9

Liberty of Conscience

"In the tribunal of conscience the plea is between man and God, whereas in the outward tribunal it is between man and man." —Thomas Aquinas[1]

I. Statement of the Question

One issue that may have nagged the reader is the question of conscience. Doesn't Christian nationalism, as I've presented it, violate the freedom of conscience? Does Christian nationalism recognize the sanctity of conscience? Asking these questions is fair and expected, since I have called for public institutions and culture to be Christian. But, in most cases, these questions arise from serious confusion about classical Protestant political theology and from

1. Aquinas, *ST, Supplement*, 22.1.

ignorance on how Protestants justified civil action for true religion. Contrary to popular belief, liberty of conscience is not original to our modern era, or to the Enlightenment, or even to the Baptists. The 16th- and 17th-century Reformers universally affirmed the sacred liberty of conscience, even while insisting that civil magistrates protect and support true religion and suppress false religion. Were these brilliant men wildly, blatantly, absurdly inconsistent? No. Neither the outward suppression of false religion nor the public exclusivity of Christianity violates the sacredness of conscience, as I demonstrate in this chapter.

Compelled Religion

It is common today, even among Christian academics, to improperly state the question concerning civil government, religion, and conscience. This error goes back centuries. In the 17th century, Samuel Rutherford complained of "ignorant Anabaptists" who claimed that the issue centers on "internal liberty." The question, to their mind, was "whether the magistrate can force men with the sword to [religious] opinions and cudgel them out of some [and] into other contrary judgments in the matters of God."[2] Rutherford joined the Anabaptists in denying such compulsion. From the early days of the Reformation, magisterial Protestant thinkers emphatically insisted that magistrates must not, and indeed *cannot*, compel faith. Every man has an internal liberty. The Reformed confession produced by the Bern Synod of 1532 reflects this early consensus: "[N]o magistrate should compel the conscience, or

---

2. Rutherford, *Against Pretended Liberty of Conscience*, 46. A modern Baptist, Russell Moore, recently wrote that some would "pretend to enforce the kingdom [of God] with tanks or guns. . . . " Quoted in Walker, *Liberty for All*, 32.

command and forbid with respect to anything more than what is outward."[3] All attempts to coerce belief is unjust, for no one can be coerced to believe something. As Rutherford said, no one can "offer violence to mind, understanding, will or affections of love, fear, joy, because all these elicit acts cannot flow from any principle but the internal and vital inclinations of the soul." Thus, the statement of the question is "whether the magistrate can compulsorily restrain the external acts of the outward man in religion."[4] This is an accurate but incomplete statement of the question. The rest of this section clarifies and completes it.

The chief dispute between classical and modern Christians on the liberty of conscience centers on the relationship of external religion and internal religion. My contention is that proponents of religious liberty have asserted a *non sequitur* for centuries, arguing that since true inward religion cannot be forced but is a matter of persuasion, the magistrate cannot use coercive power to suppress external false religion. The conclusion, however, does not follow, because it fails to distinguish what Richard Baxter called the "liberty of tongue and practice" and the "liberty of conscience."[5] The differences between these two liberties will become more evident as I proceed.

---

3. "The Bern Synod (1532)," in *Reformed Confessions of the 16th and 17th Centuries in English Translation*, ed. James T. Dennison, vol. 1, *1523–1552* (Grand Rapids: Reformation Heritage Books, 2008), 231.

4. Rutherford, *Against Pretended Liberty of Conscience*, 46.

5. Richard Baxter, *A Holy Commonwealth* (London, 1659), 278. He continues: "Men's consciences are not under inspection or cognizance of the Magistrate. He that will be an Infidel, must have liberty of conscience to damn himself, and then to torment himself whether the Magistrate will or no: But if he have liberty to infect and seduce others, the Magistrate shall answer for it."

Internal Religion

Internal religion refers to religious acts of the inward man, such as belief, faith, hope, and love. Only God can see these acts directly; they are in themselves completely invisible to men, and they fall outside human jurisdiction, given the kind of thing they are. Thus, no civil authority can compel one to perform them. The question, therefore, is not whether civil authority can compel internal religion.

The conscience cannot be subordinated to any external entity—whether civil, social, familial, or ecclesiastical—such that these entities dictate to it the judgments concerning internal religion. No man can defer to them or treat their authority as sufficient grounds to affirm some proposition of faith. Internal religion is grounded in knowledge that one affirms by referencing Scripture, not by referencing a mediating authority. Certainly, we came to be believe many things from others, but we do not ground our religious belief in our trust of them, as if they are authorities that mediate truth to us. They were instruments in showing us the truth of Scripture. Thus, the question is not whether one ought to defer to the judgment of an external truth-mediating authority for internal religious beliefs.[6] No civil government (or ecclesial institution or society at large) can mediate religious truth such that its subjects or members can or must defer to its judgments concerning what one affirms inwardly. One must be convinced in his own mind by his encounter with the deposits of truth, both in Scripture and the book of nature. The church's duty is to teach true religion, and the civil government must ensure that truth is taught and that harmful false

6. We can defer to reliable teachers on matters that we have not resolved ourselves, such as answers to questions on the Trinity. But the principal role of these authorities is instrumental—to demonstrate these truths to you from Scripture. That is, their authority does not ground your belief; rather, the authority of Scripture, which they point to, grounds your belief.

teaching is restrained, but each person is responsible before the Governor of the Universe for affirming and embracing what is religiously true, and his mind must be left free to do so.

An internal belief in itself, being visible only to God, affects only the one who holds it. That is, a belief as a belief—considered only as an internal thing—can bring neither good nor evil to another. Thus, civil authority has no concern with true or false belief *in itself*, for civil authority concerns itself directly only with outward good and evil. As Francis Turretin states, "Coercive power does not apply to internal faith, but is concerned with external acts, over which the magistrate has power. For as an opinion of the mind is not to be punished, still neither is a pestilent and impious profession to be endured."[7] Civil authority has neither cognizance of nor jurisdiction over, nor interest in beliefs themselves. False belief itself must never be the basis of civil punishment.[8] False religion *externalized* is the only principled object of punishment. Hence, the question is not whether civil authority can punish one on the basis (in whole or part) for false belief itself. Furthermore, since civil power cannot reform hearts, we deny that the direct intent of civil punishment for false religion can be inward reformation.[9]

Nor is the question whether civil rulers can "prosecute crimes against [God]" (as Jonathan Leeman suggests about this position).[10]

---

7. Turretin, *IET*, 3:18.34.34.

8. This precludes any government-run inquisition whereby authorities force people to profess their beliefs and then punish them on account of their alleged falsities.

9. To be sure, this can be an indirect effect of civil action, but it cannot serve as the ground or direct object for civil action.

10. Jonathan Leeman, *Political Church: The Local Assembly as Embassy of Christ's Rule* (Downer's Grove, IL: InterVaristy Press, 2016), 204. Quoted in Walker, *Liberty for All*, 55. David VanDrunen repeats this confusion as well. *Politics after Christendom*, 202.

It is true that some Reformed writers spoke of punishment for "tak[ing] away from God his own honor," as Calvin said. But Calvin also said that such people "destroy souls . . . corrupt pure doctrine . . . [and] confound the whole order of the Church."[11] As I'll argue below, false religion is a crime against God, *and* it can cause harm to one's fellow man. Hence, one can reject the view that magistrates ought to punish the dishonoring of God and still coherently affirm that magistrates can restrain false religion in the interest of public good.

External Religion

External acts of religion are of a different nature than internal acts of religion. External religion includes professions of faith (vocal or written), ceremonies of worship, teaching, etc. These are outward and visible and can affect others, and so external religion belongs to the kind of things that external authorities can regulate. Most importantly, such external acts, unlike internal ones, can affect others both internally and externally, for good or for ill, which I will elucidate and demonstrate in the next section. All appropriate civil action against false religion is directed at its *external expression* in order to suppress external false religion and thereby prevent harm to the public, both to souls and to the body politic. Suppressing false religion is a *means*, not an end in itself. Thus, the question is not whether the suppression of external false religion by civil government is a good in itself or ought to be pursued for its own sake; nor is the question whether civil government ought to prosecute *all* expressions of false religion regardless of their consequences and circumstances; nor is the question

---

11. Calvin, *Commentaries on the Twelve Minor Prophets*, 4:383 [on Zech. 13:3].

whether civil power can force one to speak outwardly what is true, for that would cause one to lie.[12]

Final Statement of the Question

Given these clarifications and conclusions from previous chapters, I can offer the fundamental point of division between classical and modern views on the liberty of conscience.

> The question is whether a Christian magistrate, having civil rule over a civil society of Christians,[13] may punish (with civil power) false teachers, heretics, blasphemers, and idolaters for their external expressions of such things in order to prevent (1) any injury to the souls of the people of God, (2) the subversion of Christian government, Christian culture, or spiritual discipline, or (3) civil disruption or unrest.

Modern religious liberty advocates deny this and I affirm it.

II. Principle

Affirming this question requires me to demonstrate both that civil rulers can *in principle* punish such people and that it is *prudent* to do so, at least in some circumstances. Something may be permissible

12. However, as my argument demonstrates below, the magistrate can compel one not to speak or practice falsehood. Also, positive affirmations of doctrine can be conditions for civil office or for outsiders who seek residence, since these are voluntary actions.

13. The civil regulation of religion assumes both that the civil rulers are Christians (at least with regard to profession and church membership) and that the principal part of the people are Christian. Thus, the question is not whether civil rulers are required to regulate religion in all demographical circumstances. The regulation of religion is in the service of Christians, not absolute duty that the civil ruler fulfills in every set of circumstances.

but never prudent. This allows me to address the various issues and objections by type, some concerned with principle and others with practical considerations. This section concerns the principle.

Public Harm

Those in the denial camp typically affirm that civil government ought to regulate outward religious actions that cause public harm. But they limit public harm to *physical* harm. Andrew Walker states, for example, that "only forms of worship that physically harm others should be restrained or punished."[14] He then cites Leeman, who writes, "The God of the Bible gives governments authority to prosecute crimes against human beings, not the authority to prosecute crimes against himself. As long as people remain unharmed, false religion should be tolerated publicly and privately."[15] As far as I can tell, Walker and Leeman limit the extension of public harm to *physical* harms on the unstated assumption that external false religion cannot cause internal harm or harm to the soul. Since it only harms God, it is not subject to civil action. I do not see how the argument would work otherwise.

I will grant here that civil authorities should not prosecute crimes solely against God, as if civil punishment right wrongs committed against him. But the assumption that external false religion does not harm souls is clearly false. Christians widely acknowledge that outward false religion can harm others. Indeed, we praise families and churches that protect themselves from false teaching, because we know that such teaching can harm people's souls. Thus, the proper

14. Walker, *Liberty for All*, 54.

15. Jonathan Leeman, *Political Church: The Local Assembly as Embassy of Christ's Rule* (Downers Grove, IL: InterVarsity Press, 2016), 204.

extension of public harm includes harms to the soul, for public actions, such as heretical teaching, can harm the soul.[16]

Thus, by Walker's stated major premise—namely, that magistrates may punish those whose actions harm or threaten to harm one's fellow man—magistrates are permitted to punish external false religion, for it can harm fellow humans. These actions are crimes against God *and* fellow man, and thus they are subject to punishment (at least) on account of the latter.

So my argument is as follows:

> (1) Any outward action that has the potential to cause harm to others is rightfully subject to civil restraint or punishment (in principle).
>
> (2) External false religion has the potential to cause harm to others.
>
> Therefore, (3) external false religion is rightfully subject to civil restraint or punishment.

The major premise extends to all actions that cause harm, including those outward acts that express inward religious beliefs, because there is no good reason to limit it. It cannot be, "You cannot compel the conscience," for the conscience is not compelled, since only external expression is targeted. Nor can it be, "You cannot punish beliefs," for the belief itself is neither the ground of the civil action nor the object of the action. Nor can it be, "People ought to be able to express their beliefs," for this would require us, for example, to tolerate inciters of political violence. Expressions of false religion

16. In other words, all public actions that cause harm are public harms; some public actions that cause harm are actions that harm the soul; therefore, some public harms are actions that harm the soul.

are outward, and so they are subject to civil jurisdiction as to the kind of action; and because they can harm others, they are in principle subject to civil restraint and punishment.

As for the minor premise, there is no question that those who actively and outwardly espouse damnable error can lead people astray, especially when they have skill and personality. Even those who are eternally secure—those "kept by the power of God" (1 Pet. 1:5)—can be diverted from the path of righteousness. Christian parents regularly act to keep their children from such people, ordering the household into an exclusively Christian space. Within the extent of their powers and vigilance, they eliminate anti-Christian influences so that children are raised in the fear of the Lord. Civil authorities, having civil power over civil space, can and ought to do likewise.

Principled Cognizance

One might acknowledge the soundness of the syllogism but claim that the conclusion is actionable only if civil government has cognizance of what would be good for the soul. That is to say, the statement "false religion is rightfully subject to civil restraint or punishment" is true, but it remains unactionable because civil government has no ability to identify the extension of "false religion" (or "true religion") and thus has no concrete objects to restrain and punish. Though this might appear to be a prudential question, it is actually a question of principle. The question here is not whether one can expect a magistrate to have reliable judgments concerning religious and spiritual things but whether civil rulers can have principled cognizance of such things.[17] Here are my responses:

17. "Principled cognizance" (or "principled access") refers to one having a principled basis for possessing certain knowledge and acting on it. Though a civil magistrate as a man can

1. The fact that the objects of civil action for the magistrate are outward things does not limit his knowledge as a magistrate only to outward things. He can know what is good inwardly and can order outward things to that good. The magistrate is (typically) not a mental health therapist, and he cannot cure by civil command those who suffer from poor mental health. But he can know (from his own experience and by consulting therapists) what constitutes a healthy and tranquil mind. And with that knowledge, he can order outward things in the interest of mental health. Therefore, the magistrate, though he can only affect outward things, can know what is good inwardly and order outward things to inward good.

2. As most Reformed political theologians affirm today, civil magistrates ought to enact civil law derived from the natural law as summarized in the Second Table of the Ten Commandments (i.e., our duties to fellow man). Thus, civil magistrates can have principled cognizance of our duties to our fellow man. Many deny that the civil magistrate can know and act on the natural law summarized in the First Table (i.e., our duties to God). But this is false. If the civil magistrate has principled cognizance of any part of the natural law *as law*, then he logically can know of the Lawgiver, for all law has a lawgiver. Thus, civil magistrates as magistrates can know of God as the fountain of law. Now, if the magistrate can know of God, then he can know God's nature, at least in principle. But knowledge of God's nature rationally leads to the First Table, for God's nature makes him worthy of

know his duties to God, this does not necessarily mean (as many argue) that the magistrate *as magistrate* knows these duties. A magistrate as such having "principled cognizance" of man's duties to God means that he can have such knowledge and act on that knowledge.

the highest praise, reverence, and worship. It follows that the magistrate can have principled cognizance of the First Table. In other words, since the civil magistrate has cognizance of Second Table precepts, he can have cognizance of First Table precepts, for the Second Table presupposes God's existence, and his existence rationally leads to the First Table. So, at least with regard to natural religion, the magistrate can have principled cognizance of true and false religion as captured in the First Table of God's law. The Second Table-onlyists are thus refuted.

3. Lastly, since a civil magistrate as a man can know true religion and can order his personal life to religion, he can know it as a civil magistrate. While we might want to restrict some personal knowledge from actionability in civil office, these restrictions are exceptions and thus require an explicit reason for the restriction. Since no good reason for an exception can be brought forward to exclude personal knowledge of true religion, then it is not excluded from actionable knowledge in civil office.

But what about supernatural knowledge? One might agree that we can have a nation under God, referring to God the creator, and civil leaders who enforce only the demands of natural religion, not those of revealed religion. The argument goes something like this: Since supernatural revelation is adventitious to nature and civil government is founded on nature, civil government has no principled cognizance of supernatural revelation such that it can adjudicate competing claims concerning that revelation. Or one might say that since the principles of civil government are natural, it cannot act in light of supernatural knowledge, even if in principle civil magistrates could have supernatural knowledge. Put differently, a civil ruler who is Christian may know Christian truth but cannot order his people to that truth, because his principles of action are entirely natural and so have only natural objects. Lastly, one might claim that doctrinal adjudication is a matter for the church, not the state, and thus the state cannot adjudicate between competing claims with regard to supernatural revelation.

These arguments can be addressed in a few ways:

1. Scripture is originally a possession of the people of God; it was not originally handed to ministers but to the people. This is evident in the fact that, as Turretin said, "[T]he ministry is posterior to the church. . . . [T]he church precedes the ministry and produces it."[18] The instituted church teaches the Word not because the Word was given directly to ministers from God but because they are entrusted with a sacred teaching function among the people of God—a people who already have the Scriptures. Now, since the knowledge contained in Scripture is a possession of the people of God, civil rulers have principled access to this knowledge,[19] for civil rulers are installed by and from the people of God. And since the people of God erect civil government for their good, both body and soul, the civil ruler can act according to this knowledge for their good. It makes little sense that a man, having been installed by and for a people with a certain type of knowledge, will lose principled access to that knowledge, especially when it is necessary for ordering them to their complete good.

18. Turretin, *IET*, 3:18.24.10.

19. See two earlier notes for a definition of "principled access."

2. If civil rulers can determine the truth or falsity in natural revelation, nothing precludes them (in principle) from determining truth and falsity in special revelation, for both revelations
are knowledge, and they differ only in the *means to* knowledge.
They differ in this regard only to the extent that philosophy
differs from theology. Anyone who can reason to natural truth
can *a fortiori* interpret Scripture to supernatural truth or be
teachable concerning the truths therein. It would be quite odd
for Protestants to elevate the magistrate's abilities in unaided
reason while downgrading his abilities in theology. In addition,
scriptural revelation is a *public* deposit of truth, meaning in effect that it is not the instituted church's deposit, as if it is for
ministers' access only. It is accessible by all and for all, including
by and for the magistrate. As a public knowledge, it is intended
for all. And the magistrate, with consultation and instruction of
church ministers (serving as instruments, not mediators), can
decide upon supernatural truth for civil purposes.

3. Natural commands are not limited to natural content. As with
all the commandments, the first commandment is a natural
command. It instructs us to acknowledge and worship the
true God alone.[20] The referent of "true God" in our worship
is revealed by nature *and* Scripture. By natural revelation, man
knows that God is one. Special revelation tells us that God is
Triune. This latter revelation neither eliminates nor undermines natural revelation but rather assumes and completes it.

---

20. Question 46 in the Westminster Shorter Catechism states, "The first commandment
requireth us to know and acknowledge God to be the only true God, and our God; and to
worship and glorify him accordingly."

Scripture completes our knowledge of the same God. Still, the command itself remains a natural command. Thus, worshipping God according to the fullness of revelation—worshipping the Triune God—fulfills the natural command to worship the true God. Therefore, when the civil magistrate enforces the First Table, he is not limited only by what is revealed by nature (e.g., that God is one); he can enforce the fullness of God as revealed; and in so doing, he is not fulfilling a command of grace but of nature, even though some of the content is of grace (e.g., Trinitarianism). It follows that the magistrate may regulate external actions in accordance with the Christian religion.

4. Since the natural ends of civil government are fixed and immutable and one of those ends is ordering the people to their supernatural end, civil government ought to order the people according to the means available to meet that end. Since Christ the redeemer is the sole means to obtain man's supernatural end, civil government ought to order the people to him and thereby meet its own natural end.

5. Though Christian magistrates do not arise from the instituted church or by the sanction of ministers, they are members of the instituted church and under the teaching ministers of the church. The magistrate is the first among the people of God who sit under the instituted teaching ministry that they have constituted. These ministers are the ordinary means by which the magistrate comes to know the articulation and formulations of sound doctrine and faithful gospel ministry to which he orders the people to their eternal good. A civil magistrate

is no less a member of the church as magistrate than a man is a member as husband or father; and just as men can be instructed as fathers, so too can the magistrate be instructed as magistrate.

6. If the father, who rules over the natural family, can know and act on supernatural knowledge *as father*—ordering his household to Christ—then so too can the magistrate know and act on supernatural knowledge *as magistrate* and thereby order civil society to Christ. This argument is effective because the arguments used to deny the consequent require one to deny the antecedent, for the father and magistrate are sufficiently similar to each other. For example, if one were to deny that Christian magistrates can adjudicate between true and false religion for civil society, insisting that this is the prerogative of the instituted church only, then the father in his household cannot adjudicate between true and false religion either, because his household is not the church, and all fathers lead their homes as fathers, not as pastors.[21] To deny the possibility of a Christian magistrate entails denying the possibility of a Christian father. But since there are Christian fathers, there can be Christian magistrates.

The question of whether civil magistrates can adjudicate competing claims of supernatural truth needs some clarification. The ministers of the Word are charged with "hold[ing] fast the form of sound words" (2 Tim. 1:13) and with issuing authoritative (though not infallible) judgments concerning theological truth and error. Ministers pronounce *positive* judgments. The civil rulers, however, having only

---

21. All fathers who are pastors in the instituted church lead their homes not as pastors but as fathers.

civil law to work with, legislate a *negative*—viz., criminalizing only what is false. Declaring a negative does not always require antecedent knowledge of a positive (for one can know what is false before he knows what is true), but magistrates may base their negatives on positive knowledge. For example, he can base his suppression of anti-Trinitarianism on his knowledge of Trinitarian doctrine.

Hypocrisy

The accusation that restraining and punishing heresy will produce hypocrisy goes back at least to the 16th century. We hear today that people will "live a lie." But this objection assumes a principle that, when applied broadly, has practically absurd results. The principle is, *all have the right to express outwardly what they affirm inwardly*. If they don't have this right, then they are forced into hypocrisy, as the claim goes. Advocates of religious liberty almost always limit the application of this principle to religion. But this is arbitrary. Criminalizing sins of the Second Table—such as murder, adultery, theft, and defaming character—also makes men hypocrites. One might inwardly want to murder his enemy and even believe sincerely that killing him would be just, but the fear of civil punishment might lead him to act like a friend. This is indeed hypocrisy—his inward state does not match his outward action. While we do not approve of inward hatred towards others, we would say that in this case civil law is fulfilling one of its functions, viz., restraining outward sin that causes public harm. Why are these examples of hypocrisy acceptable but not hypocrisy with regard to false religion? Should the civil magistrate not punish murder, since the threat of punishment makes hypocrites out of those who would otherwise commit it? Since civil law can restrain murder, it can restrain false religion.

To avoid this, one would have to claim that the sins of the First Table and those of the Second Table are different. But what might that difference be? It cannot be sincerity, for people have sincere though erroneous convictions on civil justice. It cannot be harmfulness, for public heresy can be harmful. Certainly, one can think of prudential reasons to treat them differently (which I address below), but what is the difference in *principle*? There is none. If one finds Second Table hypocrisy acceptable as a consequence of civil law, then he must also find First Table hypocrisy acceptable as a consequence of civil law.

One of the early Reformed confessions—the Bern Synod (1532)—directly addressed the issue of hypocrisy with the "temporal magistrate":

> It is true that whenever Christ himself is not at work, your [i.e., the magistrate's] work, your service and your power touching the gospel only makes men hypocrites, and has always done as much. . . . But this must not deter you, for the ministry of Moses respecting the law of God is likewise capable of nothing more, though it is a law of life. He may not forbear, but is obliged to carry out his office, though the flesh is all the while making the law of life into a dead letter and into wrath and death itself. This is because God throughout the ministry of Moses gave the people no understanding heart. . . . It should make no difference with your excellencies as to how it will be received. For even though the world take it to be mere hypocrisy, the intention of your excellencies through your service is to bring everyone to the truth and to remove public scandal, as when Moses sought to carry the people on to God, and to preserve among them a

pious and corrected pattern of conduct. Thus though neither you nor any authority is able to produce a good conscience before God, yet the service performed by your excellencies procures the preaching of the pure Word of God among your subjects, and ensures that His grace will be heralded with clarity. The people are directed to the fountain from which alone the water of salvation is drawn, namely our Lord Jesus Christ who is our only mediator. He receives whom He will.[22]

This speaks more to what I call "sins of omission," which I address later. But it relies on the same underlying reasoning. You cannot fault civil power for not performing what it cannot perform. Civil power—when by itself—will occasion (not cause) hypocrisy; by God's decree, civil power can touch directly only the outward man. The inward man is an entirely separate domain and is ordered by different means. Hypocrisy is the fault of the hypocrite, not the one commanding outward duty. And, as I've stressed throughout this work, civil power is only one power of an organic set of powers, ordained by God, for man's good. Civil power ought to support the spiritual power as the body supports the soul. It cannot legislate a good conscience, but it can create outward conditions for the spiritual power to do its work on the conscience.

Stating the Principle

Moving away from an elenctic method, I'll state the principle directly:

The civil magistrate may restrain outward expressions of false religion that, in his judgment, (1) can injure souls, (2) are

22. "Bern Synod (1532)," in *Reformed Confessions*, 231–32.

subversive to Christian civil government, Christian culture, and sacred ministry, or (3) threaten civil disruption and unrest; and he restrains in order to establish or maintain the best outward conditions for his people to live "a quiet and peaceable life in all godliness and honesty" (1 Tim. 2:2).

I have sufficiently demonstrated the truth of this principle. But I'll offer some clarifying remarks. First, the magistrate "may" do this because all civil action is a matter of principle *and* prudence (as I discuss below). Second, the "best outward conditions" are conditions that prepare for faith, order people to the means of grace, eliminate distractions from faith and worship, secure sacred ministry, and normalize Christianity. Third, in addition to inward harm, false religion can also cause *outward* harm. As we see in the next chapter, the New England authorities in the 17th century acted against people like Roger Williams and the Antinomians in part from fear that their religious teachings might undermine Christian civil authority and threaten civil discipline. Fourth, public heresy or profanation might ignite righteous indignation among the people and thereby bring about public unrest.

III. Prudence

The Necessity of Prudence

Prudence is relevant because all civil action is a means to an end, and the means must conduce to that end. The effectiveness of means depends on the circumstances in which the means operate. Althusius recognized this in the early 17th century. Here he is discussing how religious diversity limits the extent to which the magistrate can enforce true religion:

> [T]he magistrate who is not able, without peril to the com-
> monwealth, to change or overcome the discrepancy in religion
> and creed ought to tolerate the dissenters for the sake of public
> peace and tranquility, blinking his eyes and permitting them to
> exercise unapproved religion, lest the entire realm, and with it
> the household of the church, be overthrown. He shall therefore
> tolerate the practice of diverse religions as a skilled navigator
> bears with diverse and conflicting winds and clashing waves.
> Just as amidst these winds and waves the navigator brings his
> ship safely into the harbor, so the magistrate directs the com-
> monwealth in a manner that keeps it free from ruin for the wel-
> fare of the church.[23]

The principle I demonstrated in the previous section does not demand an absolute and universal set of policies that eradicate *all* false religion. Suppressing false religion is not an end in itself but a *means* to a godly and tranquil public life. As Althusius points out, suppressing false religion to the degree that the commonwealth itself is threatened may violate the very end of such suppression, for the false religionists may overthrow the state and attack the church.

Suppressing false religion in one's own land can be called a "holy war," for the intended effect is the elimination of sacrilege. But it differs from the sort of holy war that God commanded the Jews to conduct. The Jews were to conduct that war as if it were an end in itself—simply as obedience to God—though of course clearing the land of idolatry was a means in God's plans for the Jews and the land. In our time, the suppression of false religion is not an end in

23. Althusius, *Politica*, 174 [28.66]. This passage also shows that religious diversity hinders the ability for civil rulers (and society itself) to order the people to true religion.

itself but a means and a matter of prudence; and such actions are prudent only if they conduce concretely to the good of the church. The church is ordinarily not well served by inciting powerful and destructive rage against it. In all situations, Christian civil rulers must set their eyes on the end, for as Jeremiah Burroughs said, "Many think they do great service to Christ, the Church and State, if they can stir up Magistrates to suppress whatsoever they conceive are errors; it may be their hearts are upright in the main, they aim at peace, but certainly they cause much disturbance in Church and State."[24] This caution should not undermine the resolve of magistrates to perform their duty, nor should it serve as an excuse for passivity under the pretense of irenicism and civil peace, both of which (like suppressing false religion) are means to human good, not ends in themselves.[25]

The idea that Reformed magistrates had no flexibility with regard to religious diversity is a myth. Indeed, in the 16th and 17th

24. Jeremiah Burroughs, *Irenicum to the Lovers of Truth and Peace* (London, 1653), 56.

25. Though civil peace is an end of civil government, it is a means to the public good. Peter Martyr Vermigli wrote, "Wherefore for as much as the one or the other is to be chosen, the whole and uncorrupted worshipping of God ought rather to be wished for than the commodity of outward peace. For the end of cities and public-wealths is to obey God and rightly to worship God, that is by his word and prescribed rule. For to have a city or public-wealth quiet and peaceable, is not by it self necessary, but to obey God, to believe his word, and to worship him as he hath prescribed is the sum and end of all human things, and therefore it is to be preferred above all good things." *The Commentary of Master Peter Martyr [Vermigli] upon the Book of Judges* (London: John Day, [1575?]), 124. Vermigli is speaking here about Christians choosing to worship God rightly despite the fact that it will disturb civil peace. But the principle assumed here also applies to governments acting against false religion. Civil peace is a good, but civil disturbance is acceptable in the event of suppressing false religion, if the disturbance does not threaten the commonwealth, for the temporary suspension of civil peace serves a higher good, namely, establishing or maintaining the true worship of God. Civil peace can at times (and especially in our time) allow idolatry and degeneracy to spread unhindered.

centuries, inflexibility was a common Roman Catholic position, particularly among Jesuits. Althusius states, for example, that "Franz Burckhard therefore errs, and the Jesuits with him, who think that the magistrate is not able to tolerate diverse religions."[26] This rigid position is natural enough for Roman Catholic theology, which asserted (or asserts) that it is the one true visible church and that anyone who claims Christianity but rejects the bishop of Rome's supremacy is heretical. But in Protestantism the church is essentially invisible and composed of the elect by faith, and belonging to that church is not conditioned on or grounded in one's outward belonging to a visible, centralized, and global communion. Thus, Protestants of different doctrinal persuasions and practices can mutually recognize their shared faith. This is the basis for principled toleration and religious liberty in Protestant commonwealths. Indeed, the unfolding of Protestant principles—not Enlightenment or Roman Catholic "doctrinal development"—is what led Americans to affirm religious liberty in the 18th century, which I demonstrate in the next chapter. The point here is that Protestant magistrates ruling a Protestant people have principled flexibility when faced with religious diversity. Denominational unity might be the best situation, but achieving harmony among differing Protestants is good enough. How a Christian magistrate navigates this complexity requires wisdom, prudence, and resolve.

---

26. Althusius, *Politica*, 174 [28.65]. Burckhard, a Roman Catholic professor at Ingolstadt, is reported to have said, "What more just than to cut off the heads of all these villains of Lutherans!" Quoted in J.H. Merle D'Augbigne, *History of the Reformation in the Sixteenth Century*, trans. Henry Beveridge (Glasgow: William Collins, 1846), 3:130. Burckhard wrote a book titled *De Autonomia* (1586) that called for Roman Catholics to rescind the Peace of Passau (1552), which granted religious freedom to Lutherans within the Holy Roman Empire.

The necessity of prudence raises another set of objections to my argument. Even if we conclude that civil government has a duty to advance the Christian faith, perhaps it does this best by not privileging Christianity. Maybe it serves the church best by maximizing religious liberty, by confining religious instruction and institutionalized Christianity to churches, and by adopting some version of the late-20th-century model of church-state relations in the United States.

Epistemic Limitations

One might, for example, say that the magistrate, even if he is a godly Christian, is practically in no epistemic position to decided disputes between competing religious claims. That is, even if he has the power to act in principle, there is no reason to believe that his judgments will be reliable. He is just as likely to oppose truth as to oppose error. It is better, therefore, never to use this power and to leave religion to civil society. I will address two aspects of this objection. The first is the epistemic and the other is a matter of historical experience.

The godly Christian magistrate, who reigns by the consent of a Christian people, will have reliable knowledge of Christian doctrine. Here is why. As I've said, the First Table is inscripturated natural law. These precepts are, therefore, natural to man as man and are for his good. Scripture clarifies our natural duties to God, telling us to worship him alone, to worship him how he desires to be worshipped, to revere him and all his works, and to set aside a time for his worship. We can expect a Christian magistrate, having this inscripturated clarification, to understand the most basic principles of man's duty in natural religion and to know what clearly violates those duties, namely, (1) atheism, polytheism, and idolatry; (2) strange and profane rites; (3)

blasphemy and sacrilege; and (4) profanation of the Sabbath. These principles and their violations should be indisputable to a Christian magistrate, since they are known (at least vaguely) by natural reason and conscience and clarified in Scripture. Therefore, the Christian magistrate has good and confident epistemic ground to act against those who violate natural religion.

Moving to things of grace, we should distinguish fundamentals and secondary matters. Fundamentals, being necessary for true faith, are perspicuous in Scripture, at least with regard to clear demonstration from Scripture. These are essential to the certitude of faith and so must be knowable with a high degree of confidence, even among the unlearned. How can we insist that regular Christians have confidence in Trinitarian doctrine, justification by faith alone, and the infallibility of the Scriptures and yet deny that confidence to Christian magistrates? And presumably, the Christian magistrate (though not a theologian) would be no regular Christian but educated. He is, therefore, in a good and confident position to decide between disputes as to fundamentals. Thus, a godly civil magistrate will have competence to decide on what pertains to mere Christian orthodoxy.

But what about secondary doctrines? Secondary doctrines are secondary not because we necessarily hold them with less confidence but because they are not absolutely essential to salvation. Thus, one can affirm at least some secondary doctrines with the same degree of certainty as fundamentals, and so the Christian magistrate can determine at least some of them with confidence. Moreover, Protestant principles, when properly applied, will mitigate the harm caused by established errors in secondary doctrines. The most important of these principles is this: Every true believer has an equal right to the means of grace from any true church.[27] This is not a concession or a prudential action but a matter of strict Protestant principle. *All* Christians—those who have a credible profession of faith—have rights to the means of grace upon examination by ministers. Dissenters who are genuine believers cannot be excluded based on disagreement over secondary matters. Indeed, it is a great evil to deny membership to a brother in Christ for no reason but such disagreements. Even the 17th-century Congregationalists of New England, for example, admitted credobaptists into their established churches as *full* members, giving them unhindered access to the means of grace. Of course, I believe that paedobaptism is biblical, so I am not using this as an example of mitigated error. My point is that *if it were false*, its establishment would not separate Baptists from the means of grace. Ensuring equal access to the administration of grace mitigates the consequences of established error. Thus, an established church that is in error on a secondary matter is dangerous to Christian brethren only if that establishment denies dissenting believers access to the means of grace.[28] Further mitigation might include extending toleration to dissenting Christians, allowing them to erect their own churches.

Given these considerations, the prudent Christian magistrate ought to be more willing to risk an error on secondary matters than to remove himself from the Christian religion entirely and risk undermining the Christianity of the commonwealth. An established

---

27. Of course, churches have a right to establish vetting processes for membership. But they should not exclude anyone from that process on account of a disagreement over a secondary matter.

28. This is one reason why forced conformity to adiaphoristic ceremonies and practices proves troublesome to a commonwealth and should be avoided.

church that is a true church, though erroneous on something secondary, is better for a people than having an embattled church or no church at all.

One might point to historical experience to question the wisdom of giving magistrates power in religion. It is true that civil rulers have terrorized consciences and oppressed brethren. False religion and uniformity of adiaphoristic ceremonies have been forced upon peoples, and wars have been fought over doctrine. We should not disregard this experience, but our response should not be to surrender to "neutrality" or political atheism or secularism, which will only spiral civil society into despair, malaise, and a will to die. There is no prudential line from past religious conflict to adopting political atheism or to an incoherent Second Table-onlyism. If the arguments in this book are correct, then a secularist or "neutral" civil government or one that has no cognizance of eternal things *must be bad for people*. Isn't the moral insanity of our time proof enough? As Richard Baxter once said, "It is a *mad commonwealth* . . . that is without a church ministry."[29] Non-religious regimes make earthly things the ultimate end. They make politics a sort of religion—into an abstract, transcendental vision of the good, which is forcibly immanentized into earthly life. By eliminating public religion, secularism generates its own ultimate commitments that are false, idolatrous, and harmful to all but especially and most importantly harmful to the church.

The plausibility of secularism or a "common" public space depends on what Aaron Renn has called the "Neutral World." Renn argues that the "story of American secularization" has three stages:

---

29. Baxter, *A Holy Commonwealth*, 269.

the Positive World (pre-1994), the Neutral World (1994–2014), and the Negative World (2014–present).[30] In the Neutral World, "Christianity no longer has privileged status but is not disfavored . . . . Christianity is a valid option within a pluralistic public square."[31] It is no surprise that within this neutral period several Reformed writers published books calling for Christians to disengage from Christian-oriented political struggles, such as Michael Horton's *Beyond Culture Wars* (1994), D.G. Hart's *A Secular Faith* (2006), and the rise of a novel approach to two-kingdoms theology represented by David VanDrunen's *Living God's Two Kingdoms* (2010). This neutral-world Reformed theology is false in its distinctives, given my arguments in this book (and according to the Reformed tradition itself), but it is increasingly less plausible now that we've entered the Negative World. In this world, says Renn,

> Being known as a Christian is a social negative, particularly in the elite domains of society. Christian morality is expressly repudiated and seen as a threat to the public good and the new public moral order. Subscribing to Christian moral views or violating the secular moral order brings negative consequences.[32]

The "neutral" or "common" space lasted only about twenty years, which shouldn't surprise us: the most common human arrangements in history for public space are decidedly *not* neutral.

---

30. Aaron M. Renn, "The Three Worlds of Evangelicalism," in *First Things*, February 2022, accessed May 28, 2022, https://www.firstthings.com/article/2022/02/the-three-worlds-of-evangelicalism.

31. Ibid.

32. Ibid.

It is a shame that we treated this neutral world as normal and universal and, subsequently, developed dubious theologies around it. Now that we're in the negative world, political theology is predictably moving in neo-Anabaptist directions in an attempt to recover neutrality by neutralizing true religion as a threat to the secularist establishment.

Experience over the last decades has made evident that there are two options: Christian nationalism or pagan nationalism. The totality of national action will be either *Christian*, and thus ordered to the complete good, or *pagan*—ordered to the celebration of degeneracy, child sacrifice (e.g., abortion), mental illness, and idolatry. Neutrality, even if it was real for a time, will never hold, because man by his nature infuses his transcendent concerns into his way of life and into the place of that life. The pagan nationalist rejection of neutrality is correct *in principle*, and Christians ought to abandon their foolish commitment to neutrality, contestability, and viewpoint diversity. In their place, Christians should assert the godly direction for this natural principle, namely, Christian nationalism. Neutral World political theology is simply irrelevant to our new world; it is obsolete. And it did little but encourage people to invest sentiment in what would ultimately turn on them and their children. It instilled patterns of thought that ill-prepared Christians to confront what was coming. It is now a political theology for the historian, not for the theologian or political theorist.

The arguments against Christian nationalism from history are prudential arguments, concluding that secularism is better for Christians than a Christian commonwealth. With the prevailing degeneracy and anti-Christian hostility of our time, this conclusion is at best naive, if not utterly foolish. Hostile liberalism, which is what we're facing now, will do far greater damage to the visible church than a Protestant commonwealth.

Christians have hundreds of years of experience from which to pull to make prudential decisions. In the next chapter, I'll present some of that experience, demonstrating the possibility for a pan-Protestant political order. The early American republic had it right, in my view. But the future Christian nationalism is not a wholesale return to some "golden age," nor is it about conserving the vestiges of Christian morality and culture from past decades. It is a great renewal according to timeliness Christian political principles.

Let the Best Argument Win

Another holdover from the neutral world is the argument that religious liberty or a neutral or "contestable" public square will allow the space for the best argument to win. *If you think that your conclusion is true and that you have the best argument, then what are you afraid of? Why do you have so little confidence in your faith? Let the best argument win the day.* There are several problems with this argument. The first is that it assumes that those participating in the public square have an equal commitment to contestability in that square. The last few decades have shown, however, that only the political conservative cares about contestability, while the political left is very willing to exploit the conservative in order to capture most of the West's institutions. As a result, the left now effectively excludes conservatives from positions of influence and power. Free speech, openness, and contestability were all *means to power* for the left, not principles. But most intellectual conservatives today, naively proclaiming their commitment to principle, continue the same losing struggle for "viewpoint diversity." Most on the left have little interest in it and so conservatives continue to lose. Perhaps the chief end of the conservative is losing with principle.

But let's give the left some credit: They are acting according to good principles. If one is serious about some robust conception of the good, then he should seek to exclude from the public square those whom he deems harmful to that good. To be sure, this praise assumes too much of the left, since their pursuits are likely rooted more in resentment, mental illness, narcissism, and hatred of beauty than in principle. Left-wing politics is the politics of self-harm and "taking revenge against God for the crime of being," as Jordan Peterson once said.[33] But granting them more than they deserve, I'll say that they correctly reject the possibility of neutrality. Most public institutions—such as public education—cannot avoid thick moral norms and narratives and value socialization. Furthermore, the left is correct that disagreement in public discourse must be bounded within an acceptable range of acceptable opinion.

Today, that range happens to exclude all but a few conservatives of the "center-right." These conservatives are acceptable not only because they are the controlled opposition, who provide the appearance of two sides, but because they are active participants in policing the cordon of acceptable opinion. They dutifully denounce anyone to their right. When the left shrieks about the "alt-right," the center-right obediently joins in the shrieking. The conservatives indeed have an acceptable range of discourse, and it just happens to overlap with that

---

33. Andy Ngo, "ANTIFA: The Rise of the Violent Left," interview by Jordan Peterson, *The Jordan B. Peterson Podcast*, March 28, 2022, https://youtu.be/FE_UjbQSf2w.

of the left.[34] Progressive liberalism determines the acceptable range of opinion today, demanding that acceptable pundits on the right focus their efforts on attacking the "far right." They must also have the same general concerns as the left (e.g., "democracy," racial justice, and LGBTQ rights), though they are allowed to have more "free market" solutions. The American regime is tolerant of a few regime-faithful "center-right" Christian pundits who are anti-abortion, because they know that being anti-abortion is necessary to operate as an insider among conservative Christians, and being an insider allows them to critique "their own" from secularist publications on behalf of the regime. The left-right fights in popular media give the appearance of wide disagreement, but this is a show, an illusion. The "liberal democratic" regime that we live in today has a narrow range of acceptable opinion, because it is ordered according to a secularist notion of the good. "Legitimate," "credible," "good faith," and "winsome" speech is speech that, in one way or another, is ordered to the secularist vision of the good. The constraints for this vision are difficult to see because we are all enmeshed in them.

Christian nationalism does not deny the good of viewpoint diversity. But, as with the American regime, the acceptable range ought to be bounded by principles of inclusion and exclusion. One of those principles is the primacy of Christian peoplehood, and so Christian nationalism will exclude at least the following from acceptable opinion and action: (1) political atheism, (2)

---

34. There is only a superficial difference between left and center-right on enforcing this range. The conservatives will say that *legally* we ought to have maximal freedom of speech, but they have little concern over the *de facto* regulators of acceptable opinion, such as big-tech companies, the mainstream media, and academic institutions, who regularly "cancel" right-wing speech. Practically speaking, center-right legal principles do very little to protect any speech to the right.

subversion of public Christianity, (3) opposition to Christian morality, (4) heretical teaching, and (5) the political and social influence of non-Christian religion and its adherents. Of course, the range and type of diversity allowed is a matter of prudence and collective experience. The purpose here is not to stifle public debate but to maintain conditions for public debate to serve a Christian people. Public debate is a means, and as such it ought to conduce to what is good. I affirm, therefore, that there ought to be freedom of speech and, as with all societies and institutions, that freedom must be bounded prudently such that public discourse conduces to what is good.[35]

The fact that the Protestant tradition considers persuasion to be essential to the advancement of the Gospel does not require a neutral or contestable public square of purely disinterested minds

---

35. As for the free speech clause in the First Amendment, I agree with Joseph Story, the great commentator on the US Constitution, that it "was intended to secure to every citizen an absolute right to speak, or write, or print, whatever he might please, without any responsibility, public or private, therefor [sic], is a supposition too wild to be indulged by any rational man. . . . It is plain, then, that the language of this amendment imports no more, than that every man shall have a right to speak, write, and print his opinions upon any subject whatsoever, without any prior restraint, so always, that he does not injure any other person in his rights, person, property, or reputation; and so always, that he does not thereby disturb the public peace, or attempt to subvert the government. . . . But to punish any dangerous or offensive writings, which, when published, shall, on a fair and impartial trial, be adjudged of a pernicious tendency, is necessary for the preservation of peace and good order, of government and religion, the only solid foundations of civil liberty. Thus, the will of individuals is still left free; the abuse only of that free will is the object of legal punishment. Neither is any restraint hereby laid upon freedom of thought or inquiry; liberty of private sentiment is still left; the disseminating, or making public of bad sentiments, destructive of the ends of society, is the crime, which society corrects. A man may be allowed to keep poisons in his closet; but not publicly to vend them as cordials." See his *Commentaries on the Constitution of the United States* (Boston: Hilliard, Gray, 1833), 3:731–32, 736.

exchanging reasons for this or that belief. Neutrality or hostility to the faith is not a prerequisite for genuine persuasion, and it is typically a hindrance. Prejudice for Christianity, being preparative, is a great help in persuading one to Christianity. And since the public square can never be neutral, for it will always dispose people to beliefs (whether true or false), a Christian public square—reflecting a normalized Christianity—eliminates the abuse of social power for satanic ends and orders people rightly to trust in Christ.

They Will Use It Against You

The best version of this objection, which is rarely articulated well, is that the power we use to suppress heresy or secularism will eventually be used *against* orthodoxy, because we have set a precedent for that use of power. Of course, the abuse of a thing does not negate the thing itself. But that reply misses the point. The objection affirms the permissibility but denies the prudence of using such power. My response is simple: The power in question is already being used in the West to exclude religion from public life, culture, and institutions. The precedent is already set. Furthermore, the fact that power could be used for evil is trivially true. The power to restrain murderers could be used to aid murderers. At this time, power is wielded against the church. Let us wield power in support of the church.

IV. Specific Groups

This section applies my discussion of principle and prudence to specific groups, namely, heretics, non-Christians, dissenting Christians, and conforming Christians.

Heretics

Heretics are those who profess the Christian religion but have religious opinions that are either soul-damning or, if not in themselves damning, dangerous to the soul. As I've said, the magistrate as magistrate has no interest in heretical belief itself (as an inward error) but only public heresy (the outward expression of error). The belief itself harms no one except the man who holds it, which is a matter between him and God. But public heresy has the potential to harm other's souls by causing doubt or distraction or by disrupting public peace. The magistrate, who must care for the souls of his people, may act to suppress that heresy.

The Reformed tradition has a long and widely acknowledged practice of ministers admonishing and disputing with heretics prior to magistrates exercising the sword. This practice recognizes a few things: (1) the exclusive and effective power of the Word to convict and reform hearts; (2) a care for the heretic's soul; and (3) that teaching, correcting, and admonishing with regard to spiritual things are duties of ministers, not magistrates. "In vain," writes Calvin, "will the magistrate employ the sword, which undoubtedly he must employ, to restrain wicked teachers and false prophets ... unless this sword of the word go before"[36] and elsewhere, "Now both prudence and gentleness is [sic] to be exactly preserved by us, there is no doubt that a mild and religious knowledge of doctrine

36. Calvin, *Commentary on the Prophet Isaiah*, 1:381 [on Isa. 11:4]. Similarly, Althusius writes, "Those who err in religion are therefore to be ruled not by external force or by corporal arms, but by the sword of the spirit, that is, by the Word and spiritual arms through which God is able to lead them to himself. They are to be entrusted to ministers of the Word of God for care and instruction. If they cannot be persuaded by the Word of God, how much less can they be coerced by the threats or punishments of the magistrate to think or believe what he or some other person believes." *Politica*, 172–73 [28.64].

ought to go before judgment."[37] If these efforts fail and the heretic publicly persists, then the magistrate may take steps to punishment him. But his direct intent is neither to punish false belief itself nor to reform the heretic's soul but to safeguard the souls of the spiritually weak or to eliminate some outward evil such as subversion. As Turretin states,

> Although [the magistrate] does not have a right over the soul, he has [a right] over the tongue, as over the hand; and he can punish the heretic teaching another doctrine no less than the thief who steals another's property, or the robber who kills a man, because he corrupts society, the care of which the magistrate ought to have.[38]

Recoiling from the idea of civil action against heretical teaching, modern Christians might ask, "Doesn't Christian kindness call for radical forbearance?" In reply, I ask, "What principle backs this question? By what principle do we treat the harm of public heresy differently than Second Table harms? Do we forbear murderers or rapists?" While gentleness and respect are required when addressing the error, it does not sheath the magistrate's sword, if a real harm is expected. "Cruel is the mercy," writes Turretin, "which exposes the sheep as a prey that the wolf may be appeased."[39]

The degree and type of response depends on the type of heretic. We have all encountered Christians who speak serious error out of ignorance or youthful zeal. Theodore Beza wisely says,

37. John Calvin, quoted in Turretin, *IET*, 3:18.34.43. See also Bullinger, *Decades*, 1:360–63 [Second Decade, Sermon viii].

38. Turretin, *IET*, 3:18.34.34.

39. Ibid.

> Far be it from us to arm the magistrate against those who sin
> even from simplicity rather than from wickedness, without in-
> juring others and without old blasphemy. We are not so foolish,
> nor do we divest ourselves of all feeling of humanity; nay, we
> wish all milder remedies to be first applied even to contagious
> and moral diseases and to be directed to the glory of God and
> the love of our neighbor.[40]

Reformed theologians of the 16th and 17th centuries considered themselves the moderates with regard to action against heretics. Of course, by today's standards, they were extremists. But they regularly distinguished themselves from Roman Catholics, whom they accused of homicidal persecution. One might cite the shameful persecution of the Albigensians and the Waldensians in which hundreds were tortured by fire and other means by order of the bishop of Rome. Francisco Suárez, a Spanish Jesuit, laid down principles that justify such persecutions: (1) "That all heretics, who after sufficient instruction and admonition, still persist in their error, are to be without mercy put to death"; (2) "That all impenitent heretics, though they profess to be Catholics, being convicted of heresy, are to be put to death"; and (3) "That relapsing heretics, though penitent, are to be put to death without mercy."[41] Turretin rightly accused Roman Catholics of

> barbarity and cruelty [which] is repugnant to the spirit of
> Christianity and the design of the gospel, which is to save,

40. Theodore Beza, *De haereticis a civili magisratu puniendis* (1554), quoted in Turretin, *IET*, 3:18.34.43.

41. Francisco Suárez, quoted in George Gillespie, *Wholesome Severity Reconciled with Christian Liberty* (1645; Dallas: Naphtali Press, 1997). This is Gillespie's translation of lines from Suárez's *De triplice virtute theologia*, tract. 1, disp. 23, sec. 2.

not to destroy; to allure men to the faith by the word, but not to compel them by the sword; to destroy errors and vices, but to spare persons as far as possible. It belongs to Mohammed to advance with slaughter and blood and to establish his empire by cruelty and torments. But Christ reigns in us by the Spirit of grace and love. He seeks the salvation of men, not their blood.[42]

One might be surprised to read that Calvin himself distinguished "three grades of errors": some deserving "pardon" on account of ignorance and weakness; others who require a "moderate chastisement"; and some that require "capital punishment."[43] The Reformed position on civil action against heretics is not akin to crusading, or to some divinely commanded holy war, or to an inquisition. It is based on practical considerations of public harm caused by public error and on the limitations of civil action for spiritual reformation. Only the sword of the Spirit reforms hearts. The civil sword can act against heretics but not as an instrument of vertical divine justice upon the enemies of God; rather it acts as a means to safeguard the souls of those under the magistrate's care. Hence, the practice of suppressing heresy, according to Reformed political theology, is flexible—a matter of prudence, not a matter of rigid duty and brute divine command.

To be sure, Reformed writers generally approved of capital punishment for heresy, but they reserved this punishment only for the fanatically determined sort, what they called the "arch-heretics." Calvin writes,

42. John Calvin, quoted in Turretin, *IET*, 3:18.34.36.
43. Ibid, 18.34.33.

> Where religion is torn from her foundations, detestable blasphemies against God are indulged in, souls hurried to destruction by impious and pestiferous doctrines, finally where defection from the sole God and pure doctrine is openly essayed, it is necessary to descend to that extreme remedy that such poison may spread no farther.[44]

Arch-heretics are publicly persistent in their damnable error and actively seek to convince others of this error, to subvert the established church, to denounce its ministers, or to instigate rebellion against magistrates. For this reasons, they can be justly put to death.[45] This is a remedy to stop the "poison," as Calvin said. Turretin cites a great number of Reformed theologians who supported capital punishment for arch-heretics: Zanchi, Becanus, Bullinger, Beza, Franciscus Junius, Danaeus, Gerhard, Bucer, and Melanchthon.[46] This is not to say that capital punishment is the necessary, sole, or desired punishment. Banishment and long-term imprisonment may suffice as well. And perhaps a Christian people may consider some heretics harmless, or they might conclude that suppressing heresy is, in at least some cases, more harmful than the heresy itself. The crucial point here is that civil action against heretics is justified in principle but the practice of it requires considerable discernment, care, gentleness, and prudence. I say this not to place doubt on the action but simply to establish the appropriate principles and heart toward error and the proper process in addressing it.

44. John Calvin, quoted ibid.
45. Turretin writes, they "not only pertinaciously defend the errors which they cherish, but also whenever as opportunity is presented, strive to spread them against admonitions and prohibition often repeated, polluting heaven and earth by their horrible blasphemies, and who under this pretext excite disturbances and seditions in the state." Ibid., 18.34.31.
46. Ibid., 18.34.48.

Non-Christians

Those who do not profess Christianity and yet actively proselytize their non-Christian religion or belief system or actively seek to refute the Christian religion are subject to the same principles outlined above. They are not technically heretics, but they are doing the same class of actions and, for that reason, are subject to the same process and punishments. The purpose is neither to compel faith nor to punish them for their rejection of Christianity but rather to suppress or eliminate any influence they may have upon Christian society. This is not because Christians lack confidence in Christian truth but because the Christian commonwealth sets preparative conditions for the reception of Christian faith and encourages people in that faith.

The political status of non-Christians in a Christian commonwealth is a matter of prudence. Since civil society is a human institution, it must guarantee equal protection and due process with regard to human things for all people. That is, it must guarantee justice and secure natural rights. But this does not entail equal participation, status, and standing in political, social, and cultural institutions. Only Christians can be expected to take an interest in conserving the explicit Christian character and ends of these institutions and of society. Furthermore, non-Christians may exercise natural rights insofar that their exercise coheres with the common good, and the common good includes the Christian religion. This limitation on exercising rights is true of *all* people as to principle, regardless of religion, though non-Christians are more limited in application due to their rejection of Christianity. Thus, they are guaranteed a basic right to life and property (the absence of which would harm the common good), but they may be denied by law to conduct certain activities that could exploit or harm Christians or the Christian religion.

This position, though fairly standard in the Christian tradition until recently, will be received with controversy today, and few would stomach any *legal* discrimination on the basis of religion. But even in the absence of legal distinctions, the cultural norms of a Christian nation will require non-Christians to be the exceptions to the norm. Thus, for example, were a public school to put on a Christmas play, non-Christians might be exempted by request though not necessarily granted a publicly funded alternative.

Dissenting Christians

Dissenting Christians are true Christians who dissent from the established church. They are not heretical, for their differences are not damnable, nor do they place the soul in serious danger. Yet they disagree on some key or important doctrines. The best example would be the Particular Baptists living in Congregationalist New England, which I discuss in the next chapter.

As with heretics and non-Christians, it would be wrong to punish dissenters for no reason but that they have erroneous opinions. Indeed, this would properly be called "persecution." And since their views are not heretical, the justification to suppress them must not be protecting Christian souls from damnable error. There must be something about the error that harms the particular arrangements of society, its good order and discipline, or the administration of the churches properly established. Appropriate action with regard to dissent depends on circumstances, such as the particular character and ends of the civil society and the constitution of the civil polity. Active suppression at times might be appropriate (e.g., early New England), while complete toleration might be more suitable at other times (e.g., early American republic).

Wide toleration is desirable, in my view, for it displays the beauty of Protestant theology—that differing brethren can recognize their mutual union with Christ and live together in peace. Burroughs reminds us that "certainly in the variety of the practices of Brethren in such things as we are speaking of, tuned with brotherly love one towards another, there will be a sweet harmony."[47] We are, after all, fellow Christians and ought to exercise love and forbearance. As John Davenant once wrote, "The bond of the brotherly communion of Christian Churches ought not to be dissolved upon every difference of opinion, but only for the denying or opposing Fundamentals."[48]

Protestant harmony amid diversity does not require disestablishment. But granting religious liberty to all orthodox Christians, if deemed suitable, would effectively end dissension, as I've defined it, and create a sort of pan-Protestant civil society. This is precisely what I hope for future arrangements in North America. Still, there are times when establishment is necessary and good.[49]

47. Burroughs, *Irenicum*, 17.

48. John Davenant, *Exhortation to Brotherly Love amongst Churches*, chap. 10, and quoted in and translated by Burroughs in *Irenicum*, 56. Burroughs rightly said, "In things controversial and doubtful amongst godly and peaceable men, though there should be a declaration of difference of judgement, and some different practice, yet there is to be a forbearance of compulsory violence; we must not be to one another in such things as these are, as that Giant we read of, who laid upon a bed all he took, and those who were too long, he cut them even with his bed, and such as were too short, he stretched them out to the length of it. Verily this is cruelty, God hath not made men all of a length nor height; men's parts, gifts, graces differ; men's tempers, apprehensions, educations are various, and if there be no suffering one another in things not clear, all the world must needs be quarrelling, there will be strengthening interests, sidings and opposing one another continually, except not only men's bodies and estates, but their very souls also be brought under sordid slavery" (p. 55).

49. For example, the public funding of church ministry ensures that sparsely populated and poorer areas have qualified ministers.

Conforming Christians

Magistrates punish sins of commission and sins of omission with regard to external religion. The former applies both to those who profess and do not profess the Christian religion. My discussion so far has dealt with these people. But sins of omission pertain to public actions expected of Christians, such as attending church. In punishing omissions, the magistrate has not claimed the authority to force men positively to the external worship of God. Indeed, as Rutherford said, "[T]he magistrate as the magistrate does not command these outward performances as services to God,"[50] for civil power cannot command man to an inward end, which is required to truly serve God in external worship. Worship is, as Tertullian said, "by will not by force."[51] Rather, the civil magistrate forbids these omissions negatively, viz., he punishes them for being detrimental to Christian society. The flagrant violation of Christian duty is a poor example to others and it harms Christian civil community. In other words, the magistrate punishes for the violation not of failing to worship itself but because the failure to attend violates a fundamental norm of Christian civil community. The magistrate's ultimate goal, as with all his commands, is ordering his people to eternal life, but the object of and reason for the command is maintaining Christian civil community.

There is a legitimate question about who can be subject to punishment for sins of omission, for such people are presumed to be Christians. This requires some theology that I'd prefer left to the theologians. But I will say that the Presbyterian and Anglican models, in which the baptized are presumed to be part of the *corpus Christianum*, better cohere with and make possible a stricter and

50. Rutherford, *Free Disputation Against Pretended Liberty of Conscience*, 51.
51. Tertullian, quoted by Rutherford in ibid., 50-51.

closer church-state relation. Also, all the baptized would seem to be able to commit sins of omission, and so punishment is not limited to confirmed members but to nonmembers as well. We can then distinguish between full participants and mere attenders, the former being those who are approved to participate in the Lord's Supper and the latter are those who attend only for the sermons. Magistrates can require that everyone who is baptized will attend, even those who are unconfirmed by the church and not allowed to participate in the Supper. They, after all, are baptized into the visible church with obligations to the people of God.

V. Conclusion

I will stress for the last time that the central point of this chapter is an outline of principles, not a blueprint for action. This follows my principle throughout this work, that each people-group must decide for themselves how they will govern and arrange themselves. Making these decisions requires people to consider their experience as a people and the circumstance in which they find themselves. The next chapter will get more people specific. I will show that principle concerning religious liberty at the American founding was both Protestant in principle and Anglo-Protestant in application, and thus the American political tradition, as least in its early era, is consistent with and a resource for an American Christian nationalist project today.

10

The Foundation of American Freedom: Anglo-Protestant Experience

"In the United States the influence of religion is not confined to the manners, but it extends to the intelligence of the people.... Christianity, therefore, reigns without any obstacle, by universal consent." —Alexis de Tocqueville[1]

I. Introduction

The theoretical argument of this work being complete, I now turn to my country. Throughout this book I've suggested that we must return to the old Protestant principles of our spiritual forefathers and that we must apply them, with prudence and resolve, according

1. Alexis de Tocqueville, *Democracy in America*, trans. Henry Reeve (New York: Bantam Dell, 2004), 1:354.

to our own particularity and circumstances. Many American Christians, however, question whether there can be an American Christian nationalism. Does the American political tradition permit a Christian self-conception, Christian governments, and church establishments? One popular narrative is that the American founding was anti-establishment and secularist and reflects the influence of "Enlightenment philosophy." How can we get Christian nationalism out of that? But that narrative is false, as this chapter shows. This chapter is not, however, an attempt to answer the question, "Is America a Christian nation?" It is evident enough that for most of United States history Americans thought of themselves as a Christian people. Historian John Fea, who himself is no fan of Christian nationalism, said that

> [t]hose who believe that the United States is a Christian nation have a good chunk of American history on their side. . . .
> Christians believed [throughout the 19th and 20th centuries] that they were living in the Christian nation. A close look at the historical record suggests that they were probably right.[2]

---

2. John Fea, *Was American Founded as a Christian Nation? A Historical Introduction*, rev. ed. (Louisville: Westminster John Knox Press, 2016), 245. He also states that "[t]oday's Christian nationalists have a good portion of American history on their side. . . . Christianity, and particularly Protestant evangelicalism, defined the culture [between 1789 and 1861]" (4); "The idea that the United States was a 'Christian nation' was central to American identity in the years between the Revolution and the Civil War" (p. 4); "As the people of the United States entered the twentieth century, they never abandoned their commitment, dating back over one hundred years, to the proposition that the United States was a Christian nation" (42); "Those who argue that the United States is a Christian nation have some strong historical evidence on which to rely" (56); and "When it comes to the individual states [at the time of the founding], today's defenders of Christian America have a compelling case" (246).

"Is America *now* a Christian nation?" is a question I'll reserve for another time. Certainly there is at least one Christian nation in America. Here I want to show that the American political tradition can support Christian nationalism and provide resources for an American Christian nationalist project.

Since so much of the concern over Christian nationalism is how religion relates to civil government, this chapter shows (1) that the American political tradition, at least as it concerns religious liberty, is based in Protestantism, not secularism or the Enlightenment; and (2) that the development of religious liberty, which culminated in the founding era, constitutes a unique and principled Anglo-Protestant development of classical Protestant principles. Thus, this principled development is both Protestant and American, and it permits an American version of Christian nationalism. American Christian nationalists, therefore, do not need to reject their origins or their political tradition (at least not entirely). The Anglo-Protestant experience that culminated in the American founding is a resource for ideas, political arrangements, pride, and the spirit for return.

Views at the Founding

Though the American founding fathers were unanimous in supporting religious toleration, their unanimity on the government's role in religion ended there. There were two seemingly contrary views. The question in the founding era on religious liberty was, to put it simply: establishment or non-establishment? This language of "establishment" in the American context referred not to the old Erastian kind—with the magistrate as the ruler over the church. Rather, establishment typically referred to "plural establishment" in which all (or property-owners only) pay taxes that support the denomination of each person's choosing. This led to the *de facto* establishment of the majority's denomination, albeit with the right of free exercise for others. In my estimation, the majority position in the founding generation affirmed some form of establishment at the colony-state level. A few important founders, such as Madison and Jefferson, took the minority position: strict separation by non-establishment (viz., no public support for any denomination). The minority position has received the most attention in scholarship and in American jurisprudence, and the most common opinion among scholars is that Enlightenment philosophy (especially Lockean) is what most shaped founding-era discourse on religious liberty. This betrays several confusions, most of which I cannot address here.

Both the majority and minority positions rely on standard positions in historic, classical Protestantism. Indeed, contrary to most accounts, the founders even applied the *same* principles as their Puritans forefathers, and the majority position (as to it principles) is thoroughly consistent with classical Protestantism.[3] This might be surprising, since the New England Puritans suppressed dissenters, and the founders affirmed wide toleration or liberty. But this reflects only a discontinuity of application, not of principles. The expansion of religious liberty in the late 18th and early 19th centuries was a product of Anglo-Protestant experience, constituting an unfolding (not undermining) of Protestant principles. Thus, the American tradition of religious liberty, at least into the founding era, reflects a people-specific development—a particularity arising from a people applying universal principles

3. The minority position is largely consistent as well, though it breaks with the past by conflating inward liberty and outward liberty. I show this below.

for themselves over time. To show this, we begin with the New England Puritans.

II. Puritan New England and Free Expression

Consistent with the Reformed tradition, the New England Puritans denied that civil government can punish anyone simply for erroneous belief, and they denied that it can coerce the conscience for any reason, including to reform it.[4] Religious belief was a matter of persuasion, not coercion, even after baptism and church membership. This is why church ministers, armed with the Word, were always first to attempt the reformation of erring minds and hearts, and civil authorities would step in only if they remained publicly obstinate and a disruption to the ordinary life of the community.[5] The 1649 *Platform of Church Discipline*, written in part by New England minister John Cotton, states that "[t]he objects of the power of the magistrate are not things merely inward, and so not subject to his cognizance and views: as unbelief, hardness of heart, erroneous opinions not vented, *but only such things as are acted by the outward man*."[6] Cotton denied

---

4. John Cotton writes, "Nor doth the civil state in such punishments attend so much how to procure the conversion of heretics, or apostates, or such like scandalous turbulent offenders: as how to prevent the perversion of their sounder people." *Bloudy Tenent Washed*, 1.20, spelling modernized.

5. This is precisely what happened in the Antinomian Controversy. The clergy debated the issues in 1636. Only when acrimony was at its highest did the General Court of the Massachusetts Bay Colony step in, ordering a fast-day in January 19, 1637—the day on which John Wheelwright gave a sermon that, at least in the eyes of the New England authorities, was seditious. This sermon ultimately led to his and Anne Hutchinson's banishment.

6. John Cotton, Richard Mather, and Ralph Partridge, "A Platform of Church Discipline," in *The American Republic: Primary Sources*, ed. Bruce Frohnen (Indianapolis: Liberty Fund, 2002), 63, emphasis added.

that magistrates can "compel their subjects to become church-members." They can restrain all outward "idolatry, blasphemy, [and] heresy," for these ordinarily disturb "the peaceable administration and exercise of the worship and holy things of God."[7]

In every famous incident in which New England authorities "persecuted" dissenters—Roger Williams, Antinomians, Quakers, and Baptists—the authorities claimed to have good *civil* grounds to suppress the expression of dissenting religious belief. Roger Williams was sectarian and seditious.[8] The Antinomians were subversive and undermined civil obedience and discipline.[9] The Quakers were wild and disruptive.[10] The Anabaptists undermined ecclesi-

7. Ibid.

8. Roger Williams claimed that he was banished for affirming that "the civil magistrate's power extends only to the bodies, and goods, and outward estates of men." Cotton flatly denies this, saying that such people "are tolerated not only to live in the commonwealth, but also in the fellowship of the churches," making this "no cause at all" for his banishment. John Cotton, "A Reply to Mr. Williams His Examination; And Answer of the Letters Sent To Him," (London, 1643), in *Bloudy Tenent Washed*, 2.26, spelling modernized. Cotton insists that Williams was banished mainly because he publicly and relentlessly denounced the patent for the colony issued by King Charles I in 1629. The New England authorities concluded that Williams's manner of publicizing his views "subverted the fundamental state, and the government of the country" (II.28). The second reason for his banishment was his preaching against taking a civil oath of loyalty, claiming that it violated the third commandment. The New England authorities concluded, according to Cotton, that his views were "dangerous, because they tended to unsettle all the kingdoms and commonwealths of Europe" (2.29).

9. In John Winthrop's official account, he states that "this case was not [a] matter of conscience, but of a civil nature." The chief concern, and what motivated the New England authorities to act, was the threat of civil war. He writes, "The wars in Germany for these hundred years arose from dissentions in religion, and though in the beginning of the contention, they drew out only the sword of the spirit, yet it was soon changed into a sword of steel." *A Short Story of the Rise, Reign, and Ruin of the Antinomians, Familists, and Libertines That Infected the Churches of New-England* (1644; London: Tho. Parkhurst, 1692), 48, 56.

10. Cotton Mather, who was against "hereticide," said that the Quakers "manifest[ed] an intolerable contempt of authority, and needlessly pull upon themselves a vengeance"

astical discipline. In their accounts of these events, New England authorities denied that they conducted persecution; rather, they suppressed those who (in their minds) disturbed the peace of the church and the state.

Doctrinal purity was not required to join the New England churches, and indeed these churches regularly extended the benefits of spiritual administration to dissenters, including full membership. New England churches received Antinomians and Baptists into Congregationalist churches, and Presbyterian churches had their own ministries.[11] This justified their refusal to allow dissenters the right to constitute their own churches: New England ministers recognized them as brothers in Christ (except the Quakers) and made the means of grace available to them. Though New England denied Baptists from constituting their own religious assemblies (at least in some places), they never denied any Christian, including credible believing Baptists, full access to the ordinary means of grace. In this way, New England was able to retain an exclusive establishment, while also ensuring that all credible believers were spiritually fed.

and thus they deserved some kind of civil correction. *Magnalia Christi Americana: Or, the Ecclesiastical History of New-England* (1702; Hartford: Silas Andrus, 1820), 2:453. Samuel Sewall wrote in his diary that "a female quaker, Margaret Brewster, in sermon-time came in, in a canvas frock, her hair dishevelled loose like a Periwig, her face as black as ink, led by two other quakers, and two other quakers followed. It occasioned the greatest and most amazing uproar that I ever saw." *The Diary of Samuel Sewall* (New York: Farrar, Straus, and Giroux, 1973), 1:44 [July 8, 1677].

11. Cotton writes, "Nor is it true, that we suffer no man of any different conscience or worship to live in our jurisdiction. For not to speak of Presbyterians, who do not only live amongst us, but exercise their public ministry without disturbance, there be Anabaptists, and Antinomians tolerated to live not only in our jurisdictions, but even in some of our churches." *Bloudy Tenent Washed*, 1.165, spelling modernized.

Baptists in Congregationalist New England

Baptists in Puritan New England played an important role in early American experience. Baptists today like to claim that their arguments for religious liberty won the day in the 18th century. But, in my view, this is false. Baptists convinced the paedobaptist core not by argument but by actions that they could be safely brought into a Protestant political order. It wasn't Baptist theology but the capacious principles of classical Protestantism that led to the widespread acceptance of toleration and religious liberty. Here is a brief summary of how that happened.

The conflict between paedobaptists and credobaptists in 17th-century New England was less about credobaptist belief itself than about the sort of ecclesiology entailed in credobaptism. While the paedobaptist churches could acknowledge the baptism of the credobaptist—since paedobaptists baptize infants *and* adults—the credobaptist could not reciprocate. The credobaptist could not acknowledge the legitimacy of any infant baptism, and so they could not acknowledge the baptism of most paedobaptists in New England. And since baptism is required for church membership and participation in the Lord's Supper, the credobaptist could not admit to full membership or have full communion with those who were baptized as infants.

This important difference led many credobaptists to "unchurch all the faithful upon the earth besides themselves," as Cotton Mather said, for only properly administered baptism can mark off the "visible saints." Since they "declared infant baptism to be a mere nullity, . . . with them therefore our churches were no churches of the Lord Jesus Christ, nor are there any visible saints among us." Mather states that "they would not own" that "the churches of

New-England [are] true churches." Credobaptists were, therefore, not only unable to admit into their churches those baptized as infants; they were unable to reciprocate ecclesiastical communion, even informally. They would not recognize the established churches as true churches. The established New England churches, however, would let Baptists "enjoy all the ordinances in the fellowship of our churches," states Cotton Mather. But many credobaptists refused because they could not "communicate with [one who was baptized as an infant] at the table of the Lord." That is, since the Lord's Supper is only for the truly baptized, the credobaptist could not share the table with those who were baptized as infants. But in the mind of Cotton Mather and other New England ministers, the Congregationalist churches made ecclesiastical unity possible, for they were able to accommodate credobaptist beliefs. The nature of the disagreement made established Congregationalism more suitable for civil union and stability. Cotton Mather even says that he was willing to permit Baptists to "withdraw when an infant was baptized."[12]

New England authorities concluded that the existence of credobaptist churches threatened civil unity. Denying the legitimacy of your fellows' baptism might undermine the credibility of the ecclesiastical and civil leadership. Baptists churches might also consider themselves purer than the established church, leading to sectarianism and civil discord. New England had learned quite a lot from their disputes with Roger Williams, whose radical views of church purity generated contention in Boston and Salem. For these reasons, laws against preaching credobaptism were justified on grounds of civil unity and peace.

12. All the quotes in this paragraph are from Mather, *Magnalia Christi Americana*, 2:533.

The conflicts between Baptists and the New England authorities are most visible from 1665 to 1679. The dispute culminated in the published *Narrative* by John Russel, who was a church officer in a Baptist church in Boston, and in a published reply to the narrative written by Samuel Willard (prefaced by Increase Mather, Cotton Mather's father). The narrative and reply follow a familiar pattern from previous incidents: The dissenters claim that they were persecuted for their beliefs, and the authorities deny it. In the reply, *Ne sutor ultra crepidam* (published in 1681), Increase Mather and Willard are evidently exasperated at the charge of persecution. Increase claims that the Baptists' narrative is "fallacious" and has "grievously offended God," for its errors and misrepresentations were easily avoidable: "[R]ight information was easy to have been obtained."[13]

A letter attached to the narrative charges the New England churches with "molestation" against Baptists "merely for supposed error about the subject of baptism" and "for one Protestant congregation . . . persecut[ing] another."[14] Increase states that in the "twenty years" of his ministry in New England, he never saw "any of those that scruple infant-baptism . . . met with molestation from the magistrate merely on the account of their opinion." He says that he "would speak to them as unto brethren . . . whom I love." According to Increase (and Willard), the magistrates acted against the Baptists on this occasion because the Baptists accepted into membership those whom the established churches had excommunicated for "moral scandals." Willard provides the details. Increase states that

13. Increase Mather, "To the Reader," in Samuel Willard, *Ne sutor ultra crepidam* (Boston: S. Green, 1681), n.p., spelling modernized.

14. "Christian Reader," in John Russell, *A Brief Narrative* (London: J.D., 1680), n.p.

should men of any other persuasion whatsoever have done the like, the same severity would have been used towards them. . . . [I]f any men, either of the Presbyterian or Congregational . . . persuasion in matters referring to church-discipline should behave themselves as the Anabaptists in Boston, in New-England, have done, I think they would have deserved far greater punishment than any thing that to this day that been inflicted upon them.[15]

Increase, therefore, denies that the magistrates persecuted the Baptists for religious beliefs, and he expects that all would agree that their actions were appropriate or at least understandable.

Increase asks the Baptists to consider the New England perspective, providing us an insightful passage on the possibilities of toleration and religious uniformity in New England Puritan thought. It is worth quoting in full:

It is evident that toleration is in one place not only lawful, but a necessary duty, which in another place would be destructive; and the expectation of it irrational. That which is needful to ballast a great ship, will sink a small boat. If a considerable number of Antipaedobaptists should (as our fathers did) obtain liberty from the state to transport themselves and families into a vast American wilderness, that so they might be a peculiar people by themselves practicing all and only the institutions of Christ: if now paedobaptists should come after them, and intrude themselves upon them, and when they cast men out of their society for moral scandals, entertain them: Surely they

15. Samuel Willard, *Ne sutor ultra crepidam* (Boston: S. Green, 1681), n.p., spelling modernized.

would desire such persons either to walk orderly with them, or to return to the place from whence they came. And if they would do neither, they would think that such paedobaptists were blame-worthy: let them then do as they would be done by; and deal by us, as they would have us to deal by them; were they in our case and we in theirs.[16]

Besides making a strikingly Christian nationalist statement, Increase acknowledges that tolerating dissenting religion is sometimes both right and necessary, but only if the circumstances call for such toleration. The metaphor of the two ships is instructive: what makes a large ship seaworthy will sink a small one. A large and religiously diverse people require wide toleration to maintain civil peace. Imposing religious uniformity on such people would result in civil disturbance and possibly even revolution. But when the community is small and religiously homogeneous, the same degree of toleration will destroy civil stability and tranquility. The same civil end—peace—requires different policies in different circumstances.

Increase may have had in mind a letter sent to New England clergy in 1669 from important English Congregationalists, John Owen and Thomas Goodwin, who urged New England to adopt toleration. Owen and Goodwin, along with the Baptists, faced persecution in England following the interregnum period. Increase admits that these Congregationalists "plead for Anabaptist liberty as for their own." He even agrees with them to a point: "That they plead for liberty and indulgence to be extended towards those that differ from them only in that point of paedo-baptism, I believe: when I was in England, I did so my self; and if I were their [sic] now, I

16. Ibid.

would do so again." But England is not New England. Denying toleration is necessary for New England, a "peculiar" people who traveled across the Atlantic "to walk orderly" in a particular way.[17]

We see that Increase affirms (1) that political arrangements must conform to and adjust with circumstances, and (2) that opposing policies (e.g., toleration and non-toleration) can be consistent applications of the same principle. Presumably, if religious diversity increased in New England (contrary to his wishes), Increase would not oppose the expansion of religious toleration; and as we will see, it does and so he comes to support toleration. He is willing to extend "liberty" to the Baptists in New England, given the right conditions; but the conditions in New England in the 1670s and 1680s required restriction of free exercise in the interest of the community.

We should also notice that Increase's argument assumes a sort of Christian nationalism—that a particular people have a right to their particularity, and outsiders wishing to reside with them must conform to their way of life. If they don't, the whole order can collapse or suffer. Increase appeals to a universal principle: that outsiders ought to respect the communities they enter, which further assumes a right of difference and a right of exclusion based on the good of particularity.

Ordination of Elisha Callender

A few decades later, Cotton Mather, the son of Increase Mather, is giving the ordination sermon for a Baptist entering Baptist ministry in a Baptist church. Affixed to this sermon upon its publications is a preface written by none other than Increase, who approved of his son's actions and was present at the ordination. Cotton's

17. Ibid.

participation in the 1718 ordination of Elisha Callender (a Boston native) is an important event in American history, representing a change in sentiment from earlier generations.[18]

Near the end of the sermon Cotton Mather states that "good men, alas, good men have done such ill things as these," that is, "inflict[ed] uneasy circumstances" upon dissenters. "Yea, few churches of the Reformation have been wholly clear of the iniquities. New England also has in some former times, done some things of this aspect." He continues, saying that the people of New England no longer "approve" such actions and that they "dislike . . . everything that has look'd like persecution in the days that have passed over us."[19]

But Cotton Mather still insists that civil magistrates should not tolerate blasphemy, profaneness, and vices, which all "directly disturb the peace of human society." The magistrate can "punish the breaches of the peace." He can forbid "papists" and atheists—the former for their "declared principle" to persecute the moment they have civil power and the latter for "dissolv[ing] the ligaments of all human society." Suppressing these things through civil actions is consistent with the "liberty of conscience," which he calls a "native right of mankind."[20] Cotton's view reflects adherence to a classical Protestant principle: religious toleration depends on whether one's external religion harms civil society. The Mathers had come to

18. See Jeffrey A. Waldrop, *The Emergence of Religious Toleration in 18th Century New England* (Berlin: De Gruyter, 2018), 100–112.

19. Cotton Mather, *Brethren Dwelling Together in Unity. The True Basis for an Union among the People of God, Offered and Asserted; in a Sermon Preached at the Ordination of a Pastor, in the Church of the Baptists at Boston in New-England* (Boston, 1718). Increase Mather wrote the preface for the publication.

20. Ibid.

believe, as with much of New England apparently, that the Baptists were no longer (or never had been) a threat to New England civil and ecclesiastical order. No longer are credobaptists and paedobaptists adversarial and mutually suspicious; no longer is the strict unity of outward confession required for civil unity. Cotton Mather's chief motivation was their "fraternal union"—they were brothers in Christ. Toleration was *not* based on common humanity, or inviolable human dignity, or the *imago dei*; it was based on "an union in piety."[21] Cotton had not discovered some abstract human principle. He applied an old Protestant one.

Thus, the Mathers were still in continuity with the principles of John Cotton and John Winthrop and classical Protestantism. They simply applied those principles differently, recognizing that spiritual brothers who disagreed on secondary matters could not only co-exist but could also cooperate in a civil project. We can conclude that it was not the Enlightenment, Lockean philosophy, or Baptist theological arguments that convinced Cotton and Increase Mather that a pan-Protestant political order was possible; it was experience with that diversity that produced the requisite imagination to see its possibility.

III. Religious Liberty in the Founding Era

Let us now jump to the founding era. We see that the founders assumed distinctively Protestant principles—the *same* principles as their Puritan forefathers. Religious liberty in the founding era was not opposed to the classical Protestant tradition but a principled development of it.

21. Ibid.

THE CASE FOR CHRISTIAN NATIONALISM

Religion is Necessary for Civil Happiness

The founders were unanimous in the belief that religion is necessary for civic morals and public happiness. This is important for a couple reasons. First, it is a point of continuity with the Reformed political tradition (though contrary to Roger Williams). Second, it assumes (contrary to much 20th-century thought) that religious associations are different in species from other public associations as to their *necessity* for public happiness.[22] That is, churches were distinguished from other associations by their necessity for the public good.

Even those who held the minority view on religious liberty— those who wanted to disassociate civil government entirely from religion—considered flourishing religion to be necessary for a well-regulated and happy society. This is why they almost always argued that religious establishment is bad for religion and that strict separation is good for it. For example, in his famous "Memorial and Remonstrance against Religious Assessments," Madison states that establishment "is adverse to the diffusion of the light of Christianity."[23] And in 1833, nearing the end of his life, Madison writes approvingly to Jasper Adams that his advocacy for disestablishment led to "greater purity & industry of the pastors & in the greater devotion of their flocks."[24]

The evidence that most of the founders, including the "key" founders, believed that religion had an essential role in political order

22. Put more precisely, religious associations (viz., churches) belong to the same genus, public association, but are distinctive in relation to all other public associations as *necessary* associations for public happiness.

23. James Madison, "A Memorial and Remonstrance against Religious Assessments," 1785, in Dreisbach and Hall, *The Sacred Rights of Conscience*, 312.

24. James Madison, "Letter from James Madison to Jasper Adams," in *Sacred Rights of Conscience*, 613.

is well-established and widely acknowledged. Gregg Frazer makes it a basic feature of theistic rationalism, a label he thinks best characterizes the key founders' religious beliefs.[25] Mark David Hall says that

> with few, if any exceptions, every founding-era statesman was committed to the proposition that republican government required a moral citizenry, and that religion was necessary for morality. . . . [W]hen America's founders spoke about "religion," virtually all of them—even those most influenced by the Enlightenment—meant Christianity.[26]

John Adams, Benjamin Rush, Gouverneur Morris, James Madison, Roger Sherman, Alexander Hamilton, James Wilson, George Washington, and John Hancock affirmed the necessity of religion for public happiness.[27] John Witherspoon best summarizes the consensus: "[V]irtue and piety are inseparably connected, [and so] to promote true religion is the best and most effectual way of making a virtuous and regular people."[28] At issue, then, is not whether the arrangements of civil society ought to promote religion but *how* it

25. See Gregg L. Frazer, *The Religious Beliefs of America's Founders: Reason, Revelation, and Revolution* (Lawrence, KS: University Press of Kansas, 2012), 179–85. Of course, orthodox Protestants universally affirmed that true religion improves the morals of civil society.

26. Mark David Hall, *Did America Have a Christian Founding?* (Nashville: Nelson Books, 2019), 31.

27. The "key founders," according to Frazer, believed that "[m]orality was needed to get men to live in civil fashion without coercion in a free society; and religion was the best source of morality." *Religious Beliefs*, 179.

28. John Witherspoon, "Lectures on Moral Philosophy," in *Selected Writings of John Witherspoon*, ed. Thomas Miller (Carbondale, IL: Southern Illinois University Press, 1990), 212. Madison writes of the "God all powerful wise & good . . . as essential to the moral order of the world." Quoted in Frazer, *Religious Beliefs*, 180.

ought to promote religion. Some founders believed that strict separation best promoted religion; many (or most) disagreed.

John Witherspoon

In his *Lectures on Moral Philosophy*, given to his students at the College of New Jersey (later Princeton University), John Witherspoon discusses the role of government in religion. Though his comments are brief, Witherspoon affirms classic Protestant principles, but he denied the old 17th-century applications. He discusses the government's role in religion after asking how to maintain the "general disposition of a people" to observe civil laws. He writes that the "strict and rigorous execution" of the laws by civil authority is not enough, for when a people are "against the laws, they cannot long subsist." What is the best way to "make the people of any state virtuous?" His answer is piety. He writes,

> If . . . virtue and piety are inseparably connected, then to promote true religion is the best and most effectual way of making a virtuous and regular people. Love to God and love to man is the substance of religion; when these prevail, civil laws will have little to do.[29]

But acknowledging this leads to a problem: How far ought the magistrate "interfere in matters of religion"? After all, "religious sentiments are very various" and one "natural liberty" is that "everyone should judge for himself in matters of religion."[30] This latter point, which one could misinterpret, simply reflects the fundamental

---

29. Witherspoon, "Lectures," 212.
30. Ibid.

Protestant view that the Gospel and religious belief cannot be coerced; it is a matter of persuasion, and one must decide for himself. It is not a distinctive supposition of Enlightenment philosophy.

Witherspoon addresses the problem of religious diversity with four points. The first is that the magistrate "ought to encourage piety by his own example." In doing so, however, he is not required to maintain neutrality but may "promote . . . men of piety" and "discountenance those whom it would be improper to punish." The second point reflects Protestant experience in government and religion. Witherspoon writes that (1) "the magistrate ought to defend the rights of conscience," and (2) "tolerate all in their religious sentiments that are not injurious to their neighbors." Defending the rights of conscience requires the magistrate to keep the peace between those whose religious sentiments are "essentially repugnant one to another." He must ensure that no one is harassed simply on account of belief. As I've shown, this is a standard right (though not always designated as such) in the Reformed tradition. But Witherspoon's point is more about circumstances than principle. He writes that "at present *as things are situated* . . . the magistracy [must] protect the rights of conscience."[31] The religious diversity of America requires greater deliberation on how to keep the peace between potentially conflicting denominations.

As for toleration, Witherspoon appeals to experience. He acknowledges that some sects "hold tenets subversive of society" and that withholding toleration is "just . . . in way of reasoning," for they might "threaten ruin to others." He specifically mentions Roman Catholics, whom many accused of "subjection to a foreign power,

31. Ibid., 213.

the see of Rome." Though he affirms the principle that undergirded past civil policies that withheld toleration, Witherspoon denies that it usually works in application. He writes,

> [W]e ought in general to guard against persecution on a religion account as much as possible because such as hold absurd tenets are seldom dangerous. Perhaps they are never dangerous, but when they are oppressed. Papists are tolerated in Holland without danger to liberty.[32]

Witherspoon has not denied that civil governments can, in principle, withhold toleration from subversive sects. Rather, he denies that withholding toleration is effective, since subversion is often its consequence.[33]

The third point is that the "magistrate may enact laws for the punishment of acts of profanity and impiety." Witherspoon's concern is civil peace, for various religious sentiments could lead to "such acts as any of them count profane." This would presumably include speech and actions contrary to natural religion, which would justify the prohibition of blasphemy. This places Witherspoon in line with Cotton Mather. For the fourth point, Witherspoon states that there is "a good deal of reason" to "make public provision for the worship of God" so that the "bulk of common people" have instruction.[34] The assumption here is that most people are either unwilling or unable to fund religious instruction; and since religion is necessary

32. Ibid.

33. Even by the early 17th century, experience with tolerance and intolerance had its effects on Reformed thought. Althusius, for example, argued that magistrates ought to "tolerate the dissenters for the sake of public peace." *Politica*, 174 [28.66].

34. Witherspoon, "Lectures," 213.

for civic morals, it follows that government can and should provide public funding for Christian ministry.

Witherspoon's view on the role of government in religion is no different than Cotton Mather's. He acknowledges the possibility that religious sects can be subversive and, therefore, are legitimate objects of government suppression, but he demurs on the need for it. Why? Because experience teaches that suppression of religious dissent makes matters worse. Still, civil government cannot neglect religion and so should provide publicly funded instruction "in such manner as is agreeable to the great body of the society."[35]

Massachusetts Constitution (1780)

The Massachusetts Constitution, largely written by John Adams and ratified by voters in 1780, offers another example of both full toleration and establishment. In the first part, the constitution states that all have a "right" and "duty" to worship the "SUPREME BEING."[36] It then grants toleration for all to worship "in the manner and season most agreeable to the dictates of his own conscience; or for his religious profession of sentiments." But it then adds the classic proviso: "provid[ing] he doth not disturb the public peace, or obstruct others in their religious worship." A few paragraphs later, it states that "every denomination of Christians, demeaning themselves peaceably, and as good subjects of the commonwealth, shall be equally under the protection of the law."[37] The principle and proviso are the same as in the 17th century. The difference is in the range of expressions tolerated.

35. Ibid.
36. "Massachusetts Constitution (1780)," in Dreisbach and Hall, *Sacred Rights of Conscience*, 246.
37. Ibid.

The document next justifies the power of the legislature to require local bodies to "make provision, at their own expense, for the
institution of the public worship of God, and for the support and
maintenance of public Protestant teachers." It is for the "happiness
of the people," for the "good order and preservation of civil government . . . depend upon piety, religion, and morality." This provision
ensures that the "public worship of God, and . . . public instruction"
are "diffused through a community."[38]

The common elements of these pro-establishment voices are
(1) the necessity of organized religion for public happiness and
civil order, (2) the effectiveness of religious establishment to
provide religious instruction throughout society, (3) a proviso
stating that toleration is conditioned on peaceful assembly and
support for the civil government, and (4) that civil government
should suppress violations of natural religion, such as blasphemy
and impiety, and prevent one sect from harming another. The advocates for establishment in the founding era and Cotton Mather
share the same principles.

Protestant Premises

The content of the founding-era debates on religious liberty were
not mere assertions of Enlightenment reason or intellectual light
that cast away centuries of darkness. The content was public argument—the use of premises, thought to be well-received or generally
believed, to demonstrate a satisfactory conclusion. Eighteenth-century Americans were Protestants, and so debates relied heavily on
Protestant premises. Take Isaac Backus's arguments, for example, in
his 1774–1775 *History of New England*. He writes,

38. Ibid.

It may now be asked, *What is the liberty desired?* The answer is: As the kingdom of Christ is not of this world, and religion is a concern between God and the soul, with which no human authority can intermeddle, consistently with the principles of Christianity, and according to the dictates of Protestantism, we claim and expect the liberty of worshipping God according to our consciences.[39]

The premises of his argument are thoroughly Protestant. "The kingdom of Christ is not of this world" not only alludes to John 18:36 but is a common proof-text for two-kingdoms theology. That "religion is a concern between God and the soul" affirms the basic Protestant doctrine that there is no earthly mediator between God and man. Backus is appealing to *Protestant* premises, not Enlightenment ones. Why would he do this? Because he is addressing fellow Protestants immersed in Protestant tradition.

Elisha Williams, another advocate of disestablishment, assumes Protestant premises as well: "[T]he sacred scriptures are the alone rule of faith and practice [sic] to a Christian, all Protestants are agreed in" and so all "must therefore inviolably maintain, that every Christian has *right of judging for himself* what he is to believe and practice."[40] True Christian belief is not based in mere assent to ecclesiastical authority or any other earthly authority. It is about genuine and immediate conviction of the objects of faith themselves—the Scriptures offering *immediate* and *sufficient* reasons for

39. Isaac Backus, *A History of New England* (Newton, MA: Backus Historical Society, 1871), 2:201n1. Quoted in Philip B. Kurland and Ralph Lerner, eds., *The Founders' Constitution*, vol. 5, Amendments I–XII (Indianapolis: Liberty Fund, 1987), 65.

40. Elisha Williams, "The Essential Rights and Liberties of Protestants," in Dreisbach and Hall, *Sacred Rights of Conscience*, 175.

belief in those objects. These are not Enlightenment premises but basic Protestant ones.

In his draft for what became the Virginia Declaration of Rights (1776), George Mason wrote that "Religion, or the Duty which we owe to our divine and omnipotent Creator, and the Manner of discharging it, . . . [is] governed by Reason and Conviction, and not by Force or Violence."[41] Again, this is a Protestant premise: namely, that religious belief is always a matter of unmediated persuasion based in reasons to believe the supposed objects of faith; external force and coercion are incapable of persuading. Here is the draft in full:

> That as Religion, or the Duty which we owe to our divine and omnipotent Creator, and the Manner of discharging it, can be governed only by Reason and Conviction, not by Force or Violence; and therefore that all Men shou'd enjoy the fullest Toleration in the Exercise of Religion, according to the Dictates of Conscience, unpunished and unrestrained by the Magistrate, unless, under Colour of Religion, any Man disturb the Peace, the Happiness, or Safety of Society, or of Individuals. And that it is the mutual Duty of all, to practice Christian forbearance, Love and Charity towards Each other.

Implicitly recognizing the inner/outer distinction, Mason's draft reflects the old principles. The premise—that religion is "governed by Reason and Conviction"—concerns an inner reality: namely, that one's reconciliation or relation to God is immediate and a matter

---

41. George Mason, "Mason's Draft (May 1776)," in Dreisbach and Hall, *Sacred Rights of Conscience*, 241.

between the person and God. But inner beliefs accompany or produce *outer* or external expressions, and so the beliefs become public in a way. As such, they can clash or conflict with others' activities; they can contribute to or degrade public happiness; and they can secure or threaten public safety. Mason's draft reconciles the inward/outward dimensions, recognizing that religious expression must come under some degree of civic regulation. To this end, he includes the classic proviso: "unless, under colour of Religion, any Man disturb the Peace, the Happiness, or Safety of Society, or of Individuals."

These are just a handful of innumerable examples of classic Protestant premises used in founding-era documents on religious liberty. This should surprise none of us, because the founders and the American people were largely Protestant. But more importantly, it demonstrates that the American political tradition, at least from the colonial period into the early American republic, *assumed* basic Protestant beliefs upon which to support their positions; and, in addition to Protestant principles, the founders brought Protestant *experience* to bear upon their reasoning as well.

The Influence and Importance of James Madison

In June 1776, Madison's revision of Mason's draft won in the Virginia legislature—a win for the minority camp on religious liberty. The revision replaced "fullest toleration in the exercise of religion" with "equally entitled to free exercise of religion," and Madison removed the proviso.[42] Madison's version contains Protestant assumptions,

42. Here is Madison's version: "That religion, or duty which we owe to our CREATOR, and the manner of discharging it, can be directed only by reason and conviction, not by force or violence; and therefore, that men are equally entitled to enjoy the free exercise of religion, according to the dictates of conscience, unpunished and unrestrained by the magistrate, Unless the preservation of equal liberty and the existence of the State are man-

but it follows his usual pattern of implicitly conflating inward opinion and its outward expression—a distinction affirmed not only by
his opponents but also by the Protestant tradition. As that tradition
insisted, opinions when expressed or acted upon become public
and visible. They are no longer merely opinions but public actions
and so are subject to civil jurisdiction.

Madison explicitly uses this reasoning in his *Memorial and Remonstrance*, which he wrote in opposition to a bill proposed in the
Virginia legislature by Patrick Henry that would tax property owners to fund church ministers from all denominations. In his first of
fifteen reasons, Madison writes that "[r]eligion then of every man
must be left to the conviction and conscience of every man, and it
is the right of every man to exercise it as these may dictate. . . . It is
[an] unalienable [right] because the opinions of men . . . cannot
follow the dictates of other men."[43] Again, Madison seems to rely
on Protestant premises concerning the inward nature of belief and
man's immediate relation with God.[44] But he jumps from there to
an "unalienable" right to express those beliefs. He then says that
legislatures lack "jurisdiction" over religious belief, having "limited"

---

ifestly endangered; And that it is the mutual duty of all to practice Christian forbearance,
love, and charity towards each other." "Final Version (June 12, 1776)," in Dreisbach and
Hall, *Sacred Rights of Conscience*, 241.

43. James Madison, "Memorial and Remonstrance," in Dreisbach and Hall, *Sacred Rights
of Conscience*, 309. Muñoz notes that Madison "takes these theological premises as giv-
en." Vincent Phillip Muñoz, *God and the Founders: Madison, Washington, and Jefferson*
(Cambridge: Cambridge University Press, 2009), 30. Madison makes no attempt to defend the premises because they are not controversial among Protestants.

44. Muñoz recognizes this as well. He says that Madison's "immediate (though certainly
not his only) intention was to persuade a largely Protestant audience. Although the political context is not decisive in itself, it should not surprise us that Madison employed
arguments that appealed to his immediate audience." *God and the Founders*, 31.

authority.[45] But, without logical justification, Madison extends the restriction of civil jurisdiction over the inner man to the outward man. In so doing, he not only fails to make the crucial and classical inward/outward distinction, but he is also led into a practical absurdity: that people have a right to outwardly express *all* inward religious beliefs, even when they are publicly harmful.[46]

But we might reasonably ask, "How important is Madison in the founding era with regard to religious liberty?" Despite the attention he has received from scholars and jurists, Madison's view was extreme for his time, going past even John Locke in seemingly rejecting the classic proviso and in speaking of religious liberty as an "unalienable right." For Locke, as he argued in *A Letter Concerning Toleration*, the civil magistrate is not required to tolerate "opinions contrary to human society, or to those moral rules which are necessary to the preservation of civil society."[47] Neither atheists nor Roman Catholics sufficiently passed these requirements, according to Locke. As one scholar, Vincent Phillip Muñoz, recent commented, "Madison breaks from Locke on this point; his principle of noncognizance is uniquely his own."[48]

Madison's importance in the founding era on religious liberty is exaggerated. His importance for jurisprudence today does not necessarily demonstrate his importance in the founding era.

45. Madison, "Memorial and Remonstrance," in Dreisbach and Hall, *Sacred Rights of Conscience*, 309.
46. I am sure that Madison would deny this, but it seems to follow from his reasoning. And if he would deny it, then he has to affirm some version of the classical proviso—that outwardly expressed religious beliefs are, in principle, subject to civil jurisdiction and can be restrained by civil coercion.
47. John Locke, *A Letter Concerning Toleration* (n.p.: J. Brook, 1796), 53.
48. Muñoz, *God and the Founders*, 29.

The Supreme Court did not rely on Madison's *Memorial and Remonstrance* until the mid-20th century.[49] Mark Hall states that he "could find no record of any civic leader being influenced by, or appealing to, Madison's *Memorial* prior to the ratification of the Bill of Rights."[50] George Washington refused to sign Madison's *Memorial*, saying that he was not "so much alarmed at the thoughts of making people pay towards the support of that which they profess."[51]

We might ask the same questions about Thomas Jefferson's influence. His Virginia Statute, which he wrote in 1779 and was signed into law in 1786, has received far more attention after the founding era than it received at the time. Hall argues that "mostly, it was ignored," despite its wide distribution in the 1780s by Jefferson's own diligence. Indeed, the importance of Virginia on religious liberty in the founding era has been exaggerated. Throughout the 1780s, as the colonies revised their constitutions, they adopted language not from the Virginia Statute but from the Massachusetts Constitution of 1780, which I discussed above. New Hampshire in 1784, Connecticut in 1784, Vermont in 1786, and the Northwest Ordinance of 1787 adopted language from this constitution. Hall concludes, "[T]here is no record of civic officials utilizing the Virginia Statute as a model for a constitutional provision or law prior to the adoption of the First Amendment . . . [and] there is little reason to conclude that Jefferson influenced the views of the men who drafted, debated, and ratified the First Amendment."[52]

49. Ibid, 2.
50. Hall, *Did America Have a Christian Founding?*, 72.
51. Ibid, 72.
52. Hall, *Did America Have a Christian Founding?*, 66.

Thus, in the founding era prior to the ratification of the Bill of Rights, neither Jefferson's Virginia Statute nor Madison's *Memorial* significantly influenced public opinion or state constitutions. The majority view of the founding era rejected Madison's and Jefferson's strict separationism. Even after the founding, several states had church establishments, including Vermont, Connecticut, New Hampshire, Maine, and Massachusetts.[53]

The First Amendment

As for the First Amendment, there is no evidence that Madison was its sole author. Muñoz writes that "although Madison certainly had influence, he was not the sole author and, hence, not solely responsible for the adopted text."[54] Hall states that Madison

> was not a god among men imposing his personal views on cowed colleagues. Approximately eighty-seven representatives and senators participated in the debates and voted for or against what became the First Amendment. And a list of those who played significant roles must include, besides Madison, Roger Sherman, Oliver Ellsworth, Benjamin Huntinton,

---

53. Ibid., 94–95. American society moved more towards Madison's vision as the 19th century progressed, even among orthodox Reformed Christians. In his *Systematic Theology* (1871), the stalwart Reformed theologian Charles Hodge of old Princeton Seminary affirmed religious liberty. He writes, "All are welcomed; all are admitted to equal rights and privileges. All are allowed to acquire property, and to vote in every election, made eligible to all office, and invested with equal influence in all public affairs. All are allowed to worship as they please, or not to worship at all, if they see fit. No man is molested for his religion or for his want of religion. No man is required to profess any form of faith, or to join any religious association. More than this cannot reasonably be demanded." *Systematic Theology*, vol. 3, *Soteriology* (1871; New York: Charles Scribner's Sons, 1887), 345–46. Robert Dabney, a Southern Presbyterian and theologian, asserts a similar position in chapter 48 of his *Systematic Theology*.

54. Muñoz, *God and the Founders*, 35.

Abraham Baldwin, Elias Boudinot, William Patterson, Samuel Livermore, Charles Carroll, and Fisher Ames.[55]

Jefferson took no part in the process. He was in Paris and returned two months after the ratification.[56] One important member of the amendment committee was Roger Sherman, who was in agreement with Witherspoon, Washington, Patrick Henry, and other founders on the role of government in religion.[57] With Richard Law, he wrote a new state code for Connecticut that included a section on religious liberty similar in content to the Massachusetts Constitution. Yet Sherman's is even stronger, stating that it is the *"duty* of the civil authority to provide for the support and encouragement" of "piety, religion, and morality."[58] Since Sherman and many like him helped draft, deliver, or ratify the First Amendment, one cannot read it strictly through a Madisonian lens. Indeed, the opposite lens is likely more accurate. The First Amendment does not reject establishment in principle. How could it, when so many involved in drafting and ratifying it explicitly affirmed establishment for their own states? Rather, the First Amendment reflects the unsuitability of establishment at the federal level and the imprudence of permitting Congress to interfere in the exercise of religion in the states.

Muñoz recently demonstrated, using other sources, that the original purpose of the Establishment Clause in the First Amendment was to "quell" the concerns of the Anti-Federalists who feared

---

55. Hall, *Did America Have a Christian Founding?,* 75–76.

56. Hall reports that despite Jefferson's complete absence from the process, Supreme Court justices have cited him 112 times in their rulings on the First Amendment's religion clauses. Madison is cited 189 times. *Did America Have a Christian Founding?,* 76.

57. Hall identifies Sherman as a "latter-day Puritan" (ibid.).

58. Roger Sherman, quoted in Hall, *Did America Have a Christian Founding?,* 92–93.

that "the new Congress would impose one form of church-state relations throughout the nation."[59] Muñoz cites a Massachusetts author, "Agrippa":

> Attention to religion and good morals is a distinguishing trait
> in our [Massachusetts's] character. It is plain, therefore, that we
> require for our regulation laws, which will not suit the circum-
> stances of our southern brethren, and the laws made for them
> would not apply to us. Unhappiness would be the uniform
> product of such law; for no state can be happy, when the laws
> contradict the general habits of the people, nor can any state
> retain its freedom, while there is a power to make and enforce
> such law.[60]

Notice that the concern is not over establishment itself but establishment at the federal level. Since Massachusetts has its own "general
habits," as do the other states, religion should be left to the states.

Another Anti-Federalist writer, "Deliberator," expressed concern over the term *general welfare* in the preamble, that it might justify establishing "uniformity in religion." Others expressed concern
over the "necessary and proper" clause.[61] The fear, however, was not
religious establishment itself. As Muñoz states, "Most Anti-Federalists did not object to religious establishments per se."[62] They
feared that Congress, under the guise of national welfare, would

59. Vincent Phillip Muñoz, "The Original Meaning of the Establishment Clause and the
Impossibility of Its Incorporation," *University of Pennsylvania Journal of Constitutional Law*
8 (2006): 604.

60. Quoted in ibid., 615–16.

61. Quoted in ibid., 615.

62. Ibid.

seize control over what rightly belongs to the states. Though it is unlikely that Congress would have enacted religious uniformity, it is at least theoretically possible, since all founders thought that religion was necessary for and contributed to the welfare of the people. Whether their concerns were rational or irrational, the Anti-Federalists forced the first Congress to expressly curtail their powers in establishing religion. The motivating principle, however, was not anti-establishment; it was federalism. Given religious diversity between the states, the promotion and regulation of religion was best left to the states.

The "godless" Constitution

There is a legitimate question concerning the absence of religious language and declared Protestantism in the Constitution. I will not address that issue fully here.[63] But I will say, as scholar Stephen Botein has argued, that those in the founding era who stressed the importance of religion for civil stability and happiness did not see the federal government as the sort of political entity that needed religion. The states alone required a "religious dimension," and only around the mid-19th century did "the federal government [begin] to reveal enough attributes of a true state to warrant some semblance of [an] official religious identity."[64] Resolving the questions

---

63. See Hall, *Did America Have a Christian Founding?*, 21–56.

64. Stephen Botein, "Religious Dimensions of the Early American State," in *Beyond Confederation: Origins of the Constitution and American National Identity*, ed. Richard Beeman, Stephen Botein, and Edward C. Carter (Chapel Hill: University of North Carolina, 1987), 325. Donald L. Drakeman writes, "Church-state issues were simply not seen by the framers as contentious federal issues; all of the various areas of continuing disagreement were being left for the states to work out." "The Antifederalists and Religion," in Daniel L. Dreisbach and Mark David Hall, eds., *Faith and the Founders of the American Republic* (New York: Oxford University Press, 2014), 137.

of church and state concerned one's state citizenship—to be resolved by deliberating with those residing in one's state.

Even if the framers should have included explicit Christian language in the Constitution (and I agree that it was a mistake not to), it says little in itself about the political tradition operating at the founding. Firstly, the general consensus at the time was that religion ought to be left up to the states, and so the absence of religion in the Constitution says nothing about the American nation as a whole or about the political-theoretical questions about the role of civil government vis-à-vis religion. It speaks only about the federal government's suitability to regulate religion, given the circumstances. Secondly, several states had establishments well into the 19th century, as I've said, and the rest of the states were unmistakably religious and Protestant. We should not overemphasize the "founding" of the American founding, as if every consideration used to construct the federal government is generally applicable, reflecting some universal arrangement for *all* governments. In other words, despite the fact that the Constitution lacks Christian language, we cannot forget that the American people in the founding era and early American republic were Protestant Christians, animated by religious concerns, who viewed themselves as a Christian people and relied on Protestant principles and biblical argumentation. If anything, the absence of Christianity from America's constituting documents diverges from American principles; it did not establish an American secularist principle of civil government.

Americans in the 19th century, for example, who wanted to Christianize the Constitution with a Christian amendment sought not to overthrow secularist principles embedded in the Constitution but to *correct a mistake of omission* and thereby bring the

Constitution fully in line with American principles.[65] Christian-izing American civil institutions is simply making explicit what is already implicit in them. For example, after agreeing to place "In God We Trust" on US coinage, James Pollock, the director of the US Mint, wrote, "We claim to be a Christian nation—why should we not vindicate our character by honouring the God of Nations in the exercise of our political Sovereignty as a Nation?"[66]

IV. Conclusion

In this chapter, I have argued that, despite appearances, the majority view on religious liberty in the founding era shared the same princi-ples as the 17th century New England Puritans. The apparent discon-tinuity found in the historical record is a product of Anglo-Protestant experience, which informed the imagination on the possibilities of public order amid Protestant religious diversity. Among the found-ers, all believed that a religious people were necessary for civic mor-als, public happiness, and effective government, and most (if not all) thought that Christianity provided something distinctive in this re-gard. Most believed that government had a role in promoting, sup-porting, and protecting true religion, even particular denominations, though not at the expense of full toleration. Most believed that vio-lators of natural religion could be censored and that religious expres-sions that "disturb the Peace, the Happiness, or Safety of Society" (as

---

65. Reformed theologians led this movement, seeking to add "Jesus, the Messiah, the Saviour and Lord of all" to the preamble. A.A. Hodge was an active supporter of the amendment. Despite Abraham Lincoln's interest in the amendment, Congress failed to vote on it.

66. James Pollack, quoted in Gillis J. Harp, *Protestants and American Conservatism* (New York: Oxford University Press, 2019), 95–96.

Mason wrote)[67] could be suppressed. And most founders explicitly grounded their principles of religious liberty in Protestant principles. What was new about the new American political order was not principle but prudential arrangements that reflected the culmination of Anglo-Protestant experience.

As a resource for Christian nationalism, this development is suitable only for a people whose core is Protestant—those who can affirm God's sole reign over the conscience and the freedom of individuals from external coercion, and who at the same time can affirm an outward Christian order that directs people to their complete good. We cannot expect non-Protestants to receive an Anglo-Protestant tradition or even all Protestants. Let's claim and assert what is ours and utilize it to renew our land.

I am not advocating a return to late 1780s America; this is not a return-to-the-founding project. The religious liberties in the founding era were not necessarily better than the policies in prior eras in early America. I am not offering a Whig narrative of progress. The point is that religious liberty in the American founding era, though reflecting universal Protestant principles, was a particular development by a people—particularly an Anglo-Protestant people. As such, the whole tradition—between the early settlements to the early American republic—is an American, ethno-cultural inheritance that must be reclaimed and serve as an animating element of American Christian nationalism and a resource for American renewal.

67. George Mason, quoted in Dreisbach and Hall, *Sacred Rights of Conscience*, 241.

Epilogue:
Now What?

"God grant that there may come a reaction, and that the great principles of Anglo-Saxon liberty may be rediscovered before it is too late!" —J. Gresham Machen[1]

The reader has likely asked himself, "Okay, but what we do now? How do we recover Christian nationhood? Where do we find this 'Christian prince' you speak of? Is any of this feasible in our situation?" These questions and others came to mind repeatedly while writing this book. I will try to give us a way forward, to the extent that I can. But this book is not an action-plan. It is a justification of Christian nationalism, and we are early in recovering the movement. Every movement needs its intellectuals, pamphleteers,

---

1. Machen, *Christianity and Liberalism* (1924; Moscow, ID: Canon Press, 2020), 13.

strategists, organizers, and foot soldiers. This book belongs in the first category, and perhaps in the future I can contribute in other ways. Let each have his role.

However, I feel obligated to speak freely about our situation. Many of these thoughts apply specifically to the place I know best: America. Our problem in the West is fundamentally psychological, and so I focus on patterns of thought and our rhetorical framing of things. The style of this conclusion is different than most. I offer a sort of fragmented conclusion, a series of loosely organized aphorisms. This is only the beginning.

I. The New America

1.

The Christian nationalist project is not "conservative." Post-WWII conservatism is inadequate for our situation. I have no interest in conserving the liberalism of the 1980s or 1990s or the militaristic adventure-imperialism of the "compassionate" conservatives of the 2000s. American conservatism has operated under the assumption that our institutions are still fundamentally ours—still basically *for us.* But our institutions are not only captured by the left; they have become fundamentally oriented against us. The conservative cannot fathom this. He is an institution man, the sort who lined up against Donald Trump to "protect the institutions." But what if the meaning of America produced by these institutions—its myths, symbols, monuments, and story—is actually against you, not for you? What if the "America" of these institutions casts you as the villain? What then? Are you going to conserve these institutions to your own destruction?

The left in America are now the true conservatives. This isn't a compliment but a statement of fact. The institutions are theirs and they now conserve them; they protect these institutions from the enemies of the New America. *But,* the conservative might say, *they are the "progressives"; they don't conserve.* What an old and obsolete conservative dichotomy! In our world today, conserving and progressing are *not* opposites; they are complementary. Progressives conserve the institutions that further progress. Progress means that these institutions are working, not failing.

Thus, we are past the time of "conservative principles." People conserve what they know and love. How can you love institutions that hate you? Why would you want to "conserve" them? The solution is *renewal,* not conservation. What we need is the *instauratio magna,* the Great Renewal.

2.

The American ruling class are true Americans in the New American way. This is understandably hard to stomach for Americans whose hearts lie in an older heritage. According to old conservatism, today's ruling class is un-American and unpatriotic, and it hates America. There is truth to this; they do indeed hate *that* America and want it obsolete, dead, destroyed.

But eventually, self-identified conservatives will break out of these simplistic frames and see that "America" as they understand it no longer exists. Not the conservative but the progressive in America will look around and see the left's image reflected in its institutions, monuments, national celebrations, and special months. In the New America, the ground of patriotic sentiment is progress *away* from the Old America. Thus, civic holidays, national heroes, memorials, and patriotic events are all colored according to the grand narrative of progress, and each is considered true, good, and beautiful only to the extent that it celebrates that narrative.

Conservatives love narratives of progress. But the New American narrative insists that *this is only the beginning*—there is still much work to be done. Progress *is* our tradition, they claim. Thus, the narrative of America as embodied in our institutions today is relentlessly hostile to Old America. That means that New America is relentlessly hostile toward *you*. Every step is overcoming *you*. Ask yourself, "What sort of villain does each event of progress have in common?" The straight white male. That is the chief out-group of New America, the embodiment of regression and oppression.

3.

Conservatives say that "education should be patriotic." This is true in principle. But the conservative thinks that the left disagrees with this: *They want unpatriotic education*, they'll say. But if America is a narrative of progress, why not ground patriotism in progress? The true patriot *is* the progressive—one who is proud of past acts of resistance, who praises murderous John Brown and celebrates the great struggles against Old America.

The conservative's patriotic history is also fundamentally a story of progress. It goes something like this: The US was founded on principles of equality, freedom, and individual rights, though we didn't live up to them. But a promise was made by them, and over time through civil war, labor struggles, immigration, fighting fascists, more immigration, more noble foreign wars, civil rights for blacks, gay rights, more immigration, and so on it was finally realized. The conservative teacher of US history is the champion of the previous stage of progress, politely asking, "Can we please stop?" But why would it stop? Progress is patriotic. America is progress. Let's fight on for a "more perfect union," both here and abroad.

It is nearly impossible to detach the conservative from his progressivist narrative of US history. In this mind, his country is good because it was founded on good values that became progressively realized over time; and to the conservatives' minds, they were the ones who did it. Yes, the conservatives indeed did it; only they *could* do it. But what was the reward for your blood, sweat, and tears? To be called "racists" by the Squad, to be denounced as the source of all bad social outcomes, and to be passed over by the incompetent and neurotic. You fought the fascists abroad and then at home only became the fascists of New America.

4.

I was in the military back when the Don't Ask, Don't Tell (DADT) policy was rescinded by the Obama administration. Prior to the policy change, the military sent teams to military installations to "listen" to concerns of service members. It became clear that the intent was to convince everyone that DADT was a backward policy. The rhetoric employed for persuasion appealed entirely to progress. After pointing to the inclusion of women and racial integration in the armed forces, the team claimed that ending DADT was just another step in that progress. Logically, the argument doesn't work, but can logic defeat such a compelling American story? The story was not new; it assumed the conservative narrative of progress. These people were clever. They knew that their audience was full of southerners from conservative communities, so they tapped into the conservative narrative of progress. Advancement in diversity and inclusion is the American story. Why not allow homosexuals to serve openly? To be a good American—committed to one's national story—one has to be progressively inclusive. This rhetoric has worked time and time again, and it will work again.

5.

The United States military provides a good example of how conservatives are duped into fighting for causes that harm them. The military is full of patriotic young Americans, largely from the American South—the sort of people whose grandfathers fought in World War II, whose fathers or uncles served, and who felt the duty to fight for their country. The impulse to serve is itself commendable, deserving of great praise. But this love of country was exploited, and young men were sent across the world to fight for "freedom" in places that had never heard of John Locke or James Madison—and didn't care. "Make the world safe for democracy," they told us. We then see the rainbow flag in Kabul and NGOs advocating for transgender rights and gender studies programs. That's "democracy," and we are here to kill and die for it. Get blown up in the name of liberal imperialism; shed blood to open up markets for Netflix and Pornhub; make the world safe for dudes in dresses.

Politicians have made the US military the most exploitative institution in the United States. In 2021, George W. Bush—the man who sent young men on a pointless liberalizing crusade in Iraq—had this to say to service members:

> The cause you pursued at the call of duty is the noblest America
> has to offer. You have shielded your fellow citizens from danger.
> You have defended the beliefs of your country and advanced the

rights of the downtrodden. You have been the face of hope and
mercy in dark places. You have been a force for good in the world.[2]

You "defended the beliefs of your country." He is right in a way:
you've defended the beliefs of New America—feminism, homosexuality, gender fluidity, secularism, porn, and base entertainment.
But the conservative mind does not think about these things when
it hears about the "call of duty" in defense of the "downtrodden."
The conservative thinks about fighting fascists in the 40s; that's who
his grandfather fought. Is it any surprise that for years we called Islamic fighters the "Islamo-fascists"?

But the "American way of life," which the military fights for today, is not to work hard, go to church, call your mother—it is a
man in a miniskirt threatening you for not using his preferred pronouns. It is coming home from war to hear that your kid learned
in school that he and his family are racists. It is being forced to
acknowledge that men can get pregnant. It is saying over and over
again "diversity is our strength." It is listening to a US congresswoman born in a failed foreign country safely denounce your
country as evil, to her party's praise. You fight the fascists abroad
only to be called a fascist at home. You fight Communists far from
home to be spit on by Communists at home. It is invade the world,
invite the world. It is returning to your homeland, after all those
lost years fighting for "democracy," to recite enforced speech by
the mentally ill, resentful, and malicious. But conservatives will

2. George W. Bush, "Remarks by President George W. Bush at the Flight 93 National
Memorial in Shanksville, Pennsylvania," (speech, September 11, 2021) accessed May 30,
2021, https://www.bushcenter.org/about-the-center/newsroom/press-releases/2021/09
/remarks-president-bush-shanksville-9-11.html.

continue to funnel some of their best into the military, thinking that the military is still *ours*, that deep down its mission is just, and that it serves Americans.

The conservative support for the military is emblematic of the conservative mind and political practice: that they will fight and die for universal ideas, assuming a universal "love for liberty," and—upon failing to force Western liberty upon non-Western peoples—they then invite the world to their country only to suffer explicit contempt, vitriol, and ingratitude. Why do the conservatives continue to do this?

6.

The US military serves what some have called the "globalist American empire" (GAE). The GAE is centered in Washington, DC, and wields US diplomatic, military, and economic power to advance modern liberal ideology across the globe. All Western nations are in the GAE to one degree or another, and together they advance international liberalism. To see the effect of this, consider Ukraine. It has been a battleground (both literally and figuratively) of the GAE. The election of Volodymyr Zelenskyy in 2019 was instantly celebrated as a victory for liberalism. In an article by Yaroslav Trofimov, a foreign affairs analyst for the *Wall Street Journal*, we read that Zelenskyy promises to move Ukraine "decisively in embracing an inclusive, almost American, model of nationhood," such that "ethnic Ukrainian has become obsolete in mainstream life." Trofimov speaks of a "cultural boom, with new globally-minded art centers, bands, film production outlets and fashion design studios." Some of the new music "combines rap, hip-hop and folk." In moving away from "ethnicity," Ukraine is "heading to the civilized world," and the Ukrainian people are "part of a world-wide civilizational process." Ukraine has gone "in a more liberal direction," having "gay pride events in Kyiv" that shows a shift from "religious conservatism." Trofimov ends the article by quoting a woman "entrepreneur" who started a fashion company: "[W]e can actually achieve something. . . . We're out to conquer the world."[3] All this is reported without question, as if it is a natural step in the evolution of nations.

This liberalizing is largely a product of the GAE, with its allure of liberal decadence and promises of mass consumption and "freedom." Ukraine will become just another mass of restlessness, full of consumers of GAE products, talking about GAE entertainment, and orienting their lives around GAE fandom. Those who oppose the GAE will be deemed "right-wing extremists" and marked for elimination. When it is too late, however, Ukrainians of the older sort—after waking from a drunken slumber induced by GAE consumption—will learn that they chose not a new identity but a sort of liberal, soft occupation.

7.

America is just as much under the GAE as countries like Ukraine. America itself, or at least its older sort, is not an imperial nation; rather, it is the centralized location of GAE imperialism. Thus, Americans live under an implicit occupation; the American ruling class is an occupying force. The rulers are largely Americans by geographical birthplace but are better understood as cosmopolitans or "nowheres." We might call them liberal internationalists. The intent

3. Yaroslav Trofimov, "Ukraine Tries to Build a New Identity," *The Wall Street Journal*, October 11, 2019, accessed October 10, 2022, https://www.wsj.com/articles /ukraine-tries-to-build-a-new-identity-11570809736.

of the occupation here, as it is everywhere, is to impose modern liberal norms upon Americans, particularly sexual deviancy. This was evident in early 2022, when the American ruling class vociferously denounced Florida republicans for prohibiting instruction on sexual orientation and gender ideology in kindergarten through third grade. They also prohibited schools from withholding information to parents concerning their children's expressed gender identity at school. Even the CEO of Disney, Bob Chapek, met with Governor DeSantis to express concern. Why are large corporations, the entertainment media, academic institutions, educational institutions, social media companies, and other powerful entities so interested in sexualizing and injecting gender questioning among kids five to eight years old? Whatever the answer might be, the GAE—which extends beyond political institutions—is indeed imposing these things upon our children. Few people actually want this; parents never asked for it. If the people advocating for it did not look or sound like us, we'd think they were foreign occupiers trying to impose their strange rites and barbaric values on us. But no, these people represent "democracy," and those who oppose them are "authoritarians." The fact that they look and sound like us does not mean they are of us.

Why is the GAE so interested in kids? Here's the simple answer: They want child warriors. Kids with gender confusion is to the GAE what a child with an AK-47 is to third-world warlords. They fight their battles and lose their souls, but they also pledge life-long loyalty.

Whether or not you want to call it an occupying force, we are nevertheless subjected to transformative efforts *as if* under a sort of cultural revolutionary force. It is a soft revolution, for it appears to exist by consent. And the revolutionaries have an easier time at it, since they control America's institutions and the information apparatus. They can swiftly enforce the demands of the next social movement and quickly shift the people to the new "current thing." This was not so in Afghanistan. Under its occupation, it saw its first gender studies program at Kabul University. Indeed, the US government spent $787 million on gender equality programs in Afghanistan. (Ironically, neither the Dari nor Pashto languages have words to distinguish "gender" and "sex.") At the insistence of the US, the Afghanistan lower house had a 27 percent quota for women representatives. Several other programs attempted to impose gender equality. Of course, it didn't take in Afghanistan, but it did in the United States. There are significant differences between Americans and Afghanis, but *both* received the GAE imposition under their respective occupations. One fought back and won.

The *Obergefell* decision, which forced homosexual marriage on all states, is an imperial imposition. So too was the Immigration and Nationality Act of 1965, which opened the floodgates of non-Western immigration into the United States, despite assurances that it wouldn't. The occupiers have let criminals run rampant through cities and neighborhoods and then prosecute those who stand up to them.[4] They teach critical race theory and white self-hatred in secondary education. They encourage gender ideology and the "exploration" of one's gender identity. The onslaught is a transformative operation imposing an unwelcome ideology on the people.

---

4. See my article, "Anarcho-Tyranny in 2022," *Im—1776*, accessed May 28, 2022, https://im1776.com/2022/03/18/anarcho-tyranny.

THE CASE FOR CHRISTIAN NATIONALISM

8.

Christian nationalists need to know what they're up against. The Russia-Ukraine war is instructive here. One does not need to be pro-Putin to be alarmed at the intense anti-Russia propaganda in the West and how quickly the entire Western world turned their vitriolic ire away from the unvaccinated to the Russians. Ukrainian propaganda flourished as Western media pushed the propaganda as fact. Facebook and Instagram explicitly allowed calls for violence against Russians on their platforms.[5]

Any promising Christian nationalist movement would face the same degree of opposition. The GAE will see no difference between Putin's Russia and any Christian nationalist movement. To them, we're like the Taliban of the West. Christians nationalists threaten liberalism; they see us as regressive and authoritarian. Since Christian nationalists in the West exist within the reach of the state, we can expect civil authorities to punish Christian nationalists at every opportunity.

In addition to sanctions, Russians were punished by multinational corporations. Credit-card companies, Apple, and Google stopped servicing transactions. And Westerners were very willing to suffer higher gas prices to punish Russia. One poll indicated that almost 80 percent of Americans supported a Russia oil embargo. The point is that the most powerful forces of the world, which happen to possess almost all the available force, will treat us like Putin, the Taliban, and perhaps worse. This is not something

5. Munsif Vengattil and Elizabeth Culliford, "Facebook Allows War Posts Urging Violence against Russian Invaders," Reuters, March 10, 2022, accessed September 21, 2022, https://www.reuters.com/world/europe/exclusive-facebook-instagram-temporarily-allow-calls-violence-against-russians-2022–03–10.

to take lightly. And, of course, the most vociferous critics will be GAE-affirming Christians.

9.

The early days of the Russian-Ukraine war disclosed a fascinating phenomenon occurring among Western countries: the Marvelization of reality. The object of modern life's attention is an imagined reality, often composed of heroes and villains that keep us engrossed to our screens to cheer on our side. Thus, President Zelenskyy is "Captain Ukraine," and there is a "ghost of Kyiv" killing Russians, alongside an assault-rifle wielding, kick-ass supermodel with perfect hair and makeup.

George Orwell captured this phenomenon in *Nineteen Eighty-Four*. He called it the "Two Minutes Hate"—propaganda repeated day after day, bringing people to a sort of ritualistic frenzy in opposition to whatever the people were told to hate. It was so powerful that even the more self-aware took part. He writes,

> The dark-haired girl behind Winston had begun crying out "Swine! Swine! Swine!" and suddenly she picked up a heavy Newspeak dictionary and flung it at the screen.... In a lucid moment Winston found that he was shouting with the others and kicking his heel violently against the rung of his chair. The horrible thing about the Two Minutes Hate was not that one was obliged to act a part, but, on the contrary, that it was impossible to avoid joining in. Within thirty seconds any pretense was always unnecessary. A hideous ecstasy of fear and vindictiveness, a desire to kill, to torture, to smash faces in with a sledge hammer, seemed to flow through the whole group of people like

an electric current, turning one even against one's will into a grimacing, screaming lunatic. And yet the rage that one felt was an abstract, undirected emotion which could be switched from one object to another like the flame of a blowlamp.[6]

The bulk of late-modern Western man sits on his couch watching Fox News or CNN (it doesn't matter which) enmeshed in the Breaking News, as if watching the latest Marvel movie. He lives vicariously through the heroes, while remaining fat and passive on the sofa and tweeting with the latest hashtag. Reality is thus fandomified—modern man projecting his need for adventure, productivity, and confident action upon an imagined reality supplied to him by the regime.

It is only a matter of time before Christian nationalists become the villains in the next imagined reality, and our fellow believers, who are just as enmeshed in this world as their secularist neighbors, will join in the Two Minute Hate. But let *us* remain free in mind, be the true liberals. The mind is its own place.

10.

"For thus you speak: 'Real are we entirely, and without belief or superstition.' Thus you stick out your chests—but alas, they are hollow!" wrote Nietzsche in *Thus Spake Zarathustra*.[7] He was right in this regard: Modern life drives mankind to passivity, to "little pleasure[s]," keeping warm, and utter boredom. Thus, people "have a regard for

6. George Orwell, *Nineteen Eighty-Four*, ed. John Bowen (Oxford: Oxford University Press, 2021), 13.

7. Friedrich Nietzsche, *Thus Spoke Zarathustra: A Book for None and All* (New York: Penguin, 1978), 120.

health" and live a long time, but pursuing higher life is too risky and achieving dominion is too burdensome. This is the "last man."[8]

Some political theorists fear that modern liberalism, by pathologizing any way of life besides the last man, offers no outlet for what Francis Fukuyama called "megalothymia"—viz., striving for superiority, the passion for a higher life.[9] But, perhaps, the Marvelification of reality is the terrifying solution. One can passively consume and feel like an active participant in the latest drama. He can consume and tweet, consume and tweet, consume and tweet . . . and still make it to an Applebee's for dinner. The need for action, love, and hate; for good to fight evil; for busty blondes to stomp in heads— all is provided. Everyone is caught up in the latest target of GAE passion. The imagined, Marvelized reality is perhaps the evil solution to the instability of the last man. If it is, then the modern world will be in permanent crisis mode—one state of fear after another. And Christian nationalism will eventually be part of that drama.

11.

Modern life deadens the will; we seek, as Nietzsche said, warmth and comfort. There is little exertion of will. The modern world teaches us to say, "We have become happy" with base pleasure and entertainment. But we're bored, barely alive, with nothing to contend for except the latest "cause" thousands of miles away. Our will is not here but there and not for us but for them. This is modern nihilism, the "death of God" at work, the disenchantment of life, a desperate plea for meaning. But Christian nationalism is the pursuit of higher life—both the life to come and a life on earth that images

8. Ibid., 17, 18.

9. Francis Fukuyama, *The End of History and the Last Man* (New York: Free Press, 1992), 182.

that life to come. Christians should look upon the world as their inheritance—it is indeed ours by inheritance in Christ. The will for what is ours in Christ is the true revolt against the modern world. Let us passionately assert that Christian nationalism is the recovery of a Christian *megalothymia*—a collective will for Christian dominion in the world.

II. Gynocracy

12.

We live under a gynocracy—a rule by women. This may not be apparent on the surface, since men still run many things. But the governing virtues of America are feminine vices, associated with certain feminine virtues, such as empathy, fairness, and equality. All of life now is subjected to credentialism, institution-conferring "expertise," risk-aversion, and strict rules of conduct that disincentivize masculine, competitive expression. Since men are naturally animated by rugged individualism and natural hierarchy formation—that is, they are capable of agonistic self-organization that often disregards or demotes women—gynocracy pacifies men by eliminating independent agency and suppressing competitive, spontaneous coordination. This ensures a "fair" and "cooperative" system of organization. In the end, men can succeed only if they are effeminate or female-adjacent (viz., they participate under feminine terms), defer to women at every turn, praise and elevate not the accomplished but the "victim," and tip-toe around the authorities constructed to maintain feminine space and advantage. The male aggression-in-reserve—i.e., the resolve to defends one's own cause—is pathologized and replaced by "the authorities."

Women are, by their nature, more personally dependent on others than men in terms of protection and security, mainly because of their size and because they are vulnerable when bearing children. Traditionally, the "protector" was the husband or father, and that remains theoretically the chief role of men for complementarians. The woman's natural dependence creates another vulnerability for them: they are vulnerable to the men they depend on. A husband might abuse his wife in a variety of ways. For this reason, women by nature are prone to seek out *third parties* as interjecting powers to check their husbands. The civil state does this with domestic violence laws and law enforcement, the church with pastoral intervention,[10] and brothers and fathers in less civilly sanctioned ways. These powers equalize the home, providing the weaker party (the woman) some power, usually operating in reserve, over the stronger party (the man). I am not criticizing this appeal to third parties in itself. As I said in another chapter, *ad hoc* measures that equalize can mitigate the abuse of natural hierarchies. It is understandable that women are like this.

But the feminine natural instinct for third-party power makes women prone, especially when having institutional power, to subject *everything* to rules and credentials that equalize the sexes and even favor women. Thus, feminized spaces tend to subject all actions to procedure and process, and all grievance, no matter how slight, is delivered to the authorities whose job it is to act on the grievance. This institutionalizes passive-aggression, effectively overpowering and suppressing overt aggression and even natural masculine agonism. The masculine agonistic impulse to compete and self-sort and to spontaneously

---

10. I often wonder whether men are less interested in church because they sense that their wives want them under church authority simply to "fix" them for their own interests. And the way that many pastors speak about men in sermons would give some credence to this.

harmonize into hierarchies threatens women in most spaces. Thus, gynocracy pathologizes masculinity, making "successful" men essentially panderers to women and subjected to processes that hinder their ability to succeed in ways most natural to men.

This is why women tend to be more invested in the modern state than men. The state ensures their independence; it is the ultimate third-party. It renders personal dependence on men entirely optional. The state is their father, brother, and husband. The modern state makes possible a woman's independence and equality in society. The price for it is pathologizing masculinity.

13.

Though feminine space might seem ideal to some, the gynocracy inevitably enacts practical contradictions. I call these "gynocratic contradictions." Feminine empathy is good in itself, but its virtues arise only when constrained. Untethered empathy in society leads to policies that harm women and indeed everyone. The most obvious is transgendered "girls" in girls' sports, which women support more than men. Consider also urban crime. Urbanite white women vote for Democrats in huge numbers. Urban Democrats are those who want to "defund the police" and exercise "prosecutorial discretion" that frees criminals. Urbans areas are thus full of unchecked crime, making the streets more dangerous for women. Women are also the most susceptible to woke discourse, which guilts them into "allyship." Are you a minority and have a grievance? Signal displeasure to white women, even *blame* them for your pain, and women will shower you with money and retweets.

Empathy is vital for tender understanding, but it is easily exploited, and it can even rationalize self-harm. Take the bizarre celebration of obesity today. It makes little sense apart from unconstrained feminine empathy. Or what about hoards of mainly single, able-bodied men from patriarchal nations who have migrated to Western borders? The West lets them all in and then has to conceal the spike in sexual assaults, and women will only quietly acknowledge their fear of going out in public.[11] Consider also child transgenderism, which seems to be facilitated in large part by over-empathetic and sometimes deranged mothers.

The most insane and damaging sociological trends of our modern society are female-driven. The gynocracy is self-destructive and breeds social disorder. Feminine virtues *greatly* benefit individuals and society; they are indispensable. But they operate for good only when complemented with masculine leadership.

14.

I once saw an effeminate and flamboyant military officer address a formation of soldiers. He was relaying mundane information, but the manner of his delivery (which was light and gay) made the female soldiers giggle, as if they were with their gay friend having casual conversation. The male soldiers were mainly stone-faced, though some responded instinctively to their female soldiers around them. If the formation were exclusively male and they were not constrained by higher administration, the men would find ways to rid themselves of this officer.

11. See Douglas Murray's *Strange Death of Europe: Immigration, Identity, Islam* (London: Bloomsbury, 2017), chap. 12, for bizarre and heartbreaking examples of how native European women have responded to injustices perpetrated on them by immigrant men. He describes a German woman who, after being sexually assaulted by a migrant, "lied about the identities of her attackers because she did not want to 'help fuel aggressive racism.'" She even wrote an open letter *apologizing to them*! (197–98).

15.

For decades, women have sought equality in public discourse—to be treated as a person whose ideas should receive recognition. The request that every argument should receive a fair hearing is easy to accept. But many men hesitate to fully integrate women in high-level discourse, because they suspect that inclusion will heavily gender the discourse. The concern is not that women will take disagreement personally. Men do this as well. The fear is that women will take disagreement personally *and* frame the disagreement as an oppressor silencing the oppressed. Disagreement is interpreted as a male obsession with excluding women from high-level discourse, whose credentials qualify her (in her mind) to be there and to be believed.

Embodying the rules of this gendered discourse, some men defend the offended woman with a semblance of masculinity: They protect her against the attacking men. Thus, the "discourse" is now centered less around objectivity than the subjective feelings of the woman. The defending male faction, who are often called the "white knights," hover around these women, affirming them and denouncing their detracting men as jerks or worse. This is a sort of pseudo-chivalry, which shields the women from male criticism, and in effect it strengthens the feminine nature of the discourse. It also undermines high-level discourse. Thus the "white knights" are supporting a gynocratic contradiction—that women, in the interest of equality in high-level discourse, will promote (via white-knighting men) the sort of discourse that undermines argumentative standards and justifies shoddy work. For these reasons, many men have quietly refused to even *engage* most women in spirited debate. It is not worth the cost. The few men who dare to criticize the work of women have to litter their criticism with so much effusive praise or genuflection that the criticism is all but worthless; and in the end, the pandering is not enough to avoid the ire.

As academic institutions cater to and graduate more and more women, credentialism is on the rise. The academic institution is an authority—a third-party—that confers "expertise" on an individual. This is why women place their credentials—"Dr." or "PhD" or "Professor," or even "MA in theology"—in their social media name: They serve as institution-conferred markers that position them above those who lack the title. Thus, the "credibility" of a statement, no matter how contestable, depends more on one's relationship to credibility-conferring institutions than on the soundness of the claim in itself. Even if you have the credentials, you may not have proper "training" in some narrow specialty, or you haven't taken a specific gender studies seminar in graduate school with a specific professor. And then there is "tone" in one's criticism. The tone of "critical" reviews of works written by women have to treat the author as if she were royalty or an infallible goddess. Any perceived slight sends you to the gallows.

16.

Men and women do not have to live like this. A masculine society is preferred because it harmonizes the individual and hierarchy for the common good. Masculine societies are not threatened by the feminine virtues but complement them, neither eliminating nor suppressing but ordering them to the common good. Without masculine leadership, feminine virtues will inevitably become disordered and self-destructive. Masculine virtues are ordered not directly by the feminine virtues but in the leadership of them. To be sure, a masculine society is not a male-only society but rather a society whose principal institutions embody masculine virtues, and the feminine virtues operate through them. Women are necessary and vital for the common good, and I say this with no pandering intent. It is true. But the pursuit of gender equality will produce more harm than good.

Christian nationalists must affirm and restore gender hierarchy in society for the good of both men and women. I've focused an entire section on gynocracy because gynocracy will resist Christian nationalism. Our claims of exclusivity are contrary to untethered empathy and gynocratic norms. The rise of Christian nationalism necessitates the fall of gynocracy.

III. Universalism

17.

In modern life, truth and error are so subordinated in our minds to sentiments of good and bad that to affirm what is actually true often requires you to endure the feeling of being bad for affirming it. In other words, we have been so conditioned to affirm what we *feel* to be good that that feeling determines for us what is true. Conversely, we deny any thought that we feel is bad. We like to think that our minds are free from social influence, but they are not. Some beliefs are *psychologically* (not merely socially) easier to hold than others. This is not bad in itself. This is the principal role of cultural Christianity as a mode of religion. But in a fallen world, the mental structures that make some beliefs easier to affirm than others is subject to corruption, and we can be led by society to affirm subjectively what is objectively false.

Many thoughts cause us psychological discomfort, even when we know they are true; and we often try to find ways—frequently absurd, irrational, and contrary to experience—to suppress that discomfort. We are all moderns in mind; we all have these psychological pressures that draw us to the social flow, to acquiesce to things we know are false or suspect. The side of error in our time looks comfortable, warm, and tranquil. It is no surprise that de-conversion accounts often include pictures of the de-converted smiling in some tranquil nature scene. He dove straight into the calm social pond and became elated at the release of psychological conflict and at society's affirmation. His mind is now at ease, as he waves the "current thing" flag. Of course, this is not courageous: it is mental weakness and last-man psychology.

Christian nationalists hold beliefs that run contrary to the prevailing norms of Western society, and thus a Christian nationalist must have the strength of will to affirm what is true, even if it doesn't feel good to him. This is the main reason why I emphasized the *will* throughout this book. We often have to act against our psychological inclinations; we have to run from cognitive comforts and from the embrace of modern society; we have to retrain the mind by the strength of will. We might *feel*, for example, that it is wrong for public space to be exclusively Christian, but it still ought to be. Remember that most of our spiritual forefathers had the opposite feeling. We must overcome ourselves.

18.

In evangelical discourse, the audience of our "moral witness" is not the mid-America nominal Christian. The audience is the coastal elites. Thus, when examining social and political issues, most evangelicals argue for or against some position according to the sensibilities of the secularist ruling class. Our "loving" arguments against transgenderism, for example, devote a lot of space to empathy, non-judgmentalism, the recognition of purported evils against them, "good faith," and the denunciation of (sometimes imagined) enemies who wish them harm. But when evangelicals write against "racists" or "xenophobes," they go in with all guns blazing, lacking any sense of empathy, understanding, or even rational consideration of arguments. In every case, the manner they go about addressing some topic is determined by ruling-class sentiment towards that topic. This is true even when we address fellow Christians. Thus, "good faith" discussions between Christians about same-sex attraction look very different from the unequivocal denunciation of anything with a semblance of "kinism." Evangelicals are rhetorically enslaved to the sentiments of coastal elite, even when they are not being addressed. These elites are the Big Brother always watching and judging in the shadows.

But the ruling class's hold on rhetoric must be critiqued and discarded. Christians must overcome a psycho-rhetorical hurdle and affirm the dangerous thought that their political vision has no room for the secularist elite. We do not need to frame our positions as if they are watching. Free yourselves from their enslavement. There is no convincing them of our side, unless they were to convert to Christ. There is no robust common ground here. There is no credibility we can establish with them. Unavoidably, we are threats to their regime. Christian nationalism is an existential threat to the secularist regime. They are enemies of the church and, as such, enemies of the human race.

19.

You denounce *this*; you disclaim *that*; you distance yourself from [insert the uncouth]; you love your country, but you're not a fascist; you disagree with homosexuality, but you're not homophobe; you're patriotic but recognize our "checkered" national history; you're not woke, but "God hates racism" ... Okay, we get it. You're not a baddie.

Let's stop trying to establish credibility by denouncing the deplorable and listing all our disclamations. "Racist," "bigot," "xenophobe," "homophobe," "transphobe"—these terms are simply socio-rhetorical devices used to curtail speech, and our attempts to avoid them are a mental *habit*. It is a product of socialization. By habit, we preface statements with, "Now, I'm not a racist, but . . ." as if that makes any difference to the left. Any hint of some bad perception or connotation, and our mental programming kicks in: "Now, to be clear, I denounce so and so" or "I find this or that abhorrent, but . . ."; or, "It is not homophobic to say . . . ." We're constantly trying to wedge our views within a narrow window of credibility by checking off all these rhetorical boxes. We waste pages and pages trying to keep socio-rhetorical power at bay: "If I give this disclaimer or affirm their (likely imagined or fake) hate crimes, maybe he won't call me a homophobe or racist."

Once you *feel* this habit in your own writing or speaking, you can begin to squash it. And once you're aware of it, you will see how it operates in discourse. We're playing a rhetorical game, one that is rigged against us. Don't play the game.

20.

The Western mind has a universalizing tendency. The root of this tendency seems to be our emphasis on the human over the ethnic. Try to imagine how you would view the world if you had no comprehension of the concept "human," no universalizing concept of man. One ethnicity to another would be as dogs are to cats. Think about how that would frame one's sense of duty and his good. Or perhaps consider C.S. Lewis's science fiction novel *Out of the Silent Planet* in which three different sentient species—the hrossa, séroni, and pfifltriggi—live in harmony on the same planet but have very different bodies, interests, activities, and strengths. Ethical reflection among each species would dwell not on what is universally good and obligatory; rather, each would concern itself mainly with the good of their own species. Their thoughts would center on their own kind, for each is very different. Imagine how different one's framing of duty and goodness would be if we shared a planet with sentient species as different as the hrossa, séroni, and pfifltriggi.

Now, we don't live in that sort of world; there is only one species of man. But the Western mind thinks almost entirely in terms of humankind, in terms of universal humanity. We universalize our ethics, patterns of thought, altruism, and conceptions of the good. We even universalize our universalism—we ascribe universal thinking to non-Westerners. We assume that *all* people affirm that universal human duty overrides any ethnic duty. We assume that all have a universal altruism. We assume, in short, that they view the world like Westerners—in a humanistic rather than an ethnic frame. But I suspect that this is the West ascribing its own *particular* tendencies to all people. Universalizing has helped the United States justify wars to replace dictatorships with "democracy," presumably thinking that Middle Eastern dictators are holding down that universal urge in every man and women to adopt the "natural" virtues of Western political life. But these virtues are products of centuries of Western political life. Our own universalizing is a particular Western thing.

Non-Western peoples do not think like this. They do not invade other countries in the name of some universal, abstract ideals. Universality is far less prevalent among non-Westerners, who tend toward a more ethno-centric frame of what is good. That is, they view other ethnic-groups not in terms of common humanity (though certainly they have a conception of humanity) but in terms of ethnicity—in terms of ethnic in-group/out-group. At one level, we implicitly know this and show little concern about it, which is why Japan's restrictive immigration policies do not trouble Westerners. They are, well, Japanese: Japan is for the Japanese. The same policy in any Western country would horrify Western elites because it violates their universalistic frame.

My point is not to attack non-Westerners but to highlight that they are normal; indeed, *they are right*. The Majority World is more ethno-centric than the Minority World. The West is weirdly sensitive about these things. But we should join the Majority World: lighten up and learn from them. The various Western ethnicities should view the world more through an ethnic frame. Or, put differently, they must stop universalizing their ethics, ways of life, patterns of thought, and sense of what is good and become more exclusive and ethnic-focused.

IV. Dominion

21.

The chief end of men is not protecting women. Thinking otherwise is a product of modern urban and suburban life, in which the home is only a place of consumption and the family does not take part in a productive project. But the *man* is given the mission from God and the woman is made his helper, and his mission is not directed at the woman but outside himself—to the world. The woman is an object of protection because she is integral to the mission, not because she *is* the mission or the chief agent of that mission. Masculinity is justified not on grounds of protecting women or even in fighting evil men. Masculinity makes possible the necessary competencies for leading the household to exercise dominion in this world. Indeed, given the nature of the mission, masculine virtues are principal and feminine virtues are ancillary.[12]

22.

Attempts to resist modern life in practical ways are often derided as LARPing, or live-action role playing—that one's anti-modernity is superficial, imaginary, and made possible by modernity itself. There is some element of truth to this. Modern homesteading, for example, often requires supplemental income from modern sources. But many of the things ridiculed as LARPing are simply good choices for living well in this world. A woman who makes food from scratch from her own garden is not only offering her family healthy options but also exercising praiseworthy skills and passing those skills on to her children. The variety of skills that our ancestors mastered to survive are now unnecessary and obsolete, and the products of those skills are now readily available at stores. But certainly something important for living well has been lost as a result, as we've lost the ability to make and fix things for ourselves and to intimately bring something from soil to the table. LARPing is, in the best sense, mastering inefficient and old skills and practices that attune one to the natural world, that break you free in part from modern life.

The world of sustenance farming is over for the West, for now, but some of the crafts and skills of that world need to be recovered. This requires intentional actions, deliberate inefficiencies. You have to LARP a little, to endure some rugged austerity, and to relearn

12. By "ancillary," I mean *necessary* for the mission but supplemental to it.

what Walmart and the grocery store have made obsolete. I'm not going to tell you how far to go in this, but it is both good for you and your family *and* it prepares for a better future. I expect that the most committed Christian nationalists will be farmers, homesteaders, and ranchers. Why is that? They understand from experience that the good of this world doesn't come simply from good will or from waiting on fate, but from actively asserting one's will in the world and contending for good.

23.

Nature is so thoroughly controlled by modern technique that contending with nature is, for most people, rarely a feature of daily concern. Our single-family homes are mini-aristocratic estates with front-yards well-manicured and easily managed that represent our leisure and freedom from labor. We no longer directly assert our will upon animals and the land to bring forth fruits for human life; we do not have *productive* property. Everything is designed for physical comfort, ease, and convenience. Now, I am not going to rant against the suburbs; the suburbs are a refuge in our time. The world you grew up in no longer exists. I understand why people move into HOA-controlled track housing. When you live in a low-trust society that is constantly moving about and undergoing demographic transformation outside your control, you need artificial stability and order, and you need low-risk, retainable home value for when you must flee from the latest government-sponsored transformation. I don't fault anyone for preferring the suburbs.

But let us consider how suburbia shapes our relationship to dominion. The suburbs are well-ordered, but the power of human will is concealed behind modern technique, which renders our wills fat and dependent. We cannot help but want order, but it comes about through contracted third-parties, many of which are bureaucratic (e.g., HOA). We no longer know what it takes to tame the wild. We no longer have the competencies, or even the desire, to stake a claim for ourselves and contend for it. We have a spirit for order in a way, but not for dominion—no spirit to inscribe one's will into a piece of dirt, to stand at its boundaries and with resolve say *mine* to both fellow man and the wild.

24.

The revival of natural law thinking among Protestants today has led many to see in nature more than the Hobbesian "red in tooth and claw." This is a positive development. But let us not fall into the opposite error—into the Disneyfied view of nature in which benevolence alone domesticates nature, somehow making the crops grow and wild animals prance and dance around us. John Smith was better attuned to nature than Pocahontas. The human will tames the wild so that nature is put into use for us. However, we do not thereby transcend nature but complete it and complete ourselves.

We usually treat the human-developed environment as if it were separate from nature. We "leave" the developed world to go on a "nature walk," for example. This distinction certainly works for us, but it might also conceal an important truth. If humans are natural and if exercising dominion over non-human creation is natural, then human development is neither unnatural nor non-natural. Our development, though a product of choice, is natural to creation; it perfects creation. Thus, the developed landscapes and towns (and perhaps even cities) are natural. This should shape *what* we develop on the land and *why* we develop it.

More importantly, we should consider that nature *as wilderness* is something man must tame. It is not "untrammeled" or "pure." Our dominion over nature requires the imposition of human will upon wilderness. By nature, man tames the wild. I am not suggesting that *all* wilderness ought to be tamed, as if taming it is an end in itself.

Since dominion necessitates masculine virtues, masculine virtues are not postlapsarian but essential to our design and to achieve the intended earthly end of creation. Without a frontier, masculine virtues sustain dominion, for wilderness has a habit of encroaching and returning. It resists. Pre-modern circumstances offered sufficient opportunities to exercise these virtues, since most people had to contend with domesticated animals and dangerous wildlife. However, in the modern world, in which the state governs every square inch with maximal power, most traditional skills are made obsolete by mass production; the masculine virtues don't have an outlet. Indeed, the system is so designed for an ease of activity and separation from nature that masculinity is seen as a threat, and so it is pathologized.

The growing homesteading movement in the US seems to represent a move back to at least a semblance of these pre-modern conditions. It offers the opportunity to domesticate. This exaggerates a bit what most people are doing, and there are socio-economic class factors here. But it is, nevertheless one way that people can relearn about human life in the world—that it requires imposing one's will on a stubborn, sometimes violent wilderness. Most people cannot be homesteaders, of course, but we ought to think of ways to experience "nature" in a dominion-oriented way. A life that contends with nature learns to contend for higher goods.

25.

A few years ago, I told my wife that I would like our boys to become white-collar professionals of some sort. I was not interested in them maintaining some social station. I reasoned that since we have resources for it to happen, becoming anything else would seem to be a squandering of resources. But I've changed my position entirely. What I care most about is their future independence and autonomy—not from me but from liberal totalization. The bureaucratized workforce is increasingly ruled by social justice advocates who enforce rules of belief and behavior that force people to assert both moral absurdities and self-repudiation. I say now, "Find a career that maximizes your autonomy from the forces of the secularist ruling class."

If you are a white, heterosexual, cis-gendered male, then the world will not offer you any favors. Indeed, your career advancement depends on sacrificing your self-respect by praising and pandering to your inferiors who rule over you. Even the CEOs, in the end, are dominated by the woke scolds. Ponder well the demeaning demands of "greatness" in our time. Imagine spending forty years of your life in the military to become a general only to learn about "white rage" and oversee, by the order of some ditsy and lecturing congresswoman, a program to integrate transgenderism into the military. How many of us conservatives have entered these timeless professions and strove for greatness in them only to find ourselves in the middle of a clown show and enforcing policies that lead to the destruction of the military, or worse: seeing it set its sights on Old America?

As an alternative, young people should find a path that maximizes their independence, especially from HR departments, DEI standards, woke administrators, government mandates, etc. Learn skills that provide services to people directly, both locally and online. We should praise independence more than college degrees, and Christians should provide support networks for independent and autonomous employment. To be clear, this does not preclude Christians from pursuing white-collar jobs or public professions (e.g., political office). I am not saying that we should retreat from these important professions. But having skills and backup resources for autonomy is the very thing that makes such pursuits viable and wise. You may be forced out of your profession.

Along these lines, American parents should no longer expect their children to leave the house after graduating high school. This was once a good rule, since there were opportunities for young adults and people could be normal. But times have changed. Staying home into one's twenties provides a safe, secure place to chart a path for independence, though parents should have zero tolerance for laziness and encourage independence.

26.

The Christian trend of attacking "individualism" is a mistake. There is certainly an unhealthy individualism, either the fake expressivist variety or the libertarian version that denies pre-political ties and unchosen bonds. But healthy individualism expands each person's possibilities for action and development. It sets the goal at greatness. It encourages an active life of competence, self-command, and a command of nature. The collectivist fear of individualism is that it isolates man from man or sets people in destructive opposition. But this falsely assumes that individuals pursuing mastery cannot spontaneously generate hierarchy. In such hierarchies, skills are synchronized under authority for a common mission.

Masculine individualism is not opposed to but *seeks* harmonious hierarchy. Men are not averse to an inferior station. A man readily accepts another's superiority, *if* he is recognized as a man among men, having a skill that contributes to the whole. In this way, masculinity harmonizes equality and hierarchy such that the individual is empowered to serve the good of the whole. Masculinity provides a necessary ingredient for natural hierarchy formation: agonism. Men contend with each other and compete, and they can achieve respect as an individual in a group. Individualism and hierarchy are opposites only in a feminized society.

Anti-individualism subjects everything to processes and rules in the name of "fairness" and "equity." For kids, all play must be "structured" and minutely supervised. The naturally superior has to play a game rigged against him, becoming great only by being the best at calling everyone equal. Self-respecting people will not make it. The result is organizational incompetence, mediocrity, the suppression of greatness, and an artificial hierarchy. No one is a man among men, but a person among persons; and your standing among others is not because of something you've achieved but simply by virtue of the fact of existence, or by being superior at congratulating everyone for their existence or empathizing with another's "trauma."

The promise of the "American dream" was not that anyone can become a millionaire if he tries hard enough. That negative characterization is a widespread lie. The American dream was that each person's striving can attain him a respectable place among fellow Americans. That is, you will likely not be fabulously wealthy, but you can achieve mastery in something that will earn you recognition as a man among men. And in that recognition, you have a place of your own. Your dignity was once tied to what you did and to what you *could* do when called to do it. Unfortunately, this sort of striving today is degrading and futile in most areas of the economy. We work for woke corporations that hate you and that force you to adopt an ideology of self-loathing and self-incrimination. Your only self-worth is grounded in the worth you ascribe to other people's delusions about themselves.

The return to true American individualism will require local networks of counter-economies in which each family can aid others with practical skills for necessary goods. A renewed individualism will resist the blobbing and softness of modern manhood, will reject the talk of "universal dignity," will pursue timeless competencies, will cultivate martial virtues, will reject the "warmth" of modernity, and will repel the schoolmarms in our institutions who want to smother vitality, self-mastery, and achievement. It may be difficult to achieve collective self-sufficiency in these relations, but pursuing it is a start.

27.

Christian households in American should form local networks of production and exchange. These are people you can trust who share your Christian beliefs and your vision. They will not join in "cancelling" you when the rest of society might but will support and encourage you. The goal is not a commune but an anti-fragile counterculture and countermarket of personal connections and mutual service. Perhaps each household can have its unique contribution. This requires intentional effort and some degree of household production, and it will not be possible for all Christians in our modern day. Still, all should be able to support such networks. At the very least, we should have like-minded Christian nationalist friends in real life.

Men must take the lead in this. Be the true heads of households. Make it part of your household vision. Adopt a plan and talk to the men in your churches.

28.

The need for a connection of people and place is natural and good. The Gospel did not "critique" or eliminate this. We should seek out forms of living that make that life possible. Many of my readers already do, and they should help the rest of us sort out the way to achieve this. It starts with families staying put and committing themselves to a place for good. Truly rooted people have nowhere else to go, no country to which they can flee in rough times; they dig their heels into their soil and fight for their place.

29.

It is important to remember that Christian nationalism is a means, not an end in itself. Let us not serve an ideology. I say this not to suppress action for Christian nationalism but to remind us of the purpose of it—the earthly and heavenly good of the people of God. In the near term, Christians may be unable to restore explicit Christian nationhood. But instead of despairing, we can seek other means for that good, such as the networking I spoke of above. Many of my readers likely live among Christian people who need their people-hood brought to consciousness. Whatever role we play, let us trust in but not wait on providence. Let us help ourselves by grace.

Political theologies that are stated in eschatological terms can easily fall into a sort of waiting mode. This includes even the more positive theologies, such as post-millennialism. Their adherents often fail to recognize the necessity of action and the right social conditions for establishing a Christian commonwealth. If it is going to happen, we have to make it happen. I'm often asked whether I'm a post-millennialist. I answer that my political theology is based more in human nature than eschatology.[13] Christian nationalism, in light of grace, is most natural to the Christian human being. Thus, the precursor to any Christian nationalism is a people intentionally seeking their natural good according to man's nature. We neither seek a Christian commonwealth for its own sake nor wait on providence for it to spontaneously appear. Rather, we seek our good, and when possible, we arrange ourselves politically for that good.

30.

Men are generally drawn to the sort of labor in which one's inputs ordinarily produce their intended effect: an output. That is, they want to exert will on material to produce something. But leading the home in spiritual life does not work that way. No man has the power to produce a spiritual effect, and the effect is not immediately seen. Still, men *must* lead their families in spiritual life. It is your responsibility, as the head of household, to order your home to God in Christ.

Lead the family in family worship. Keep it simple, but make it the priority.

31.

Christian nationalism should have a strong and austere aesthetic. I was dismayed when I saw the attendees of a recent PCA General Assembly—men in wrinkled, short-sleeved golf shirts, sitting

---

13. Of course, theological anthropology is not divorced from eschatology, as this book has made clear. My point is that the emphasis on eschatology often distracts us from what is (to my mind) more fundamental—what is the nature of restored humanity?

plump in their seats. We have to do better. Pursue your potential. Lift weights, eat right, and lose the dad bod. We don't all have to become bodybuilders, but we ought to be men of power and endurance. We cannot achieve our goals with such a flabby aesthetic and under the control of modern nutrition. Sneering at this aesthetic vision, which I fully expect to happen, is pure cope. Grace does not destroy T-levels; grace does not perfect testosterone into estrogen. If our opponents want to be fat, have low testosterone, and chug vegetable oil, let them. It won't be us.

32.

Churches and pastors are integral to the spiritual health of the Christian nationalist movement. But since it is a political movement, pastors as pastors should not take the lead. Pastors are to political movements what chaplains are to military commanders: they advise and serve people's spiritual needs, but they do not lead, nor are they decision-makers. Pastors *as fellow Christians* can be involved in non-pastoral matters, but pastors *as pastors* should be more like chaplains. We are Christians pursuing Christian things outside the sphere of the instituted church. The instituted church is not a hub of Christian activism or the "embassy" of godly political rule. The people of God arrange for themselves their own civil rule, and it doesn't proceed from the ecclesiastical order or from the approval of ministers. For too long, we have looked to fiery political sermons to satisfy our concerns over the "culture." We listen and then walk out the door thinking, *The secularist culture got it good!* and we are satisfied. Meanwhile, the culture continues going to hell. This exaggerates things a bit, but still Christians have treated Sunday as their weekly political meeting. It should be no such thing, and practically speaking, turning it into a political church hinders Christian political movements. We must form civil associations outside the ecclesiastical sphere, and without pastoral leadership.

33.

The "Have more babies; save the world" argument needs to go away. I understand the idea: we can't win now, but if we outbreed them, then we'll win. Whatever truth there is in this, we should not pass the struggle on to future generations: "We had fun making and raising you; now, do what we wouldn't do ourselves." Remember, a Christian nation is not merely a nation of Christians but a nation with a Christian self-conception and a willingness to act for itself. Producing numbers will not make a people, especially when the secularists actively try to steal them from us. Having babies is only one part of a greater project. Let us not be passive in things we can accomplish now.

34.

The benefit of being right-wing is that you can recommend that people read old books without including caveats, or warnings, or dangers. Not everything in old books comports with Christian truth or wholesomeness, but old books are far less harmful than practically *any* channel on television and most school curricula. And many of the truths taken for granted in the past are now "based" right-wing views and cancelable opinions. So read all the old books, especially the epics—Homer and Virgil. Take the advice of Philip Melanchthon: "I would consider anyone who is not charmed by reading Homer lacking in any sense of humanity: an animal, not a man."[14]

14. Philip Melanchthon, "Preface to Homer," in *The Great Tradition: Classic Readings on What It Means to Be an Educated Human Being*, ed. Richard M. Gamble (Wilmington, DE: ISI Books, 2007), 420–21.

In order to renew our institutions, we have to set them straight according to ancient principles. We cannot lose the timeless wisdom, prudence, and knowledge of our Western heritage. To this end, we cannot reject classical literature; we must be grounded in it. Again, listen to Melanchthon:

> I consider in my mind these admirable gifts of God, namely the study of literature and of the humanities—and apart from the Gospel of Christ this world holds nothing more splendid nor more divine and I also consider, on the other hand, by what blindness the minds of men are enveloped in unnatural and Cimmerian darkness; they spurn these true and greatest gifts, and with great effort they pursue means for their wishes and desires that are not only inferior but also ruinous and destructive to themselves. When I weigh these things in my heart, I am violently moved, for it comes to my mind by what dense darkness and, so to speak, black night the hearts of men are surrounded. I am not further astonished, if men are blind in things that are divine and beyond human understanding, when I see them thus treading under foot these their own and personal goods for which they are intended by divine providence, and which they could have comprehended and cherished.[15]

The American founders, though revolutionaries, were able to build after the revolution ended. Why? They cherished their Western inheritance. We must follow their example. The will and ability to resist is not enough. Our education should develop statesmen and peace-time leaders—men of knowledge, patriotism, and

15. Ibid.

prudence. Eventually, we will have to enact a positive vision, and so we must be grounded in the classical texts of the Western canon. We must prize morally formative education.

V. America is Not Lost

35.

In the United States, the civil power of state governors is not derived from the federal government but comes immediately from God, as I described in chapter 7. State governors are deputies of God, not deputies of the federal government, and their power from God is for good, not for evil. Thus, they must resist and nullify unjust and tyrannical laws imposed on the people by the federal government. No unjust federal law is an ordinance of God, and so it is not backed by a power of God. Therefore, a state governor resisting an unjust law of the federal government is not resisting God but the tyranny of men. Resistance to such tyrannical laws—which are not laws at all—is obedience to God, for they *harm* the people, and the state governors have the power of God to eliminate what harms the people. State governors must recall their duties to God and fight against injustices of the federal government.

36.

At the Federal Convention of 1787, which produced the United States Constitution, Oliver Ellsworth (a delegate from Connecticut) gave a speech that emphasized the importance of the states for securing one's rights and happiness. Governors today should heed his words. The following is James Madison's summary of Ellsworth's speech:

Mr. ELLSWORTH: Under a national government, he [Ellsworth] should participate in the national security, as remarked by Mr. King but that was all. What he wanted was domestic happiness. The national government could not descend to the local objects on which this depended. It could only embrace objects of a general nature. He turned his eyes therefore for the preservation of his rights to the state governments. From these alone he could derive the greatest happiness he expects in this life. His happiness depends on their existence, as much as a new born infant on its mother for nourishment. If this reasoning was not satisfactory, he had nothing to add that could be so.[16]

We should look again to the states. Christian nationalists ought to elect Christians into state office, especially those who are willing to be the lesser magistrate against an unjust federal government.

37.

This conclusion might suggest to the reader that America is lost. But America is not lost. It is better to say that the *United States*, as a whole, is lost; the GAE has captured it. But parts of America are certainly not lost. Hundreds of counties in the United States have a majority of conservative Christians, as do several states. There is no reason why Christian nationalist movements cannot find success in these places, and we should organize and support Christian political visions for towns, counties, and states. In many places, our success or failure is not a matter of numbers but a matter of whether we have the *will* for success.

16. Oliver Ellsworth, summarized in James Madison, *Notes of Debates in the Federal Convention of 1787 Reported by James Madison* (1840; Athens, OH: Ohio University Press, 1966), 230 [June 30, 1787].

38.

Many claims in this book will worry many American conservative Christians. I've said that political governments can suppress false religion, establish a church, even require people to attend church. I also wrote about a "Christian prince," which is not the sort of political title one would find in America. I will not walk back those arguments; I affirm my conclusions as good and true *principles*. But I have demonstrated that Christian nationalism can and should look different in different places, for all principles are *applied* according to the concrete situation. One application that is righteous in itself is not necessarily suitable for all situations. The means by which a Christian people achieve their good depend on their identity, their experiences, and their way of life.

An American Christian nationalism would acknowledge the old American sense of liberty—one that predates World War II. And we must reject the idea that American liberty is universal and merely human. It is particular and American. Let us embrace it as ours. And let us, by grace, submit ourselves to the law of nature and nature's God, actively working in the holiness of Christ for the great renewal of our country, to the glory and advancement of Christ's kingdom.

Acknowledgments

An impulse of post-war conservatism is to disavow whatever accusation the left hurls at you. When "Christian nationalism" became the Current Thing—the new thing that perpetuates the state of fear—many nationalist Christians saw it as a gift. It was revelatory in a way. *We are Christians and nationalists,* we said to ourselves, *but we are more. We are Christian nationalists.* I must, for this reason, recognize the anti-Christian nationalists, who assumed that Americans would flee from whatever the left decries as bad. You woke many from their dogmatic slumber that kept "Christian" and "nationalism" apart for so long, and more are awakening each day.

But my praise is mainly reserved for the Christian nationalists, who have overcome themselves or, more precisely, have by the force of will eradicated the secularist dogmas that were preached into them and have denounced the modern cult of ugliness. My hope is that this book helps you to articulate what is already present in your spirit and to love even more what is beautiful.

The editors at Canon are exceptional—Jake McAtee, Brian Marr, and Brian Kohl. Their comments throughout this project helped me greatly improve the clarity and content of my argument. I also appreciate the liberty they granted me to say what needed to be said. My errors, whether they be factual or moral, are my own, however.

Several friends have encouraged and supported me in this project. To let them chart their own path, I will leave them unnamed. But I thank you all.

If I were unmarried and childless, I would not have written this book. This book is not an intellectual exercise, nor intended simply to "contribute to the field" of Christian political theory. It is personal. It is a vision of the future, and my family is a part of that future. My motivation was not abstract justice or humanity but *real* people whom I love. The love for my own—and my family most intensely—animates this whole work.

Made in the USA
Middletown, DE
21 November 2022

15608745R00291

THE AGNOSTIC AGE

THE AGNOSTIC AGE

LAW, RELIGION, AND THE

CONSTITUTION

PAUL HORWITZ

OXFORD
UNIVERSITY PRESS

Oxford University Press, Inc., publishes works that further Oxford University's objective of excellence in research, scholarship, and education.

Oxford   New York
Auckland   Cape Town   Dar es Salaam   Hong Kong   Karachi   Kuala Lumpur   Madrid   Melbourne
Mexico City   Nairobi   New Delhi   Shanghai   Taipei   Toronto

With offices in
Argentina   Austria   Brazil   Chile   Czech Republic   France   Greece   Guatemala   Hungary   Italy
Japan   Poland   Portugal   Singapore   South Korea   Switzerland   Thailand   Turkey   Ukraine
Vietnam

Library of Congress Cataloging-in-Publication Data

Horwitz, Paul.
  The agnostic age : law, religion, and the Constitution / Paul Horwitz.
    p. cm.
  Includes bibliographical references and index.
  ISBN 978-0-19-973772-7 ((hardback) : alk. paper)
1. Freedom of religion—United States. 2. Religion and law--United States.
3. Agnosticism—United States. 4. Liberalism (Religion)—United States. I. Title.
  KF4783.H67 2011
  342.7308'52—dc22
                                                    2010032098

  2 3 4 5 6 7 8 9
Printed in the United States of America on acid-free paper

Note to Readers
This publication is designed to provide accurate and authoritative information in regard to the subject matter covered. It is based upon sources believed to be accurate and reliable and is intended to be current as of the time it was written. It is sold with the understanding that the publisher is not engaged in rendering legal, accounting, or other professional services. If legal advice or other expert assistance is required, the services of a competent professional person should be sought. Also, to confirm that the information has not been affected or changed by recent developments, traditional legal research techniques should be used, including checking primary sources where appropriate.

(Based on the Declaration of Principles jointly adopted by a Committee of the American Bar Association and a Committee of Publishers and Associations.)

You may order this or any other Oxford University Press publication by visiting the Oxford University Press website at www.oup.com

To my parents, Marvin and Yvonne Horwitz

CONTENTS

ACKNOWLEDGMENTS

I owe a debt of gratitude to many people and institutions for bringing this book to life. I must begin by thanking the University of Alabama School of Law, where this book was written. Dean Kenneth Randall and my faculty colleagues have been unstinting in their support, including the opportunity for an early teaching leave. I am grateful to the Bounds Law Library, particularly its staffers Penny Gibson and Paul Pruitt, for their time and patience. Not least, I greatly appreciate the support of Oxford University Press.

At the Law School, Jennifer Michaelis of the Class of 2009 served as my research assistant in the early stages of this project. Martha Rogers of the Class of 2011 was my research assistant during the drafting and editing of the book, and offered exemplary service. Both of them kept me organized and on track in spite of myself. I am also grateful to Donna Warnack for clerical assistance.

Suzy Hansen provided freelance editing services of the highest order. The book benefited immeasurably from her light and, when necessary, heavy touch. (She has not edited these acknowledgments, which is why they are so prolix, and why I have gotten away with the use of the word "prolix.")

Portions of this book were presented at workshops at Columbia Law School, Emory Law School, and St. John's University School of Law, and I am grateful to my questioners on those occasions. The first and last chapters were also given a thorough going-over at the first annual Law and Religion Roundtable, which featured a stellar cast of senior and rising scholars in the field. I am grateful to those scholars, to Rick Garnett and Nelson Tebbe, my co-organizers for this conference, and to Brooklyn Law School for hosting it.

Many friends and colleagues offered useful comments on portions of the manuscript and illuminating conversations about the book, including Bill Brewbaker, Marc DeGirolami, Mary Jean Dolan, Rick Garnett, Fred Gedicks, Kent Greenawalt, Abner Greene, Jessie Hill, Philip Hamburger, Dan Joyner, John Kang, Andrew Koppelman, Jeffrey Lipshaw, Chip Lupu, Marcus Mierle, Mark Modak-Truran, Michael Perry, Frank Ravitch, Shannon Riordan, Micah Schwartzman, Steve Shiffrin, Steve Smith, Amy Uelman, Laura Underkuffler, Robert Vischer, and John Witte. To all of them, I owe my thanks and admiration, both for their own work and for their help and friendship on this and many other occasions. I am especially grateful to Andrew Koppelman and Micah Schwartzman for pressing me to think more carefully about the relationship between constitutional agnosticism and liberalism.

I must single out Kent Greenawalt, who has been a friend and mentor ever since I took his law and religion class as a graduate student at Columbia Law School in the fall of 1996. Kent's brilliance in the field is known by all who have read his work. Equally apparent to me are his kindness and generosity, expressed many times but notably in his early invitation to present a portion of this book at Columbia. For this and much else besides, I owe him a debt beyond words.

My family bore a large burden in their support of this book. My wife, Kelly Riordan Horwitz, carved out endless time for me to write and think, despite the demands of her own thriving legal and political career. Her love, strength, and wisdom infuse this book, as they do my life. My children, Samantha and Isaac, were too young to appreciate why I was so immersed in my writing, but I offer this book to them with love. I hope that when Isaac is old enough to read the passages about Abraham and Isaac, he will forgive my somewhat latitudinarian views on child sacrifice.

But for my parents, Marvin and Yvonne Horwitz, this book would never have been written. There is nothing agnostic about their faith in me. Their love and support has sustained me over a lifetime. I dedicate my first book to them with love and gratitude.

INTRODUCTION

What is truth? said jesting Pilate, and would not stay for an answer.

—*Francis Bacon*[1]

It is a sad thing for the human race that Pilate went out without waiting for the answer; we should know what truth is.

—*Voltaire*[2]

Most scholars of law and religion have something important in common with Pontius Pilate, and an important difference. Here is the common point: Like Pilate, they throw up their hands at the question: "What is truth?"[3] And here is the difference: At least Pilate was willing to ask the question. Not so with today's leading theorists on freedom of religion. Indeed, if there is any single question they are most likely to flee, it is the question of religious truth—the question of the nature of the universe, the existence of God, and our own fate after death. That question, and how to approach it, is the subject of this book.

This is, perhaps, a somewhat sour note on which to begin a book about law and religion. There are, after all, perfectly good reasons to avoid this question. If the state is not in the business of declaring religious truths, these scholars might say, neither are they. Their job is to explore the boundaries between law and religion. That job is hard enough already. To take on the confounding question of what religious truth *is* would doom them to failure from the start. Any question that has managed to challenge all of us across the whole span of human existence is surely too deep for mere lawyers.

Better, then, to lay the question to one side and focus on the practical questions that already occupy us: What role does the state play in people's religious lives? When can a religious individual seek or win an exemption from laws that apply to others, but that would severely restrict his or her own religious practices? When can the state endorse religious ideas and practices, and when must it fall silent? When can it subsidize religious groups, and when are these groups forbidden to seek the same privileges that any other group may win in the political process?

---

1. Francis Bacon, *Of Truth*, in *The Essays* 61 (John Pitcher, ed., Penguin Books 1985) (3d ed. 1625).

2. *Voltaire, Voltaire's Philosophical Dictionary* 282 (2007) (1764).

3. John 18:38. In general, quotes from the Bible in this book are taken from the King James Version.

Against this practical justification for deferring the question of religious truth, however, there is an opposing concern. Questions of religious freedom ultimately cannot be satisfactorily answered without at least some attempt to grapple with the broader question of religious truth. In this simple fact lies much of what we have seen in the realm of law and religion scholarship: dissatisfaction, approaching a state of utter misery.

The Religion Clauses of the First Amendment are deceptively simple. They read, in just sixteen words, "Congress shall make no law respecting an establishment of religion, or prohibiting the free exercise thereof." But these two clauses—the Establishment Clause and the Free Exercise Clause—have occasioned endless debate and confusion. It is so common and so obligatory nowadays to begin any serious work on law and religion in the United States by describing this confusion that the computers of American law and religion scholars might as well come with a macro key to save them the time and trouble of hunting down the usual sources. Instead, a keystroke would vomit forth words and phrases like "incoherent,"[4] "chaotic, controversial and unpredictable,"[5] "in shambles,"[6] "schizoid,"[7] "confused,"[8] and "a complete hash."[9] And that is just what law and religion scholars are likely to say when they are feeling generous. On bad days, they may say something *really* unpleasant.

It is our happy fate as legal scholars to have a very convenient scapegoat for this state of affairs: the United States Supreme Court. The Court cooked this dog's breakfast, we may say; we're just serving it up. The Court's members, when they're especially candid (or when they are describing each other's work), are happy to shoulder the blame. So Justice Antonin Scalia has said of his brethren that they have "made such a maze of the Establishment Clause that even the most conscientious government officials can only guess what motives will be held unconstitutional."[10] Justice Stephen Breyer has attempted to make a virtue of necessity, arguing that the Supreme Court's opinions on religion form a landscape riddled with inevitable "difficult borderline cases" in which there is

---

4. Mark V. Tushnet, *Red, White, and Blue: A Critical Analysis of Constitutional Law* 247 (1988).

5. Michael W. McConnell, *Neutrality, Separation and Accommodation: Tensions in American First Amendment Doctrine*, in *Law and Religion* 63, 64 (Rex J. Adhar ed., 2000).

6. Christopher L. Eisgruber & Lawrence G. Sager, *The Vulnerability of Conscience: The Constitutional Basis for Protecting Religious Conduct*, 61 U. Chi. L. Rev. 1245, 1246 (1994).

7. Ronald Y. Mykkeltvedt, *Souring on Lemon: The Supreme Court's Establishment Clause Doctrine in Transition*, 44 Mercer L. Rev. 881, 883 (1993).

8. Mary Ann Glendon, *Law, Communities, and the Religious Freedom Language of the Constitution*, 60 Geo. Wash. L. Rev. 672, 674 (1992).

9. Christopher L. Eisgruber & Lawrence G. Sager, *Unthinking Religious Freedom*, 74 Tex. L. Rev. 577, 578 (1996).

10. *Edwards v. Aguillard*, 482 U.S. 578, 636, 640 (1987) (Scalia, J., dissenting).

"no test-related substitute for the exercise of legal judgment."[11] For a Supreme Court Justice, that is the politely worded equivalent of Bette Davis's famous warning in *All About Eve*: "Fasten your seat belts—it's going to be a bumpy night."[12]

But we should not blame the courts. The incoherence of religious freedom jurisprudence is just a symptom of a disease suffered equally by law and religion scholars and the Supreme Court. To be more specific, the disease is an allergy: an allergy to questions of religious truth.

It is certainly not the case that law and religion scholars avoid questions of religious truth because they all share the same religious viewpoint. Nor, despite frequent accusations to the contrary, is it that law and religion scholars, even at our most liberal law schools, all share an aversion to religion. There is plenty of diversity among law and religion scholars. Their primary tendency is neither religious belief nor hostility to religion. It's a reluctance to talk about religious truth *at all*.

THE AGE OF CONTESTABILITY

Outside the legal academy, in contrast, contemporary public dialogue is bursting with talk about God and religious truth. In recent years, a number of best-selling polemical writers have argued against the existence of God and for the absurdity and irrationality of religious belief. The argument advanced by these writers has been labeled "the New Atheism."[13] Proving the Newtonian literary dictum that for every argument in publishing that sells well, there will be an equal and opposite reaction, the New Atheists have been met at the ramparts by an equal number of vociferous defenders of religious belief. Call them the "New Anti-Atheists."[14] These critics argue that what is new about the New Atheists is mostly how little they know about religion, and how impoverished their arguments are in comparison to those of the "old" atheists—influential writers like Freud, Feuerbach, Marx, and others. In any event, the battle between the New Atheists and the New Anti-Atheists has been well and truly joined in the contemporary public square.

---

11. *Van Orden v. Perry*, 545 U.S. 677, 700 (2005) (Breyer, J., concurring in the judgment).

12. *All About Eve* (20th Century Fox 1950).

13. *See, e.g.*, Christopher Hitchens, *god is Not Great: How Religion Poisons Everything* (2007); Richard Dawkins, *The God Delusion* (2008); Daniel C. Dennett, *Breaking the Spell: Religion as a Natural Phenomenon* (2006); Sam Harris, *The End of Faith: Religion, Terror, and the Future of Reason* (2004). Because I am averse to undue cutesiness, I will generally refer to Hitchens' book as *God is Not Great* from now on, ignoring his insistence on using a small-case "g."

14. *See* Chapter Four. For the use of the label "New Anti-Atheists," see The New Yorker, August 31, 2009, at 8 (table of contents description of a book review published in this issue by James Wood, *God in the Quad*, at page 75).

Public interest in the question of God's existence hasn't been this hot since *Time* Magazine prematurely published His obituary over 40 years ago.[15]

What are the reasons for the sudden resurgence of public interest in the ultimate question of God's existence? There are two principal causes for this explosive growth. One is the complex status of religion and religious belief in what Charles Taylor has called our "secular age."[16] The phrase, as used here, does not mean that God has disappeared from the stage and we are all living in a post-religious environment. Whatever *Time* Magazine, along with many serious academics of the mid-1960s, may have thought would happen to religious belief in America, the United States remains, by and large, a resolutely religious country.

What has changed is the social context in which religious belief exists. If Western society was once a milieu in which "it was virtually impossible not to believe in God," in our own age, "faith, even for the staunchest believer, is [now only] one human possibility among others."[17] We live in an age in which religion is very much alive, but also highly contestable. On the one hand, the profusion of faiths within the American landscape gives an extraordinarily rich picture of what it means to be religious. On the other hand, it is now possible to imagine life without religious belief at all. Three centuries of post-Enlightenment thought and liberal democratic development have made it possible—indeed, unexceptional—for people to be securely atheistic in their worldview, or, if they do believe in God, to give the matter little thought in their daily lives. In individual lives, God may be everything from a delusion to a bit player to a constant and powerful presence. In society as a whole, however, God is merely an option.

Surprisingly, the very fact that religion is now just an option makes it all the more important. In a society like our own, in which religion was once part of the common social fabric, and most people subscribed to relatively tame variants on what we have come to call "Judeo-Christianity," the very fact that our religious beliefs were so shared and widespread made them relatively unimportant, or at least uncontroversial.[18] But religion plays a very different role in what we might call "an age of contestability."[19] In this environment, precisely *because* religion is of fading importance to some people, it is of increasing importance to others. The very question of religious belief has become a flashpoint. Religious truth, once relegated to the background, is now firmly in the foreground of public discussion.[20]

---

15. *See Time*, April 8, 1966 (asking, on the front cover, "Is God Dead?").

16. Charles Taylor, *A Secular Age* (2007).

17. *Id.* at 3.

18. *See generally* Paul Horwitz, *Religion and American Politics: Three Views of the Cathedral*, 39 U. Memphis L. Rev. 973 (2009).

19. *Id.* at 976.

20. *See id.; see also* Mark Lilla, *The Stillborn God* 3 (2007) ("[W]e are again fighting the battles of the sixteenth century—over revelation and reason, dogmatic purity and toleration,

Although law and religion has not yet done much to confront the question of religious truth, it has been greatly affected by the question of religion's fate in an age of contestability. Law is one of the main areas in which Americans fight over what it means to be religious or irreligious. Once, Americans were widely religiously observant, and the struggles were largely internecine disputes over whether the state could redistribute income from one (Christian) denomination to another. It was a time in which James Madison could argue forcefully against the taking of so much as "three pence . . . for the support of any one [religious] establishment."[21]

Now, after several decades of struggle on and off the courts, a delicate détente prevails, and there is, relatively speaking, less controversy over this issue than there once was.[22] The primary battleground has shifted to questions of religious symbolism.[23] When can the Ten Commandments be placed on public property?[24] Does their erection require the same access to public space for other religious

---

inspiration and consent, divine duty and common decency."). *Cf.* Christian Smith, *American Evangelicalism: Embattled and Thriving* (1998) (arguing that evangelicalism in the United States has grown not in spite of, but because of, its engagement and struggle with our increasingly pluralistic society).

21. James Madison, *Memorial and Remonstrance Against Religious Assessments,* reprinted in 5 *The Founders' Constitution* 82, 82 (Philip B. Kurland & Ralph Lerner eds., 1987).

22. Much of this controversy reached its denouement when the Supreme Court ruled in favor of the possibility of "vouchers" for religious schools, and for evenhanded distribution of federal funds to religious schools, in two cases early in this century. *See Zelman v. Simmons-Harris,* 536 U.S. 639 (2002); *Mitchell v. Helms,* 530 U.S. 793 (2000). These cases were the culmination of two decades of Court decisions focusing increasingly on equality as the lodestar of Establishment Clause decisions involving funding questions. The voucher decisions leave many questions to be decided. *See, e.g.,* Ira C. Lupu & Robert W. Tuttle, *Zelman's Future: Vouchers, Sectarian Providers, and the Next Round of Constitutional Battles,* 78 Notre Dame L. Rev. 917 (2003); Mark Tushnet, *Vouchers After Zelman,* 2002 Sup. Ct. Rev. 1. It is fair to say, however, that the caselaw in this area is more stable now than it has been for some time, and less controversial.

23. *See, e.g.,* Ira C. Lupu, *Government Messages and Government Money: Santa Fe, Mitchell v. Helms, and the Arc of the Establishment Clause,* 42 Wm. & Mary L. Rev. 771, 771 (2001) (arguing that the "emerging trend" in Establishment Clause litigation is "away from concern over government transfers of wealth to religious institutions, and toward interdiction of religiously partisan government speech"); Kenneth L. Karst, *The First Amendment, the Politics of Religion and the Symbols of Government,* 27 Harv. C.R.-C.L. L. Rev. 503 (1992).

24. *See, e.g., Van Orden v. Perry,* 545 U.S. 677 (2005); *McCreary County v. ACLU of Ky.,* 545 U.S. 844 (2005).

monuments?[25] When can students,[26] lawmakers,[27] and others pray in school, at legislative sessions, and in other public places? When can government display religious symbols on its own land, and when will either the speech or the property be treated as private?[28] When can universities deny sponsorship to student groups with strong religious beliefs?[29]

And the list goes on. In an age of religious contestability, the most heated battles are being fought not over how government spends, but over what government *says* about the role of religion in public life. Both those who believe that religion is a fiction and those who believe it is a vital force are caught up in a battle of symbols over these beliefs.

All of these legal battles are ultimately only one front in a larger cultural war. These individual skirmishes are both a part of that war and a reflection of it. The war is a larger debate about the relationship between religion and liberal democracy. Should religious arguments be forbidden in public political debate? Does their persistent presence in our public political dialogue demonstrate that we live under the threat of a looming theocracy, as some believe? Or does what some see as the exclusion of religious arguments from public discussion demonstrate the creeping hold of "secularism" over public debate, with the consequence that religious believers are (or believe they are) excluded from polite society and left at the mercy of an increasingly degraded culture?

This cultural war is often fought by proxy. For example, in book after book, Americans argue over the religious beliefs of the Founding Fathers and what those beliefs say about the religious or secular nature of the United States.[30]

---

25. *See, e.g., Pleasant Grove City v. Summum*, 129 S. Ct. 1125 (2009).

26. *See, e.g., Santa Fe Independent School District v. Doe*, 530 U.S. 290 (2000); *Lee v. Weisman*, 505 U.S. 577 (1992); Paul Horwitz, *Demographics and Distrust: The Eleventh Circuit on Graduation Prayer in* Adler v. Duval County, 63 U. Miami L. Rev. 835 (2009).

27. *See, e.g., Marsh v. Chambers*, 463 U.S. 783 (1983). For cases involving legislative prayers at the local level, demonstrating the unsettled nature of this area, see, *e.g., Pelphrey v. Cobb County*, 547 F.3d 1263 (11th Cir. 2008); *Hinrichs v. Bosma*, 440 F.3d 393 (7th Cir. 2006); *Simpson v. Chesterfield County Bd. of Supervisors*, 404 F.3d 276 (4th Cir. 2005); *Wynne v. Great Falls*, 376 F.3d 292 (4th Cir. 2004); *Snyder v. Murray City Corp.*, 159 F.3d 1227 (10th Cir. 1998). *See generally* Christopher Lund, *Legislative Prayer and the Secret Costs of Religious Endorsements*, 94 Minn. L. Rev. 972 (2010).

28. *See, e.g., Salazar v. Buono*, 130 S. Ct. 1803 (2010) (upholding the display of a Latin cross atop Sunrise Rock in Mojave National Preserve, on land transferred by federal legislation to a private organization); *Capitol Square Review & Advisory Bd. v. Pinette*, 515 U.S. 753 (1995) (upholding the display of a cross by a private organization on public land).

29. *See Christian Legal Soc'y v. Martinez*, 130 S. Ct. 2971 (2010).

30. *See, e.g.,* Steven Waldman, *Founding Faith: Providence, Politics, and the Birth of Religious Freedom in America* (2008); Jon Meacham, *American Gospel: God, the Founding Fathers, and the Making of a Nation* (2006); David L. Holmes, *The Faiths of the Founding Fathers* (2006); Alf Mapp, *The Faiths of Our Fathers: What America's Founders Really Believed* (2005).

Some argue that we always have been and remain a "Christian nation."[31] Others argue that, whatever the individual beliefs of the founding generation may have been, ours has always been a "Godless Constitution."[32] Still others argue that whether or not we were once a Christian nation, the profusion of religious beliefs and nonbeliefs in our own age means we are one no longer—and they proceed to argue over whether this is cause for celebration or concern. The legal battles over religious symbolism are thus just a reflection of a wider argument over the relationship between religion and liberal democracy.

But there is another reason for the resurgence of interest in all these questions, and it adds extra fuel to a fire that would already have burned quite well on its own. That is the fact that we are now living in a post-9/11 world. Whatever compromises Americans had reached over religion, and however trivial or symbolic their debates may have seemed, the fall of the Twin Towers made clear that religion is hardly a spent force. To be sure, the causes of terrorism are complex. But there can be no doubt that religion helped inspire and direct the forces that tore a hole out of New York City and Washington, D.C. The events of September 11 were a reminder of just how powerful religion can be in shaping people's lives and actions, for good or ill. The fallout from that day has shown us how fraught and fragile the relationship between religion and liberal democracy can be.

This is not just an American dilemma. If anything, the fact that religious wars in the United States are still largely fought only on symbolic grounds is a testament to just how well the American cultural landscape has weathered the rise in tension between the claims of religion and those of secularism. But ours is not the only corner of the world in which those controversies occur. As events across the world—from Western Europe to the Middle East—have shown, Americans are living through only one piece of a global dilemma.[33]

That dilemma has turned our thoughts back to questions of religious truth. For example, Sam Harris, who was an anonymous graduate student before his best-seller *The End of Faith* catapulted him to notoriety, traces the genesis of his book directly to 9/11.[34] Susan Jacoby, the author of the New Atheist tract *Freethinkers*, says much the same thing.[35] Indeed, the very fact that these books sold so well demonstrates powerfully just how much 9/11 helped redirect our public conversation toward questions of religious truth. If we are fighting a religious war, after all, it would help to know on whose side God stands, if any—or

---

31. *See* Stephen McDowell, *America, A Christian Nation?* (2005).

32. *See* Isaac Kramnick & R. Laurence Moore, *The Godless Constitution: A Moral Defense of the Secular State* (2005).

33. *See, e.g.*, Jürgen Habermas, *An Awareness of What is Missing*, in Jürgen Habermas et al., *An Awareness of What is Missing: Faith and Reason in a Post-secular Age* 15, 19 (2010).

34. *See* Harris, *supra* note 13.

35. *See* Susan Jacoby, *Freethinkers: A History of American Secularism* 2–3 (2004).

whether, as John Lennon sang, there would be "nothing to kill or die for" if we could imagine "no religion."[36]

In short, public attention in our age of religious contestability has not only focused on an array of issues concerning the nature of religion and its relationship to liberal democracy, but more fundamentally still on questions of religious truth itself. But if the urgency of these questions has reached a fever pitch, their intractability has not changed at all. That more people may be willing to argue over whether God exists, and that more people now see this as a valid question rather than an unthinkable one, does not give us any greater traction in figuring out whether he (or He—or She, They, or It) does, in fact, exist. Thousands of years of experience, reflection, debate, and sometimes bloody conflict have barely even sharpened the terms of the debate,[37] let alone resolved it.

WHY TRUTH MATTERS (EVEN TO LAWYERS)

In fairness, there *are* good reasons for law and religion scholars to avoid the subject of religious truth. We law and religion scholars can play at theology and philosophy if we have to, but at bottom we are, like all lawyers, primarily pragmatists and problem-solvers, not dealers in abstraction. (This may explain why most law and religion scholars are so haphazard in their understanding of theology or philosophy—and why, in fairness, theologians and philosophers are often equally clumsy in their understanding of law.) We are plainly in no better position than anyone else to resolve the ultimate questions of life. Anyway, that is not our job. Our job is to try to reach workable solutions to the problems of the day.

Indeed, a law and religion scholar might say our job is to come up with suggestions about how best to deal with conflicts between religion and the social order without even *attempting* to answer those deeper questions. Constitutional lawyers are proceduralists: good at coming up with rules and standards, not so good on deep and imponderable questions like the existence of God. So our marching orders are clear: We should try to arrive at a reasonable lawyerly way of addressing conflicts between law and religion, and leave the deep thoughts about God to our colleagues in religious studies departments, or to the individual conscience.

The problem is that unless and until we are willing to confront the questions of religious truth that lie at the heart of our public struggles over the relationship

---

36. John Lennon, *Imagine, on Imagine* (Capitol Records 1971).

37. For an example of this, see Jennifer Michael Hecht's history of religious doubt, which demonstrates how long the primary arguments for and against God's existence have been around, and how little they have changed. *See* Jennifer Michael Hecht, *Doubt–A History: The Great Doubters and Their Legacy of Innovation from Socrates and Jesus to Thomas Jefferson and Emily Dickinson* (2004).

between law and religious belief, our inheritance will be the very incoherence, the hollowness, that we are apt to find in the pages of Supreme Court decisions and law reviews.

Both courts and scholars have attempted to get around questions of religious truth—but, finally, without much success. For example, we may try to avoid some of these questions by simply giving a broad definition to religion, making it little different from any other strong system of belief.[38] At that point, however, religion can mean anything at all and nothing in particular. Moreover, any definition that broad is likely to result in a watered-down set of legal protections for religious belief.

Similarly, we could try to turn the discussion away from matters of religious truth by arguing that religion is nothing special. We could reject the notion "that religion is a constitutional anomaly, a category of human experience that demands special benefits and/or necessitates special restrictions."[39] We could prefer the seeming doctrinal elegance of some general legal principle that is untethered to religion itself, and rely on it to do all our work in a neat fashion. Such is the case with Christopher Eisgruber and Lawrence Sager, who have argued that the Religion Clauses can be rationalized under a principle of "equal liberty."[40] But this solution, which suggests that the best way to think about law and religion is not to think much about religion at all, ends up feeling like *Hamlet* without the Prince.[41] In any event, it cannot satisfy everyone. Some poor soul (so to speak) in the audience is bound to raise her hand and ask, "But what if religion *is* a unique, and uniquely deserving, category of human experience? What if it is *true*?"

In short, religious truth cannot be swept under the rug. All the warps and woofs in the fabric of religious freedom, all the inconsistencies that lead us to exclaim that law and religion jurisprudence is incoherent, stand as a silent but implacable reproach to all of us, judges and scholars alike, who toil in this field. They are an unstated but stark reminder that, in the end, we cannot help but confront Pilate's question.

---

38. *See, e.g., United States v. Seeger*, 380 U.S. 163 (1965) (interpreting a statutory provision concerning conscientious objectors which required a belief "in relation to a Supreme Being" to include any sincere belief that "occupies a place in the life of its possessor parallel to that filled by the orthodox belief in God of one who clearly qualifies for the exemption"); *United States v. Welsh*, 398 U.S. 333 (1970) (treating moral and ethical beliefs as qualifying for the same statutory exemption).

39. Christopher L. Eisgruber & Lawrence G. Sager, *Religious Freedom and the Constitution* 6 (2007); *see also* Brian Leiter, *Why Tolerate Religion?*, 25 Const. Comment. 1 (2008).

40. *See* Eisgruber & Sager, *supra* note 39.

41. *See, e.g.,* Chad Flanders, *The Possibility of a Secular First Amendment*, 26 Quinnipiac L. Rev. 257, 258 (2008).

CONSTITUTIONAL AGNOSTICISM

That is the project of this book. Lest I be struck by lightning or worse (say, book critics) for my presumption, let me be clear. I cannot and do not attempt here to answer the question of God's existence, let alone assign him to a particular denomination. Similarly, although I will have a good deal to say about the arguments of both the New Atheists and the New Anti-Atheists, I do not take a side in that battle once and for all, aside perhaps from finding it increasingly tedious. Although the title of this book is *The Agnostic Age*, and it has much to say about agnosticism and its role in the current debate over religious truth, this is still primarily a book for lawyers and citizens who are interested in how to reach a workable accommodation between law and religion, and between religion and liberal democracy—an approach I call "constitutional agnosticism." I hope the book will also be of interest to students of religion, not least because it argues that the questions those students ask are of crucial importance to the conflicts between religion, law, and liberal democracy. But it does not presume to tell the individual what he or she should believe about God.

Instead, this book is about how the individual—especially public officials like judges and legislators, but individual citizens as well—should think about religion *as* an officeholder or citizen. This is ultimately a book about religion's place in the public sphere, and it offers conclusions about how we, as participants in that sphere, should think about religion and its relationship to law and politics. Our views as citizens and officeholders may correspond to our own religious views, but they need not do so. We can assume that when Justice Scalia, who is politically conservative, defended the First Amendment right to burn the American flag,[42] he was not hoping to put a torch to Old Glory on the steps of the Supreme Court at the earliest opportunity.[43] In the same way, we can reach conclusions about how we should think about religion and religious truth as citizens and public officials that may not match up exactly with our own deepest conclusions about religious faith. This book is an argument about the importance of religious truth, but it is not an argument for or against some particular religious truth. Instead, it is about the best way of thinking about religion and religious truth as *constitutional* actors: as judges, public officials, and citizens.

That takes care of the "constitutional" part of constitutional agnosticism. Now for "agnosticism." The argument of this book is that public officials and others should adopt what I call an "agnostic habit" with respect to questions of religious

---

42. *See Texas v. Johnson*, 491 U.S. 397 (1989).

43. Not that he could, under prevailing Supreme Court precedent. *See United States v. Grace*, 461 U.S. 171 (1983) (permitting expressive activities on the sidewalks surrounding the Supreme Court, but not on the grounds of the Court itself).

truth, and their relationship to the conflicts between the obligations of religion and the demands of the wider society.

What agnosticism means is a tricky question. The English writer T.H. Huxley, who is generally credited with coining the term, offered an early and influential definition, although, as we will see, it is not the one we will use here. Huxley's definition treated agnosticism as the principle that because we *cannot* know whether God exists or not, we should neither believe nor disbelieve in him.[44]

This form of agnosticism has often been viewed as a decidedly tepid thing. In the popular understanding, it is just the "middle ground between theism and atheism,"[45] a way station and nothing more. One writer has suggested that an agnostic might be one whose position is taken "out of mere politeness or in some circumstances from fear of giving even more offence."[46] If so, it is a remarkably unsuccessful strategy. The middle of the road is, after all, the place where you can be hit by traffic from both directions. So it is with agnosticism. For anyone who has taken a strong position for or against the existence of God, nothing can arouse contempt more easily than a person who seems only to be refusing to fish or cut bait.

Huxley's definition of agnosticism, however, is *not* the definition that animates this book. There is more to the brand of agnosticism I describe in this book—what I call the "new agnosticism"—than that. The new agnostic's refusal to venture a final conclusion on the existence or nonexistence of God is not just a passive deferral, or a failure to screw one's courage to the sticking place. It is an adamant position of its own.

There are varieties of agnosticism, of course, just as there are varieties of theism and atheism. Some agnostics *are* just lukewarm atheists; others *are* just theists with commitment issues. But the brand of new agnosticism I champion here is different. If we are to find its meaning, we must look beyond philosophy to literature, in which doubt finds some of its most resonant and pregnant possibilities. At least since the Romantic era, agnosticism has in fact been one of the characteristics of great art, and the artist has been an agnostic par excellence.[47]

---

44. *See generally* T.H. Huxley, *Agnosticism and Christianity and Other Essays* (Prometheus Books, 1992).

45. Steven D. Smith, *Our Agnostic Constitution*, 83 N.Y.U. L. Rev. 120, 128 (2008).

46. J.J.C. Smart, *Atheism and Agnosticism, in Stanford Encyclopedia of Philosophy*, http://plato.stanford.edu.entries/atheism-agnosticism.

47. Which means, in fairness, that the "new agnosticism" is not entirely new. I call it by that label partly to distinguish it from other forms of agnosticism, such as the nineteenth century brand of agnosticism advocated by writers like Huxley; partly to set it against the New Atheists and the New Anti-Atheists; and partly to emphasize the particular qualities of the new agnosticism, such as its emphathetic capacity, that I argue are particularly well-fitted to contemporary conditions, and that I draw on in defining and arguing for constitutional agnosticism. As this book makes clear, however, the "new agnosticism" draws on deep sources in history and tradition, both religious and otherwise. *See* Chapter Three.

Indeed, the primary text for the new agnosticism is not that of a philosopher or a theologian, but a poet.[48] The new agnosticism I argue for here draws on John Keats, who argued that the artist must display what he called "negative capability"—the ability to remain "capable of being in uncertainties, Mysteries, [and] doubts."[49] The artist who displays true negative capability is nimble at "entertaining and even multiplying doubts indefinitely"; he "manages to project himself sympathetically into the positions occupied by his many and varied characters[,] . . . to be all of them and none of them, to be nowhere and everywhere."[50] This capacity to remain in a state of suspension has been called "an element of intellectual power[,] . . . of seeing the full force and complexity of the subject."[51] It has been described as a quality that "is essential for any creative artist, whether writer, poet, composer or painter."[52]

But the same quality of negative capability can be an equally essential element of great judgment, political leadership, or citizenship. Above all, it denotes the ability to occupy, as fully and empathetically as possible, the varied worldviews of our fellow citizens, even at those moments when their worldviews come into the sharpest conflict with each other and with our own perspectives. The result, when we carry the lessons of the new agnosticism forward into the realm of law and religion, is what I call *constitutional agnosticism*: a sense of the capacity of judges, public officials, and citizens to engage empathetically with their fellow citizens' perspectives on questions of religious truth, rather than trying to avoid those questions altogether—and the *necessity* of their doing so. As with the new agnosticism, it requires intellectual power. It is no easy task. But it may be a crucial one, if we are to negotiate the fault lines between law and religion without prematurely taking one side or the other, or disappearing into the crevasses between them.

I discuss the new agnosticism in greater detail in Chapter Three, and constitutional agnosticism in greater detail in Chapter Five. For now, I offer four central points by way of preview and for the sake of emphasis.

First, in arguing for *constitutional* agnosticism, I am not arguing that we must become *religious* agnostics. This book is primarily about the relationship between law and religion, and between religion and liberal democracy, not about religion itself. Because these subjects, in my view, cannot be discussed meaningfully

---

48. Not for nothing did the poet Percy Bysshe Shelley call poets the "unacknowledged legislators of the world," although it is just possible that a hint of self-regard had something to do with it as well. *See Percy Bysshe Shelley, A Defence of Poetry and Other Essays* 45 (2004) (1840).

49. John Keats, *Letters of John Keats* 43 (Robert Gittings ed., 1970).

50. Stanley Fish, *Unger and Milton*, 1988 Duke L.J. 975, 1005.

51. Daniel J. Kornstein, *The Double Life of Wallace Stevens: Is Law Ever the "Necessary Angel" of Creative Art?*, 41 N.Y.L. Sch. L. Rev. 1187, 1280 (1997).

52. *Id.*

without confronting questions of religious truth, I do contribute to those larger debates. I argue that the agnostic perspective has been given too little attention in the pitched battle between the New Atheists and the New Anti-Atheists. Too often, these antagonists have traded volleys across a vast no-man's land without stopping to consider whether that middle ground has something to offer. Readers who have come to this book out of an interest in the larger questions of religious truth, and who are unsatisfied by both poles of the current debate, might find something attractive about the vigorous and empathetic new agnosticism I argue for here.

But I am still ultimately arguing only for *constitutional* agnosticism. Constitutional agnosticism ought to be attractive to citizens and officials who want to find a workable common ground between the needs of the church and those of the state. Crucially, it ought to be attractive *regardless* of their individual religious beliefs. This is an ecumenical book, and I hope to reach two audiences in particular. The first is what we might call conventional liberals: those who either have a residual sense that religion is untrue, or who believe that there is or may be a religious truth, but see that question as either irrelevant or best avoided where church-state issues are concerned. In those cases, according to this view, we must reason together while laying questions of religious truth aside. I hope to convince those readers that we *cannot* avoid those questions—that given the plural nature of the beliefs that abound in our own age, we must confront the issue of religious truth, and that any approach that relies on a purported common ground of "reasonableness" in fact ends up smuggling in a host of religious truth-claims. Just as important, however, is my other audience: readers with strong religious views for *or* against the existence of God, who after all constitute a majority of the population. To those readers, I say that it should be possible to come away convinced by the arguments of this book without altering one's own religious beliefs or disbeliefs.

Second, the brand of constitutional agnosticism I argue for here *is* a kind of conclusion about questions of religious truth. It would be teasing, at least, to argue that law and religion needs to address questions of religious truth, and then offer up a position that seems to back away from doing just that. (Although law and religion scholars are experts at precisely this kind of two-step.) The constitutional agnosticism I argue for here *does* offer a distinct perspective on questions of religious truth. This perspective holds that these questions cannot be answered with finality. But that is *not* the same as avoiding them altogether. It is precisely that strategy of avoidance, I argue, that characterizes most judges' and legal scholars' approach to religious truth, and that has led to the state of confusion and dissatisfaction that permeates the theory and practice of the Religion Clauses of the First Amendment. Constitutional agnosticism believes that these questions have to be confronted head-on rather than avoided, even though it argues that the best way to confront them is with the capacity to live with and among uncertainties, mysteries, and doubts that Keats extolled.

Third, in many respects, constitutional agnosticism best responds to the spirit of our own age. We live in an age of contestability, an age in which we not only see a variety of responses to questions of religious truth—different faiths, atheism itself, and so on—but in which we are aware that each of these responses is *possible*. Charles Taylor calls this a secular age. As the title of this book suggests, however, it might be more appropriate to call it an *agnostic* age. Perhaps more than we may realize, constitutional agnosticism offers a way of thinking about questions of religious truth, and about the conflict between church and state, that is better suited to our own age than the conventional approaches to these questions.[53]

Finally, constitutional agnosticism is *not* the current position of the courts, or of most legal scholars. For decades, both courts and legal scholars in the area of law and religion have used buzz words that, at first glance, might resemble the agnostic perspective. Words and phrases like "equality," "neutrality," and "equal liberty" are the coins of the realm in current law and religion jurisprudence. A writer arguing from one of these perspectives might be tempted to put down this book at once, concluding that she is *already* a constitutional agnostic.

She would be wrong to do so. (Although, if she has already paid for the book, I'm willing to live and let live.) Prevailing approaches to law and religion that purport to be neutral, or to hold religious and non-religious beliefs alike in equal regard, routinely fail to do anything of the sort. The perspective they ultimately offer tilts clearly, if (sometimes) unconsciously, in favor of the secular. Faced with the difficult conflicts that form the "hard cases" of law and religion—questions such as how we are to treat a parent who, for religious reasons, wishes to withhold lifesaving medical care from a minor child—they ultimately decide in favor of the state, in a way that privileges a distinctly secular vision of human goods. Sometimes they are candid about what they are doing. More often, they are blind to the full implications of their decision. They believe they have remained staunchly "neutral" when they have actually favored one side of the debate.

Such a decision might be the right one. But it is not neutral. What, from the perspective of constitutional agnosticism, ought to be genuinely wrenching decisions, "hard cases," are from this perspective all too easy. The state wins, and not an ounce of doubt, uncertainty, or regret is involved. One thing readers of this book should take away is a deepened sense of the tragic choices involved in conflicts between law and religion.[54] Readers of this book should gain a renewed

---

53. In her book *Working on God*, Winifred Gallagher offers a somewhat similar observation, arguing that "neoagnostics"—"well-educated skeptics who have inexplicable metaphysical feelings"—are "America's most subdued, neglected religious group, yet they are one of its most powerful." Winifred Gallagher, *Working on God* xiii–xiv (1999).

54. Marc DeGirolami has written valuably on this point in an as-yet unpublished manuscript. *See* Marc O. DeGirolami, *Tragic Historicism* (draft manuscript, 2010).

appreciation for the kinds of conflicts that really are, or should be, hard cases in law and religion.

Hard means *hard*. It does not mean we should always reach the opposite conclusion. It may be that the constitutional agnostic will reach the same results as the resolutely liberal or secular judge. The state *may* still intervene to give a sick child a blood transfusion or other lifesaving medical assistance. It *may* still deny some claims of conscience by religious believers, no matter how deeply and sincerely they are held. I think some results *should* change, and at times I will argue strenuously that the courts have gotten the balance between church and state wrong. Still, even under a regime of constitutional agnosticism, one that emphasizes the importance of the possibility that religious claims that come into conflict with the needs of the state are not only important, but *true*, the religious believer will still sometimes lose.

And that, too, is a lesson of this book. For, although the individual agnostic can refuse indefinitely to reach a final conclusion on questions of religious truth, judges, lawmakers, and citizens do not have the same luxury. Judges must judge; lawmakers and citizens must make decisions, in real time. The kind of empathetic negative capability that comprises constitutional agnosticism will require the state to accede to religious needs more often than the state currently does. But in any viable system of liberal democracy, at times the state and its largely secular needs will have the final word.

What constitutional agnosticism suggests is that, like the agnostic who fully appreciates the compelling arguments of both atheism and theism even as she refuses to join one side or the other, we should be clear about the tragic choices this position entails. We may conclude on some occasions that the state must prevail without believing that the state is *right*. Constitutional agnosticism argues for a new way of thinking about the balance between law and religion, and between religion and liberal democracy more broadly. In some cases, it counsels in favor of different outcomes with respect to church-state conflicts than the ostensibly "neutral" courts might reach today. But it also concludes that there may be no perfect, final agreement between church and state. Constitutional agnosticism is an important and valuable ideal, and it has many important and achievable implications in practice. Like all ideals, however—and perhaps like agnosticism itself—it is tortuously difficult and perhaps impossible to attain in full. That, too, can be an important lesson.

THE PLAN OF THE BOOK

Part One of this book lays the ground for constitutional agnosticism. In Chapter One, we examine in detail the dilemma that religion faces in liberal democracies like our own. Our society has reached an uneasy accommodation between religion and the state by relying, sometimes explicitly and sometimes implicitly, on general liberal principles. We might think of liberalism as a treaty, a way of reaching a truce between the forces that engaged in bloody religious conflict in Europe for centuries. What I call the "liberal treaty" or the "liberal consensus" has come under pressure, however, and that accommodation has become increasingly fragile.

The liberal consensus has come under attack from both the religious and the secular sides of the divide. Religion's pressure on liberal democracy has grown dramatically in recent years. That is apparent when we look at some of the obvious sources of this pressure: domestically, the rise of Christian evangelism and the so-called "Christian right,"[55] and globally, the rise of radical forms of Islam and the violence that has come in their wake. But liberal democracy is under pressure as well from many of what we might consider the more "moderate" faiths, whose renewed vigor and increasing interest in taking public stands on controversial political questions has contributed to what José Casanova calls the "deprivatization" of religion in modern life.[56]

At the same time, the liberal consensus is under attack from the liberal or secular side of the divide as well. Liberal democracy has long sought an accommodation with religion by avoiding questions of religious truth and focusing instead on values like religious "freedom" and "neutrality." But the rise of public religion has led some liberals to call for a redrawing of the boundaries between religion and state. We see this, for example, in France and the Netherlands, where liberal states have argued for an increasingly militant form of secularism and sought, literally and figuratively, to strip the veils that insulate religion from the mandates of the state. The New Atheism itself, with its more direct attack on religion and its combative stand on questions of religious truth and toleration, is another symptom of the unraveling of the liberal consensus. Finally, the liberal tradition is under a more subtle and far-reaching attack from with its own borders, as thoughtful writers from within the liberal tradition have called liberalism into question and explored its limits and pretensions.

In describing the collapse of the liberal consensus, I may be accused of launching a full-scale attack on the political philosophy of liberalism. I will indeed have many critical things to say about the difficulties of the liberal project along the way. That is not my primary aim, however. As I make clear in Chapter One, my main target here is not liberalism at the abstract level of political philosophy, but the liberal consensus as it has been widely, and crudely, understood and employed in public discussion.[57] At that level, even committed

---

55. And, potentially, the religious "left" as well. *See, e.g.*, Steven H. Shiffrin, *The Religious Left and Church-State Relations* (2009).

56. *See generally* José Casanova, *Public Religions in the Modern World* (1994); *see also* José Casanova, *Public Religions Revisited*, in *Religion: Beyond a Concept* 101 (Hent de Vries, ed., 2007).

57. *See* Mark Tushnet, *A Public Philosophy for the Professional-Managerial Class*, 106 Yale L.J. 1571, 1572–73, 1586–89 (1997).

philosophical liberals may well agree that there are many reasons to think that the liberal consensus is in a weakened state. Whether more sophisticated forms of liberal philosophy are stronger than the general public understanding of liberalism, or whether those forms of liberalism are also fatally flawed; whether those sophisticated forms of liberalism are, in fact, wholly consistent with constitutional agnosticism, or whether, regardless of the virtues or flaws of various forms of liberalism, there are reasons to prefer the language of "constitutional agnosticism" to the usual language of academic debates over liberalism—all of these are important questions. But I put them off until the last chapter. For now, it is enough to say that Chapter One's description of liberalism's fragile state is directed at liberalism as it is popularly understood, not as its most sophisticated advocates may understand it.

Chapter Two narrows the focus to law and religion itself. It surveys the central doctrinal approaches to the Free Exercise and Establishment Clauses of the First Amendment, and argues that these approaches, whatever their practical merits, are intellectually inconsistent and ultimately incoherent. It examines the theories of religious liberty proposed by some of the most prominent law and religion scholars. Most of these writers have tried to bring consistency to law and religion by focusing on a single liberal principle like liberty or equality. A few *have* offered specifically religious justifications for religious freedom, although those justifications are unlikely to command widespread support. Others have offered a more eclectic grab-bag of approaches. This chapter shows that they have ultimately been unsuccessful in bringing order to the landscape of law and religion—or have purchased order at too high a price. For these writers, the worm at the core of the apple is religious truth. Unless we are willing to confront more directly the question of religious truth that lies at the heart of our struggles over law and religion, our proposals will be built on a fractured and flawed foundation.

Part Two introduces constitutional agnosticism to the mix. Chapter Three starts off this discussion by describing religious agnosticism itself. The brand of "new" agnosticism I offer here is not a form of disbelief, or even simply of refusal to believe. Instead, it argues that certainty on matters of religious truth *may* (not *must*) ultimately be unattainable, and that one approach to this prospect is to suspend judgment on these questions, or at least to introduce a note of doubt and humility to one's conclusions.

This strategy is not unique to agnostics themselves, and committed religious believers and nonbelievers should not flinch at it too quickly. As I show in this chapter, a rich tradition of doubt and agnosticism flows through Western culture. One important part of this tradition is its manifestation not just in philosophy, but in art and literature, in which we have inherited an especially rich, complex, and empathetic form of agnosticism from the Romantic artistic tradition. Another important contribution to the agnostic tradition can be found within religion itself, which, despite the way in which the New Atheists present it, has often made doubt a central part of its own tradition. In short, there are reasons to conclude that the kind of new agnosticism I describe here is well within the reach of most citizens in our own age, whatever their religious beliefs may be.

Chapter Four offers a brief but important digression. It surveys the heated debate between the New Atheists and the New Anti-Atheists. The New Atheists, commendably, confront directly the central questions of religious truth that lie at the heart of our debates over the role of religion in a liberal democracy. Unfortunately, that's about where the applause ends. The New Atheists have taken an astonishingly counter-productive approach to these questions. Far from bringing about the civil peace that they insist is their ultimate goal, the New Atheists' strident writing, and their monolithically negative views on religious belief, threaten to make the debate all the more protracted and bitter. Some of the evidence for this can be found in the responses of their opponents, who regularly meet shrillness with shrillness. What should be an enlightening dialogue is becoming a tedious standoff. Agnosticism deserves its own round in this debate, rather than being treated with barely disguised contempt or condescension by both sides. On a broader social level, if not at the level of individual belief, agnosticism, or at least the form of new agnosticism I describe, can be a sounder approach, one that calms the waters without avoiding the vital question of religious truth.

At the very least, the empathetic brand of agnosticism I describe in this book acknowledges a truth about human experience that some of the most strident New Atheists, and their opponents as well, either stumble over or deny. Most of us, including many atheists, are able to acknowledge and appreciate the importance of spirituality and religion in individual life, and sometimes to make a meaningful imaginative leap into the mental space of religious believers (and vice versa). Anyone who is capable of appreciating the profound presence of the sublime in our lives—whether in religious experience or through art, literature, poetry, and natural beauty—is capable of sharing the sense of awe and mystery that lies at the heart of religious belief. That imaginative leap dissolves the borders between theism and atheism, between belief and unbelief.

It is a virtue of our often fragile status as people living in the midst of an agnostic age that we are capable of making these leaps, of flitting back and forth over the increasingly permeable borders of belief. As destabilizing and disorienting as this can be, it also gives us the gift of being able to experience something of the inner lives of others. Agnosticism, empathetically and sensitively practiced, thus not only disclaims any conclusions about religious truth, but is capable of understanding and sharing a sense of the profundity of religious belief as religious individuals experience it—and, conversely, of seeing the stark and lonely beauty of a world without God. This perspective respects the fervor of the combatants in the war over religious truth. But it offers the possibility of a truce, or at least a cooling of tensions, in our long-running culture war.

Chapter Five builds on this vision of empathetic agnosticism, and begins the work of putting it together with law and religion, to form what I call constitutional agnosticism. Our focus shifts from agnosticism as a personal belief system to *constitutional* agnosticism as a working rule for judges, lawmakers, and citizens in a pluralistic liberal democracy who face conflicts between religion and the state. I argue that, rather than subscribing to particular truth claims about religion, and instead of trying to avoid and evade these questions altogether, public actors in our society should cultivate an agnostic habit. That is, when approaching questions of church-state conflict, they should attempt to remain genuinely agnostic on questions of religious truth, but in a manner that attempts to make the imaginative leap into the mind of the other (usually the religious believer, but potentially the nonbeliever too) that Keats had in mind in his description of negative capability. This chapter also demonstrates the ways in which the current approach of the courts and many law and religion scholars is not truly agnostic, but rather either shies away from questions of religious truth altogether or smuggles in a set of conclusions that ultimately give an unfair advantage to secular interests.

Although constitutional agnosticism is especially important for judges, it is not a rule for judges alone. In many circumstances, lawmakers, too, might benefit from the agnostic habit in public deliberation and decision-making. They are not required to abandon or set aside their own religious views—something that has been proposed by some liberal theorists but that is contrary to our constitutional values and counterproductive. Still, lawmakers often face competing interests in their public deliberations, interests that involve deep claims of religious belief or nonbelief. An agnostic habit might enable them to negotiate this treacherous terrain in a way that is ultimately more successful and more respectful to everyone.

Similarly, private citizens emphatically should not be required to leave their religious (or irreligious) beliefs at the door when entering the public square. Like everyone else, however, they need to find ways of coexisting in a deeply diverse and religiously pluralistic society. Adopting the agnostic habit may enable them to enter into a richer and more sensitive public dialogue with their fellow citizens. It may help them to consider controversial questions and conflicts from the perspective of the other, without having to sacrifice their own beliefs.

Part Three puts constitutional agnosticism to work. My principal focus here is on the Religion Clauses—the Free Exercise Clause and the Establishment Clause—of the First Amendment.[58] Although I will point to some controversial cases that I think were wrongly decided, I do not argue in these chapters for a wholesale rewriting of current Religion Clause doctrine. That doctrine, on the

---

58. "Congress shall make no law respecting an establishment of religion, or prohibiting the free exercise thereof . . ." U.S. Const., amend. 1.

level of results if not reasoning, as often as not gets things right, albeit for ultimately unsustainable reasons. Rather, I argue that constitutional agnosticism
can lead us to a smarter, stronger, richer, and more sensitive understanding of
what is going on in these cases.

Chapter Six considers the law of the Free Exercise Clause of the First
Amendment, which prohibits Congress (and, through the Fourteenth
Amendment, state and local governments as well) from infringing on the free
exercise of religion. Perhaps the most controversial development in the Free
Exercise Clause in the last twenty years has been the Supreme Court's shift
away from a legal regime that—in principle, if not always in practice—gave substantial protection to religious believers whose faith-based obligations come into
conflict with the law, even if the law was not directed at those religious believers.
In a controversial 1990 case, the Supreme Court held that any "neutral" and
"generally applicable" law that incidentally placed a burden on the exercise of
religious belief would no longer present a basis for a free exercise challenge.[59]

It is fair to say that most law and religion scholars consider this case to have
been a disaster for religious liberty. I agree with them. It is also fair to point out
that a number of law and religion scholars have come to believe that the Court
was right. They argue that the Free Exercise Clause does not require, and society
could not long tolerate, a legal regime that gives religious believers an "out"
where any generally applicable law is concerned, allowing them, say, to ingest
peyote or refuse to pay taxes. The Court's decision in this case is still controversial. It has been met with a vigorous, if not completely successful, response from
Congress and the state legislatures, which have provided additional protections
for religious believers in limited areas, even where generally applicable laws are
involved.

Despite those defenses of a regime of "neutrality" toward religion, a constitutionally agnostic approach to the Free Exercise Clause counsels in favor of strong
constitutional accommodations for religious belief. At the very least, this
approach helps us to understand the full weight of the pressures felt by our
fellow citizens who confront laws that conflict with their religious beliefs and
practices. If we do not try to occupy and appreciate the perspective of those who
face these conflicts, we will not be able to comprehend just why these believers
find even some generally applicable laws impossible to obey, and we will not be
able to properly balance their needs against the genuine—if often exaggerated—
needs of the state. Those who have argued that there is no place for empathy in
the judicial role are wrong;[60] if judges are to understand the stakes involved in

---

59. *Employment Division v. Smith*, 494 U.S. 872 (1990).

60. Most recently, that argument has been made by those who opposed the confirmation of Supreme Court Justice Sonia Sotomayor. *See Nomination of Judge Sonia Sotomayor
to be an Associate Justice of the United States Supreme Court: Hearings Before the Senate
Committee on the Judiciary*, 111th Cong. (2009).

free exercise cases, they must understand those claims from *within* the believer's perspective, not just from a narrowly secular perspective.

At the same time, constitutional agnosticism is not for judges alone. It is equally important that citizens and lawmakers adopt the agnostic habit. If they adopt a genuine and empathetic habit of agnosticism, imagining the needs of religious believers from those believers' own perspective, they might be more willing to grant legislative accommodations to religious believers, and thus reduce the tension between religious obligations and generally applicable laws without the courts having to step in.

Beyond this general topic, the Free Exercise Clause involves a wide range of conflicts between religious and legal obligations, and this chapter explores a number of them. I move here from what we might label the "easy" free exercise cases to the "hard" cases. Constitutional agnosticism offers an important change in perspective on these issues. The current approach of courts and legal scholars sometimes privileges secular values while purporting to remain "neutral" on questions of religious truth. This leads them to view what should be easy cases as hard ones, and what should be hard cases as easy ones.

An example of the latter category is the set of cases dealing with blood transfusions and other life-saving medical treatment for children, ordered against the religious objections of their families. This is an area in which, understandably, the law heavily favors the state. The medical treatment cases are viewed as easy cases from the perspective of the average judge or citizen.

From the constitutional agnostic's perspective, however, these are among the hardest cases confronted by the courts (and by lawmakers, who face the question whether to grant exemptions from general laws concerning manslaughter and child abuse or neglect). A long tradition, stretching back at least to God's command to Abraham to sacrifice his son Isaac, shows the power of the conflict between the needs of the state and the needs of one's faith at the borderlands of life and death. For the constitutional agnostic, these are cases in which the stakes are just as high for the religious believer as for the state. I do not argue that religious believers should always win in these cases, although I do believe courts should do all that they can to avoid setting these cases up for total conflict and an inevitable victory for the state. But I do suggest that if courts and lawmakers took seriously their obligation to remain agnostic with respect to questions of religious truth, these cases would be far more difficult, and involve far more tragic choices, than they are currently understood as presenting.

Chapter Seven moves from free exercise conflicts back to the world of money and symbols that constitutes one of the primary battlegrounds in our modern culture wars. This is the world of the Establishment Clause of the First Amendment, which forbids any law "respecting an establishment of religion." The Establishment Clause is perhaps the primary field in which questions of religious truth are contested in our legal and political culture. It is also the area of legal doctrine that has been most vulnerable to charges of incoherence and inconsistency.

In the Establishment Clause, there are two primary concerns: issues of government funding for religion, and cases involving symbolic alliances between religion and government, such as cases involving the Pledge of Allegiance, public displays of the Ten Commandments, and school prayer. The current state of the law, more or less, allows government to aid religious organizations financially so long as those groups are treated on an equal basis with non-religious groups, but is much more strict in barring any effort by government to come down symbolically on the side of one religious "truth" or another.

I agree with many of the decisions in both areas. But I argue in this chapter that a constitutionally agnostic approach makes better sense of these cases, and brings more coherence to the field, by confronting rather than avoiding the question of religious truth. Although I largely affirm the current state of Establishment Clause law, I argue that some decisions—particularly those involving longstanding practices like the inclusion of the phrase "under God" in the Pledge of Allegiance—may be impossible to justify when viewed from a constitutionally agnostic perspective.

If Part Three moves from a general perspective on religious truth and church–state conflict to the more specific legal issues raised by the Religion Clauses of the First Amendment, Part Four draws together the lessons of the book by moving the focus outward again. This Part examines the potential problems with the constitutionally agnostic approach to law and religion.

These concerns deserve serious consideration. No approach to law and religion can resolve once and for all the tensions between law and religion. But a soundly constitutionally agnostic approach—one that does not avoid questions of religious truth but instead seriously, empathetically, and *agnostically* confronts them—may still have many benefits. It can bring greater consistency and coherence to our resolution of the pressing controversies surrounding church–state relations. More broadly, it may help ease the tensions that have arisen in the broader public debate over the role of religion in public life—tensions that are evident not only in the war between the New Atheists and the New Anti-Atheists, but more generally in the endless struggle between religion and liberal democracy.

In the final analysis, while constitutional agnosticism can help ease the tensions in our public and legal dialogue, it is not a panacea. Ultimately, we must look beyond specific issues in law and religion to the central and unavoidable question for any liberal democracy, particularly in our own age: whether religion and liberal democracy are simply irreconcilable, and whether questions of religious truth are doomed to prove unresolvable, even in a society whose officials and citizens do their level best to adopt the agnostic habit.

Although an agnostic approach promises to lend a good deal of clarity and calm to these difficult questions, it is still only a partial and imperfect solution. Religion remains in serious conflict with both law and the broader claims of the liberal democratic state. Religious belief makes claims that ultimately cannot achieve a perfect compromise with the needs of the state. Conversely, liberal democratic states have needs that cannot be perfectly reconciled with those of religious believers. These tensions are written into the DNA of liberal democracy. They cannot be completely resolved without remaking society itself—if, that is, they can be resolved at all. We must resign ourselves to the fact that we live in an imperfect world, filled with unbridgeable conflicts and tragic choices.

Still, we need not live utterly without hope and without any prospect of reaching a better, more sensible and sensitive way of talking about and dealing with these conflicts. By confronting rather than avoiding the question of religious truth, constitutional agnosticism promises to salve the wounds of our culture wars, offers sounder resolutions of the many conflicts between church and state, and helps us to coexist, imperfectly but better than we do now, in a pluralistic society that is filled with endless varieties of religious and non-religious experience.

PART ONE

THE END OF THE WORLD AS WE KNOW IT: THE COLLAPSE OF THE LIBERAL CONSENSUS IN LAW AND SOCIETY

1. RELIGION UNDER ATTACK, LIBERALISM UNDER ATTACK

In this chapter, I describe a fragile consensus and its collapse. The story I tell here is our story. It is the story of the society we know and the one we are coming, however uneasily, to inhabit. It is an oft-told tale. But if we are to follow our path to a new world of constitutional agnosticism, we must begin with the way we live now. We must start with the foundations—or, maybe, the ruins—of the current order.

Our story is about the liberal consensus in Western liberal democratic society. It is the story of how, after centuries of bloody religious strife, and more centuries of political, philosophical, and theological debate—sometimes calm and reasoned, sometimes inflamed and impassioned—different forms of religious belief and disbelief came to coexist more or less peaceably in the common space we call the liberal democratic order. It is also the story of whether this peace can prevail much longer.

This is rich and complicated terrain. The picture I draw here of liberal democracy and its discontents will be a simple and stylized one, omitting at least as much as it includes. It will focus on liberalism as what we might call a "public philosophy," emphasizing liberalism as it is generally understood rather than as its most sophisticated academics might describe it.[1]

Even so, trying to capture the liberal consensus, even at a single moment in time, cannot help but be an exercise in partiality and incompleteness. Imagine trying to photograph a waterfall—to freeze Niagara Falls in a single snapshot. The photo might be panoramic and magnificent. But it could not contain within itself the fluid movement of water from source to source, the prodigious energy that drives and is created by the onrush, the way that what seems massive and stable is actually a collection of droplets that all came from somewhere and are going somewhere. Nor, to take a longer view, could such a photo capture the eons of geological time, of accretion and erosion, that make a rivulet a waterfall, and the forces that will, perhaps, reduce it back to a rivulet a million years hence. We could not, in short, capture its dynamism, its impermanence, its fluidity.

---

1. *See, e.g.,* Mark Tushnet, *A Public Philosophy for the Professional-Managerial Class*, 106 Yale L.J. 1571, 1572–1573 (1997) ("A public philosophy is not a form of systematic political philosophy. Rather, it is the philosophy 'implicit in our practices and institutions.'") (quoting Michael J. Sandel, *Democracy's Discontent: America in Search of a Public Philosophy* ix (1996)).

Similarly, liberal democracy at present may have describable features, but it is more accurate to think of it in terms of change than stability. The liberal consensus emerged only after centuries of change and debate, and the terms of the compromise are constantly undergoing a host of molecular negotiations and renegotiations.

Let me offer, then, a modest sketch of the liberal consensus as it stood, in a roughly fixed and stable sense, in the twentieth century and up to the present day. As we will see, this consensus is under attack from all sides.

THE LIBERAL CONSENSUS AS TREATY

The liberal consensus, or compromise, answers the question of how we can all live together under conditions of diversity and pluralism without coming to blows. The difficulty of arriving at a workable answer is testified to by centuries of history written in blood. Nevertheless, the liberal consensus attempted to provide an answer to this question. In many respects, it did its job well.

Strictly speaking, however, the liberal consensus is not an answer at all. It is less a formula or proposition and more like a treaty or pact, or, even better, a détente between the warring sides. It is a *modus vivendi*, one that allows all sides of the conflict to lay down their arms and live together in an uneasy peace.

Viewing the liberal consensus as a treaty has its perils, of course. It may overemphasize the degree to which each side was able to maintain its prior views. Two nations fighting a boundary dispute might agree to put the controversy before a neutral international tribunal without waiving their right to continue pressing their competing claims about where the boundaries lie. The liberal consensus is different. It is a treaty whose terms ended up redrawing the borders of one or both sides of the dispute.

In our own day, we might tend to believe that the subtle perceptual shifts worked by the terms of the liberal consensus between the religious and the secular orders had a more significant impact on the views of the religious side of the debate than it did on the secular side. Many have argued that the liberal revolution changed religion itself. Religion in the post-Enlightenment era became more privatized, relegated to the devotional margins of existence rather than the center of public life. Its adherents became more tolerant of views they once strongly believed were both false and harmful to the souls of individuals and to society itself. In this sense, religious individuals and groups might argue that the treaty failed, that the secular side of the battle actually won a victory by degrees and by stealth. On the other side, secularists might argue that the increasing primacy over time of secularism and "public reason" represented the foreordained outcome of an intellectual contest in which the religious side was badly overmatched. They might describe the slow shift in, and away from, religious belief not as victory by stealth, but as the inevitable winnowing away of false beliefs when confronted by the truth.

We need not resolve these questions here. We can note, however, that the argument that liberalism and secularism have won out over religion is increasingly out of fashion—and rightly so. It assumes that religion changed its views on matters such as toleration and the voluntary nature of belief by *force majeure*, or that any change in religious belief generated by a confrontation with secular ideas or influences was necessarily secular in nature, not religious. It neglects the possibility that religious views about toleration evolved for *religious* reasons. Responding and adapting to conditions in the world is simply what religion as a living tradition *does*, and it is no more "secular" for that.[2] Just as important, although the changes in position might, from a modern perspective, seem more pronounced on the religious side of the conflict, we are increasingly aware that the influences ran both ways. Many of the ideas we think of as the "secular" foundation of the liberal consensus—ideas like toleration, liberty, and rights themselves—also had deep religious roots, and much of what we now view as secular ideas about liberal democracy have their provenance in religious thought.[3] Finally, the idea that secularism is slowly winning out over religion, that society is in the grips of a long and steady process of secularization, has been refuted by the increasing numbers and vitality of religious groups and individuals across the world. If secularism seemed for a time to be quietly winning the hearts and minds of society, it would appear that the secularists declared victory prematurely.

Still, despite its flaws, the metaphor of the liberal consensus as treaty is important and useful. It captures the idea that the liberal consensus was not a final answer to the question how we can coexist in a pluralistic society, but a *process* by which we managed to do so, despite our differences and perhaps despite ourselves.

ROOTS OF THE LIBERAL CONSENSUS

Although this is a snapshot and not a narrative history, we may better understand the terms of the current liberal consensus if we consider its development over centuries of debate, discussion, and evolution. The struggle between

---

2. *See, e.g.,* John T. Noonan, Jr., *A Church that Can and Cannot Change: The Development of Catholic Moral Teaching* (2005); Richard W. Garnett, *Assimilation, Toleration, and the State's Interest in the Development of Religious Doctrine*, 51 UCLA L. Rev. 1645 (2004); Kif Augustine-Adams, *The Web of Membership: The Consonance and Conflict of Being American and Latter-Day Saint*, 13 L.J. & Religion 567 (1998-1999); Frederick Mark Gedicks, *The Integrity of Survival: A Mormon Resonse to Stanley Hauerwas*, 42 DePaul L. Rev. 167 (1992).

3. *See, e.g.,* Michael J. Perry, *Toward a Theory of Human Rights: Religion, Law, Courts* (2008); Michael Allen Gillespie, *The Theological Origins of Modernity* (2008).

religion's demands and those of the state could be traced back to antiquity. Or we could begin at the dawn of Christianity, with early Christian debates about Jesus' injunction to "render . . . unto Caesar the things which be Caesar's, and unto God the things which be God's."[4] But it may be more fruitful to begin somewhat later, with the birth of modern controversies over the allocation of power between the earthly and divine powers represented by the Investiture Controversy of the eleventh and twelfth centuries, in which papal and royal authorities battled over who had the right to select bishops within a king's realm.[5]

These struggles were heightened when the church itself was fractured by the Protestant Reformation. Protestantism's spread had a theological basis. It involved doctrinal disagreement about fundamental religious propositions. It also had a basis in church reform, given widespread concern over the corruption of the church represented by, among other things, the brisk trade in indulgences. But it also had a political basis. It suited a number of temporal powers to enlist in the Reformation, and forswear their allegiance to Rome, because doing so would "eliminate a competing source of authority in their domain" and allow them to "consolidate their power."[6]

A momentary détente was signaled by the Peace of Augsburg, in 1555. Its guiding principle was *Cuius regio, eius religio*—"Whose region, his religion." Under this principle, the religion of a region's leader would constitute the religion of the people of that region. It ended the dispute between warring Catholic and Lutheran forces within the Holy Roman Empire by allowing the ruling authority of a region to determine the religion that would govern. Other models, distinct but similar, arose at roughly the same time to provide the basis for church–state relations elsewhere in Europe. In Geneva, John Calvin taught that both church and state constituted separate authorities, each of which had distinct responsibilities and neither of which enjoyed absolute dominance. In France, the Edict of Nantes, which was declared in 1598, gave the French Calvinists, the Huguenots, the right to "worship in and control their immediate territory."[7]

None of these arrangements constituted a genuine *separation* of church and state as we think of the term today. Nor were these compromises stable. The Edict of Nantes was rejected within sixty years by King Louis XIV of France; the Peace of Augsburg shattered with the Thirty Years War in 1618. The result was

---

4. Luke 20:25.

5. *See, e.g.,* Brian Tierney, *The Crisis of Church & State 1050–1300* (1964).

6. Douglas Laycock, *Continuity and Change in the Threat to Religious Liberty: The Reformation Era and the Late Twentieth Century,* 80 Minn. L. Rev. 1047, 1052 (1996).

7. Carl H. Esbeck, *Dissent and Disestablishment: The Church-State Settlement in the Early American Republic,* 2004 B.Y.U. L. Rev. 1385, 1403; *see also* Laycock, *supra* note 6, at 1053–54.

the Treaty of Westphalia, which left the continent divided between Catholic rule in southern Europe and Protestant rule in the north.

So the early church–state struggle was marked by a set of jurisdictional compromises, in which religious orthodoxy followed the political flag of the ruler. This reduced some of the internecine bloodshed, but hardly eliminated it. Every royal succession, as the twists and turns of English history demonstrate, was fraught with the possibility of a changeover in the reigning religion and a "stripping of the altars," both literal and figurative, as power changed hands.[8]

Another sort of jurisdictional compromise between church and state was proposed by the English writer John Locke,[9] whose influence was deeply felt by the founding generation in the United States. In his famous *Letter Concerning Toleration*, Locke argued for a principle of religious toleration *within* the boundaries of temporal kingdoms. Locke's argument for toleration was partly religious and partly political. Politically, Locke argued that the commonwealth served limited purposes, primarily the protection of life, liberty, and property, and that any more invasive conception of the state would violate the consent of the people who had agreed to this social contract. This limited scope for state authority suggested that matters of conscience would lie outside the boundaries of state power, provided that conscience-driven beliefs did not interfere with others. Religiously, Locke argued that God had vested individuals with an indefeasible religious conscience. The state had no power to compel religious belief, and individuals had no right to delegate the power to choose a religious belief to anyone else. To impose religious beliefs on others would be, "in effect, to command them to offend God."[10] In Noah Feldman's words, "true faith must flow from free choice."[11] The state must respect the right of individuals to form their own consciences and religious beliefs, "so long as they [do] not infringe on the government's responsibilities to keep the peace and protect the basic natural rights of others."[12] Given their religious roots and the stage in history at which he wrote, Locke's ideas on toleration were not as thoroughgoing as the modern liberal democratic conception of toleration. He did not believe toleration applied to atheists, who posed a threat to the state, or to religionists, such as Catholics, who owed primary allegiance to a "foreign power" such as the Pope. Still, Locke's views on toleration were an important step in the formation of the liberal democratic consensus on church–state matters.

---

8. *See, e.g.,* Eamonn Duffy, *The Stripping of the Altars: Traditional Religion in England, 1400–1580* (1992).

9. To be clear, I am not referring here to the character from the television show *Lost*.

10. John Locke, *A Letter Concerning Toleration* 43 (1990) (1689).

11. Noah Feldman, *Divided by God: America's Church-State Problem—And What We Should Do About It* 30 (2005).

12. *Id.* at 31.

These religiously based justifications for religious toleration sowed the seeds for more secular arguments for freedom of religious conscience, and for the principle of non-establishment that was said to flow from this freedom.[13] These arguments flowered in the development of religious freedom in the early American Republic. The religious views of the champions of religious toleration among the early colonists and, later, the Founders, varied greatly, from the deeply religious arguments of Roger Williams to the far more secularist views of Thomas Jefferson.[14] But all were children of the Enlightenment, and their arguments for religious freedom clearly made reason one of the key foundations for a theory of religious freedom and non-establishment. Jefferson, for instance, counseled his nephew to "question with boldness even the existence of a God; because, if there be one, he must more approve of the homage of reason than that of blindfolded fear."[15]

One of the strongest statements for religious freedom and non-establishment in the new American Republic can be found in James Madison's *Memorial and Remonstrance Against Religious Assessments*. It was written in opposition to a Virginia bill that would have given Christian churches tax money, while allowing the individual taxpayer to either designate the church of his choice to receive the tax or, if he did not do so, send his portion of the tax revenues to support schools. Madison's argument against the bill was neither wholly religious nor wholly secular. Rather, it combined "religious arguments designed to appeal to Evangelical Christians and secular arguments designed to appeal to Enlightenment Lockeans."[16]

Madison opens the *Memorial and Remonstrance* with a religious claim that would be familiar to Locke: "It is the duty of every man to render to the Creator such homage, and such only, as he believes to be acceptable to him. This duty is precedent both in order of time and degree of obligation, to the claims of Civil Society."[17] But its arguments are not only religious. Madison also appeals to history, arguing that the centuries have shown that religious establishment is disastrous for both religion, which is corrupted by the influence of the state that holds

---

13. *See also* Jürgen Habermas, *Intolerance and Discrimination*, 1 Int'l J. Con. L. 2, 4 (2003) ("[P]hilosophical justifications for religious toleration in the seventeenth and eighteenth centuries paved the way for the secularization of the state and the switch to a secular legitimation of the state").

14. *See, e.g.*, David L. Holmes, *The Faiths of the Founding Fathers* (2006); Alf Mapp, *The Faiths of Our Fathers: What America's Founders Really Believed* (2005).

15. Letter from Thomas Jefferson to Peter Carr (August 10, 1787), in *The Life and Selected Writings of Thomas Jefferson* 429, 431 (Adrienne Koch & William Peden eds., 1944).

16. Andrew Koppelman, *Corruption of Religion and the Establishment Clause*, 50 Wm. & Mary L. Rev. 1831, 1875–76 (2009).

17. James Madison, *Madison's Remonstrance*, in *The Documentary History of the Struggle for Religious Freedom in Virginia* 256 (Charles F. James, ed., 1900) (1785).

the purse strings, and government, because religious establishments end up "upholding the thrones of political tyranny."[18] We thus see in the *Memorial and Remonstrance* evidence of the expansion of religious toleration, both in its justifications, which move from purely religious to a combination of religious and secular, and in its scope, which moves from a narrow principle of non-interference with religious conscience to the view that *any* state subsidy of religion necessarily constitutes a threat to freedom of conscience.

Madison's robust defense of religious freedom and non-establishment also represented a change in view about toleration itself. By advocating non-establishment, Madison moved beyond a simple Lockean defense of toleration, which requires freedom of religious conscience but does not prohibit the state from promoting a particular religious faith. He did not simply argue that the state might ally itself with the "true" religious faith while leaving a space open for other religious beliefs. He argued more vigorously that establishment itself offended religious conscience, and that the state must be prevented from advancing the interests of any one faith. Thus, when George Mason proposed in 1776 that the bill of rights for Virginia should protect the "toleration" of religion, Madison argued for a more full-throated protection of equal treatment of *all* religions.[19] This was an early version of what became the "familiar modern criticism" of toleration: "[T]olerance is too insipid or unambitious a goal for a 'liberal' society."[20] Similarly, Thomas Paine, who was far more hostile toward religion than many of his colleagues in the struggle for American independence, and whose views and manner ultimately pushed him to the margins of that struggle, insisted that "[t]oleration is not the *opposite* of intoleration, but is the counterfeit of it."[21] A century later, John Stuart Mill's famous "harm principle," which argued that the only basis on which the state can interfere with the opinions or actions of another is to "prevent harm to others,"[22] would complete the move from religious to secular arguments for toleration. Mill's vigorous, and quite non-religious, arguments for toleration would ultimately "permeate[] across all aspects of liberal theory and practice."[23]

We thus come to the next stage in the development of the liberal consensus: the move from "the liberalism of tolerance in which there is an orthodoxy but no repression of dissent" to "the liberalism of neutrality and equality in which there is not even an official orthodoxy."[24] This is the modern liberal regime in brief.

---

18. *Id.* at 259.

19. *See, e.g.,* Steven D. Smith, *Getting Over Equality: A Critical Diagnosis of Religious Freedom in America* 12 (2001).

20. *Id.* at 6.

21. *Id.* at 11.

22. John Stuart Mill, *On Liberty* 11 (Michael B. Mathias, ed., 2003) (1859).

23. Catriona McKinnon, *Toleration: A Critical Introduction* 10 (2006).

24. Steven D. Smith, *The Restoration of Tolerance*, 78 Cal. L. Rev. 305, 308 (1990).

It is captured in one of the more famous passages in the Supreme Court's First Amendment jurisprudence: Justice Robert Jackson's statement, in *West Virginia Board of Education v. Barnette*, that "[i]f there is any fixed star in our constitutional constellation, it is that no official, high or petty, can prescribe what shall be orthodox in politics, nationalism, religion, or other matters of opinion or force citizens to confess by word or act their faith therein."[25]

The no-orthodoxy position is clearly leagues away from the starting point of this brief tour of the historical development of the liberal consensus. It is not a jurisdictional settlement, under which both church and state retain coercive power within their own realms, or in which religious orthodoxy follows the flag. Nor is it toleration, which by its very nature implies an orthodoxy from which dissenters are free to depart. Rather, it is at least ostensibly a position of genuine neutrality, in which the state is to take no position at all, whether on matters of religious truth or anything else. From this position follow ineluctably both a protective view of individual religious freedom and a proscription against government establishment of religion. It is, somewhat paradoxically,[26] the "orthodoxy" of the modern First Amendment.

THE LIBERAL CONSENSUS DESCRIBED: TERMS OF THE TREATY

This has been a decidedly short history, but it will help us to sketch some of the basic principles that form the liberal consensus. Returning to our earlier metaphor of the liberal consensus as treaty, we can ask: What are the basic terms of the détente between warring sides—especially between members of different religions, and between religion and the state—that comprises the liberal treaty as it is generally and popularly understood? And what implications follow from these terms?

Neutrality

The idea that "government should be neutral on the question of the good life" has been called the "central idea" of liberalism.[27] According to this view, liberalism is "a form of government where political decisions are, so far as possible, 'independent of any particular conception of the good life or what gives value to

---

25. *West Virginia Board of Education v. Barnette*, 329 U.S. 624, 642 (1943). How seriously this passage can be taken is, at least implicitly, the concern of much of this chapter. For a perceptive critique, see Steven D. Smith, Barnette's *Big Blunder*, 78 Chi.-Kent L. Rev. 625 (2003).

26. *See* Smith, *id.*

27. Michael J. Sandel, *Freedom of Conscience or Freedom of Choice?*, in *Articles of Faith, Articles of Peace* 74, 75 (James Davison Hunter & Os Guiness, eds., 1990).

life.'"[28] Liberal democracies "respond[ ] to modern conditions of conflict among private values by striving to remain evenhanded, neither promoting nor disfavoring one or another of the comprehensive commitments that vie for citizens' allegiance."[29] The liberal consensus thus strives to maintain peace among warring factions by remaining neutral on the fundamental questions that divide them. Whether it succeeds in this—whether it is an impartial referee or an active player in the game—is a question we will take up in due course.

Democracy

One means by which the liberal consensus maintains its neutral stance while quelling the discord between contending groups is by providing a process by which these groups can coexist without bloodshed. That process, in a word, is democracy. Liberalism and democracy are thus intimately related: democracy is both a liberal good and a process by which liberalism interposes itself between what might otherwise be violently opposed groups. As Carrie Menkel-Meddow writes, "[B]ecause we are unlikely ever to reach any real, uniform consensus on what constitutes the 'substantive good' in a deeply pluralist and divided world, perhaps we can, at best, arrive at some close-to-universal principles for processes that enable us to live together within these differences."[30] Democracy is one mechanism by which this stance of liberal neutrality is achieved. Every side in the battle of all against all has an opportunity to convince others of the rightness of its positions. Those positions may in turn suffer political reversal, and the outs may become the ins. No side is granted an absolute victory. Democracy is a form of "controlled revolutionary activity,"[31] in which the revolution is bloodless and always incomplete.

Individual Rights

There is an important caveat to democracy as a term of the liberal consensus as treaty. That is the notion of individual rights. Whether they are described as "trumps,"[32] "side-constraints,"[33] "shields" against government action,[34] vehicles

---

28. Stanley Fish, *The Trouble With Principle* 177–78 (1999) (quoting Ronald Dworkin, *A Matter of Principle* 191 (1985)).

29. Nelson W. Tebbe, *Excluding Religion: A Reply*, 157 U. Pa. L. Rev. PENNumbra 283, 286 (2009).

30. Carrie Menkel-Meddow, *Peace and Justice: Notes on the Evolution and Purposes of Legal Processes*, 94 Geo. L.J. 553, 557 (2006) (discussing Stuart Hampshire, *Justice is Conflict* (2000)).

31. Jean Hampton, *Democracy and the Rule of Law*, in *Nomos XXXVI: The Rule of Law* 34 (Ian Shapiro, ed., 1994).

32. Ronald Dworkin, *Taking Rights Seriously* xi (1977).

33. Robert Nozick, *Anarchy, State, and Utopia* 29 (1974).

34. Frederick Schauer, *A Comment on the Structure of Rights*, 27 Ga. L. Rev. 415, 428–31 (1993).

for "representation-reinforcement,"[35] or some other label, the meaning is the same. Any given side of the conflict between contending views is not only prevented from winning an absolute victory by virtue of the ongoing contest of democracy, it is prevented from winning even a *temporary* victory on some issues.

Individual rights serve two functions. First, they preserve the freedom of conscience: the freedom to make one's own choices on fundamental questions without fear of being compelled to say or believe something simply because one side in the ongoing battle of views has a temporary legislative majority. Second, they "clear[] the channels of political change."[36] In order to ensure that one side cannot entrench itself indefinitely in power, individuals enjoy the right to speak out against that side, to an equal vote along with everyone else, and to be treated equally. In this way, contending viewpoints are aired, and no one side can subject its adversaries to unequal treatment from its temporary perch in the seat of government.

Religious Freedom

Religious freedom, obviously, is one of the individual rights that act as a side-constraint on democracy, but for our purposes it deserves its own focus. This is so not just because the subject of this book is law and religion, but because, as we have seen, the liberal consensus is at bottom a response to the relationship between religion and the state. Religious freedom entails, at a minimum, the right to believe, practice, and profess the faith of one's choice, subject to some constraints on religious practices that pose a significant threat to the interests of others. Whether this freedom can be invoked against any law that even incidentally intrudes upon religious practices, or whether it only embraces those laws that are directly or indirectly targeted at religion, has been a controversial topic at least since 1990, when the Supreme Court in *Employment Division v. Smith*[37] forthrightly took the latter position.

Whether the liberal consensus demands non-establishment of religion in addition to individual freedom to practice one's religion is a more difficult question. Madison's *Memorial and Remonstrance* and the First Amendment, of which he was the principal draftsman and leading proponent, show that the American view embraces a principle of non-establishment, although its precise meaning is debated to this day. But other nations that clearly dwell within the heart of the liberal consensus do not take this position. England, for example, protects individual religious freedom but also enshrines the Church of England as its established church. Perhaps the most we can say is that the liberal consensus does not necessarily prohibit religious establishments, but does set limits on their ability to coerce individual beliefs and practices.

---

35. *See generally* John Hart Ely, *Democracy and Distrust* (1980).
36. *Id.* at 107.
37. 494 U.S. 872 (1990).

Equality

Another central term of the liberal treaty is equality. It plays a prominent part in the *Memorial and Remonstrance*, which declares that "all men are to be considered as entering into Society on equal conditions."[38] Indeed, in the Enlightenment, equality "became the touchstone of political life and thought."[39] In the United States, the principle of equality, in theory if not always in practice, took center stage from the nation's very inception, with the Declaration of Independence's eloquent if unfulfilled statement that "all men are created equal."

The principle of equality is closely linked to the principle of religious freedom, although, as American debates over race, gender, and a host of other issues have demonstrated, it is hardly limited to that subject alone. Thus, the *Memorial and Remonstrance* goes on to say that, "[a]bove all," human beings are "to be considered as retaining an equal title to the free exercise of Religion according to the dictates of conscience."[40] At the outset of the American experiment, then, and long before the promise of equality had been cashed out for women, African-Americans, and others, equality at least meant that all religions stood on equal footing. We can see here the ways in which equality unites both the principle of individual religious freedom and the principle of non-establishment, by declaring that there should be no privileged religious class. In recent years, equality has taken an increasingly prominent role in the Supreme Court's rulings on the Religion Clauses of the First Amendment.[41]

Public Reason

The last clause of the liberal treaty that deserves mention is somewhat more controversial. This is the principle of public reason. It demands that public debate about political issues avoid any reliance on comprehensive doctrines like religion, and instead speak in terms that can be understood and agreed upon by everyone. Arguments must be framed in terms of "accessible" reasons—reasons that "appeal to political values shared by all reasonable inhabitants of a liberal democracy."[42] In modern times, it has been closely associated with, and most fully developed by, the political philosopher John Rawls,[43] who described public reason as part of "a conception of a well ordered constitutional democratic

---

38. Madison, *supra* note 17, at 256.

39. Martha C. Nussbaum, *Liberty of Conscience: In Defense of America's Tradition of Religious Equality* 73 (2008).

40. Madison, *supra* note 17, at 258.

41. *See* Chapter Seven.

42. Aaron-Andrew P. Bruhl, *Public Reason as a Public Good*, 4 J.L. in Soc'y 217, 218 (2003).

43. *See* John Rawls, *Political Liberalism* (1993).

society," and as "part of the idea of democracy itself."[44] There is a close link between the requirement of public reasons in political debate among citizens and the principle of neutrality. The requirement of public reason is the neutrality rule made manifest in public discussion. It is the neutral "language" or "grammar" by which "politics is to be conducted."[45] Just as the state must remain neutral on fundamental questions of the good, so public discussion on political issues must take place in terms that do not appeal to particular conceptions of the good, but instead rely on terms of argument that are available to everyone.

Whether public reason is, in fact, a central tenet of liberal democracy—whether, indeed, it is even *possible*—has been the subject of vigorous and ongoing debate.[46] Still, there is no doubt that some form of the public reason principle has figured prominently, if controversially, in modern liberal democracy. Its traces are evident, for instance, in the Supreme Court's willingness to strike down laws, such as those banning the teaching of evolution[47] or requiring a moment of silent prayer or meditation in public schools,[48] that are based primarily or exclusively on religious beliefs rather than on reasons that are shared by all citizens. This requirement is captured by the Court's insistence in its Establishment Clause jurisprudence that every law must serve a "secular purpose."[49]

These are the key terms of the liberal treaty. No doubt others would offer a slightly different list, but it will do for our purposes. What remains is to consider some of the assumptions that underwrite this treaty, or that follow from it.

Individualism

One premise that seems to follow from many of the terms of the liberal treaty is a strong orientation toward the individual and individualism. The state's neutrality as between conceptions of the good, and the belief that each person is entitled to freedom of religious conscience, imply that the individual is at the center of human experience. He or she makes choices as an individual, and questions of the good must ultimately be resolved by him or her alone. This individualism has deep roots in Protestantism, with its belief that the individual conscience is, by God's ordinance, at the heart of religious faith.[50] These religious roots

---

44. John Rawls, *The Idea of Public Reason Revisited*, 64 U. Chi. L. Rev. 765, 765 (1997).

45. Patrick McKinley Brennan, *Political Liberalism's Tertium Quiddity: Neutral "Public Reason,"* 43 Am. J. Juris. 239, 243 (1998).

46. *See, e.g.,* Kent Greenawalt, *Public Conscience and Private Reasons* (1995).

47. *See, e.g., Epperson v. Arkansas,* 393 U.S. 97 (1968).

48. *See, e.g., Wallace v. Jaffree,* 472 U.S. 38 (1985).

49. *See, e.g., Lemon v. Kurtzman,* 403 U.S. 602 (1971); *see also* Andrew Koppelman, *Secular Purpose,* 88 Va. L. Rev. 87 (2002).

50. *See, e.g.,* Noah Feldman, *The Intellectual Origins of the Establishment Clause,* 77 N.Y.U. L. Rev. 346, 350 (2002).

contributed to a secular worldview that placed the individual, and individual free-dom, at the center of the political order. Although this perspective obviously differed from, say, Catholicism, which was more communal and authoritarian in nature, Catholic thought itself came to recognize the primacy, in many respects, of individual conscience—influenced, not incidentally, by American Catholic writers such as John Courtney Murray.[51] Thus, the liberal consensus, for both religious and secular reasons, is pervaded by a highly individualistic worldview.

Voluntariness

Along with individualism comes a related principle: voluntariness. Religious choices, among other decisions about fundamental beliefs, are treated as just that: *choices*. An individual's religious beliefs may be influenced by those of family, friends, community, or society, but they are ultimately a matter for his or her own independent decision. Each person must decide for himself where he stands on these fundamental questions. Although religion may be experienced as something foreordained, or whose truth and power is such that there seems to be no choice involved at all, on a worldly level these are still treated as choices that are not compelled, at least by any temporal authority. Both non-establishment and individual religious freedom work in concert to clear a space in which those voluntary choices can manifest themselves in word and deed. The principle of voluntariness is thus both important and perhaps inevitable under the conditions of religious pluralism and doubt in which the modern liberal democratic state exists.[52] In enshrining freedom of conscience and neutrality, the liberal consensus emphasizes a vision of belief as voluntary, as a matter of choice for each individual, one that cannot be taken away by church *or* state.

Bracketing Religious Truth

Here we come to a premise of the liberal consensus that will figure centrally in the constitutional agnostic's critique of the current order. By remaining neutral on the nature of the good and on fundamental religious questions, liberalism effectively attempts to take questions of religious truth off the table altogether. Instead of giving itself over to interminable and potentially bloody conflicts over religious truth, liberalism makes Pontius Pilate's shrug its signature gesture. It brackets questions of religious truth entirely.[53] Although individuals are free to

---

51. *See, e.g.,* John Courtney Murray, *We Hold These Truths: Catholic Reflections on the American Proposition* (1960).

52. *See, e.g.,* Charles Taylor, *A Secular Age* (2007); Roger Lundin, *Believing Again: Doubt and Faith in a Secular Age* (2009).

53. *See, e.g.,* Mark Lilla, *The Stillborn God* 7 (2007) ("The novelty of modern political philosophy was to have relinquished . . . comprehensive claims [about religious truth] by disengaging reflection about the human political realm from theological speculations about what might lie beyond it.").

make their own choices about what constitutes religious truth, the state remains scrupulously neutral on these questions. This stance is manifested in a host of terms of the liberal treaty, from religious freedom and other individual rights, which constrain the state from attempting to impose answers on anyone, to the requirement of public reason, which in its strongest form erects a prohibition on bringing these questions to bear at all on matters of public debate.

The Possibility of Public Reason

We have already seen that the requirement of public reason is a key term, albeit a controversial one, in the liberal consensus. That it persists suggests another premise that appears to follow from the liberal consensus: namely, that public reason is possible in the first place. If the liberal consensus is that the state must remain neutral on questions of the good, and if the effort to separate questions of religious truth from public discussion is to succeed, it follows that it must be possible to hold productive and meaningful discussions that do not rely on fundamental conceptions of the good or of religious truth. It must be possible, in other words, to hold discussions using common terms of agreement and argument that are available to everyone regardless of their own beliefs. We must be able to discuss and debate whether government should take particular actions or enact particular policies without referring to these broader religious questions or turning the debates into arguments over the existence of God or the nature of the good. That implies that there is something left *on* the table when questions of religious truth are taken *off* the table. If, to take Rawls' famous concept, we were to be placed behind the "veil of ignorance,"[54] if we were to be separated from all the fundamental beliefs and thickly rooted aspects of our identity—race, gender, class, family, and so on—and asked to reason from within that realm of limbo, it would still be possible for us to hold meaningful discussions about how to establish our social order. An important premise of the liberal consensus is thus that there remains something to talk about, and a common language with which to discuss it, when we remove religious beliefs and other fundamental views from the equation.

Public and Private Spheres

Another crucial aspect of the liberal consensus is the division of our social life into public and private spheres. The idea of a public sphere "is a central feature of modern society."[55] It is a relatively recent phenomenon, one that can be traced back to the Enlightenment.[56] It may be distinguished from the social map of earlier societies, in which the line between public and private life was less distinct.

---

54. John Rawls, *A Theory of Justice* 10 (1971).
55. Taylor, *supra* note 52, at 185.
56. *See id.* at 187; Jürgen Habermas, *The Structural Transformation of the Public Sphere* (1989); Michael Warner, *The Letters of the Republic* (1992).

The public sphere is now treated as lying "outside power," as a space in which the contending voices "strive for a certain impersonality, a certain impartiality."[57] It is a public space in which discussion is supposed to take place within "a discourse of reason."[58]

Just as important is what the division between the public and private spheres implies for the private sphere. The private sphere is the sphere of the home, the family—and religion. In our age, this division may seem entirely natural. The idea of a private sphere so pervades our lives, with our assumptions about a "right to privacy" and our discussions about how to strike a balance between work and "private life," that it may be difficult to conceive of any other way in which life could be lived. But the distinction is not simply a natural one. It depends on the conditions under which we live, in which individuals can participate together in common tasks such as work and politics, while still repairing to homes, churches, and other separate spaces to speak in our own idiosyncratic languages and cultivate our own views about what constitutes a good life. In this sense, the idea of a private sphere is both a cause and a product of many of the terms of the liberal treaty. It is part and parcel of our structuring of social life around the idea of individualism and voluntariness. It suggests that each of us is free to make our own "private" choices about what life means, while treating those choices as separate from our dealings with each other within a common, public space.

Perhaps the most important aspect of the division of life into the public and private spheres, for our purposes, is the way it affects our picture of religious life. The centripetal force of the division of life into public and private spheres, the ways in which it distinguishes between our "public" and "private" selves, has a strong influence on how we think about religion and religious truth. Because the public sphere is stripped bare of fundamental beliefs about God and other higher concerns, because it is a place in which we all talk in terms of public reason, religion is pushed to the private spaces of our lives. We are permitted to hold strong beliefs on these questions, but they are made a matter for private life alone. They belong at home, in church, and in other enclaves, but not in the public sphere. This idea is apparent in Justice William O. Douglas's pronouncement that "our Constitution decrees that religion must be a private matter for the individual, the family, and the institutions of private choice."[59] Religion may continue to be important after the emergence of a public sphere, but it is, as it were, zoned for residential uses only.

---

57. Taylor, *supra* note 52, at 190.
58. *Id.*
59. *Lemon v. Kurtzman*, 403 U.S. 602, 625 (1971) (Douglas, J., concurring).

Secularism?

The division of social life into the public and private spheres, along with the implicit treatment of religion as falling within the private sphere alone, can be taken together with the premise that public reason is both possible and necessary for the maintenance of the liberal consensus. These assumptions, when combined, raise the question whether we must add one final item to our list of liberal principles: Is liberal democracy fundamentally secular in orientation? Is the liberal order a secular order?

Some individuals have argued that liberal democracy *is* and must be secular. The United States Constitution, they assert, establishes a "secular public order."[60] The Constitution is distinctly a product of the Enlightenment, and it embodies the triumph of "rationalism and empiricism" over "religious faith and mysticism."[61] It represents the Founders' "general Enlightenment secularism with its preference for reason over faith."[62]

This is not the only way to understand what the Founders had in mind when they ratified the First Amendment and its Religion Clauses. Certainly, as we have seen, early Enlightenment arguments in favor of freedom of religion were often deeply influenced by specifically *religious* arguments for religious toleration, such as Locke's religious argument for the necessity of freedom of conscience. Even those who may have favored freedom of religion for more secular reasons, such as Madison, made common cause with religious minorities, who, because they feared for their future as religious believers in any society in which they were outnumbered by adherents of other sects, were eager to embrace a policy of religious freedom for instrumental as well as spiritual reasons.[63] Certainly many aspects of the liberal treaty would appear to argue against too strong an assertion that the liberal order was meant to enshrine a principle of secularism. Foremost among these is the principle of neutrality, which, in theory if not always in practice, requires the liberal democratic state to remain neutral as to conceptions of the good rather than taking sides in favor of a distinctly secular view.

That does not completely settle the question, however. More than one understanding of secularism could be at work in our understanding of what the liberal

---

60. Kathleen M. Sullivan, *Religion and Liberal Democracy*, 59 U. Chi. L. Rev. 195, 201 (1992).

61. Suzanna Sherry, *Enlightening the Religion Clauses*, 7 J. Contemp. Legal Issues 473, 483 (1997).

62. *Id.* at 489.

63. *See, e.g.*, Vincent Blasi, *School Vouchers and Religious Liberty: Seven Questions From Madison's Memorial and Remonstrance*, 87 Cornell L. Rev. 783, 793–97 (2002); John T. Noonan, Jr., *The Lustre of Our Country: The American Experience of Religious Freedom* 78 (1998); Douglas Laycock, *Religious Liberty as Liberty*, 7 J. Contemp. Legal Issues 313, 344–47 (1996).

consensus demands. Charles Taylor has written compellingly on this point in his book *A Secular Age*. As he rightly points out, religion continues to thrive in the United States.[64] That suggests that the liberal state's neutrality as to conceptions of the good, combined with the creation and protection of both public and private spheres, leaves a fertile space for religious belief and practice. The state, in this view, really *is* neutral as to religion, not secular.

There are other understandings of secularism, however. One of them is clearly evident in the treaty terms we have examined so far. Consider what it means to think of religion as centered in the individual and as being a matter of voluntary choice. Given the conditions of pluralism in which we live, and the increasing numbers of people who profess no faith at all, we might redefine secularism as a state of affairs in which "faith, even for the staunchest believer, is one human possibility among others." We may, in short, live in an age in which "[b]elief in God is no longer axiomatic."[65] If it goes too far to say that we live in an age of religion as a "hobby,"[66] it is still the case that we live in an age in which religious belief is not inevitable, but rather is a choice or an option, and just one of many at that. In this sense, we might argue that the liberal consensus creates the conditions in which secularism, or at least a form of pluralism in which secularism stands on equal grounds with religious belief, can flourish. In this sense, liberal democracy does indeed furnish us with a secular order.

The second important point to consider is that, whether or not the liberal order purports to be secular, its treatment of religion as one choice among many, which is intimately linked to the values of individualism and voluntarism that undergird the liberal consensus, may have the effect of *bringing about* a secular order. This is true in two possible senses. The first is sometimes summarized in the sociological concept of the "secularization thesis." This is the idea that, in an order in which secularism and religious belief compete, secularism will drive out religion. Secularity will thus consist of "the falling off of religious belief and practice, . . . people turning away from God."[67] Although the secularization thesis no longer commands consent among the sociologists who coined the term,[68] many diehard secularists continue to believe in it, most prominently the New Atheists.[69] Whether the secularization thesis is true or not, however, the very fact

---

64. Taylor, *supra* note 52, at 2.

65. *Id.* at 3.

66. Stephen L. Carter, *Evolutionism, Creationism, and Treating Religion as a Hobby,* 1987 Duke L.J. 977; *see also* Stephen L. Carter, *The Culture of Disbelief: How American Law and Politics Trivializes Religion* 23–33 (1993).

67. Taylor, *supra* note 52, at 1.

68. *See, e.g.,* Peter Berger & Anton Zijderveld, *In Praise of Doubt: How to Have Convictions Without Becoming a Fanatic* (2009).

69. *See* Chapter Four.

that we live in an age of religion as one choice among many can itself influence the nature of religious belief. Even if the liberal state remains neutral as to conceptions of the good, the absence of its support, and the degree to which it throws its lot behind the idea that religion is merely an option, may deprive religion of some of the social solidarity it needs in order to thrive. Left to their own resources, religions may find that their adherents drift into unbelief, or treat religion as a private matter that takes an ever-diminishing role in an age that is lived so much in public. In this sense, too, it may be that the liberal consensus, no matter what its aims, leads to secularism.

The division of life into public and private spheres may affect the move toward secularism in another way. We have just noted the possibility that religion will lose some of its vital force as people live their lives in an increasingly public space and religion is pushed into private life. To this we must add the liberal premises that public reasons are both required and possible in public debate, and that the state must referee these debates neutrally and in publicly accessible language. These features of the liberal consensus also support the argument that the liberal state erects a specifically secular order.

Most importantly, for our purposes, it suggests that when the state is required to make decisions, and especially when it is required to weigh the competing interests of church and state, it will render its judgments in specifically *secular* terms. If forced, for example, to consider whether the legislature can enact a law requiring parents to have their children vaccinated against deadly diseases, it will balance these interests by addressing the dispute in explicitly secular terms, which inevitably gives the edge to secular interests. Measuring the risk of an epidemic of disease against what the religious claimant argues is the risk of religious damnation for allowing vaccination will register as no contest at all, because there will be little or no secular language by which to gauge the interests of the religious claimant. If there *is* any secular language available with which to measure these claims—if, for instance, the state treats the religious interest against vaccination as a matter of individual "conscience" rather than religious truth—the religious claim will come off as far weaker than the secular interests at stake, which can be more easily measured and agreed upon by all parties.[70]

So we can say that, in a social order in which the state requires publicly accessible reasons for particular decisions and rules, secular arguments will necessarily have the advantage. This will be especially true if the state is unaware of just how thoroughly it has diminished or privatized the religious side of the argument. If the state believes it is remaining neutral as between different conceptions of the good, it may simply fail to see how much it has actually privileged secular reasons. It is that very blindness to the richness and force of religious arguments that will be the subject of much of this book. In short, in refusing to

---

70. *See* Chapter Six.

consider questions of religious truth, the liberal consensus may in fact be privileging secular arguments, if not erecting a secular state. Secularism may not be the *goal* of the liberal consensus, but it may prove to be its inevitable result.

THE LIBERAL CONSENSUS DISSOLVES

So far, I have offered a fairly straightforward description of the development and terms of the liberal consensus, conventionally and popularly understood. It arose as a form of compromise or treaty between different religious groups forced to coexist in the same society and seeking to do so without endless bloodshed, and between those who hold religious beliefs and those whose beliefs are secular in orientation. The liberal consensus sought a means by which all sides of the endless dispute over fundamental values could find some basis for living together that would prove more effective and enduring than the kinds of compromises that had clearly failed in the centuries of Western history that preceded them.

The liberal "treaty" we laid out has a number of fundamental terms. They include: (1) neutrality as to conceptions of the good; (2) democracy; (3) individual rights, especially (4) religious freedom; (5) equality; and (6) the requirement of public reason. And these terms imply or give rise to a number of fundamental premises that animate the liberal consensus: (1) the centrality of individualism and (2) voluntariness; (3) the bracketing of questions of religious and other fundamental truths in public discussion; (4) the possibility of finding publicly accessible terms with which to fulfill the liberal requirement of public reason; (5) the division of life into public and private spheres; and (6) the emergence of secularism, either as a mandatory principle of liberalism or as a byproduct of life in a society teeming with different beliefs, in which religious beliefs are only one option among many.

These are the terms of our working compromise, the basis on which we manage to live and work together without being too much at each others' throats. Most of what political philosophers like to call "reasonable" people might well agree that the compromise has worked very well for us.[71] Whatever other kinds of wars we have fought within the Western world in the last several centuries, few of them have been openly religious or sectarian. Open nonbelievers have rarely reached positions of high political power in the United States,[72] but at

---

71. *See, e.g.,* Lilla, *supra* note 53, at 304 ("[C]ontemporary liberal democracies have managed to accommodate religion without setting off sectarian violence or encouraging theocracy, which is a historic achievement.").

72. Oral Argument of Michael A. Newdow, *Elk Grove United School Dist. v. Newdow,* No. 02-1624, 542 U.S. 1 (2004).

least some of them—Jefferson, for example—have clearly not been especially committed religious believers, if they were believers at all. More importantly, the terms of debate in which leaders of all religious stripes have carried out public discussion and implemented public policy have been of a decidedly secular cast. One could praise or condemn, say, the presidency of John F. Kennedy without ever mentioning his Roman Catholic faith.

There is, as I said earlier, some danger in treating the liberal consensus as ever having been too fixed or stable. Nevertheless, we can say that something like the liberal consensus as we recognize it today achieved a relative degree of stability sometime in the last 150 years, and remained fairly stable throughout that time. On the surface, things were relatively calm. This was just the world we all grew up with, roughly from Beethoven through Beyonce, and it served us well— or reasonably well, if you are "reasonable," or at least a fan of Beyonce. (One can, of course, be both.)

This is the world that has increasingly appeared to come under attack. I say "appeared" because, as I have stressed, the liberal consensus has always been subject to revision. But to the extent that we have enjoyed a long and relatively happy day in the sun of liberal democracy, as certain that it would last as that the sun itself would rise tomorrow, we are now in the twilight of the liberal consensus as we have known it. It may survive, with important revisions. Or it may collapse altogether, and new prophets will arise to predict what will come after it. One thing, however, seems certain: The liberal consensus that emerged after the Enlightenment, gelled in the nineteenth century, and reached a more or less stable form in the twentieth century, cannot last much longer as a basic, unquestioned assumption about the way we live. From within and beyond its borders, the liberal consensus is under attack. On all sides, we are hearing calls, sometimes measured and sometimes shrill, for a revision or an outright rejection of the terms of the liberal treaty. We can identify three trends in particular that signal the fragility of the liberal consensus today.

LIBERALISM UNDER ATTACK BY RELIGION

The first attack on the liberal consensus comes from the religious side of the religious–secular divide. As we have seen, the liberal consensus creates public and private spheres, and relegates religion to the private sphere. That settlement may have suited many religious believers and institutions for a long time. It cost them a more vital role in the public sphere, but it also protected them. For religious minorities in particular, the benefits of accepting the privatization of religion were significant. It allowed them to survive despite their minority status without being swallowed up by either the state or majority faiths.

Religion is no longer content with this compromise. Increasingly, "many religious traditions have been making their way, sometimes forcefully, out of the private sphere and into public life."[73] As José Casanova argues, our era has seen a trend toward the "deprivatization of religion."[74] Across the globe, religious groups "are refusing to accept the marginal and privatized role which theories of modernity as well as theories of secularization had reserved for them."[75] Religious groups no longer accept "the reigning structures that have long organized understandings of religious and secular life: state and civil society; the private and public domains; religion and secularism; faith and reason; belief and action."[76] They increasingly insist that they have a role to play in public as well as private life, on their own terms and in their own language.

This trend is visible at a global level as well as in the United States, in established liberal democracies and emerging democracies alike. Two examples of the deprivatization of religion and its challenge to the liberal order have been especially visible: the emergence of radical global Islamism, and the rise within the United States of Christian fundamentalism.

The growth of radical strains of Islam has complicated roots and explanations. But its growth, and thus its status as a challenger to liberal democracy, has been evident for the past three decades, at least since the Iranian revolution in 1979. In an increasing number of societies, radical Islamists have either taken political power and enforced their views through the imposition of harsh and anti-liberal strains of Islamic law, or have by their very presence forced the ruling regimes in nations such as Saudi Arabia to check secularizing trends within their borders and at least pay lip service to more radical Islamic sects.

With the rise of global terrorism and the events of 9/11, radical Islam has come to be seen as posing a direct threat to the well-being, if not the survival, of the liberal democracies of the West. Obviously, the United States has been the target of much of this anti-Western sentiment. Not coincidentally, however, radical Islam has almost entirely failed to take root in the United States. The American tradition of religious pluralism has made Muslim immigrants welcome and woven Islam into its fabric, and thus reduced the likelihood that American Muslims will turn to violent and destructive strains of Islamism.[77]

Elsewhere in the West, however, radical Islam has been viewed as an *internal* threat to the liberal consensus. A number of incidents have revealed the extent to which Europe faces an internal population of radical Muslims who reject the

---

73. Rosalind I.J. Hackett, *Rethinking the Role of Religion in Changing Public Spheres: Some Comparative Perspectives*, 2005 B.Y.U. L. Rev. 659, 662.

74. José Casanova, *Public Religions in the Modern World* (1994).

75. *Id.* at 5.

76. Ruti Teitel, *Vouchsafing Democracy: On the Confluence of Governmental Duty, Constitutional Right, and Religious Mission*, 13 Notre Dame J. L., Ethics, & Pub. Pol'y 409, 414 (1999).

77. *See, e.g.*, Spencer Ackerman, *Why American Muslims Haven't Turned to Terrorism*, The New Republic, Dec. 12, 2005, at 18.

social contract offered by liberal democracy. Dutch filmmaker Theo van Gogh was murdered for collaborating with the Somali-born politician Aayan Hirsi Ali on a film critical of the Muslim treatment of women; Hirsi Ali also suffered death threats and ultimately left the country. Violence ensued after a Danish newspaper published satirical cartoons featuring the image of Muhammad, an act seen as blasphemous by many Muslims.[78] These threats in turn propelled European efforts to crack down on Muslim customs that would occasion little serious protest in the United States.

In France, for example, ongoing debates over whether Muslim schoolgirls can wear the *hijab* in French schools have intensified efforts to enforce the French concept of *läicité*. *Läicité* may be broadly defined as "the character of religious neutrality, independent with regard to all churches and confessions."[79] In practice, it involves a far thicker conception of secularism than the same language would suggest in the United States. It sees the state as taking an active role in "protecting citizens from the excesses of religion."[80] Thus, although France in principle treats the wearing of religious garb as consistent with *läicité*, in practice it views the *hijab* as a threat to its secular tradition—as "ostentatious or combative" behavior that threatens to "disturb public order."[81]

Similar controversies have arisen across Europe, leading to increasing discussion about what it means for Europe to absorb and protect the rights of Muslim immigrants without sacrificing what is thought of as a largely secular liberal establishment. One hardly needs to take sides in these controversies to see that they represent a destabilization of the liberal consensus that reigned in Europe in the latter half of the twentieth century.

Whether the rise of radical Islam within Europe represents an existential threat to the West, or instead demonstrates the extent to which the liberal consensus there privileged existing Christian faiths and became an issue only when Europe was faced with the presence of the "other,"[82] can be debated. But

---

78. *See, e.g.,* Jytte Klausen, *The Cartoons That Shook the World* (2009).

79. *Dictionnaire de L'Academie Francaise* 7 (9th ed. 1992), *translated in* Holly Hinkley Lesan, *The Muslim Foulard in France's Public Sphere: Current Conceptions of* L'Ordre Publique, Läicité, *and* Religious Liberty (May 8, 2004) (unpublished manuscript) (cited in Frederick Mark Gedicks, *Religious Exemptions, Formal Neutrality, and Läicité*, 13 Ind. J. Global Leg. Stud. 473, 475 (2006)).

80. T. Jeremy Gunn, *Religious Freedom and Läicité: A Comparison of the United States and France*, 2004 B.Y.U. L. Rev. 419, 420 n.2.

81. Seyla Benhabib, *Another Cosmopolitanism: Hospitality, Sovereignty, and Democratic Iterations* 54–55 (Robert Post, ed., 2006) (quoting *Avis du Conseil d'Etat*, Nov. 27, 1989, No. 346893) (quoted in Patrick Weil, *Why the French Läicité is Liberal*, 30 Cardozo L. Rev. 2699, 2700 (2009)).

82. The French legal scholar Michel Troper, for instance, observes that it is impossible "to give a good account of French positive law by merely saying that it means absence of influence of religion on the State," because French law in fact allows for a significant state

these questions are less important than the fact that Islam's rise was, and is, *perceived* as a threat.[83] The European reaction is significant, regardless of whether it is proportionate to a real or perceived threat, because it suggests that liberal democracy itself *believes* it does not possess the tools to maintain itself—that, if it is to survive, it cannot rely on the liberal consensus itself, but must actively enforce that consensus, in ways that strain the principles of toleration and religious freedom, perhaps to the breaking point.

If the United States has been relatively untouched by the rise of radical Islam from within, it is in a very different position from Europe with respect to the other major religious response to the liberal consensus: the rise of fundamentalist and evangelical forms of Christian belief. These also pose a direct, if less violent, challenge to the liberal consensus. "The fundamentalist challenge to 'secular humanism' and 'liberalism,'" writes Nomi Stolzenberg, "represents an attack on the entire worldview of modernity—a worldview that emphasizes the ascendancy of reason over social conditioning and 'superstition.'"[84] In its own way, it thus also challenges the liberal consensus.

Although the rise of politically active fundamentalism is often traced back to the Supreme Court's decision in *Roe v. Wade*,[85] which brought abortion to the top of the public agenda and helped lead to the politically active Moral Majority movement, fundamentalist Christianity in fact is a response to a century of developments in liberal democracy *and* religion. It began as a challenge to the theological trend of "higher biblical criticism" in the late nineteenth and early twentieth centuries, which championed modes of biblical interpretation that called into question the authenticity and divine authorship of the Scriptures.[86] The response initially took the form of a series of volumes produced by the Bible League of North America called *The Fundamentals*, which emphasized "the doctrine of biblical inerrancy," and "the refutation of higher biblical criticism" and "modern scientific method."[87] Fundamentalism ultimately evolved into a broader challenge to the liberal consensus and its ostensible neutrality on questions of religious truth.

---

influence on and support of (Christian) religion, as is evidenced by the fact that France's Minister of the Interior is also called the "minister of religions." Michel Troper, *Sovereignty and Läicité*, 30 Cardozo L. Rev. 2561, 2563 (2009).

83. *See, e.g.,* Talal Asad, *Formations of the Secular: Christianity, Islam, Modernity* (2003).

84. Nomi Maya Stolzenberg, *"He Drew a Circle That Shut Me Out:" Assimilation, Indoctrination, and the Paradox of a Liberal Education*, 106 Harv. L. Rev. 581, 614 (1993).

85. 410 U.S. 113 (1973)

86. *See* Stolzenberg, *supra* note 84, at 616.

87. Ralph C. Chandler, *The Wicked Shall Not Bear Rule: The Fundamentalist Heritage of the New Christian Right*, in *New Christian Politics* 41, 43 (David G. Bromely & Anson Shupe, eds., 1984).

Fundamentalists enjoyed an early victory in the Scopes "Monkey Trial," in which John Scopes was convicted for violating an anti-evolution law in Louisiana. But it was a pyrrhic victory. The fundamentalist side, represented in court by former presidential candidate William Jennings Bryan, was made a laughingstock by the national press.[88] Its response was to retreat to the private sphere.[89] Jerry Falwell, who later became a leading figure in the rise of public fundamentalism, wrote in 1965 that fundamentalists had "few ties to this earth."[90] The 1970s and 1980s, however, witnessed the resurgence of Protestant fundamentalism as a significant social movement. This movement was based on the fundamentalists' desire to pose a serious challenge to the terms of the liberal consensus in which they lived, and on their belief that religion was being forced inward to a vanishing point by the privatizing impulse of liberal society. It was a response to the view that "external forces [were] encroaching upon the separatist fundamentalist life world," and that fundamentalists were obliged to retake the public stage if they were to weather the cultural threat to their existence.[91] The result was the forging of a political coalition that reshaped American politics for at least a decade, and whose influence is still felt strongly, especially in the Republican Party.[92]

Others have written at length about the fundamentalist movement, and debated the extent of its influence. For now, what is important is the challenge it poses to the liberal consensus. It rejects the premise that religion should be purely a matter of "quiet faith,"[93] and that public discussions must be held according to the requirement of public reason. It contends that the bargain struck between religion and the state which pushed faith groups to the margins of public life was wrong. It has resulted in the takeover of the public sphere by liberal and secular values. Some fundamentalists have argued for the revival of Christianity in public life and devotion—returning prayers to the public schools, displaying the Ten Commandments on public property, and so on—in ways that pose a direct challenge to existing Establishment Clause jurisprudence. This suggests that they reject views about the separation of church and state that were once settled principles within the liberal consensus.

---

88. *See* Edward J. Larson, *Summer for the Gods: The Scopes Trial and America's Continuing Debate Over Science and Religion* (2006).

89. *See* Stolzenberg, *supra* note 84, at 619.

90. Steve Bruce, *The Rise and Fall of the New Christian Right: Conservative Protestant Politics in America, 1978–1988* 138 (1988).

91. Casanova, *supra* note 74, at 151.

92. Although a resurgent religious left has, with less success, sought a more prominent position in modern Democratic Party politics. *See generally* Steven H. Shiffrin, *The Religious Left and Church-State Relations* (2009).

93. Richard W. Garnett, *A Quiet Faith?: Taxes, Politics, and the Privatization of Religion*, 42 B.C. L. Rev. 771 (2001).

These are only a few examples of the ways in which religion has come to question the liberal consensus. They are emblematic of a larger religious challenge to the terms of the liberal treaty. They represent the leading edge of a broader questioning of whether the principles that underwrite the liberal consensus are even possible, let alone advisable. On this view, religious voices must take a stand against a "culture of disbelief"[94] that pushes religion to the margins of public life in the name of neutrality and public reason, and in so doing demands that the religious individual "annihilate [] essential aspects of his very self."[95] Whether these forces are right about what the liberal consensus demands is less important than the fact that they believe it to be so. Whether their conception of the liberal consensus is right or wrong, what matters is that they are not simply content to live under its terms. They insist that it must be revisited and, if necessary, rejected.

RELIGION UNDER ATTACK FROM WITHIN LIBERALISM

Another attack on the liberal consensus comes from the other side of the liberal–religious divide. On this view, the problem with the liberal consensus is not that it is too intolerant of religion, but that it is too *tolerant*. Some secularists, not content with an uneasy détente in which religion is treated as one among many legitimate beliefs, argue that religion is not legitimate at all, and that the liberal consensus is wrong to accord it equal respect.

This is the province of the New Atheism. A rash of books and authors argue that religion is pernicious and harmful, a hangover from earlier and more superstitious times. It would do us all a favor if it shuffled off the stage. Although the New Atheists may describe themselves as operating squarely within the heart of the liberal consensus, their attack on religion makes them every bit as hostile to the liberal treaty as the religious fundamentalists. Indeed, in their belief that religion should be written off in favor of a robust view of secular truth, they *are* fundamentalists.

Sam Harris's best-selling book *The End of Faith* is a model of the secular attack on the liberal treaty. Harris begins by arguing that intolerance is a peculiarly religious flaw. Although "all faiths have been touched, here and there, by the spirit of ecumenicalism," the fundamental view of all religious faiths is that all other faiths are wrong.[96] "Intolerance is thus intrinsic to every creed. . . . Certainty about the next life is simply incompatible with tolerance in this one."[97]

94. Carter, *supra* note 66.
95. Michael Perry, *Morality, Politics, and Law: A Bicentennial Essay* 182 (1988).
96. Sam Harris, *The End of Faith: Religion, Terror, and the Future of Reason* 13 (2005).
97. *Id.*

This is, of course, simply wrong. As Harris quickly admits, some religious individuals "remain fully committed to tolerance and diversity."[98] (It should be noted that many religious traditions, including post-Vatican II Catholicism, believe in religious tolerance for *religious* reasons: they believe no one can come to the truth unless they do so freely and voluntarily. Harris refuses to accept this possibility, arguing instead that religious moderates merely plagiarized their moderation from the secularists.[99]) Even this admission is offered grudgingly. Those "religious moderates" who champion toleration, he suggests, are either mistaken about the implications of their religious views or fail to see that they have given cover to violent religious extremists. "The very ideal of religious tolerance" is thus "one of the principal forces driving us toward the abyss."[100]

Harris's prescription for what he sees as the inevitability of religious intolerance, combined with his view that religious belief itself is false and leads to calamities such as the events of 9/11, is—more intolerance. He does not demand the active suppression of religion or the extermination of its adherents. But he looks forward to a day "when faith, without evidence, disgraces anyone who would claim it."[101] He sees no reason to tolerate ideas that he believes are simply false and that only lead to violence and terror. Any principle of toleration that forms part of "the larger set of cultural and intellectual accommodations we have made to faith itself" ultimately comprises "the greatest problem confronting civilization."[102] So, just as the religious fundamentalists challenge a fundamental term of the liberal treaty from the side of religious belief, Harris and other New Atheists challenge it from the secular side. If society has agreed to set aside questions of fundamental truth, then so much the worse for society.

Like the religious fundamentalists, Harris also challenges the division of life into public and private spheres. He shares a common cause with his adversaries in believing that the distinction is false. "It is time we recognized," he writes, in language that could just as well have been written by a religious fundamentalist, "that belief is not a private matter; it has never been merely private."[103] By sheltering religious belief within the private sphere, we are simply providing a space in which the flames of religious extremism can be tended until they erupt in a conflagration that sweeps over us all. If "every belief is a fount of action *in potentia*," then the actions that ended in the destruction of the Twin Towers began with beliefs carefully nourished in private spaces.[104] Here, too, we see an outright rejection of the terms of the liberal treaty.

---

98. *Id.* at 14.
99. *See id.* at 18–19.
100. *Id.* at 15.
101. *Id.* at 48.
102. *Id.* at 45.
103. *Id.* at 44.
104. *Id.*

Richard Dawkins is perhaps the best-known of the New Atheists, and his book *The God Delusion* is one of the key texts of the movement. He is no wallflower. Like Harris, Dawkins condemns the "widespread assumption," shared by both religious and non-religious individuals, that all views on matters of fundamental truth, including religious views, are entitled to equal respect.[105] Toleration, he argues, has become lopsided: secular arguments may be made against secular beliefs, but religion is effectively immune from public criticism. (In its own way, this too is an example of the New Atheist challenge to the separation of the public and private spheres.)

Dawkins argues that society displays an "overweening respect for religion."[106] He does not question toleration absolutely—although one will search the index of his book in vain for the word—but he argues that society must get over its "unparalleled presumption of respect for religion."[107] Like Harris, he is not content to confine his sallies to religious extremism. He argues that religious moderation ultimately shares the same unprovable belief in the absolute that leads to religious absolutism. The "take-home message" of acts of extreme religiously motivated violence like terrorism, he argues, "is that we should blame religion itself, not religious *extremism*—as though that were some kind of terrible perversion of real, decent religion."[108] Dawkins is but a step away, albeit a large step, from Diderot's famous comment, in the period leading up to the French Revolution and its bloody aftermath, that men will never be free until the last king is strangled with the entrails of the last priest.

In short, the New Atheists "seek[ ] to resolve religious-secular tensions" within the liberal consensus by attempting to "convinc[e] believers to abandon faith."[109] They reject the liberal consensus because it gives far too much respect to a set of beliefs that are not only false, but that constitute a "moral and intellectual emergency" for society.[110] They do not believe that religion can simply be relegated to the private sphere, and they view "moderate" religious beliefs not just as delusional, but as lending aid and comfort to violent religious extremism. In the short run, they may agree that these beliefs should only be refuted, not suppressed. In the long run, they see religion's death as both necessary and inevitable. If, like most others in a world in which religious belief has proliferated rather than faded away, they do not think of the secularization thesis as a sure bet, they will do their best to improve the odds of its coming true. They are militant atheists, anti-believers rather than live-and-let-live nonbelievers; their

---

105. Richard Dawkins, *The God Delusion* 42 (paperback ed., 2008) (2006).

106. *Id.* at 43.

107. *Id.* at 50.

108. *Id.* at 345.

109. Alan E. Garfield, *Finding Shared Values in a Diverse Society: Lessons From the Intelligent Design Controversy*, 33 Vt. L. Rev. 225, 231 (2008).

110. Sam Harris, *Letters to a Christian Nation* xii (2006).

marching song just happens to be John Lennon's "Imagine," not "Onward Christian Soldiers." Like the utopians of the French Revolution, their battle cry is Voltaire's *ecrasez l'infame*—"crush the infamous" forces of religion.

Liberal democracy is no place for either militants or utopians. So it can be said that the New Atheists, whatever genuine fealty or lip service they pay to liberal values such as toleration and freedom of conscience, ultimately are as destabilizing to the liberal consensus as religious militants. They are as unsatisfied with the long-standing compromise between the secular and spiritual realms as their rivals. Although, for secular reasons, they believe that religious individuals must come to unbelief voluntarily, they do not doubt that the "end of faith" is the goal they seek. They reject the peace between contending sides of the debate over religious truth represented by such liberal values as toleration, except in a narrow legal sense, and the separation of life into public and private realms. Not all of them urge the state to take a side in this contest. Nevertheless, their stringent view of the limits on the state's support for religious belief places a thumb on the scales in favor of an actively secular state.

THE LIBERAL CONSENSUS ITSELF UNDER ATTACK

So far, we have seen the liberal consensus under attack from both sides of the secular–religious divide. Religious individuals believe that the liberal consensus does not give enough room to religious truth, and that a public square stripped of religion and forced to operate according to "public reason" leads not just to secular*ization*, but to a thorough-going ideology of secular*ism*. Conversely, the New Atheists believe that the liberal consensus gives "unearned respect"[111] to a set of false and pernicious opinions with no warrant for reasoned belief. They wonder why we should tolerate any set of religious beliefs, moderate as well as extremist, that can ultimately lead only to violence. They would erase the distinction between the public and private realms—not to allow religion more breathing room, but so they can get at it and throttle it.

Neither side, it must be said, necessarily wants to utterly destroy the liberal consensus. Religious opponents of liberalism are not necessarily enemies of voluntarism and freedom of conscience; the New Atheists, in turn, want to vanquish faith by winning an argument, not by putting it to the sword. But in refusing to simply live peaceably within the liberal consensus under conditions of compromise, both sides put the liberal consensus under serious pressure.

Both sides thus argue that liberalism leads to bad results—that it leads to too much secularism, or too much religion—without necessarily challenging the liberal consensus, although their attacks threaten to undo the consensus.

---

111. Dawkins, *supra* note 105, at 20.

But another set of arguments seeks to undermine it altogether. They are not combatants in the war between faith and liberalism itself. Instead, these insurgents want to attack the referee itself. They argue that the liberal treaty is and always has been nonsense. Liberalism, these writers argue, "rests on a bedrock of illiberalism,"[112] and the liberal consensus represents a "mission impossible."[113] We can get a good look at this argument for the impossibility of the liberal consensus by examining two of the most prominent proponents of this argument within the field of law and religion: Stanley Fish and Steven Smith.

Fish opens his argument in typical barnstorming fashion, asserting that "[a]ll of liberalism's efforts to accommodate or tame illiberal forces fail, either by underestimating and trivializing the illiberal impulse, or by mirroring it."[114] What Fish means can be seen by referring back to our discussion of the liberal consensus, which largely tracks Fish's own description. Liberalism, he says, was "born of the desire to escape the conflicts generated by religious disputes."[115] It does so by separating life into public and private spheres and attempting to maintain the public sphere in a state of neutrality as to particular conceptions of truth or the good life.[116] The problem is that some people, particularly some religious people, insist on views that defy this compromise. From within their worldview, there is no "neutral" position on truth and the nature of the good.

Liberalism's response to this, Fish writes, is ultimately to rig the game without admitting that it is rigged, by excluding views that cut against the liberal consensus while pretending to remain neutral. He writes:

> If you begin by acknowledging the inevitability of difference and the desirability of preventing the conflicts that will erupt if proponents of opposing religious and moral viewpoints are left to vie for control of the state and its coercing mechanisms, you have only three alternatives: (1) institute a regime of tolerance and face the difficulty of a system of government (hardly government at all) without the power to constrain and punish what it thinks wrong; (2) institute a regime of power and recommend it as an alternative to the chaos everyone fears; (3) institute a regime of power but don't identify it as such—instead, claim for it the status of an impersonal law tied to the interests of no one but capable of safeguarding the interests of everyone.[117]

---

112. Larry Alexander, *Illiberalism All the Way Down: Illiberal Groups and Two Conceptions of Liberalism*, 12 J. Contemp. Legal Issues 625, 625 (2002).

113. Stanley Fish, *Mission Impossible: Settling the Just Bounds Between Church and State*, 97 Colum. L. Rev. 2255 (1997).

114. Fish, *supra* note 28, at 162.

115. *Id.* at 177.

116. *See id.* at 177–78.

117. *Id.* at 185.

"Pretty much all liberals," Fish claims, "go for option three, with the result that almost every interesting question has been answered (or evaded) in advance and all that is left are in-house debates about just who or what to exclude and how best to package the exclusions so that they will appear to have been directed by universal principles."[118] At least as long as liberals want to argue that their regime really is what it purports to be—that it really *is* neutral toward questions of religious truth—this is what they *have* to do. In order to keep *almost* everyone on the reservation, liberalism will have to kick *some* people off. Because doing so is inimical to liberalism in theory, however, "those who institute such a regime will do everything they can to avoid confronting the violence that inaugurates it and will devise ways of disguising it, even from themselves."[119]

An example will help here. In a case well known to law and religion scholars, *Mozert v. Hawkins County Board of Education*,[120] the United States Court of Appeals for the Sixth Circuit confronted the case of some parents who objected to the use of a set of public school readers that was designed to teach critical reading and thinking. The problem, said the parents, was that the readers depicted activities and values that posed a threat to their children's Christian development and worldview. For example, one parent objected to a poem called "Look at Anything," because it suggested "that by using imagination a child can become part of anything and thus understand it better," an idea she believed amounted to the "occult practice" of "us[ing] imagination beyond the limitation of scriptural authority."[121] The plaintiffs also objected to the depiction of magic and other supernatural phenomena (phenomena which the books did not endorse). The broader problem with the readers, the parents complained, was that they "expose[d] their children to other forms of religion and to the feelings, attitudes and values of other students that contradict the plaintiffs' views without a statement that the other views [were] incorrect and that the plaintiffs' views [were] the correct ones."[122] In other words, "the plaintiffs objected to the very values—tolerance and evenhandedness—traditionally used to justify liberal education."[123] And, we might add, to justify liberalism itself.

In a fractured set of opinions, all three appellate judges rejected the plaintiffs' claims. If for no other reason than that the school system would be impossible to administer under the terms set by the plaintiffs—a reason that convinced at least one of the judges[124]—the court's decision was arguably reasonable. But it was *not* "neutral."

---

118. *Id.*
119. *Id.* at 167.
120. 827 F.2d 1058 (6th Cir. 1987).
121. *Id.* at 1062.
122. *Id.*
123. Stolzenberg, *supra* note 84, at 591.
124. *Mozert*, 827 F.2d at 1073 (Kennedy, C., concurring).

Both the school board and, ultimately, the court hastened to assure the parents that simply being exposed to different points of view was not the same thing as an endorsement of those points of view. But this response has two problems. First, it rests on a premise—that there is a distinction between being exposed to something and being indoctrinated into it—that the parents rejected. In their view, the very point that the court took as dispositive of the case—that the mind can and should "remain[ ] unaffected by the ideas and doctrines that pass before it, and its job is to weigh and assess those doctrines from a position distanced from and independent of any one of them"—was inimical to their own understanding of how the mind works.[125] Second, because there is ultimately no getting around this fundamental difference, the court does not—really, cannot—provide a public space in which the religious parents can function without what they perceive as an injury to their religious beliefs. So the court does what it must: It excludes. It tells them to either play by the rules or go elsewhere—to a private religious school, for instance. The court is sensitive to the plaintiffs' claims, but in the final analysis its answer to the parents can be summed up in Ring Lardner's immortal words: "'Shut up,' he explained."[126]

Mozert, Fish would say, is liberalism in a nutshell. Liberalism promises a public sphere that is scrupulously neutral as to conceptions of the good, but that conception is underwritten by a non-neutral understanding of the good. When individuals or groups challenge it, the referee tosses them out of the game, perhaps by calling their views "unreasonable," but without admitting that the referee is playing the game too.[127] To the extent that liberalism upholds a sphere of public reason that is accessible to all but rejects some positions as unreasonable, there is a failure to acknowledge one of its own fundamental and uncomfortable realities: "[W]hile adhering to 'common ground' is proclaimed as the way to side-step politics and avoid its endless conflicts, the specifying of common ground is itself a supremely political move."[128]

In short, Fish argues that liberalism has set itself an impossible task. Its neutrality is nothing of the sort, and it could not long survive if it were. The problem is not so much that liberalism chooses sides, but that it refuses to *admit* that it does. For Fish, liberalism cannot even be compared to a casino where the game is ostensibly fair but the odds ultimately favor the house. It's more like a game of three-card monte in Times Square, in which the dealer wins by pretending he's not playing while rigging the hell out of the game. Fish would rather be robbed by honest thieves.

---

125. Fish, *supra* note 28, at 197.

126. Ring Lardner, *The Young Immigrunts*, in *The Ring Lardner Reader* 411, 426 (Maxwell Geismar ed., 1963).

127. *See, e.g.*, Paul F. Campos, *Secular Fundamentalism*, 94 Colum. L. Rev. 1814 (1994).

128. Fish, *supra* note 28, at 170.

Fish's critique of liberalism goes to the heart of "the entire liberal project to which the distinction between church and state is basic."[129] The law professor Steven Smith has focused on critiquing liberalism specifically with respect to law and religion, but his critique and its implications are much the same. His sunny optimism about the future of liberalism and the values that undergird it can be seen in the titles of his books, which have cheery titles like *Foreordained Failure* and *The Disenchantment of Secular Discourse*. (Presumably he would have gone with *Abandon All Hope, Ye Who Enter Here*, if it had not already been snapped up by Dante.) But Smith makes a strong case that the liberal project, with respect to issues of law and religion and well beyond that, is in deep trouble.

Smith argues that "insofar as scholars seek to derive the Constitution's principle of religious freedom from political or legal theory, they are consigned to continuing frustration," because religious freedom, "like many other matters of both personal and political concern, . . . cannot plausibly be confined to or regulated by 'theory.'"[130] This is so, at least if we read "theory" as "liberal theory" popularly understood, because "any account of religious freedom will necessarily depend on—and hence will stand or fall along with—more basic background beliefs concerning matters of religion and theology, the proper role of government, and 'human nature.'"[131]

To take some examples from law and religion jurisprudence, whether we tolerate and protect different kinds of religious conduct—from seemingly innocuous behavior like wearing a yarmulke in the military[132] to what liberals view as easier cases for state interference, such as forbidding someone to sacrifice his child because God commands it—will depend on controversial value choices, such as the acceptability of child sacrifice or the importance of wearing or not wearing religious headgear while in uniform. It will also depend on the needs and values of the state with respect to such matters as military order, social stability, and the value of life itself. There is no neutral ground. "[A] theoretical account of religious freedom cannot be assessed in the abstract; it must be considered with the background beliefs that support it, and it will be convincing only insofar as those supporting beliefs are themselves convincing."[133]

Moreover, what constitutes a "convincing" belief depends on where one stands. If the liberal state is to preserve its own values, such as its belief that individual rights end where individual actions cause harm to others, it must choose among possible values and outcomes. But the "adopting or preferring of

---

129. *Id.* at 177.

130. Steven D. Smith, *Foreordained Failure: The Quest for a Constitutional Principle of Religious Freedom* 16 (1995).

131. *Id.* at 63.

132. *See Goldman v. Weinberger*, 475 U.S. 503 (1986).

133. Smith, *supra* note 130, at 67.

one religious or secular position over its competitors is precisely what modern theories of religious freedom"—and of liberalism more generally—"seek to avoid."[134] Or, as Smith writes, "To say that a theory of religious freedom requires the theorist to determine which of the conflicting religious or secular positions within a society is most plausible or attractive seems to defeat the purpose that prompted the theorist to seek a theory of religious freedom in the first place."[135] For liberals, that purpose is to be neutral, to avoid taking stands on matters of truth. Ultimately, that is just what the liberal position cannot avoid doing.[136]

In his book *Getting Over Equality*, Smith is even more adamant in his attack on the liberal consensus. [137] He identifies the principles of equality and autonomy as "the foundation of modern understandings . . . of religious freedom."[138] But neither of these values can do the work that liberal theory demands of them. Autonomy is underwritten by a belief in individual choice unchained from the commands of any "alien authorities," and thus in an important sense it excludes religion right from the start.[139] In any event, "autonomy" is too muddy a concept to offer any clear marching orders. Moreover, in the final analysis, the liberal consensus's view of what constitutes a proper or improper invocation of autonomy looks suspiciously like liberalism's preservation of its own values and preferences.[140] Similarly, equality is an "empty" concept: It tells us that we should treat like things alike, but it does not tell us how to figure out whether and in what respects things are relevantly alike or different. (To take a trivial example, are the shoes I am wearing right now "alike" in both being shoes, or footwear more generally, or are they "unalike" in being *left* and *right* shoes, or in the fact that one is a sandal while the other is an army boot? Nothing in the word equality answers the question.) Thus, "claims about equality are conclusions to be *argued for*, not premises to be *argued from*."[141] Like Fish, Smith complains that invoking the idea of equality will thus obscure the degree to which "equality is being used to smuggle in (or, more often, exclude) more substantive values or criteria

---

134. *Id.* at 68.

135. *Id.* at 71–72.

136. *See also* William E. Connolly, *Belief, Spirituality, and Time*, in *Varieties of Secularism in a Secular Age* 126, 140 (Michael Warner, Jonathan VanAntwerpen, and Craig Calhoun, eds., 2010) ("Commentators who purport to avoid [substantive] judgments indirectly express them anyway in the terms of art they use and the modes of description they offer, for ordinary language regularly folds moral appraisals into terms of description"); Michael J. Sandel, *Political Liberalism*, 107 Harv. L. Rev. 1765, 1777-78 (1994).

137. *See* Smith, *supra* note 19, at 4–6.

138. *Id.* at 7.

139. *Id.* at 29.

140. *See id.* at 42–43.

141. *Id.* at 13; *see* Peter Westen, *The Empty Idea of Equality*, 95 Harv. L. Rev. 537 (1982).

without any careful attempt to provide justification."[142] It is nothing more than a form of "cheating," or "deception, or self-deception."[143]

Smith therefore questions whether a "theory" of religious freedom is even possible.[144] And his criticisms are ultimately not just directed at law and religion alone. Rather, "one might argue that the discourse of religious freedom is itself merely an example in miniature of the modern discourse of 'liberal democracy,' which a critic might view as a massive project in question-begging based on the empty notions of equality or, sometimes, neutrality."[145]

Critics like Fish and Smith are hardly alone.[146] They represent not so much a friendly critique of liberalism from *within* liberalism—we might indeed describe such critics as liberals, although some of them would describe themselves instead as anti-liberals, communitarians, postmodernists, and so on—as a critique of the *possibility* of liberalism, one that proceeds by taking conventional liberalism's claims seriously and pushing them to their breaking point. They are, in a sense, liberal critiques of liberalism, because they argue in fairly straightforward liberal terms and take a relatively neutral view that Thomas Nagel calls the "view from nowhere."[147] But they press this methodology into the service of its own destruction, arguing that there *is* no "view from nowhere," and that liberalism's pretenses to the contrary are a charade. In fact, liberalism has strong substantive values that are not neutral at all. In pretending to mediate between different views without having one of its own, liberalism is the ultimate act of bad faith. What it actually does is take sides, excluding those who disagree with it by treating them as "unreasonable" or summarily suppressing them, while pretending that it is above the fray and not in it.[148]

---

142. Smith, *supra* note 19, at 14.

143. *Id.*

144. *Id.* at 45.

145. *Id.* at 19.

146. For strong similar arguments, see Larry Alexander, *Liberalism, Religion, and the Unity of Epistemology*, 30 San Diego L. Rev. 763 (1993).

147. Thomas Nagel, *The View From Nowhere* (1986).

148. It bears emphasis that not all forms of liberalism operate this way. Some forms of liberalism purport to be neutral on fundamental questions, but others openly adopt a "comprehensive" set of beliefs. The basic distinction is set forth most prominently in Rawls, *supra* note 43, at xxv-xxviii. *See also, e.g.*, Bruce M. Landesman, *The Responsibilities of the Liberal State: Comprehensive vs. Political Liberalism*, 2010 Utah L. Rev. 171; Ronald C. Den Otter, *Can a Liberal Take His Own Side in an Argument?: The Case for John Rawls's Idea of Political Liberalism*, 49 St. Louis U. L.J. 319 (2005); Douglas G. Smith, *The Illiberalism of Liberalism: Religious Discourse in the Public Square*, 34 San Diego L. Rev. 1571 (1997); Stephen Gardbaum, *Liberalism, Autonomy, and Moral Conflict*, 48 Stan. L. Rev. 385 (1996); Miriam Galston, *Rawlsian Dualism and the Autonomy of Political Thought*, 94 Colum. L. Rev. 1842 (1994). As I said at the outset of this chapter, however, my concern here is with liberalism popularly and crudely understood as a public philosophy—a "treaty" of sorts. The criticism offered in the text seems to fairly apply to this brand of liberalism. I deal

The point is not necessarily that liberalism is a lie, although some critics might say exactly that. Surely many liberals have recognized the contradictions that Fish, Smith, and others point out. Indeed, it might be said that the project of more sophisticated forms of modern liberal political philosophy, at least since Rawls, has been to frame a response to these problems—to achieve liberalism without embarrassment. We will turn to the question whether they have succeeded in Chapter Eight. For now, however, our concern is less with developments in the understanding of liberalism in rarefied academic circles, but with the liberal consensus or treaty as it is popularly understood. And there, the problems are evident. For, notwithstanding what may be going on in liberal philosophy in the refined precincts of the university, on the ground liberalism does indeed purport to remain neutral with respect to questions of the good and ultimate truth. Its critics say this is impossible. Not only is liberal neutrality itself false or unattainable, but *all* the terms of the liberal treaty—autonomy, individualism, public reason, the division between the public and private spheres, and so on—are ultimately substantive and controversial values, in a way that undermines the ambitions of the liberal project itself.

CONCLUSION: LIBERALISM TODAY

In this chapter, we have examined the development and entrenchment of a liberal consensus—a "treaty"—that promised to keep the peace between eternally warring views on fundamental values, and still hopes to do so. It does so by offering a stance of neutrality, equality, and democracy, with individual rights serving as a backstop. Fundamental views of religious truth and the nature of the good are shunted off to the private sphere, and public reason serves as the *lingua franca* in which the liberal conversation between the contending sides is supposed to proceed. This, in a nutshell, has been the compromise under which liberal democratic society has proceeded for the last couple of centuries.

The problem is that the treaty is now under serious attack from all sides. Under these conditions, to offer the obligatory quote from Yeats, "the center cannot hold." Religion no longer accepts its own marginalization. It no longer accepts its relegation to the private sphere, or the idea that its adherents must equip themselves with a "public reason" phrasebook in order to participate in public discussion. It is reclaiming its right to be a comprehensive worldview with comprehensive reach.

On the other side, the New Atheists and other stringent nonbelievers are no longer content to simply coexist with a congeries of views and values they believe

---

with more philosophically sophisticated forms of liberalism in (slightly) greater detail in Chapter Eight.

are both false and dangerous. They are not ready (and, to be fair, not willing) to break out the stakes and kindling, but neither are they satisfied to live and let live or to treat religious views with what they believe is an unearned respect. They, too, question the division of life into public and private spheres. They would let religion out of its pen in the private sphere—not to liberate it, but so they can flush it out and hunt it down.

Finally, rather than attacking each other and hitting the referee in the process, other critics are aiming directly *at* the referee. Their problem is not that liberalism is unfairly tilted in favor of secularism or religion, which suggests the possibility of reform, but that liberalism itself is either impossible or fraudulent—or both. They believe neutrality and other liberal values cannot succeed as treaty terms not because they have been misused, but because the terms themselves were always meaningless. There is nothing but the play of politics, and liberalism is just one more competitor on an already crowded field.

As Smith points out, it is true that "life has to go on."[149] Unless we want to return to an earlier age of bloodshed, we are unlikely to abandon some form of the liberal consensus altogether. Liberals, religionists, and anti-liberals alike will continue to invoke and practice some form of liberalism, in practice if not always in theory.

But that is not saying very much. Life will go on, yes, but under increasing conditions of uncertainty and change. That is the state the liberal consensus finds itself in today. It is a working compromise, not a theory—and a fragile one at that. This is not new: the liberal consensus has always been in a process of flux, and has never been as fixed or stable as theoretical discussions may make it appear to be. But two hundred years of *relative* stability is no small thing. That era may now be coming to an end.

One reason the liberal consensus may be coming to an end, or at least may be reaching a critical stage of insecurity, has been implicit in this discussion, even though we have not yet directly addressed it. It has to do with the key move in the liberal consensus: its effort to bracket larger questions of *truth*, to remain scrupulously neutral on fundamental questions such as whether God exists and what the good life consists of. That same move is equally essential to most modern attempts to achieve a theory of religious freedom. Whether that effort has enjoyed any greater success, or whether it is equally doomed to fail, is the question we turn to next.

---

149. Smith, *supra* note 19, at 4.

2. PILATE'S SHRUG: THE SAD SAGA OF MODERN LAW AND RELIGION THEORY

The last chapter argued that liberalism is under attack from outside and inside its own borders. It is time to focus more narrowly on theories of law and religion. Our focus here will be on the Religion Clauses of the First Amendment, and their interpretation within the American legal academy.

The discussion currently taking place in this field has been especially lively and energetic. The question, however, is whether that energy is moving us forward, or whether the debate over law and religion exhibits the pointless excitability of a dog chasing its own tail. Are we making progress, or just moving in circles, to the point of exhaustion? Steven Smith, whose skepticism about liberalism's answers to the dilemmas of law and religion we saw in the last chapter, has argued that law and religion, and indeed the whole "Western tradition of carefully reasoned discourse about the relations between religion and government," may be entering a twilight period, one characterized by a sense of "decadence or exhaustion," an "inner decay that infects modern theorizing about religious freedom."[1] It may be that the energy level of current writing about law and religion exists not despite, but because of, the sense of enervation, of reaching an end to the conversation, that Smith describes. Not everyone in the field would agree with Smith's prognosis, and even those who do may quarrel about the reason for this sense of exhaustion. So the question before us is largely one of diagnosis. *Is* the patient sick or dying? Why? And what, if anything, can or should be done?

In this chapter, we shall examine some of the leading theories of religious freedom in contemporary American legal scholarship. What I suggest in these pages is that the fundamental problem that ails us is not just a problem with modern theories of religious freedom. It is symptomatic of the larger fragility of the liberal consensus, and it is rooted in the same fundamental problem.

Theorists of religious freedom differ in the concepts and principles they bring to bear on religious freedom issues, and the results they recommend. But what ties most of them together is their studious reluctance to place the truth at the center of their theories.[2] Like liberalism itself, these theorists understandably

---

1. Steven D. Smith, *Discourse in the Dusk: The Twilight of Religious Freedom?*, 122 Harv. L. Rev. 1869, 1906–1907 (2009).

2. As always, there are exceptions, which we will examine below, but this is an accurate description of the general tendency of law and religion scholarship. Even those theorists who do confront the question of religious truth do not necessarily do so in the sense I recommend in this book.

seek an answer to the endlessly perplexing debates over religious freedom that will enable us to coexist in a pluralistic society, one in which religious believers of all kinds live cheek by jowl with equally committed nonbelievers. This leads them to search for process-oriented values that do not require them to take a stand on fundamental questions of religious truth.

This is understandable. But it is also fatal. The refusal to fully confront these questions is exactly what makes each of these theories of religious freedom ultimately unsatisfying and unsuccessful. This will become evident over the course of this chapter, as we examine some of the central modern theories of religious freedom—theories centered around now-familiar terms like "neutrality," "equality," and "liberty"—and find that each of them ultimately falls short on the theoretical level, the practical level, or both.

My aim is not just to repeat the standard attacks on these theories. I do not want simply to show that these theories ultimately fail, which is no great surprise given the ever-present gap between theory and practice. Instead, I want to show that these theories fail for a particular *reason*, and that this reason has everything to do with religious truth. For the most part, the major theories we examine below attempt, in keeping with the rules of the liberal consensus, to avoid answering—or even asking—questions of religious truth. As I observed at the outset of this book, they treat Pontius Pilate's shrug and his rhetorical question, "What is truth?," as a model, a necessary element of any acceptable theory of religious freedom in a liberal democracy. No matter how understandable this strategy may be, however, religious truth remains the skull at the liberal banquet, reminding them of the futility of their efforts to run from it. Because it cannot be avoided, it must be confronted.

I should say at the outset that there is nothing set in stone about the particular categorization of theories I have used in this chapter. Theories that focus primarily on, say, neutrality, do not necessarily utterly neglect equality, and vice versa. If anything, many of these theorists are eager to persuade their readers that the particular value they focus on also happens to be the best means of serving other values. For example, a theorist who argues for an equality-centered understanding of religious freedom may argue that this is the best means of ensuring that the values of neutrality or liberty are also honored. Whether these arguments succeed is another question.

Finally, although most prominent theories of religious freedom adopt the fatal strategy of avoiding questions of religious truth, not everyone who has entered this arena does. Some writers instead refuse to adopt any theory at all, acknowledging the hopelessly complex and multifactored nature of religious freedom. These writers have been called the anti-theorists of religious freedom.[3] Although they disclaim any theory of religious freedom, these writers believe,

---

3. Thomas C. Berg, *Religion Clause Anti-Theories*, 72 Notre Dame L. Rev. 693, 694 (1997).

with varying degrees of optimism, that we can nevertheless continue to protect religious freedom on a prudential, case-by-case basis. Although I am somewhat in sympathy with them, I will argue that the anti-theorists, to the extent that they truly run from theory, are left with nothing; and to the extent that they supply *something*, they must be relying on a theory.

Still other writers have simply chosen to forego the terms of the liberal consensus and rely on specifically and openly religious arguments for religious freedom. These writers, admirably, are willing to confront, and *admit* that they are confronting, questions of religious truth. But that does not mean they have provided the right answer to the dilemma of religious freedom, one that will succeed in our own agnostic age.

NEUTRALITY-ORIENTED THEORIES

"Perhaps the most pervasive theme in modern judicial and academic discourse on the subject of religious freedom is 'neutrality.'"[4] Although it has been around for at least as long as the modern jurisprudence on law and religion,[5] in recent years it has become even more central to Religion Clause doctrine. In interpreting the Free Exercise Clause, the Supreme Court has made neutrality the primary measure of religious rights.[6] Similarly, under the Establishment Clause, a raft of recent cases have made it clear that the central question for church–state separation issues is whether the law in question is neutral between religious and other beliefs and institutions.[7] If it is, there is no Establishment Clause violation, even if the effect of the law is to grant to religion the kinds of financial benefits Madison railed against in his *Memorial and Remonstrance* .[8]

Neutrality has become the Supreme Court's tool *du jour*, and a leading concern of law and religion scholars, despite—or perhaps because of—the fact that neutrality remains a protean term, a "coat of many colors," in the words of Justice

---

4. Steven D. Smith, *Foreordained Failure: The Quest for a Constitutional Principle of Religious Freedom* 77 (1995).

5. *See, e.g., Everson v. Bd. of Educ.*, 330 U.S. 1, 15 (1947) ("Neither [a state nor the federal government] can pass laws which aid one religion, aid all religions, or prefer one religion over another").

6. *See, e.g., Employment Division v. Smith*, 494 U.S. 872, 881 (1990).

7. *Cf.* Dhanajai Shivakumar, *Neutrality and the Religion Clauses*, 33 Harv. C.R.-C.L. L. Rev. 505, 505 (1998) ("The language of the Supreme Court's most recent opinions indicates that neutrality has replaced the separation of church and state as the guiding metaphor for American secularism.").

8. *See, e.g., Zelman v. Simmons-Harris*, 536 U.S. 369 (2002); *Good News Club v. Milford Central School*, 533 U.S. 98 (2001); *see generally* Frank S. Ravitch, *A Funny Thing Happened on the Way to Neutrality: Broad Principles, Formalism, and the Establishment Clause*, 38 Ga. L. Rev. 489 (2004).

John Marshall Harlan.[9] Its application is uncertain largely because, in law and religion as in the broader world of liberalism, the very meaning of the word "neutrality" is fluid and unclear.[10] That discussions about neutrality and religious liberty inevitably devolve into arguments about what neutrality *means* suggests something of the frailty of this value as a solution to church–state problems. We can see this more clearly by examining some of the leading neutrality-centered theories of religious liberty.

Formal Neutrality

One version of neutrality theory takes neutrality in its most formal sense, and has therefore been labeled formal neutrality.[11] In legal scholarship on law and religion, it is closely associated with the work of the late Philip Kurland, who wrote that the Religion Clauses should be interpreted to "prohibit classification in terms of religion either to confer a benefit or to impose a burden."[12] Although it has relatively few modern advocates—outside, perhaps, of Justice Scalia, whose name admittedly is rarely invoked in the same sentence as the word "modern"— it has been championed by a few legal scholars, including Mark Tushnet[13] and, perhaps most vociferously, Marci Hamilton.[14]

Formal neutrality's main attraction is its seeming simplicity, elegance, and fairness. It requires that religion be treated no better or worse than anyone or anything else. Government simply cannot treat religion as a relevant factor, whether in singling out religion for particular benefits or in imposing special burdens on it. The principle of formal neutrality thus seeks to wipe out any conflicts between the two Religion Clauses—free exercise and non-establishment—and instead reads them together as offering the First (and Only) Commandment: thou shall not treat religion as a special category for purposes of the law. Thus, Hamilton reads the Religion Clauses as issuing two complementary instructions. Religious entities, like any other entity, "can be forestalled and prohibited from harming others and thus can be made to obey a myriad of laws," but they must not be "subjected to laws that are hostile or motivated by animus toward religion in general or any sect in particular." Nor can they be made the special favorite of the law.[15]

---

9. *Bd. of Educ. v. Allen*, 392 U.S. 236, 249 (1968) (Harlan, J., concurring).

10. *See, e.g.*, Andrew Koppelman, *The Fluidity of Neutrality*, 66 Rev. Pol. 633 (2004).

11. *See, e.g.*, Douglas Laycock, *Formal, Substantive, and Disaggregated Neutrality Toward Religion*, 39 DePaul L. Rev. 993, 999–1001 (1990).

12. Philip Kurland, *Of Church and State and the Supreme Court*, 29 U. Chi. L. Rev. 1, 96 (1961).

13. *See* Mark Tushnet, *Of Church and State and the Supreme Court: Kurland Revisited*, 1989 Sup. Ct. Rev. 373.

14. *See* Marci A. Hamilton, *God vs. the Gavel: Religion and the Rule of Law* (2005).

15. *Id.* at 210–11.

Formal neutrality would not require, and in some versions would positively forbid legislatures to provide, special exemptions from generally applicable laws that happen to incidentally burden religious belief and practice. It would also prohibit government from giving religion privileges under the law that are not enjoyed by others. It balances this out by prohibiting government from subjecting religion to special disabilities on account of hostility toward religion in general or particular religious beliefs.

This approach seems superficially attractive. Lawyers like rules that are—or seem—fair and easy to apply. And yet, formal neutrality has few defenders. One reason for this is that, despite its claims to fairness, formal neutrality almost immediately runs into serious difficulties at the level of results. A classic example is the use of sacramental wine during the Catholic Mass, or the consumption of wine during the Jewish Passover seder. The National Prohibition Act, which outlawed the consumption of alcohol, carved out an exemption for the use of sacramental wine. A formal neutrality approach would conclude that because the Prohibition law treated everyone alike in a formal sense, no such exemption was required. A stringent view of formal equality would even forbid the legislature from creating such an exemption. This alone would be enough to rule out formal neutrality for many: A law that "barred the sacred rites of Catholics and Jews . . . could not be reconciled with any concept of religious liberty worthy of the name."[16] Conversely, and in a way that in fact predicts the course that an increasingly neutrality-oriented Court has taken with respect to the controversial issue of school vouchers,[17] formal neutrality might require the government to "give unlimited amounts of aid to religious schools," in seeming violation of the Establishment Clause, provided that such aid was also given to secular schools.[18] Not everyone would agree on which of these implications are outrageous, but most people would conclude that at least one of them is. Hence, Douglas Laycock writes, formal neutrality "has something to offend everybody."[19]

That a theory is likely to displease everyone is a pretty good indication that it is a non-starter in the real world. But the fact that everyone agrees that a particular theory is untenable in practice doesn't make it a bad *theory*. Perhaps our practice is at fault, not our theory. After all, past generations would have greeted the thought that the law should treat all races as formally equal under the law with the same incredulity. So what renders formal neutrality troublesome as a *theory*?

The simple answer is that it is not a theory—or, at least, not a self-sufficient one. Imagine that a legislature declares that everyone, without exception, should be subject to anti-discrimination laws that forbid any employer from treating

---

16. Laycock, supra note 11, at 1000.
17. *See, e.g., Zelman v. Simmons-Harris*, 536 U.S. 639 (2002).
18. Laycock, *supra* note 11, at 1001.
19. *Id.*

people differently on the basis of sex. On its terms, this law would require the Roman Catholic Church to start stocking its priesthood with women. (Of course, some would like to see this happen.[20]) Although many would object to this result, we cannot say that it would not be formally neutral. Right?

Well, that depends. Some would argue for exactly this outcome. Others would argue that neutrality, even formal neutrality, requires us to treat the Church's belief that women are not eligible for the priesthood as a relevant distinction between that entity and other entities, which at least in theory maintain no such belief. Or suppose that a legislature enacted a law that provided that everyone shall work on Sunday. Again, this law is formally neutral, but many would respond that nothing prevents us from recognizing, for purposes of judging such a law's neutrality, that many people consider themselves religiously forbidden to work on Sundays.

How do we resolve these issues? By arguing about the *baseline* from which we measure neutrality. If we chose, we could put that discussion in terms of neutrality, and argue about what the term requires. But what we would really be doing is arguing about something *outside* of neutrality. We would be arguing over the background assumptions about what constitutes fair, equal, or neutral treatment. We would be arguing a substantive and not a formal question. And there is the rub. Formal neutrality is ultimately parasitic on substantive arguments. It does not rest on its own bottom.

We could try to argue that neutrality is sufficient if it is based on a non-controversial principle. Hamilton, for instance, insists that the baseline for legislation should be whether "the public good has been properly served."[21] So, for example, a law that prohibits children from carrying dangerous weapons into the schools would presumably serve the public good, and thus satisfy Hamilton's test, even if it would prevent a Sikh child from carrying a *kirpan*, the ceremonial knife that Sikh males are required to carry.[22]

But, of course, there is nothing uncontroversial, let alone neutral, about a capacious term like "the public good."[23] What constitutes the public good is a *substantive* question. It rests on controversial assertions about the nature of the good—precisely the sorts of assertions that liberalism is supposed to avoid. Even the attempt to short-circuit the debate by arguing that only secular and not religious reasons can form part of our discussion of the "public good" is a substantive move. Formal neutrality, in short, is an empty theory.

---

20. *See, e.g.,* Mary E. Becker, *The Politics of Women's Wrongs and the Bill of "Rights": A Bicentennial Perspective,* 59 U. Chi. L. Rev. 453 (1992).

21. Hamilton, *supra* note 14, at 279.

22. *See id.* at 114–18.

23. *See generally* Marc O. DeGirolami, *Recoiling From Religion,* 43 San Diego L. Rev. 619 (2006).

Substantive Neutrality

Some writers—most prominently Douglas Laycock—have argued that where formal neutrality fails, a more "substantive" form of neutrality, one that looks past the mere use of formal categories in the law, may succeed in offering a more attractive theory of religious freedom.[24] Laycock defines substantive neutrality as requiring that the state "minimize the extent to which it either encourages or discourages religious belief or disbelief, practice or nonpractice, observance or nonobservance," so that religion is as much a matter of "private choice as anything can be."[25] Substantive neutrality "insists on minimizing government influence on religion. Minimizing government influence leaves religion maximally subject to private choice, thus maximizing religious liberty."[26]

How does substantive neutrality work in practice? Take our example of the question whether a law prohibiting the consumption of alcohol constitutionally permits or requires an exemption for people who use alcohol in religious ceremonies such as the Catholic Mass or the Passover seder. A proponent of formal neutrality would argue that it does not. She might believe that the legislature *could* create such an exemption if suitably neutral grounds could be found for doing so, or she might believe that the Establishment Clause, as seen through the lens of formal neutrality, positively forbids such an exemption. But she would not find the underlying law itself to be a violation of religious liberty, properly understood.

In contrast, a regime of substantive neutrality would positively permit or even require an exemption. Banning a significant religious practice in the name of formal neutrality would, in substance, create a major disincentive to the decision whether or not to practice that faith. On the other hand, creating such an exemption would provide a minimal incentive to join that faith. It takes a pretty dedicated churchgoer to get drunk on communion wine. Better, then, to enact an exemption, or require one as a matter of constitutional law, which would leave individuals free to decide for themselves what religious path to tread.[27]

Looking at the Establishment Clause from the perspective of substantive neutrality, we would take the same approach, asking whether a law that implicates the Establishment Clause creates undue incentives or disincentives to practice or refrain from practicing a particular religion. Thus, school prayer is not substantively neutral because it involves government taking positions on religion that

---

24. *See* Laycock, *supra* note 11; Douglas Laycock, *Substantive Neutrality Revisited*, 110 W. Va. L. Rev. 51 (2007). Michael McConnell, formerly a judge on the United States Court of Appeals for the Tenth Circuit, is also one of the major advocates of a theory of substantive neutrality. *See, e.g.*, Michael W. McConnell, *Religious Freedom at a Crossroads*, 59 U. Chi. L. Rev. 115 (1992).

25. Laycock, *supra* note 11, at 1002.

26. Laycock, *supra* note 24, at 65.

27. *See, e.g., id.* at 55.

will influence religious belief and practice; conversely, equal funding for religious and secular schools, as in the voucher cases, *is* substantively neutral, because "it creates no incentives to choose religious or secular education," and thus "protects individual choice" for each family.[28]

For many, substantive neutrality offers a far more attractive theory of religious freedom, both at the abstract level and in practice, than formal neutrality. Because it does not simply assume that the law on the books is the whole story, and instead looks behind formal categories to ask whether religious beliefs are being served or disserved by facially neutral laws, it can honor private religious choice in a more meaningful way. It does a better job of ensuring that the choices people make on matters of fundamental religious truth are their own, unaffected by government pressure one way or the other. Substantive neutrality has many champions in the legal academy; on the Supreme Court, Justice David Souter was one of its most vocal advocates.[29] In many respects, I find it an attractive approach myself.

But the question remains whether substantive neutrality is a coherent *theory* of religious freedom, or whether it is "not neutrality at all," but just "mere verbal wordplay."[30] The problem, again, is one of baselines. What constitutes a "neutral" position from which to evaluate "substantive neutrality?"

Laycock has an answer to this question. He "recognizes that substantive neutrality must be substantively neutral about *something*, and that something is individual autonomy, choice, voluntarism, the separation of church and state, or what he simply describes as liberty."[31] Those are excellent choices for a baseline. Certainly liberals should welcome them, for they are familiar terms of the liberal treaty. But they are still *choices*, and any religious individual who does not understand his or her religious tradition in terms of "choice," or "voluntarism," or "separation" of church and state, will immediately recognize them as such. This is where questions of religious truth come in. Although a writer coming from Laycock's perspective might well view religion as a question of choice—might, indeed, say that everyone has the freedom to "choose" what is true, religiously speaking—from other perspectives it is not clear that anyone has any "choice" as to what is true, or that, if some religious belief *is* true, anyone ought to be free to reject it. Thinking of questions of religious truth as a matter of personal and private choice, the kind of choice that government ought not be involved in, is itself a substantive move. As Steven Smith observes, "Laycock's version of

---

28. *Id.* at 71.

29. *See, e.g., Church of the Lukumi Babalu Aye, Inc. v. City of Hialeah*, 508 U.S. 520, 561–62 (1993) (Souter, J., concurring); *Lee v. Weisman*, 505 U.S. 577, 627 (1992) (Souter, J., concurring).

30. Laycock, *supra* note 24, at 55.

31. Marc O. DeGirolami, *Tragic Historicism*, draft of Sept. 30, 2009, at 115 (quotations and citations omitted).

'neutrality' may be attractive, but it clearly is not 'neutral' with respect to potential background beliefs that might inform one's views about religious freedom."[32]

In fairness, Professor Laycock recognizes this, and is clear that particular value judgments inform his version of substantive neutrality.[33] I happen to be sympathetic to those value judgments, for the most part. But seeing them as such means we can, perhaps, call this a substantive theory, but not a theory of neutrality. It suggests that any theory of religious liberty that attempts to remain neutral on questions of religious truth will either fail on its own terms, or be forced to unmask itself and admit that it *is* making a judgment on those questions.

EQUALITY-ORIENTED THEORIES

Another theory of religious freedom emphasizes a similar but distinct value. Instead of taking neutrality as the benchmark by which questions of religious freedom are to be judged, it focuses on equality as the central value of religious freedom. The two are remarkably similar values, and often will come out the same in practice. But while neutrality focuses on the importance of governmental non-interference with private religious choices as such, equality focuses on government's obligation not to treat individuals and groups differently on the basis of their religious beliefs and practices. To be sure, that will often mean giving equal regard to religious choices. In that sense, neutrality and equality will tend to overlap. But the focus is different. It is a matter of non-discrimination rather than a matter of private choice as such.[34]

Like neutrality, equality has taken center stage for many theorists of religious freedom, and is prominent in the modern church–state jurisprudence of the Supreme Court. One area in which this focus on neutrality is especially apparent is the Establishment Clause. An example of this is the Court's recent decision upholding the use of educational vouchers for private schools, religious or secular.[35] From both the equality oriented perspective and the neutrality oriented perspective, these decisions were uncontroversial. Of *course* religious schools should be treated no better and no worse than secular schools. But to read Justice Souter's impassioned dissents in this and related cases, which argue that the decisions of the Court "break[ ] fundamentally with Establishment Clause principle,"[36] and to compare these decisions with prior decisions by the Court on

---

32. Smith, *supra* note 4, at 81; *see also* Ravitch, *supra* note 8, at 505 ("Professor Laycock's substantive neutrality . . . approach has a lot of substantive value, but no neutrality.").

33. *See, e.g.,* Laycock, *supra* note 11, at 994, 996, 1004–05.

34. *See, e.g.,* Nelson Tebbe, *Free Exercise and the Problem of Symmetry*, 56 Hastings L.J. 699, 711–12 (2005).

35. *See Zelman v. Simmons-Harris*, 536 U.S. 639 (2002).

36. *Mitchell v. Helms*, 530 U.S. 793, 869 (2000) (Souter, J., dissenting).

Establishment Clause issues, gives one a sense of just how much the Court's approach has changed in recent years under the influence of the equality principle.

Although there are several distinguished advocates of an equality-oriented theory of religious liberty, the most prominent are Christopher Eisgruber and Lawrence Sager.[37] In their book *Religious Freedom and the Constitution*, Eisgruber and Sager argue for a theory of the Religion Clauses that they label Equal Liberty. Equal Liberty consists of two principles. First, an equality principle: No one should be "devalued on account of the spiritual foundations of their important commitments and projects."[38] This in turn entails that apart from being protected from discrimination, religion should not be treated "as deserving special benefits or as subject to special disabilities."[39] Second, a liberty principle: In general, constitutional liberties, including "rights of free speech, personal autonomy, associative freedom, and personal property," should be vigorously protected, an approach which will "allow religious practice to flourish" but does not do so for religion's sake.[40]

What these rules make clear is that one of the primary goals of Eisgruber and Sager's work is to deny religion any special or distinctive place in the constitutional firmament. They write that the "dominant way of thinking about religious freedom in the United States," "remarkably," "insists *both* that the Constitution should confer special benefits like regulatory immunity on religious practice *and* that the Constitution should impose special disabilities on that practice."[41] This position is ill-conceived, in their view, because it treats religion as having "distinctive virtues that entitle it to special constitutional status."[42] They will have none of this.

Instead, Equal Liberty "denies that religion is a constitutional anomaly, a category of human experience that demands special benefits and/or necessitates special restrictions." "Aside from our deep concern with equality," they write, "we have no reason to confer special constitutional privileges or to impose special constitutional disabilities upon religion."[43] Theirs is a resolutely egalitarian theory of religious liberty. Indeed, in many respects it's *not* a theory of *religious* liberty as such, but a theory of egalitarianism, of which religious liberty is just

---

37. *See* Christopher L. Eisgruber & Lawrence G. Sager, *Religious Freedom and the Constitution* (2007). In giving pride of place to Eisgruber and Sager, I do not mean to neglect other important recent equality-oriented approaches to religious freedom, such as that of Martha Nussbaum. *See* Martha C. Nussbaum, *Liberty of Conscience: In Defense of America's Tradition of Religious Equality* (2008).

38. Eisgruber & Sager, *supra* note 37, at 5.

39. *Id.* at 52.

40. *Id.* at 52–53; *see also id.* at 4.

41. *Id.* at 5.

42. *Id.*

43. *Id.* at 6.

a by-product. It seeks to "focus[ ] attention on equality and remov[e] it from imponderable questions about the goodness of religion."[44] In its single-minded focus on egalitarianism, to the point of denying religion any distinctive role in the Constitution, *Religious Liberty and the Constitution* is a little like a guide on how to grill meat, written by friendly but quizzical vegetarians.

This is not to say that Equal Liberty, or other egalitarian accounts of religious liberty, cannot be vigorously protective of religious freedom. "To deny that religious projects are entitled to a unique constitutional immunity from otherwise valid laws," Eisgruber and Sager write, "is not to deny that such endeavors are entitled to robust constitutional protection."[45] It is fair to say they make good on this promise. Even its critics acknowledge that the scope of protection provided to religion by the theory of Equal Liberty is "robust indeed."[46] This protection is achieved largely by Eisgruber and Sager's strong reading of what equal treatment for religion demands. They write that "minority religious practices, needs, and interests must be as well and as favorably accommodated by government as are more familiar and mainstream interests."[47] In theory, the word "minority" in that sentence is the giveaway that their concern is with equality, not with religion as such. But in practice, given the wide range of accommodations made by legislatures for a host of non-religious interests, it means that religion will usually be protected. For example, Eisgruber and Sager argue that a Muslim police officer who is religiously obliged to wear a beard should be exempted from a police department policy that requires its officers to be clean-shaven, if that policy also creates secularly based exemptions, such as exemptions for officers whose medical conditions make it painful to shave.[48]

They would apply this rule "even in the absence of ready-made comparisons" like the one in the case of the beard regulation.[49] Thus, in *Lyng v. Northwestern Indian Cemetery Protective Association*,[50] the Supreme Court upheld the decision of the United States Forest Service to build a road through federal lands in a way that threatened to desecrate the holy site of a Native American religion. It held, in a formal neutrality-oriented way, that any burden imposed on the religion was incidental to a decision made on secular grounds—specifically, the necessity of building federal roads. Eisgruber and Sager suggest that if one asks the "implicit counterfactual question lurking in the background" of the case—namely, whether

---

44. *Id.* at 20.

45. *Id.* at 13.

46. Ira C. Lupu & Robert W. Tuttle, *The Limits of Equal Liberty as a Theory of Religious Freedom*, 85 Tex. L. Rev. 1247, 1249 (2007).

47. Eisgruber & Sager, *supra* note 37, at 13.

48. *Id.* at 90–91; *see Fraternal Order of Police Newark Lodge No. 12 v. City of Newark*, 170 F.3d 359 (3d Cir. 1999).

49. *Id.* at 91.

50. 485 U.S. 439 (1988).

the government would have acted the same way if it would have had a similar effect on a popular and well-organized group, religious or secular—then Equal Liberty insists on the wrongness of the government's action in that case.[51] Equal Liberty can, in short, be a strong tool for protecting religious freedom, even if its concern is for equality rather than for religion itself.

Equal Liberty should be attractive to many modern liberals. In many respects, it *is* modern liberalism, stripped of its religious roots. It "seems to carry stronger resonances of the political philosophy of John Rawls than of traditional concerns about the free exercise or nonestablishment of religion."[52] Whereas liberalism arose in large part to address the distinctive question of religion, this is a decidedly up-to-date version, one that is so reluctant to privilege particular notions of the good or of religious truth that it denies "the constitutional distinctiveness of religious commitments and religious institutions" altogether.[53] The Rawlsian liberal nature of Equal Liberty is apparent in its authors' view that "it is a sign of America's progress in the domain of religious freedom that most Americans prefer to defend their views on grounds that assume or are at least consistent with the equal status of all believers and nonbelievers, rather than on the ground that some subset of believers should enjoy a preferred constitutional status."[54]

Of course, not everyone agrees with this version of liberalism, as we saw in the previous chapter. So, from the outset, Equal Liberty is making particular substantive choices about what counts, about what should be the lodestar of liberal theory in general and religious liberty in particular. We *could* accept Eisgruber and Sager's own selection of equality as the central liberal value. But this raises serious questions about whether Equal Liberty rests on solid ground as a theory of religious liberty.

For one thing, there is the question whether equality, like neutrality, is ultimately "substantively empty, incapable of generating answers to particular controversies."[55] Does equality, that is, do any serious work in the theory of Equal Liberty? *Can* it? If, for instance, the concern for Equal Liberty is whether religion has been treated the same as other deeply held beliefs, then the discussion will necessarily shift to the question of what makes particular activities the same or different for purposes of comparison.[56] As Thomas Berg has observed, "In any case involving accommodation of a religious interest, numerous other personal commitments and interests arguably are comparable, and

---

51. Eisgruber & Sager, *supra* note 37, at 92.

52. Lupu & Tuttle, *supra* note 46, at 1249.

53. *Id.* at 1250.

54. Eisgruber & Sager, *supra* note 37, at 21.

55. *Id.* at 59; *see also* Peter Westen, *The Empty Idea of Equality*, 95 Harv. L. Rev. 537 (1992).

56. *See, e.g.,* Abner S. Greene, *Three Theories of Religious Equality . . . And of Exemptions*, 87 Tex. L. Rev. 963, 1003 (2009).

the government typically accommodates some and not others."[57] Eisgruber and Sager, for instance, would hold that a police officer must be allowed to wear a beard for religious reasons if the police department grants exemptions from the regulation for medical reasons. But what if, as was the case, the department did not exempt "those who [wore beards] to mark an ethnic identity or follow the model of an honored father?"[58]

Eisgruber and Sager respond by assuming that religious claims to accommodation should be compared with accommodations for "serious mainstream . . . secular interests."[59] But how to determine what qualifies as a "serious" secular interest is neither clear nor self-defining. Equal Liberty is thus "entirely indeterminate—even incoherent—unless it somehow specifies which interests to compare to religion."[60]

Conversely, Equal Liberty's egalitarian insistence that religion should not be treated as a constitutionally distinct or significant matter leads rather quickly into the weeds. In Free Exercise cases, why, if religion is not distinctive, is it treated the same as the *weightiest* secular concerns, rather than being compared to *all* secular concerns? In Establishment Clause cases, if religion is no different from any other belief system, why is the government prohibited on a theory of Equal Liberty from advancing religious views, when it regularly argues in favor of a number of secular positions, in public schools and elsewhere?

Eisgruber and Sager's fallback here seems to be a substantive one. For example, in arguing that government can make certain kinds of statements— say, that a town is a "Nuclear-Free community"—and not others, such as that a town is a "Christian community,"[61] they assert that the distinction is warranted by a host of background features of religion that distinguish the religious statement that a town is a "Christian community" from the secular statement that it is a nuclear-free zone. These include the "comprehensive" nature of religious belief, its tendency to involve "large, expansive webs of belief and conduct," and the "momentous" stakes involved in religious belief, such as "being saved and slotted for eternal joyous life or condemned to eternal damnation."[62]

Thus, at the same time that they deny that religion is distinctive, Eisgruber and Sager "tell us how religion is experienced by many Americans as a distinctive form of belief and practice."[63] That they do so in the service of equality, rather than for the sake of religion itself, does not change the fact that this

---

57. Thomas C. Berg, *Can Religious Liberty Be Protected as Equality?*, 85 Tex. L. Rev. 1185, 1194 (2007).

58. *Id.*

59. Eisgruber & Sager, *supra* note 37, at 90.

60. Berg, *supra* note 57, at 1195.

61. Eisgruber & Sager, *supra* note 37, at 124.

62. *Id.* at 125.

63. Greene, *supra* note 56, at 979.

approach "raise[s] the inevitable question" whether the factors they point to show, in fact, "precisely why . . . religion has two clauses all its own" in the First Amendment.[64] "Time and again," Eisgruber and Sager fall back on "arguments that rest on the special vulnerability of religious identity to state-authored disparagement and discrimination."[65]

Perhaps those of us who think religion *is*, in fact, distinctive should not complain too loudly about this. But their tendency suggests that religion *does* involve a distinctive, and distinctively important, set of beliefs and practices. That seems to conflict with Eisgruber and Sager's insistence that the distinctiveness of religion is something "that Equal Liberty cannot countenance."[66] This is just the age-old question of whether it is possible to talk about equality without ultimately talking about substance. As Steven Smith says, "The notion of 'equal regard' has a tone of fairness, benevolence, [and] sagacity." But it also results in "inevitable question-begging" about the substantive choices one is making, and leads Equal Liberty to "smuggle[ ] in . . . substantive criteria under which 'deep' commitments are relevantly like each other and unlike other commitments."[67] The "obliging rhetoric of 'equality'" cannot obscure the fact that these choices are being made.[68] Indeed, as Smith observes, this is another example of the ways in which theories of religious freedom can be "an example in miniature of the modern discourse of 'liberal democracy,' which a critic might view as a massive project in question-begging based on the empty notions of equality or, sometimes, neutrality."[69] In short, the impossibility of evading important substantive choices about what constitutes "equality" in the context of the Religion Clauses, and about whether and why religion is in fact distinctive, suggests that "Equal Liberty should not be, cannot be, all there is to the Religion Clauses."[70]

Another question posed by egalitarian accounts of religious freedom is whether they can redeem one of their central promises: to offer an easily administered method of addressing questions of church–state conflict. It seems likely instead that, once we descend beneath the surface pleasantries represented by terms like

---

64. *Id.*

65. Lupu & Tuttle, *supra* note 46, at 1267.

66. *Id.* at 1250; *see also* Berg, *supra* note 57, at 1188 ("[A]lthough they reach many normatively attractive results[,] . . . [Eisgruber and Sager] can only do so by surrendering a primary focus on equality and nondiscrimination."), 1190 (Eisgruber and Sager "want both liberty and equal treatment. And they add a fair amount of liberty to the equation— but at the cost of surrendering many of their objections to treating religious commitments differently from other deep commitments.").

67. Steven D. Smith, *Getting Over Equality: A Critical Diagnosis of Religious Freedom in America* 18 (2001).

68. *Id.* at 19.

69. *Id.*

70. Kent Greenawalt, *How Does "Equal Liberty" Fare in Relation to Other Approaches to the Religion Clauses?*, 85 Tex. L. Rev. 1217, 1234 (2007).

"equality," we will find this approach no more capable than others of providing a pellucid method of resolving these conflicts.[71]

To take an example, consider *Epperson v. Arkansas*.[72] There, the Supreme Court invalidated a state law that forbade any teacher in a state-supported school from teaching the theory of evolution. The Court stated that the law "select[ed] from the body of knowledge a particular segment which it proscribe[d] for the sole reason that it [was] deemed to conflict with a particular religious doctrine."[73] This violated the First Amendment's rule of "governmental neutrality between religion and [other] religion[s], and between religion and nonreligion."[74] But public schools regularly take positions on all kinds of controversial subjects, teaching (or not teaching) such matters as sexual abstinence, women's equality, and so on.[75] Why, then, can the state not similarly declare that evolution will be an out-of-bounds topic? Why is this distinct from the many decisions that schools make every day in designing and teaching a curriculum?

One possible answer to this is that religion is somehow special, rendering state intervention less appropriate. That raises questions about how we are to know when this value is implicated. Doesn't a health class that teaches abstinence, for instance, potentially raise these same comprehensive concerns? In any event, this approach, again, entails making a substantive decision that religion *is* distinct. That means abandoning the egalitarian project.

Another answer—the one Eisgruber and Sager adopt—is to say that *Epperson* was rightly decided, but for reasons having nothing to do with religion.[76] Instead, the case should be understood as standing for the proposition that the state has no power to declare orthodox opinions.[77] On this view, "the best understanding of the outcome in *Epperson* is not that the statute was impermissibly religious, but that the statute abused the state's educational power by attempting to impose an orthodoxy (religious or not)."[78] Because the state "imposes" orthodoxy all the time, however,[79] this approach would require us to revisit and presumably strike down any number of common practices by public schools.[80] Or we could invoke some thicker value to help us distinguish between acceptable and

---

71. This is the primary focus of Greenawalt's critique of Eisgruber and Sager; *see id.*

72. 393 U.S. 97 (1968).

73. *Id.* at 103.

74. *Id.* at 103–04.

75. *See, e.g.,* Greenawalt, *supra* note 70, at 1234. For a startling example, see *Brown v. Hot, Sexy & Safer Prods., Inc.,* 68 F.3d 525 (1st Cir. 1995).

76. *See* Eisgruber & Sager, *supra* note 37, at 191 ("[W]e believe that the best way to defend *Epperson* does not invoke religious liberty in a direct sense at all.").

77. *See, e.g., West Virginia Board of Education v. Barnette,* 329 U.S. 624, 642 (1943).

78. Eisgruber & Sager, *supra* note 37, at 193–94.

79. *See, e.g.,* Steven D. Smith, *Barnette's Big Blunder,* 78 Chi.–Kent L. Rev. 625 (2003).

80. *See* Greene, *supra* note 56, at 983–84.

unacceptable "orthodoxy," allowing schools, for instance, to teach students that they ought to treat each other as equals, but not to restrict the teaching of the theory of evolution. But that again depends on the kinds of substantive choices about the distinctiveness of religion that an egalitarian account is supposed to forswear. These questions of application suggest that egalitarian accounts of religious liberty are no more capable of resolving questions of religious freedom clearly and consistently, and without recourse to other substantive values, than other theories of religious freedom.

The point here is not that egalitarian theories of religious freedom cannot be highly protective of religious practice and belief. To frame the question in this way assumes the very point of contention: that there is a particular vision of religious freedom that is "good" and that can be reached without deciding questions of religious truth. That is the problem that confronts egalitarian theories of religious freedom. They cannot avoid questions of religious truth, but can only disguise, defer, or, finally, confront them directly.

Thus, Eisgruber and Sager argue that the problem with non-egalitarian theories of religious freedom is that they ultimately take the view that "any viable theory of religious freedom must endorse one or another controversial definition of religion," and that this "self-defeating" approach leads to the dilemma that "you cannot protect religion without knowing what it is, but once you say what religion is, you have undone religious liberty."[81] But they have not escaped the horns of this dilemma either. Even an egalitarian account ultimately entails making some of the same judgments. On the one hand, it may lead the egalitarian to take the controversial view that religion is no different from any other belief: that from an internal perspective there is no reason to assume that "religious convictions exercise a more powerful grip upon the individual psyche than do deeply felt secular conviction[s]," and from an outsider's perspective "there is no reason to assume that any specific religious practice . . . is *really* commanded by God."[82] On the other hand, if one attempts to *avoid* "the dubious enterprise of finding some ground from which to make sweeping metaphysical or phenomenological comparisons between religious and secular commitments,"[83] the effort will fail. One will invariably be forced to make just these sorts of substantive judgments when it comes time to apply egalitarian theory in the real world. For egalitarians as for every other liberal theorist of religion, questions of religious truth are unavoidable.

---

81. Christopher L. Eisgruber & Lawrence G. Sager, *Does it Matter What Religion Is?*, 84 Notre Dame L. Rev. 807, 810–11 (2009).

82. Eisgruber & Sager, *supra* note 37, at 103.

83. *Id.* at 104.

LIBERTY-ORIENTED THEORIES

Another possible approach to religious freedom is to focus not on equality or neutrality, but on freedom itself. Although we have considered Douglas Laycock's theory of religious freedom under the rubric of neutrality, another article of his bears a title that gives the flavor of this approach: "Religious Liberty As Liberty."[84] A liberty-centered view of religious freedom holds that neutrality (formal neutrality, at least) and equality may be valuable sorting mechanisms, but they neglect the fundamental fact that religion, and religious freedom, *matters*. The important thing about religious freedom is not whether it treats people neutrally or whether people are at risk of discrimination, but that it "guarantees that each citizen in a free country may believe as he will about the existence and characteristics of God and about the role of faith."[85]

On its own terms, this "theory" of religious liberty approaches tautology. If we treat liberty and religious freedom as synonymous, then naturally a theory of religious freedom should champion religious liberty. Its focus can, perhaps, distinguish it from theories built on formal neutrality or on equality, both of which are about religion's relative status rather than its absolute status.[86] Although that is an important distinction, however, it does not tell us *what* religious liberty consists of, or why it is worth protecting.

Moreover, religious liberty is not the same as religious license. One could in theory imagine a theory of religious freedom that amounts to an absolute right to do whatever one wants in the name of religion—kill one's enemies, sacrifice oneself or one's children, or seize the reins of political power and establish a theocracy. Aside from the fact that one would still need a substantive theory as to *why* this license was required or advisable, this is not an approach that answers any practical questions about how society is to manage in a state of religious pluralism. It should therefore not be surprising that this is not what anyone means by a liberty-centered theory of religious freedom.

Once we have established that limits are needed, however, the game is up. The everyday language of religious freedom in the courts, just like the language of constitutional law in general, is replete with tests and formulas that purport to tell us how to balance the needs of different individuals with the needs of other individuals and of the state: "rational basis," "compelling interest," "least

---

84. Douglas Laycock, *Religious Liberty As Liberty*, 7 J. Contemp. Legal Issues 313 (1996).
85. *Id.* at 313.
86. *See, e.g.*, Michael A. Paulsen, *Religion, Equality, and the Constitution: An Equal Protection Approach to Establishment Clause Adjudication*, 61 Notre Dame L. Rev. 311, 333 (1986).

restrictive means," and many more.[87] But they cannot offer us a "view from nowhere" about what tests to select or how they are to be applied. Every effort to balance rights against their restrictions necessarily plunges us into normative questions about what we should value and how.[88] We might operate—the courts often do—from a secular perspective, privileging the state's understanding of its own interests from a point of view that is shorn of religious belief. Or we might adopt the view that religious belief and practice is in some important sense true and therefore should outweigh the state's claims. But there is no neutral ground.[89] Thus, like its competitors, a theory of religious liberty as liberty does not rest on its own bottom, but instead depends on a series of controversial conclusions about what is permitted and what is prohibited, each of which necessarily implicate involve questions of religious truth. Liberty will do very little work of its own here.

Furthermore, in particular areas of the religious freedom debate—particularly the question of what constitutes an impermissible "establishment" of religion—liberty leaves open some serious questions. Locke, for example, advocated a wide scope for religious liberty, but he also believed that the state could literally establish a particular church as part of the apparatus of government. Suppose that the federal government replaced the statue of "Freedom" that sits atop the U.S. Capitol with a representation of the Hindu god Shiva, and proclaimed, "From now on, this is a Hindu nation, and we encourage everyone to follow our lead. Of course, you are free to believe whatever you wish." This would not require anyone to *do* much of anything in response. But, on some liberty-oriented views of religious freedom, this action would still violate that principle, because it would gently encourage citizens to adopt Hindu beliefs and practices. It would thus interfere with each person's ability to "believe as he will" on questions of religion.[90] That view, however, depends on contested questions about the centrality of voluntariness to individual decisions about religion, as well as the meaning and scope of voluntariness in relation to the formation of religious belief. One might well share these intuitions. But, again, "liberty" itself does little of the work here. Thus, as much or more so than the neutrality- or equality-oriented approaches, a liberty-centered approach to religious freedom cannot avoid substantive questions of religious truth.

---

87. *See, e.g.,* Richard H. Fallon, Jr., *Implementing the Constitution* (2001); Morton J. Horwitz, *Foreword: The Constitution of Change: Legal Fundamentality Without Fundamentalism,* 107 Harv. L. Rev. 30 (1993); Robert F. Nagel, *The Formulaic Constitution,* 84 Mich. L. Rev. 165 (1985).

88. *See, e.g.,* Richard A. Posner, *Constitutional Law From a Pragmatic Perspective,* 55 U. Toronto L.J. 299 (2005).

89. *See generally* Frederick Mark Gedicks, *The Rhetoric of Church and State: A Critical Analysis of Religion Clause Jurisprudence* (1995).

90. Laycock, *supra* note 84, at 313.

NON-THEORIES OF RELIGIOUS FREEDOM

Neutrality, equality, and liberty round out the collection of usual suspects when it comes to theories of religious freedom. But they by no means exhaust the methods, principles, or terms that have been used in discussing the theory of the Religion Clauses. What distinguishes these theories, however, is that they are just that: theories. By contrast, the principles we examine below might be called *non*-theories of religious freedom, in the sense that they are tools for interpretation rather than robust stand-alone attempts to provide principles for the resolution of church–state controversies.

One candidate, probably the most well-known for most readers, is originalism. In brief, originalism is the view that the Constitution, including the Religion Clauses of the First Amendment, ought to be interpreted according to some understanding of the original meaning of the Constitution. There are, as it turns out, many versions of originalism, although the most widespread version in current use requires the Constitution to be interpreted according to the public meaning of the words of the constitutional text at the time of the ratification of the document (or, according to some versions, at the time of the ratification of the Fourteenth Amendment).[91]

In the case of the Religion Clauses, for example, scholars have argued over whether the Free Exercise Clause should be understood, according to its original public meaning, as requiring exemptions for religiously compelled conduct in the face of generally applicable laws, or whether no such exemptions are required.[92] Both of these positions happen to track, fairly closely, the contending positions of most non-originalist scholars of the Free Exercise Clause. Debates over the original meaning of the Establishment Clause can have more radical implications, because some views of that clause would reject its incorporation, through the Fourteenth Amendment, against the states,[93] and instead hold that the Constitution only prohibits *federal* establishments of religion.[94] Even originalists

---

91. *See, e.g.,* Antonin Scalia, *A Matter of Interpretation* (1997). On originalism and the Fourteenth Amendment, *see, e.g.,* Bret Boyce, *Originalism and the Fourteenth Amendment,* 33 Wake Forest L. Rev. 909 (1998); Akhil Reed Amar, *The Bill of Rights and the Fourteenth Amendment,* 101 Yale L.J. 1193 (1992).

92. *Compare* Michael W. McConnell, *The Origins and Historical Understanding of Free Exercise of Religion,* 103 Harv. L. Rev. 1409 (1990) (arguing that it does), *with* Philip A. Hamburger, *A Constitutional Right of Religious Exemption: An Historical Perspective,* 60 Geo. Wash. L. Rev. 915 (1992) (arguing that it does not). For a useful survey of the debate, see Vincent Philip Muñoz, *The Original Meaning of the Free Exercise Clause: The Evidence From the First Congress,* 31 Harv. J. L. & Pub. Pol'y 1083 (2008).

93. *See Everson v. Bd. of Educ.,* 330 U.S. 1 (1947).

94. *See, e.g., Elk Grove Unified Sch. Dist. v. Newdow,* 542 U.S. 1, 49–50 (2004) (Thomas, J., concurring in the judgment); Steven D. Smith, *The Jurisdictional Establishment Clause: A Reappraisal,* 81 Notre Dame L. Rev. 1843 (2006).

who are unwilling to go this far, or who accept the incorporation of the Establishment Clause against the states as a done deal for all practical purposes, nevertheless can mine the original understanding of the Establishment Clause to draw conclusions about the breadth or narrowness of its scope.[95]

This is not an originalist book, although I hope it is sensitive to the claims of history. But the debates over originalism in general, or the original meaning of the Religion Clauses in particular, need not detain us long here. For originalism is not a *theory* of the Religion Clauses at all. It is, rather, a *method* of interpreting them. (The same could probably be said for originalism as a theory of the Constitution more generally. For most of its users, it is more of an interpretive method than a normative theory.[96]) Its attraction, for most originalists, consists largely in its purported ability to provide an answer to questions of constitutional interpretation that is both legitimate and, equally important, clear and predictable. Whether it achieves those aims is another question.[97] For our purposes, originalism, in its ideal state, would partake of a mechanical quality of application that has little to do with theory as such, and everything to do with the availability and usefulness of the historical evidence.

In practice, of course, that evidence is often complex and controversial. The fierce debate over the original meaning of the Free Exercise Clause and whether it requires religious exemptions is only one example. At that point, however, the debate over the historical meaning of the Religion Clauses quickly, if not inevitably, turns into a debate over the nature and meaning of the *values* that underlie the Religion Clauses. Once we reach this juncture, the values, not the theory, do all the heavy lifting. Thus, for our purposes, originalism can be treated as a non-theory of the Religion Clauses and largely set aside.

Other interpretive principles that have been mustered to make sense of the Religion Clauses include *separationism*, the belief that the Religion Clauses must be understood as erecting a high wall between church and state, which for decades was the primary lens through which the Establishment Clause was viewed,[98] and *accommodationism*, the view that the Religion Clauses require the accommodation of the needs of religious believers.[99] Like separationism, accommodationism had a long run in the Supreme Court. It may raise a few hackles to describe both separationism and accommodationism as non-theories of the

---

95. *See, e.g.*, Robert G. Natelson, *The Original Meaning of the Establishment Clause*, 14 Wm. & Mary Bill of Rts. J. 73 (2005).

96. *See* Kurt T. Lash, *Originalism, Popular Sovereignty, and Reverse Stare Decisis*, 93 Va. L. Rev. 1437, 1440 (2007) ("[O]riginalism is an interpretive method and not a normative constitutional theory").

97. *See, e.g.*, Mitchell N. Berman, *Originalism is Bunk*, 84 N.Y.U. L. Rev. 1 (2009).

98. *See, e.g.*, Ira C. Lupu, *The Lingering Death of Separationism*, 62 Geo. Wash. L. Rev. 230 (1993).

99. *See, e.g.*, Michael W. McConnell, *Accommodation of Religion*, 1985 Sup. Ct. Rev. 1.

Religion Clauses. I do not mean to cast aspersions on either approach. In calling them non-theories, I simply mean that they are more often "augmenting concepts," to use Frank Ravitch's words, rather than genuine stand-alone theories of religious freedom.[100] They usually serve as a means of realizing some other, broader value or theory, such as neutrality, equality, or liberty, not as independent theories of religious freedom. As such, all of the now-familiar criticisms of those theories examined above also hold true for separationism and accommodationism.

In particular, they face the same issues with respect to questions of religious truth. Separationism, for instance, can be seen as an approach that seeks to dig a trench between government and private religious choice, or that views religion as either beyond the competence of the state or so divisive a subject that it should be set aside from issues of democratic governance.[101] But these justifications either depend on questions that cannot be answered absent a judgment about religious truth—for example, whether and why government is not competent to make claims about religious truth, or why private choice is a more appropriate path to the discovery of religious truth—or make an ultimately fruitless effort to avoid them altogether. Similarly, accommodationism can be justified as necessary for the private formation of religious belief. But this again raises questions about whether and why this is the best means for individuals or communities to arrive at religious truth. In short, both of these approaches are best treated as non-theories of religious freedom, in the sense that they rely on and are adjuncts to larger theories like equality or neutrality. As such, they are just as subject to the problem of religious truth as those larger theories are.

ANTI-THEORIES OF RELIGIOUS FREEDOM

By now, it should come as no surprise that some writers have given up on the theory game altogether. These are the anti-theorists of religious freedom;[102] we examined two prominent advocates of this approach, Steven Smith and Stanley Fish, in the last chapter.[103] The milder form of Religion Clause anti-theory argues

---

100. *See* Ravitch, *supra* note 8, at 497; *see also id.* at 537 (observing that accommodationism, like separationism, "can arguably function both at the level of a broad principle and as a narrow principle, or as a facet of a doctrinal test").

101. *See, e.g.,* Richard W. Garnett, *Religion, Division, and the First Amendment,* 94 Geo. L.J. 1667 (2006).

102. *See generally* Berg, *supra* note 3.

103. We could also add Frederick Gedicks and Larry Alexander to the ranks of anti-theorists. *See, e.g.,* Gedicks, *supra* note 89; Larry Alexander, *Good God, Garvey! The Inevitability and Impossibility of a Religious Justification of Free Exercise Exemptions,* 47 Drake L. Rev. 35, 38–39 (1998).

that "at present, there is no single viable principle or approach available for courts to use to decide cases under the Religion Clauses." The stronger form argues that we should delete the words "at present." On this view, "no coherent form of religious freedom is possible and even desirable."[104] Recall the pessimistic banners under which these writers march: a theory of religious freedom is a "mission impossible" or a "foreordained failure."

Given this chapter's argument that theories of religious freedom run aground on the shoals of religious truth, I am tempted to cut short my review of the anti-theorists with a simple, "Right on!" But it is worth observing the ways in which Religion Clause anti-theory, too, ends up confronting the difficulties that questions of religious truth pose for any attempt to offer a coherent approach to religious freedom.

Religion Clause anti-theorists offer three basic responses to the impossibility of a theory of religious freedom. One we might call Hamlet's strategy: "The rest is silence."[105] If the theory of religious freedom founders on the problem of religious truth, then we should face up to this fact manfully (or, perhaps, personfully), and do and say nothing more. This is a respectable response, but also a rather unattractive one. Hamlet, after all, *dies*. Judges do not have that luxury; the cases keep coming and must be decided. Nor, in a sense, do academics. If we were to stop writing about religious freedom, we might have to find something else to do. (Perish the thought!) In fact, Religion Clause anti-theorists demonstrate a remarkable capacity to keep writing despite their skepticism, both because there is always another Religion Clause theorist to cut down to size and because, as Hamlet's death suggests, it beats the alternative.

Another response is to argue that in the absence of a coherent theory of religious freedom, as long as we continue to be confronted with church–state conflicts, we must all just do our best to muddle through as best we can. Smith, for example, argues that judges deciding Religion Clause cases "can and should promote prudence over principle."[106] His prescription finds an echo in Justice Stephen Breyer's suggestion that in the "difficult borderline cases" that inevitably arise under the Religion Clauses, there is "no test-related substitute for the exercise of legal judgment."[107] This is a realistic response, and in fact judges are rather good at muddling through. But it is also incomplete. It is not clear that there can be such a thing as "prudence" without at least *some* principle to ground it. In deciding cases involving church–state conflict, *something* must inform our pragmatic analysis, and that something will ultimately be a conclusion or intuition

---

104. Berg, *supra* note 3, at 693–94.
105. William Shakespeare, *Hamlet*, act 5.sc. ii.
106. Smith, *supra* note 67, at 6.
107. *Van Orden v. Perry*, 545 U.S. 677, 700 (2005) (Breyer, J., concurring in the judgment).

about what constitutes a sound outcome.[108] However submerged it may be, a prudential approach to the Religion Clauses will ultimately appeal to conclusions about the nature and status of religion and religious liberty that imply some answer to the question of religious truth.

The final response is *force majeure*. If there is no perfect theory of religious freedom, or at least no theory of religious freedom that can avoid the question of religious truth, then we should unflinchingly face the reality that with each decision we *are* imposing a vision of religious truth. Thus, Larry Alexander writes bluntly (for a legal philosopher) that "at the apex of one's philosophical system, one's own point of view is what matters, not in the postmodern sense that point of view is everything, ontologically, but in the epistemic sense that there is no other vantage point from which one can adjudicate."[109] And Stanley Fish writes bluntly (for *anyone*) that liberalism cannot wish away the conflicts that arise over questions of religious truth. Conflict is simply "the name of our condition"; the only thing to do is play the game and "play it to win."[110] This is simply a way of saying that when the rubber hits the road, we must confront *and decide* questions of religious truth. The anti-theorist who takes this stark position may find grim or even gleeful satisfaction in it. But she will not be able to settle any issues. Indeed, the very point of the position is that these disputes must be visited and revisited again and again through the play of politics. So the questions of religious truth that lie unavoidably at the heart of the liberal state, although settled by force at any given moment, will always rise again to confront us.

ANTI-RELIGIOUS AND ANTI-LIBERAL THEORIES OF RELIGIOUS FREEDOM

Two final families of theories of religious freedom remain to be considered. Their approaches may seem to be diametrically opposed. But in many respects, they share more in common, from the perspective of religious truth, than they do with any of the other theories we have seen so far. Both of them, unlike virtually all of the theories examined above, actually seek to *answer*, rather than *avoid*, the fundamental questions of religious truth that lie at the heart of the modern liberal order in general, and our legal regime of religious freedom in particular. They just happen to reach contrary conclusions.

---

108. *See, e.g.,* Michael Sullivan & Daniel J. Solove, *Can Pragmatism Be Radical?: Richard Posner and Legal Pragmatism*, 113 Yale L.J. 687, 693–96 (2003).

109. Larry Alexander, *Liberalism, Religion, and the Unity of Epistemology*, 30 San Diego L. Rev. 763, 796 (1993).

110. Stanley Fish, *Mission Impossible: Settling the Just Bounds Between Church and State*, 97 Colum. L. Rev. 2255, 2330, 2332 (1997).

SECULARISM: AN ANTI-RELIGIOUS THEORY OF RELIGIOUS FREEDOM

The first theory, or family of theories, is secularism. In many respects, secularism is liberalism's handmaiden. As Benjamin Berger writes, it is "the main conceptual means by which Western Liberal societies deal with the expression of religious conscience."[111] Although it can be "a confusing and slippery term,"[112] in general it refers to the belief that in a liberal society, legal choices must "be based on secular public reasons, i.e., reasons accessible to all, irrespective of their religious belief."[113] It can take stronger or weaker forms, although the insistence on "the possibility of a reason-based political society"[114] is common to secularism in all its forms. Secularism need not be anti-religious, and may in fact believe that it remains scrupulously "agnostic" on questions of religious truth[115]—although Part Two of this book will offer a version of constitutional agnosticism that is worlds away from the secularist version. But stronger versions of secularism, in their stringent exclusion of religious beliefs and justifications from all but the private corners of our lives, cannot help but be viewed, by both religious believers and many nonbelievers, as not just agnostic to religion, but hostile.[116]

Secularism is often associated with neutrality. It "requires that government remain neutral between religious sects and between religion and non-religion generally."[117] It achieves this goal through a set of rules that are both principles of secularism and tools for its enforcement. In particular, secularism maintains itself through the enforcement of the division of life into public and private spheres, in which the public sphere is to remain exclusively secular. In this manner, it can "marginalize religion without having to eliminate it."[118]

The secularist insists that this division is just "simple neutrality."[119] For some religious believers, however, it is nothing of the sort. It is in that difference of opinion that we can see the ways in which secularism in fact takes a position on matters of religious truth. Secularism ultimately rests on a "deeply rooted

---

111. Benjamin Berger, *The Limits of Belief: Freedom of Religion, Secularism, and the Liberal State*, 17 Can. J. L. & Soc'y 39, 49 (2002).

112. Kent Greenawalt, *Secularism, Religion, and Liberal Democracy in the United States*, 30 Cardozo L. Rev. 2383, 2383 (2009).

113. Andras Sajo, *Constitutionalism and Secularism: The Need for Public Reason*, 30 Cardozo L. Rev. 2401, 2401 (2009).

114. *Id.*

115. *See, e.g.,* Steven G. Gey, *Unity of the Graveyard and the Attack on Constitutional Secularism*, 2004 BYU L. Rev. 1005, 1021–22.

116. *See, e.g.,* Iain T. Benson, *Considering Secularism*, in *Recognizing Religion in a Secular Society* 83, 90 (Douglas Farrow, ed., 2004).

117. Gedicks, *supra* note 89, at 12.

118. *Id.* at 31.

119. *Id.* at 27.

normative [position] about how church and state should interact."[120] That position is one in which religion is private, in which public reasons are genuinely possible and available, and in which the religious individual should have no complaint about checking her religious beliefs, no matter how comprehensive, at the door. Secularism makes a fundamental judgment of religious truth: "Secular knowledge" is "objective" and "religious belief" is "subjective."[121] But those categories only make sense from a secularist perspective. To a religious believer, they may be wrong, or even incoherent.

That does not mean secularism is wrong or bad, although I tend to think it is. As a practical matter, one might argue that it is the best we can do in a pluralistic society, at least if we want the trains to run on time. From a constitutional perspective, it could just be the case that, as some have argued, our Constitution in fact creates a secular legal and political order.[122] This is an argument about authority, of course, not a theory; but in the real world, authority matters. As a matter of theory, too, we cannot say that secularism is *wrong* as such. If one accepts its premises, then it can be perfectly coherent.

One thing we cannot say about secularism, however, even in its gentler forms, is that it is *neutral*. By carving up the world in particular ways, ways that are not self-defining but rest on a host of assumptions about the nature of the world and of human nature—that there is a distinction between public and private and that religion belongs on the private side of the divide, that there is such a thing as "reasoned" public argument, and so on—secularism takes a firm stand on questions of religious truth. Secularists who insist otherwise should consult their local truth-in-advertising laws.

RELIGIOUS JUSTIFICATIONS FOR RELIGIOUS FREEDOM; OR, ANTI-LIBERAL THEORIES OF RELIGIOUS FREEDOM

Like secularism, our final theory of religious freedom also takes a forthright stand on questions of religious truth. Like Religion Clause anti-theory, this approach rejects the idea that liberal theory can offer a coherent approach to religious liberty. It also agrees with the argument I have been making here that any theory of religious freedom ultimately must confront questions of religious truth. But this theory takes a somewhat different approach from my own. It simply grasps the nettles and adopts an explicitly *religious*, and often—perhaps

---

120. *Id.* at 26.

121. *Id.* at 32.

122. *See, e.g.,* Susanna Sherry, *Enlightening the Religion Clauses,* 7 J. Contemp. Legal Issues 473 (1996); Isaac Kramnick & R. Laurence Moore, *The Godless Constitution: A Moral Defense of the Secular State* (2005); Kathleen M. Sullivan, *Religion and Liberal Democracy,* 59 U. Chi. L. Rev. 195 (1992).

inevitably—sectarian, theory of religious freedom. A leading version of this argument has been offered by John Garvey, whose views are summarized in the title of his article, "An Anti-Liberal Argument for Religious Freedom."[123]

Garvey argues that the standard liberal justifications for religious freedom fall short. One standard liberal argument for religious freedom treats it as a component of individual autonomy. This sentiment animates substantive neutrality, for instance. The problem, Garvey argues, is that it tends to treat the autonomous individual as "a kind of free-floating self."[124] This is "a view of human nature that many religious people would reject."[125] For many religious individuals, particularly many committed Christians, we cannot be unencumbered selves. We no more "choose" to believe in and obey God than we "choose" to obey the laws of gravity. Indeed, for some "Christian[s,] freedom consists not in making our own choices but in obeying the law of God."[126]

Moreover—and this is the question on which Eisgruber and Sager's egalitarian account of religious freedom arguably stumbles—an argument for liberty (religious or otherwise) that is based on autonomy, by treating all personal claims and choices as equally valuable and potentially worthy of protection, offers us no yardstick by which to evaluate such claims. It leaves open the possibility of protecting everything in the name of autonomy, or nothing. It offers religious choices presumptive protection—but it is equally an argument for the "right" to smoke, snort cocaine, or do something genuinely irrational and harmful, like watching Michael Bay movies. As a practical matter, Garvey argues, "What we need is an argument that protects religion while leaving unprotected many other activities that we do not support as strongly."[127] Another standard argument is "political rather than ethical": religious freedom is necessary to avoid civil strife of the kind that characterized Europe's wars of religion.[128] But this argument does not tell us "why we should prefer freedom to other means of bringing peace," such as suppressing faith altogether.[129]

Against these arguments, Garvey asserts that we should protect religion "on the assumption that religion is a good thing."[130] He assumes that religion is true, that living out our religious commitments may in fact lead us to the truth, and that we may experience the need to worship as a genuine compulsion from God.

---

123. John H. Garvey, *An Anti-Liberal Argument for Religious Freedom*, 7 J. Contemp. Legal Issues 275 (1996). This article was later reprinted in Garvey's book, *What Are Freedoms For?* (1997). I cite here to the article rather than the book.

124. *Id.* at 277.

125. *Id.* at 279.

126. *Id.*

127. *Id.* at 278.

128. *Id.* at 280.

129. *Id.* at 282. For further criticism of this argument, see Garnett, *supra* note 101.

130. Garvey, *supra* note 123, at 283.

These arguments, Garvey says, rest finally on "religious premises," such as that "faith is a gift" and "revelation is progressive."[131] He concedes that these arguments rely "upon reasons that only some people find convincing."[132] Nevertheless, given the many problems with any theory of religious freedom that purports to avoid questions of religious truth, Garvey argues that the religious justification for religious freedom "is the most convincing explanation for why our society adopted the right to religious freedom in the first place."[133]

After our slog through liberal theories of religious freedom, Garvey's approach is bracing, at least. It is a pleasure to see someone wearing his heart on his sleeve. Like secularism, the religious justification for religious freedom is not shy about confronting and answering questions of religious truth. Of course, like secularism, the religious justification for religious freedom is also unlikely to satisfy everyone. Nonbelievers and individuals from different faith traditions may well object to it, not just because it adopts a justification based on a particular understanding of religious truth, but because they disagree with some of its premises, such as that religious belief is necessarily a matter of individual faith or revelation. As I will argue at greater length in the next chapter, in our own agnostic age, one in which both different religious beliefs and belief in religion itself have become both varied and optional, there is good reason to think that, as a practical matter, Garvey's proposal will lack enough support to get it off the ground.

These objections are not a basis for rejecting Garvey's theory as incoherent. As Larry Alexander writes, "It is . . . no objection to Garvey's account of religious freedom that it is religiously partisan. For that is exactly the kind of account Garvey purports to be offering and that he maintains is necessary."[134] One may indeed reject it, but not because it does not make sense, *if* one accepts its premises.

But there are other objections to Garvey's account. Larry Alexander, for instance, has suggested that from any point of view that takes religious truth-claims seriously, "[C]omplying with one's conception of God's duties is a good thing only if that conception is correct. . . . There is nothing generally good about complying with imagined religious duties."[135] From the perspective of those who believe that Jesus Christ is the way, the truth, and the light, it is not clear why someone should be entitled to exemptions from generally applicable laws that conflict with, say, the practices of Scientology.

---

131. *Id.* at 285.

132. *Id.* at 289.

133. *Id.* at 291.

134. Alexander, supra note 103, at 38–39.

135. *Id.* at 41; *see also* Dennis C. Mueller, *Reason, Religion, and Democracy* 362 (2009) ("Indeed, it is difficult to see how a truly religious person can be tolerant of other religions"), 397 ("Religions are inherently intolerant of one another and of secularism").

Alexander is unconvinced by Garvey's response, namely, that since "revelation is progressive" from his religious point of view, we must allow individuals to come to the light as a matter of their own free will, even if there is a risk that they will fall into religious error. He points out that, given the consequences of the legal regime Garvey proposes, we would end up creating potentially hazardous exemptions for what, from some religious points of view, would count as patently false religious beliefs.[136]

I am not convinced by Alexander's riposte. A religious individual could certainly believe that, given the centrality of the individual quest for religious freedom, even harmful activity based on a false religious belief is entitled to protection. But Alexander's broader point seems correct: Garvey's theory runs into some of the same limits he criticizes in other theories. If the religious justification for religious freedom that Garvey offers protects individuals in searching for their own truths, even when they are in error, then it is not clear how we can effectively keep out the harmful activities that Garvey wants to exclude from protection as *religious* liberties—that is, how we can conclude that a particular practice, such as smoking or watching *Pearl Harbor*, is motivated by something other than religious belief. Conversely, if we believe that religion should be protected because it is *true*, then why should the state's interests *ever* trump religious interests?[137] In short, despite the admirable candor of Garvey's theory, those who do not reject it because it is too partisan may still reject it for being either too bold or too timid.

* * * * *

The purpose of Part One has been to clear the ground. We saw in Chapter One that the liberal consensus, at least as it is popularly understood, is at risk of collapsing under the weight of its own presuppositions, which are difficult if not impossible to maintain. Just as the effort to avoid the question of religious truth is at the heart of the liberal order, so it is at the heart of liberalism's failure as a theory. Liberalism cannot avoid questions of religious truth. It can run from them, only to find that it has not managed to escape their clutch. Or it can take an openly partisan position on those questions, in which case it violates its own rules.[138]

The same is true of theories of religious freedom. Liberal theories of religious freedom, like neutrality, equality, and liberty, and their non-theory adjuncts, like separationism and accommodationism, face an unavoidable baseline problem. We cannot say that they guarantee "neutrality" or "equality" without answering

---

136. *See* Alexander, *supra* note 103, at 40–41.

137. *See id.* at 41–43.

138. At least under the popular view that liberalism refuses to take sides on questions of religious truth and the nature of the good. For a discussion of other forms of liberalism that are more openly comprehensive in their view of the good, see Chapter Eight.

the question: From *what* perspective? In this and many other ways, these theories ultimately cannot avoid the need to confront questions of religious truth. Anti-theories of religious freedom, to the extent that they do not just remain on the sidelines but actually attempt to resolve ongoing church–state controversies through some kind of prudentialism, or Justice Breyer's "exercise of legal judgment," will have to rest on some substantive ground, which brings us back to the same fundamental questions of religious truth.

Anti-liberal theories of religious freedom, like Garvey's religious justification for religious liberty, or anti-religious theories of religious freedom, like secularism, escape these criticisms. They *do* acknowledge and confront the necessity of facing up to questions of religious truth. The problem with these theories is not that they are incoherent, although secularism flirts with incoherence when it pretends that it is mere neutrality. The question for these theories, instead, is whether they are the best we can do. Many religious believers, and nonbelievers for that matter, will reject a forthright secularism because, in their view, it not only rests on false premises but ultimately slights an aspect of human existence that is of vital importance and should not be shunted aside and treated as a merely private habit, little better than a personal eccentricity. Similarly, many nonbelievers, and for that matter many religious believers, will reject one or another form of religious justification for religious freedom, either because they reject its premises in general, or because they reject the premises of some *particular* religious justification for religious freedom, or because they believe it will lead to incorrect or outrageous outcomes.

The question still remains: Can we find a better theory of or approach to religious freedom? Answering that question is the burden of Part Two of this book.

PART TWO

GETTING TO MAYBE:
THE AGNOSTIC TURN

3. EMPATHETIC AGNOSTICISM

O babbling Gnostic! Cease to beat the air. We yearn, and grope, and guess, but cannot know.
—*John Tyndall*[1]

THE DILEMMA RESTATED—AND THE BEGINNING OF THE WAY OUT

Here is the dilemma we have seen thus far in looking at the relationship between liberalism, law, and religion. Liberalism, according to the conventional understanding of the term, aims to create a way for us to coexist without reaching violent confrontation over the potentially divisive question of what constitutes the ultimate truth about the world. Its primary response to this problem is to simply take truth off the table. Liberalism purports to favor neither religious belief nor unbelief. Instead, it treats the question of religious truth as out of bounds. The same approach is evident in one of liberalism's major tributaries, law and religion. The shared quest of most of the prevailing theories of law and religion has been for a principle—neutrality, equality, and so on—that can mediate between religious and secular claims without having to enter into the debate over religious truth itself.

The problem is that the strategy of avoiding the question of religious truth is now widely seen as fatally flawed. It has had a good run, to be sure. We have managed, more or less, to coexist within the liberal state for the past two centuries without major eruptions of bloodshed over religious questions. The benefits that the liberal consensus has bequeathed us shouldn't be shrugged aside too quickly.

As a matter of both practice and principle, however, things are now more precarious. It is widely agreed that liberalism cannot justify itself in a thoroughgoing, persuasive way without embroiling itself in the very question it seeks to avoid. Every effort to write religious truth out of the equation altogether fails. The need to confront questions of ultimate truth can be deferred for a while—perhaps a long while—or shunted off to the side. At some point, however, the bill comes due.

The same thing is true for theories of law and religion. It is ultimately impossible to arrive at a theory of law and religion that does not either rest on

---

1. John Tyndall, *A Morning on Alp Lusgen*, in *Fragments of Science* (1896). *See* Francis O'Gorman, *John Tyndall as Poet: Agnosticism and "A Morning on Alp Lusgen,"* 48 Rev. Eng. Stud. 353 (1997).

a contestable conclusion about religious truth, or founder because it fails to take a stand on the issue. Certainly every theory that operates from *within* the liberal consensus runs up against this problem. Law and religion scholars can fell entire forests arguing over whether liberty, neutrality, equality, or some other high-sounding principle offers the best prospect of refereeing between church and state. But the whole enterprise has come to seem increasingly dubious.

A few theories of law and religion come from *outside* the liberal consensus, and purport to squarely confront questions of religious truth. John Garvey, for instance, refuses to play the liberal game, and argues instead for an explicitly religious and essentially Christian resolution of First Amendment questions about law and religion. Theories like his are in many respects more honest and coherent than liberal efforts to arrive at a principle that avoids the question of religious truth.

But that does not mean they are the *best* theories. If our goal is to come up with a theory of law and religion that is not only conceptually coherent and honest, but that can, at a practical level, command a broad degree of public support, this approach may not be up to the task. Answering the question what religious freedom means and why we value it by saying, "Because God says so" is little different, on this level, from saying, "Because our conception of neutrality, or equality, or autonomy, says so." In either case, the response to this explanation will be Tonto's rejoinder to the Lone Ranger: "What do you mean *we?*"

That answer doesn't change just because our society is predominantly religious. Under current conditions of religious pluralism, any sectarian religious theory of religious freedom will begin with a seriously deficient subscriber base, just as liberal or secular theories do. However flawed liberal theories of religious liberty may be, moreover, they have pervaded our worldview for two centuries, and they may be more prevalent among even religious citizens than an advocate like Garvey might suppose. An open and unapologetic religious theory of religious freedom is thus unlikely to command a substantial consensus in society at large. In short, openly religious accounts of religious freedom will be a nonstarter with most secular theorists of law and religion, and it is not clear that they will fare much better among non-secular theorists and citizens, who will either prefer liberal theories or disagree over *which* religious theory should prevail.

We can further clarify our dilemma, and point the way toward a possible resolution, if we look a little more closely at Garvey's religious theory of religious freedom. Our question here is not so much what he is *for*, but what he is *against*. Garvey writes that standard liberal theories of religious freedom "make no assumptions about the truth or value of religious decisions," but instead "view such questions from an agnostic standpoint."[2] He does not define the "agnostic

---

2. John H. Garvey, *An Anti-Liberal Argument for Religious Freedom,* 7 J. Contemp. Legal Issues 275 (1996).

standpoint," but he does describe it. The agnostic standpoint, he suggests, is one that privileges choice. It believes that people are capable of "step[ping] back" from their own religious beliefs, "assum[ing] an agnostic stance, and mak[ing] a fresh start."[3] Agnosticism is thus less a belief system than it is "a device . . . for securing everyone's agreement."[4] Not coincidentally, he links it to the Rawlsian veil of ignorance, behind which no one has *any* religious beliefs.[5]

Garvey's definition of agnosticism thus entails taking, at best, no point of view about religious freedom. It is, in his view, really just another label for the liberal viewpoint on religious freedom–one that tries to take the question of religious truth off the table altogether. Indeed, Garvey comes close to equating the agnostic viewpoint with a *secular* viewpoint, or at least one that devalues the strength and importance of religious belief. "The only real hard question," he writes, "is why an agnostic would support special treatment for religious people who want to comply with a moral or ceremonial code."[6] For Garvey, then, the "agnostic viewpoint" is the antonym of the believer's viewpoint, and is almost synonymous with unbelief. It adopts the strategy of attempting to minimize questions of religious truth altogether. In other words, it is just the standard liberal approach to religious freedom with a different label.

Garvey's frequent and loaded invocation of the word "agnostic" deserves the response of Inigo Montoya in *The Princess Bride*: "You keep using that word[.] I don't think it means what you think it does."[7] *Is* agnosticism what Garvey thinks it is? Are there better ways to understand the concept? And do they provide us with better answers to the dilemma of religious truth that confronts liberalism, and law and religion, at every turn?

An agnostic has been defined by the *Merriam-Webster Dictionary* as a person "who holds the view that any ultimate reality (as God) is unknown and probably unknowable," and more broadly as "one who is not committed to believing in either the existence or the nonexistence of God or a god."[8] The *Oxford English Dictionary* defines an agnostic as "[o]ne who holds that the existence of anything beyond and behind material phenomena is unknown and (so far as can be judged) unknowable, and especially that a First Cause and an unseen world are subjects of which we know nothing."[9] These definitions tell us much about the mixed reception of agnosticism in our culture, about common misunderstandings of the concept, and about the failure to fully appreciate its depths. Both definitions treat agnosticism as the conclusion that we can know *nothing* about

---

3. *Id.* at 277.
4. *Id.* at 289.
5. *See id.*
6. *Id.*
7. William Goldman, *The Princess Bride* 102 (25th anniv. ed., 1998) (1973).
8. *See Merriam-Webster Online*, http://www.merriam-webster.com.
9. *See Oxford English Dictionary Online*, http://www.oed.com.

the existence of anything beyond the material world—not that we know nothing *for sure*, but that we *can* know nothing *at all*. The *OED* definition tends to treat the agnostic as a thoroughgoing materialist. And *Merriam-Webster* insists that the essence of agnosticism is a *lack* of commitment to questions of religious truth, rather than a different *kind* of commitment.

And these are relatively gentle treatments of agnosticism. The list of those who think still less of agnosticism is too long to give in full, although a few examples may suffice. In his history of agnosticism, Bernard Lightman observes that many writers have treated it as if it were synonymous with anti-religious beliefs.[10] Others have suggested that agnosticism might simply be impossible.[11] Many critics have suggested that it is ultimately no different from atheism— indeed, it's worse, because the agnostic is simply a "timid atheist[ ]."[12] Most common, however, is the suggestion that agnosticism is not even timid atheism—just timidity, pure and simple. It is nothing more than "a halfway point between theism and atheism," a kind of waiting room of the mind.[13] The "great cop-out," as Joseph Levine calls it.[14]

That is not the brand of agnosticism that drives this book, and that helps underwrite constitutional agnosticism in particular. Constitutional agnosticism is humble, but not half-hearted. Like the agnosticism described by John Tyndall in the epigraph that opens this chapter, it "yearn[s], and grope[s], and guess[es]," even if it reaches the tentative conclusion that "we cannot know" for sure.

Before we can understand what *constitutional* agnosticism consists of, how-ever, and what it suggests about freedom of religion, we must reach a clearer understanding of *agnosticism*, or at least the form of it I describe here—what I call the "new agnosticism." That is the subject of this chapter. It is important to the rest of what follows in this book, and deserves to be laid out at length. I hope readers will approach this argument in a spirit of patience, imagination, and empathy, and with a cautious willingness, if not to believe that this kind of agnos-ticism is absolutely right or absolutely attainable, then at least to see how it *might* be attainable and why it *might* be attractive. If they do, they will be more than halfway home, for that very spirit is the essence of the new agnosticism.

I open the argument by defining the "new agnosticism." I then compare it with some of its competitors and some of the main criticisms of agnosticism, asking, for example, whether agnosticism is just a faint-hearted form of atheism.

10. Bernard Lightman, *The Origins of Agnosticism* (1987).

11. This is one reading of William James's classic essay *The Will to Believe*, although it is not the only possible reading. William James, *The Will to Believe and Other Essays* (2006) (1897).

12. David Novak, *Law: Religious or Secular?* 86 Va. L. Rev. 569, 574 (2000).

13. Lightman, *supra* note 10, at 17.

14. Joseph Levine, *From Yeshiva Bochur to Secular Humanist*, in *Philosophers Without Gods: Meditations on Atheism and the Secular Life* 17, 29 (Louise M. Antony, ed., 2007).

As we will see, the new agnosticism that is the subject of this book is not simply a negative strategy, a method for deferring the questions of religious truth that pose a seemingly insurmountable problem for liberalism in general and liberal theories of religious freedom in particular. It is, instead, a *positive* strategy: a productive, generative, and *empathetic* one.

The new agnosticism is a form of confronting the question of religious truth head-on. It is true that it answers the question by saying, not yes or no, but maybe.[15] But this eternal maybe is a way of viewing the world that continually *confronts* the question of religious truth, rather than seeking to avoid it. Unlike those forms of agnosticism that amount to a belief that the question of religious truth is not important, the new agnosticism sees this question as central to our existence. It shares with William James the view that "so far as man stands for anything and is productive or originative at all, his entire vital function may be said to have to deal with maybes."[16]

In the second part of the argument, our focus broadens. I will show that agnosticism is not just the province of more or less secular philosophers and writers. To the contrary, religion itself has always made room for the kind of questing skepticism and doubt that the new agnosticism demands. Christianity, Buddhism, and many other faiths that are central to our religious tradition are not just places of certainty, let alone dogmatism. They have always incorporated what Stephen White calls *agnosis*, or "a space for unknowing."[17]

An important corollary of religion's history of agnosis, or doubt, is that nothing I say here about agnosticism should be viewed as alien or hostile to faith itself. *Some* atheists and *some* religious believers may share an understanding of religious truth that makes agnosticism seem like a forbidden or unacceptable move. For reasons I explore more fully in Chapter Five, even those thinkers need not reject *constitutional* agnosticism out of hand. For now, however, my point is different: Religious believers, who after all constitute a majority of our population, need not think of agnosticism as falling outside mainstream religious tradition, let alone as anti-religious.

But agnosticism is not just a *possible* strategy for confronting questions of religious truth. It is an eminently attainable one. More than that, the new agnosticism I describe here may be the most natural and attractive approach to

---

15. In thinking about this issue, I am reminded of a story in the humor newspaper *The Onion*, in which God is said to answer the prayers of a dying boy. Unfortunately, his answer is "a resounding no." *See God Answers Prayers of Paralyzed Little Boy: "No," Says God*, The Onion, Dec. 9, 1998, available at www.onion.com/content/node/28812. Like the divine non-intervention in that story, agnosticism can be seen as providing an answer to the question of religious truth, even if it is not necessarily the answer one might have expected or hoped for.

16. *See* James, *supra* note 11.

17. Stephen White, *A Space for Unknowing: The Place of Agnosis in Faith* (2007).

questions of religious truth in our "secular age,"[18] or what I have called our agnostic age: an age whose profusion of belief and non-belief habituates us to see God, and the transcendent, neither as an absolute certainty nor a dead impossibility, but as a constant, vital, living option. In our faiths, in our relationships with others, and especially in the appreciation of nature, art, and the sublime that is our inheritance from the Romantic tradition, we are, in an important sense, all agnostics now. With the poet John Keats, we all live in a state of "negative capability"—of life in and amidst "uncertainties, Mysteries, [and] doubts."[19] Our secular age is, in many respects, an agnostic age.

DEFINING AGNOSTICISM

Our definition of agnosticism begins where this book did: with the fundamental question of religious truth. We can begin by saying that an agnostic is one who is *at least provisionally committed to believing in neither the existence nor the non-existence of God*. Before we add to this definition some of the qualities that distinguish the *new* agnosticism, this basic definition of agnosticism needs to be unpacked a little.

Begin with the nonexistence of God. Here, to be clear, I do not mean God with a capital G, He of the flowing white beard (or, to be fair, She of the flowing white dress, and so on).[20] Nor do I even necessarily mean *a* god, with a lower-case *g*. I am not referring to anything we might think of in more or less anthropomorphic terms. I mean any non-natural, transcendent being or principle that is above, beyond, outside, or interfused with the material world. The gods of the mainstream world religions fall into this category, but so does anything, including Buddhist cosmology, that is not strictly material in the common understanding of the word. The agnostic looks around his world and is not committed to believing that it is *not* all there is.

Why doesn't the agnostic believe? The usual answer—and it's a good one—is that the agnostic thinks there is no convincing evidence in favor of belief. But to this I need to add two important qualifications, which may differ from some forms of agnosticism. T.H. Huxley, along with other nineteenth-century agnostics,

---

18. *See* Charles Taylor, *A Secular Age* (2007).

19. *John Keats: The Poems* 80 (John Blades, ed., 2002).

20. That acknowledgment made, I will generally refer to God as "he," without the capital G—that seems too strong a commitment for a book about agnosticism!—but also without an endless repetition of he, she, it, or they. I trust that readers will remember that my references to God as "he" are not intended to suggest any conclusions about the gender (if any) or number of the deity or deities—or even whether this deity *is* a deity, as opposed to something more encompassing and less rooted in personality, as in some versions of Buddhist spirituality.

insisted that it is wrong to believe anything for which one cannot produce evidence that supports the certainty of that belief.[21] What he meant by evidence, however, was not evidence of *any* kind, but evidence of a logically and empirically verifiable kind. In other words, scientific evidence.[22]

For our purposes, we can speak more broadly than this. The agnostic need not insist on scientifically verifiable evidence for the existence of God. God could be proven scientifically, in a rigorous manner that is capable of confirmation or falsification through experiment. Or he could be proven through some extraordinary experience: a voice thundering from the heavens, "Horwitz, stop dithering and *believe!*" He could even be proven by something more ineffable, such as an experience of the Buddhist sensation of nirvana, a sudden and powerful disintegration of personal identity and a strong sense of the transcendent All. For the kind of agnosticism I am discussing here, belief does not require peer review.[23] Whatever kind of proof the agnostic might accept, however, the point is moot, because none is, as yet, forthcoming.[24]

At the same time, if my agnostic does not demand scientific proof of God, neither is God simply a self-improvement program, like Pilates or jazzercize. The French philosopher and mathematician Blaise Pascal famously argued that we must all wager for or against the existence of God, and that the smart money favors betting on God.[25] One version of this argument asserts that whether or not God exists, faith in his existence can at least, by giving us a moral foothold and a measure of comfort about the life to come, make us better and happier people. Even many people who do not believe in God accept that religious belief may have significant moral or emotional benefits, although they would argue that these benefits can also be found elsewhere.[26]

That may be so, but for our agnostic it is not enough. Agnosticism is a stance in relation to a belief in something *true*, a fact of the matter about the universe. It is not simply a moral guide. An agnostic may agree that religious belief tends

---

21. *See, e.g., The Agnostic Reader* 11 (S.T. Joshi, ed., 2007).

22. *See, e.g.,* Lightman, *supra* note 10, at 15 (describing Huxley's argument for agnosticism as epistemological in nature and restricted to the phenomenal and provable realm of knowledge).

23. *See generally* William P. Alston, *Perceiving God: The Epistemology of Religious Experience* (1991).

24. I stress the words as yet. As I write this, the world is still caught up in the controversy over Tiger Woods's car accident and family troubles. An agnostic who finds himself saying, "Man, I'm glad I'm not Tiger Woods," may have cause to revisit his agnosticism. He may be forced to conclude that any world in which one could be glad *not* to be Tiger Woods is one that cannot possibly operate purely by the laws of logic or nature—and therefore that God not only exists, but has a perverse sense of humor.

25. *See, e.g.,* Jeff Jordan, *Pascal's Wager: Pragmatic Arguments and Belief in God* (2006).

26. *See, e.g.,* Marcia Homak, *An Aristotelian Life,* in *Philosophers Without Gods, supra* note 14, at 133, 134.

to conduce to self-betterment without being persuaded that a religious belief is *true*. A story about Huxley's own life makes this point eloquently. Huxley's son Noel died suddenly in 1860, at the age of four. Huxley's friend, Charles Kingsley, a minister, wrote to comfort him and to offer hope that the event might cause him to turn to God for succor. Huxley responded in a powerful letter thanking Kingsley but rejecting faith as an answer. He wrote:

> What! because I am face to face with irreparable loss, because I have given back to the source from whence it came, the cause of a great happiness, still retaining through all my life the blessings which have sprung and will spring from that cause, I am to renounce my manhood, and, howling, grovel in bestiality? Why, the very apes know better, and if you shoot their young, the poor brutes grieve their grief out and do not immediately seek distraction in a gorge.[27]

The agnostic, in short, is unwilling or unable to believe simply because belief will ease her mind or make her a better person. She seeks the answer to the question whether God exists or not, and is not yet persuaded that he does.

So the agnostic is not committed to religious belief. Neither, however, is she committed to *non-belief*. Unlike the atheist, who is committed to the nonexistence of God, the agnostic has not seen sufficient evidence to convince her that God does *not* exist.

The reasons for this can vary greatly. Some of them are rooted in a deep epistemological and existential skepticism—a skepticism about what we know, how we know it, and what we can *possibly* know. On this question, the agnostic leans toward the view that the existence of God is "beyond the ability of reason to prove or disprove."[28] The agnostic may believe that scientific methods of arriving at knowledge are useful on a day-to-day, practical basis. She may believe that the laws of physics provide a pretty compelling reason why she should not jump out of a moving car, or expect her coffee to remain in her cup if she upends it. But she does not think that science can *prove* the nonexistence of God. Whatever it may explain about the world, it cannot demonstrate conclusively that there is nothing beyond this world. Science has its own magisterium, to use Stephen Jay Gould's term,[29] its own realm of authority. But that realm does not extend to the deep mysteries that surround the possible existence of some transcendent being or principle.

Moreover, as a skeptic, the agnostic may be uncertain whether science itself *is* authoritative. She may believe it has immense practical value, but she is convinced only of its usefulness, of its seeming descriptive accuracy, and not of its abiding correctness as a method of amassing full knowledge of the world.

---

27. *The Major Prose of Thomas Henry Huxley* 360 (Alan P. Barr, ed., 1997).
28. See Levine, *supra* note 14, at 35.
29. *See* Stephen Jay Gould, *Rocks of Ages: Science and Religion in the Fullness of Life* (1999).

She is aware, as John Polanyi pointed out, that there is an irreducible element of faith in science itself: that scientists must operate in a world in which they know that some of their conclusions about how the world works will eventually be "proven" wrong, but cannot know which of those conclusions will suffer that fate.[30] That does not put her in an adversarial position with respect to science, but it does caution her against putting all her eggs in that basket. She believes that "our science is a drop, our ignorance a sea."[31] She is not persuaded, in the final analysis, that science can provide the last word on the nonexistence of God.

Beyond this, there are other reasons why the agnostic is not committed to the nonexistence of God, reasons that have a little to do with knowledge and just as much to do with, if I dare use the world, a sense of *hope*, or at least of *possibility*. One of these is her awareness that many people—countless people throughout history, but just as important, countless people in her own community, people she finds trustworthy—*do* believe in God. The presence of these traditions cannot convince her that they are right. Other traditional beliefs have been proved wrong or cast into serious doubt. Nor does the presence of reliable neighbors who do believe in God convince her that they are right. They may be misguided or deluded. Still, the knowledge that many people do believe in God provides *some* basis for her not to commit to his nonexistence.

She is also, perhaps, alive to a sense of *something* in her life that seems larger than her immediate material surroundings. Perhaps she has experienced awe in the sight of nature, or the birth of a child, or romantic love; perhaps she has experienced a sense of fullness and joy that came on her unawares and left her trembling in its wake; perhaps she has experienced a sense of mystery in the stunning richness of life or the awful suddenness of death. Whatever has moved her, she believes that she has experienced something of the ineffable that is the wellspring of so much religious sentiment in others. That feeling could be nothing more than chemical and electrical activity in her brain, or it could simply be a human reaction to a world that, no matter how beautiful, awful, awesome, or strange, is still all there is. But she is not willing to count this experience out altogether. She does not know the source of the richness and mystery of life, but she is unwilling to chalk it up to simple material causes. She cannot believe, but she cannot *not* believe either.

This, then, is the starting point for the version of agnosticism I am exploring here: The agnostic is provisionally committed to believing in neither the existence nor the nonexistence of God. I say "provisionally" because the agnostic does not assume that her answer counts for all time. She is unable to commit to belief in God's existence or nonexistence right now. But she is unwilling to say

---

30. *See* Alister E. McGrath, *The Twilight of Atheism: The Rise and Fall of Disbelief in the Modern World* 95 (2006).

31. *See* James, *supra* note 11.

with certainty that something might not change. Perhaps scientific advances will shed some more definitive light on the subject; perhaps advances in religious thought will do the same.[32] Or perhaps she will have some experience—a personal communication from God, an overwhelming revelation, or, conversely, a near-death experience that reveals nothing, no bright light at the end of a tunnel or welcoming heavenly choir—that will sway her in one direction or the other. Until then, however, she provisionally cannot commit to either God's existence *or* his nonexistence.

This is the provisional conclusion that the agnostic draws about the central questions of religious truth. So far, most agnostics, and most of agnosticism's critics, will likely agree with my description of what it means to be an agnostic. The next move, however, is to ask: What *stance* does the agnostic, or at least the "new agnostic" I am interested in here, take? What is the *spirit* with which the new agnostic approaches these fundamental questions?

Here, many agnostics, and many critics of agnosticism, might tend to describe agnosticism as a negative or, at best, neutral stance. This view of agnosticism sees it, not as *committed* to a state of neither belief nor non-belief, but as *noncommittal* on the question of religious truth. As Andre Comte-Sponville describes it, the agnostic "check[s] the no opinion box" in the "great metaphysical opinion poll."[33] This view sees agnosticism not as a passionate commitment to and struggling with questions of religious truth, but as a refusal to engage those questions, one that ultimately settles into indifference. Popular views of agnosticism today, Stephen White writes, think of it as "a feeling not only that we cannot know but that there is no point in trying to know."[34] Agnosticism, viewed from this perspective, is "nothing more than a negatively-charged spiritual laziness."[35] We can see, from this perspective, why William James likened the agnostic to a general who tells his soldiers that it is better to avoid battle altogether rather than suffer the risk of a single wound. To this, James offered the powerful rejoinder that "the universe will have no neutrals in these questions."[36]

This kind of indifferentism may accurately describe some forms of agnosticism, but it is emphatically not the agnosticism I am interested in. The new agnosticism is not a negative or disinterested standpoint with respect to questions of religious truth, but one that is deeply engaged and involved in these questions. Even if it is not or cannot be committed to a definitive answer on one side of the line between belief and unbelief, it is still deeply committed to asking

---

32. *See, e.g,* J.L. Schellenberg, *The Wisdom to Doubt: A Justification of Religious Skepticism* 94 (2007).

33. Andrew Comte-Sponville, *The Little Book of Atheist Spirituality* 74 (Nancy Hudson trans., 2008).

34. White, *supra* note 17, at 57.

35. *Id.*

36. James, *supra* note 11, at 25, 88–89.

and exploring these questions. It is a distinctly *positive* approach to the question of religious truth, albeit one that does not finally commit to an answer to that question beyond *maybe*. It is passionately, we might say *religiously*, interested in what, if anything, lies beyond the limits of our seeing. Max Weber described himself as "religiously unmusical."[37] By contrast, our questing agnostic "cultivate[s] [a] musical sensitivity" toward religion.[38]

The stance of this sensitive agnostic is characterized by three features: active interest, openness, and an empathetic, imaginative, and humble perspective. Interest is what distinguishes our agnostic from those who do not believe or disbelieve, but who also don't care. The new agnostic remains deeply involved in the question of religious truth, even if he is unable to cast his lot with one party or the other. He experiences a "wonderment about the world," a wonderment that is "not reflexive but proactive."[39] He has a profound sense of "the limits of our knowledge, of silence, reticence, and awe" in the face of the universe.[40] Far from being indifferent to questions of religious truth, or putting up an agnostic front[41] as a buffer between himself and the ineffable, he sees these questions as "something of inexhaustible beauty and interest, something you could think about and pay attention to constantly and for your whole life without ever finding [them] boring or uninteresting."[42] With Einstein, he believes that "the most beautiful and deepest experience a man can have is the sense of the mysterious," that those who fail to live fully in its thrall are, "if not dead, then blind."[43] His patron saint is not those who write with certainty about God or those who write with certainty *against* his existence, but Søren Kierkegaard, the philosopher of "doubt that yearns to believe."[44]

That the new agnostic is unconvinced of the existence of God does not mean that he is not deeply impressed with the importance of the question; that he may never find an answer to the question does not stop him from asking it. He is alive to doubt but also enlivened by it. He may not believe that God exists, but he understands in his depths that delightful German compound word: to be

---

37. Taylor, *supra* note 18, at 435.

38. J.L. Schellenberg, *The Will to Imagine: A Justification of Skeptical Religion* 156 (2009).

39. Peter Berger & Anton Zijderveld, *In Praise of Doubt: How to Have Convictions Without Becoming a Fanatic* 111 (2009).

40. Karen Armstrong, *The Case for God* xviii (2009).

41. Not to be confused with Agnostic Front, the hardcore band.

42. Anthony Simon Laden, *Transcendence Without God: On Atheism and Invisibility*, in *Philosophers Without Gods*, *supra* note 14, at 121, 123.

43. Jennifer Michael Hecht, *Doubt—A History: The Great Doubters and Their Legacy of Innovation from Socrates and Jesus to Thomas Jefferson and Emily Dickinson* 447 (2004).

44. *Id.* at 399.

Gottbetrunken, "obsessed with a craving for God."[45] He may be too thoroughly agnostic, too caught in equipoise between belief and non-belief, to *crave* God. But he understands what it means to live amidst the inexpressible and inexhaustible mystery of life, and to keep asking questions for which he believes there may be no answers. Like the early agnostics of Victorian England, he may be "unable to believe in any of the old [religious] formularies," but he remains "overwhelmed by the moral seriousness and mystery of life."[46] God may or may not exist, but for the agnostic he never gets old.

With this active interest comes a stance of genuine openness to experience, to a multiplicity of religious and non-religious perspectives, and to the buffeting winds of doubt. In his classic essay, *The Will to Believe*, William James writes that we "stand on a mountain pass in the midst of whirling snow and mist, through which we get glimpses now and then of paths which may be deceptive."[47] Charles Taylor calls James "our great philosopher of the cusp," who describes "what it is like to stand in that open space and feel the winds pulling you now here, now there."[48] Taylor observes that to stand in this "Jamesian open space" requires us to "actually feel some of the force of each opposing position." But he believes that "so far apart are belief and unbelief, openness and closure, that this feat is relatively rare."[49]

I think this stance is more common than Taylor does. In any event, it aptly describes the perspective of the new agnostic. Although poised between belief and unbelief, he is not paralyzed but open, capable of living in what Keats called "negative capability": the ability to remain "capable of being in uncertainties, Mysteries, [and] doubts."[50] He experiences his life in "a spirit of doubt, uncertainty, and openness to new ways of thinking and living."[51] As Taylor writes, he explores meaning, including spiritual meaning, with his "ontological commitments as it were in suspense."[52] In other words, he does not settle on a determined course of belief or unbelief, but he continues to mine these deep existential questions even in the absence or suspension of a settled commitment, occupying a "kind of middle space, neither explicitly believing nor atheistic, but

---

45. A.O.J. Cockshut, *The Unbelievers: English Agnostic Thought 1840–1890* 143 (1964). Cockshut takes the word from Mrs. Humphry Ward's bestselling late nineteenth-century novel of agnosticism, *Robert Ellsmere* (1888).

46. A.N. Wilson, *God's Funeral: The Decline of Faith in Western Civilization* 199 (1999).

47. James, *supra* note 11, at 33.

48. Charles Taylor, *Varieties of Religion Today: William James Revisited* 59 (2002).

49. Taylor, *supra* note 18, at 549.

50. John Keats, *Letters of John Keats* 43 (Robert Gittings ed., 1970).

51. Tina Beattie, *The New Atheists: The Twilight of Reason and the War on Religion* 124 (2008); *see also* Hecht, *supra* note 43, at 472 (quoting Rick Fields' description of doubt as "a state of openness and unknowing" that "allows us to explore things in an open and fresh way").

52. Taylor, *supra* note 18, at 351.

a kind of undefined spirituality."[53] Some might not describe this stance as one of spirituality, but it *is* profoundly spiritual, and I suspect many of the new agnostics I am describing would not balk at the word. The new agnostic aspires to A.N. Wilson's description of Benjamin Jowett, who had the "rather attractive mixture" of being "a person of profound religious feeling and a sceptical cast of mind."[54]

It is sometimes assumed, as Taylor does in describing the Jamesian "open spaces," that this is an unsteady perch. This kind of doubt can be unsettling or agitating. The more committed religious believer or nonbeliever may assume that the agnostic feels the pull of belief and wants to convert his doubts into certainty.[55] But the new agnostic experiences his condition neither as paralyzing nor as compelling him to move toward the certainty of belief or unbelief. To the contrary, it is the very fact that his ontological commitments are suspended that gives him a sense of openness to other perspectives, and the potential value and enrichment that this openness can bring. If, like Kierkegaard, he yearns to believe, he also believes that the yearning is all. He "glorie[s] in the sacredness of uncertainty."[56] As such, he remains ready to learn from any person, text, thing, or experience that can help him to explore belief, unbelief, and the vast open spaces between them. He aspires to a "higher ignorance," a state in which one "acquire[s] the art of seeing the unknown everywhere, especially at the heart of our most emphatic uncertainties."[57]

Openness to doubt and uncertainty leads to the final major characteristic of the new agnostic. He has a capacity for and interest in cultivating an *empathetic* sense of religious belief or non-belief. In his grappling with questions of religious truth, he attempts to cultivate, not so much a neutral view or a "view from nowhere,"[58] but an empty view, one that is pregnant with possibility: an open space from which he can attempt to occupy, as best as he can, the perspectives of others on questions of religious truth.[59] The agnostic may be incapable of or

---

53. *Id.* at 360.

54. Wilson, *supra* note 46, at 120.

55. Schellenberg, *supra* note 32, at 95.

56. Lightman, *supra* note 10, at 30.

57. James P. Carse, *The Religious Case Against Belief* 3 (2008).

58. *See* Thomas Nagel, *The View From Nowhere* (1986).

59. It has been suggested to me, in helpful comments by Elizabeth Emens, that we might draw a parallel between this empathetic and imaginative approach and that of the feminist political philosopher Susan Moller Okin, who argued that we might rethink the famous "veil of ignorance" described by John Rawls in his classic book *A Theory of Justice* in a way that treats it as "a model of empathy—or at least as a model for understanding the world from others' perspectives." Marion Smiley, *Democratic Citizenship v. Patriarchy: A Feminist Perspective on Rawls*, 72 Fordham L. Rev. 1599, 1607 (2004); *see* Susan Moller Okin, *Justice, Gender, and the Family* 89–109 (1989). Under this approach, the veil of ignorance is not so much a view from nowhere, but a space from within, in which we can take turns imagining different perspectives on the world. Whether Okin's reconstruction

unwilling to settle on belief or unbelief, but he wants deeply to know what it *means*, what it *feels like*, to live in a state of belief or unbelief. Again and again, when confronting himself with the ultimate questions of existence, he does not so much inquire what he himself believes, but asks instead what *others* believe from a multitude of perspectives. He is interested in living in "other possible worlds," in leaping the perspectival chasm to "explore those worlds, and try to understand how they look[ ] from the point of view of the people who inhabit[ ] them."[60]

The agnostic's tutor in this enterprise is the Romantic poet John Keats. Keats believed that the most direct and successful route to a deeper truth about the world was not what he called consecutive reasoning, the kind of data-driven analysis that ends up killing what it seeks to understand, like a scientist who takes apart an animal to examine its constituent parts.[61] Instead, the poet "is unobtrusive in character and by negating his own identity capable of entering into the soul of his subject."[62] The poet's imaginative leap, in an "intuitive and immediate" fashion, dissolves the barrier between the poet and his subject "through the momentary identification of the imagination with its object through sympathy."[63] One must, Keats wrote, "make up one's mind about nothing," and "let the mind be a thoroughfare for all thoughts."[64] Keats identified this imaginative capacity most closely with Shakespeare, whose plays succeed not by imposing a grand authorial perspective on their subjects, but by describing fully each character and his innermost thoughts and feelings, so that one comes away convinced that one understands what it means to *be* Othello, or Hamlet, or Rosalind. Shakespeare, for Keats, epitomized what he labeled negative capability, the capacity of "being in uncertainties, Mysteries, [and] doubts."[65]

The agnostic, like Keats's Shakespeare, gets at the truth imaginatively and empathetically, not by keeping his mind perpetually empty but by filling it with an array of possible perspectives, trying on each one and seeing fundamental questions of religious truth now from this viewpoint and now from that one. To be in the midst of uncertainties, mysteries, and doubts does not entail paralysis or inaction, but impersonation. It involves attempting to understand the truth

---

of Rawls is true to his own account is explored in Smiley, *id*. But I agree, without necessarily accepting Rawls or Okin's entire structure, that my empathetic agnostic shares common traits with this position. I am grateful to Professor Emens for pointing me to this literature, although I do little more with it here.

60. Daniel Garber, *Religio Philosophi*, in *Philosophers Without Gods*, *supra* note 14, at 32, 33.

61. Walter Jackson Bate, *Negative Capability: The Intuitive Approach in Keats* 15 (1976).

62. *Id.* at 25.

63. *Id.*

64. *Id.* at 18.

65. Keats, *supra* note 50, at 43.

of the matter not by adopting a single perspective, but by entering into a multitude of perspectives. It is not the passive, negative, permanently suspended stance that many identify with agnosticism, but a highly active and engaged stance, one that accepts "the intensity that lies within the particular and is its truth."[66] "What shocks the virtuous philosopher," Keats writes, "delights the [chameleon] poet."[67]

Keats's concept of negative capability finds a parallel in many depictions of religious doubt, and of the modern human condition—depictions that are close to the imaginative and empathetic new agnosticism I have described here. They all involve efforts to understand the perspectives of others, and to use those perspectives as a means of wrestling with larger questions of religious truth. Tina Beattie writes that "[w]e have no hope of understanding our fellow human beings unless we try to understand those whose views of the world are different from our own."[68] David Bentley Hart argues that it is "bizarre" to believe that one can judge another's experiences "from the outside"; if we want to understand faith, we must "attempt to enter the actual world of belief to weigh its phenomena from within."[69] And Charles Taylor writes eloquently that disengagement can be the wrong way of increasing our understanding of the world and of other human beings. We must be "open to the person or event." We should not seek meaning by "tak[ing] things in through [the] bleached language of social science," but rather "must allow ourselves to be challenged by the ways that new insights fail to fit our recognized range of meanings."[70] We do so by imagining ourselves into different identities and perspectives, asking again and again, "[W]hat would it be like if I were . . .?"[71]

All of these suggestions are second nature for the new agnostic. His suspension of ontological commitments and his cultivation of negative capability are not directed toward the end of maintaining an objective neutrality, but of imagining and occupying a wide range of subjectivities. He asks what it is like to believe, or not believe: how the world looks seen through different lenses of religious or non-religious commitment, what implications each worldview has for one's behavior, how it helps one to grasp the larger questions of religious truth, and how it enables one to experience the ineffable. His world is now enchanted,

---

66. Bate, *supra* note 61, at 66.
67. *Id.* at 31.
68. Beattie, *supra* note 51, at 15.
69. David Bentley Hart, *Atheist Delusions: The Christian Revolution and its Fashionable Enemies* 11 (2009).
70. Taylor, *supra* note 18, at 285.
71. *Id.* at 149. There are links between this approach and what Hans Vaihinger called the "philosophy of as if," although I do not mean to overstate them. *See generally* Hans Vaihinger, *The Philosophy of "As If": A System of the Theoretical, Practical and Religious Fictions of Mankind* (C.K. Ogden, trans., 1949).

now disenchanted; now Christian, now atheist, now Buddhist; now numinous and now dark; now circumscribed by science and now alive with miracle. It is, in a sense, sequentially and simultaneously *all* of these things.

This kind of agnosticism is not simply the act of checking "no opinion" on the "great metaphysical opinion poll."[72] Nor is it a mere waiting room of the mind. It is not an ending but a beginning, a kind of metaphysical Grand Central Station from which the agnostic departs repeatedly to enter into other modes of thinking and seeing, returning to the state of ontological suspension only to venture forth again. From Walt Whitman, the agnostic takes the injunction, "Now voyager sail thou forth to seek and find," even if the "finding" is for him never a final state.[73]

Nor, to be clear, is this sort of imaginative, empathetic spirit simply a synonym for the non-specific spirituality that so often characterizes the modern age: the cafeteria religiosity that picks one item from Christianity, another from Buddhism, and so on.[74] Although this kind of mix-and-match spirituality is often sneered at by writers on religion, the agnostic is less troubled by it—necessarily so, since he cannot, from within his state of suspension of ontological commitment, say that the truth does *not* lie in the middle, that it does *not* partake of a little of all these beliefs. He sees the possibility, even the potential virtue, of this perspective.[75] But, with Keats, he also delights in specificity. In wrestling with questions of religious truth, he wants to know what it feels like to experience the truth through different *particular* perspectives. And so he does not so much borrow from each of his favorites among the vast menu of spiritual options, including non-belief, but rather asks what each of these particular perspectives feels like from within.

To summarize, the stance of the new agnostic is characterized by three main qualities. Her suspension of belief or non-belief is not *indifferent* to questions of religious truth, but deeply and intensely *interested* in exploring them. She is not closed off to religious belief or non-belief, but endlessly open and alive to its possibilities—its doubts, mysteries, and uncertainties. She does not seek to cultivate a neutral viewpoint, but attempts to get at the truth through the imaginative, empathetic adoption of a dizzying array of *different* viewpoints. She is an ardent practitioner of negative capability, a poet of spiritual possibility. She may only be a "visitor" or "voyeur" in these possible worlds and perspectives, but she finds a "visceral pleasure" in visiting them.[76] More than that, she is *sustained* by these visits. If she cannot rest on a single truth, she nevertheless believes that these imaginative leaps help her to understand what the truth looks like, or

---

72. Comte–Sponville, *supra* note 33, at 74.
73. Walt Whitman, *Leaves of Grass* 534 (2006) (1855).
74. *See, e.g.*, Taylor, *supra* note 18, at 513.
75. *See id.*
76. Garber, *supra* note 60, at 34.

might look like, when viewed from multiple perspectives. She is never settled but ever hopeful.[77]

COMPETITORS, CRITICS, AND QUESTIONS

Having set out at some length what the new agnosticism is, it is also important to emphasize what it is *not*. Agnosticism has been subject to many criticisms and assumptions, both about its essential nature and about its very *possibility*. In some cases, those criticisms are almost certainly wrong about agnosticism in general; in most cases, they are definitely wrong about *this* brand of agnosticism. Examining these common misconceptions about agnosticism will help place the new agnosticism in further relief.

Agnosticism as Atheism or Rationalism

Perhaps the most common misconception about agnosticism is that it is simply warmed-over atheism, that the agnostic is simply a disguised rationalist or materialist.[78] Bernard Lightman's history of nineteenth-century English agnosticism observes that many people today are "accustomed to thinking of agnosticism as hostile toward religion and especially Christianity."[79] Many theists, and not a few atheists, have returned the favor by seeing agnosticism as a less straightforward form of atheism. The point is put forward confidently—and wrongly—by David Novak, who manages to enlist both theists (namely, himself) and atheists in making this argument:

> Despite the attempt to create a neutral position called "agnosticism," one can show that agnostics are actually timid atheists, those who have not yet taken moral responsibility for their contrary stance regarding God. Thus I am reminded of the time I asked the president of a leading society of atheists what the difference between an atheist and an agnostic is, and he said "guts."[80]

Similarly, Christine Niles suggests that agnosticism is simply "another word for secularism." Agnostics "may claim that they do not know whether certain religious truth claims are true, but they live as if they know they are not true. . . . The man who says 'I do not know' with his mouth declares with his life the

---

77. *Cf.* Beattie, *supra* note 51, at 171 (describing faith, not as "an answer to life's questions," but as "a willingness to inhabit the darkness of knowing that there are some things we cannot know").

78. *See, e.g.,* 1 *The Encyclopedia of Unbelief* 4 (Gordon Stein, ed., 1985) ("[s]ome say that an agnostic is really a subtype of atheist").

79. Lightman, *supra* note 10, at 16.

80. Novak, *supra* note 12, at 574.

opposite."[81] On this view, "self-styled agnostics [are] actually just polite or perhaps self-deceived atheists."[82]

Niles is right that agnosticism is not simply neutral. But she and other critics of agnosticism are wrong to say that it is simply polite or self-deceiving atheism, secularism, or rationalism. Agnosticism declares atheism neither true nor untrue. In contrast with atheism, it "requires only the Scottish verdict on the status of God's existence: not proved."[83] Although it may be easy to confuse the two, there is a world of difference between believing that the right answer to a question is to be neutral, and simply holding the answer in abeyance. The agnostic may be unable or unwilling to commit to a final answer on the question of God's existence or nonexistence, but he is *not* neutral on the question, if by neutral we mean indifferent. Rather, he is passionately interested in exploring the question. He believes there *is* an answer, although he is not certain that he can know what the answer is at present.

Nor are the charges of moral abdication, or a lack of guts, that critics like Novak and Niles hurl at agnostics accurate. A Scottish juror (not that I have spoken to any lately) who renders a verdict of "not proved" is not blinking her moral responsibility. She is making a morally serious judgment that the evidence she possesses does not point convincingly in one direction or the other. She does so with a full sense of her moral responsibility for that conclusion. Since the agnostic holds herself accountable for her judgment, and knows that she may be made to answer for it in some higher realm, or right here on earth by both theists and atheists, "guts" have nothing to do with it.

It is also untrue that agnosticism necessarily involves acting as if God does not exist. Although this is surely true of some agnostics, it fails to recognize the particular nature of the empathetic and engaged agnostic who is the subject of this chapter. An agnostic, particularly one who believes that the evidence strongly favors the nonexistence of God, may indeed choose to live as if there is no God despite holding out some doubt on the final answer to this question. But she may also decide to live as though God *does* exist—whether by orienting her moral compass around religious teachings, engaging in religious practices, or in some other way—even if she is unwilling to commit absolutely to God's existence.[84]

---

81. Christine L. Niles, Note, *Epistemological Nonsense? The Secular/Religious Distinction*, 17 Notre Dame J.L. Ethics & Pub. Pol'y 561, 574 (2003).

82. Steven D. Smith, *Our Agnostic Constitution*, 83 N.Y.U. L. Rev. 120, 131 (2008) (setting out this claim but disagreeing with it).

83. Rob Atkinson, *Connecting Business Ethics and Legal Ethics for the Common Good: Come, Let Us Reason Together*, 29 J. Corp. L. 469, 530 (2004).

84. *See* Smith, *supra* note 82, at 135 ("On the operational level of belief-informed conduct, the agnostic might decide to live as if God does exist. She might go to church, pray, and participate in sacraments. . . . Even so, on a more purely cognitive level, she might confess complete uncertainty about whether or not God exists.").

As the agnostic philosopher Anthony Kenny writes, "Being agnostic does not mean that one cannot pray. In itself, prayer to a God about whose existence one is doubtful is no more irrational than crying out for help in an emergency without knowing whether there is anyone within earshot."[85]

More than that, however, the imaginative and empathetic agnostic may live both as if God does exist *and* as if he does not. In attempting to enter into the believing and non-believing perspectives of others, she may experience a variety of responses to the world, some decidedly secular and some distinctly religious. At the very least, she may often experience a sense of awe and stillness in the face of what she considers life's unanswerable mysteries that is hard to distinguish from a sense of religious awe. It may be a partial, inconsistent, and temporary form of religious experience, but it is still unmistakably religious.

In short, both those theists and those atheists who want to add agnostics to the ranks of nonbelievers, or who believe that agnostics are simply secularists or rationalists, are wrong. The new agnostic may on occasion *long* to be an atheist (or, equally, yearn to believe in God), but she is not committed to the nonexistence of God.

Agnosticism as Pyrrhonism

Agnosticism can also easily be misidentified with the ancient Greek philosophy of Pyrrhonism. Pyrrhonism's founder is said to be Pyrrho of Ellis, who lived in the fourth or third century B.C., but it is typically more closely identified with the second century B.C. philosopher Sextus Empiricus. Pyrrhonism is one of the earliest forms of skeptical philosophy. It shares with many forms of agnosticism the view that competing truth-claims are exceedingly hard to come by, and that the best response to this is simply to suspend one's judgment on questions of truth. The Pyrrhonist met every claim with a counterclaim, every proposition with a competing proposition, until no side of the argument could enjoy the final advantage.[86]

In many respects, this is close to the conclusion that many agnostics might draw on fundamental questions of religious truth. But our new agnostic is not simply a thorough-going Pyrrhonian skeptic, doomed to be caught forever betwixt and between. For one thing, the agnostic's unwillingness to commit to a particular truth-claim on the question of God's existence or nonexistence is only a *provisional* one. In principle, if not in practice, she believes that a final answer to these questions exists. Although she may find herself suspending her own conclusions for her entire life, she never suspends her search for the truth.

---

85. Anthony Kenny, *What I Believe* 64 (2006).

86. *See, e.g.,* Leo Groarke, *Ancient Skepticism,* in *Stanford Encyclopedia of Philosophy,* available at http://plato.stanford.edu/entries/skepticism-ancient.

Another important difference between agnosticism and Pyrrhonism is the attitude that each takes toward what Taylor calls the suspension of ontological commitments. For the Pyrrhonists, balancing doubt against doubt served as the "basis for a life of exceptional equanimity and contentment."[87] The Pyrrhonists sought a "condition of stable suspense of judgment in the interest of peace of mind."[88] This led them to turn *away* from the search for truth, and to find stability and tranquility instead in their suspended condition.[89] They wanted to achieve happiness by "stand[ing] aloof from life" and its mysteries.[90]

The new agnostic, by contrast, seeks *fulfillment*, not contentment, and she does so in the act of searching for the truth rather than calling off the search. Although she finds a sense of richness and meaning in that search, and in her imaginative efforts to see these questions from a multitude of points of view, it is unlikely that this could rightly be called equanimity. It would be more accurate to say that she finds meaning *in* doubt, and specifically in her attempts to address this doubt through different religious and non-religious perspectives, than that she finds contentment by ceasing either to doubt or believe, and instead treating skepticism as a final resting-place.

One final difference between agnosticism and Pyrrhonism, although it is a more controversial one, is the *scope* of the questions that are subject to the suspension of ontological commitment. Pyrronhism's skeptical gaze encompassed everything. Under its doubting lens, *any* proposition, from the deepest questions of religious truth to the most banal observations—that I am sitting at a table, that the table has four legs, and so on—was open to question. As such, Pyrronhism was as fatal to beliefs about even plain natural phenomena as it was to beliefs about headier matters such as the existence of God. This was not the case for the early English agnostics, whose views still influence modern agnosticism. Their skepticism centered only on the transcendental realm, not on the realm of observable empirical fact. Indeed, if they placed their faith in anything, it was in science. These agnostics "drew on Kant, not Pyrrho."[91]

Whether this position is tenable or not, whether agnosticism can confine itself to the transcendental without casting doubt on the everyday, is a difficult question. I am not certain our agnostic agrees that it *is* possible to make this distinction. For now, however, we can simply conclude that there are important differences between agnosticism and Pyrrhonism, of which one may be the

---

87. *Id.*

88. Gideon Rosen, *Problems in the History of Fictionalism*, in *Fictionalism in Metaphysics* 14, 19 (Mark Eli Kalderon ed., 2005).

89. *See, e.g.*, Hecht, *supra* note 43, at 41; Schellenberg, *supra* note 32, at xi (observing that the Pyrrhonists "were inclined to turn away from inquiry altogether").

90. Hecht, *supra* note 43, at 41.

91. Lightman, *supra* note 10, at 19.

distinction between all-encompassing doubt and doubt only about the existence or nonexistence of God.

Agnosticism as Passivity

Another charge against agnosticism is that it is passive. We see this in David Novak's repetition of the witticism from the head of a "leading society of atheists" that the difference between agnostics and atheists is "guts."[92] Apart from demonstrating that atheist societies are places where senses of humor go to die, this is false, at least for the new agnostic. Agnosticism is not a respite from the search for truth. It is an active and engaged approach to the fundamental questions of religious truth, one that "lives with and in doubt that is troubled by faith."[93] It may be wrong, or jejune, but it is not passive.

Agnosticism as Timidity, and *The Will to Believe*

A related charge is that, whether the agnostic is passive or not, he is timid. He is like a gambler seated at the betting table who is asked to make Pascal's wager, and simply refuses to bet. He may think he loses nothing, but neither does he gain anything. Moreover, the argument goes, because the question of God's existence is a "forced option,"[94] one that does not simply "consist of abstract or detached propositions about which we can suspend judgment," but instead "offers normatively and existentially laden propositions" whose consequences demand that we cast our lot *now*,[95] the agnostic is wrong to think he risks or loses nothing by not wagering. In fact, he stands to lose everything. Atheists and theists alike see themselves as lions in the metaphysical wilderness, and agnostics as lambs.

From the atheist side, we can see this spirit in Joseph Levine's dismissal of agnosticism as a "great cop-out,"[96] or Andre Comte-Sponville's rather condescending description (he *is* French) of agnostics as simply leaving the question of God's existence "up in the air" rather than settling it once and for all.[97] It is also implied by atheists' perception of themselves as trading "the security and comfort of religion" for "a hard logical look at the universe."[98] The atheist scientist Steven Weinberg exemplifies this trait. "Living without God isn't easy," he says. "But its very difficulty offers one other consolation—that there is a certain honor, or perhaps just a grim satisfaction, in facing up to our condition without

---

92. Novak, *supra* note 12, at 574.
93. Berger & Zijderveld, *supra* note 39, at 109.
94. James, *supra* note 11, at 21.
95. Smith, *supra* note 82, at 132.
96. Levine, *supra* note 14, at 29.
97. Comte-Sponville, *supra* note 33, at 69.
98. Stewart Shapiro, *Faith and Reason, the Perpetual War: Ruminations of a Fool*, in *Philosophers Without Gods*, *supra* note 14, at 3, 16.

despair and without wishful thinking."[99] Atheists, Charles Taylor writes, see in "scientific materialism" not so much a sense of its "cogency" as of its "epistemo-logical and ethical stance"—one of "maturity, courage, manliness," one that is "ready to face unvarnished reality."[100] Atheists positively *preen* about their own courage. For some atheists, their contempt for theism carries a whiff of admira-tion: At least theists take a stand, even if it's the wrong one. On this view, agnostics are neither as brave as the atheists nor as forthright as the theists.

The same sentiment can be found in the writing of theists. The strongest expression of this criticism, however, comes not from a theist, but from what we might call a would-be believer. William James's essay *The Will to Believe* was written in response to the arguments of some of the most prominent agnostics of the Victorian age, including T.H. Huxley, who coined the term. James's fierce criticism of that early generation of agnostics is still powerful, and deserves some attention.

The target of James's ire was the insistence of some agnostics, especially William Clifford, that "it is wrong always, everywhere, and for anyone, to believe anything upon insufficient evidence."[101] For James, this position was too intolerant.[102] It was symptomatic of the early agnostics' fascination with science and scientific and logical methods of proof, which became a sort of agnostic dogma.[103] By insisting that a question could only be settled by scientific and materialist methods, the agnostics "imposed scientific values" on the realm of religious concerns.[104] The agnostics, James argued, were free to choose to sus-pend their judgment in light of what they thought of the available evidence; but they should not dictate this choice to the rest of us.[105]

In saying so, James was not opposed to scientific methods of proof. He thought they were important and accepted their "relative objectivity," although he believed agnostics placed too much faith in them.[106] The problem was that agnostics misunderstood the nature of the choice between belief and non-belief, and failed to understand that refusing to place a bet is the same thing as betting, and perhaps worse. For one thing, James believed the choice between

---

99. Steven Weinberg, *Without God*, N.Y. Rev. Books, Sept. 25, 2008.

100. Taylor, *supra* note 18, at 365.

101. 2 William Kingdon Clifford, *The Ethics of Belief*, in *Lectures and Essays* 177 (1879), reprinted in *Philosophy of Religion: Selected Readings* 65, 70 (Michael Peterson et al. eds., 1996). Huxley and other nineteenth-century agnostics spoke in similar terms. *See* James, *supra* note 11, at 77; Joshi, *supra* note 21, at 25; Noel Annan, *Leslie Stephen: The Godless Victorian* 234–35 (1984).

102. *See, e.g., Introduction*, in James, *supra* note 11, at xv.

103. *See, e.g.*, Lightman, *supra* note 10, at 146–47; James C. Turner, *Without God, Without Creed: The Origins of Unbelief in America* 190 (1986).

104. *Introduction*, in James, *supra* note 11, at xv.

105. *See id.*

106. *Id.* at xx.

belief and non-belief was a "forced option," one in which the stakes were so high that one could not simply defer making a choice—as one may, say, suspend a final conclusion about the truth of quantum mechanics without suffering any personal disadvantage. For another, he believed the choice was a "live" option: The hypothesis that God exists (or doesn't) is a real possibility, one that demands a decision.[107] Because the agnostics placed such supreme faith in the scientific method, their suspension of judgment was a false choice, because "the religious hypothesis wasn't a live one for them."[108] Their agnosticism thus flew under false colors; it "was not only equivalent to atheism in practice but was a thinly disguised variant of it."[109] Against this, James argued for the "will to believe," a phrase he later said should really have meant the "right to believe."[110] Nothing, he said, rightly prevented someone from making a considered choice to believe in the existence of God or the transcendent.

All of this led James to accuse the agnostics of timidity. His language is characteristic of the post-Civil War thought of a number of American figures, including his friend, the future Supreme Court Justice Oliver Wendell Holmes, Jr.[111] It is infused with a sense that manliness and honor consist in the willingness to risk one's all on the great struggles of life and on the uncertain bet that those struggles have meaning, a demand for courage, and a contempt for those who remain in the rear and avoid the battle.[112] The agnostics, James wrote, believe that through the scientific method "they shall escape all danger in regard to truth." But neither that method nor any other provides a certain guide "by which men can steer between the dangers of believing too little or too much. To face such dangers is our duty and to hit the right channel between them is the measure of our wisdom." Picking up the martial theme that runs through the essay, James continues, "It doesn't follow because recklessness may be a vice in soldiers that courage ought never to be preached to them."[113] And later: "Clifford is like a general telling his soldiers it's better to keep out of battle forever than to risk a single wound. Not so are victories gained."[114]

---

107. See James, supra note 11, at 14.

108. Introduction, in James, supra note 11, at xv.

109. Id.; see also id. at 21 ("When the Cliffords tell us how sinful it is to be Christians on insufficient evidence, insufficiency is the last thing they have in mind. They already think the evidence is sufficient in the other direction. Christianity is a dead option for them.").

110. Id. at xxii.

111. See generally Louis Menand, The Metaphysical Club: A Story of Ideas in America (2002); Edmund Wilson, Patriotic Gore: Studies in the Literature of the American Civil War (1962).

112. See also Walter Kaufmann, Critique of Religion and Philosophy 116 (paperback ed. 1978) ("James makes a virtue of wishful thinking: courage, to be specific.").

113. James, supra note 11, at 7.

114. Id. at 25.

For James, this timid approach neglected two vital considerations. First, it failed to account for the "passional" nature of mankind: the emotions and passions that drive us to make one choice or another, to stand by one belief or another, including the belief in the scientific method. The agnostics failed to see that *every* choice, including the decision to rely on scientific materialism, unavoidably involves the human play of passions, and thus failed to see that they were operating from an emotional perspective, not an Olympian remove. "Pretend what we will," James wrote, "the whole man is at work within us when we form philosophical opinions, including passions."[115]

Second, the agnostics' timidity led them to miss the forced nature of the bet they faced, and its grand stakes. James wrote, "Believe truth! Shun error! These are two different laws, and by choosing between them we end by coloring differently our intellectual life."[116] The agnostics did not see that rather than searching for truth, they were actually attempting to avoid error. By being "willing to keep [his] mind in suspense forever rather than incur the awful risk of believing something false," the agnostic was blind to the possibility that "the risk of error is small compared with the blessings of real knowledge," that one might "be ready to be duped many times rather than postpone indefinitely the chance of guessing true."[117] The agnostic, like a coward in war,[118] prefers not fighting to either winning big or losing big.

This view was wrong, James argued. The agnostic did not truly avoid the option that faced him. Rather, by shying away from being wrong, he chose the "option of a certain kind of risk," the view that says, "better the risk of loss of truth than chance of error."[119] In thinking that he is refusing to choose, the agnostic "is actively playing his stake just as much as the believer is, backing the field against the religious hypothesis."[120] Even if the agnostic cannot be said to bet *against* the religious hypothesis, his bet is still on the table, and he stands to lose as much as the person who *does* bet against it. He risks not only being *wrong*, but all the goods that might come with being *right*: spiritual gain, fulfillment, heavenly reward, and so on. "In the total game of life," James wrote, "we stake our persons all the while."[121]

Thus, in James's view, to say that belief on insufficient evidence was immoral not only neglected the "passional" nature of *every* important choice that confronts

---

115. *Id.* at 77.

116. *Id.* at 24.

117. *Id.*

118. A theme that certainly ran through the literature of the Civil War, including much of Holmes' writing and much of the literary fiction that came out of that war. *See, e.g.,* Stephen Crane, *The Red Badge of Courage* (1895).

119. James, *supra* note 11, at 30.

120. *Id.*

121. *Id.* at 78.

us, but failed to understand that deferral was not a real option. "We stand on a mountain pass," he wrote, with the grim sense of life's terrible stakes that characterized the era, "in the midst of swirling snow and mist through which we get glimpses now and then of paths which may be deceptive. If we stand still we will freeze to death. If we take the wrong road we may be dashed to pieces. *We must still act.*"[122] The acting is all: the only choice we have, if we are to stand for anything at all, is to wreak ourselves on a world of "maybes."[123] "He who commands himself not to be credulous of God may be no different from he who dogmatically denies him," James wrote. "The universe will have no neutrals in these questions. We are doing volunteer service for one side or the other."[124]

The Will to Believe is a justly celebrated essay.[125] James scored many points on his generation of agnostics. Charles Taylor aptly calls him "our great philosopher of the cusp."[126] James shows us what it means to stand in the lonely open spaces, at the center of some wind-blown Arctic wilderness, confronting choice on all sides. And he shows us that there can be no absolute deferral of that choice—that to choose nothing is a choice in and of itself, one that carries all the risks of opting for or against belief. James may ultimately be arguing only that one is not *required* to be agnostic.[127] But a strong current runs through his work of seeing choice as, if not necessary, then at least the fullest expression of courage, and the deferral of choice as the act of someone whose blood has ceased to course through his veins. Although it is in some sense written from an agnostic perspective that does not *insist* on belief, *The Will to Believe* can also be read as a strong statement of the theist accusation that agnostics are ultimately timid creatures.

James's essay is worth such sustained attention not only because it so eloquently expresses the criticism that many theists and atheists alike have raised about agnosticism's timidity, but because it warns the agnostic against tempting but erroneous paths. It counsels against the dogmatic faith in science that characterized Huxley and Clifford; it lays bare the "passional" nature that drives and guides each of our possible steps out of the dilemma of religious truth; and it reminds us that every choice, including the decision not to choose, has its costs. Even in an age that carries less of the emphasis on courage and manliness that characterized James's own time, there is still something bracing about this work.

---

122. *Id.* at 33 (emphasis added).

123. *Id.* at 53.

124. *Id.* at 88–89.

125. For discussions of James's essay, see, *e.g.*, Taylor, *supra* note 48; Jeffrey Jordan, *Pascal's Wagers and James's Will to Believe*, in *The Oxford Handbook of Philosophy of Religion* 168 (William J. Wainwright, ed., 2005); James C.S. Wernham, *James's Will-to-Believe Doctrine: A Heretical View* (1987).

126. Taylor, *supra* note 48, at 59.

127. *See id.* at 58.

It has lost very little of its power. Indeed, James may speak even more clearly to our present age than he did to his own.

Are James's volleys well aimed at the kind of *new* agnostic we have in mind, however? I think not. To the contrary, in many respects James might find a kindred spirit in the kind of engaged, open, empathetic agnosticism that is the subject of this chapter.

To begin with, if he is committed to nothing else, the new agnostic is certainly committed to the passionate nature of his belief system. James criticizes the agnostics of his day because they fail to recognize that one cannot keep one's passions out of one's commitments.[128] Far from denying this, the new agnostic practices what we might call a distinctly "passional" form of agnosticism. The role of passion and emotion play out in the new agnostic's life in two ways. First, unlike the agnostic described (or caricatured) by James, he is well aware of the role that passion plays in his life. Indeed, for our agnostic, passion provides another reason *not* to commit to either belief or non-belief in the existence of God. This agnostic is aware that passion is an inextricable aspect of *every* choice, that none of us are pure, logic-driven Vulcans. That gives him reason to hesitate before signing on whole-heartedly to either a position of belief or one of non-belief. He knows that *either* position may be distorted by the play of passions and emotion, that *both* of them involve an emotionally driven faith commitment, either to the presence of the transcendent or to purely materialistic rules of evidence.

At the same time, and somewhat contrary to James's vision, our agnostic experiences agnosticism *itself* as a passional standpoint. The universe may have no neutrals on questions of religious truth, but the new agnostic's stance of unwillingness to commit to a final answer is very different from an attempt to reach a state of neutrality or a "view from nowhere." Rather, she is strongly engaged in exploring questions of religious truth, not from a neutral perspective but from a welter of different faith perspectives or positions of non-belief. In making the imaginative leap into these perspectives that negative capability calls for, she *commits* herself, on a deep if temporary and provisional level, to those perspectives.

It is true that she does so in a complicated way. As Steven Smith observes, the agnostic's "mental life is complex, operating on more than one level."[129] On one level, James is right to describe the agnostic as suspended in doubt. On other levels, however, her life is not suspended at all, but deeply, imaginatively committed to exploring questions of religious truth from an engaged perspective. At times, she may "live[ ] as if she believes there is no God,"[130] not because she finally *does* believe this, but because she is, so to speak, trying on this perspective

---

128. *See id.* at 50–51.
129. Smith, *supra* note 82, at 134.
130. *Id.*

for size, attempting to enter into it as fully as possible and imagine what life looks like under conditions of non-belief. At other times, she "might decide to live as if God does exist,"[131] exploring that perspective just as fully and with a sort of Keatsian absence of self, a spirit that "is unobtrusive in character and by negating [her] own identity capable of entering into the soul of [her] subject."[132] Given the layered nature of the human mind, she may, in fact, occupy these and other perspectives not just serially but *at the same time*. But the point of the imaginative leap, the essence of the poet's—and the new agnostic's—stance of negative capability, is that one should live these commitments, however provisionally, as if they are *one's own deepest commitments*.

Our agnostic's perspective suggests that there are very different ways to view agnosticism than James himself (or theists who share something of his perspective) does. With a little work, it is easy to imagine a passional agnosticism. James is thus wrong to equate agnosticism absolutely and necessarily with the kind of timidity and unwillingness to stake one's all that he scorned in early agnostics like Clifford and Huxley. Our agnostic is not someone who is unwilling to bet on life and its mysteries. To the contrary, like a compulsive gambler, she cannot tear herself away from the table. It is true that she does not make a final, all-in bet. But she views the activity of throwing herself into the fray again and again, now from this perspective and now from that, as one of the central aspects of her life and her identity. To pursue James's military analogy, far from being a rear-guard coward, she is a jack-of-all-trades, fighting the "battle" with religious truth in different ways and with different weapons. Now she is a general, now a private; sometimes she fights from the heights and sometimes from the thick of the field; sometimes, perhaps, she fights for the other side, so to speak. But one thing she is *not* is a coward. She may dismay the generals, whether atheist or theist, who want her in a fixed position throughout the battle. But she is still decidedly a combatant.

At the same time, the new agnostic is fully aware that her stance of refusal to make a final commitment to belief or non-belief *is* a stance, and one that carries potential costs. She knows intimately what it means to stand in the mountain pass, buffeted by the winds coming from all directions, venturing out along different paths, any of which may lead to disastrous error. Like James, she may well believe that truth demands risk, that belief demands that you meet it halfway; in a sense, this is one of the purposes of her empathetic leap into different religious and non-religious perspectives. But she is also aware that by failing to commit fully and finally to one belief or another, she may end up stranded, even damned. She knows this, even if her view of the equipoise of the evidence surrounding

---

131. *Id.* at 135.
132. Bate, *supra* note 61, at 25.

the mysteries of religious truth ultimately compels her *not* to make a final commitment.

And she accepts the potential consequences of her viewpoint. She knows that she may be only "a passionately interested observer" of other people's faith or lack of faith, "not a genuine participant,"[133] and that this outsider's status may prevent her from experiencing fully those perspectives, or carry serious consequences if it turns out that the Eternal does demand an absolute commitment. As passionate as her involvement in the questions of religious truth may be, and as hard as she may try to live fully each of the experiences into which she makes the imaginative leap, she takes James's point that the universe may in the final analysis demand more. But she is willing to pay the price for her suspension of ontological commitment. Thus, there is nothing cowardly, timid, half-hearted, or neutral about a "passional" agnosticism. James may have been right about the agnostics he was describing,[134] but the new agnostic has learned a few things since then.

Agnosticism as Impossible

The last objection to the kind of agnosticism I am describing is in some ways the most powerful. This objection is that agnosticism of the kind we have seen here is at best difficult to achieve, and at worst simply impossible. It is impossible in two important senses. First, it is not possible to truly enter into anyone else's perspective, especially a religious belief and especially without a strong faith commitment. Second, the agnostic position, if taken seriously, requires such thorough-going skepticism about *everything* that the agnostic is caught in an infinite regress of doubt and is doomed either to spend the rest of his life in a state of paralysis, watching television on the couch and eating Ring-Dings while waiting to make up his mind (which doesn't sound *so* bad), or to just implode, like a robot on *Star Trek* that has been caught up in some logical contradiction by Captain Kirk (which *does* sound bad).

Neither form of this objection is fatal as a practical matter. The first form of the objection—that it is impossible to enter into anyone else's perspective—may simply be wrong, or at least wrong enough for the agnostic to get by. The second form of the objection—that skepticism about God's existence or nonexistence must eventually become a viral skepticism about *everything*—probably is not worrisome on a day-to-day basis. On a conceptual level, however, it is a far more powerful objection. To see this, we must explore both forms of what I will call the impossibility objection.

---

133. Garber, *supra* note 60, at 34, 40.

134. Although even this is open to debate. *See Introduction*, in James, *supra* note 11, at xxi (arguing that James failed to accurately describe the "volitional commitments" of the "strong agnostic").

The first form of the impossibility objection has to do with the difficulty or impossibility of genuinely entering into the perspective of another of some religious believer or nonbeliever. It says, more or less, that negative capability, as Keats described it, is bunk. "We live, as we dream, alone," Joseph Conrad wrote.[135] Or, to quote the film *Miller's Crossing*, "Nobody knows anybody. Not that well."[136] The individual is "imprisoned in her subjectivity, and there appears to be no exit."[137] Even Shakespeare, Keats's model of negative capability, had to imagine his characters in order to create them, and they were ultimately only multifaceted reflections of Shakespeare himself. Any historical figures on whom those characters were based had a real inner life that was beyond his capacity to imagine in all its richness: the real Henry V was necessarily more complex than *Henry V*. We are who we are, and we cannot know what is like to be someone else and to believe as they do.

On this view, the agnostic who strives to enter imaginatively into other people's perspectives is well meaning but deluded. Whatever he *thinks* he is experiencing, it remains inescapably his own perspective and not someone else's. At best, he may arrive at a pale shadow of what it feels like to believe (or not believe) as someone else might; at worst, the whole thing is a fantasy. One can no more imagine what it is like to be someone else, with all the physical, emotional, and biographical experiences that go into that mix, than one can imagine what it is like to be a bat.[138]

This criticism may be particularly powerful from a religious perspective, one in which an intimate knowledge of God requires a commitment of faith that in turn alters one's view of every experience. A religious believer might well say that trying to "imagine" what it is like to believe in God is as hopeless as a blind man trying to imagine a rainbow. A life charged by religious revelation is one that is so different from one without it that no imaginative leap to that state is possible. Even a life of faith, untouched by revelation, requires and acts on the whole self, and cannot be the subject of a momentary and provisional effort to "enter" this perspective. You're either in or out.

The new agnostic cannot say that this criticism is wrong; he cannot say that he *can* enter perfectly into the perspective of a particular faith commitment or that of a nonbeliever. On a practical level, he is aware of how difficult it is to fully inhabit another self or to see life through someone else's eyes. But he thinks— and for good reasons, which we will explore more fully below—that he may be able to make an imaginative leap that is, shall we say, good enough for government work. We may each ultimately be imprisoned within our subjectivity, but

---

135. Joseph Conrad, *Heart of Darkness* 30 (2005) (1902).

136. *Miller's Crossing* (20th Century Fox 1990).

137. Drucilla Cornell, *Toward a Modern/Postmodern Reconstruction of Ethics*, 133 U. Pa. L. Rev. 291, 301 (1985).

138. *See* Thomas Nagel, *What is it Like to Be a Bat?* 83 Philosophical Rev. 435 (1974).

the bars are neither so high nor so strong that we cannot, through imagination, share *something* of what it is like to be someone else and to think as that person does. If we cannot plumb those depths completely, if we are merely visitors in other possible worlds, we can still experience at least a sense of the ways in which other people live and think. Our condition may be inescapably subjective, but it is also the *shared* human condition, and we are not so alone in experiencing that condition that we cannot appreciate what others go through. Although revelatory experiences *may* be impossible to imagine fully, we can taste something of what it is like to make a faith commitment and to see the world from that perspective.

Moreover, from the agnostic perspective, just as one cannot say that the argument from impossibility is *wrong*, one also cannot say that it is *right*. The agnostic makes no final judgment as to whether God or the transcendent exists or not. He does not *know* that a religious revelation is anything other than a delusion, or a completely human experience of awe and mystery. Nor does he *know* that the world looks any different viewed through the eyes of faith than it does through the eyes of a human being rooted completely in the material world. His suspension of ontological commitment makes it impossible for him to rule out either possibility. In the meantime, he can at least try to imagine, bringing his own sense of the ineffable to the enterprise of what it means to see the world as either invested with divine meaning or simply filled with human sensation, thought, and desire. He certainly ought to bring a strong sense of humility to this imaginative work. In the layered way that is part of the agnostic mindset, he may remind himself with one part of his consciousness that his imaginative leaps may land him nowhere in particular, while yet another part of his mind tries to occupy the space of a believer or nonbeliever as fully as possible. But he does not believe the experiment is doomed from the start.

The second and more powerful form of the impossibility argument is broader. It is not so much about the impossibility of escaping our subjectivity as it is about the corrosive effects of doubt on *all* experiences and beliefs, including our own. This criticism stems from an assault on the nineteenth-century thinkers who helped define and popularize agnosticism. By privileging scientific methods of proof, the charge went, these thinkers were opting for a particular belief system every bit as much as religious believers did. On a practical level, the scientific method appears to have a high cash value; it provides seemingly justified confidence that the earth will not wobble off its axis tomorrow, at least not without a pretty good scientific explanation.[139] Still, scientific methods of knowledge

---

139. We should not overstate this point, however. The scientific method is of recent vintage, and its predictive successes have improved only fairly recently. I would be better off taking instruction from a physician or physicist today than I would have been 50 or 150 years ago. What seems like the strong predictive accuracy that science and the current scientific method enjoy today might look closer to guesswork when viewed from the

are just working hypotheses, subject to revision or complete replacement. There is, Henry Sidgwick observed early on in the history of agnosticism, "no coherent theory of knowledge [on] an empirical basis."[140] Thus, those agnostics, like Clifford and Huxley, who demanded of religious belief a degree of evidential certainty and unassailability that they were unwilling or unable to impose on their scientific beliefs, ultimately "took science on faith."[141]

This is a just criticism, but it is less fairly aimed at the new agnosticism that is the focus of this chapter. Our agnostic knows that she does not know, in a final sense. She does not demand of religious truth that it justify itself according to a specifically scientific or materialist evidentiary standard of proof. She is willing to accept, say, a personal revelation or a one-time supernatural occurrence as convincing evidence. She understands that "justifications must come to an end somewhere, generally in some kind of faith."[142] But she feels the same way about science. She may sign on to it provisionally, but she acknowledges that her confidence in science and logic may not be justified in the final analysis.

That does not make our agnostic a complete skeptic about science and the material world on a day-to-day basis. Her confidence in it may be provisional, but it can be strong at any given moment. In this, she is in no different position from most theists. If anything, it is the *religious believer's* day-to-day faith in the laws of science that is puzzling. Even a theist who believes that the laws of science are part of God's order for the universe[143] generally believes in the possibility of miracles. The universe *could*, at any moment, act in a way that defies scientific law. Yet the religious believer does not walk gingerly along the street for fear of rising off the pavement in temporary violation of the laws of gravity, or mutter "Inshallah" under her breath every time she calculates the rate of speed of falling bodies.[144] That attitude really ought to pose greater questions for theists than it does for agnostics. Our agnostic's faith in science, like her faith in everything else, is provisional, not nonexistent.

---

perspective of a future that is not too far off—say, 500 years from now. The agnostic is well aware of this. *See also* Schellenberg, *supra* note 32, at 25 (discussing the importance of using a broad time horizon when comparing the successes of both religious and scientific arguments).

140. Lightman, *supra* note 10, at 161.

141. *Id.* The same point can be made against atheism itself. *See, e.g.,* McGrath, *supra* note 30, at 180–81.

142. Terry Eagleton, *Reason, Faith, and Revolution: Reflections on the God Debate* 124 (2009).

143. Setting aside deists, like Jefferson, Voltaire, and other figures from the early Enlightenment, who believed that God never interferes with the laws of nature that he set in motion.

144. *See* Richard A. Posner, *The Problematics of Moral and Legal Theory* 62 (1999) ("Virtually no one rejects scientific theory in those areas in which science impinges on everyday life.").

But there is an even deeper form of this version of the impossibility argument. It does not simply attack agnostics for having undue confidence in science. It asks how an agnostic can believe in *anything*. If the agnostic is a skeptic on the question of the existence or nonexistence of God, why doesn't he extend this skepticism "to *all* knowledge?" Once we "listen to the siren song of skepticism, how are we to avoid being drawn into radical doubt?"[145] Why do we not end up in a state of "almost total scepticism about human knowledge?"[146] Why do we not question, say, the occurrence of the Holocaust,[147] or the tangible solidity of the table in front of us? Why is the agnostic not "checking every five minutes to make sure there are no cobras under [her] bed?"[148]

The new agnostic has some provisional answers to this question. The first is to say that there is a difference between maintaining a position of doubt on religious matters and on what we might think of as mundane, everyday matters, like the law of gravity, or whether Namibia or my wife exist. The theologian Paul Tillich famously identified religion with "ultimate concern[s]."[149] So, we could say, the agnostic retains a sense of skepticism about ultimate concerns but not about mundane ones.

This answer works well on a practical level. Whether she recognizes it or not, it is probably the same answer the theist would give when asked why she goes about her day with so little apparent concern for the possibility of intrusively supernatural events. At a deeper level, however, it is much more problematic. From a religious perspective, or from an empathetic agnostic one, there is no clear dividing line between ultimate concerns and everyday ones. The agnostic cannot say that God is only *out there*, that everything is not suffused with his presence in a direct way. Moreover, from the agnostic perspective, the scientific method itself is at bottom a matter of faith, despite its relative predictive success. Although there is practical value in believing in, say, the accuracy of the law of gravity on a day-to-day basis, there is no philosophical foundation for treating that commitment any differently than one's answers to ultimate questions of religious truth. So the agnostic cannot, on this basis, justify the distinction between her doubt with respect to religious questions and her provisional faith with respect to mundane questions.

Another possible answer is, again, an essentially practical one. It argues that, if we are to be "inquirers at all, we must suppose that there is a real world to be

---

145. Schellenberg, *supra* note 32, at xii.

146. P.J. McGrath, *Atheism or Agnosticism*, 47 Analysis 54, 55 (1987).

147. *See* Eagleton, *supra* note 142, at 115 (raising this example by way of arguing that it is "a romantic myth that there is a moral superiority about people who refuse to make up their minds because the evidence is not 100 percent compelling").

148. *Id.* at 124.

149. Paul Tillich, *What Faith Is*, in *The Essential Tillich* 13, 13–15 (F. Forrester Church ed., 1999).

examined and worth examining."[150] If we are not to be stuck on the sofa amid *Gilmore Girls* reruns and old Frito-Lay wrappers, we must reach some kind of accommodation with the "real world." If we are to venture forth at all and ask the questions worth asking about the ultimate state of our universe and ourselves, we must "strike a balance," one that allows us to be "skeptics on the general matters in which religion deals" while still maintaining our grasp on the immediate and tangible.[151] This answer, too, has its attractions, but it ultimately runs into the same questions.

There is another answer, though, one that is more philosophically sophisticated than this pragmatic approach but without sacrificing practical value. It is suggested by the philosophical school of fictionalism, and it should be highly agreeable to the new agnostic we have been discussing in this chapter. On this view, in a sense the agnostic *is* a skeptic all the way down. She may have different confidence levels about different phenomena, remaining fairly certain about the law of gravity or the existence of Namibia, say, but much more ontologically "suspended" on the question of the existence or nonexistence of God or the soul. But in the end, *all* her beliefs are provisional. She does not "believe" mundane claims about existence, "but *accepts* them in some sense."[152] If you were to ask her whether God exists, she might answer, "I don't know," while if you asked her whether Disneyland exists, she would say, "Yes." But if you could shine a magic flashlight on her thoughts, you would find that her answer was closer to, "Yes, as far as I know," or "I am willing to conform my conduct to the assumption that Disneyland exists, but in a deeper sense, I don't know."

Thus, the agnostic, like the fictionalist, places "significant weight on the distinction between acceptance and belief in his account of his own practice[s]."[153] He does so with respect to both mundane *and* ultimate matters, although in different ways. As to mundane matters, he accepts standard material facts as a strong working hypothesis, one so strong that he would not scruple to call them facts even if, with a tiny residual part of his self, he might be said to be crossing his fingers. With respect to transcendent matters, his position is more openly provisional. He does not *believe* in God, or *disbelieve* in God, with the same confidence with which he believes in the first law of thermodynamics or his own physical existence. And, hearkening back to James, he is aware that not doing so is itself a commitment of sorts—that he might be better off betting his all on the existence (or nonexistence) of God, just as he regularly bets his all on the laws of physics. But he finds that it is easier to function in this suspended state when it comes to ultimate matters than when it comes to mundane or material ones.

150. Schellenberg, *supra* note 32, at xii.

151. *Id.*

152. Rosen, *supra* note 88, at 19 (emphasis added).

153. *Id.*

More to the point, he finds he is unable to function any other way when it comes to religious questions.

Still, although the agnostic does not *fully* commit to belief or non-belief where ultimate questions are concerned, neither, as we have seen, does he *never* commit. Rather, he commits a *part* of himself *all the time*, entering imaginatively into a series of commitments to religious belief or non-belief, and ultimately jumping out of those commitments and back to his state of ontological suspension. It is, to be sure, a peripatetic life, and one whose only real constancy lies in its provisional nature. But it is still a form of commitment, different in degree but not entirely in kind from the way the agnostic approaches mundane questions.

So there are several ways to respond to the impossibility argument against agnosticism. Those responses are especially strong on a practical level. It is certainly possible to be agnostic on the larger questions without falling into paralytic doubt about *everything*.[154] Whether that response is philosophically convincing is another matter. It may be that the best answer to this conundrum is the fictionalist one. The agnostic, like most theists, accepts as working hypotheses many things that he may not absolutely believe, although his acceptance of certain mundane matters, like gravity, is closer to genuine belief than his provisional, imaginative, and shifting acceptance of a variety of religious perspectives.

Still, the impossibility objection at least demonstrates that "skepticism is a two-edged weapon" and a "dangerous" one.[155] Once we begin to doubt, it is difficult to know where to stop doubting. This is one reason the modern agnostic, unlike the Huxleyan agnostic, is not so much a thorough-going skeptic as he is a doubter who yearns to believe, one who acknowledges the partial and incomplete nature of his knowledge at every step and turns to the imaginative leap to try to fill that void. He is conscious of Wittgenstein's warning that "[i]f you tried to doubt everything you would not get as far as doubting anything."[156] He may more or less escape this dilemma on a day-to-day basis, but whether he can truly avoid it in the long run and at a deeper level is a question that will haunt not only the new agnostic, but constitutional agnosticism in general—and every other treatment of church–state conflict as well.

---

154. This calls to mind Mark Twain's response to the question whether he believed in infant baptism: "Believe in it? Hell, I've seen it done!" Tom Quirk, *Mark Twain and Human Nature* 1 (2007).

155. Lightman, *supra* note 10, at 9.

156. Ludwig Wittgenstein, *On Certainty* § 115 (G.E.M. Anscombe & G.H. von Wright eds., Denis Paul & G.E.M. Anscombe trans., 1974).

AGNOSTICISM WITHIN RELIGION

Thus far, we have defined a particular brand of agnosticism. It begins with an unwillingness to commit finally to either the existence or nonexistence of God, or what Charles Taylor calls a suspension of ontological commitment. But that doubting stance is not a negative or passive approach to the ultimate questions of religious truth. To the contrary, the new agnostic is actively interested in questions of religious truth. She is open to the possibility that, as they used to say on *The X-Files*, the truth is out there. She is continually journeying amidst possible truths, taking an imaginative, empathetic stance in which she attempts to understand and occupy as best as she can the perspectives of other actual or possible religious believers and nonbelievers and asks what those perspectives tell her about the universe. Like Keats, she is alive to life's mysteries, uncertainties, and doubts, living richly among them by making her mind a thoroughfare for all manner of approaches to these mysteries. She is *in* doubt, but not paralyzed by it.

The agnostic is also aware that she may need to risk her all in order to find the truth, and of the possibility that her commitment to doubt will leave her doubting everything. Nevertheless, she is "willing[ ] to inhabit the darkness of knowing that there are some things we cannot know,"[157] and she finds fulfillment in this stateless mode of existence. Like Rick Blaine in *Casablanca*, she is a citizen of all possible worlds and a permanent resident of none.[158]

Many people today may find this perspective attractive. Others may find it sad, lonely, even disturbing. To be a citizen of all possible worlds may seem to be indistinguishable from belonging in none of them. A stateless state of being is also an unrooted one, without the ultimate sense of community and comfort—even the cold comfort of the ostentatiously "courageous" stance of some atheists—that a more definitive state of religious commitment may bring.

Moreover, from some religious perspectives, agnosticism may seem alien and false. The religious individual may believe that to hold one's ontological commitments in suspense is a direct path to nothingness, and that no imaginative leap, no attempt at negative capability, no matter how heroic and well-intentioned, can fill the need for religion—or at least the *true* religion. He may think that the agnostic who attempts to imagine what life is like from within a religious perspective, but without a final faith commitment, sees nothing but his own delusions, or sees through the glass so darkly that he ultimately lacks the faintest conception of what a true life of faith means. Conversely, the atheist may believe that the agnostic who goes traipsing through various faith perspectives is

---

157. Beattie, *supra* note 51, at 171.

158. *See Casablanca* (Warner Bros. 1942) ("Major Strasser: What is your nationality? Rick: I'm a drunkard. Captain Renault: That makes Rick a citizen of the world.").

engaged in self-delusion, refusing to face the truth directly and taking refuge in a pleasant fiction.

Although I will argue below that these criticisms are overstated, for our purposes they are less important than one might initially assume. This book is, after all, *not* a brief for religious agnosticism itself. As we will see in Chapter Four, this vigorous brand of agnosticism may still be a valuable response to the endless debate between the New Atheists and their antagonists, in which absolute belief or absolute unbelief are treated as the only possible options. Our version of agnosticism may at least convince others that there is room for a middle position, and with it a cooling off of the culture wars. Still, I would be perfectly content if no one walked away from this book as a convert to *religious* agnosticism. Rather, this book is an argument for *constitutional agnosticism*—a strategy for dealing with the flashpoints of church–state relations. This chapter has been necessary because it is impossible to fully appreciate what *constitutional* agnosticism offers without first understanding what *agnosticism*, or at least the new agnosticism, involves. But it is not necessary that anyone ultimately become a religious agnostic to appreciate the merits of constitutional agnosticism.

Nevertheless, there may be some value in reassuring religious readers that agnosticism itself is not foreign or hostile to religious belief itself. That is the goal of this section. I hope to show religious readers that doubt is itself a deep part of religious tradition.

A natural place to start, given our focus on the Western liberal tradition and its expression in the law of the First Amendment, is with Judaism and Christianity. In his valuable study of religious doubt, or what he calls agnosis, Stephen White observes that "[a]gnosis is probably not the first concept which springs to mind when we think of the Jewish understanding of faith and experience of God in the Old Testament."[159] Yet it is there just the same. Alongside the voice of "divinely ordered certainty" which runs through what Jews call the Torah and the other pre-Christian Scriptures, there is "another voice," quieter but "always present as a questioning counter-melody to the headlong rush of the dominant theme,"[160] one that speaks in terms of doubt and hesitation.

Consider the Book of Ecclesiastes, with its constant refrain, "all is vanity"—or, even more strikingly in some translations, "[e]verything is meaningless."[161] "No-one can comprehend," Ecclesiastes writes in language that continues to ring true for our agnostic, "what goes on under the sun. Despite all his efforts to search it out, man cannot discover its meaning. Even if a wise man claims he knows, he cannot really comprehend it."[162] Ecclesiastes offers a believer's perspective, but he makes doubt a central part of religious practice and of one's

---

159. White, *supra* note 17, at 13.
160. *Id.*
161. *Id.* at 17.
162. *Id.* at 18 (quoting Eccl. 8:17).

understanding of the world. He continually grapples with religious truth, and is continually left with an abiding sense of the mystery at the heart of existence.

Perhaps the most famous voice of doubt in the Jewish Scriptures is found in the Book of Job. Job's story is a mystery whose solution is yet another mystery. A good and pious man blessed with earthly joy and success, Job becomes the subject of a bet between God and Satan over whether he would be good even without those blessings. Over the course of the tale, he is stripped of his livelihood, his home, and every last one of his children, and is subjected to intense physical suffering. His wife begs him to "[c]urse God and die," but he refuses.[163] Only when three of his friends come to comfort him, and end up offering him shallow reassurances of God's ultimate justice, has he had enough. *Then* Job speaks out, questioning God's justice and righteousness, and the inexplicable grief of life and death. In effect, Job becomes the spokesman for two of the standard arguments against God. The first is the argument from theodicy, the idea that the existence and persistence of evil and suffering in this world counts as an argument against God altogether, or against a perfectly just and loving God. The second is the argument from divine hiddenness, the idea that a just God would not hide his face from humanity and give it no clear sign of his presence.[164]

As it turns out, God does show up to answer Job's criticisms. But he answers doubt with doubt, questioning Job's knowledge of things that necessarily lie beyond his ken. "Where were you when I laid the foundations of the earth?" he asks Job. "Have the gates of death been opened to you? Where does light come from? And where darkness?"[165] And so on, in a crescendo of questions whose unanswerability cast Job into a state of surrender and humility: "Therefore have I uttered that I understood not; things too wonderful for me, which I knew not."[166]

For many people, religious or not, the Book of Job would be just as powerful if God had been left out of it altogether. Certainly the fact that God does appear to answer Job means that this story, like Ecclesiastes, is ultimately a story of belief. But Job remains one of the richest and most studied books of the Bible, for three reasons. First, it demonstrates that, within the Jewish tradition at least, a rich relationship with God need not be one that accepts him in absolute faith and need not be worshipful; to the contrary, like Abraham and Moses' own relationship with God, Job's relationship with God has a distinctly antagonistic quality. This may ring powerfully not only for those who are steeped in the Jewish tradition, but also for new agnostics, who are less interested in committing to a final

---

163. Job 2:9.
164. *See, e.g., Divine Hiddenness: New Essays* (Daniel Howard-Snyder & Paul Moser eds., 2001); J.L. Schellenberg, *Divine Hiddenness and Human Reason* (1993).
165. Job 38: 4, 17, 19.
166. Job 42:3.

faith perspective and resting comfortably in it than they are in wrestling with questions of religious truth.

Second, as Jack Miles has pointed out, God's answer to Job is also the last time God speaks in the Jewish Scriptures.[167] From this moment on, he becomes a *deus absconditus*, an unknowable or hidden God. "God may seem to silence Job," Jennifer Hecht writes, "but Job silences God."[168] In a sense, this silence suggests that doubt can be so powerful a tool, so compelling a predicament, that God either must answer it by invoking other, still more unanswerable mysteries, or must himself remain silent.

Third, God's silence has not prevented religious believers from entering into an ongoing dialogue with him. This illuminates doubt's role in religious tradition. God's answers to Job's questions have not spared God from being challenged, even by those who believe in him with their whole hearts. This antagonistic, adversarial relationship with God can continue even if we believe in him—and, the agnostic would add, even if we do not believe or are not sure. Both from within and from beyond any particular faith perspective, we can continue poking at what Sartre called the "god-shaped hole in human consciousness," whether we are certain it was ever filled by his presence or not.[169] As the Jewish-German philosopher Margarete Susman wrote, even after God becomes a *deus absconditus*, "[t]he dispute with [him] cannot cease even now." Although God is now silent, "the process against God must take a new shape . . . a version in which God is all silence and man alone speaks. And yet, though His name is never mentioned, only He is addressed."[170] For religious believers as for new agnostics, the debate with God, the endless struggle with questions of ultimate truth, persists in the face of life's mysteries, and need not end even if one is certain of his existence.[171]

This is not, of course, the end of the agnostic tradition within Judaism. It continues in medieval Judaism, in such works as Maimonides' classic *Guide for the Perplexed*.[172] And in many respects, the Jewish relationship with God has become both more doubt-ridden and more intimate and questioning in the wake of the Holocaust, whose immense suffering and loss of life make it the starting point for questions of theodicy across many faith traditions today.

Although God does not speak in the Jewish Scriptures after the book of Job, he not only speaks but is incarnated in the New Testament. So it is

---

167. Jack Miles, *God: A Biography* 329 (1995).

168. Hecht, *supra* note 43, at 73.

169. Armstrong, *supra* note 40, at 287.

170. Hecht, *supra* note 43, at 465.

171. Andre Comte-Sponville remarks, too broadly but with a note of truth, that for Jews, "believing or not believing in God is not the main issue." Comte-Sponville, *supra* note 33, at 35.

172. *See generally* Hecht, *supra* note 43, at 239–50.

understandable that for many Christians, their own faith would seem to be an even more unlikely breeding ground for agnosis.[173] But although Jesus' existence, and his insistence that he was "the way, the truth, and the life,"[174] have placed a premium on belief rather than doubt in mainstream Christian belief,[175] Christian thought has always made a room for a rich and abiding sense of doubt and an unceasing quest for religious truth.[176]

Indeed, Jesus himself, in one of the many paradoxes of incarnation, is wracked with profound—and profoundly human—doubt, despite his knowledge of his own divine nature, his awareness that he is literally his father's son. Among the most wrenching of the final scenes of Jesus' life are his wish, on the eve of his crucifixion, to have his burden pass from him, and his dying words on the cross: "My God, my God, why hast thou forsaken me?"[177] The New Testament, G.K. Chesterton wrote in one of his powerful apologetics for Christianity, "portrays a god who, by being wholly present in the dying cry of Jesus, even doubted and questioned Himself."[178]

One of the most powerful expressions of agnosis within Christian experience, one that echoes across a range of other faiths, is the concept of *kenosis*: emptying out, or self-emptying. It can refer on one level to Jesus' own "laying aside of divine attributes," his forgoing of divine immunity from pain and suffering in order to share the human condition to its bitter end.[179] But it can also refer to an experience shared by many religious individuals, one in which the individual empties himself out, casting aside aspects of self—pride, self-regard, the desire for glory, and a rootedness in the physical—and makes himself receptive to God's spirit and to the mysteries of existence. One lets go of "illusory 'certainties' which are then replaced with a faithful unknowing which places itself more humbly, because of its emptiness, in the hands of God."[180]

The concept of kenosis runs through the history of Christian thought, and especially the rich tradition of Christian mysticism.[181] For Meister Eckhart, kenosis brought its practitioner to the "'silence' and desert' of the intellect," to a place where he could "eliminate the images, concepts, and experiences that [he] used to fill [his] inner emptiness and, as it were, dig out an interior vacuum that would

173. *See* White, *supra* note 17, at 27.

174. John 14:16.

175. *See* White, *supra* note 17, at 42 (arguing that the "marginalizing of agnosis has been, sometimes directly and sometimes indirectly, the cause of (or at least a significant factor in) many of the church's severest problems").

176. *See, e.g.,* Herbert McCabe, *Faith Within Reason* 33–40 (Brian Davies, ed., 2007).

177. Matthew 27: 45–46.

178. David Dark, *The Sacredness of Questioning Everything* 19 (2009).

179. White, *supra* note 17, at 159; *see also* Phil. 2:6.

180. White, *supra* note 17, at 48.

181. *See, e.g., The Essential Writings of Christian Mysticism* (Bernard McGinn, ed., 2006).

draw God into the self."[182] "To be full of things is to be empty of God," he wrote. "To be empty of things is to be full of God."[183] For the anonymous author of *The Cloud of Unknowing*, the believer who asks how he is to think of God, and what God is like, must be told, "I cannot answer you, except to say 'I do not know!'"[184] The would-be believer must instead enter a "cloud of unknowing," a darkness in which there is nothing save "a simple, steadfast intention reaching out towards God."[185] Similarly, the sixteenth-century mystic St. John of the Cross writes of the believer's "dark night of the soul," a state of sensual and spiritual purification that simultaneously casts the believer into a profound sense of silence and abandonment and prepares his cleansed soul to be filled by God.[186] For all of these thinkers, the first step to enlightenment is unknowing: a letting go of beliefs, perceptions, and certainties. Just as the Keatsian poet finds meaning by living in doubts, mysteries, and uncertainties, so the Christian mystic believes "radical unknowing to be the beginning of illumination."[187]

Nor is this sense of doubt unknown to Christianity outside mysticism. A similar approach can be found in the longstanding Christian tradition of negative or apophatic theology, or the "via negativa," in which it is argued that God is ineffable, incapable of being defined or understood by mere humans, so that, as Saint Cyril of Jerusalem said, "[I]n what concerns God[,] to confess our ignorance is the best knowledge."[188] This tradition of uncertainty resurfaced in the same period during which agnosticism itself emerged as a freestanding philosophy. Just as the scientific revolution and the ascendance of Darwinian theory helped trigger agnosticism, the rise of science also triggered a *Christian* response that was rich with doubt. The *Lux Mundi*, an important collection of essays from Anglo-Catholic theologians that appeared toward the end of the nineteenth century, was different from some Christian responses to science and evolution in that it neither sought to frame religion in scientific terms nor denied the claims of science altogether. Instead, it "allow[ed] all manner of previously hallowed

---

182. Armstrong, *supra* note 40, at 155.

183. Meister Eckhart, *About Disinterest*, in *German Mystical Writings* 86 (Karen J. Campbell, ed., 1991).

184. Armstrong, *supra* note 40, at 156, quoting Anonymous, *The Cloud of Unknowing* (Clifton Wolters, trans., 1980).

185. *Id.* at 156.

186. *See* St. John of the Cross, *The Dark Night of The Soul* (2007).

187. White, *supra* note 17, at 48.

188. Cyril, Archbishop of Jerusalem, *Catechetical Homilies* VI § 2, in 7 *Nicene and Ante-Nicene Fathers, Second Series* 33 (Philip Schaff, ed., 1994); *see also* Armstrong, *supra* note 40, at 133 (noting the "apophatic conviction" of St. Anselm "that any idea that human beings could conceive of [concerning] God would inevitably fall short of the reality"). Apothatic theology remains central to Eastern Orthodox Christianity, as opposed to other Christian denominations, which tend to stress cataphatic or positive theology, or the knowableness of God.

certainties to fall away, leaving [the authors] to face, in a genuinely agnostic faith, the discoveries and theories of their own generation."[189]

There is room for doubt even within those religious traditions that, in our own time, have been viewed as especially dogmatic in their approach to faith. Islam provides an excellent example. Although Islam is treated by some New Atheists as the exemplar of how unquestioning religious faith can easily turn to violence,[190] the reality is more complicated. The history of Islam in the early medieval period, during the Islamic empire's long reign in Spain, also saw the rise of skeptical and proto-agnostic theories within Islamic theology and philosophy. Those theories were influenced by the Muslims' reading of the ancient Greek philosophers, whose work was largely unknown in the Christian West in this period, and they both fed and were fed in turn by similar developments in Jewish and Christian philosophy—perhaps unsurprisingly, given the polyglot nature of the Islamic empire during this period.

As with Jewish and Christian skepticism and doubt, this movement was controversial, and its proponents sometimes suffered a terrible price for their doubts. Many members of the eighth-century circle of *zindiq* writers, who publicly doubted the accuracy of some of Muhammad's statements and the tales of his resurrection, were executed.[191] Later figures, however, still occupy a revered, if uneasy, place within the history of Islamic thought. The ninth-century figure Abu Bakr el-Razi, for instance, was called both "the greatest nonconformist in the whole history of Islam" and one who was "frequently denounced and disapproved as a heretic in the subsequent history of Islamic thought," but he was also "beloved" for his services to the community as a doctor.[192] Abu Ali ibn Sina, better known in the West as Avicenna, did not deny the truth of Islam, but found a place alongside it for rationalist philosophy of the kind practiced by Aristotle.[193] Abu Hamid al-Ghazzali, whose skepticism was so deep that it led him to a psychological breakdown, pushed the Islamic strain of doubt "so far that he became not only a doubter in the rationalist tradition but also a doubter in the tradition of the dark night of the soul."[194] Ibn Rushd, or Averroes, as he is known in the West, was led by Aristotle to advance a form of Islam that privileged demonstrable rational proofs and argued that any scripture that plainly contradicted those proofs must be treated as allegory rather than believed as fact.[195]

---

189. White, *supra* note 17, at 51.

190. *See, e.g.,* Sam Harris, *The End of Faith: Religion, Terror, and the Future of Reason* (2005).

191. *See, e.g.,* Hecht, *supra* note 43, at 222–23.

192. *See id.* at 227 (quotations and citations omitted).

193. *See id.* at 230–31.

194. *Id.* at 233.

195. *See id.* at 237–39.

Modern doubters and skeptics continue to operate within the Islamic tradition to this day.[196]

The traces of what White calls agnosis are even stronger in a host of other religious traditions, particularly Eastern religions like Hinduism, Buddhism, and Confucianism. Few doubt that Buddhism is a religious philosophy, and many Buddhist sects expressly believe in a divine being. Nevertheless, Buddhism places doubt and uncertainty at the heart of religious practice, making it difficult for some to categorize it as a religion at all. The Buddha himself, when asked whether there was life after death, said he did not know.[197] The Zen Buddhist tradition "urge[s] keeping oneself in a constant state of unknowing" and "generating an attitude of questioning that is sustained and vivid in its wonder, yet blank and unhopeful in relation to answers" to ultimate religious questions.[198] Like some strains of Christian thought, both Buddhism and the *Upanishads*, one of Hinduism's central texts, emphasize kenosis—emptying one's self and one's conviction in right answers in order to let in a deeper truth. Confucianism, like some forms of Buddhism, is a religion without a distinct belief in what Westerners would call religious truth or certainty. When pressed on those questions, Confucius "tended to be agnostic and dismissive," saying about the question of immortality, "We don't yet know about life, how can we know about death?"[199]

This is a decidedly brief tour. But it demonstrates that doubt, or agnosis, is hardly unknown within religious tradition. The major faiths in religious history have always grappled with questions of doubt at the same time that they emphasized faith and belief. In many cases, their leading figures made doubt a central part of their thought. Even when believing—perhaps *especially* when believing—many of them emphasized that the road to true knowledge must lead first through doubt and the emptying of one's own convictions. Viewed from this perspective, the new agnosticism need not be seen either as alien to the tradition of religious faith or as a threat to it.

OUR AGNOSTIC AGE

But is agnosticism *more* than that? I want to suggest that it is. *Constitutional* agnosticism, I have emphasized, is consistent with religious agnosticism, but not the same as it; one can be a constitutional agnostic without being a religious agnostic. Still, the argument for constitutional agnosticism may be easier to appreciate if we first understand that the new agnosticism, whatever attractions it may or may not hold for the reader, is eminently *possible*. More than that, it is,

---

196. *See id.* at 424–29.
197. *See, e.g.,* Carse, *supra* note 57, at 209.
198. Hecht, *supra* note 43, at 214.
199. *Id.* at 117.

in many respects, simply our modern condition. Despite my words earlier in this chapter, it is too strong a statement to say that we are all agnostics now. But it is much closer to the truth to suggest that, in important ways, many people are more agnostic than they may realize, and that even those who are not have been bequeathed by our culture with the background and the tools to make agnosticism both understandable and, to a large degree, capable of being practiced and experienced.

That this is true, and *why* it is true, has to do with a confluence of influences that have combined to make the agnostic spirit the spirit of our age. That story is too complex to do justice here.[200] For our purposes, we can focus on just a few of these developments.

We can begin where many atheists probably would as well: with the rise of the modern scientific worldview and our complex response to it. It is frequently argued that science and religion do not conflict, either because science answers only the questions of the "what" and "how" of the universe, not the "why," or because science does not answer the questions of morality to which religion is devoted. Science and religion are, in the late paleontologist Stephen Jay Gould's words, non-overlapping magisteria: separate and distinct realms of understanding.[201]

That *may* be true from the present perspective, but any such statement lacks a sense of history. Whether it meant to or not, science, with its profound explanatory power, has over time colonized much of the realm that once belonged solely or principally to religion. Concurrent with that colonization has been not only a rise in the sophistication and standardization of the scientific method, but the widespread adoption of scientific modes of reasoning by most people in their daily lives, such as the way we think about causality. Although science is now the realm of professionals and not amateurs, as it once was,[202] its lessons and habits pervade modern thought.

In many respects, the rise of science is consistent with what sociologists of religion have called the secularization thesis: the idea that the rise of science, along with other social changes, will necessarily bring about "secularization," or "the progressive decline of religion in society and in the minds of individuals."[203] This thesis has been rejected by most experts,[204] and for good reasons. A larger number of people have adopted a secular worldview in the past century and a half than ever before, to be sure; indeed, such a move once would have been

---

200. This story is told masterfully in Charles Taylor's *A Secular Age. See* Taylor, *supra* note 18.

201. *See* Gould, *supra* note 29; *see also* Huxley, *supra* note 27; Homak, *supra* note 26.

202. See, *e.g.,* Richard Holmes, *The Age of Wonder: How the Romantic Generation Discovered the Beauty and Terror of Science* (2009).

203. Berger & Zijderveld, *supra* note 39, at 3.

204. *See id.* at 4.

simply unthinkable.[205] But it should be evident from the events of the past few years that we have not lost our taste for God. If anything, what we have seen in the past half-century points more to the revival and "deprivatization" of religion than to its inevitable demise.[206] In short, the rise of science has led not only to an increasing sense of doubt about what were once religious verities, but also to a resurgence in religious faith and, from both sides of the divide, a continued interest in questions of religious truth.

This leads to the second and third factors that characterize our age: the growth of pluralism and the pluralizing effects of globalization. Modernity has not led to secularization, but to plurality.[207] We live in an age in which "diverse human groups (ethnic, religious, or however differentiated) live together under conditions of civic peace and in social interaction with each other."[208] Our neighbors may be Jews or Christians, Muslims or Sikhs, Buddhists or atheists, agnostics or (in Hollywood, anyway) Scientologists. Or they may subscribe to a less specific spirituality, one that refuses to march under a sectarian banner, or purports to belong to one faith but draws freely from others.[209] They may be consumed by belief or ardent in their non-belief. And all of these are just the *religious* aspects of the diversity of our age. In combination with this variety of religious experience, we also see a profusion of other identities, including ethnicity, nationality, and ideology.

Even when our immediate neighbors do not display this incredible diversity,[210] our more distant neighbors will. And that distance is narrowing. Between air travel, mass culture, the Internet, global immigration patterns, and other factors, our society is increasingly a global one.[211] That observation has become banal, but its influence is still profound. It makes religion itself "more dynamic and

---

205. *See, e.g.,* Turner, *supra* note 103, at xii.

206. José Casanova, *Public Religions in the Modern World* (1994).

207. Berger & Zijderveld, *supra* note 39, at 7.

208. *Id.* at 7. Berger and Zijderveld helpfully distinguish between what they call the phenomenon of plurality and the ideology of pluralism, which sees plurality as a positive good rather than simply describing it as a state of affairs. In using the phrase pluralism in the text, I am referring mainly to the phenomenon, and not to any ideology that presumptively favors plurality.

209. *See* Robert N. Bellah, *et al., Habits of the Heart: Individualism and Commitment in American Life* 221 (1996) (1985) (noting the widespread presence of individualized forms of religion in the United States, which they called "Sheilaism" after one of their subjects, named Sheila, who described her faith as "just my own little voice," and raising the prospect of "over 220 million American religions, one for each of us").

210. *See* Paul Horwitz, *Demographics and Distrust: The Eleventh Circuit on School Prayer in* Adler v. Duval County, 63 U. Miami L. Rev. 835 (2009).

211. *See, e.g.,* William E. Connolly, *Belief, Spirituality, and Time,* in *Varieties of Secularism in a Secular Age* 126, 137–38 (Michael Warner, Jonathan VanAntwerpen, and Craig Calhoun, eds., 2010).

diverse,"[212] as far-flung faiths encounter and respond to each other. And it makes our awareness of these differences more salient.[213] For increasing numbers of humanity, our lives are lived in a "global context" in which, even if we are fixed in our own beliefs and share them with many of our friends and neighbors, each of us is "very aware of the options favoured by the others, and cannot just dismiss them as inexplicable exotic error."[214]

To this profusion of *religious* diversity and plurality, we can bring the rise of scientific worldviews back in as another source of diverse identities. The addition of these nonbelievers to the social mosaic makes doubt or outright non-belief another available option, where not so long ago it would have been unthinkable to many people. These people are our friends, family, neighbors, or *us*; if we do not know any nonbelievers personally (an increasingly unlikely scenario), we surely are aware of their existence as something other than a breed apart. Even those who "stand in the heart of belief . . . sense that there is nearby another vantage-point."[215]

Nor do religious individuals need to look elsewhere to capture a sense of what it is like to see the world through a non-religious lens. Both the rise of science and liberalism's privatization of religion have, in important respects, made secularism our *lingua franca*. Most of us, for much of each day, live lives that are rooted in secular activities and modes of thought and expression.[216] "Today," Ronald Aronson writes, "even intensely religious lives are mostly secular most of the time."[217] An intensely religious individual might respond that her sense of the sacred encompasses the mundane aspects of her life, that she experiences nothing as purely "secular." She might be right; the agnostic certainly would be in no position to tell her otherwise. Still, it is fair to observe that many people who are quite religious *do* experience stretches of their lives primarily within the "secular" realm. They can at least *imagine*, on the basis of those mundane activities—waiting for elevators, exchanging business cards, putting cover sheets on their TPS reports[218]—what it is like to live in a purely material or disenchanted realm.[219]

---

212. Beattie, *supra* note 51, at 49.

213. *See, e.g.,* Taylor, *supra* note 18, at 148.

214. *Id.* at 21.

215. Roger Lundin, *Believing Again: Doubt and Faith in a Secular Age* 7 (2009).

216. Put differently, Charles Taylor suggests that we have all become used to seeing the world at different times from both an "engaged" and a "disengaged" perspective, a view from somewhere *and* a view from nowhere. Taylor, *supra* note 18, at 12.

217. Ronald Aronson, *Living Without God: New Directions for Atheists, Agnostics, Secularists, and the Undecided* 29 (2008).

218. *See Office Space* (Twentieth Century-Fox 1999).

219. These are, I should add, unfair examples to the purely secular individual, who would point out that in addition to pushing elevator buttons, he experiences any number

This does not make other points of view *good*, from the point of view of one who does not share them. The believer may wish to reject the purely material landscape of the secularist; the confirmed atheist may wish to reject the faith-laden worldview of his neighbor; the Hindu may see the Christian living halfway around the world or halfway down the block as misguided in her beliefs. But it makes these points of view *available* to each of us in a way that they once would not have been.

In many cases, of course, the view is not so grim. Knowing and trusting our neighbor as we do, and catching a glimpse of the role that belief or non-belief plays in his life, we may appreciate that he remains both knowable and trustworthy, that he is not so different, or that his differences in some ways enhance his character. Then the imaginative leap into his perspective becomes easier and less threatening. In any case, these changes have made it much easier for us to acknowledge the possibility of different ways of seeing the world, and to imagine what those ways look like from the inside. "There are no more naïve theists or atheists," writes Charles Taylor. It is "harder and harder to find a niche in which belief or unbelief go without saying."[220] Instead, we "live in a pluralist world in which many forms of belief and unbelief jostle and fragilize each other"[221]—in which the line that divides what is "thinkable" from what is "unthinkable" has blurred almost to a vanishing point.[222]

Taken together, these features of our modern social, cultural, and mental landscape make agnosticism in many respects the perfect representative of our age—*not* atheism, despite the rise of science and the widespread habit of thinking on a day-to-day basis in material terms, and *not* theism, despite the resurgence of religious beliefs. Both of those belief systems undoubtedly are vibrantly alive today. Certainly, as we shall see in the next chapter, atheism and theism continue to dominate the terms of public debate. But the spirit of our times is most truly the spirit of William James. It is the spirit of the cusp, the spirit of standing in the open spaces and feeling the winds push us to and fro. Ours is an age in which a range of options for belief or non-belief are available without being unthinkable; in which, however deeply rooted in their religious identities and beliefs particular individuals and communities may be, they are at least aware of the possibility that there might be a *choice* in the matter.

Nothing betrays that fact better than the virulent passions that some atheists display toward religious belief—the degree to which they continue to wrestle with it, like Jacob with the angel, and even the sense of stubborn courage in the face of the void for which they so often congratulate themselves. For these are

---

of other, more meaningful experiences, from the love of his children to his appreciation of the sunset, on a secular level.

220. Taylor, *supra* note 18, at 30, 437.
221. *Id.* at 531.
222. *Id.* at 556.

all stances *with regard to religion*. They are so vehement precisely because they still see religion as a live option in many respects, and religious questions as important questions. From the early English agnostics down to our own age, there remains a "sense of loss" in the "despair of modern skepticism," a sense of "longing."[223] Even for the atheist, we are not in a post-religious age; we are in an age of plurality and possibility. Many still feel their "hearts aching for the God they no longer believe in."[224] The spirit of our times is, in short, the agnostic spirit.

AGNOSTICISM, ART, AND NEGATIVE CAPABILITY

One more ingredient plays a vital role in making ours an agnostic age, and in making both religious believers and nonbelievers aware of the possibilities of agnosticism. That is art. We live in a post-Romantic age, one that remains deeply influenced by the strains of thought that inspired the Romantic view of art. Indeed, Romanticism was in large measure driven by the same forces that created a crisis in religious belief and inspired the early agnostics: the rise of science and the social changes wrought by industrialization. It has also, in the longer run, been a response to liberalism's privatization of religion, which eliminated a shared cultural space in which we could experience a sense of mystery and awe.

The Romantic notion of art is expressive rather than imitative. It represents a move to an understanding of art that "stresses creativity."[225] The artist does not simply draw on existing pictures of reality, or for that matter on religious symbols. Rather, he creates new symbols and a new "self-constituting and self-sustaining" reality.[226] He does so not through imitation but through imagination—the same kind of imaginative leap into other perspectives, into nature, or into other possible worlds that animates Keats's negative capability. And the reader, listener, or watcher of that art takes a similar leap, temporarily exiting her own perspective and entering a different one, leaving something of herself behind while enriching herself at the same time. Through the Romantic conception of art, we experience something of ourselves, something of other selves, and something that seems to lie outside the self altogether.

The Romantic conception of art, which is still largely our own conception of art (the rise and fall of modernism and postmodernism notwithstanding), has multiple implications for our agnostic age. For one thing, it offers a substitute

---

223. Lightman, *supra* note 10, at 2.

224. Wilson, *supra* note 46, at 245.

225. Taylor, *supra* note 18, at 352.

226. Earl R. Wasserstrom, *The Subtler Language: Critical Readings of Neoclassic and Romantic Poems* 4 (1964).

for religious experience.[227] That was especially important to the early English agnostics, who had lost their belief in God but not their craving for awe and mystery. Art allowed them to continue searching for and experiencing something that at least seemed to stand outside themselves, without having to commit to any religious belief system.[228] Art became a place to "recover a sense of transcendence."[229]

The universality of that experience is also important. In some sense, we are "all romanticists" now.[230] Art is a place, alongside religion itself, in which we experience the sublime—the sense of vastness, of unbridgeable spaces and unfathomable mysteries, that seems to resonate so strongly at the heart of the human condition.[231] The contemplation of art, like the appreciation of nature, is a way to try to "express the inexpressible."[232] As with religious practice, the empathetic appreciation of art or nature requires us to cultivate "different modes of consciousness,"[233] in which "embodied feeling can open up to something higher."[234] It is unsurprising, then, that the poet or artist occupies a central role in the modern imagination, almost that of a substitute priest or mystic, or that Shelley called poets "the unacknowledged legislators of mankind."[235]

This Romantic vision of art as a sort of substitute for religion can be subjected to critiques from both sides of the divide between believers and nonbelievers. The atheist may insist that art only takes us more deeply *into* ourselves—necessarily, if there is nothing else out there.[236] Conversely, the theist may argue

---

227. *See, e.g.,* John Stuart Mill, *Autobiography* 118–22 (1989) (1873); Alan Millar, *Mill on Religion,* in *The Cambridge Companion to Mill* 176, 194, 200 (John Skorupski, ed., 1998).

228. *See, e.g.,* Turner, *supra* note 103, at 352.

229. Beattie, *supra* note 51, at 17. *See also* M.H. Abrams, *Natural Supernaturalism: Tradition and Revolution in Romantic Literature* (1973) (arguing that poetry and novels became a place in which religious ideas could be adapted for and experienced within a secular worldview); Sander Van Maas, *Intimate Exteriorities: Inventing Religion Through Music,* in *Religion: Beyond a Concept* 750 (Hent de Vries, ed., 2008); Regina Mara Schwartz, *Sacramental Poetics at the Dawn of Secularism: When God Left the World* (2008); Pericles Lewis, *Religious Experience and the Modernist Novel* (2010).

230. Lundin, *supra* note 215, at 7.

231. *See, e.g.,* Friedrich von Schiller, *On the Sublime,* in *Naïve and Sentimental Poetry and On the Sublime: Two Essays* 193 (Julius A. Elias, trans., 1966) (1801).

232. Kenny, *supra* note 85, at 17; *see also* Lundin, *supra* note 215, at 39 (describing the poetic as "the presence of inexhaustible, indeterminate enormity comprehended in a [discrete] place"); Compte-Sponville, *supra* note 33, at 182 (beauty is "infinity represented in a finite way").

233. Armstrong, *supra* note 40, at 10.

234. Taylor, *supra* note 18, at 288.

235. McGrath, *supra* note 30, at 50.

236. *See, e.g.,* Simon Blackburn, *Religion and Respect,* in *Philosophers Without Gods, supra* note 14, at 179, 191 (arguing that art and music "can take us out of ourselves but

that it is impossible to fully appreciate religious art (to whose charms the atheist himself is not immune[237]) *without* a sense of the religious spirit that moves it.[238] Indeed, she may wonder whether we can "make sense of being moved by beauty in art and nature" *at all*, "in an ontology excluding the transcendent."[239] Or she may argue that whatever glimpses of the sublime are vouchsafed us through art, which ultimately is a human creation, these are mere shadows of what religion offers, just "ersatz transcendence."[240]

From the agnostic perspective, one of these criticisms may be true—but it is difficult to say *which* one. That ought to make us humble about our conclusions. We cannot be sure that art takes us to transcendent places that are genuinely outside ourselves, or that it does not. We cannot be certain that art is truly the equivalent of religious experience, but neither can we conclude with certainty that it isn't.[241] Given how difficult it is to completely assume another's perspective, those judgments are hard to make.[242] The jury is out on this question— possibly for good.

But neither should we overstate the point. Many people, both atheists and religious believers, find a strong kinship between religious and artistic experience.[243] There may be a few individuals like Sigmund Freud, who said that "[m]ysticism is as inaccessible to me as music."[244] But the reverse is also true: There are many people for whom both art and religion invoke powerful responses that verge on the mystical.[245] The new agnostic himself is unwilling to draw

---

they don't take us anywhere else"); Comte-Sponville, *supra* note 33, at 180 (beauty "can give us access to the absolute, but it's not the absolute").

237. *See* Richard Dawkins, *The God Delusion*, ch. 9 (paperback ed., 2008) (discussing Dawkins' appreciation of religious art).

238. *See, e.g.*, Beattie, *supra* note 51, at 156.

239. Taylor, *supra* note 18, at 606.

240. Eagleton, *supra* note 142, at 83.

241. For a sensitive treatment of the relationship between religion and art, specifically poetry, see Kaufmann, *supra* note 112, at 360–68.

242. *See, e.g.*, Taylor, *supra* note 18, at 606 (noting the difficulty of making such inter-subjective assessments).

243. *See, e.g.*, Armstrong, *supra* note 40, at 245 (noting Horace Bushnell's observation that religion has more in common with poetry than with science); Kenny, *supra* note 85, at 17; White, *supra* note 17, at 106 (arguing that art should be a "partner with religion in agnosis"), 113 ("[M]usic is the realm in which I find some of my most profound experiences of God").

244. Comte-Sponville, *supra* note 33, at 154.

245. *See, e.g.*, Taylor, *supra* note 18, at 359 (arguing that nothing in the experience of art "rules out" the possibility that beauty "reflects God's work in creating the world"). This is why Eagleton's description of art as "ersatz transcendence" strikes me as too strongly put. Eagleton, *supra* note 142, at 83. Eagleton seems eager to trace religion back to a divine source and art to a human one. But a religious person might just as readily assume that all artistic inspiration is ultimately divine in origin.

strong conclusions about the relative comparability and authenticity of religious and artistic experiences. He acknowledges that the seeming "genuineness of [the] experience of wonder [through art] doesn't exclude the possibility that something even richer might be recovered in the register of religious belief."[246] But he still believes that art may have *something* to teach him about what it means to encounter the ineffable.

What is important here is that the post-Romantic experience of art suggests that agnosticism is truly the modern condition. We have become accustomed by both pluralism and Romanticism to view the world in the way that the new agnostic I have described in this chapter does. We are all at least aware of the possibility of this experience. Even the most committed theist or atheist may betray the possibility of the agnostic stance by doing something as unremarkable, but quintessentially modern, as reading a novel. As Terry Eagleton observes, reading fiction "involves a degree of 'ironic credulity,' believing and not believing at the same time."[247] One enters the novel as a willing participant, one who is willing to experience it as a real thing—think of the hoards of readers at the docks, waiting to find out the fate of Dickens's Little Nell—but at the same time maintains a distance from complete belief, knowing that the tale is not true. These "flexible mental states" are "the sine qua non of modern subjectivity."[248] To live in a world in which both belief and non-belief are both plausible options, and in which our culture and our experience of our communities, our world, and our artistic heritage train us to see things from other perspectives, is to live, if not in an agnostic age, then in an age in which agnosticism is a strongly available option. It may, indeed, be the modern default position.

SUMMARY

Agnosticism, as we have seen, is a term that is thrown around with abandon, often by way of cheaply equating it with a cowardly form of atheism. I hope the falsity of this view is now clear.

Even those who use the term less pejoratively may have something different in mind than the brand of "new agnosticism" I have described in this chapter. The new agnosticism has a strong respect for mystery and for the possibility of a transcendent religious truth, without being willing to commit absolutely to that position. In that respect, it is different from, say, the more skeptical and disenchanted agnosticism championed by the later Huxley. Although he initially shared a sense of the potential of what Herbert Spencer called the

---

246. Taylor, *supra* note 18, at 607.
247. Eagleton, *supra* note 142, at 146.
248. *Id.* at 147.

"Unknown," later in life Huxley refused even to use the term, calling it "the waste of a capital U."[249] The new agnostic is not as willing as Spencer to assume the existence of an Unknown.[250] Unlike Huxley, however, he is willing to spare a capital letter or two as a tribute to the power of its *possible* existence.

The new agnostic is not committed to either belief or non-belief in the existence of God or some spiritual or transcendent realm. Although she is unwilling to make a final commitment, however, she is hardly passive. She experiences her agnosticism as an active, positive, and enriching force. She is deeply interested in struggling with questions of religious truth, not indifferent to them. Rather than simply resting contentedly in the open spaces, she takes her suspension of ontological commitments as an opportunity to imagine, as best as she can, what the "truth" looks like from a variety of perspectives. Like Keats, she does not experience this "negative capability" as nothingness, but as an erasure of the barriers between herself and others—both believers and nonbelievers. Whatever else she is, she is neither a half-assed theist nor a cowardly atheist. She is something else altogether.

In this, she represents our agnostic age: an age in which a variety of forces have coalesced to make agnosticism deeply *possible*. Not everyone in our age is a new agnostic, to be sure. But many people, perhaps without realizing it, are quite capable of understanding what it means to be one. Most of us, at one time or another, have made agnostic moves in our own lives, in ways that may be as simple as experiencing art or trying to see things from our neighbors' perspective. We might think that these imaginative leaps are unremarkable. In fact, they are extraordinary. They are strong evidence of just how firmly we are embedded in an agnostic age.

---

249. Lightman, *supra* note 10, at 136.

250. A.N. Wilson, arguing that "[q]uestions of faith and doubt and religion, despite seeming eternal, are actually very different from one generation to another," adds that "[n]othing enforces this view as poignantly as the complete evaporation of Herbert Spencer from human consciousness." Wilson, *supra* note 46, at 155. This overstatement makes a valuable point. Our agnostic need not, and perhaps may not, make the same pseudo-mystical assumptions about the Unknowable as Spencer did because, in our age of plurality and suspension of ontological commitment, she stands in a very different relation to both religion *and* science than Spencer and his generation did.

4. THE NEW COMMISSARS OF ENLIGHTENMENT: THE NEW ATHEISTS, THE NEW ANTI-ATHEISTS, AND THE NEW AGNOSTICISM

INTRODUCTION

If agnostics, or new agnostics, are the representative figures of our age, they sure are quiet about it. Instead of Ten Commandments displays and ads touting atheism on the sides of buses,[1] where are the folks erecting a large question mark on top of a building, or marching with banners proclaiming, "I'm Not Sure; Check Back With Me Later?" Agnostics don't seem quite the type for shouting from the rooftops, but mightn't we expect at least a little tentative murmuring from doorways?

In general, the agnostic voice is a relatively quiet one in our society.[2] Agnostics are not religious enough to get elected to Congress,[3] but not atheist enough to get elected to the Berkeley City Council.[4] Theirs is a largely excluded middle voice. Instead, what we get from both ends of the spectrum is—war.

In particular, in recent years we have witnessed the revival of open combat over questions of religious truth. The opening salvo was fired by four authors: Sam Harris, in *The End of Faith*; Richard Dawkins, in *The God Delusion*; Daniel Dennett, in *Breaking the Spell*; and Susan Jacoby, in *Freethinkers*. They were joined by Christopher Hitchens, whose *God is Not Great*[5] appeared a couple of years later.[6] Of course, there have been others, although they often write from a less perfervid perspective.[7] Inevitably, a host of more or less religious authors

---

1. *See, e.g.*, Sarah Lyall, *Atheists Send a Message, on 800 Buses*, N.Y. Times, Jan. 6, 2009, available at http://www.nytimes.com/2009/01/07/world/europe/07london.html.

2. *But see* Ron Rosenbaum, *An Agnostic Manifesto*, Slate, June 28, 2010, available at http://www.slate.com/id/2258484/.

3. *See, e.g.*, Oral Argument of Michael A. Newdow on Behalf of the Respondent, at 24, *Elk Grove Unified School District v. Newdow*, 542 U.S. 961 (No. 02-1624).

4. I actually have no idea about the religious affiliations of the members of the Berkeley City Council. But I'm sure you get my drift.

5. To be precise, the book is showily titled *god is Not Great*, with a small g. As I noted earlier, I cannot bring myself to follow suit.

6. Terry Eagleton, writing about the New Atheism, focuses on Dawkins and Hitchens and, in an excess of cuteness, bundles them together as "Ditchkins." Terry Eagleton, *Reason, Faith, and Revolution: Reflections on the God Debate* 2 (2009).

7. *See, e.g.*, Ronald Aronson, *Living Without God: New Directions for Atheists, Agnostics, Secularists, and the Undecided* (2008); Andrew Comte-Sponville, *The Little Book of Atheist*

have written impassioned rebuttals. They include Tina Beattie, Alistair McGrath,[8] David Bentley Hart, Terry Eagleton, and a number of others.[9]

This is just a paper war. No one has put Harris's head on a spike or packed McGrath off to a re-education camp. In that sense, the war between the New Atheists and what we call the New Anti-Atheists can seem charming, a little quaint, and certainly a far cry from the religious wars of old. These days, the combatants meet with pens, not swords, and the battlefields are the *New York Times* best-seller list, C-SPAN, and the bloody proving grounds of the Frankfurt Book Fair.

There have been genuine outbreaks of religious violence over these issues in recent times, of course. One should not forget that the very real events of 9/11 gave many of the New Atheists the impetus to speak out.[10] But religious terrorists don't write bestsellers. The actual perpetrators of religious violence in our own age are, by and large, noncombatants in this particular battle. If your last name happens to be Barnes or Noble, it's a splendid little war.

Of course it's a *little* more serious than that. For one thing, the contest between the New Atheists and the New Anti-Atheists is a front in the seemingly endless culture wars: the struggle between contending sides to claim the culture for themselves—to define its terms, police its boundaries, and banish its transgressors.[11] Like all wars, it has its casualties. In the case of the culture wars, the main

---

Spirituality 74 (Nancy Hudson trans., 2008). In fairness, Dennett's contribution to the New Atheist literature, *Breaking the Spell*, is often (and deservedly) treated, even by its adversaries, as a far more even-tempered book than, say, Dawkins's screed. *See, e.g., The Future of Atheism: Alister McGrath & Daniel Dennett in Dialogue* 28 (Robert B. Stewart, ed., 2008) (remarks of Alister McGrath).

8. In addition to Alister E. McGrath's *The Twilight of Atheism: The Rise and Fall of Disbelief in the Modern World* (2006), see, *e.g.,* Alister E. McGrath & Joanna Collicutt McGrath, *The Dawkins Delusion?: Atheist Fundamentalism and the Denial of the Divine* (2007).

9. *See, e.g.,* John F. Haught, *God and the New Atheism: A Critical Response to Dawkins, Harris, and Hitchens* (2008); Michael Novak, *No One Sees God: The Dark Night of Atheists and Believers* (2008); Scott Hahn & Benjamin Wikes, *Answering the New Atheism: Dismantling Dawkins' Case Against God* (2008); Timothy Keller, *The Reason for God: Belief in an Age of Skepticism* (2008); Eric Reitan, *Is God a Delusion?: A Reply to Religion's Cultured Despisers* (2008).

10. *See, e.g.,* Sam Harris, *The End of Faith: Religion, Terror, and the Future of Reason* 18 (2005). Others began writing in the wake of September 11, but with less violent examples in mind. *See, e.g.,* Susan Jacoby, *Freethinkers: A History of American Secularism* 2–3 (2004) (describing President Bush's presiding over "an ecumenical prayer service in Washington's National Cathedral" following September 11 as one of the incidents that inspired her book).

11. *See, e.g.,* James Davison Hunter, *Culture Wars: The Struggle to Control the Family, Art, Education, Law, and Politics in America* (1991).

casualty is often our culture itself. Furthermore, although the debate between the New Atheists and the New Anti-Atheists excludes the genuinely violent figures in our current global struggles over religion and religiously motivated terrorism, that background looms over the debate and raises its stakes considerably.

Finally, the battle between ardent believers and nonbelievers says something about our culture itself: about the role that questions of religious truth play in our culture, the benefits and flaws of liberalism, and, not least, why the extremes in the debate so often define its terms. For all those reasons, it is worth spending some time considering the debate between the New Atheists and the New Anti-Atheists, and the role that agnosticism might play in mediating between the extremes of this argument.

In one sense, this chapter is incidental to the broader subject of constitutional agnosticism that is at the heart of this book. As Chapter Five emphasizes, it is possible to be a *constitutional* agnostic without being a *religious* agnostic. One may enlist on one side or the other of the New Atheist–New Anti-Atheist struggle without giving up the right to be a constitutional agnostic, or losing a sense of the value of constitutional agnosticism.

Nevertheless, this book probably would not have been written if it were not for this very prominent debate between believers and nonbelievers. The nature of the debate, with its oddly overheated quality, and the fact that it is so often driven by its extremes, says something about both legal debates over church–state relations and broader debates over questions of religious truth and their role within a liberal democracy. For the social debate, it suggests that we are at a particularly fragile moment in the liberal consensus, one in which the old arguments over the role of religion within our society have returned to the foreground.[12] The fact that the debate swirls around questions of religious *truth* suggests that those questions remain important. For the legal debate, it suggests that the poles of that debate are still formed around belief and non-belief.[13] As Chapter Two argued, despite the best efforts of the most prominent legal theorists of religious freedom, we cannot escape the need to directly confront questions of religious truth. This is the dilemma to which constitutional agnosticism is a response.

To see this, we must do three things. We need an overview of the nature of the debate between the New Atheists and the New Anti-Atheists. We must consider why this debate is so unsatisfying. And we must ask what role the New Agnosticism might play in this debate.

---

12. *See* Chapter One.
13. *See* Chapter Two.

THE NEW ATHEISTS AND THE NEW ANTI-ATHEISTS

What is the core of the New Atheist argument? What, if anything, is "new" about it? The arguments raised by the New Atheists can be summarized briefly:[14]

- The standard arguments for God's existence, such as the ontological argument offered by St. Anselm or St. Thomas Aquinas's five proofs of the existence of God, are all fatally flawed. This gives us good reason to doubt God's existence.[15]
- Science provides strong, if not conclusive, evidence for the nonexistence of God or, indeed, any truly supernatural or transcendent explanations for the nature of the cosmos and human life.
- Science and the scientific method provide the proper approach to these questions. Belief that is not based on evidence, defined in scientific and empirical terms, is not *justified* belief.
- Belief in God, moreover, is unnecessary. We can subsist and thrive without it by finding meaning and moral purpose in the material world.
- Religion faces and fails the test of evil. The presence of evil in the world, both from natural calamities like cancer or tsunamis, and of our own human devising, like the Holocaust, defies the idea that a perfectly loving God could possibly exist.[16]
- Religion confronts a final problem: that of its *own* evil. Religion has been and continues to be a source of great violence and cruelty in the world, from the burning of heretics by St. Thomas More to the suicide bombers of modern extremist Islam.

This is the standard New Atheist bill of indictment of religion. Some version of it can be found in all of the most popular New Atheist works. The list makes pretty clear that little is really new about the New Atheism.[17] All of these points have been debated, both inside and outside religious communities, for almost as long as religious faith itself has been around. The Scottish philosopher David Hume wrote of the problem of evil, ages before Richard Dawkins was a gleam in

14. *See, e.g.,* Haught, *supra* note 9, at xiii–xiv; Reitan, *supra* note 9, at 4.

15. A brief summary of these arguments and counter-arguments, embedded in a charming novel, can be found in the appendix to the philosopher and novelist Rebecca Goldstein's book *36 Arguments for the Existence of God: A Work of Fiction* (2010). For a short, accessible introduction, see Torin Alter & Robert J. Howell, *The God Dialogues: A Philosophical Journey* (2010).

16. A similar concern is that of divine hiddenness: a perfectly loving God would want to make his presence and love felt to his creation, rather than hiding outright or making it difficult to find him. *See, e.g., Divine Hiddenness: New Essays* (Daniel Howard-Snyder & Paul K. Moser, eds., 2001). This argument is important, but is not raised much by the New Atheists, who do not generally operate at this level of sophistication.

17. *See, e.g.,* Haught, *supra* note 9, at xi ([T]heologians have "seen it all before.").

his father's eye: "Is [God] willing to prevent evil, but not able? Then he is impotent. Is he able, but not willing? Then he is malevolent. Is he both able and willing? Whence then is evil?" Hume himself was paraphrasing Epictetus, who died some 1700 years earlier.[18] Nor, oddly enough, is Christopher Hitchens the first person to notice that the Spanish Inquisition was not a good thing.

That does not make these arguments unconvincing. Indeed, the fact that both religious believers and professional theologians have grappled with them for centuries suggests that they are profoundly important and difficult questions—even if, as some of the New Anti-Atheists suggest, many New Atheists show little awareness that anyone *has* been thinking about these issues.[19]

What *is* new, then, about the New Atheism? In essence, there are two new aspects, one a matter of style and one a matter of substance. The style is one of harshness and ridicule toward religion. Even this, of course, is not completely novel. The scorn heaped on religion in the pages of the New Atheists' books pales next to what we have seen in the past, although the worst historical examples of anti-religious sentiment were less a product of out-and-out atheism than of anti-clericalism, which was often grounded in religious faith and concerns about church corruption.

But the New Atheists are not just anti-clericalists. They train their guns on religion as a whole, and they fire as long and gleefully as a character in a Quentin Tarantino movie. Thus, for Richard Dawkins, an English evolutionary biologist and author of popular atheist tracts, bringing up one's children in a religious faith is a form of child abuse.[20] For the atheist novelist Martin Amis, "[r]eligious belief is without reason and without dignity, and its record is near-universally dreadful."[21] Sam Harris announces that "all reasonable men and women have a common enemy," a "deceptive" one that "threatens to destroy the very possibility of human happiness." You will already have guessed the ending: "Our enemy is nothing other than faith itself."[22] Harris reserves special hostility for Islam, writing that "any notion of a fundamentally peaceful Islam that has been corrupted by a wicked few is wrong, because most Muslims are *utterly deranged by their*

---

18. Reitan, *supra* note 9, at 186–87.

19. *See, e.g.*, Karen Armstrong, *The Case for God* 308 (2009) (concluding that it is difficult to argue effectively with the New Atheists because their knowledge of theology is so "rudimentary"); Tina Beattie, *The New Atheists: The Twilight of Reason and the War on Religion* 7–8 (2008) (arguing that the New Atheists have failed to keep up with developments in modern theology). Terry Eagleton, as usual, says it best: "An atheist who has more than a primitive understanding of theology is as rare as an American who has not been abducted by aliens." Eagleton, *supra* note 6, at 49.

20. *See* Beattie, *supra* note 19, at 2.

21. *Id.* at 3.

22. Harris, *supra* note 10, at 131.

religious faith."[23] Ultimately, he believes this is true of all faith: It is "the devil's masterpiece" among those "demons" that "lurk inside every human mind."[24]

It is difficult to know where to begin with Hitchens. At least he writes with a zeal and wit that, before it curdles, briefly entertains. But his arguments are facile. With his typical flair for offering a stale insight as if he had invented it, he says, "it is not arrogant of me to claim that I had already discovered . . . before my boyish voice had broken" that religion is, among other things, "both the result and the cause of dangerous sexual repression."[25] Religion, he argues, has led "innumerable people . . . to award themselves permission to behave in ways that would make a brothel-keeper or an ethnic cleanser raise an eyebrow."[26] His book concludes with a plea for a "new Enlightenment," but its closing words are as much inspired by a lurid combination of Thomas Cromwell, the Hellfire Club, and *Playboy* Magazine as by Voltaire or Jefferson. He identifies "the enemy" as a set of "gnarled hands which reach out to drag us back to the catacombs and the reeking altars and the guilty pleasures of subjection and abjection."[27] Terry Eagleton writes of Dawkins and Hitchens that the principal difference between them is that Hitchens's *God is Not Great* is "stylish, entertaining, splendidly impassioned, [and] compulsively readable," while Dawkins's *The God Delusion* "merits none of these epithets."[28] Eagleton is a literary critic, and may be blessed with greater powers of discernment than mine. In any event, the New Atheists by and large are "distinguished by their outrage" toward religion in general.[29]

The other new aspect of the New Atheism is more worrisome. The old saying goes that there are no atheists in foxholes. For the New Atheists, there are no moderates in churches. Or, if there are, even religious moderation is still pernicious. "While all faiths have been touched, here and there, by the spirit of ecumenicalism," Harris writes, every faith ultimately believes that every other faith is wrong; "[i]ntolerance is thus intrinsic to every creed."[30]

This argument has the unfortunate flaw of being garbled at best and specious at worst. Harris may be right that "faith" must mean a belief in something in particular, not in nothing at all. But that is not saying much. One can believe that God exists, but remain unsure whether any description of God that has yet been offered is accurate. Even if we take a more stringent definition of faith—suppose, for example, that one believes in Christianity, with all the necessary assumptions

---

23. Sam Harris, *Letter to a Christian Nation* 85 (2006). In case the sentiment is unclear, Harris helpfully supplies his own italics.

24. Harris, *supra* note 10, at 226.

25. Christopher Hitchens, *God is Not Great: How Religion Poisons Everything* 4 (2007).

26. *Id.* at 6.

27. *Id.* at 283.

28. Eagleton, *supra* note 6, at 3.

29. Reitan, *supra* note 9, at 3.

30. Harris, *supra* note 10, at 13.

about the historical existence of Jesus and the truth of his divinity, crucifixion, and resurrection—that simply means one believes those who have reached different conclusions are *wrong*. It doesn't mean one refuses to tolerate them. I doubt that my Protestant neighbors share the same views on Christian doctrine as my Catholic wife, and I *know* that they do not share the views that I would hold with greater conviction if I were a more of an observant Jew. And yet, Harris's warning to the contrary, so far they have graciously restrained themselves from burning down my house. Maybe they are just very good neighbors or very bad Christians. But I don't think that's quite it.

It is perhaps less important that Harris is wrong here. After all, he has a point of sorts. Faith in a particular creed generally involves believing that there is a particular fact of the matter, and beliefs that contradict it are wrong. What is important is the relationship between this argument and the broader view shared by the more vituperative New Atheists: that *all* religion is a potential threat and should be viewed as such. Harris gladly concedes that there are religious moderates as well as religious extremists. But he argues that we have failed to give enough attention to the idea that "religious moderates are themselves the bearers of a terrible dogma; they imagine that the path to peace will be paved once each of us has learned to respect the unjustified beliefs of others."[31] We must realize that "the very ideal of religious tolerance . . . is one of the principal forces driving us toward the abyss."[32]

To the extent that there are religious moderates, Harris says, that moderation is merely a "capitulation" to "the many hammer blows of modernity that have exposed certain tenets of faith to doubt."[33] Religious moderation is not itself religious: it is "the product of *secular* knowledge and scriptural *ignorance*"; it "has no bona fides, in religious terms, to put it on a par with fundamentalism."[34] So religious moderates are either misguided atheists or sloppy believers. Harris concludes that as long as we fail to call "the core dogmas of faith" into question, "religious moderation will do nothing to lead us out of the wilderness."[35]

Similar sentiments crop up elsewhere in the New Atheist literature. "[E]ven mild and moderate religion helps to provide the climate of faith in which extremism naturally flourishes," Richard Dawkins argues.[36] What is "really pernicious" is the belief that "faith itself is a virtue."[37] As long as we persist in this view, no matter how moderate the brand of faith we are dealing with, "it is hard to withhold

---

31. *Id.* at 14–15.
32. *Id.* at 15.
33. *Id.* at 19, 20.
34. *Id.* at 21.
35. *Id.*
36. Richard Dawkins, *The God Delusion* 342 (paperback ed., 2008).
37. *Id.* at 347.

respect from the faith of Osama bin Laden and the suicide bombers."[38] We should not warn people against religious extremism, but "against faith itself."[39]

Again, there is a valid point concealed within these intemperate arguments, one that would be entirely evident to the new agnostic. Unless we stack the definition of God with a variety of caveats meant to avoid extremism—which, we will see, is just what some of the New Anti-Atheists do—then any faith-claim that follows a consistent internal logic will be hard to distinguish from other faith-claims, even if one leads to mass destruction and the other to, say, an especially bland form of ecumenicalism, like Unitarianism on steroids. (Most of us would prefer Unitarianism to the apocalypse, but a few would probably ask for a moment to think about it.) From an agnostic perspective, it is impossible to prefer the truth of the statement that God would appreciate your calling your mom every week to the statement that God commands us to kill the unbeliever unto the last generation. We might have a *moral* preference between the two, but we cannot say that our moral preferences correspond to what happens to be *true*. Stacking the deck in this way, concluding without further thought that the peaceful forms of religious doctrine are necessarily truer than the unpleasant or horrific ones, ultimately does a disservice to the genuine effort to seek religious *truth*, rather than just believing what happens to suit us.[40] For this reason, there are genuinely difficult questions concerning when, whether, and why we should tolerate at least *some* forms of religion, and more broadly what it means to "tolerate" something we think is either factually or morally wrong, simply because it involves religious belief.[41]

Those questions are worth considering. But the New Atheists wield an axe, not a scalpel. So these important questions are obscured by the broader argument that religion *itself*, in all its forms, is a danger. It is best addressed not by moderation or toleration, but by *intolerance*, in certain respects, of *all* religious faith. New Atheism is a snazzy label, and perhaps the New Atheists are not looking for another one.[42] If they are, though, they might look to the early Soviet government, which established a People's Commissariat for Enlightenment.[43]

---

38. *Id.* at 345.

39. *Id.* at 346.

40. *See, e.g.,* James Tappenden, *An Atheist's Fundamentalism,* in *Philosophers Without Gods: Meditations on Atheism and the Secular Life* 104 (Louise M. Antony, ed., 2007).

41. *See, e.g.,* Simon Blackburn, *Religion and Respect,* in *Philosophers Without God, id.,* at 179; Brian Leiter, *Why Tolerate Religion?,* 25 Const. Comment. 1 (2008).

42. If they are, they will have to do better than Brights, a term suggested by Daniel Dennett, *see, e.g.,* Daniel C. Dennett, *Breaking the Spell: Religion as a Natural Phenomenon* 21 (2006). Even some of the New Atheists will have no truck with that one. *See* Hitchens, *supra* note 25, at 5 (rejecting the "cringe-making proposal" of Dennett and Dawkins "that atheists should conceitedly nominate themselves to be called 'brights'").

43. I am indebted to A.N. Wilson's charming book *God's Funeral* for introducing me to this factoid. *See* A.N. Wilson, *God's Funeral: The Decline of Faith in Western Civilization* 95 (1999).

Given their brutal take on religion as a whole, we might rename these writers the New Commissars of Enlightenment.

One might argue that some of the New Anti-Atheists deserve the same label. The New Anti-Atheists give as good as they get. So, in the words of just one of those critics, David Bentley Hart, Richard Dawkins is a "tireless tractarian" with an "embarrassing incapacity for philosophical reasoning."[44] Daniel Dennett offers an argument based on "pure intuition, held together by tenuous strands of presupposition," resulting in a book that is "utterly inconsequential," "something of an embarrassment," and "trivial."[45] Sam Harris's *The End of Faith* is "an extravagantly callow attack on all religious belief," a book that "is little more than a concatenation of shrill, petulant assertions, a few of which are true, but none of which betrays any great degree of philosophical or historical sophistication," one that "displays an abysmal ignorance of almost every topic he addresses."[46] Harris's real adversary is Christian fundamentalists, "but he does not even get *them* right."[47] And Christopher Hitchens has produced, in *God is Not Great*, "a book that raises the wild non sequitur almost to the level of a dialectical method."[48]

And those are just the remarks of one theologian(!) and philosopher. At times, the New Anti-Atheists, with their intemperate language, seem to confirm the New Atheists' claim that godliness is no guarantee of gentleness. Terry Eagleton, a literary critic of great slashing vigor, outdoes himself in describing what he sees as the ungodly (so to speak) ignorance of Hitchens and Dawkins. He argues in a crescendo of metaphors that they, and other New Atheists, assume that religion primarily serves the function of explaining the nature of the world, and ignore the significance of religion's deeper morality and rituals. In doing so, they miss the point of the whole enterprise. Thus, Dawkins and Dennett, by assuming that religion "is a kind of bogus theory or pseudo-explanation of the world," are "rather like someone who thinks that a novel is a botched piece of sociology."[49] Dennett commits the "blunder of believing that religion is a botched attempt to explain the world, which is like seeing ballet as a botched attempt to run for a bus."[50] Dawkins and Hitchens think "that all Christians are fideists, holding that

---

44. David Bentley Hart, *Atheist Delusions: The Christian Revolution and its Fashionable Enemies* 3,4 (2009). Dawkins, whose harsh tone regularly provokes this kind of reaction, really brings out the stylistic best in his critics. Elsewhere, Andrew Brown writes of Dawkins's *The God Delusion*, "It has been obvious for years that Richard Dawkins had a fat book in him, but who would have thought him capable of writing one this bad?" Beattie, *supra* note 19, at 3.

45. Hart, *supra* note 44, at 6–7.

46. *Id.* at 4, 8.

47. *Id.* at 8 (emphasis added).

48. *Id.* at 4.

49. Eagleton, *supra* note 6, at 5.

50. *Id.* at 50.

reason is irrelevant to faith, which is rather like believing that all Scots are stingy."[51] Hitchens' argument that, because of the telescope and the microscope, religion no longer has anything important left to explain fails to see that "Christianity was never meant to be an *explanation* of anything in the first place. It is rather like saying that thanks to the electric toaster we can forget about Chekhov."[52] This is what the New Anti-Atheists are like when they are in a *good* mood. The rest of the time they can be as condescending as the New Atheists, addressing their antagonists in a more-in-sorrow-than-in-anger tone—a kind of *esprit de* Joseph Lieberman.

That the New Anti-Atheists are sometimes harsh in their writing does not mean they do not score important points—although it does tend to revise one's mental image of what a faculty meeting must be like at a divinity school. Among other things, they argue convincingly that the New Atheists offer a crabbed definition of religion and a narrow understanding of theology.[53] They argue powerfully that the New Atheists' reductionism, even when it purports to pay tribute to a sense of mystery or awe as a purely human phenomenon, does not do justice to this sensibility, and thus cannot do justice to the reasons for choosing a life of religious faith.[54] And they suggest that many of the New Atheists give short shrift to the individual religious experiences that many, from famous mystics to ordinary people, have described.[55] Of course, these experiences are difficult to replicate or verify. But, the New Anti-Atheists insist, they are at least *some* kind of evidence, which the New Atheists sweep under the rug.

Many of the New Anti-Atheists, without trying to conceal the long historical record of evils committed in the name of religion, point out the many ways in which the New Atheists either fail to acknowledge the equally long record of good committed in its name or dismiss such actions—say, the religiously motivated work of Martin Luther King, Jr.—as not being genuinely religious. Conversely, they argue, the New Atheists often attempt to clear atheism of any similar record of evils, by arguing that anyone who committed violence seemingly motivated by atheism (for example, Hitler or the Khmer Rouge) was acting under some other compulsion, or was actually religious.

---

51. *Id.* at 53.

52. *Id.* at 7.

53. *See, e.g.,* Armstrong, *supra* note 19, at 304–08; Beattie, *supra* note 19, at 7–8, 41; James P. Carse, *The Religious Case Against Belief* 2 (2008); Eagleton, *supra* note 6, at 53–54; Reitan, *supra* note 9, at 18–22; *see also* J.L. Schellenberg, *The Wisdom to Doubt: A Justification of Religious Skepticism* 78 (2007).

54. *See, e.g.,* Wilson, *supra* note 43, at 179 ("These days even the most hard-nosed materialists, if they get themselves into conflict with the religious, find themselves wanting to say how awe-struck they are by the complexity of nature, and end up sounding like Louis Armstrong with his 'wonderful world.'").

55. *See, e.g.,* Reitan, *supra* note 9, at 39; *see also* Schellenberg, *supra* note 53, at 190.

The broadest and most important point made by many of the New Anti-Atheists is that the New Atheists, even if they get *somewhere* in their critiques of religion, do not get us to *atheism*. They fail for three reasons. First, their definition of what counts as evidence for or against God's existence is so driven by science, by a narrow slice of what can be proven or experienced or replicated, that they stack the deck in favor of atheism.[56] By assuming that the proofs for or against God's existence must be played out only in the scientific realm, they take as a given what ought to be cause for debate: *how* one proves or disproves God's existence.

Second, they fail to recognize that science is, in its own way, also a matter of faith.[57] To be sure, it is a particular kind of faith—namely, a faith in replicable results, observable phenomena, convincing proofs, and so on. But it is also a *provisional* belief, a belief that is always ready to be superseded by what tomorrow's evidence might bring. And it is a faith in its own kind of explanatory and evidentiary process, one that rests on a belief that science provides the best means of explaining the world so far, but that does not rest firmly on a self-sufficient argument of its own.

Finally, they say, even if we accept that the combat should take place on this narrow ground, the New Atheists still fail. It is not true that "science has advanced sufficiently to be able to make a definitive statement on the existence or nonexistence of a God having the attributes that are traditionally associated with the Judeo-Christian-Islamic God,"[58] let alone the existence or nonexistence of a supernatural force with less specific attributes. It is not clear that science will *ever* be able to do so. Science can provide strong descriptions and explanations of the natural world, but it cannot refute the possibility of a supernatural world. It can say much about the *how* of our world, but not much about the *why*. Even its cosmological explanations of the universe, at least at present, bottom out at the Big Bang, at a moment in which the nascent universe was compressed in space and time, without being able to tell us much about how this focal point came to exist.[59]

This is what led Stephen Jay Gould to write of science and religion as non-overlapping magisteria,[60] and what convinces Alister McGrath that "there is no

---

56. As Charles Taylor puts it, "God is set up to flunk the atheist exam." Charles Taylor, *A Secular Age* 389 (2007). *See also* Reitan, *supra* note 9, at 36–37, 84–86; Armstrong, *supra* note 19, at 279; Haught, *supra* note 9, at 4–5.

57. *See, e.g.,* Armstrong, *supra* note 10, at 301; Haught, *supra* note 9, at 17; McGrath, *supra* note 8, at 95–97.

58. Victor J. Stenger, *God: The Failed Hypothesis: How Science Shows That God Does Not Exist* 11 (2007).

59. *See, e.g.,* William Lane Craig, *In Defense of Theistic Arguments*, in *The Future of Atheism, supra* note 8, at 67.

60. *See generally* Stephen Jay Gould, *Rocks of Ages: Science and Religion in the Fullness of Life* (1999). *See also* Peter B. Medawar, *The Limits of Science* 66 (1985) (arguing that

watertight way of arguing from the observation of the world to the existence or nonexistence of God."[61] Even if science displays great explanatory power, such as its use of fossil evidence to demonstrate the age of the earth, it cannot prove that God exists or does not exist (although it can challenge some religious accounts of the origins and development of both the universe and humanity, such as Bishop Ussher's famous "proof" that the universe was created in 4004 B.C). "The fact that empirical reality seems seamless," Eric Reitan writes, "is not evidence against God, if God is transcendent and capable of creating a seamless empirical reality."[62] Similarly, Daniel Dennett's argument that religion is an entirely natural phenomenon, an offshoot of evolutionary psychology, does not mean religious belief is not *true*. It means only that the religious impulse, and evolutionary psychology, are part of God's design.[63] Evolutionary and religious accounts of religion are not mutually exclusive.[64]

STALEMATE

In significant ways, then, atheism and belief are at an impasse when it comes to offering a final answer to the ultimate questions of religious truth: the nature of the universe and the existence or nonexistence of God.[65] One may believe that one side of the argument or the other is *right*. But neither side is likely to score a knockout blow any time soon. It is little wonder that Alister McGrath writes, "Final adjudication on the God question lies beyond reason and experiment. Maybe T.H. Huxley was right: agnosticism is the only credible option here."[66]

A number of the more thoughtful antagonists in this debate, without necessarily professing agnosticism, reach similar conclusions. McGrath provides an example on the theist side. Similarly, Daniel Dennett, while remaining as convinced of his atheism as McGrath is of his theism, acknowledges the fruitless nature of much of the debate between atheists and theists on the question of God's existence.[67] Even Richard Dawkins, who heaps scorn on what he cutely

---

questions about the meaning of life and its ultimate causes and origins are "questions that science cannot answer, and that no conceivable advance of science would empower it to answer.").

61. McGrath, *supra* note 8, at 181.

62. Reitan, *supra* note 9, at 85–86.

63. *See* Hart, *supra* note 44, at 8; Robert Wright, *The Evolution of God* (2009).

64. *See* Haught, *supra* note 9, at 87; *see also* McGrath, *supra* note 8, at 180–81.

65. *See, e.g.,* McGrath, *id.* at 182–83.

66. *Id.* at 183.

67. *See* Dennett, *supra* note 42, at 27; *see also* Robert B. Stewart, *The Future of Atheism: An Introductory Appraisal,* in *The Future of Atheism, supra* note 7, at 1, 7.

calls "Permanent Agnosticism in Principle"[68] for failing to take sides on questions on which he thinks the evidence overwhelmingly favors the nonexistence of God, concedes that a range of agnostic responses may be appropriate in particular circumstances. He writes, dismissively but plainly, that the fact that "you cannot prove God's nonexistence is accepted and trivial, if only in the sense that we can never absolutely prove the nonexistence of anything."[69]

And yet, this is not a conclusion that most of the New Commissars of Enlightenment, on either side, are especially happy to sign on to. To the contrary, they are still at it—hammer, tongs, book tours, and all. Both sides recognize the nature of the stalemate. Yet both sides keep their voices raised, their tongues sharp, and their arguments fierce—and, sometimes, dubious. Both sides of the debate use dodges and devices that cannot prove terribly convincing to anyone who has not already signed onto their major assumptions, or who approaches the debate with a genuinely open mind (an empty one, some of them might reply).

On the New Atheist side, as we saw, the trick lies in loading the word "evidence" with a host of scientistic assumptions about just what counts as evidence.[70] For the New Anti-Atheists, the loaded word is "God." By smuggling into that word a host of assumptions—that God is not only all good and all-powerful, but that he is good and powerful in a way that coincides with our own human understanding of goodness and power—the New Anti-Atheist writers attempt to avoid the New Atheist critiques about the nature of evil in the world, or about the consequences of belief in God.

Eric Reitan, for example, attempts to refute some of the charges against religion's potential for violence by arguing that religion is only divisive and violent when it is not what he calls *true* religion, when it has "lost touch with the *substance* of the original religious feeling, thereby ceasing to be authentic religion at all."[71] Similarly, he argues against Harris and Dawkins's view that religious toleration leads as surely to suicide bombers as the Salvation Army by asserting that we should only tolerate those who have "authentic religiosity"; this rules out "those who behave in ways utterly at odds with what anyone moved by religious piety would do."[72] Reitan gives away the game by complaining that Dawkins, by "excluding goodness from his definition of God," has "excluded from his concept of God the very thing that can guard the concept from abuse."[73]

---

68. Dawkins, *supra* note 36, at 70. The acronym spells out "PAP." This, alas, is what passes for wit in Dawkins's writing.

69. *Id.* at 77.

70. *See, e.g.,* Haught, *supra* note 9, at 4–5.

71. Reitan, *supra* note 9, at 25.

72. *Id.* at 29.

73. *Id.* at 64.

Reitan may sincerely believe that God must, by definition, be good. For one who adopts a genuinely agnostic perspective, however, this stance is unavailable. From an agnostic perspective, we cannot say whether God, if he exists in the sense of being something transcendent that falls outside human comprehension, meets the human definition of good or evil. Even if she *wants* to believe that God is necessarily good, the agnostic will not assume that she has cornered the market on understanding what divine goodness means, lest she be faced by God's reply to Job: "What do *you* know about it, bub?" If one is squarely prepared to face God (or the potential existence of God) as a genuine mystery with sweeping implications, moral and otherwise, then one must be prepared to accept the possibility that God loves a sacrifice, that he wants those who do not rotate their crops in the approved manner to be punished—even that he favors or accepts, in some circumstances, the slaughter of innocents. Religion is not for the fainthearted. There are reasons why so many of the saints and prophets were not especially cuddly figures.

From a genuinely agnostic perspective, neither side in the battle of the New Commissars of Enlightenment is completely convincing. Both seem quite willing to make arguments that cannot satisfy those who have not accepted certain highly contestable premises, premises that need to be proved rather than asserted—and that may not be *capable* of proof.

COOLING THE CULTURE WARS

This does not mean both sides should settle on agnosticism as a kind of happy medium. After all, agnosticism is a creature of its own, not simply a midpoint between belief and non-belief. From a genuinely agnostic perspective, one that is concerned with questions of religious truth, one ought to respect the fact that both sides insist on the truth of their own beliefs.

What *is* surprising is that these extremes have succeeded so very well in setting the terms of the debate. Why is the debate over religious truth, at least in its popular form, so often one in which each side preaches to its own ranks of converts? What has happened to the middle ground? Why do even those New Atheist or New Anti-Atheist writers who acknowledge the nature of the stalemate, and concede that agnosticism might have something to offer to the discussion, so quickly dismiss it and fall back on the usual arguments wholly in favor of belief or non-belief?

A few explanations are possible. Charles Taylor argues that although many people, and possibly a majority in our age, may fall in between the extremes, "[P]eople take up a stance of this kind in a field which is polarized by the two extreme perspectives; they define themselves in relation to the polar opposites, whereas the people in polar opposition don't return the favour, but usually define themselves in relation to each other, ignoring the middle (or abusively assimilating it to the other side)."[74] Certainly there is good evidence for this. Theists, we have seen, often describe agnostics as timid atheists, and atheists often describe agnostics as timid theists.

Another possible explanation is that both belief and non-belief, by virtue of the very fact that neither can simply be assumed any more, have become mutually "fragilized."[75] The fact that both sets of beliefs have passionate advocates and equally passionate critics makes both sides feel simultaneously vindicated and embattled, triumphant and under siege. It is striking how many books on both sides begin by disagreeing on what ought to be simple factual questions, such as whether religion today is thriving or dying as a matter of simple demographics. In our pluralistic age, both sides of the argument are forced to justify themselves. This very demand simultaneously inspires a sense of righteous conviction on both sides and convinces both the atheists and the theists that the world is hostile to their beliefs.

There is an even simpler explanation: Extremes, especially in a fragmented cultural marketplace, sell. Their adherents are reliable cultural consumers; they are more easily reached than those who occupy the middle ground, vast though it may be. When Fox News and MSNBC's commentators raise their rhetoric to fever pitch and thereby garner new viewers, their *combined* viewership is still only a fraction of the major networks' viewership some 30 years ago. News, opinion, and cultural outlets today are fighting for market *fragments*, not the whole market, and so they rely on the relatively inexpensive expedient of plucking the low-hanging fruit.

These are all different explanations for the dominance of the extremes in our cultural conversation. Yet each in its own way speaks to the same underlying phenomenon: the pluralistic nature of our age. We live in an age in which there is a profusion of views—cultural, political, and most certainly religious. Belief *and* unbelief can be found everywhere in modern Western society. Even if our next-door neighbors believe (or disbelieve) as we do, we are aware of the profound varieties of belief and unbelief that can be found one street over, or one state over, or a continent away. In such an age, it is understandable that the extremes will drive the debate. Both the New Atheists and the New Anti-Atheists may have some basis for feeling embattled in our pluralist culture, and both sides may shout all the more loudly, both to galvanize their own supporters and to be heard by their opponents across the vast middle ground.

Furthermore, these extremes may be all the more attractive to some in our pluralistic landscape. In an agnostic age, one that can be as dizzying and unsettling

---

74. Taylor, *supra* note 56, at 431.
75. *Id.* at 675.

as it is liberating, the extremes of conviction and belief at least offer a sense of stability, certainty, and comfort. The very fact that they feel embattled drives these extremes to ever greater heights of fervor and certitude in their arguments. They are all the more driven to advocate their views because of their unshakeable sense that they are *right*, and their frustration that some people just can't see it. Anyone who has chosen otherwise or, perhaps worse, who has not chosen a side at all, poses a threat to their existence.

It is unsurprising that in such a fragmented and pluralistic world, the more extreme believers or nonbelievers will be the easiest people to reach. Our culture-makers may prefer the certainty of a small but committed audience to the risk and expense of trying to carve a market share out of the vast middle of our society.

Not that the venerated strategy of going for the lowest common denominator has disappeared, of course; just consult your local movie listings. It is unclear whether this strategy can work as well with books, magazines, and other sources of serious public discussion, however. Overall readership has declined, although books, magazines, and newspapers remain the venues in which much of our cultural dialogues occur.[76] Much of our cultural discussion has thus become oriented toward the most convinced, loyal, and extreme groups, rather than the segment of the population that falls in between the extremes.

This is what we find when we look at both the New Atheists and the New Anti-Atheists. Both sides emphasize the most extreme arguments rather than the middle ground. They are more interested, in many respects, in speaking to themselves than to each other or to the undecided. The leading writers on both sides may be intemperate, but they are not stupid. They recognize the gaps in their arguments. They know that their most important conclusions—that God definitely *does* exist, or that God definitely does *not* exist—cannot win by argument alone. In their quieter moments, they acknowledge the limits of their position, in footnotes or sentences tucked away here and there that begin, "Of course, . . ." or "One must admit that . . ." They may even concede, as McGrath does, that agnosticism, whether in the sense in which I have used it or in the weaker sense of refusing to be firmly and finally convinced by either side, may be the "only credible option."[77]

To the extent that the New Atheists and the New Anti-Atheists are intent on shoring up their own side rather than reaching anyone in the middle or on the

---

76. By contrast, movies, in which the lowest-common-denominator strategy still succeeds, are cultural *experiences*, not conversations. One does not generally enter into dialogue with a movie about a tough but tender cop and his plucky dog. Nor do I mean to neglect the role of the Internet. But the Internet, by its very nature, tends to be a fragmented place, a place driven by enclaves of the like-minded rather than conversations among and between the agnostic cultural middle.

77. McGrath, *supra* note 8, at 183.

other side, however, those occasional admissions are mere asides. They *do* believe what they believe, even if they acknowledge that argument alone cannot demonstrate the rightness of their beliefs. And so the usual round of thrust and parry, argument and counterargument, jibe and insult, begins all over again.

* * * * *

Surely we can do better. The culture wars are real and important. But they are not the whole story.

We do not need to deride or dismiss the views of those who fervently believe or disbelieve in God. Nor need we conclude that we have nothing to learn from either side or both sides—that, simply because there is a middle ground, the extreme views cannot be true or important. To the contrary, a true agnostic would begin by acknowledging that one of the extreme views might just be *right*.

But we also know that ours is an age of possibility and uncertainty, one in which it is possible to change our minds, to suspend our own ontological commitments, to see things from other perspectives. More than ever, we know that there *are* other perspectives. And we know that the people who hold them are reasonable—are, often enough, our friends, neighbors, and loved ones. From this perspective, we can see that although the culture wars are important, they neglect the complex views of a vast cross-section of our population, one that includes many believers *and* nonbelievers and certainly embraces those in between the two.[78]

Despite the high stakes, we can hope for a better approach to the question of religious truth, just as we hope for better solutions elsewhere in the culture wars. Indeed, precisely *because* these questions are so important, it is essential that we do better than just trading canned arguments and accusations about the knavery or stupidity of the other side. Too many people whose views are *not* defined by the extremes of the religious culture wars are interested in grappling with these fundamental questions to allow the debate to be defined and captured by those extremes.

That is why it has been important to provide a clear account of the new agnosticism and connect it to larger currents in our own age. It is vital that we understand what this brand of agnosticism looks like: its suspension of absolute commitments, its openness, its interest in questions of religious truth, and its willingness to plumb these mysteries by living in a state of negative capability in which one makes an imaginative leap into others' perspectives. And it has been necessary to show that, in many respects, the agnostic spirit is the spirit of our age: an age that is deeply pluralistic, in which a wide variety of beliefs and

---

78. *See generally* Morris P. Fiorina, Samuel J. Abrams, & Jeremy C. Pope, *Culture War?: The Myth of a Polarized America* (3d ed. 2004).

unbeliefs are viewed as genuine and not unthinkable possibilities, and in which the imaginative leap into others' perspectives is both a possible and, in many contexts, a commonplace move. It is important not only because the qualities that characterize the new agnostic, transposed into a different register, are the same ones that underwrite constitutional agnosticism. It is also important because it tells us something about our culture itself, one of pluralism and religious contestability, and about why constitutional agnosticism may be both possible and attractive in such a culture.

What all this suggests is that agnosticism is an unfairly neglected perspective in the religious culture wars. That does not mean that anyone must or should become a religious agnostic. But it does mean that in the endless debates between the New Atheists and the New Anti-Atheists, an important perspective is missing. There is room for a different and perhaps attractive perspective that falls between the poles of the usual debate. In between an emphatic *Yes* or *No*, there is room for an impassioned *Maybe*.

Our culture wars might proceed very differently if they were conducted in an agnostic spirit. Although agnostic voices themselves could contribute usefully to this debate, an agnostic spirit would be useful even if there were no agnostic voice as such in the religious culture wars, if the debates were still conducted primarily between staunch believers and nonbelievers. Even if the agnostics remain on the sidelines, the religious culture wars might be a lot different if they were conducted in a spirit of humility and doubt, or what Stephen White calls agnosis.

A debate conducted in this spirit would be one in which both sides of the debate carefully and humbly set out their own beliefs, but also subjected them to searching self-criticism. It would be one in which they shared what it is that makes them so strongly convinced of the final rightness of their beliefs. For believers, that would include a sense of the divineness of the world, of the awe and mystery at the heart of the universe, and of the sacredness of the lives within it. For nonbelievers, it would include a sense of life's "sacredness" as arising precisely from its contingent and impermanent nature, and of the poignant beauty of human life and feeling in a finite and mortal universe. But they might also candidly discuss their doubts as well as their certainties.

If nothing else, it would be a debate conducted in a spirit that is informed by humility rather than a sometimes overweening confidence. It might well convince both sides that in addition to sharing their own perspective, they might also devote some time to genuinely attempting to understand the perspective of the other—not from a critical outside perspective, but from an empathetic and imaginative inside perspective.[79]

---

79. *See, e.g.*, David Tracy, *Plurality and Ambiguity* (1987); David Tracy, *The Analogical Imagination* (1981).

Such a perspective might offer the New Atheists a sense of the power of faith in individual lives, and of the ways in which even religious people live in a state of doubt and constant reassessment, and are thus more nuanced and mature than the childish caricature of religious belief that many New Atheists insist on drawing. It might also impel them to acknowledge the ways in which a sense of faith may encourage good works rather than violence, that faith underwrote the civil rights movement and not just the Inquisition.

Conversely, it might lead the New Anti-Atheists to acknowledge the ways in which faith *can* lead to violence. They might treat this as an essential and troubling aspect of the religious experience, one that raises genuine questions about God's will, rather than brushing aside examples of religious violence because they supposedly lack "authentic religiosity." It might also lead them to appreciate the ways in which atheism too can coexist with a sense of awe and mystery, an appreciation for one's fellow human beings, and a genuine moral sense.

None of this need turn people away from belief or non-belief and toward agnosticism. One of the lessons of our agnostic age is that one can adopt a *spirit* of agnosticism without abandoning one's own deepest convictions on the ultimate questions. We live in an age of "fragilized" beliefs, not one of no beliefs at all.

The point is that we need not give in to the fear that if we openly discuss questions of religious truth, we must necessarily have a polarized, vacuous, sometimes vicious debate. We need not choose between either having an apocalyptic culture war or refusing to have any discussion of religious truth *at all*. There is a middle ground, and its benefits are considerable. By giving agnosticism a greater role in the debate over the ultimate questions of religious truth, and by encouraging a greater agnostic *spirit* on the part of all those who are engaged in the discussion, we might come to better appreciate the strengths *and* weaknesses of the many different possible perspectives on these questions. We might come to a stronger sense of our own uncertainties and limitations as well as our convictions.[80]

It is probably going too far to hope that such an approach might lead us closer to the actual *truth*—although the agnostic, as usual, cannot rule out that possibility. There is every reason to think that the search for religious truth will continue indefinitely, and that fierce debates and even culture wars will continue to be

80. *Cf.* William E. Connolly, *Belief, Spirituality, and Time*, in *Varieties of Secularism in a Secular Age* 126, 136–37 (Michael Warner, Jonathan VanAntwerpen, and Craig Calhoun, eds., 2010) (advocating a form of "deep pluralism" consisting of "the readiness to defend your creed in public while acknowledging that it so far lacks the power to confirm itself so authoritatively that all reasonable people must embrace it"); Jeffrey Stout, *Democracy and Tradition* 85 (2004).

a part of that search. But perhaps a little more of the agnostic spirit will help cool down our culture wars a little. As we continue to grapple with the ultimate questions of religious truth, perhaps it is possible to bring a little more charity and generosity to our dealings with each other, a little more light and a little less heat to our discussion, and a little more common ground to our divided and diverse community.

5. CONSTITUTIONAL AGNOSTICISM

INTRODUCTION

It is time to shift our focus away from *religious* agnosticism and toward what I call *constitutional agnosticism*. Constitutional agnosticism is similar to what I call the new agnosticism, but it is not the same thing. It speaks to the same currents in the culture wars. But constitutional agnosticism is aimed at a narrower, albeit significant, set of concerns. If religious agnosticism is one (but not the only) answer to the question of how we should confront the human condition as individuals, constitutional agnosticism is about the practical question of how we can collectively coexist and govern ourselves in a fragmented and pluralistic society. As Part Three will show, its primary payoff is for law and religion, the legal rules that govern our attempt to strike a balance between personal religious obligations and the shared needs of citizens in a pluralistic liberal state.

In this chapter, I describe what constitutional agnosticism entails, and why we ought to make the move toward constitutional agnosticism. I will then talk about what constitutional agnosticism is *not*. In particular, although some commentators have argued that we already have an agnostic Constitution, the kind of contemporary approach to law and religion issues they are talking about is not constitutional agnosticism, properly understood. If anything, it is closer to secularism.

Having thus laid the ground, I will discuss constitutional agnosticism itself in more detail. It raises several important questions. First, to *whom* does constitutional agnosticism apply? Does it apply only to judges, or does it also have something to say about the approach of both public officials and citizens with respect to church–state issues? Second, does one have to be a *religious* agnostic to be a *constitutional* agnostic? The answer is that one does not. Constitutional agnosticism draws on the lessons that the new agnosticism offers, but it is a political and jurisprudential strategy, not a religious belief system.

Constitutional agnosticism also raises a couple of subsidiary issues. First, I will argue that constitutional agnosticism is consistent with the text, history, and traditions of the First Amendment. Second, I will ask what happens when constitutional agnosticism runs out. What happens when constitutional agnosticism cannot fully resolve a question of church–state conflict? That question will be previewed in this chapter, and fleshed out over the rest of the book.

WHY CONSTITUTIONAL AGNOSTICISM?

Even if our current state of affairs is rightly viewed as posing a genuine predicament for liberalism in general and law and religion in particular, why should we turn to constitutional agnosticism? How does one move from discussing *religious* agnosticism to arguing for the value of *constitutional* agnosticism? In particular, if one is already committed to a position of belief or non-belief with respect to religious truth, why might one still conclude that constitutional agnosticism is the best approach to the questions of church–state conflict that haunt us?

The answer lies primarily in the agnostic spirit of our age, and the failure of the standard approaches to religious liberty—openly secular approaches, openly religious approaches, or liberal approaches—to satisfy the conditions of that age. The "strange and complex conditions of belief"[1] in our own time are such that these standard approaches can no longer succeed. To live in our agnostic age does not require that one become a religious agnostic; one can still be a believer or a nonbeliever. But one can no longer be a believer or nonbeliever in a "naïve" fashion, in a way that is blind to the "awareness that one could change one's preferences."[2]

Once we acknowledge this, a number of options that might once have been available are foreclosed as a practical matter, no longer capable of commanding widespread agreement. Neither openly secular nor openly religious approaches to religious freedom are likely to be convincing in our age. We are too aware of the ways in which both positions are mutually "fragilized,"[3] as Charles Taylor puts it, for either option to be fully satisfactory to a sufficient portion of the population. They certainly will not convince their opponents. In an age in which we are aware of the presence of other perspectives and the potential mutability of our own beliefs, they may no longer fully convince even their proponents.

The liberal perspective on religious freedom purports to differ from both of these approaches. It claims to proceed from a position of neither belief nor unbelief, arguing instead that we should simply set aside fundamental questions of religious truth, leaving them for the private realm. Despite the successes it has enjoyed, however, this approach no longer suffices. Liberals may continue to argue that their approach, by sidelining questions of religious truth, respects both religious belief and non-belief, and offers the best hope for an approach to religious liberty that will avoid miring us once more in the sectarian wars that

---

1. Charles Taylor, *A Secular Age* 727 (2007).

2. Peter Berger & Anton Zijderveld, *In Praise of Doubt: How to Have Convictions Without Becoming a Fanatic* 111 (2009).

3. Taylor, *supra* note 1, at 30, 675.

made liberalism necessary in the first place. But that prospect seems ever more fragile.

The problem, as we have seen, is that liberals are no longer sure that their justifications for liberal values, including the value of religious toleration, stand on neutral ground. They are not sure that it is possible to justify religious liberty *without* addressing questions of religious truth. Indeed, some advocates of religious justifications for religious liberty, like John Garvey, as well as some critics of liberalism, like Stanley Fish, are *certain* it is impossible. As the rise of the New Atheists suggests, some nonbelievers believe that religious toleration itself is dangerous, because its protection of religious moderates ends up giving cover to violent religious extremists. They argue that we must finally have it out on the question of religious truth. And individuals from all of these perspectives believe that the liberal strategy of damping down conflict by relegating questions of religious truth to the private realm is incoherent at best, and an unjustifiable form of hegemony at worst.

In short, questions of religious truth stubbornly persist, try as we might to avoid them or put them on the sidelines. The hope that we might craft a stable, coherent, and lasting approach to political liberty and religious freedom without confronting questions of religious truth has become increasingly doubtful.

That conclusion is not just a matter of reasoned argument. It is also a matter of numbers. In an agnostic age, the conventional liberal position inevitably will command the loyalty of a diminishing number of people. It is also a question of what Charles Taylor calls our social imaginary:[4] the worldview that shapes and reflects our times, and that influences what arguments we are likely to find plausible, attractive, and worthy of deep loyalty. Whatever their merits, liberalism and liberal justifications for religious freedom simply do not occupy the same privileged status in our modern social imaginary that they did even a short time ago. The pull of opposing forces, the breadth of social and religious pluralism that liberalism must accommodate, the sense that liberalism itself is only one among many possible choices, the number of individuals who are unwilling to live under the demands that the liberal treaty imposes—all are too great. We have no choice but to confront questions of religious truth; but neither believing nor unbelieving answers to those questions are likely to prevail in an age in which both sides are mutually fragilized.

Constitutional agnosticism is the solution to this dilemma. It is the approach that is best suited to our agnostic age, that best occupies the shifting ground on which we stand. It is the hardiest and fittest occupant of the Arctic middle spaces of which William James wrote. It is a constitutional philosophy of the cusp, for an age of the cusp.

---

4. Charles Taylor, *Modern Social Imaginaries* (2004).

Although, as I have been at pains to point out, constitutional agnosticism is not a religious belief system, agnostic or otherwise, it is, like the new agnosticism, a response to the conditions of our age, one that draws on many of the same lessons and shares many of the same empathetic, imaginative, and questing qualities. Like the new agnosticism, constitutional agnosticism refuses to shy away from questions of religious truth, recognizing the futility and unsustainability of this strategy. Rather, it engages them. It treats these questions as central to the human condition. It insists that unless we try to address them, we can arrive at no lasting compromise, no coherent or widely accepted solution to the questions of church–state conflict that confront us. It places these ultimate questions squarely in the foreground of our thought rather than seeking to defer or ignore them. At the same time, its very unwillingness to offer a final *answer* to these questions, and its eagerness to explore and imagine what the truth looks like from a variety of possible perspectives, makes constitutional agnosticism the approach that is most capable of mediating among and between these different perspectives.

It cannot do so with absolute success, to be sure. As we will see in Chapter Eight, *no* approach to church-state conflict can completely redeem such a promise. Nevertheless, because constitutional agnosticism is the approach that best reflects the conditions, the spirit, and the "social imaginary" of our agnostic age, it stands the closest chance of offering a coherent and widely acceptable approach to questions of religious liberty. In keeping with what we have learned about that age, it acknowledges the centrality of questions of religious truth to questions of religious liberty and church–state conflict, rather than shunting them aside. It is not antagonistic toward belief; to the contrary, it assumes that religious beliefs may be *true* in a final sense. Neither is it antagonistic toward non-belief, to which it accords the same assumption. It does not, as some liberal approaches to religious liberty might, disserve *both* sides by treating questions of religious truth as purely private matters. And, of course, it gives due recognition to agnosticism itself. It recognizes that agnosticism is an approach to religious belief shared by an increasing number of individuals in our society. It understands the value of agnosticism as an imaginative frame of mind, a response to the pluralism of our age and the sense of belief (and non-belief) as a live option—one that is widely shared today by confirmed religious believers *and* nonbelievers, as well as by agnostics themselves.

WHAT CONSTITUTIONAL AGNOSTICISM IS NOT

Before describing constitutional agnosticism in more detail, one last important objection must be addressed. This is the objection that constitutional agnosticism is nothing new—that it is just the standard liberal approach to questions of religious liberty with a new paint job.[5] According to this argument, the liberal state (including the courts) already assumes neither the truth nor the falsity of any particular religious belief. It is already solicitous of religious beliefs. It already provides the same protections that constitutional agnosticism offers. It *is* constitutional agnosticism, and vice versa.

Certainly one can find language to that effect in existing legal scholarship. Steven Smith, for example, argues that the Constitution itself is agnostic.[6] Andrew Koppelman says, in terms that resemble what I have to say about constitutional agnosticism, that under our present system, "[t]he state is agnostic about religion, but it is an interested and sympathetic agnosticism."[7] Douglas Laycock, who writes that his own "agnostic view of religion predisposes me to an agnostic explanation for religious liberty,"[8] suggests that the current approach to religious liberty is similar, although not identical, to an agnostic approach: "Agnostics have no opinion [on religious truth] for *epistemological* reasons; the government must have no opinion for *constitutional* reasons. The government must have no opinion because it is not the government's role to have an opinion."[9]

All three writers make important points, but I ultimately take issue with each of them. Of the three, Smith most clearly argues, as I do, that our Constitution *should* be agnostic, but that this agnosticism is not always reflected in the current practice of the courts. I agree with him, but will argue in a later chapter that he is mistaken about the implications of that argument for legal doctrine. By contrast, I agree with many of the substantive doctrinal points about law and religion advanced by Laycock and Koppelman. But both of them argue that the Religion Clauses of the Constitution are agnostic not only in principle, but as a matter of *current* practice. Here, I think they are mistaken. Whether it should be or not, the current liberal approach to law and religion, as reflected in the decisions of our courts, is *not* constitutional agnosticism.

What is the difference between constitutional agnosticism and the current approach to church–state conflict? It is primarily a matter of attitude and approach, although in some cases it also involves substantive differences. Consider, again, the quotes from Koppelman and Laycock. Koppelman writes that the state currently practices an "interested and sympathetic agnosticism"

---

5. In addition to what I have to say about that claim here, that question is taken up in greater detail in Chapter Eight.

6. *See* Steven D. Smith, *Our Agnostic Constitution*, 83 N.Y.U. L. Rev. 120 (2008).

7. Andrew Koppelman, *Corruption of Religion and the Establishment Clause*, 50 Wm. & Mary L. Rev. 1831, 1907 (2009) (emphasis added).

8. Douglas Laycock, *Religious Liberty as Liberty*, 7 J. Contemp. Legal Issues 313, 356 (1996).

9. Douglas Laycock, *Equal Access and Moments of Silence: The Equal Status of Religious Speech by Private Speakers*, 81 Nw. U. L. Rev. 1, 8 (1986) (emphasis added).

toward religion. Laycock, a prominent champion of religious liberty, writes that government has no opinion on religious matters, not for epistemological reasons, but because "it is not the government's role to have an opinion" on these matters.

Taken together, both perspectives explain why we cannot call the current approach one of genuine constitutional agnosticism. The courts, and the liberal state more generally, are certainly *protective* of religious freedom. But that is not necessarily the same as being genuinely *interested* in or *empathetic* toward religion. To the contrary, the standard liberal view is that government has no business taking an interest in questions of religious truth. Laycock argues that this is because the government is supposed to treat these questions as irrelevant to its primary concern; it does not want to discuss questions it believes it is incompetent to answer.[10] But the fact remains that under our current understanding of law and religion, government is supposed to be protective of the private and personal nature of religious claims, not interested in questions of religious truth as such. In other words, it is supposed to hew to the standard liberal line of refusing to confront questions of religious truth at all.

This distinguishes the current approach from constitutional agnosticism in a number of ways. At a theoretical level, the current approach is left with the same problems that we explored in Part One. The unwillingness of liberalism, and of theories of religious liberty that draw on liberalism, to confront questions of religious truth leaves them unmoored and unclear: untethered to any substantive value, prone to smuggle in substantive values without saying so, and bereft of the resources to justify those values. This is different from constitutional agnosticism, which *does* confront questions of religious truth, directly and sympathetically, although it ends up provisionally suspending its ontological commitments on those questions.

The unrootedness of the current approach tends, moreover, to have predictable and unfortunate consequences. The liberal approach to religious liberty tends to skew toward a distinctly non-religious or secular perspective. Both secularists and religious believers are aware of this tendency.[11] Given our current limited vocabulary, however, we are unable to acknowledge and address this

---

10. Something of this epistemological modesty is evident in the Supreme Court's attitude toward cases involving potential religious fraud and sincerity, in which it is reluctant to delve too deeply into the question whether a particular religious claimant is using religious claims to his own financial or personal advantage, or whether he is "accurately" stating a religious claim according to the tenets of a majority of believers of that faith. *See, e.g., Thomas v. Review Board,* 450 U.S. 707 (1981); *United States v. Ballard,* 322 U.S. 78 (1944). I address those issues in the next chapter.

11. To be sure, it is possible to be a secularist without being a nonbeliever. As I will argue in the text, however, an openly secularist approach tends toward policies and conclusions that lean in the direction of non-belief rather than genuine neutrality as between belief and non-belief.

problem in a candid and productive way. This is what leads John Garvey to conclude from a religious perspective that the liberal approach toward religious liberty (which, as we saw, he confuses with a genuinely agnostic approach) does not fully recognize the importance of religious belief.[12] Similarly, it is what persuades Stephen Carter that the liberal state fails to recognize the powerful force of religious obligation, and instead treats religion as a "hobby."[13]

From the opposite end of the spectrum, the same tendency has not only been acknowledged, but praised, by those who favor a purely secular approach to religious freedom. Many secularists might characterize their approach to church–state conflict as "agnostic," or argue that the Constitution itself is "godless."[14] Examined more carefully, however, their arguments betray a fierce brand of secularism. Proponents of this view argue that the state must remove religion from every place except the private realm, including the elimination of religious language from public debate and the maintenance of a high wall of separation between religion and the state. This may not be atheism, but, at least in the eyes of many religious believers, it amounts to atheism by default.

Despite the widespread use of religious language in the public square, we are closer to this secular default in American politics than we may realize. The current attitude of the state, political officials included, is often one of nominal piety and actual secularism. American politicians, by and large, *campaign* as Christians and *govern* as secularists. There are exceptions to this rule, of course. But it is still a striking tendency, and one that has not received enough attention. Whatever their own beliefs may be, the language with which public officials deliberate and govern remains that of the liberal state.

When that is our language, serious religious claims will be viewed as deficient when compared to the needs of the secular public order. One need only consider the Supreme Court's decision in *Employment Division v. Smith*. There, the Court rejected the argument that the Free Exercise Clause requires exemptions for religious believers from any general law that incidentally burdens religious practices. Instead, it held that any law that is not aimed at religion, but only incidentally burdens religion, is subject to no real Free Exercise scrutiny at all, no matter how heavy the burden may be. Why? Because such a right would "court[ ] anarchy" by threatening, among other things, the nation's *traffic* laws.[15]

In short, the prevailing approach to religious liberty is not the same as constitutional agnosticism, although the results they prescribe will often overlap.

---

12. *See, e.g.,* John H. Garvey, *An Anti-Liberal Argument for Religious Liberty,* 7 J. Contemp. Legal Issues 275, 279 (1996).

13. *See* Stephen L. Carter, *The Culture of Disbelief: How American Law and Politics Trivialize Religious Devotion* (1993).

14. *See, e.g.,* Isaac Kramnick & R. Laurence Moore, *The Godless Constitution: A Moral Defense of the Secular State* (2005).

15. *Employment Division v. Smith,* 494 U.S. 872, 888–89 (1990).

The liberal approach that generally prevails in much common thinking about the Religion Clauses is unwilling to directly confront and consider questions of religious truth. That unwillingness ends up bending the law in favor of secularism. What is missing from this approach is a genuine sense of living in and amidst mystery, uncertainty, and doubt, while remaining deeply engaged in questions of ultimate religious truth. Constitutional agnosticism, in sum, is *not* what we have now.

WHAT IS CONSTITUTIONAL AGNOSTICISM?

"The spirit of liberty," Judge Learned Hand famously said, "is that spirit which is not too sure that it is right."[16] This is a somewhat dangerous way to begin a description of constitutional agnosticism. Hand's remark has become a red flag for constitutional lawyers. Professor Philip Kurland once wrote that whenever a court quotes Chief Justice Marshall's famous line in *McCulloch v. Maryland*— "[W]e must never forget that it is a constitution we are expounding"[17]—"you can be sure that the court will be throwing the constitutional text, its history, and its structure to the winds in reaching its conclusion."[18] Hand's dictum has achieved a similar status. When someone tells you that the spirit of liberty "is not too sure that it is right," as often as not you can be certain you are in the presence of someone who is pretty damn sure he *is* right— or who simply has no idea what he means at all. Either way, you would be wise to keep your hand on your wallet.

Nevertheless, Hand's quote is exactly the right one for the occasion. (Just don't say you weren't warned.) The spirit of constitutional agnosticism *is* a spirit that is not too sure it is right.

Constitutional agnosticism is, in a sense, the new agnosticism in a different register. It is an approach to religious liberty that reflects the spirit of our agnostic age. In many respects, it builds on the phenomena we saw in Chapter Three: the suspension of ontological commitments, and the capacity for negative capability that has become ingrained in modern thought. Unlike either openly secular or openly religious approaches to religious freedom, it does not stake its all on a positive claim about religious truth.

At the same time, unlike the conventional liberal approach to religious liberty, it does not seek to avoid questions of religious truth. Instead, like the new agnosticism itself, it takes a positive and genuinely committed approach to

---

16. Learned Hand, *The Spirit of Liberty*, in *The Spirit of Liberty: Papers and Addresses of Learned Hand* 190 (Irving Dilliard, ed., 2d ed. 1953).

17. *McCulloch v. Maryland*, 17 U.S. (4 Wheat.) 316, 407 (1819).

18. Philip B. Kurland, *Curia Regis: Some Comments on the Divine Right of Kings and Courts to Say What the Law Is*, 23 Ariz. L. Rev. 582, 591 (1981).

these questions. It remains open to the possibility that there is some truth out there to be reached, although it does not reach a conclusion about what that truth is. Almost paradoxically, it takes the position that we cannot achieve a coherent approach to religious liberty without simultaneously striving to formulate an answer to the ultimate questions of religious truth *and* suspending any ultimate resolution of those questions.

Perhaps the most important contribution that constitutional agnosticism makes to questions of religious liberty is its emphasis on the importance of the imaginative leap. It refuses to take the stand-pat approach of assuming that a religious claim may be true but simultaneously discounting the importance of that possibility. All too often in liberal discourse, especially legal discourse, assuming the truth of a religious claim is just a prelude to assuming it away. Deflationary approaches of this kind treat the truth of a religious claim as a relative triviality, and move quickly to a discussion that speaks in essentially secular terms, pitting my "conscience" against your "compelling state interests." Even if they begin by assuming that religious claims are true, they end by concluding that whether they are true or not isn't really that important.

That is not the spirit of constitutional agnosticism. Instead, constitutional agnosticism asks of a religious claim, "What if this belief is true?"—and *means* it. In the spirit of negative capability, it attempts to enter a religious claim from an internal perspective rather than an external one.

To take an extreme example, consider God's command to Abraham to sacrifice his son, Isaac.[19] In the biblical narrative, God promises Abraham that, despite his advanced age and that of his wife, Sarah, he will become "exceedingly fruitful," the "ancestor of a multitude of nations."[20] Sarah, who is 90 years old when

---

19. This text, which appears in the twenty-second chapter of Genesis, is of central importance in the Judaic tradition, and its implications have been explored in a rich literature, of which one of the most important works is Søren Kierkegaard's *Fear and Trembling* (C. Stephen Evans & Sylvia Walsh, eds., Sylvia Walsh, trans., 2006) (1843). For other treatments of this story, *see, e.g.,* Shalom Spiegel, *The Last Trial on the Legends and Lore of the Command to Abraham to Offer Isaac as a Sacrifice: The Akedah* (Judah Goldin, trans., 1967); Larry Powell, *Holy Murder: Abraham, Isaac, and the Rhetoric of Sacrifice* (2006); Carol Delaney, *Abraham on Trial* (2000). For discussions in the legal literature, *see, e.g.,* Caleb E. Mason, *Faith, Harm, and Neutrality: Some Complexities of Free Exercise Law,* 44 Duq. L. Rev. 225 (2006); Andrew J. Demko, Note, *Abraham's Deific Defense: Problems With Insanity, Faith, and Knowing Right From Wrong,* 80 Notre Dame L. Rev. 1961 (2005); Grant H. Morris, *"God Told Me to Kill": Religion or Delusion?,* 38 San Diego L. Rev. 973 (2001); Suzanne Last Stone, *Justice, Mercy, and Gender in Rabbinic Thought,* 8 Cardozo Stud. L. & Literature 139 (1996); Sanford Levinson, *The Multicultures of Belief and Disbelief,* 92 Mich. L. Rev. 1873 (1994); Henry J. Abraham, *Abraham, Isaac, and the State: Faith-Healing and Legal Intervention,* 27 U. Rich. L. Rev. 951 (1993). As an aside, my own young son is named Isaac, so this story has a special resonance for me.

20. Gen. 17: 4–7.

this assurance is made, delivers a son, Isaac, who—with Ishmael, Abraham's son by Sarah's Egyptian slave Hagar, already having been shuffled out of the story and into Islamic legend—is destined to become one of the Jewish patriarchs. Despite God's promise, when Isaac is still young, God tells Abraham, "Take your son, your only son Isaac, whom you love, and go to the land of Moriah, and offer him there as a burnt offering on one of the mountains that I shall show you."[21] Abraham dutifully takes Isaac into the mountains, bidding him carry the wood for the burnt offering while "he himself carrie[s] the fire and the knife."[22] At the appointed place, Abraham binds Isaac and "reach[es] out his hand and [takes] the knife to kill his son."[23]

Only then does God intervene. In Woody Allen's modern retelling of the story, the divine one tells Abraham, "Doth thou listen to every crazy idea that comes thy way? . . . I jokingly suggest thou sacrifice Isaac and thou immediately runs out to do it. . . . No sense of humor. I can't believe it."[24] In the original narrative, however, God steps in and provides a ram as a substitute offering in Isaac's place.[25]

The story of the binding and abortive sacrifice of Isaac is one of great power and horror. It is understandable that religious believers and nonbelievers alike seek to deflect some of the power of the story by repurposing it. Religious believers assume that God would never require such a sacrifice, and that the story's true lesson lies in his provision of a substitute offering.[26] Nonbelievers treat the story as an example of the horrors of religion, and the importance of thinking for oneself.[27] Few—Kierkegaard being an important exception—are willing to confront the story on its own terms.

Certainly no prosecutor or judge operating under the prevailing liberal approach to religious freedom would be troubled by a case like Abraham's. She would assume Abraham's sincerity, dismiss the importance or relevance of his religious claim, and promptly clap him in jail. At most, if she took the claim seriously, it would be as evidence of his insanity.[28]

---

21. Gen. 22:2.
22. Gen. 22:6.
23. Gen. 22:10.
24. Woody Allen, *Without Feathers* 27 (1975).
25. Gen. 22:11–18.
26. *See, e.g.,* Robert Adams, *Finite and Infinite Goods: A Framework for Ethics* 284 (1999).
27. *See, e.g.,* Stewart Shapiro, *Faith and Reason, the Perpetual War: Ruminations of a Fool,* in *Philosophers Without Gods* 3, 10 (Louise Antony, ed., 2007) ("I cannot help seeing this episode as a refutation of rationalism. . . . For me at least, the message of the story is clear, and I reject it with all my being.").
28. *See* Adams, *supra* note 26, at 284 (describing how he asks his students, "What would you think if you asked your neighbor why he was building a large stone table in his backyard, and he said, 'I'm building an altar, because God has commanded me to

Of course, one can sympathize with this conclusion. Most of us would con-clude that just about everyone in Abraham's position must be in the grip of a delusion, not a genuine revelatory experience. (An atheist would say that *anyone* who makes such a claim is delusional.) The real mystery comes from the fact that so many *religious* people, including those who believe Abraham's story is *true*, would unhesitatingly take the liberal approach to the problem, either dis-missing Abraham's claim or treating it as largely irrelevant in the face of the overpowering state interest in preserving life. The modern response to the Abrahamic story is a tribute to the optional quality of religious belief in our agnostic age and, in a broader sense, to the cognitive dissonance that lies at the heart of the relationship between religion and liberalism.

A religious agnostic, of course, could not assume that a person making Abraham's claim was either deluded *or* the subject of a genuine communication from God. A *constitutional* agnostic would operate from something of the same perspective. He would make an imaginative leap, putting himself in Abraham's shoes (or, I suppose, sandals) and asking: What if Abraham was telling the *truth*? What stakes would such a claim raise? And could the state justifiably interfere with such a claim if it *were* true?

I have deliberately chosen a provocative example here, to remind us of the high stakes involved on both sides. Many religious claims raise far lower stakes, both for religious believers and for the state. A constitutionally agnostic approach may thus, in most cases, safely recommend a wide scope for religious liberty without raising the same concerns presented by Abraham's case. If only for personal reasons, I am certainly not suggesting that we declare open season on children named Isaac.

The point is that a constitutionally agnostic approach to a religious claim would *engage* that religious claim, seriously and imaginatively. It would give full weight to the possibility that such a religious claim could be true, and ask what followed from that possibility. It could not help but consider the serious state interests involved, but it would not be satisfied with any approach that failed to take into account the seriousness of the stakes on *both* sides. It would find some-thing pallid and insufficient in a mere balancing of a claim of "conscience" against secular state interests, as if the potential *truth* of that claim added noth-ing to the scales. Like Judge Learned Hand, a constitutional agnostic would be reluctant to conclude that a religious claim that raised such serious stakes was true in fact; but he would also be reluctant to conclude that it was *not* true. Like Keats's description of negative capability, his approach would proceed from within a state of mystery, uncertainty, and doubt. This analysis might lead to very

---

sacrifice my son as a whole burnt offering. Won't you come to the ceremony tomorrow morning?' All agree that the neighbor should be committed to a mental hospital.").

different results from the ones we see in the courts today, or to the same results. But its spirit would be very different.

Hearkening back to our earlier discussion of William James's *The Will to Believe*, the one unavailable answer to the kinds of dilemmas raised by such a religious claim is to do nothing. In law, we *are* faced with forced options, and any resolution of the claim—accepting it, rejecting it, or attempting to squirrel out of it altogether by one means or another—is a real action with serious consequences. Every choice we make in these circumstances cannot help but speak to the questions of religious truth raised by the case, and how we weigh their importance.

Constitutional agnosticism is in no different position on this point than any other approach to religious liberty. It will make decisions, some of which will favor religious claimants and some of which will not. But it will do so in a very different spirit. It will be an open, empathetic, and imaginative spirit: one that acknowledges the mysteries that lie at the heart of any church–state conflict and takes moral responsibility for them, that tries to fully account for the importance of the questions involved even as it suspends its own ultimate conclusions about the truth of those competing claims.

TO WHOM DOES CONSTITUTIONAL AGNOSTICISM APPLY?

In the popular New Atheist book *Freethinkers*, Susan Jacoby bridles at President George W. Bush's decision, after the September 11 attacks, to speak at an ecumenical service at Washington National Cathedral. Jacoby treats the speech's religious location and content as evidence of "the erosion of America's secularist tradition," and a "gross violation of the respect for separation of church and state constitutionally required of the nation's chief executive."[29]

This is a very common move, and an unsurprising one, in a nation in which the language of constitutionalism tends to pervade public discussions about policy and morality. But it is not good enough. As with any other theory of religious liberty, our treatment of constitutional agnosticism must consider whether and how that approach applies to a variety of individuals and institutions acting in different ways. Thus, we might distinguish between the President himself, judges, legislators, executive officials, and private citizens. Even within these categories, further questions arise. For example, is there a distinction between a legislator who acts in a way that touches specifically on religion, such as voting on a decision whether to erect a Ten Commandments display, and a legislator who acts on a matter of public policy that does not directly involve religion—say,

---

29. Susan Jacoby, *Freethinkers: A History of American Secularism* 3 (2004).

an appropriation for agricultural subsidies—but invokes religious reasons for his vote?

These are rich and complex questions.[30] Let us consider whether and how constitutional agnosticism might apply to various categories of public and private actors. My general answer is that constitutional agnosticism is appropriate for *all* of these categories of institution or individual, but it plays a somewhat different role in each case. It is not mandatory for elected officials or citizens, but should be a preferred approach. It is more strongly recommended, if not mandatory, for judges. The reasons for this vary according to the role involved.

The argument for judges adopting constitutional agnosticism is the most straightforward. Among public officials, judges are most in need of a general approach to questions of religious liberty, and least in need of a position that corresponds to their own views on religion and religious truth. They require a position that allows them to mediate between the diverse positions on religious truth held by different individuals and groups in society, and the generally secular reasons offered by the state to justify regulating different forms of private or public religious conduct. It is too late in the day to argue that judges must occupy a "neutral" position; indeed, a central argument of this book is that the liberal conception of neutrality is not as neutral as it purports to be and, in any event, is ill suited to our agnostic age. Constitutional agnosticism offers an approach that, while it should not be called "neutral," does not ground itself on an absolute position of religious belief or non-belief. No approach that a judge takes with respect to controversial church–state questions can satisfy everyone, and certainly no outcome in a particular case can. But constitutional agnosticism, by acknowledging the importance of religious truth, is most likely to satisfy more people more of the time, and least likely to display disregard for the deeply held positions on either side. Although it would be a mistake to call this "neutrality" in the sense in which it is generally used in standard liberal language, constitutional agnosticism is, in a sense, the closest one can come to an engaged and empathetic "neutrality" in an agnostic age.

Legislators are in a different position. Legislators are not obliged to be religious agnostics. Moreover, the respect that agnosticism demands for the possible truth of deeply held beliefs on questions of religious truth leads to a reluctance to conclude that legislators must either suppress their religiously held beliefs or, as a rule, provide publicly accessible reasons alongside any religious arguments

---

30. In this area, I am indebted to the careful work of Kent Greenawalt, who has written the most complete treatment of these issues over the course of several books. *See* Kent Greenawalt, *Religious Convictions and Political Choice* (1988); Kent Greenawalt, *Private Consciences and Public Reasons* (1995); 2 Kent Greenawalt, *Religion and the Constitution: Establishment and Fairness*, ch. 23 (2008).

for a particular policy.[31] That does not mean legislators might not *choose* to offer such reasons, if for no other reason than to capture popular support for that position.[32] But no strict rule of this sort is required by constitutional agnosticism. That does not mean that there are no limits on what legislators can *do* through official collective action. Those limits are supplied by the Religion Clauses themselves, as we will see when we discuss the Establishment Clause in Chapter Seven. But they have to do with the effects of the legislation itself, not the language in which they deliberate about it.

Nevertheless, constitutional agnosticism is still a good idea for legislators. Courts are not the only forum, or even necessarily the final one, in which questions of religious liberty are argued and decided. Indeed, ever since the Supreme Court narrowed the scope of protection for religious conduct under the Free Exercise Clause in *Employment Division v. Smith*,[33] some of the most important actions protecting religious exercise have taken place in Congress[34] and the state legislatures.[35] Legislators are regularly faced with questions of whether and how to accommodate religious liberty, to provide (or not provide) funding to religious groups, or to make or refrain from making overtly religious statements, directly or indirectly—for example, by establishing legislative prayers or requiring moments of silent prayer in public schools. As much or more than courts, they are routinely confronted with the need to balance the interests of a wide array of religious beliefs, as well as the interests of nonbelievers, against what we might generally label the secular needs of the state. Constitutional agnosticism responds to this need by counseling an open and empathetic approach to church-state conflicts, one in which the legislator, whatever his or her own position on

---

31. Such a position is taken in the later work of John Rawls. *See* John Rawls, *Political Liberalism* li–lii (paperback ed., 1996); John Rawls, *The Idea of Public Reason Revisited*, 64 U. Chi. L. Rev. 756 (1997).

32. *See* Paul Horwitz, *Religion and American Politics: Three Views of the Cathedral*, 39 U. Mem. L. Rev. 973, 1025 (2009); Jeffrey Stout, *Democracy and Tradition* 86 (2004).

33. 494 U.S. 872 (1990).

34. *See, e.g.*, Religious Freedom Restoration Act, 42 U.S.C. § 2000bb–2000bb-4 (2004). In *City of Boerne v. Flores*, 521 U.S. 507 (1997), the Supreme Court held that the act, commonly known as RFRA, could not be justified as it applied to actions by state or local governments. It has upheld the continued application of RFRA to the federal government. *See Gonzales v. O Centro Espirita Beneficente União de Vegetal*, 546 U.S. 418 (2006). The invalidation of RFRA insofar as it concerns state and local laws led Congress to draft a more narrowly tailored statute applying against the states where certain land use and prisoners' or other institutionalized persons' rights claims are involved. *See* Religious Land Use and Institutionalized Persons Act, 42 U.S.C. § 2000cc–2000cc-5 (2004), commonly known as RLUIPA. The prisoners' rights portion of the statute was upheld by the Supreme Court in *Cutter v. Wilkinson*, 544 U.S. 709 (2005).

35. *See, e.g.*, 1 William W. Bassett et al., *Religious Organizations and the Law* § 2:52 (2007) (listing so-called "state RFRA" statutes, which recreate the federal RFRA at the state level).

matters of religious truth or matters of public policy, at least attempts to enter imaginatively the perspective of the contending groups involved in any such legislation before casting his or her vote.

Indeed, some of Congress's actions in the past fifteen years or so, responding to the Supreme Court's dramatic decision in *Smith* and partially restoring a right to religious accommodation in the face of generally applicable laws that incidentally burden religion, can best be justified in terms of constitutional agnosticism. One does not need to be a Muslim prisoner, or even a religious believer, to appreciate the gravity of restrictions on Muslim prayer and diet in prison, and to balance a meaningfully empathetic understanding of those stakes against the state's asserted need for order in the prisons. A standard liberal approach to such a conflict may assume the truth of the religious claims involved, but without fully appreciating the stakes of those claims. Even if it leads to a sound outcome, that approach might not convince the individuals or groups involved that their interests have really been heard and given due weight. So, even if constitutional agnosticism is not a mandatory stance for legislators, it is still a valuable one.

Elected executive officers—the President, governors, and so on—are in a similar position to legislators. They, too, are entitled to have their own religious beliefs and to make them known. But they also govern amid a play of contending beliefs and interests, and have a strong interest in mediating fairly among those interests. They can achieve that understanding only by trying to make an imaginative leap into the perspectives of the people involved. For executive officials, as for legislators, constitutional agnosticism is the best way not only of achieving sound results, but of achieving them in a way that fully accounts for and responds to the play of interests and perspectives in a pluralistic age.

Citizens stand at one further remove from legislators and executive officials. In a pluralistic age, our assumption is that a diversity of perspectives, both on questions of religious truth and other matters, benefits our society. In any event, pluralism is just a fact about our society. Simply asserting that debates over public policy should proceed by shunting religion into the private sphere and restricting public debate to publicly accessible reasons is unlikely to be as convincing a response as it once was. Our approach to questions of religious liberty and public policy for citizens should thus be "uninhibited, robust, and wide-open,"[36] imposing no rules of dialogue and instead allowing these interests to play out as vigorously and messily as circumstances dictate. Under this system, the backstop to this no-holds-barred discussion between citizens is provided by public officials. Their constitutionally agnostic stance allows them to mediate between conflicting interests and arguments at the level of official action, subject to the constitutional constraints I discuss in Part Three.

---

36. *New York Times v. Sullivan*, 376 U.S. 254, 270 (1964).

Thus, I am not suggesting that constitutional agnosticism ought to be a *mandatory* approach for citizens, one that constrains their private views or public arguments. But that's not the whole story. As we saw in Chapter One, critics of liberalism argue that by splitting off religious sentiments from the public realm, liberalism fails to treat individuals *as* individuals, with their own religious beliefs, cultural backgrounds, and attachments. It treats us as "unencumbered selves" rather than "situated selves."[37]

This is a compelling criticism. But a competing risk is that by focusing solely on the situated self—her attachments, beliefs, or culture—we may lose sight of the fact that citizens are also part of a broader community. Our friends, neighbors, colleagues, and even our own family members often have a different set of perspectives, or encumbrances. If we are not unencumbered selves, neither are we isolated islands of identity. We live in communities in which our friends and neighbors hold different views from our own, and we are aware of the many people and communities around us, near or far, that live and think even more differently.

Our approach to both our own immediate environment and the larger community in which we live is thus not always one in which we are imprisoned by our own encumbrances and will be satisfied by nothing less than absolute victory for our own perspective. We often desire to *reach out* to others—not just to persuade them that we are right, but also because we hope to understand them better and to re-examine our own views in light of what we have learned. We are not only aware of the potential limits of our own perspective and the possible contributions that others may offer, but also of the possibility that our own perspective may change.

For these reasons, constitutional agnosticism can be a sensible and beneficial approach for citizens as well as public officials. It entails adopting what Steven Smith calls a "layered" perspective.[38] We can publicly champion our own views on questions of religious truth, religious liberty, and public policy. But we can also make an imaginative leap, asking what the same issue would look like from a different perspective.[39] We can ask what a particular policy—say, a zoning board decision that affects the ability of a mosque to build in or near our neighborhood, or a decision by the federal government to build a road through a site that is sacred to a Native American tribe[40]—looks like from the perspective of the "other," the Muslim or the Native American tribe. We can ask, from a constitutionally agnostic perspective, what role mosques play in the lives of devout Muslims, or whether some Native Americans have a very different understanding

---

37. *See* Michael J. Sandel, *Liberalism and the Limits of Justice* 11–13 (situated selves), 62 (unencumbered selves) (2d ed. 1998).

38. Smith, *supra* note 6, at 124.

39. *See* Stout, *supra* note 32, at 90.

40. *See Lyng v. Nw. Indian Cemetery Protective Ass'n*, 485 U.S. 439 (1988).

about the relationship between religious belief and sacred sites than do, say, most Christians.[41]

By making this imaginative leap, we can better understand what particular policies mean to others. We can also reconsider our own views about whether and how the beliefs of others should be accommodated in the face of, say, the cost and inconvenience of locating a new church or mosque in our community, or of redirecting the path of a federal road. We can get a clearer sense of both our own perspective and that of our friends, neighbors, family, even complete strangers. In reaching our *own* conclusions and arguing for the policies we think are best, we can better appreciate and weigh *all* the interests involved. That perspective may change our own policy views, or it may not. Even if it doesn't, it will give us a better sense of what is at stake. It will also help us to engage in a meaningful and productive dialogue with others. We need not disavow our own beliefs in arguing for some policy outcome, but we *may* alter them. Even if our views remain the same, our *arguments* may change, taking on a more sensitive, appreciative, and inclusive cast.

Constitutional agnosticism is thus an approach that is well suited to citizens as well as to public officials. It cannot dissolve disagreement, but it can offer the hope of a more sensitive approach by citizens to questions of public policy touching on religious liberty. The precise contours of constitutional agnosticism may differ according to the particular position we occupy as private citizens or as public officials. It is not simply a one-size-fits-all approach. But some form of it remains a good idea for all of us.

DOES CONSTITUTIONAL AGNOSTICISM REQUIRE US TO BE RELIGIOUS AGNOSTICS?

Although constitutional agnosticism draws on the brand of agnosticism laid out in Chapter Three, it is important to emphasize that it is *not* itself a religious belief, or even what Huxley called a "method" of examining questions of religious truth.[42] Its purpose and value have as much to do with politics as with belief, although it sees the two as intimately related. It is a method for achieving a proper understanding of the play of interests in a pluralistic age.

Why devote so much time, then, to a discussion of the new agnosticism in Chapter Three? If constitutional agnosticism is *not* religious agnosticism, why set out the nature of the new agnosticism at such length? What is the relationship between constitutional agnosticism and religious agnosticism?

---

41. *See, e.g.*, Martin Ball, *People Speaking Silently to Themselves*, 26 Am. Indian Q. 460 (2002); Vine Deloria, Jr., *God is Red: A Native View of Religion* (2003).

42. *See, e.g.*, Karen Armstrong, *The Case for God* 250 (2009).

One answer to these questions is the broad point that this book has made on a number of occasions: There is simply no escaping the question of religious truth. That is obviously true for those who wish to confront such questions directly—which, in our own age, is an increasing number of people. But the resurgence of interest in the ultimate questions, and the conflicts they provoke in our liberal democracy, also demonstrate that these questions cannot be avoided at the broader social level. The effort of the liberal consensus to avoid those questions has foundered, as more people have expressed an unwillingness to sign on to that consensus and an increasing number of critics have argued that no such consensus, or at least no "neutral" consensus, is truly possible— that we are caught in a debate over values, and their relationship to religious truth, all the way down. The dilemma of religious truth is thus common to both our individual relationship with these questions and our collective social effort to coexist in spite of them. It requires us to frame both an individual religious response to the dilemma and a broader social, political, and legal response.

A related answer, one that speaks to both the need to discuss the new agnosticism and the relationship between the new agnosticism and constitutional agnosticism, is that these questions are especially salient in our own age— our agnostic age, as I have called it. It is an age in which a vast array of religious beliefs and nonbeliefs are both present and imaginable, widely viewed as at least an option. In such an age, no single totalizing approach to these questions, or the church-state conflicts they raise in our society—a wholly and conventionally liberal one, a wholly secular one, or a wholly sectarian one—is likely to succeed. It is also an age, as we have seen, in which the very fact of our pluralism, and the imaginative capacity we have inherited from the Romantic tradition, make an empathetic and imaginative approach to our neighbors both possible and increasingly important. Just as the old agnosticism was a response to the currents of its own age, to the rise of science and the fading confidence in the old religious verities, so the new agnosticism is a response to the currents of our own agnostic age.

Constitutional agnosticism is a similar response to the same conditions. By understanding the new agnostic response to those conditions, we may better understand constitutional agnosticism: what it means, why it may be necessary, what it offers us, and why it may succeed where its competitors cannot. Again, constitutional agnosticism does not require us to be religious agnostics; but understanding the that role religious agnosticism can play in individual lives may help us to understand the part that constitutional agnosticism can play in our collective public lives.

This last point may also help us to better understand both the connections and the contrasts between religious agnosticism and constitutional agnosticism. The new agnosticism is fundamentally an *individual* and *religious* response to the conditions of our age, and to the questions of religious truth that recur in this or any other time. It is about how we, as individuals, might choose to approach questions of religious truth in a pluralistic age, at least in the absence of person-ally convincing evidence with respect to the existence or non-existence of God. Even for those who *are* personally convinced that God does or does not exist, it is a way of bringing to our religious lives a spirit of humility and imagination, an openness and responsiveness to life's mysteries.

Constitutional agnosticism draws on many of the same currents and takes many of the same lessons from them. In contrast to religious agnosticism, how-ever, it is a *collective* and *public* response, one that does not necessarily entail a particular belief or lack of beliefs in particular religious truth-claims. It is less about what and how we should *believe*, and more about how we can *coexist* given the varieties of beliefs that we encounter in our society. It is a coping mechanism for citizens in a pluralistic and agnostic age: a new form of consensus, similar in some ways to the old liberal consensus but different in other important respects, not least the spirit of engagement rather than avoidance that it brings to questions of religious truth, and its refusal to relegate those questions to the margins of private life.

In short, constitutional agnosticism does not require anyone to abandon his or her own deeply held beliefs, no matter what his or her position in society may be. It may come close to this rule for judges. But even judges are not required to shed their own perspective completely. How could they? They are required only to take a consciously constitutionally agnostic stance toward questions of religious liberty, to approach these questions from the judicial layer of their identity—not to shed the other layers. Citizens, legislators, and other public officials are even less formally constrained by constitutional agnosticism. They remain free to retain their own religious beliefs, and to argue in openly religious language.

Up to a point, anyway. Although constitutional agnosticism does not—and could not, given its respect for the possibility that some particular religious belief or unbelief is actually true—entail abandoning one's own beliefs, it does call for a certain imaginative capacity, a willingness to see important questions of religious belief and religious liberty from different perspectives. It asks the con-stitutionally agnostic citizen or official to keep in mind, as Learned Hand might say, that even if she "knows" she is right, she may not be absolutely *certain* that she is right. She should at least be aware that, as St. Paul said, we see through a glass darkly.[43] Even if she *is* certain she is right, she should be aware that other people in our pluralistic age, people acting in good faith, are equally certain that *they* are right, and that their views matter.

In this sense, to draw the circle closed, we can see that constitutional agnos-ticism has to do with both the politics and jurisprudence of religion, and with religious belief itself. It is, most fundamentally, a response to the peculiar

---

43. *See* 1 Corinthians 13:12.

pluralistic conditions of our age; as such, it is necessarily about law and politics as well as belief. It is a response to pluralism in the sense that it responds to the modern condition of being aware of God as an option, of the existence of a wide spectrum of possible commitments with respect to belief and non-belief. But it is also a response to pluralism in a narrower and more practical sense, one that directly implicates the law and politics of religious liberty. It is a strategy: a way of coexisting with others, openly, imaginatively, and in a fully engaged way, in the face of pluralism and disagreement.

CONSTITUTIONAL AGNOSTICISM AND THE RELIGION CLAUSES

Two subsidiary questions are worth considering. The first is an important but in many ways an easy one: Is constitutional agnosticism consistent with the Constitution itself, and specifically with the text, history, jurisprudence, and traditions surrounding the Religion Clauses?

Textually, nothing in the text of the First Amendment's Religion Clauses, which state that "Congress shall make no law respecting an establishment of religion, or prohibiting the free exercise thereof,"[44] conflicts with constitutional agnosticism. It is simply a method for interpreting and implementing the Religion Clauses in light of our present condition of pluralism. It offers a view on how we should implement the Religion Clauses; it does not conflict with them.

That answer is too simple, of course. To say that constitutional agnosticism is a method of interpreting the Religion Clauses does not tell us whether that interpretation does violence to the "true" meaning of the clauses. Language does not exist in a vacuum; it must be interpreted. One means of interpreting language is by putting it in its relevant historical context. We can ask what the words could reasonably have been intended to mean at the time, either by the author or by his or her assumed audience. So, in asking whether constitutional agnosticism is consistent with the meaning of the Religion Clauses, we could ask how the language of the clauses would have been understood, at a more or less abstract level, by a contemporary audience at the time that they were ratified.[45]

---

44. U.S. Const., amend. I.

45. I am skipping over some complications that are the stuff of standard debates over the original understanding of constitutional language. For example, in asking what the Religion Clauses would originally have been understood to mean, we could ask what particular conduct their contemporary audience would have understood them to permit or prohibit. Or we could ask what implication that original understanding of the Religion Clauses should carry under changed circumstances. For example, the Church of Scientology did not exist in the late eighteenth century; but we could still ask how the Religion Clauses as understood back then would affect claims made by or about Scientology

As Kent Greenawalt observes, for "someone who believes that the original understanding, in one form or another, is determinative," this question will "be the most important in the book as far as constitutional principles are concerned."[46] Others will be less concerned with the original meaning of the Religion Clauses as such, and more concerned with whether constitutional agnosticism is consistent with how the clauses have been interpreted over the grand sweep of American constitutional history, not only at its inception but as it developed over time in politics, jurisprudence, and the public understanding.

Whole volumes have been written on the initial and subsequent history of the Religion Clauses.[47] I will not attempt to settle the matter here, because I do not believe the original understanding is absolutely determinative of the appropriate interpretation of the Religion Clauses today.[48] I will confine myself to three observations.

First, even those who do not believe that history is determinative of constitutional meaning can certainly believe that it is an important source of constitutional meaning. If nothing else, it can "teach us about our society's values and lines of division, and it can illumine pitfalls and possibilities"[49] in how we interpret the Religion Clauses. Second, that history is not limited to the moment at which the Religion Clauses were drafted and ratified,[50] but includes both

---

today. At a more abstract level, we could ask whether the Religion Clauses should be understood as conveying a fixed message to their contemporary readers, or whether their authors, their audience, or both would have thought the language was intended to communicate something broader to "Our Posterity," as the preamble to the Constitution puts it.

46. 1 Kent Greenawalt, *Religion and the Constitution: Free Exercise and Fairness* 14 (2006).

47. *See, e.g.*, John Witte Jr., *Religion and the American Constitutional Experiment* (2d ed. 2005); Daniel L. Dreisbach, *Thomas Jefferson and the Wall of Separation Between Church and State* (2002); Philip Hamburger, *Separation of Church and State* (2002); John T. Noonan, Jr., *The Lustre of Our Country: The American Experience of Religious Freedom* (1998); Leonard L. Levy, *The Establishment Clause: Religion and the First Amendment* (2d ed. 1994); Arlin M. Adams & Charles J. Emmerich, *A Nation Dedicated to Religious Liberty: The Constitutional Heritage of the Religion Clauses* (1990); Thomas J. Curry, *The First Freedoms: Church and State in America to the Passage of the First Amendment* (1986); Robert L. Cord, *Separation of Church and State* (1982); Mark DeWolfe Howe, *The Garden and the Wilderness: Religion and Government in American Constitutional History* (1965). *See also* Michael W. McConnell, *The Origins and Historical Understanding of Free Exercise of Religion*, 103 Harv. L. Rev. 1409 (1990).

48. For arguments in support of this position, *see* Paul Horwitz, *The Past, Tense: The History of Crisis—and the Crisis of History—in Constitutional Theory*, 61 Alb. L. Rev. 459 (1997).

49. 1 Greenawalt, *supra* note 46, at 11.

50. Or the moment at which the Fourteenth Amendment was drafted and ratified. *See, e.g.*, 1 Greenawalt, *supra* note 46, at 25–27; Kurt T. Lash, *The Second Adoption of the Free*

prior and subsequent historical developments, all of which contribute to the tangled skein of constitutional meaning, for the Religion Clauses as for any other provision of the Constitution.[51]

Finally, our history contains many strands of thought and writing, many ideas about the meaning of the Religion Clauses. Each of these strands has its own substantial pedigree, its own advocates, its own influence on the development of the Religion Clauses. Some of them have faded from prominence or respectability. Few people today, for example, would champion an openly anti-Catholic interpretation of the Religion Clauses, just because anti-Catholicism happened to play a significant part in the history of the Religion Clauses.[52]

Constitutional agnosticism is, in my view, consistent with the broad currents of history and thought that contributed to the historical development and current meaning of the Religion Clauses. This is a very general statement but, I am confident, an accurate one. That does not mean constitutional agnosticism is the necessary consequence of our constitutional history, or that it is consistent in all ways with *all* of the intellectual and historical currents that contributed to the Religion Clauses. But it does mean that constitutional agnosticism is not hostile to or broadly inconsistent with the gloss that history may place on the meaning of the Religion Clauses.

We can reach the same conclusion about the jurisprudence and traditions surrounding the Religion Clauses. Of course, constitutional agnosticism makes its own claims about how we should interpret the Religion Clauses, and not all of those will track the current state of the law as the Supreme Court has interpreted it. But just as religious agnosticism has roots that reach deep into the history of Western thought, so constitutional agnosticism can be seen as both a part of and a response to developments in constitutional thought, past and present. Whether it is a good approach or a flawed one, constitutional agnosticism cannot be ruled out on the grounds that it is inconsistent with the initial history or subsequent development of the Religion Clauses.

Originalists may find this statement insufficient. Non-originalists may be indifferent to the question. This is not an originalist book. But those of us who believe that history is an important source of meaning for the Religion Clauses, but not the only source—that there is room to argue over the meaning of the Religion Clauses in our time, but that this inquiry should be undertaken with due regard for the historical origins of the Religion Clauses and their subsequent

---

Exercise Clause: Religious Exemptions Under the Fourteenth Amendment, 88 Nw. U. L. Rev. 1106 (1994).

51. *See, e.g.*, Horwitz, *supra* note 48; Barry Friedman & Scott B. Smith, *The Sedimentary Constitution*, 147 U. Pa. L. Rev. 1 (1998); Michael C. Dorf, *Integrating Normative and Descriptive Constitutional Theory: The Case of Original Meaning*, 85 Geo. L.J. 1765 (1997).

52. *See generally* Hamburger, *supra* note 47.

development—will not find anything in that inquiry which stands sharply in the path of constitutional agnosticism.

WHAT HAPPENS WHEN CONSTITUTIONAL AGNOSTICISM RUNS OUT?

Our last question is what happens when constitutional agnosticism runs out. To put it differently, what happens when constitutional agnosticism is not enough—when it does not come up with a perfect answer to a question of church–state conflict?

This could occur in a number of ways. Consider again the extreme example of Abraham's sacrifice of Isaac. Let us treat it as a legal question: Does Abraham have the right to sacrifice Isaac because, according to him, God instructed him to do so? Should that right trump the usual operation of the criminal laws, which would lead to his being charged with murder or (if God or chance provided a sacrificial ram at the last moment, after Abraham had already lifted his knife to strike) attempted murder?

Constitutional agnosticism might not provide us with sufficient tools to resolve this question. It might run out before reaching a sound resolution. The constitutional agnostic would proceed by assuming, in an engaged and empathetic way, the truth of Abraham's statement that the sacrifice was commanded by God, simultaneously taking care not to be too sure that Abraham was right. And then . . . . What? What could he say at this point? In Jamesian terms, the constitutionally agnostic judge faces a forced choice at this point, and must decide. But how?

More broadly, the constitutional agnostic faces what has been called the problem of incommensurability.[53] Let us say that the constitutionally agnostic judge has imaginatively entered Abraham's perspective and asked what it would mean if God had actually ordered him to sacrifice Isaac. She might well conclude that the command was absolute, its stakes of the highest order, and that this

---

53. *See, e.g.*, Brett G. Scharffs, *Adjudication and the Problems of Incommensurability*, 42 Wm. & Mary L. Rev. 1367 (2001); Jonathan M. Barnett, *Rights, Costs, and the Incommensurability Problem*, 86 Va. L. Rev. 1303 (2000); Symposium, *Law and Incommensurability*, 146 U. Pa. L. Rev. 1169 (1998); Cass R. Sunstein, *Incommensurability and Valuation in Law*, 92 Mich. L. Rev. 779 (1994); Symposium, *When is a Line As Long as a Rock Is Heavy?: Reconciling Public Values and individual Rights in Constitutional Adjudication*, 45 Hastings L.J. 707 (1994); Steven L. Winter, *Indeterminacy and Incommensurability in Constitutional Law*, 78 Cal. L. Rev. 1441 (1990). *See also Incommensurability, Incomparability, and Practical Reason* (Ruth Chang ed., 1997); John Kekes, *The Morality of Pluralism* (1993). Marc DeGirolami has drawn on these and other sources to offer a superb discussion of the incommensurability problem in law and religion in his unpublished manuscript, *Tragic Historicism* (2010). I return to the problem of incommensurability in Chapters Six and Eight.

counseled in favor of allowing Abraham to slay Isaac, or insulating him from criminal punishment if he had already done so.

On the other hand, she would confront an obvious state interest in the preservation of life and order. She might be reluctant to conclude that those interests should prevail in the face of an *actual* instruction from God to offer a human sacrifice. In the absence of a final ontological commitment to the truth of that assertion, however, she would obviously be far more willing to stop Abraham. In addition, she would be aware that even if God *sometimes* asks his people to sacrifice human life, he does not always do so, and that many people who act on those grounds are misled, insane, or lying.

How could the constitutionally agnostic judge resolve these two competing claims? It would be difficult to do so in the best of circumstances. It would be still more difficult if she was not absolutely committed to the truth or falsity of Abraham's claim, but thought that the claim *mattered* in a deep sense, that it should have an important influence on how we weigh the competing interests. But how to compare the two claims—the call of God and the needs of the state? As Justice Scalia observed in another context, such a task would be "like judging whether a particular line is longer than a particular rock is heavy."[54]

Finally, no matter how sensitive the constitutionally agnostic judge might be in her treatment of the case, she could not satisfy everyone. Someone would suffer—perhaps Abraham, perhaps Isaac, almost certainly poor Sarah. No matter how imaginatively the constitutionally agnostic judge entered Abraham's perspective in weighing it against other needs and possibilities, she would still have to decide. It is rare that a legal decision leaves fewer than half of the parties before the court unhappy. Sometimes *both* sides are unhappy, even when one of them wins.

I have put the case in the starkest possible light here in order to bring out sharply the reasons why constitutional agnosticism may "run out": why it may leave us with doubts, questions, and serious problems. In many respects, the task of working through these problems will occupy the remainder of this book. The discussion here serves primarily as a preview, and I will only offer a few preliminary observations. They amount to this: have faith![55] Things are not quite as grim as they seem, and there will be a little light at the end of the tunnel— although, to be sure, there will be some darkness too.

Three things need to be said here about the limits of constitutional agnosticism. The first is that this is a general and inescapable problem of the theory of religious liberty, and constitutional theory in general. Many, if not most, attempts to offer a grand theory of religious liberty tend to be less than candid about this. They argue that their approaches to religious liberty, whether grounded on

---

54. *Bendix Autolite Corp. v. Midwesco Enterprises, Inc.*, 486 U.S. 888, 897 (1988) (Scalia, J., concurring in the judgment).

55. So to speak.

liberty, neutrality, equality, or some other value, effectively *solve* the problem of church–state conflict. This is a false hope. As we saw in Chapter Two, those theories are generally stymied by their inability to survive without smuggling in some substantive value that is itself highly controversial, whether at a theoretical level or at the practical level of application.[56] Even religiously based arguments for religious liberty, which are more open about the substantive values they champion, face difficult questions of application, and certainly cannot attain general agreement in a diverse society. We could resort to the anti-theory of writers like Steven Smith.[57] Or we could abandon the search for a single theory of religious liberty, and conclude that a mix of values, principles, strategies, and outcomes is the best we can hope for.[58] Both these approaches may have some temporary practical value. But in another sense, they simply postpone the same questions that plague every effort to arrive at a theory of constitutional liberty, or end up smuggling in controversial substantive values of their own, concealed within the "prudential" analysis they undertake.[59]

At bottom, *some* theory of religious liberty is both necessary and inevitable—and so is the insufficiency of that theory. The best response, and possibly the only response, we can make to the impossibility of a perfect theory of religious liberty is a certain measure of candor and humility. So let me at least be candid. I am not offering a perfectionist account of constitutional agnosticism here. I argue only that it offers the best possible theory of religious liberty, at least in the Churchillian sense that it is better than the others.[60] But the best is not perfect.

Constitutional agnosticism's contribution is that, unlike other approaches to religious liberty, it is actually willing to confront questions of religious truth, without which *any* theory is necessarily incomplete or incoherent. At the same time, it is unwilling to make an absolute commitment to one particular truth, which gives it the capacity to accord due respect to the multitude of perspectives that flood our pluralistic society. It is the approach best suited to our agnostic age. But no theory can absolutely resolve every problem of church–state conflict to everyone's satisfaction. Constitutional agnosticism is no exception. I hope to convince readers that it is a valuable, and perhaps the most valuable, approach to

---

56. *See, e.g.,* Thomas C. Berg, *Can Religious Liberty Be Protected as Equality?*, 85 Tex. L. Rev. 1185 (2007); Kent Greenawalt, *How Does "Equal Liberty" Fare in Relation to Other Approaches to the Religion Clauses?*, 85 Tex. L. Rev. 1217 (2007); Ira C. Lupu & Robert W. Tuttle, *The Limits of Equal Liberty as a Theory of Religious Freedom*, 85 Tex. L. Rev. 1247 (2007); *see also* Steven D. Smith, *The Disenchantment of Secular Discourse* (2010).

57. *See* Steven D. Smith, *Foreordained Failure: The Quest for a Constitutional Principle of Religious Freedom* (1995).

58. *See, e.g.,* 1 Greenawalt, *supra* note 46; 2 Greenawalt, *supra* note 30.

59. I make this point with respect to Greenawalt's work in Paul Horwitz, *The Philosopher's Brief*, 25 Const. Comment. 285 (2009).

60. Winston Churchill once observed of democracy that it is the worse form of government—except for all the others that have been tried.

religious liberty, and that it is different from the other theories we have seen. But I do not wish to convince anyone that it is a perfect strategy—only that it may be the best we can hope for in an agnostic age.

Second, we should remember that the story of Abraham, which I have offered as an example of the limits of constitutional agnosticism, is a story about the *most* difficult questions presented by conflicts of church and state, conflicts between the highest obligations of religious truth and the greatest need for secular order. In a sense, those questions may be present in *every* instance of church–state conflict, no matter how mundane. But the stakes are not always so high. Not every church–state conflict is, like Abraham's story, a case of life and death. Sometimes it is a much lower-stakes question, such as whether to permit a military officer to wear a yarmulke while on duty.[61] Church–state conflicts, at least when they show up in court, may be forced options: some decision must be reached. But their outcome will not always be as fraught as in Abraham's case.

Constitutional agnosticism offers the best possible approach to those forced options. Its results will generally be sound, sensitive, thoughtful, justifiable, and, perhaps most important, more capable of commanding consensus in a pluralistic society than many other theories. It does not promise an Edenic state of perfect outcomes and perfect agreements. But it is still the best possible way of dealing with church–state conflict in our own agnostic age, and with the broader question of how we can coexist in a pluralistic society, one in which liberalism has become just one more competing belief system and thus can no longer keep the peace as effectively as it once did.

That leads to a final point. In the end, there *are* deep questions of incommensurability, of value conflict, and of unresolvable contests between the needs of the state and the needs of religious believers or nonbelievers. Constitutional agnosticism offers a more sensitive and candid approach to these questions than the alternatives, one that is more alive and open to the questions of religious truth that other theories either try to avoid or answer with a wholly sectarian or wholly secular response, to their own peril. But the tension between religion and the state, and especially between religion and the liberal state, is an unavoidable feature of modern existence in our age. That fundamental tension will be explored in the final chapter of this book.

But we should not let the perfect be the enemy of the good quite yet. In Part Three, let us first consider what constitutional agnosticism means for the Religion Clauses of the First Amendment.

---

61. *See Goldman v. Weinberger*, 475 U.S. 503 (1986).

PART THREE

PUTTING CONSTITUTIONAL
AGNOSTICISM TO WORK

6. CONSTITUTIONAL AGNOSTICISM AND
THE FREE EXERCISE OF RELIGION

INTRODUCTION

The first testing ground for constitutional agnosticism is the American law of free exercise of religion.[1] The Free Exercise Clause of the First Amendment tells us that Congress shall pass no law "prohibiting the free exercise" of religion.[2] Depending on how one views the Establishment Clause,[3] the Free Exercise Clause is literally the "first freedom," the first individual right recognized in the Bill of Rights.[4] It has long since been treated as a right that applies equally to the states and other local government actors, as well as Congress and the executive branch.[5]

The text is simple, sparing, and sweeping. Justice Hugo Black used to say that the phrase "no law" in the First Amendment is "composed of plain words, easily understood," that speak in "absolute" terms.[6] In other words, "No law means no law."[7] If we are to believe Justice Black, this could be a very short chapter, one that calls to mind the scene in the movie *Airplane!*, where a passenger requests

---

1. I focus in this book the American law of religious freedom. What I write here should be broadly applicable to law and religion in any constitutional liberal democracy, but some systems—Israel being a prominent example—clearly face deeper and more difficult conflicts between religion and liberal democracy than the United States does.

2. U.S. Const., amend. 1.

3. Some scholars argue that the Establishment Clause is less an individual right than a structural guarantee that prohibits Congress from establishing religion while permitting states to do so. For my view that this approach, whatever its historical merits, does not accurately reflect the current meaning of the Establishment Clause, see Paul Horwitz, *Demographics and Distrust: The Eleventh Circuit on Graduation Prayer in* Adler v. Duval County, 63 U. Miami L. Rev. 835 (2009); Paul Horwitz, *Of Football, "Footnote One," and the Counter-Jurisdictional Establishment Clause: The Story of* Santa Fe Independent School District v. Doe, in *First Amendment Stories* (Richard W. Garnett & Andrew Koppelman eds., forthcoming).

4. Although, to be fair, its placement as the "first freedom" is a historical accident. *See, e.g.,* Michael W. McConnell, *Why is Religious Liberty the "First Freedom"?*, 21 Cardozo L. Rev. 1243 (2000).

5. *See, e.g., Cantwell v. Connecticut,* 310 U.S. 296 (1940) (incorporating the Free Exercise Clause against state governments through the Due Process Clause of the Fourteenth Amendment).

6. Hugo Black, *The Bill of Rights,* 35 N.Y.U. L. Rev. 865, 874, 879 (1960).

7. Hugo Lafayette Black, *A Constitutional Faith* 45 (1968).

some light reading and is handed a wafer-thin pamphlet titled "Famous Jewish Sports Legends."[8] We would not need constitutional agnosticism to help us thread our way through the Free Exercise Clause because we would not need *any* theory; anything could be permitted in the name of free exercise. Abraham could go ahead and sharpen his knife.

Of course, we don't believe Justice Black. Even *Justice Black* didn't believe Justice Black.[9] Whatever the phrase "the free exercise" of religion means, it has always been clear that its scope is not unlimited, its protections less than absolute. Instead, broadly speaking, the Free Exercise Clause has gone through different eras in which its scope has expanded or contracted, embracing or excluding a wider or narrower, but never complete, liberty to engage in religious practice. Despite the breadth of religious practice protected by the Free Exercise Clause today, we are currently in a period of relative retrenchment, an era in which the scope of free exercise of religion has been somewhat limited.[10]

Constitutional agnosticism comes neither to bury current free exercise doctrine, nor to praise it. It does argue that courts should expand the scope of current free exercise protection, restoring what used to be the law of the land: that sincere religious claimants should be able to hold the government to a high level of justification before it can restrict their right to engage in religious exercises, even if the law in question was not aimed directly at those religious practices. But constitutional agnosticism is not unique in this. Many religious liberty scholars and advocates have urged the same thing. By and large, the constitutionally agnostic approach to the Free Exercise Clause is not too far from what many liberal religious scholars argue should be the state of the law. Readers of this chapter who are hoping for a radical overhaul should look elsewhere.

What is, perhaps, more radical is the spirit with which constitutional agnosticism approaches questions of free exercise of religion. Attitude means as much as substance here. The constitutionally agnostic judge or legislator, faced with a conflict between the needs of the state and the call of a religious belief, does not avoid the question of religious truth. Rather, he attempts to enter imaginatively into the perspective of the religious claimant, asking what that claim would mean if it were *true*: what it should mean for the law if, for example, God truly requires a parent to withdraw his or her children from public school—or from

---

8. *See Airplane!* (Paramount Pictures 1980).

9. *See, e.g.,* Allan Ides, *Economic Activity as a Proxy for Federalism: Intuition and Reason in* United States v. Morrison, 18 Const. Comment. 563, 576 (2001) ("Justice Black's insistence on the sanctity of the text in the context of the First Amendment—no law means no law—dissolved when he was confronted with intuitively uncomfortable forms of communication.").

10. That is true as far as the federal courts go, anyway. State courts and legislatures, and the federal government, have sometimes taken a broader view of what counts as protected conduct in this realm.

potentially life-saving medical treatment. It does not simply ask if the claim is important or even true *for him*, but treats the religious claim as a genuine statement of fact.

That imaginative, empathetic turn is a world away from the current approach, whose relative indifference to the truth of a religious claim tends to privilege the needs of the state over the needs of the religious believer. The constitutionally agnostic approach does not necessarily prefer every religious claim over every secular assertion of "compelling" state interests; after all, the constitutionally agnostic decision maker cannot say for sure that the religious claim *is* true. These conflicts always present us with tragic and incommensurable choices. But it gives a far weightier and more sympathetic hearing to the religious claimant. It may also lead courts and legislators to rethink what it means to weigh the needs of the state against the needs of religious believers, to reconsider what we mean by phrases like "compelling state interest" or the "public good," and to strain to reach accommodations with religious believers rather than placing them on a collision course with the state.

As we will see in this chapter, courts consider some free exercise claims easy cases, and some hard cases. But they often confuse the two. Many cases currently viewed by the courts as easy cases are harder than they may seem, and many cases viewed by the courts as close calls, if not hard cases, may be easier than they tend to assume. That does not mean constitutional agnosticism will lead to different results in either case. But it does offer a very different way of looking at these cases: a perspective that is far more empathetic and humble, one that acknowledges both religious *and* secular interests, and one that tends to emphasize the tragic quality of church–state conflicts rather than sweep it under the rug.

FREE EXERCISE, THEN (SORT OF) AND NOW

To see where things stand, it is important to get a sense of where we have been. Free exercise doctrine has been a moving target. The same issues and the same contending forces have recurred in each era. But the balance between them has been like a pendulum, swinging between a more restrictive view of the scope of free exercise and a more permissive one, and back again.

The first period, which stretched out over almost a century, was one of relatively limited freedom for religious exercise. It began with one of the Supreme Court's first major free exercise cases, *Reynolds v. United States.*[11] Reynolds involved the then fairly new Church of Jesus Christ of Latter-day Saints –the

---

11. 98 U.S. 145 (1878). *Reynolds* involved what was then the federal territory of Utah, and thus fell squarely under federal law. This explains the relative scarcity of free exercise cases in the Supreme Court before *Reynolds*. The Court's freedom of religion jurispru-

Mormon Church, as it is commonly known. Reynolds was charged with bigamy for entering into a polygamous marriage, which was still a church practice at the time, and asserted the Free Exercise Clause as a defense. The Court thus faced the question "whether religious belief can be accepted as a justification of an overt act made criminal by the law of the land."[12] More specifically, since the law was ostensibly aimed at plural marriage as a general legal wrong, not a specifically religious wrong, the Court had to ask whether, in modern terms, a neutral and generally applicable legal prohibition could be trumped by someone's religious beliefs and practices.

The Court had little difficulty distinguishing between what it said "properly belongs to the church and what to the State."[13] The Free Exercise Clause prohibited to the legislature any "power over mere opinion," but left the state "free to reach actions which [are] in violation of social duties or subversive of good order."[14] In other words, the Court distinguished between religious *beliefs* and religious *practices*. Chief Justice Morrison Waite wrote in terms that drew on the same fears of chaos and disorder, and the same concern with extreme eventualities, that drive the discussion to this day:

> Laws are made for the government of actions, and while they cannot interfere with mere religious belief and opinions, they may with practices. Suppose one believed that human sacrifices were a necessary part of worship, would it be seriously contended that the civil government under which he lived could not interfere to prevent a sacrifice? Or if a wife religiously believed it was her duty to burn herself upon the funeral [pyre] of her dead husband, would it be beyond the power of the civil government to prevent her carrying her belief into practice? . . . Can a man excuse his practices . . . because of his religious belief? To permit this would be to make the professed practices of religious belief superior to the law of the land, and in effect to permit every citizen to become a law unto himself. Government could exist only in name under such circumstances.[15]

The belief–practice distinction may have been driven by a concern for these extreme cases, but it applied across the board. Certainly, despite the Court's animadversions on the evils of polygamy,[16] that practice did not involve the same

---

dence would remain scarce until the mid-twentieth century, when the Court began applying the Religion Clauses against the states.

12. *Id.* at 162.
13. *Id.* at 163.
14. *Id.* at 164.
15. *Id.* at 166–67.
16. *See id.* at 164–66 (discussing the general treatment of polygamy as "odious among the northern and western nations of Europe" and noting the concern that the practice would "fetter[ ] the people in stationary despotism").

threat to life and limb as the examples it cited. But the *Reynolds* decision stood for a broader principle than that. It meant that religious freedom existed only in one's *thoughts*, not in one's *deeds*. A legislature could prohibit *any* conduct without having to bend to the exigencies of particular religious practices. In theory, this left the Free Exercise Clause little more than a redundancy, a faint echo of the freedom already protected by the Free Speech Clause. In practice, it meant even less: In a later case, the Court would uphold the denial of the vote to an individual who refused to take an oath forswearing any encouragement of plural marriage.[17]

The pendulum swung to a much broader protection for religious exercise in 1963, with the Court's decision in *Sherbert v. Verner*.[18] *Sherbert* concerned a Seventh-Day Adventist whose religious beliefs prohibited her from working on Saturdays. The plaintiff, Adell Sherbert, sought unemployment compensation from the state and was denied, because her refusal to accept jobs that involved Saturday work did not constitute a "good cause" refusal under the statute.[19] By contrast, the statute made clear that the refusal to work on *Sunday* would not prevent a claimant from receiving unemployment, even if a "national emergency" required textile plants to stay open all week.[20]

Effectively overruling *Reynolds*, the Supreme Court held that Sherbert could continue receiving benefits. In the Court's words, it was unjust to force Sherbert "to choose between following the precepts of her religion and forfeiting benefits, on the one hand, and abandoning one of the precepts of her religion in order to accept work, on the other hand."[21] To "condition the availability of benefits upon [Sherbert's] willingness to violate a cardinal principle of her religious faith [would] effectively penalize[ ] the free exercise of her constitutional liberties."[22]

None of the arguments advanced by the state outweighed Sherbert's free exercise rights. The state insisted that some unscrupulous individuals might take advantage of such a ruling to make fraudulent religious claims, in order to obtain unemployment compensation despite the lack of good-faith reasons not to accept alternative job offers. But the Court responded that the state had not offered sufficient evidence in support of this argument. Even if it did, the state would have to show that there was no alternative means of guarding against abuse that would involve less of an infringement on the free exercise rights of claimants like Adell Sherbert. In other words, it subjected the law to a standard of "strict scrutiny"— the state would have to show that the law was the least restrictive means of achieving a compelling state interest.

---

17. *See Davis v. Beason*, 133 U.S. 333 (1890).
18. 374 U.S. 398 (1963).
19. *See id.* at 399–401.
20. *Id.* at 406.
21. *Id.* at 404.
22. *Id.* at 406.

The Court also found it significant, although it did not say it was *essential*, that state law already "expressly save[d] the [Sunday] worshipper from having to make the kind of choice which we here hold infringes the Sabbatarian's religious liberty."[23] That suggested that not only Sherbert's liberty, but her right to be treated on equal terms with other religious believers, had been violated by the state.

Whether *Sherbert* should be viewed primarily as a liberty-centered case, or whether the Sunday exemption meant that the case was really about equality, has been a subject of debate ever since.[24] In other cases, though, the Court took an explicitly liberty-oriented view of the Free Exercise Clause. Most prominently, in *Wisconsin v. Yoder*,[25] the Court held that an Old Order Amish parent could, under the Free Exercise Clause, remove his child from school after the age of fourteen, despite a state law requiring children to remain in school until they turned sixteen. The law did not single out the Amish, and no statutory exemptions provided a hook for the equality-centered argument that some readers placed at the heart of *Sherbert*. Yet the Court was emphatic in holding that the law, generally applicable though it might be, could not outweigh the parents' right to free exercise unless it was narrowly tailored and served "interests of the highest order."[26]

Sherbert and *Yoder* represent the high-water mark of the Free Exercise Clause. In a number of subsequent cases, the Court repeated its basic standard: Any law that substantially burdens the free exercise of religion must be subjected to strict scrutiny, and a free exercise claim must succeed unless the state can demonstrate that the law is necessary to achieve a compelling state interest. This rule applied whether or not the law was aimed at religion as such; even a law that only incidentally happened to burden religion would be subject to strict scrutiny. It was an era of what has been called constitutionally compelled accommodation for religious exercise, even in the face of general laws.

In theory, this regime should have seriously limited the state in its efforts to subject religious practices to direct or indirect legal restrictions. In practice, it was a different story. The rule turned out to be "strict in theory but feeble in fact."[27] Time and again, the Court balked when applying its own rule.

---

23. *Id.*

24. Christopher Eisgruber and Lawrence Sager, for instance, favor an equality-centered reading of *Sherbert*, one that turns less on the existence of the Sunday exemption and more on the argument that the state's failure to provide reasons why Sherbert's religious beliefs should not count as "good cause" meant that she was treated unequally with respect to other, secular reasons that the state did treat as good cause not to accept alternative work. *See* Christopher L. Eisgruber & Lawrence G. Sager, *Religious Liberty and the Constitution* 40–41 (2007).

25. 406 U.S. 205 (1972).

26. *Id.* at 215.

27. Eisgruber & Sager, *supra* note 24, at 43.

Two examples will suffice. In *Goldman v. Weinberger*,[28] the Court held that an Air Force officer who was also a religiously observant Jew could be required to obey Air Force regulations that prohibited him from wearing a yarmulke while on duty and in uniform. Under *Sherbert*, Goldman should have won. But the Court declined to apply genuine strict scrutiny, citing the unique context of military life, which requires reviewing courts to be "far more deferential than [when they engage in] constitutional review of similar laws or regulations designed for civilian society."[29] In the view of Justice William Brennan, the author of the Court's opinion in *Sherbert*, the Court's decision in *Goldman* "abdicate[d] its role as . . . protector of individual liberties in favor of credulous deference to unsupported assertions of military necessity."[30]

In *Lyng v. Northwest Indian Cemetery Protective Association*,[31] the Court rejected a free exercise claim brought by an Indian tribe against the government, seeking to prevent it from building a road on federal lands in an area traditionally used for religious ceremonies and treated as sacred land by that tribe. Writing for the Court, Justice Sandra Day O'Connor acknowledged the possibility that the government's action "could have devastating effects" on the tribe's religious practices, because the land itself was central to their practices.[32] The potential harm was thus graver than, say, planning a road that would run through the site of Christ's crucifixion. As sacred as that place may be to Christians, Christianity does not depend on its continued existence. That is precisely what the plaintiffs in *Lyng* asserted.

Nevertheless, the Court denied the free exercise claim. It held that any devastating effects were indirect. Because the land was federally owned, any government construction must be treated as an internal government matter. Although the project might literally lay waste to the plaintiffs' faith, they would not be directly "coerced by the Government's action into violating their religious beliefs; nor would either governmental action penalize religious activity by denying any person an equal share of the rights, benefits and privileges enjoyed by other citizens."[33] The opinion was marked by a strong sense that any other ruling

---

28. 475 U.S. 503 (1986).

29. *Id.* at 507–08. The Court took a similar approach with respect to free exercise claims brought in the prison context, one that it also saw as a rarefied and specialized environment that required courts to defer to the determinations of prison officials. *See O'Lone v. Estate of Shabazz*, 482 U.S. 342 (1987). *See generally* Paul Horwitz, *Three Faces of Deference*, 83 Notre Dame L. Rev. 1061 (2008).

30. *Goldman*, 475 U.S. at 514 (Brennan, J., dissenting).

31. 485 U.S. 439 (1988).

32. *Id.* at 451.

33. *Id.* at 449.

would wreak havoc with the state's ability to deal with the vast stretches of public land in the United States.[34]

These two examples exemplify a broader pattern following *Sherbert* and *Yoder*. What the Court gave with one hand, it took away with the other. It required strict scrutiny, but found one reason or another to soft-pedal its application of the rule. When it came time to balance the religious claims of individuals or groups against the secular needs of the state and the broader society, the Court was left without a yardstick: the competing claims were incommensurable. As a result, the Court ended up privileging the state's interests, which at least presented themselves in terms it could understand. Despite the lip service it paid in cases like *Sherbert* and *Yoder* to the importance of religious practice, it placed a thumb on the scales in favor of secular arguments. Or perhaps the Court realized all too well what strict scrutiny required, and feared opening the floodgates to religious claimants.

In 1990, the pendulum swung firmly back. In *Employment Division v. Smith*,[35] the Court retreated from the rule that had applied, at least in theory, for the previous three decades. *Smith* strongly echoed the facts of *Sherbert*. Two individuals were fired by a private drug rehabilitation center because they had used a hallucinogenic drug, peyote, as part of an Indian religious ceremony. They sought unemployment compensation and were rejected by the state of Oregon because its statute disqualified applicants who had been fired for work-related "misconduct."[36] As Adell Sherbert had, they invoked the Free Exercise Clause to seek a constitutionally compelled exemption from the statute. In this case, however, the plaintiffs' claim was rejected.

Smith effectively revived the belief–practice distinction relied on by the Court in *Reynolds*, with the addition of a non-discrimination principle. The state, said the Court, cannot "compel affirmation of religious belief" or "punish the expression of religious doctrines it believes to be false."[37] Nor can it "impose special disabilities on the basis of religious views or religious status" or take sides "in controversies over religious authority or dogma."[38] But that's it. If a burden on religious practice, no matter how severe, is "merely the incidental effect of a [neutral,] generally applicable and otherwise valid provision, the First Amendment has not been offended."[39]

Justice Scalia, writing for the majority, distinguished earlier cases like *Sherbert* and *Yoder* without overruling them, but on highly strained grounds. *Sherbert*, he

---

34. *See, e.g., id.* at 453. It may not be a coincidence that Justice O'Connor had spent much of her life in Arizona, a great deal of which is government land.

35. 494 U.S. 872 (1990).

36. *Id.* at 874–75.

37. *Id.* at 877.

38. *Id.*

39. *Id.* at 878.

suggested, really only involved unemployment compensation. It turned on the individualized assessment that every unemployment compensation applicant receives, which creates the risk that the individual government bureaucrat who evaluates each claim will discriminate because of his or her personal views about a claimant's religious beliefs.[40] *Yoder*, he asserted, involved a hybrid claim. In other words, it did not involve a free exercise claim standing alone, but was combined with an additional constitutional claim: the right of parents, under the Due Process Clause, to control their children's education.[41] Whether the free exercise claim in such cases was therefore redundant, or whether it somehow could alchemically transform two independently inadequate constitutional claims into a successful "hybrid right," he did not say. Unsurprisingly, the idea of a "hybrid right" has been widely derided, on and off the Court.[42]

Ultimately, the result in *Smith* was driven by the same concerns that had moved the Court over a century earlier in *Reynolds*. Citing that decision, Justice Scalia worried that constitutionally compelled exemptions from generally applicable laws would allow each person to "'become a law unto himself,'" a result which "contradicts both constitutional tradition and common sense."[43] It would be particularly dangerous in a religiously diverse society: "Any society adopting such a system would be courting anarchy, but that danger increases in direct proportion to the society's diversity of religious beliefs, and its determination to coerce or suppress none of them."[44] To give religious claimants the "luxury" of requiring that any law that burdens their practices meet a test of strict scrutiny would threaten the legal order itself.[45]

Thus, religious objectors to a generally applicable law effectively had no rights *at all*. This was a far cry from *Sherbert* and *Yoder*. Justice Scalia did say that religious claimants were always free to seek the aid of the political process—that is, to lobby for legislative exemptions rather than demanding exemptions from the courts. He acknowledged that minority religions might be at a "relative disadvantage" in the political process: it might be easier for the Catholic Church to win an exemption from laws prohibiting alcohol for the use of wine during

---

40. *See id.* at 882–85.

41. *See id.* at 881–82 (citing *Pierce v. Society of Sisters*, 268 U.S. 510 (1925)).

42. *See, e.g., Church of the Lukumi Babalu Aye v. City of Hialeah*, 508 U.S. 520, 566–67 (1993) (Souter, J., concurring in part and concurring in the judgment); Kent Greenawalt, *Quo Vadis: The Status and Prospects of "Tests" Under the Religion Clauses*, 1995 Sup. Ct. Rev. 323, 335 (noting that "[m]ost scholars assume" that Justice Scalia's invocation of hybrid rights "was a make-weight to 'explain' *Yoder* that lacks enduring significance"); Michael W. McConnell, *Free Exercise Revisionism and the* Smith *Decision*, 57 U. Chi. L. Rev. 1109, 1121 (1990) ("One assumes that the notion of 'hybrid' claims was created for the sole purpose of distinguishing *Yoder*.").

43. *Smith*, 494 U.S. at 885 (quoting *Reynolds*, 98 U.S. at 167).

44. *Id.* at 888.

45. *Id.*

Communion than it would for Indian tribes to win the right to use peyote.[46] But this "unavoidable consequence of democratic government must be preferred to a system in which each conscience is a law unto itself or in which judges weigh the social importance of all laws against the centrality of all religious beliefs."[47]

Smith has been the subject of vituperative criticism by law and religion scholars.[48] Douglas Laycock, one of the leading scholars of the Religion Clauses, wrote that *Smith*, "[i]n effect, repealed the substantive component of the Free Exercise Clause,"[49] that it "creates the legal framework for persecution" of religion, and that "[r]eligious liberty in this country is in very serious crisis."[50] Michael McConnell called *Smith*'s treatment of the Court's free exercise precedents "troubling, bordering on the shocking."[51] He argued that *Smith* denies "that the government has an obligation to defer, where possible, to the dictates of religious conscience," and thereby asserts "that government is, in principle, the ultimate authority."[52]

Smith's critics argue that it represents a chilling vision of statism, or what William Galston calls "civic totalism."[53] The decision "prefer[s] the interests of the regulatory state over those of the individual standing against the state," and "falsely presents statism as the only viable alternative to chaos."[54] On this view, *Smith* presents a vision in which, more or less by default, the needs of the secular world win out over any claim that draws on other sources of belief and obligation. It is liberalism as something close to tyranny, its imperial impulses laid bare. It is a world in which "statist judges [ ] become so intent on order, so insistent that

46. *Id.* at 890.

47. *Id.*

48. For early examples, *see, e.g.,* John T. Noonan, Jr., *The Death of Free Exercise?*, 42 DePaul L. Rev. 567 (1992); Douglas Laycock, *Summary and Synthesis: The Crisis in Religious Liberty*, 60 Geo. Wash. L. Rev. 841 (1992); James D. Gordon, III, *Free Exercise on the Mountaintop*, 79 Cal. L. Rev. 91 (1991); McConnell, *supra* note 43; Douglas Laycock, *The Remnants of Free Exercise*, 1990 Sup. Ct. Rev. 1.

49. Laycock, *supra* note 48, at 855–56.

50. *Id.* at 849, 850.

51. McConnell, *supra* note 42, at 1120.

52. *Id.* at 1152.

53. William A. Galston, *The Idea of Political Pluralism*, in *Nomos XLIX: Moral Univeralism and Pluralism* 95, 101 (Henry S. Richardson & Melissa S. Williams, eds., 2009); *see also id.* at 105 (describing civic totalism as the view that "if state power is exercised properly—that is, democratically—it need not be limited by any considerations other than those required by democratic processes").

54. Frederick Mark Gedicks, *Public Life and Hostility to Religion*, 78 Va. L. Rev. 671, 693 (1992). *See also* Kenneth L. Karst, *Groups and the Free Exercise Clause*, 87 Cal. L. Rev. 1093, 1095 (1999) (noting the "statism of the *Smith* rule"); Benjamin C. Zipursky, *The Pedigrees of Rights and Powers in Scalia's Cruzan Concurrence*, 56 U. Pitt. L. Rev. 283, 314 n.109 (1994) (arguing that *Smith* can be seen "as a consistent application of [Justice Scalia's] general statist framework").

only one law, the state's law, shall prevail, that the efforts and commitments of other rich sources of meaning, other normative enclaves, are needlessly limited or destroyed."[55] Scholars see this statism at work in *Lyng* as well, in which the government's secular need to build a road through its own land threatened the survival of a religious "normative enclave." Constitutional agnosticism is strongly opposed to this brand of statism.

Smith has also inspired a cottage industry of defenders.[56] In many cases, those writers defend not *Smith* itself, but the broader proposition that the Free Exercise Clause does not require an exemption from neutral and generally applicable laws.[57] They add an important set of arguments to Justice Scalia's own opinion in *Smith*, and suggest that its retreat from robust free exercise rights is not without justification.

Smith's defenders argue that courts are ill-equipped to weigh religious claims against secular justifications for state laws. As a result, they are likely to discount the claims of minority faiths as opposed to mainstream faiths, to do a clumsy job of weighing religious claims in general, and to "underestimat[e] the strength of the countervailing state interest."[58] And they argue that a strong rule of free exercise exemptions violates the principle of equality, in two ways. First, the possibility that courts will give a more respectful hearing to claims by members of majority religions than it will to claims by members of minority faiths raises an equality concern within the community of religious believers. Second, giving a religious exemption from generally applicable laws to religious believers, while forcing nonbelievers to obey the same laws, promotes "a constitutional preference for religious over non-religious belief systems."[59]

I will offer constitutional agnosticism's answer to *Smith* shortly. For now, we should note two important aspects of free exercise doctrine after *Smith*. First, the Court has tempered the worst fears of *Smith*'s critics by making clear that even after that decision, there is still some life left in the Free Exercise Clause. It has done so through the very language it used to retreat from the rule in *Sherbert*

---

55. Austin Sarat, *Robert Cover on Law and Violence*, in *Narrative, Violence, and the Law* 257–58 (Martha Minow, et al., eds., 1993).

56. *See, e.g.*, Ronald J. Krotoszynski, Jr., *If Judges Were Angels: Religious Equality, Free Exercise, and the (Underappreciated) Merits of* Smith, 102 NW. U. L. Rev. 1189 (2008); Philip A. Hamburger, *A Constitutional Right of Religious Exemption: An Historical Perspective*, 60 Geo. Wash. L. Rev. 915 (1992); Gerard V. Bradley, *Beguiled: Free Exercise Exemptions and the Siren Song of Liberalism*, 20 Hofstra L. Rev. 245 (1991); William P. Marshall, *In Defense of* Smith *and Free Exercise Revisionism*, 58 U. Chi. L. Rev. 308 (1991).

57. *See, e.g.*, Marshall, *supra* note 56, at 308–09 (defending the rule in *Smith*, but suggesting that "[t]he *Smith* opinion itself . . . cannot be readily defended. The decision, as written, is neither persuasive nor well crafted. It exhibits only a shallow understanding of free exercise jurisprudence and its use of precedent borders on fiction.").

58. *Id.* at 312.

59. *Id.* at 319.

and *Yoder*. Although *Smith* made clear that laws that are "neutral" and "generally applicable" will raise no free exercise right to a constitutional exemption, it also said that laws that are *not* neutral or generally applicable, or that are aimed directly and discriminatorily at religious practice itself, must still undergo strict scrutiny.

That was the result in *Church of the Lukumi Babalu Aye v. City of Hialeah*,[60] a case that involved a local ordinance banning the "unnecessary" killing of "an animal in a public or private ritual or ceremony not for the primary purpose of food consumption."[61] Although the statute itself did not say so, the law was transparently aimed at the practice of animal sacrifice by local adherents of the Santeria faith. The law was honeycombed with exceptions and narrowly drafted and interpreted in a way that excluded most similar acts, such as hunting, or even killing animals in accordance with Jewish kosher practices. As a result, even though the law did not single out religion in plain terms, it could be viewed as neither neutral nor generally applicable.[62] In those circumstances, the Court made clear, courts would continue to apply the rule of strict scrutiny familiar from *Sherbert* and *Yoder*.[63] A number of lower courts have followed *Lukumi's* lead, making clear that even laws that do not mention religion, but nevertheless fail to accord it the respect that they give other exemptions from an ostensibly "neutral" and "generally applicable" law, may trigger strict scrutiny.[64]

Second, despite the worries of *Smith's* critics that the political process would fail to protect minority religions while safeguarding mainstream faiths, *Smith* in fact provoked a sweeping response from Congress and the state legislatures. Soon after *Smith*, a broad coalition of religious and civil liberties groups banded together to advocate the successful passage in Congress of the Religious Freedom Restoration Act (RFRA),[65] which restored by statute a modified version of the compelling interest test that had prevailed in free exercise cases prior to *Smith*. Although the Supreme Court held the statute invalid as applied to the states,[66] RFRA continues to apply as a valid limit on federal laws that incidentally place a significant burden on religious exercise.[67] Many states have drafted similar laws,

---

60. 508 U.S. 520 (1993).

61. *Id.* at 526–28.

62. *See id.* at 533–46.

63. *Id.* at 546 ("A law burdening religious practice that is not neutral or of general application must undergo the most rigorous of scrutiny."). For commentary, *see, e.g.,* Stephen L. Carter, *The Resurrection of Religious Freedom?*, 107 Harv. L. Rev. 118 (1993).

64. *See, e.g., Trefelner ex rel. Trefelner v. Burrell School District*, 655 F. Supp. 2d 581 (W.D. Pa. 2009); *Fraternal Order of Police v. City of Newark*, 170 F.3d 359 (3d Cir. 1999); *Rader v. Johnston*, 924 F. Supp. 1540 (D. Neb. 1996).

65. 42 U.S.C. § 2000bb–2000bb-4 (2004).

66. *See City of Boerne v. Flores*, 521 U.S. 507 (1997).

67. *See, e.g., Gonzales v. O Centro Espirita Beneficente União de Vegetal*, 546 U.S. 418 (2006).

called mini-RFRAs, to restrain the operation of their own laws. And after RFRA was invalidated as it applied to the states, Congress passed a narrower statute, the Religious Land Use and Institutionalized Persons Act (RLUIPA),[68] which applies strict scrutiny to local land use decisions and the treatment of institutionalized persons such as prisoners where those decisions burden religious exercise.[69]

That is where things stand today. The Free Exercise Clause, as the courts understand it, has swung back and forth between more and less protective versions. The more protective version not only protected religious belief and practice, but also applied even to laws that are not aimed specifically at religion, but only incidentally burden it. The narrower version we have today, post-*Smith*, makes the Free Exercise Clause primarily an anti-discrimination rule. Laws aimed at religion are subjected to searching scrutiny, while neutral and generally applicable laws do not trigger the Free Exercise Clause at all, even if they impose significant incidental burdens on religious practice. That rule is moderated by the fact that courts have taken a broad view of what it means for a law to fail the test of neutrality and general applicability, and by the significant legislative response of the federal and state governments, which re-establishes a version of the *Sherbert* and *Yoder* tests in many cases, and thus gives religious claimants a statutory, but not a constitutional, right to an exemption from laws that burden religious practice.[70]

Under the current regime, then, the Free Exercise Clause and its statutory counterparts are something more than a mere redundancy, protecting only those practices that are already covered by the Free Speech and Equal Protection Clauses. But they are something less than the full guarantee of constitutionally compelled exemptions from general laws that incidentally burden religious exercise—a guarantee that was promised, if rarely fulfilled, by the rule in *Sherbert* and *Yoder*.

This leaves us with a number of questions. Is free exercise as it stands too narrow, too broad, or just right? And even if we have moved away by degrees from the straitened version of the Free Exercise Clause that *Smith* seemed to portend, how do we address the very real questions that *Smith* raises—questions about how courts should balance religious practices against the needs of the state, whether and when legislatures ought to grant such exemptions, and whether these sorts of exemptions risk anarchy?

---

68. 42 U.S.C. § 2000cc–2000cc-5 (2004).

69. *See Cutter v. Wilkinson*, 544 U.S. 709 (2005) (upholding the prisoners' rights provision of RLUIPA).

70. I have left out one other vehicle through which *Smith* has been limited: the interpretation by state courts of their own constitutions, many of which have been read to retain the rule in *Sherbert* and *Yoder* as a matter of state constitutional law.

CONSTITUTIONAL AGNOSTICISM AND FREE EXERCISE

The constitutional agnostic's approach to the Free Exercise Clause should come as no surprise by now. It is, in brief, an engaged, open, empathetic, and imaginative approach. It begins by asking how the free exercise inquiry is affected if the decision maker assumes that the religious claim in question is *true*.

In theory, that sounds little different from the current approach, at least if the Free Exercise Clause is actually triggered—which, after *Smith*, will not always be the case. In practice, however, the approach to the Free Exercise Clause employed by the courts is largely indifferent to the question of the truth of religious claims. On the one hand, the courts in relevant cases[71] treat all plausible claims that a religious practice requires a particular action as serious claims of religious conscience. On the other hand, converting these claims into matters of conscience allows courts to treat them as *mere* matters of conscience, as it were. These claims are viewed as important primarily because the person who makes those claims *believes* them to be true, not because they *are* (or may be) true. In keeping with the liberal compromise, the courts are relatively indifferent to the genuine possibility that those claims are true in fact.

In practice, that distinction matters a great deal. Despite how seriously our constitutional culture treats claims of conscience, it is much easier to disregard a claim that rests on individual conscience than one that rests on absolute truth, or to conclude that such a claim, if it rests on conscience alone, can be outweighed by more immediate and worldly considerations.[72]

To see this point more clearly, consider two examples. Suppose my daughter tells me she is convinced there are monsters under her bed. Even if I don't believe her, I will hardly be insensitive. Fear is fear, after all. In that sense, I'll take her claim seriously. I will do what all loving parents do: I'll humor her—up to a point. If it won't inconvenience me too much, I'll reassure her by "checking" under the bed, using "anti-monster spray," or switching on a nightlight. If it becomes too inconvenient, however, I will draw the line. I certainly won't let her sleep in my room. Nor will I go to the trouble of retrieving the family flame-thrower from the basement.

---

71. That is, cases that fall outside the scope of *Smith* because they involve non-neutral and non-generally applicable laws; cases that involve RFRA or RLUIPA; and other state or federal laws or rulings that follow the older regime in *Sherbert* and *Yoder*.

72. For a rich examination of conscience and its relationship to law and religion, see Robert K. Vischer, *Conscience and the Common Good: Reclaiming the Space Between Reason and State* (2009). Although Vischer is more supportive of the value of freedom of conscience than I am, his defense of conscience proceeds largely by reconstructing what conscience means, and he shares some of my criticisms of freedom of conscience as it is currently treated by the courts.

As we saw in Chapter Four, the New Atheists argue that all religious claim-ants are in precisely the position of a little girl who is scared of monsters under the bed. To them, a secular society that is too tolerant of religious claims is akin to an overindulgent parent. We should shut off the light and tell the child to go to sleep.

The standard liberal approach to Free Exercise claims is admittedly distinct from that approach. After all, we all *know* that monsters are not lurking under our children's beds,[73] and we make little or no pretense of even-handedness on the matter. The liberal is more committed to avoiding the question of the truth of religious claims than he is to saying that those claims are wrong. Still, the liberal approach is closer to my refusal to take seriously my daughter's claims about monsters under the bed than that description might suggest. It takes reli-gious claims seriously mainly because it accords them a certain dignitary value; or because it cares about the *emotional* quality of the religious claimant's beliefs; or, perhaps, because it worries that failing to take those claims seriously would disturb the civic peace that freedom of conscience provides. Or, as we saw in the equality-centered reading of religious liberty that some scholars have advocated, liberalism shifts the ground from truth to some other value, such as equality. If I would let my daughter sleep in my room when she says she saw a raccoon under her bed, it's only fair to let her sleep in my room when she says she saw a monster.

What the standard approach does *not* do is treat the religious claimant's asser-tion that his belief is *true* with the gravity that such a truth-claim demands. Like a parent who takes his child's *feelings* seriously, but not her *claim*, the standard approach balances the religious claimant's emotions, and not the claim itself, against the countervailing needs of the state. Those are very different things.

To be fair, the conscience-centered approach accords real weight to religious claims. But this approach is not much concerned about whether those claims are true; only with whether they are sincere, and how costly it will be to accommo-date them. However much our society may value freedom of conscience, when push comes to shove those claims can easily be outweighed by more tangible and immediate secular concerns.[74] That is the lesson of *Lyng*, among other cases.

We could draw a second comparison, borrowing an analogy from John Garvey. Under that analogy, the liberal approach treats religious claimants something

---

73. Or at least we *think* they are not. For present purposes, and out of respect for my daughter, I remain agnostic on that question.

74. *See, e.g.*, Stephen L. Carter, *Religious Freedom as if Religion Matters*, 87 Cal. L. Rev. 1059, 1071 (1999) (arguing that even under a compelling interest standard, "the courts in the end will be centering their concern on the needs of the state, not the needs of the religionist").

like the way we treat the insane.[75] In many respects, we are solicitous and tender toward the insane, but we do not let them run the asylum. As Michael Stokes Paulsen observes, "If religion were insanity . . ., it would be crazy to accord it special constitutional protection. . . . Why would anyone in his right mind protect the free exercise of lunacy?"[76]

Under the conventional liberal approach, of course, we *do* protect the free exercise of religion; we do not treat it as if it were purely a delusion. In a sense, though, the liberal conclusion is not that far from the conclusion that Paulsen suggests we reach about the insane. It does not draw any firm conclusions about whether or not a particular religious claim is delusional, but neither does it accord that claim as much weight as it would if it were genuinely willing to consider the possibility that the claim was true. Our sense of what constitutes a mandatory claim to accommodation, what might be a permissible claim to accommodation that a legislature could reasonably grant, and what would be an impermissible or unwise accommodation cannot help but be influenced by this approach. Religious claims are given some weight, even substantial weight, but will ultimately topple when confronted with what appear to be more immediate and easily judged competing state interests.

These examples place in clearer relief what is different about the constitutional agnostic's approach to the Free Exercise Clause. The constitutional agnostic's approach is not concerned with those claims simply because they are claims of conscience; it is concerned with them because they may be true. They are not only assertions about the feelings of the person involved, but potentially accurate descriptions concerning the fact of the matter itself. Like the religious agnostic's suspension of ontological commitments, which is not passive or indifferent to questions of religious truth but genuinely open to the possibility that there *is* a religious truth, the constitutional agnostic proceeds from a provisional assumption that there really is a God, and that God really requires a particular religious practice, even if it conflicts with the needs of the state. He is willing to treat religious claims not as if they are important only to the person involved, or to keeping the liberal peace, but as if they involve absolute, genuine, and factually true obligations. Viewed in this light, it is difficult to see how the needs of the state can possibly compare with the will of God.

---

75. *See* John H. Garvey, *Free Exercise and the Values of Religious Liberty*, 18 Conn. L. Rev. 779 (1986). Garvey's use of the analogy is somewhat different from my own.

76. Michael Stokes Paulsen, *God is Great, Garvey is Good: Making Sense of Religious Freedom*, 72 Notre Dame L. Rev. 1597, 1614 (1997). I disagree, however, with Paulsen's assertion that a religious individual's claim "that God has directed [her] to engage in conduct contrary to the usual norms prescribed by the law of the state" would be "incomprehensibl[e] to the agnostic or secularist." *Id.* at 1613. Whether that is true or not for the kind of agnosticism that Paulsen has in mind, it is certainly not true for the agnosticism I described in Chapter Three, or for constitutional agnosticism itself.

Consider an example that has yielded conflicting results from courts that have considered it.[77] Driver's licenses in the United States generally must have a photograph that clearly shows the driver's face. Some individuals, prominently including some Muslim women, object to this requirement.[78] They argue that it offends the Koran's requirement that women dress modestly in public at all times, which means wearing some form of veil or facial covering. Some courts in the pre-*Smith* era held that these regulations burdened the free exercise of religion and could not be justified by any countervailing state interests.[79] Others, both pre- and post-*Smith*, have upheld the regulations.[80] Some post-*Smith* courts have applied that test and concluded that these claims involve neutral and generally applicable laws—that is, laws that apply to everyone equally and are not aimed at religion in particular. Laws that meet this description are subject to virtually nonexistent judicial scrutiny.[81] Even where a strict level of scrutiny is considered, these courts have found a compelling state interest in these laws: "promoting public safety and security, [combating] crime[,] and [ ] protecting interstate commerce."[82] After 9/11, courts have found these interests especially compelling in light of "new threats to public safety, including both foreign and domestic terrorism."[83] In those circumstances, these courts have held, any claims of conscience asserted by people in this situation "must be subordinated to

---

77. For a recent survey of the cases, see Peninna Oren, *Veiled Muslim Women and Driver's License Photos: A Constitutional Analysis*, 13 J.L. & Pol'y 855 (2005).

78. This objection is not limited to Muslim women. In *Quaring v. Peterson*, 728 F.2d 1121 (8th Cir. 1984), *aff'd by an equally divided Court sub nom. Jensen v. Quaring*, 472 U.S. 478 (1985), similar claims were raised by a Christian woman who based her objections on "a literal interpretation of the Second Commandment," which forbids the making of graven images. *Quaring*, 728 F.2d at 1123. Quaring's objection was admittedly idiosyncratic, *see id.*, but similar claims have been made by members of ascetic Christian sects such as the Hutterites.

79. *See, e.g., Quaring*, 728 F.2d 1121; *Dennis v. Charnes*, 646 F. Supp. 158 (D. Colo. 1986); *Bureau of Motor Vehicles v. Pentecostal House of Prayer, Inc.*, 269 Ind. 361 (1978).

80. *See, e.g., Valov v. Department of Motor Vehicles*, 132 Cal. App. 4th 1113 (2005); *Freeman v. State*, 2003 WL 21338619 (Fla. Cir. Ct. June 6, 2003), *aff'd sub nom. Freeman v. Department of Highway Safety and Motor Vehicles*, 924 So. 2d 48 (Fla. App. Ct. 2006); *United States v. Slabaugh*, 852 F.2d 1081 (8th Cir. 1988) (reaching a different result from *Quaring*, which was also decided by the Eighth Circuit, in the slightly different setting of a defendant charged with a federal felony who objected to being photographed in connection with the charge); *Johnson v. Motor Vehicle Division, Department of Revenue*, 197 Colo. 455 (1979). For an example from outside the United States, see *Alberta v. Hutterian Brethren of Wilson Colony*, 2009 SCC 37 (holding, by a 4–3 vote of the Canadian Supreme Court, that the province of Alberta's requirement of photographs for driver's licenses was justified under the *Canadian Charter of Rights and Freedoms*).

81. *See, e.g., Valov*, 132 Cal. App. 4th at 1121–22.

82. *Freeman*, 2003 WL 21338619, at *4.

83. *Id.* at *7.

society's need to identify people as quickly as possible in situations in which [the] safety and security of others could be at risk."[84]

Viewed through the lens of constitutional agnosticism, such a case might come out quite differently. A decision maker confronted with such a case[85] would not simply begin and end with a general, and thus potentially easily overcome, respect for the right of conscience involved in the claim. Rather, she would attempt to place herself imaginatively in the perspective of the claimant. She would be open to the possibility that the Koran's injunction is *true*—that God does in fact demand public female modesty. That demand might involve a threat of divine punishment, or it might simply consist of a religious obligation to live virtuously. Either way, it would not be something to be lightly overcome by the state. The constitutional agnostic would occupy the worldview of the claimant as fully and empathetically as possible, appreciating the gravity of the forced choice being offered to the claimant: Obey the state, or obey God.

That does not mean the state has no interest in requiring drivers to show their faces on their licenses. But it does suggest something about how the decision maker would evaluate that interest. Given the extraordinary importance to the claimant of covering her face, any balancing of interests would heavily favor an exemption from the law. Indeed, given the divine source of the command, one might argue that the claimant's need should not be balanced against the needs of the state at all, but should prevail absolutely. Even if the constitutional agnostic does not go that far, her sense of the stakes involved for the Muslim claimant would strongly influence her evaluation of the competing state interests. She might conclude, for example, that the state's interests could not be that compelling if, as is the case, some states do not demand photographs for driver's licenses, and most states allow temporary licenses without photographs and create exemptions for other categories of drivers.[86]

Even if she did not dismiss the state's considerations out of hand, the constitutionally agnostic decision maker might try to seek alternatives that could satisfy the claimant while still meeting the state's needs. For example, she might insist that the state offer the woman an opportunity to have her photograph taken privately and only in the presence of a female state employee. In fact, in a Florida case involving similar facts, the state department of motor vehicles followed exactly that policy for Muslim women who wear veils.[87]

The very fact that this avenue of accommodation exists suggests several points. First, it suggests that constitutional agnosticism is not a matter for judges

---

84. *Id.*

85. That decision maker could be a judge, but it could also be a legislator, executive, or citizen deciding how to address such issues as a matter of policy.

86. These and other arguments were canvassed, and rejected, by the court in *Freeman*, 2003 WL 21338619, at *4–6.

87. *See id.* at *3.

alone. Citizens, and those charged with writing and executing the laws, may also, after imaginatively entering the perspective of the religiously burdened individual, strive to accommodate her religious practices. Second, constitutional agnosticism suggests that as long as such an accommodation is *possible*, it ought to be a matter of constitutional right, not just legislative discretion.

Finally, it suggests something about the constitutionally agnostic decision maker's desire to *communicate* with the religiously burdened individual. She will not treat the believer's views as a matter of individual conscience that can quickly, and with little regret, be overcome by other considerations. Nor will she brusquely dismiss the believer's interests as something that must be "subordinated" to the interests of the state. Instead, she will try to genuinely understand the claimant's plight. She will accommodate the claimant if she can, absolutely or (as in the case of Florida's provision of a private photograph session) by half-measures. If she cannot accommodate those needs, or if the half-measures are insufficient for the claimant, she may still want to *talk* to the claimant about why her needs cannot be accommodated, in language that bespeaks a genuine respect for the potential truth and gravity of those needs. She will not assume that the impersonal language of judicial decisions suffices to describe the gravity of the conflict, or that the claimant will be satisfied by arguments grounded solely in the kind of liberal language that tends to bleach out or privatize strongly held religious concerns.

That dialogic effort, that attempt to bridge a perceptual gulf, would not mean as much to the claimant as an actual victory. But it might still mean a great deal. It might represent the difference between a dictate, pronounced from on high in what might as well be a foreign language, and a sincere and empathetic attempt to talk to the claimant in her *own* language, in terms that recognize both the divine source of her obligations and the importance of her claims. Even in cases in which the claimant loses, it might represent a genuine and meaningful effort to acknowledge and grapple with the possibility of religious truth and the fact of religious pluralism.[88] That very effort would help contribute to a sense on the part of the claimant that her claims had been taken seriously and that she was a full member of the society rather than an outsider.

So far, we have neglected an important consideration. The constitutional agnostic asks herself how she should respond to a claim seeking accommodation of religious practices, whether as a constitutional right or as a matter of legislative discretion, given the *possibility* that the claim is true. But the constitutional agnostic does not conclude that the claim *is* true. She must be equally open to the possibility that the claim is false: that the God invoked by the claimant does not exist, or doesn't require the conduct the claimant wishes to engage in.

---

88. For another effort to grapple with the Free Exercise Clause in light of both the theory and the reality of pluralism, see Bette Novit Evans, *Interpreting Free Exercise of Religion: The Constitution and American Pluralism* (1997).

Does this mean the constitutional agnostic must reject the free exercise claim? Or does it put her in a position of paralysis, leaving her unable to act at all? No. It *does* mean that the constitutional agnostic's attitude toward the claim must be geared toward the *possibility* of the truth of the religious claim, not its certainty. This suggests that there *is* a role, after all, for what we might call the conscience, or the subjective experience, of the believer. Because the constitutional agnostic cannot say either that the claimant's beliefs are true or that they are false, but rather must try to place herself in the claimant's shoes and ask what it would mean if the claim were true, she will be sensitive to the feeling of religious obligation on the part of the claimant, whether or not the claimant's beliefs are ultimately true. That is still different from the standard liberal approach to conscience, which is *only* about the subjective experience of conscience and not at all about its potential truth. But it does suggest *some* common ground between the standard approach and the constitutional agnostic's approach.

Ultimately, the constitutionally agnostic position, by virtue of its suspension of ontological commitments, favors the religious claimant, even if it cannot be certain that the claims being asserted are true. Although the analogy is imperfect, the constitutionally agnostic judge in such cases is like someone confronted with Pascal's wager. If the claim is false and she accepts it nonetheless, she runs the risk of causing some disruption to the secular order and inconvenience or harm to others. Even in these circumstances, that inconvenience may still be outweighed by the social value of respecting the believer's conscience. If the claim is *true*, on the other hand, it presents obligations and consequences of a profound nature, easily outstripping the temporal needs of the state. For the constitutional agnostic, then, the balance favors the religious claimant in free exercise cases, even though he acknowledges the possibility that these claims may not be true.

That does not mean constitutional agnosticism always benefits the religious believer. As we will see in the next chapter, the picture changes when we come to the Establishment Clause. But it does suggest that constitutional agnosticism places a thumb heavily on the scales of the religious claimant in free exercise cases. This approach applies not only to judges considering religious claims as a matter of law, but also to citizens or legislators asking themselves from a constitutionally agnostic position whether to accommodate the needs of religious believers.

MOVING THE PENDULUM BACK

The constitutionally agnostic approach to the Free Exercise Clause thus counsels in favor of strong protections for religious practices. It does so not simply because they are important to the claimant, or because in some cases it is reasonably easy to accommodate those practices; and it certainly does not do so from a position of indifference to the ultimate truth of the claims that underlie those practices. Rather, it does so precisely because those claims *might be true.*

That means we must shift the pendulum away from *Smith*'s statist regime and back toward the more protective approach represented, in theory if not always in fact, by cases like *Sherbert* and *Yoder.* From the constitutional agnostic's perspective, the *Smith* approach, limiting valid free exercise claims to cases involving non-neutral and non-generally applicable laws, is too narrow. It gives undue privilege to the interests of the state, and to the very notion that the well-being of the ordered state is the lodestar around which our rights should be oriented. Against the state's interests—which, to be sure, are real matters for concern—it weighs the possibility that there are genuine religious truths and genuinely obligatory religious practices that demand serious, if not overwhelming, consideration.

For similar reasons, the constitutional agnostic is not content with the alternative arguments that have been offered for the rule in *Smith.* He thinks the Free Exercise Clause cannot be reduced to a guarantee of "equal" treatment. For one thing, as we saw in Chapter Two, that argument depends on a loaded definition of "equality": in violation of the liberal consensus, it smuggles in strong substantive commitments by filling in that empty term with particular conceptions of what constitutes equality.[89] For another, it is difficult to square with the overall structure of the Constitution, which already guarantees equality under the Fourteenth Amendment, and already protects equality of religious speech through the Free Speech Clause. For the Free Exercise Clause to avoid being redundant, it must have some separate substantive meaning.

Most important, however, the equality-oriented reading of the Free Exercise Clause, even if we put aside the problem of the substantive commitments that it inevitably smuggles in, does not fully respect the notion of religious *truth.* By treating religious claimants *equally,* but not necessarily *protectively,* so that refusal to protect *anyone* stands on equal constitutional footing with the protection of *everyone,* it fails to appreciate the force that true (or potentially true) religious claims ought to have for both religious claimants and society as a whole.

This is especially true for non-judicial decision makers. Even if the accommodation of religious claims is not constitutionally *required* (although I believe it is), that does not mean a citizen or legislator considering whether to grant such accommodations should be content to deny those accommodations just because everyone is being treated equally poorly. Instead, the citizen or legislator should project himself imaginatively into the mind of the religious believer, and ask whether an accommodation to a law that burdens religious practices is important to the believer given the possible truth of his or her beliefs.

---

89. *See* Peter Westen, *The Empty Idea of Equality,* 95 Harv. L. Rev. 537 (1982).

The constitutionally agnostic judge, too, should not rest on equality alone. Instead, she must ask what the Free Exercise Clause requires given the possible truth of the religious claims presented by believers. If we take the possibility of religious truth seriously, if we assume that a religious claimant is making a *true* claim about what God requires, it is not enough to say, "Whatever the force of your claims, all we care about is whether the law you are complaining about is neutral and generally applicable." That's like saying to my daughter, "Even if there really *is* a monster under your bed, the important thing is that we consistently follow our rules about bedtime." That is hardly an adequate response to a *true* claim. We can say the same thing about *Smith*. To be sure, consistency and generality are important values—even though, as with equality, they are vague ones. But they are not all there is. In the contest between neutrality and truth, truth ought to have the upper hand.

So, from the constitutionally agnostic perspective, *Smith*, which did away with constitutionally compelled exemptions for individuals whose religious practices conflict with generally applicable laws, must go. *Any* claim that a law, even one that is not aimed at religion as such, burdens one's religious beliefs or practices must be given strong weight. That weight must come not merely from a respect for the believer's conscience, but from an empathetic engagement with the believer's views, based on the possibility that those views are true. That kind of engagement will counsel a far broader scope of protection for religious exercise than the rule in *Smith* currently provides.

DEFINING RELIGION, AND RELIGIOUS FRAUD

The constitutional agnostic approach to the Free Exercise Clause raises some important subsidiary questions. The first is how we should define "religion" for constitutional purposes. Many attempts have been made to do so,[90] and it is not clear that any of them have succeeded.[91] Part of the problem is that "religion" is such a protean term. A further problem is that it is difficult to think about the

---

90. I canvass many of the leading definitions in Paul Horwitz, *Scientology in Court: A Comparative Analysis and Some Thoughts on Selected Issues in Law and Religion*, 47 DePaul L. Rev. 85 (1997). For some notable discussions since then, see, *e.g.*, Winifred Fallers Sullivan, *The Impossibility of Religious Freedom* (2005); L. Scott Smith, *Constitutional Meanings of "Religion" Past and Present: Explorations in Definition and Theory*, 14 Temp. Pol. & Civ. Rts. L. Rev. 89 (2004); T. Jeremy Gunn, *The Complexity of Religion and the Definition of "Religion" in International Law*, 16 Harv. Hum. Rts. J. 189 (2003); Eduardo Peñalver, Note, *The Concept of Religion*, 107 Yale L.J. 791 (1997).

91. *See, e.g.*, Andrew Koppelman, *Corruption of Religion and the Establishment Clause*, 50 Wm. & Mary L. Rev. 1831, 1905 n.370 (2009) (noting that "it appears that no jurisdiction in the world has managed to solve [the] problem" of adequately defining religion for constitutional purposes); Walter Kaufmann, *Critique of Religion and Philosophy* 100 (paperback

constitutional definition of religion without being aware of the end-game. Too broad a definition of religion risks including practices that are generally viewed as non-religious, such as Marxism. Too narrow a definition, on the other hand, risks leaving out some belief systems that we think of as uncontroversially religious, such as non-theistic versions of Buddhism.

This problem is often linked to the question of how broad the protection for religious freedom should be, although properly speaking these ought to be different questions. One might believe in a broad definition of religion but a narrow scope of protection for religious practices, and vice versa, without one conclusion turning on the other. Often, however, how we view one question will affect our treatment of the other question. Thus, one might be perfectly willing to accept a broad definition of religion, but only if the constitutional protection for religion doesn't amount to much. Those who advocate a strongly equality-oriented approach to religious freedom, for example, often end up defining religion very broadly but not protecting it much, extending protection to any strongly held view, but only a limited degree of protection.[92]

The constitutional definition of religion raises interesting questions, but it is less important than it may seem at first blush. In practice, courts have little difficulty recognizing genuine religious claims, and the cases raising potentially difficult borderline questions appear to be few and far between.[93] For the most part, we can easily recognize claims as having or not having a genuinely religious character. Usually, no single aspect of that claim will make all the difference in characterizing the claim as religious or non-religious. Instead, the claim either will involve familiar religions like Christianity, or will have a number of features that mark it as religious, such as beliefs about the supernatural or extratemporal aspects of existence, or a deity or deity-like entity, or a set of comprehensive beliefs about the world or devotional practices.[94] In short, the constitutional definition of religion generally poses no real practical problems.

That's not to say that constitutional agnosticism has no views about what ought to count as "religion" for constitutional purposes. Its starting point, we have seen, is one of concern for religious truth. That is, it is concerned with

---

ed., 1979) ("[Non-legal] [d]iscussions of religion typically begin with definitions. But not one of these definitions has won wide acceptance, nor is it likely that any ever will.").

92. *See generally* Christopher L. Eisgruber & Lawrence G. Sager, *Does it Matter What Religion Is?*, 84 Notre Dame L. Rev. 807 (2009).

93. *See, e.g.*, Koppelman, *supra* note 91, at 1907 ("[I]t is remarkable how few cases have arisen in which courts have had real difficulty determining whether something is a religion.").

94. This is the heart of the arguments for analogical or "family resemblance" approaches to the constitutional definition made by Kent Greenawalt and others. *See, e.g.*, 1 Kent Greenawalt, *Religion and the Constitution: Free Exercise and Fairness*, ch. 8 (2006); Koppelman, *supra* note 91, at 1905–08; George C. Freeman III, *The Misguided Search for the Constitutional Definition of "Religion,"* 71 Geo. L.J. 1519 (1983).

claims about the truth of the nature of the world and of human existence. Claims about what is true—about whether the physical universe is all there is, or whether there is something more—underwrite the constitutional agnostic's sense of what constitutes a religious claim. A Christian, for example, might assert that her understanding of what God requires, or views as essential to a good life, leads her to see particular actions as necessary, advisable, or forbidden. Similarly, an atheist might say that her conduct, and her sense of right and wrong, is guided by the fact of God's nonexistence. In contrast, although a believer in Marxism may be driven to behave in particular ways, she will not do so solely because of a belief about the truth or falsity of religious claims. One can be a Marxist who believes emphatically in God's existence *or* nonexistence. So a constitutional agnostic need not see *every* belief as a religious one.

In the language of religious studies, such an approach might be seen as unduly "propositional." That is, it may be viewed as overemphasizing the importance to religious communities of "assertions about the way the world is," instead of their practices and cultural values.[95] Some might object that this approach betrays a Protestant bias. That is, it is a way of thinking about religion that is linked to the Protestant tradition, in which religion depends on one's assent to a series of propositions about God rather than one's embeddedness in a set of practices and traditions.[96] This propositional orientation leaves out other traditions, other ways of being religious.[97]

Despite the dangers of thinking too propositionally about religion, this objection hits wide of the mark. Constitutional agnosticism argues that we should not ignore the truth-claims that rest at the heart of religious belief.[98] But it does not demand a direct or conscious link between one's traditions and practices and one's ultimate beliefs. The constitutional agnostic, exercising his imaginative capacity, appreciates that religious practices or traditions can rest on an implicit set of religious beliefs. Precisely because he sees these things as interlinked, he will give equal weight to both religious beliefs and the practices that, whether directly or through historical and cultural circumstances, ultimately derive from those beliefs.

---

95. James Boyd White, *Talking About Religion in the Language of the Law: Impossible But Necessary*, 81 Marquette L. Rev. 177, 185 (1998).

96. *See, e.g., id.* at 184; *see also* Rodney Needham, *Belief, Language, and Experience* (1973).

97. *See, e.g.,* David C. Williams & Susan H. Williams, *Volitionism and Religious Liberty*, 76 Cornell L. Rev. 769, 789–90 (1991).

98. *Cf.* Wayne Proudfoot, *Religious Experience* 183–84 (1986) ("A religious experience is an experience that is identified by its subject as religious, and this identification must be based, not on the subject matter or content of the experience, but on its noetic quality or its significance for the truth of religious beliefs").

The constitutional agnostic thus places truth-claims about the nature of existence at the heart of his understanding of religion. Beyond that, however, he takes a catholic approach to religion that embraces many traditions and practices. As a practical matter, this approach is unlikely to raise serious difficulties about what "religion" means for constitutional purposes, or to insist that religious claims be propositional as opposed to tradition-based.

This raises another concern, however, one that contributed to *Smith's* narrow treatment of the Free Exercise Clause. It is the concern that a broadly protective approach to religious exercise and its accommodation will open the floodgates to fraudulent or insincere demands that the state exempt ostensibly "religious" practices from the general operation of the law. What will happen to our drug laws, for example, if some newly minted "Church of Marijuana" can come along and insist on its members' right to pass around the holy hash-pipe?[99] What will happen to laws regulating fraud if every charlatan can insist that his fleecing of a naïve public is divinely ordained?[100]

The Supreme Court has provided some guidance on this question, but not very much. In *United States v. Ballard*,[101] the Court held that a prosecution for fraud in such cases should not turn on the truth or falsity of religious beliefs. Writing for the Court, Justice William Douglas said: "Heresy trials are foreign to our Constitution. Men may believe what they cannot prove. They may not be put to the proof of their religious doctrines or beliefs. Religious experiences which are as real as life to some may be incomprehensible to others. Yet the face that they may be beyond the ken of mortals does not mean that they can be made suspect before the law."[102] Without clearly addressing the issue, the Court left open the possibility that a free exercise claimant might still be convicted of fraud if the evidence showed his religiously based claim to be insincere.[103]

The question of insincere or fraudulent religious claims raises difficult issues for any nontrivial approach to religious liberty.[104] If the protection of religious exercise is more than utterly anemic, then, of course, there will be incentives to

---

99. For a case involving the "Church of Marijuana," see *United States v. Meyers*, 906 F. Supp. 1494 (D. Wyo. 1995).

100. This is what many critics have said about the Church of Scientology. *See generally* Horwitz, *supra* note 90.

101. 322 U.S. 78 (1944).

102. *Id.* at 86–87.

103. *See id.* at 84–88. In dissent, Justice Jackson argued that neither truth nor sincerity could be part of a valid inquiry in a case involving alleged religious fraud. *See id.* at 92–95 (Jackson, J., dissenting).

104. These issues are canvassed in Horwitz, *supra* note 90. *See also, e.g.*, 1 Greenawalt, *supra* note 94, ch. 7; Jonathan C. Lipson, *On Balance: Religious Liberty and Third-Party Harms*, 84 Minn. L. Rev. 589 (2000); Stephen Senn, *The Prosecution of Religious Fraud*, 17 Fla. St. U. L. Rev. 325 (1990); Marjorie Heins, *"Other People's Faiths": The Scientology Litigation and the Justiciability of Religious Fraud*, 9 Hastings Const. L.Q. 153 (1981).

dress up one's conduct in religious clothing in order to escape the strictures of the law. This problem is not unique to religious claims. *Any* statutory exemption from a law, and *any* defense to a charge of fraud, creates incentives to frame one's conduct so that it falls within the scope of the exemption or the defense, whether or not religion is involved. To the extent that constitutional agnosticism requires exemptions from the law where religious practices are burdened, however, it is true that this approach will raise concerns about insincerity or fraud.

Because constitutional agnosticism is centrally concerned with the truth of religious claims, concerns about fraud and sincerity can be both relevant and irrelevant to the constitutional inquiry in a free exercise case. On the one hand, the constitutional agnostic asks how we might evaluate a claim based on religious truth as seen from the believer's perspective. So, although the constitutional agnostic might be agnostic, so to speak, about the *truth* of a claim offered by a free exercise claimant, he might well be concerned with whether that claimant is acting *sincerely*.

On the other hand, what it means for a religious claim to count as sincere is a complicated question. Much depends on whose perspective the constitutional agnostic is adopting, and on what we mean by sincere. Consider the Church of Scientology, a so-called "new religious movement" or, according to some, a cult, originating in the writings of the science fiction author L. Ron Hubbard. Its provenance and teachings have aroused widespread suspicion and derision.[105] But even if Hubbard himself believed that Scientology's claims were pure fiction, other church officials might believe whole-heartedly in its truth. Conversely, Hubbard himself might have believed in the truth of his claims, but other church leaders might think of Scientology as nothing more than a phony enrichment scheme. Furthermore, no matter what church officials think, the average Scientologist might be utterly sincere in her beliefs. Still others, such as those who were born and raised in the church, might be in the position of many believers in mainstream faiths, who give little thought to the truth of the underlying beliefs of their faith, but who are used to the practices of their faith and find sustenance in them as a matter of habit. Others might lie somewhere in between faith and non-belief, somewhere in the realm of agnosis,[106] harboring some doubts about the truth of their faith while remaining within the fold.

To all this rich complexity, we must add a further wrinkle. From the agnostic standpoint, a religious truth-claim can be true regardless of whether *any* of the adherents of that faith believe it to be true. From the agnostic perspective, a religious truth-claim is either true or false as a matter of fact, whether anyone believes it or not. Few people today believe in the existence of the pantheon of ancient Greek or Roman gods, but that does not tell us whether they exist or not.

---

105. *See* Horwitz, *supra* note 90, at 147–49.
106. *See* Stephen White, *A Space for Unknowing: The Place of Agnosis in Faith* (2007).

Hubbard may have been a fraud who, by dumb luck or sheer coincidence, happened upon the key to existence.[107] From an external perspective, the agnostic cannot say for sure. From the internal perspective he imaginatively adopts, he can probe the internal logic of a truth-claim—questioning, for example, how one can simultaneously believe that pork is a forbidden food while insisting on his right to chow down on ribs at a barbeque restaurant. Or he can question the truth of a claim based on the epistemic grounds the believer himself subscribes to. For example, Christians base their faith on the historical existence of Jesus, a premise that is subject to confirmation or refutation based on the historical evidence. Given the mysteries, uncertainties, and doubts involved in religious claims and practices, courts will rightly resist going too far down this road.

In short, the constitutional agnostic walks a fine line on questions of religious sincerity and fraud. Some free exercise claims might be rejected by a constitutionally agnostic decision maker because the claimant himself does not believe them—not in the sense of harboring doubts about them, which is a natural human trait, but in the more direct sense that the claimant is deliberately attempting to shield his conduct by invoking a belief system he does not share in the least. But the constitutional agnostic, like the courts under prevailing law, will be reluctant to inquire too strongly or skeptically into these matters, insisting on powerful evidence of insincerity rather than eagerly interrogating the truth of those claims.

This does not really raise the stakes much in the end. Notwithstanding Justice Scalia's mutterings about the threat of anarchy in religiously pluralistic societies, the real question is what level of protection we ought to accord to *any* religious claim. The risk of fraud will be present in *any* system that protects at least some religious practices. If we limited rigorous protection to a few mainstream faiths, a fraudulent claimant could simply assert that the exemption he was seeking involved a Christian, Jewish, or Muslim belief.[108] Our key concern is thus not so

---

107. Consider Jorge Luis Borges' tale of the Library of Babel, whose infinite volumes contain "[e]verything: the minutely detailed history of the future, the archangels' autobiographies, the faithful catalogue of the Library, thousands and thousands of false catalogues, the demonstration of the fallacy of those catalogues, the demonstration of the fallacy of the true catalogue, the Gnostic gospel of Basilides, the commentary on that gospel, the commentary on the commentary on that gospel, the true story of your death, the translation of every book in all languages, the interpolation of every book in all books." Jorge Luis Borges, *The Library of Babel*, in *Labyrinths: Selected Stories and Other Writings* 51, 54 (James E. Irby & Donald A. Yates eds., 1964).

108. *See* Horwitz, *supra* note 90, at 144 n.423; Note, *Toward a Constitutional Definition of Religion*, 91 Harv. L. Rev. 1056, 1080 (1978) ("[I]f the ambit of the term "religion" were contracted in response to the fraud argument, the unscrupulous would not be prevented from swearing false allegiance to a convenient creed."). This is especially true because the courts are unwilling to second-guess religious claims, including those raised by individuals who claim to belong to mainstream faiths, simply because that individual has an

much whether religious fraud is possible under a vigorous protection of the free exercise of religion, but whether, given the importance of religious truth, the risk of fraud is outweighed by the benefits of protecting genuine and compelling religious obligations. For the constitutional agnostic, the risk of "charlatanism is a necessary price of religious freedom."[109]

FINDING THE BALANCE: WEIGHING FREE EXERCISE CLAIMS AGAINST STATE INTERESTS

The final question raised by the constitutional agnostic's approach to the Free Exercise Clause is a perennial problem in law and religion. Assuming that a constitutional decision maker gives real weight to a free exercise claim, how should she balance that claim against the countervailing interests asserted by the state in favor of the enforcement of the law? To take examples from both ends of the spectrum, how should a constitutionally agnostic decision maker weigh Adell Sherbert's demand for an exemption from the unemployment compensation laws against the state's relatively minor interest in uniformity and administrative convenience? How should she weigh Abraham's religiously compelled interest in sacrificing Isaac against the state's profound interest in preserving life?

There is no perfect answer to this question. Because the constitutional agnostic believes that religious claims are important because they may actually be true, she cannot take the easy way out by reducing such claims to a question of equal treatment and nothing more. For the same reason, she does not want to end up in the situation that applied during the *Sherbert/Yoder* era, in which free exercise claims were overcome in practice by a wide variety of asserted state interests, culminating in *Smith's* strongly statist approach. Despite the seemingly overwhelming force that must be given to a religious claim once we assume its truth, however, the constitutionally agnostic decision maker does not believe that anything goes. The Free Exercise Clause may require us to strain the state's capacity to accommodate religious practices to its limits, but there *are* limits. At some point, the genuine dangers of an overly permissive regime must be acknowledged.

We need not be as alarmist about that prospect as Justice Scalia was in *Smith*. Most cases do not involve the gravest state interests. There is a vast distance between upholding a religious claimant's eligibility for unemployment compensation despite her unwillingness to accept work on Saturdays, and a legal regime

---

unusual understanding of what that mainstream faith requires. *See, e.g., Thomas v. Review Board*, 450 U.S. 707 (1981).

109. *Church of the New Faith v. Comm'r for Payroll Tax (Vic.)*, 154 C.L.R. 120, 141 (Aust. 1983).

that protects human sacrifice. Still, even if we are reluctant to set limits in too draconian a fashion, that does not mean there should be no limits at all. A slope may be slippery, but that doesn't mean one can never dig in one's heels.[110]

Constitutional agnosticism will thus impose some limits on free exercise claims, while admitting that it is difficult to draw the line between permissible and impermissible claims. This raises hard questions about how to strike the balance between broad protections for religious freedom and the sometimes weighty interests of the state. Of course, this problem is not unique to constitutional agnosticism. It is present in *any* legal system that attempts to balance individual rights against state interests.[111] In the law, this question is the subject of a long-running debate over whether law should emphasize rules ("don't drive faster than 55 miles per hour"), standards ("don't drive at an unsafe speed, all things considered"), or a mixture of the two.[112] The complexities of this debate cannot be explored here. Suffice it to say that it is unsurprising that Justice Scalia,

---

110. Justice Oliver Wendell Holmes once responded to the argument that the power to tax is the equivalent of the power to destroy with the succinct rebuttal, "[N]ot while this Court sits." *Panhandle Oil Co. v. Mississippi ex rel. Knox*, 277 U.S. 218, 223 (1928) (Holmes, J. dissenting). *Cf.* Arnold H. Loewy, *Rethinking Free Exercise of Religion After* Smith *and* Boerne: *Charting a Middle Course*, 68 Miss. L.J. 105, 124 (1998) (quoting Holmes in response to the "all-or-nothing approach" to the Free Exercise Clause represented by the Court's decision in *Reynolds*, a characterization that applies equally to its later decision in *Smith*). *See also* Eugene Volokh, *The Mechanisms of the Slippery Slope*, 116 Harv. L. Rev. 1026, 1029 (2003) (noting the importance of slippery slope arguments, but pointing out that "slippery slope objections can't always be dispositive").

111. *See, e.g.*, Richard H. Pildes, *Avoiding Balancing: The Role of Exclusionary Reasons in Constitutional Law*, 45 Hastings L.J. 711 (1994); T. Alexander Aleinikoff, *Constitutional Law in the Age of Balancing*, 96 Yale L.J. 943 (1987); Laurent B. Franz, *The First Amendment in the Balance*, 71 Yale L.J. 1424 (1962). Some judges and scholars, especially outside the United States, have argued that this sort of balancing, which is often described under the label of "proportionality," is both possible and relatively objective. *See, e.g.*, Aharon Barak, *The Proportional Effect: The Israeli Experience*, 57 U. Toronto L.J. 369 (2007); Aharon Barak, *The Judge in a Democracy* (2006); David Beatty, *The Ultimate Rule of Law* (2004); Alec Stone Sweet, *The Judicial Construction of Europe* 243–44 (2004). They are mistaken, in my view. For criticisms of proportionality, see, *e.g.*, Jacco Bomhoff, *Balancing, the Global and the Local: Judicial Balancing as a Problematic Topic in Comparative (Constitutional) Law*, 31 Hastings Int'l & Comp. L. Rev. 555 (2008); Richard A. Posner, *Constitutional Law From a Pragmatic Perspective*, 55 U. Toronto L.J. 299 (2005); Vicki C. Jackson, *Being Proportional About Proportionality*, 21 Const. Comment. 803 (2004).

112. *See, e.g.*, Adrian Vermeule, *Judging Under Uncertainty: An Institutional Theory of Legal Interpretation* (2006); Russell B. Korobkin. *Behavioral Analysis and Legal Form: Rules vs. Standards Revisited*, 79 Ore. L. Rev. 23 (2000); Cass R. Sunstein, *Problems With Rules*, 83 Cal. L. Rev. 953 (1995); Louis Kaplow, *Rules Versus Standards: An Economic Analysis*, 42 Duke L.J. 557 (1992); Kathleen M. Sullivan, *Foreword: The Justices of Rules and Standards*, 106 Harv. L. Rev. 22 (1992); Frederick Schauer, *Playing By the Rules: A Philosophical Examination of Rule-Based Decision-Making in Law and in Life* (1991); Antonin Scalia, *The Rule of Law as a*

the author of *Smith*, favors rules.[113] As in *Smith*, these rules are often strict, in part because they draw clear lines in order to avoid (or, more accurately, to *seem* to avoid) the difficulties of the interest-balancing approach. But anyone who is committed to a level of protection for constitutional rights that is more than minimal and less than absolute will confront the same questions, whether he is a constitutional agnostic or not.

The broader problem here is one of incommensurability: the impossibility of weighing individual rights against state interests.[114] The incommensurability problem is accentuated by constitutional agnosticism, which takes seriously the possibility that a religious claim is true and thus raises questions about how any imaginable state interest could possibly overcome a divine obligation. But incommensurability is a problem for *any* rights-balancing approach. Any approach that seeks to weigh individual rights against state interests faces the problem of how we can "compare plural, irreducible, and conflicting values."[115]

Even approaches, like Justice Scalia's formalist approach in *Smith*, that attempt to skirt this difficulty by using categorical rules instead of an explicit balancing of interests still face the incommensurability problem. Bright-line rules still raise the problem of incommensurability, either because the incommensurable values are implicitly weighed at the rule-formation stage of the process rather than at a later stage, or because the press of competing values leads decision makers to create myriad exceptions to the rule once they begin applying it.[116] Bright-line rules *appear* to take the sting out of incommensurability. But they only hide the problem; they do not eliminate it.

So it is important to approach the question of how to balance religious rights against state interests, especially under a system of constitutional agnosticism that emphasizes the possible truth of religious claims, with a measure of humility. It may be that all that can be done is to provide a set of illustrations that suggest how *I* think particular conflicts between religious practice and the needs of the state should be resolved, and leave readers to draw their own conclusions. It may even be the case that we are left with the unsatisfying conclusion that Justice Stephen Breyer drew in a case involving the Establishment Clause: The

---

Law of Rules, 56 U. Chi. L. Rev. 1175 (1989); Pierre J. Schlag, *Rules and Standards*, 33 UCLA L. Rev. 379 (1985).

113. *See* Scalia, *supra* note 112.

114. *See, e.g.*, Brett G. Scharffs, *Adjudication and the Problems of Incommensurability*, 42 Wm. & Mary L. Rev. 1367 (2001); Symposium, *Law and Incommensurability*, 146 U. Pa. L. Rev. 1169 (1998); Cass R. Sunstein, *Incommensurability and Valuation in Law*, 92 Mich. L. Rev. 779 (1994); Steven L. Winter, *Indeterminacy and Incommensurability in Constitutional Law*, 78 Cal. L. Rev. 1441 (1990); *see also Incommensurability, Incomparability, and Practical Reason* (Ruth Chang, ed., 1997).

115. Scharffs, *supra* note 114, at 1372.

116. For the latter point, see, *e.g.*, Frederick Schauer, *The Tyranny of Choice and the Rulification of Standards*, 14 J. Contemp. Legal Issues 803, 804 (2005).

constitutional agnostic approach to the Free Exercise Clause will present us with "difficult borderline cases" in which there is "no test-related substitute for the exercise of legal judgment."[117]

Constitutional agnosticism should not be singled out for this criticism. *Any* approach to religious freedom or other individual rights, including an ostensibly rule-based approach, that does not eliminate the right entirely will leave us with the problem of incommensurability. Constitutional agnosticism is thus in good company: It shares this problem with every other approach to constitutional rights. But it *is* a problem. We will explore the inability of any legal order that purports to value both religion and liberal democracy to escape that dilemma in Part Four.

Still, we can say a little more than that. If we cannot, except by example, resolve the question of how a free exercise claim will be measured against the interests of the state in every case, we can at least say something about the *spirit* in which that balancing will be undertaken. Perhaps the main conclusion we can draw is that, in keeping with its general attitude, constitutional agnosticism will approach the rights-balancing question in a spirit of humility. The constitutional agnostic will be "somewhat tentative" in his balancing of rights against state interests, "open to reevaluation and reassessment," approaching the task "with an open mind, creativity, and humility."[118]

Notwithstanding that spirit of humility, the constitutional agnostic will end up placing a heavy thumb on the scales in favor of the religious claimant. This is inherent in the fact that the constitutional agnostic imaginatively and empathetically enters the perspective of the religious claimant, envisioning a world in which a religious belief is simply *true* and the practices that it entails are strongly recommended, if not mandatory. From that perspective, it will be difficult for the constitutionally agnostic decision maker to conclude that the unemployment compensation laws should not bend when confronted with the needs of a Saturday worshipper, that the drug laws should outweigh the putative fact that God is best worshipped through the peyote ceremony, or that the building of a federal road is more important than the preservation of a religiously sacred site whose survival is essential to a particular religious community. From the constitutionally agnostic perspective, *none* of these claims may be true; but so long as any of them *might* be true, that should weigh heavily in the balance against any asserted state interests.

One response that should not satisfy the constitutional agnostic, or anyone else for that matter, is the notion that a religious claim must fail when outweighed by the public good. This is the approach advocated by Marci Hamilton, whose book *God vs. the Gavel* is a spirited defense of the result in *Smith* and a frontal

---

117. *Van Orden v. Perry*, 545 U.S. 677, 700 (2005) (Breyer, J., concurring in the judgment).

118. Scharffs, *supra* note 114, at 1374.

attack on the idea that religious practices ought to qualify for special treatment as a matter of constitutional law.[119] Hamilton argues that the right rule in free exercise cases is the one offered by the Supreme Court in *Smith*: that "neutral, general laws apply to everyone, religious or not."[120] She believes that judges are incompetent to make the kinds of determinations about the public good that are implicated in constitutional claims to an exemption from generally applicable laws for religious conduct. This inquiry should be left to the legislature, which may grant exemptions only if they are "consistent with the larger public good."[121] She is not suggesting that legislatures may grant *any* exemption for religiously compelled conduct that they wish. Rather, she argues that *only* legislatures can grant exemptions, and those exemptions must be consistent with the public good.

It is difficult to say exactly what Hamilton means by the "public good." (This is further evidence, if any more were needed, that no system of protection for individual rights, whether it comes from the courts or the political process, can escape the incommensurability problem.) Her answer to this question is inconsistent.[122] For much of her book, she equates the public good with John Stuart Mill's harm principle, writing that religious exemptions from generally applicable laws are inappropriate unless the religious claimants can demonstrate to the legislature that "exempting them will cause no harm to others."[123] Elsewhere, she qualifies this claim, arguing that exemptions are appropriate if they will cause only *minimal* harm to others.[124] Later, she modifies her rule yet again, concluding that exemptions may be appropriate if the legislature finds that the exemption is justified by "the importance of respect and tolerance for a wide panoply of religious faiths," and that any harms caused by the exemption are such that they can be "tolerated in a just society."[125]

None of these standards is especially clear or self-evident, and none is satisfactory.[126] The surface attractions of the harm principle are just that.[127] The harm

---

119. *See* Marci A. Hamilton, *God vs. the Gavel: Religion and the Rule of Law* (2005).

120. *Id.* at 274.

121. *Id.* at 275.

122. *See* Douglas Laycock, *A Syllabus of Errors*, 105 Mich. L. Rev. 1169 (2007) (reviewing Hamilton, *supra* note 119). Professor Hamilton offers a spirited response to Laycock's strongly worded critique in Marci A. Hamilton, *A Response to Professor Laycock*, 105 Mich. L. Rev. 1189 (2007), and *God vs. the Gavel: A Brief Rejoinder*, 105 Mich. L. Rev. 1545 (2007).

123. Hamilton, *supra* note 119, at 5.

124. *See id.* at 275.

125. *Id.* at 297.

126. For criticisms of Hamilton's approach, see Laycock, *supra* note 122; Kent Greenawalt, *The Rule of Law and the Exemption Strategy*, 30 Cardozo L. Rev. 1513 (2009); Kathleen A. Brady, *Religious Group Autonomy: Further Reflections on What is at Stake*, 22 J.L. & Religion 153 (2006–2007); Marc O. DeGirolami, *Recoiling From Religion*, 43 San Diego L. Rev. 619 (2006).

127. *See* Laycock, *supra* note 122, at 1171.

principle is sometimes waggishly translated as the principle that freedom ends where my fist hits your face. But in a crowded society, every fist eventually meets a face. Every action has a cost. Even "routine activities both inconvenience those around us and impose significant risks."[128] Cars cause accidents; but perfectly engineered and perfectly safe cars would be tanks, so expensive and slow moving that the economy would grind to a halt and every baby would be delivered in a back seat before the vehicle could inch its way to the hospital.[129] Moreover, "nontrivial harm arguments" can be made "about practically every moral offense."[130] The harm principle makes some intuitive sense and offers valuable insights about the limits of freedom. But those insights run out pretty quickly. Beyond that point, the harm principle turns out to be surprisingly ticklish, and to smuggle in highly debatable substantive arguments about what should count as harm.[131]

None of these issues is resolved by shifting the ground from the harm principle to a standard that asks what religiously motivated conduct can be "tolerated in a just society." General concepts like "ordered liberty" or "the rule of law," which Hamilton invokes in support of her approach, "by themselves [ ] tell us very little about the substantive content of [the question] where the public good actually lies."[132] Such values are "ambiguous and unstable," and "often substitute[ ] for . . . the author's policy preferences on a variety of issues."[133] The rule of law stresses generality, among other values.[134] But that unhelpfully vague value does not exclude the possibility of making *relevant* exceptions to general legal commands. The constitutional agnostic, in keeping with the broader American constitutional tradition, *does* value religion, and specifically thinks it is profoundly relevant that a religious claim might be true. So a general invocation of the "public good" does not rule out religious exemptions. It just raises again the question whether the "public good" in fact embraces the idea of granting religious exemptions.[135]

---

128. *Id.*
129. *See generally* Guido Calabresi & Philip Bobbitt, *Tragic Choices* (1978).
130. Bernard E. Harcourt, *The Collapse of the Harm Principle*, 90 J. Crim. L. & Criminology 109, 114 (1999), quoted in DeGirolami, *supra* note 126, at 642.
131. *See* Steven D. Smith, *The Disenchantment of Secular Discourse* (2010).
132. DeGirolami, *supra* note 126, at 648.
133. *Id.* at 620.
134. *See, e.g.*, Lon L. Fuller, *The Morality of Law* 33–94 (rev. ed., 1969).
135. *See* DeGirolami, *supra* note 126, at 645 ("[A]dherence to the procedural sense of the rule of law does not necessarily explain why interests in religious accommodation are 'like' (all) other interests, and should be treated as such for rule-of-law purposes. In fact, there is prima facie constitutional evidence that religious free exercise interests are not 'like' many other interests that the law might infringe upon or protect."); *see also* Andrew Koppelman, *Is it Fair to Give Religion Special Treatment?*, 2006 U. Ill. L. Rev. 571; Michael W. McConnell, *The Problem of Singling Out Religion*, 50 DePaul L. Rev. 1 (2000).

That leaves Hamilton with a final argument, one based on comparative institutional competence. This is the argument that legislatures are better suited than courts to balance the needs of religious believers against the needs of the state, and that courts may be "incompetent" to do so.[136] There is something to this point. But Hamilton is too romantic about the capacities and real-world practices of legislatures, and too skeptical about the capacities and practices of courts.[137] Neither institution is ideal, and neither institution is utterly incapable of striking a balance; courts balance interests all the time, and by no means badly, despite the problem of incommensurability.[138] Indeed, when she gets down to cases, it is clear that Hamilton disapproves of how *legislatures* balance religious and secular interests just as much as she disapproves of how *courts* do so.[139] It is hard for Hamilton to argue for the institutional superiority of the legislature when she is constantly outraged by the decisions it reaches on questions of religious liberty.

In short, general arguments about the public good rest on deeply flawed foundations. To constitutional agnostics, the public good includes not only the importance of religion, but also the importance of the possibility of religious *truth*. This conception of the public good leads them to weigh religious claims heavily in the balance against state interests. The constitutional agnostic does not see this as a path to chaos, but as showing respect for the possibility that some religious claims are true, and therefore should not lightly be overridden by transient state interests. It is the path to a genuine "public good," in a pluralistic and agnostic age in which the conventional liberal definition of the public good is no longer assumed or shared by all citizens.[140] As he must, the constitutional agnostic will set limits on what religious rights require of the state in practice; but he will do

---

136. Hamilton, *supra* note 119, at 297. As Laycock observes, this "may just be an odd way of restating her insistence that statutes granting exemptions enact narrow rules rather than broad standards." Laycock, *supra* note 122, at 1174. As I have argued above, this rule-based approach pushes the balancing of interests back to an earlier stage in the process—namely, the rule-crafting stage—but does not dissolve the need to engage in interest-balancing when shaping that rule.

137. *See* DeGirolami, *supra* note 126, at 651 (Hamilton's "faith in the possibility of an ideal legislator, unsullied by the whispers and tugs of special interests, is perhaps the most confounding part of the book. Hamilton appears to have traded in one set of rose-colored glasses for another.").

138. *See* Greenawalt, *supra* note 126, at 1530–34; Laycock, *supra* note 122, at 1172–77; DeGirolami, *supra* note 126, at 648–52.

139. For citations to examples in Hamilton's book, see Laycock, *supra* note 122, at 1172–74; *see also* DeGirolami, *supra* note 126, at 649 (noting Hamilton's "frequent disappointment with actual legislative decisions [ ] ostensibly aimed at the public good in the religious accommodation context").

140. *See, e.g.*, Jean Bethke Elshtain, *A Response to Chief Justice McLachlin*, in *Recognizing Religion in a Secular Society* 35, 40 (Douglas Farrow, ed., 2004).

so in a spirit of humility and openness to the possibility of religious truth, not in a spirit that treats invocations of the "public good" as somehow settling the question.

That does not mean that Hamilton's point about the relative capacities of courts and other decision makers is entirely misplaced, although the constitutional agnostic does believe that courts are authorized to act in this area. As we saw in Chapter Five, constitutional agnosticism embraces both judicial decision makers and other decision makers, including legislators, executive officials, and citizens. Even where a *court* is unable or unwilling to strike a balance between religious claims and the needs of the state, the political branches, with input from citizens operating in a suitably constitutionally agnostic spirit of empathy and dialogue, are free to do so, in a way that provides significant protection for religious freedom.

An example may help illustrate how the balance should be struck between religious claims and state interests, and how both courts and legislatures may participate in a system of constitutional agnosticism. Members of the Sikh faith believe that males should carry a ceremonial dagger, known as a *kirpan*, at all times.[141] School administrators, who have a legitimate interest in safety and security, have sometimes banned Sikh children from wearing kirpans at school, setting off a conflict between religious obligations and state concerns.

Hamilton is characteristically blunt on this question. She writes that "[o]nly a flawed legal doctrine would lead [courts] out on such a weak limb. Knives are knives, and children are not safe in their presence, no matter who they are."[142] She is critical of courts that have applied strict scrutiny in such cases. In striking contrast to constitutional agnosticism, she argues that these courts err by "thinking only in terms of the needs of the believer" and by "suspend[ing] common sense," and praises a dissenting judge for "thinking beyond the believer's perspective."[143] But she thinks the legislature acted just as badly in this case. She blames the California legislature's enactment of an exemption for kirpans on pressure from "the sizable Sikh population in California," and says that when the governor vetoed the exemption, "common sense prevailed."[144]

That's not how the constitutional agnostic would view the case. For one thing, without neglecting the competing state interests, he would indeed begin by thinking in terms of the needs of the believer. He would imagine himself in the grip of a comprehensive worldview, a set of beliefs and practices, in which it

---

141. The index reference to the discussion of this topic in Hamilton's book stacks the deck by referring to it as a "Sikh sword." Hamilton, *supra* note 119, at 407.

142. *Id.* at 116. None of the examples of violence involving kirpans that she cites involve children or schools. That does not mean there is no such danger, but it does dampen her assertion that the kirpan presents a clear and present threat to schoolchildren.

143. *Id.*

144. *Id.* at 117.

would be not only a matter of tradition and culture but, in a deeper sense, a matter of religious truth and duty to wear a kirpan. For Sikhs, the kirpan is a symbol of "righteousness and justice" and a reminder of the need to protect the weak and powerless.[145] Under a strict approach to constitutional agnosticism, any such obligation would be utterly incapable of being overcome by competing state interests. Even in a constitutionally agnostic system in which religious claims *can* be overcome by compelling state interests, the constitutional agnostic would be very reluctant to favor the state's interests over those of the religious believer, given the weight and importance of the religious obligation involved. He would certainly demand more than conjecture on the part of the state. If the evidence suggested that the state's interest in security did not *require* banning the kirpan, he would refuse to allow the state to do so. Even if there were marginal evidence that the kirpan might be used violently (not necessarily by the Sikh child himself; it is possible that a non-Sikh child might seize and use a Sikh child's kirpan), that would not necessarily justify a blanket ban. We cannot make perfectly safe schools any more than we can manufacture perfectly safe cars, and a few instances of violence involving kirpans, as against, say, countless examples of school violence involving commonplace devices like compasses, would not justify an absolute bar on wearing them, given the putative truth and importance of the Sikhs' obligation.

Even if the state presented genuine and compelling interests in this case, the constitutional agnostic would still ask whether a milder alternative response was available rather than simply signing off on a blanket ban. Many Sikhs might be satisfied by a requirement that the kirpan be "blunted or dulled," for example, or that it be sewn into its sheath in order to make it more difficult to seize or use it.[146] They would at least respect the fact that the decision maker had actually attempted to occupy the Sikh perspective and made an effort to accommodate it, rather than stating dismissively, "Knives are knives." As the Supreme Court of Canada noted in just such a case, efforts at accommodation "enable[ ] [the religious claimant and the state] to reconcile their positions and find common ground tailored to their own needs."[147] Not every case might be capable of compromise, but nothing in the "public good" prevents us from trying. To the contrary, the "public good," properly understood, would be far better served by attempts at accommodation than by blunt refusals to treat such claims with the seriousness they deserve.

---

145. *See* Oxford Sikhs, *Explaining What the Kirpan is to a Non-Sikh*, Oct. 18, 2004, available at http://oxfordsikhs.com/SikhAwareness/91.aspx.

146. *Cheema v. Thompson*, No. 94-16097, 1994 WL 477725, at 4 n.7 (9th Cir. Sept. 2, 1994). A similar result was reached by the Supreme Court of Canada in *Multani v. Commision Scolaire Marguerite-Bourgeoys*, [2006] 1 S.C.R. 256 (Can.).

147. *Id.* at para.133.

Hamilton, who believes kirpans should be banned from schools altogether, rejects efforts at accommodation by both the courts *and* the legislature in such cases. This raises questions about the sincerity of her argument that legislatures are better suited than courts to accommodate religious claims. After all, California's legislature *did* weigh the public good in such cases, and concluded that it would best be served by a legislative exemption. The constitutional agnostic would take the same approach, and reach the same result, whether he was a judge, a legislator, or a citizen. There is no reason a judge could not reach this result, no special incapacity that would prevent her from weighing the serious religious concerns involved against the (less weighty, in my view) countervailing state interests as well as a legislature could.

Before the matter ever came to a court, however, legislators, school officials, and citizens would ask themselves the same questions, through the same exercise of imaginative capacity. Operating from a perspective that attempted to assume the *truth* of the Sikhs' religious beliefs and practices, and having noted the relative paucity of evidence that kirpans present a serious threat to school safety, the constitutionally agnostic legislature would make every effort to accommodate the Sikh's needs. (This is, in fact, what the California legislature did.) In a pluralistic society, encouraging every group to participate as fully as possible in our public institutions is preferable to excluding them by invoking a highly partial notion of common sense or the "public good."

Thus, it is better to accept the marginal safety risks posed by kirpans than to demand that sikh students either capitulate, thus sacrificing their own deeply held beliefs and practices, or abandon the public schools altogether.[148] Indeed, given that all the actual evidence of kirpan-related violence that Hamilton cites[149] seems to have involved insulated segments of the Sikh community and did not occur within schools or other public institutions, it may be that a pluralistic society can do far more to reduce the threat of violence by welcoming dialogue and participation, and *allowing* the kirpan to be worn in public, than by having no kirpans and no dialogue. In a constitutionally agnostic society, courts would not need to address the issue at all, because the accommodation would already have been made by the legislature; thus, the question of comparative institutional competence would not arise. Absent legislative action, however, nothing

---

148. *See* Hamilton, *supra* note 119, at 118 (arguing that Sikh families might "choose to send their children to religious schools or to home school," or "adjust to the legal requirements . . . by jettisoning the practice altogether," or that "there might be some attempt on the part of the faith to meet the law halfway," by changing its doctrine to dispense with the kirpan requirement during school hours). The last possibility seems rather more than halfway to me, and raises the question why the *state* cannot attempt to meet the *Sikhs* halfway.

149. *See id.* at 115.

should prevent the constitutionally agnostic judge from acting if the occasion demands it.

We could say the same thing about one of the most famous modern instances of religious freedom legislation: the Religious Land Use and Institutionalized Persons Act, or RLUIPA,[150] which responded to the Supreme Court's decision in *Smith* by restoring a version of strict scrutiny in, among other things, cases involving land-use decisions that burden the ability of churches to build, reno-vate, and relocate.[151] RLUIPA was necessary because the *Smith* Court had cast doubt on whether strict scrutiny should apply in such cases.[152] Under the consti-tutionally agnostic approach, which restores to courts the obligation to grant exemptions from most generally applicable laws that burden religious practices, this legislative fix would be unnecessary. But that does not mean legislatures are *forbidden* to enact these kinds of exemptions. Neighborhood residents, of course, have a reasonable interest in peace and quiet. But those concerns, for the consti-tutionally agnostic legislator or judge, pale next to the centrality to many faiths of having a thriving church, in neighborhoods where worshippers might actually be found—particularly if the legislature assumes that the church's mission is, in fact, divinely ordained.[153]

Easy and Hard Free Exercise Cases

The kirpan cases and RLUIPA serve as a useful entry point in considering the constitutional agnostic approach to the Free Exercise Clause. We can orient this discussion around two general categories: easy cases and hard cases. This is an imperfect way of categorizing these cases, but it serves two valuable purposes. First, it suggests that current thinking about the Free Exercise Clause has gotten

---

150. 42 U.S.C. §§ 2000cc–2000cc-5 (2000).

151. RLUIPA was actually the second response to *Smith*. The first, the Religious Freedom Restoration Act, codified at 42 U.S.C. §§ 2000bb–2000bb-4 (2000), was struck down insofar as it applies to the states by *City of Boerne v. Flores*, 521 U.S. 507 (1997).

152. I say "cast doubt" because *Smith* itself contains language that appears to demand heightened scrutiny for individualized determinations involving religious claimants, which is an apt characterization of many land use decisions by zoning boards and other bodies. *See Smith*, 494 U.S. at 884 (noting that the *Sherbert* test "was developed in a context that lent itself to individualized governmental assessments of the reasons for the relevant conduct"). But *Smith* did not clearly address land use decisions, and in general signaled a reluctance to expand *Sherbert* beyond the narrow field of unemployment compensation decisions.

153. Hamilton argues against exemptions for religious institutions in land-use deci-sions, on the grounds of the "seismic change" that building or expanding churches might have in "basic aspects of . . . homeowners' lifestyles," because of factors such as increased traffic. Hamilton, *supra* note 119, at 101. For a response, see, *e.g.*, Laycock, *supra* note 122, at 1171 ("The right to worship cannot exist without a space to worship in, and if any increase in traffic counts as harm, the no-harm rule [that Hamilton invokes in her book] would make it impossible to create new places of worship.").

things wrong—that it treats easy cases like hard cases, and hard cases like easy ones. Second, looking at what the constitutional agnostic thinks should be hard cases says something about both the limits of constitutional agnosticism and the tragic nature of the relationship between religion and liberal democracy.

Easy Cases

From the constitutional agnostic's perspective, many free exercise cases ought to qualify as easy cases, given the emphasis she places on the possibility of religious truth and the thumb she places on the scale on the side of religious practices when weighing them against state interests. Both the kirpan example and the land-use cases covered by RLUIPA fall within the easy category. So might a variety of other cases, many of which were decided against the religious claimant, even in the pre-*Smith* era. For example, *Goldman v. Weinberger*,[154] the case in which an Air Force captain was barred from wearing a yarmulke while on duty, surely presents a lopsided contest between religious obligations that are ostensibly based on divine command and religious custom, and a mere interest in uniform appearance.[155] *Smith* itself, which on its facts involved a narrow claim for an exemption from the unemployment compensation laws, not a broad challenge to the drug laws, is another case in which religious practices should outweigh countervailing state interests.[156]

Consider two other examples. In *United States v. Lee*,[157] Amish farmers objected to making mandatory Social Security payments on behalf of their workers, because they believe that caring for the elderly is a job for the religious community, not the government. The government denied their claims. Despite the government's substantial interest in a functioning social security system, the constitutional agnostic would have little difficulty concluding that a limited exemption was appropriate in this case. And consider again the *Lyng* case, which involved building a federal road through a sacred Indian site.[158] Although the federal government has a significant interest in controlling its own lands, if we assume that certain lands are genuinely sacred and essential to the existence of an entire religious community, that ought to easily overcome the competing state interests. The Court was wrong to hold otherwise in *Lyng*.

If anything, what seems extraordinary from the constitutional agnostic's perspective is that these cases, which present strong religious claims and relatively weak state interests, seem to be viewed as hard cases, or at least close calls, under current doctrine. To say that these cases, which may well represent the common

---

154. 475 U.S. 503 (1986).

155. Congress agreed, and subsequently changed the regulations.

156. Again, the government agreed, and changed the law.

157. 455 U.S. 252 (1982).

158. *See Lyng v. Northwest Indian Cemetery Protective Ass'n*, 485 U.S. 439 (1988) (reaching the opposite conclusion).

run of free exercise cases, should be easy ones is not to say that there is *nothing* hard about them. As cases like *Lee*, the Social Security exemption case, suggest, there are certainly worthy state interests involved in these disputes. From a constitutionally agnostic perspective, however, once we recognize the possibility that these cases are founded on genuine religious truth, mere administrative convenience, or fears about dire consequences that always seem to be lurking around the corner but never arrive, should not outweigh a religious claim so easily. Courts should not use hypothetical fears as an excuse to set the constitutional bar so high that easy cases end up as close calls. They should set the bar at an appropriate level, and deal with the harder cases if and when they arise.

Hard Cases

Despite its generally empathetic treatment of religious beliefs and practices, constitutional agnosticism has its limits. The constitutional agnostic will inevitably encounter cases in which the needs of the state are so strong that the accommodation of certain religious practices is impossible—even if, as we have seen, the incommensurability of these interests places the constitutionally agnostic decision maker in a grey area, in which clear guidance runs out and the exercise of judgment is all we have. That it is hard to set these limits in a definitive way, and that the constitutional agnostic generally prefers to err on the side of the possibility of religious truth, does not mean no limits will be set.

In this sense, the hard cases for the constitutional agnostic are those in which an irresistible force meets an immovable object—in which the decision maker is asked to compare "whether a particular line is longer than a particular rock is heavy."[159] They are cases in which a religious practice, when viewed through the lens of negative capability, presents powerful claims that it is both true and compelled, but the interests asserted by the state—life, health, the protection of third parties,[160] and other interests—rise to the highest levels of importance. In these cases, the conflict between the demands of religious truth and the needs of the state is at its apex.

Consider some examples, ranging from the ancient or legendary to the real and immediate occurrences of everyday life. We might begin with the case of Abraham and Isaac, an example we have treated as paradigmatically difficult for constitutional agnosticism.[161] From the perspective of the constitutional agnostic, Abraham presents a powerful case for the sacrifice of his son. On this view, Abraham is not sick or deluded, but the beneficiary of an awesome and awful

---

159. *Bendix Autolite Corp. v. Midwesco Enterprises, Inc.*, 486 U.S. 888, 897 (1988) (Scalia, J., concurring in the judgment); *see generally* Symposium, *When is a Line as Long as a Rock is Heavy?: Reconciling Public Values and Individual Rights in Constitutional Adjudication*, 45 Hastings L.J. 707 (1994).

160. *See, e.g.*, Lipson, *supra* note 104.

161. See Chapter Five.

communication from God, commanding him to sacrifice the thing he holds dearest in the world: his son.

Abraham is caught in a web of paradoxes. Isaac is the link to the future generations that God has promised, but he is also the sacrificial object. Moreover, in the moment of sacrifice, what is ethical is opposed to what is higher still than ethics—obedience to divine command. "[I]t is indeed this love of Isaac that in its paradoxical opposition to [Abraham's] love of God makes his act a sacrifice."[162] As one commentator has written, "there would be no test, no faith, no supreme act of religious devotion, if in any way Abraham . . . were unaware of the terrible wrongness, inhumanity, self-negation, and brutality of what [he was] commanded to do."[163] And yet, Abraham is still called upon by the most holy, whose word cannot be gainsaid, to sacrifice his son.

From the agnostic perspective, one cannot say that Abraham has *not* been given a binding instruction by God. One might want to argue that the response Abraham *ought* to make is the one Job initially made—to argue, to rebel, to suggest defiantly that God, not Abraham, should back down. It certainly would not be the only time Abraham argued with God.[164] But that is surely demanding too much. From the perspective of the religious believer who has received a direct order from God, obedience, even in an extreme case, hardly seems unreasonable.[165]

The usual way of responding to this problem is to say that Abraham has the virtue of being long dead, whereas we have to deal with the lunatics of the day— and they *are* lunatics. Where the person involved is not Abraham but Deanna Laney, a mother of three in Tyler, Texas, who "killed two of her children, and attempted to kill the third, by bludgeoning them on the head with large rocks," because she "heard God's voice in the sky commanding her to sacrifice her children" as a "final test before the apocalypse,"[166] most people conclude that only madness could have driven such an act. For many, including many religious people who purport to believe every word of Abraham's story, this is the only possible conclusion one *can* draw. In fact, the law recognizes a defense to criminal responsibility for such heinous crimes— the "deific decree" doctrine, under

---

162. Søren Kierkegaard, *Fear and Trembling* 100 (Alastair Hannay trans., 1985) (1843).

163. Caleb E. Mason, *Faith, Harm, and Neutrality: Some Complexities of Free Exercise Law*, 44 Duquesne L. Rev. 225, 262 n.116 (2006).

164. In Genesis 18, Abraham argues God down from his willingness to destroy Sodom if he cannot find fifty righteous people there, and convinces God to relent if he can find only ten righteous people in Sodom. Sodom, alas, still comes up short.

165. Of course, another possibility is to obey God—and hate him for it. This scenario is powerfully explored in the movie *The Rapture* (New Line Cinema 1991), one of the few American movies that actually bothers to take God seriously—to the likely detriment of its box-office success.

166. Mason, *supra* note 163, at 258–60.

which an instruction from God to kill is treated as "a delusional belief justifying an insanity verdict" rather than a conviction.[167]

For a constitutional agnostic, this conclusion is troubling. It is not impossible, to be sure. The constitutionally agnostic judge provisionally believes that God *could* tell someone to sacrifice her child, but she is not obliged to believe that God has done so in every such case. She does not think that *everyone* who says God told her to slay an innocent is sane. But neither can she conclude that *no one* who kills because God told her to do so is sane. Moreover, the constitutional agnostic thinks it is possible for someone to be both insane *and* the recipient of an authentic command from God; we have no reason to believe that God administers a psychological exam before deciding to communicate with someone. The constitutional agnostic could still treat independent evidence of the claimant's insanity as offering good reason to doubt the veracity of that person's assertions. But the bare statement that God had told one to kill, without additional evidence, could not be treated as conclusive evidence that this person was under a delusion. Approaching the case as she does from within "mysteries, uncertainties, and doubts," the constitutional agnostic must acknowledge that, if God in fact ordered Abraham to sacrifice his child, he could do so again.[168]

Nor would it do for the constitutional agnostic to respond, as one might under current legal doctrine, that we cannot say whether or not a person claiming to be acting under God's instruction is correct, and should therefore err on the side of caution. The constitutional agnostic would certainly agree with the first half of this proposition. But he might have a somewhat different view of what it means to err on the side of caution. He would replace the relative indifference of liberalism to the truth or falsity of the religious claim with a truth-based concern that

---

167. Grant H. Morris & Ansar Haroun, M.D., *"God Told Me to Kill": Religion or Delusion?* 38 San Diego L. Rev. 973, 977 (2001). For further discussion, see, *e.g.*, Mason, *supra* note 163; Andrew J. Demko, Note, *Abraham's Deific Defense: Problems With Insanity, Faith, and Knowing Right From Wrong*, 80 Notre Dame L. Rev. 1961 (2005); Jeanine Girgenti, *Bridging the Gap Between Law and Psychology: The Deific Decree*, 3 Rutgers J.L. & Religion 10 (2001).

168. I am not saying this would be consistent with all of the readings of the Abrahamic story in religious tradition. For example, Jewish tradition often treats the episode as marking the end of human sacrifice. *See, e.g.*, Deut. 12:31 (condemning human sacrifice by the Canaanites); *see also* George A. Butrick, 1 *The Interpreter's Bible* 164 (1952) (cited in Joan C. Williams, *Rorty, Radicalism, Romanticism: The Politics of the Gaze*, 1992 Wisc. L. Rev. 131, 137 n.29); *Pentateuch & Haftorahs: Hebrew Text, English Translation and Commentary* 201 (Dr. J.H. Hertz, ed., 2nd ed. 1985) (1963) (cited in Malla Pollack, *Prayer in Public Schools: Without Heat, How Can There Be Light?*, 15 Quinnipiac L. Rev. 163, 165 (1995)). Christian tradition, in turn, links God's staying of Abraham's hand to the crucifixion of Jesus, which constitutes God's *self*-sacrifice in human form. The constitutional agnostic's provisional willingness to assume the inscrutability and mystery of God, however, precludes a definitive conclusion that God, even the God of Judeo-Christian tradition, will never again demand another human sacrifice.

God might in fact have commanded the sacrifice. Given that possibility, the constitutional agnostic might conclude that erring on the side of caution actually requires the state to respect God's command.

None of this means that the constitutional agnostic wouldn't prevent a person from sacrificing his or her child! He would, of course. (*I* would, anyway.) The question is not so much *what* the constitutional agnostic would do in such a case, but *how* he would do it. He would favor a powerful state interest like the preservation of life—especially the life of someone other than the believer himself, and a child at that—because, as Judge Learned Hand once put it in another context, of "how importunately the occasion demands [that] answer."[169] He would acknowledge the possibility that he was acting contrary to God's will, and that worlds and souls might hang in the balance. But he would still be forced to balance that possibility against the certainty and seeming finality of death, and he would choose life, now and in this mortal realm.

So the *what* of the matter is easy. In this case, and no doubt in many others, the constitutional agnostic would reach the same answer as the committed atheist or the indifferent or statist liberal. However strongly constitutional agnosticism may urge us to take seriously the stakes involved in cases that involve the invocation of God's will, it does not demand that we go past our breaking point. If that makes constitutional agnosticism fainthearted, so be it.

The *how* of the matter is a different question, however. The constitutional agnostic's approach to cases like Abraham's would differ from the conventional approach. The constitutional agnostic, having conceded the possibility that Abraham might indeed be acting under divine command, and having imagined the force of such a command from the internal perspective of the believer and not just from an external perspective, would be alive to the high stakes of the case. He would appreciate the full measure of the conflict between the will of God and the needs of the state that arises in such crucial moments. The decision to restrain Abraham might be an easy one. But the tragic nature of that choice would be just as evident. The stark conflict between church and state, the opposition between the cherishing of life and the cherishing of things that are greater still than life itself, the incommensurability of the conflicting values, the supreme stakes involved from each perspective—all of these would be inescapable, impossible to ignore or forget.

This is the crucial difference between the constitutional agnostic's approach to questions of law and religion and the conventional approach to these questions. It lies less in the decision itself, since both would almost certainly reach the same result in Abraham's case, but in how each would understand and respond to that decision. Most liberals, and most conventional accounts of religious freedom, would say this was an easy case, not worth a moment of doubt or

---

169. Learned Hand, *The Bill of Rights* 15 (1958).

a minute of lost sleep. But they cannot tell us why. Just as the constitutional agnostic would ultimately have a hard time justifying the decision to preserve life rather than permit Abraham to proceed with his sacrifice (as I believe he would), the conventional approach would have a hard time explaining *why* this case should be an easy one—unless, perhaps, it is because such cases belie the liberal's insistence that he is refraining from drawing any conclusions about religious truth.

For the constitutional agnostic, on the other hand, even if the decision to preserve life in the face of a compelling religious claim represents a clear choice, the decision will still be accompanied by a proper sense of the tragic nature of the choice, and by a deep sense of moral regret. He will understand the moral seriousness of both claims—Abraham's *and* the state's—and the impossibility of satisfying both of them.

That does not mean he would decide differently if the occasion arose again. "Regret," the philosopher Bernard Williams wrote, "necessarily involves a wish that things had been otherwise, for instance that one had not had to act the way one did. But it does not necessarily involve the wish, all things taken together, that one had acted otherwise."[170] The constitutional agnostic would consistently choose life, health, and safety over the possibility of damnation, or of violating God's will. But, unlike most conventional accounts, he would understand the choice as a genuinely and ineluctably tragic one.

Regret may seem like no great matter. If both the constitutional agnostic and the conventional liberal decision maker would reach the same result, we might say, it is better to get a good night's sleep than to agonize over the inevitable. Judges are not usually afflicted by regret. That may surprise laypeople, who might assume that the weighty choices faced by judges will occasion some indecision and worry. But it will not surprise lawyers, and it will surprise judges themselves still less. They know that judges must make hard decisions every day, and that the judicial office would be unbearable if they agonized over each one. If judges had a motto, it would be, "Maybe in error but never in doubt."[171] Judges would not think much of any doctrine that tells them: "You should reach the right decision—but you should feel bad about it."

But regret—an appreciation of the moral seriousness of a decision, the incommensurability of the factors that go into it, and the tragic nature of the choice presented—can be a *good* thing, for both principled and pragmatic reasons. At the level of principle, the regret that accompanies the constitutional agnostic's

---

170. Bernard Williams, *Moral Luck: Philosophical Papers 1973–1980* 31 (1981).

171. *See, e.g.*, Jeffrey Rosen, *A Majority of One*, N.Y. Times Mag., June 3, 2001, at 32, 37 (noting that Justice Sandra Day O'Connor had this saying embroidered on a pillow in her chambers at the Supreme Court); Richard A. Posner, *The Problematics of Moral and Legal Theory* 197 (1999) ("Judges no more quaver at rendering judgments than surgeons quaver at making incisions.").

decisions in hard cases makes his approach more honest and coherent than the conventional liberal treatment of law and religion. He does not shrink from the seriousness of his choices by pretending that those choices aren't serious. He does not profess to respect religion, or at least to be agnostic about religious truth, while betraying his insensitivity to and borderline disbelief in religion at precisely those moments when religion's claims are at their most compelling. He understands that religion and liberal democracy may, at a fundamental level, be irreconcilable.[172] But he does not pretend otherwise. If he ultimately gives the victory to the state in some cases, it's not by sleight of hand.

The sense of regret that accompanies the constitutional agnostic's approach to hard cases involving the Free Exercise Clause also has a practical payoff. For one thing, it puts into proper perspective the common run of free exercise cases that are easy for a constitutional agnostic but closer calls for followers of the conventional approach. It reminds us that many free exercise cases are not hard cases. They present a conflict between genuinely compelling religious practices and relatively un-compelling state interests. *Goldman, Lee, Smith, Lyng*: all of these cases involve state interests in convenience and administrability, interests that should be easily overcome by the religious claims involved in those cases. Given the potential truth and importance of the religious claims at issue, the state cannot simply invoke hypothetical fears of anarchy to banish those claims.[173] Thus, the corollary of constitutional agnosticism's awareness of the tragic choices presented by the hard cases is its recognition that many free exercise claims pose no serious moral remainder. A sound resolution of those claims properly favors religious freedom over relatively insignificant or hypothetical state interests.

Even in what constitutional agnosticism views as the hard cases, there is a practical value to the sense of regret. Once we acknowledge the moral remainders caused by the conflict between the demands of religion and those of the state,[174] a great deal can be done to minimize them, to seek as much accommodation as possible before drawing the line. By treating these hard cases as easy ones, however, the conventional approach fails to fully account for the importance of the religious claims involved, and the tragic incommensurablity of the conflict between religious practices and state interests that is present in such cases. This leads it to confidently issue blunt decisions with little regard for the real stakes involved, and without any serious effort to reduce or eliminate the moral remainders involved.

This has two drawbacks. First, it substitutes fiat for dialogue. It does not attempt to explain to the religious claimant why his claim must fail, or even

---

172. *See* Chapter Eight.

173. *Cf.* Stephen L. Carter, *The Culture of Disbelief: How American Law and Politics Trivialize Religious Devotion* 133–35 (1993) (making the case for "subversive anarchy").

174. *See, e.g.*, Bernard Williams, *Problems of the Self* 179 (1973); Rosalind Hursthouse, *On Virtue Ethics* 47–48 (1999).

acknowledge that he has presented claims that are deeply meaningful to him, and potentially *true*. It responds to serious religious claimants, burdened by serious conflicts between their beliefs and the needs of the state, with curt dismissal. Perhaps this kind of knee-jerk response was acceptable in an era in which religious pluralism was at a low ebb and the liberal consensus was at its height. But in our own agnostic age, an age of religious pluralism in which the liberal consensus itself no longer commands the allegiance it once did, it will not do. Making a genuine effort to understand and acknowledge the force of religious claims, even if the decision maker must nevertheless deny those claims, may not satisfy the religious claimant. But it is far more likely to lead to a dialogue that brings outsiders back into the fold, and thus does more in the long run to respond to conditions of pluralism *and* preserve our faith in the rule of law.

Second, the constitutional agnostic, recognizing the stakes involved in the hard cases, will approach these cases in a spirit of humility. If he cannot avoid the tragic choices inherent in the hard cases, he can at least attempt to reduce the amount of conflict, bridging the gap as much as possible by accommodating the believer until he reaches the point at which no further compromise is possible. Such an approach reduces the size of the moral remainder involved, increases the amount of accommodation between church and state, and helps to encourage a dialogue among the different members of our pluralistic society rather than cut it short.

To take an example, consider the cases involving medical treatment decisions.[175] In these cases, an individual, either on her own behalf or on behalf of her minor child, refuses medically recommended treatment that might alleviate sickness or even save the patient's life. Typical examples involve Christian Scientists, who generally believe that prayer is a sounder response to illness than conventional medical care, or Jehovah's Witnesses, who "acknowledge that blood transfusions may be needed for physical recovery, but . . . believe that God's will is that they not accept transfers of blood."[176]

These cases "raise one of the most pointed conflicts between the free exercise of religion and the State's indisputable interest in protecting the health and

---

175. For an introduction to this topic, see 1 Greenawalt, *supra* note 94, ch. 21. *See also, e.g.,* Shawn Francis Peters, *When Prayer Fails: Faith Healing, Children, and the Law* (2008); Jennifer Stanfield, *Faith Healing and Exemptions to Child-Endangerment Laws: Should Parents Be Allowed to Refuse Necessary Medical Treatment for Their Children Based on Their Religious Beliefs?*, 22 Hamline J. Pub. L. & Pol'y 45 (2000); David E. Steinberg, *Children and Spiritual Healing: Having Faith in Free Exercise*, 76 Notre Dame L. Rev. 179 (2000); Jennifer L. Hartsell, *Mother May I . . . Live? Parental Refusal of Life-Sustaining Medical Treatment for Children Based on Religious Objections*, 66 Tenn. L. Rev. 499 (1999). I address these issues in Paul Horwitz, *The Sources and Limits of Freedom of Religion in a Liberal Democracy: Section 2(a) and Beyond*, 54 U. Toronto Fac. L. Rev. 1, 43–47 (1996).

176. 1 Greenawalt, *supra* note 94, at 396.

welfare of its citizens."[177] But one would not know it from the cases themselves, or from a good deal of scholarly commentary.[178] Courts permit competent adults to refuse medical treatment,[179] but this rule is grounded on the autonomy of adults in general, not on the religious nature of some individuals' objections to medical treatment. Where minor children are involved, however, the courts "have not hesitated to order treatment over the parents' wishes."[180] That is true even where the recommended course of treatment is both extremely painful and unlikely to succeed,[181] or where the treatment is necessary for the child's well-being but not his survival.[182]

The courts' attitude toward the parent's religious objections in these cases is often dismissive. These decisions suggest an underlying attitude of incredulity that anyone could prefer their child's spiritual welfare to their physical welfare. Thus, one court wrote, "The fact that the subject is an infant child of a parent who, *arbitrarily*, puts his own theological belief higher than his duty to preserve the life of his child cannot prevail over the considerable judgment of an entire people, in a case such as this."[183] Whether decisions to refuse medical treatment are right or wrong, they are not arbitrary. To the contrary, from the believer's perspective they involve profound spiritual consequences. And yet, in the common run of medical treatment cases, the courts give little or no "weight to the proposition that," for example, "accepting a transfusion will lead to eternal damnation."[184]

---

177. Steinberg, *supra* note 175, at 180.

178. For commentary that is critical of religiously based parental refusals of medical treatment for children, or of legislative exemptions to child-welfare laws that might at least shield these parents from liability for their refusal, even if the state has already intervened to provide medical attention to the child, *see, e.g.*, Henry J. Abraham, *Abraham, Isaac, and the State: Faith-Healing and Legal Intervention*, 27 U. Rich. L. Rev. 951, 986 (1993); James G. Dwyer, *The Children We Abandon: Religious Exemptions to Child Welfare and Education Laws as Denials of Equal Protection to Children of Religious Objectors*, 74 N.C. L. Rev. 1321 (1996); Ann MacLean Massie, *The Religion Clauses and Parental Health Care Decisionmaking for Children: Suggestions for a New Approach*, 21 Hastings Const. L.Q. 725 (1994).

179. *See, e.g.*, *Cruzan v. Missouri Dep't of Health*, 497 U.S. 261 (1990).

180. 1 Greenawalt, *supra* note 94, at 402.

181. *See, e.g.*, *Newmark v. Williams*, 588 A.2d 1108 (Del. 1991) (ordering medical intervention over the parents' religious objections where doctors recommended a difficult course of chemotherapy with a 40 percent chance of survival).

182. *See, e.g.*, *In re Sampson*, 317 N.Y.S. 2d 641 (Fam. Ct. 1970), *aff'd*, 323 N.Y.S. 2d 253 (App. Div. 1971), *aff'd*, 278 N.E.2d 918 (N.Y. 1972) (ordering a dangerous operation that would only partially repair a "grotesque" facial deformity on a child's face caused by neurofibramatosis).

183. *Morrison v. State*, 252 S.W.2d 97, 101 (Mo. Ct. App. 1952) (emphasis added).

184. Carter, *supra* note 173, at 220.

The standard liberal response to this possibility is to emphasize the child's autonomy: the child should be able to make his own decision about whether he wants to live or die, and if he is too young to make an informed decision he should be kept alive until he can. This ostensibly reasonable stance nevertheless smuggles in assumptions about the individual as opposed to the communitarian nature of religious belief, the status of individual autonomy, and the obviousness of the choice of life over death, even if the claimant believes that the eternal consequences for the child are graver than the threat of mere physical death.[185] Or, in keeping with the liberal premise that we ought to avoid questions of religious truth, it will be suggested that "the legal system's refusal to take account of the religious claim that the transfusion must lead to perdition is a statement not that the claim is false, but that it is irrelevant."[186] But this cannot be true. As Stephen Carter observes, "There is a logical sense in which the refusal to take account of the claim *is* to treat it as false. For if the claim is true, life eternal would seem plainly to trump the transient life available on earth."[187]

Because the constitutional agnostic prizes the possibility of religious truth, he cannot call religious objections to medical treatment, even those invoked by parents of minor children, irrelevant or arbitrary. That is not to say he will decline to order medical intervention in these cases. But it does suggest that, as in the paradigmatic hard case of Abraham, he will understand them to *be* hard cases. He will appreciate the tragic nature of these cases rather than treating them as easy ones in which the religious interest in non-intervention somehow simply evaporates. He will approach such cases humbly, in a spirit of empathetic dialogue with the religious parent and/or child that strives to reduce the moral remainder involved in these cases.

In some cases, perhaps most of them, the result will be the same. The constitutionally agnostic judge will still order medical intervention. But he will at least openly acknowledge and give due weight to the religious interests involved, thus letting the religious claimant know that he is not simply irrational, arbitrary, or a "bad" parent. That empathetic approach may not satisfy the religious claimant, given the stakes involved. But it is far less likely to make a total outsider of the claimant, to draw a circle around "proper" society that excludes the religious believer.[188]

In other cases, the balance might shift in favor of the religious claimant. Rather than assume that intervention is the only course of action, the judge will give a more meaningful consideration to all of the factors involved, including the parents' and children's religious beliefs, the likelihood the treatment will

---

185. *See* Horwitz, *supra* note 175, at 45–46.

186. Carter, *supra* note 173, at 220.

187. *Id.*

188. *Cf.* Nomi Maya Stolzenberg, *"He Drew a Circle that Shut Me Out": Assimilation, Indoctrination, and the Paradox of a Liberal Education*, 106 Harv. L. Rev. 581 (1993).

succeed, the degree of pain involved in the medical treatment, and so on. In some cases, that balancing of interests may counsel against medical intervention. This result is most likely to occur in cases involving so-called "mature minors," whose advanced age and maturity makes it more likely that the child is making an informed decision against treatment, even though the child still falls below the legal threshold for adulthood.[189]

Even in cases involving younger children, the court *might* still decide that the balance favors non-intervention. A particularly sensitive approach along these lines can be found in a Canadian case, *Re L.D.K.; Children's Aid Society of Metropolitan Toronto v. K. and K.*[190] In that case, a twelve-year-old child of Jehovah's Witnesses who suffered from leukemia wanted to forgo chemotherapy, which would involve blood transfusions. The judge in that case, having weighed all the factors involved, including the child's own reluctance to undergo chemotherapy, wrote: "With this patient, the treatment proposed by the hospital addresses the disease only in a physical sense. It fails to address her emotional needs and her religious beliefs. It fails to treat the whole person."[191] The judge declined to order medical intervention, allowing the child instead to try an alternative therapy at home, where she "would be surrounded by her family and . . . be free to communicate with her God. She would have peace of mind and could get on with attempting to overcome this dreadful disease with dignity."[192]

That does not mean the constitutional agnostic will refuse to intervene in every case. Medical intervention over religious objections, particularly in cases involving young children, will probably be the rule rather than the exception. But by treating these cases as hard cases, the constitutional agnostic advances the discussion in a number of ways. She is more honest about the competing claims involved, and so gives due recognition to the tragic nature of these cases. She leaves open the possibility of genuine dialogue with the claimants, rather than simply casting them outside of society by treating them as irrational or evil. And she will strive to reduce the moral remainder involved by doing her best to weigh seriously the competing claims and, in appropriate cases, seek the greatest possible accommodation between the religious claimant and the state, which in some instances may favor living (and dying) with dignity, secure in the embrace of a meaningful religious faith, over medical treatments that may be physically painful and spiritually and emotionally costly without promising any certain beneficial result.

---

189. *See, e.g., In re E.G.*, 549 N.E.2d 322 (Ill. 1989) (refusing to order a transfusion for a 17-year-old Jehovah's Witness).

190. 48 R.F.L. (2d) 164 (Ont. Prov. Ct. (Fam. Div.) 1985).

191. *Id.* at 169.

192. *Id.* For a sensitive treatment of the issues raised by these and other cases, see Shauna Van Praagh, *Faith, Belonging, and the Protection of "Our" Children*, 17 Windsor Y.B. Access to Just. 154 (1999).

Finally, in keeping with the argument that constitutional agnosticism is a matter for other decision makers besides judges, the constitutionally agnostic legislator or citizen would be more likely to try to minimize the moral remainder involved in these sorts of cases. For instance, a number of states have created legislative exemptions to child neglect or abuse statutes for parents who fail to seek medical treatment for their children as a result of sincerely held medical beliefs.[193] Some have argued that these statutory exemptions are wrong, because they imply that "the child's life is not all that valuable."[194]

From the constitutional agnostic's perspective, however, legislative exemptions from child neglect and abuse statutes are a reasonable attempt to acknowledge the seriousness of the religious claims involved and their potential truth, and to reduce the moral remainders involved in these tragic cases. That does not mean the decision maker should refuse to order medical treatment in appropriate cases. But adding a charge of parental abuse or neglect to that intervention would simply heap insult on top of what the religious claimant already believes is a serious injury to his faith and his eternal well-being, or that of his child.[195] It is a way of making a blanket statement that the parent, by virtue of his or her religious beliefs, is so irrational as to be neglectful or abusive, even if in every other respect he or she is a loving and tender parent. So the constitutionally agnostic legislator, citizen, or prosecutor would generally be amenable to seeing intervention itself as the most that was required, and would be inclined either to provide a legislative exemption from further legal proceedings or to exercise his charging discretion in a merciful fashion.

In sum, constitutional agnosticism offers a very different view of what constitutes an easy case or a hard case within the balancing of competing religious and state interests that the Free Exercise Clause entails. For the constitutional agnostic, those cases that receive the most attention, like *Smith*, and in which the state invokes mere concerns about administrative convenience, or hypothetical fears about anarchy or lawlessness, against compelling religious obligations would be relatively easy ones. On the other hand, the constitutional agnostic would treat as genuinely hard cases those that raise genuinely tragic choices or

---

193. *See, e.g.*, 1 Greenawalt, *supra* note 94, at 408–13; Eric W. Treene, *Prayer-Treatment Exemptions to Child Abuse and Neglect Statutes, Manslaughter Prosecutions, and Due Process of Law*, 30 Harv. J. Legis. 135 (1993); Stanfield, *supra* note 175.

194. Hamilton, *supra* note 119, at 33.

195. Thus, Kent Greenawalt observes that subsequent punishment is less necessary "so long as courts can order necessary medical intervention." If the child has already died, punishment will not help the child, and "punishing as serious criminals parents whose failure to get medical help has already brought them the worst misfortune most parents imagine is to inflict further pain on people who are already suffering terribly." 1 Greenawalt, *supra* note 94, at 411.

moral remainders—the very cases that under current doctrine are viewed as easy cases in favor of the state.

That does not mean the constitutional agnostic would necessarily reach a contrary result in those hard cases. Faintheartedly or not, constitutional agnosticism does not demand absolute license for religious practice. But it does mean that the constitutional agnostic will attempt to fully appreciate the competing claims involved in hard cases. He will do what he can, whether as a judge or as a citizen or public official, to accommodate religious practice if possible, and thus to reduce the extent of the moral remainder left over in hard cases; and he will engage in a sympathetic dialogue with the religious believer if the hard choice cannot be avoided.

CONCLUSION

In this chapter, I have offered a comprehensive discussion of what constitutional agnosticism demands with respect to the Free Exercise Clause. The most important aspect of this argument is the difference between how most conventional accounts of religious freedom treat free exercise cases and how constitutional agnosticism treats the same cases. Unlike constitutional agnosticism, the standard approach to these cases is relatively indifferent to questions of religious truth. But that indifference runs into all the problems of coherence and consistency that we saw in discussing the liberal consensus in general in Part One. Nor does constitutional agnosticism value free exercise cases primarily as matters of individual conscience. That approach has its merits, but by severing the connection between conscience and religious truth, it risks unduly privileging even relatively trivial state interests over matters of "mere" conscience.

Instead, constitutional agnosticism takes a genuine interest in the possibility that claims for exemptions from generally applicable laws for religious beliefs and practices are important precisely because those claims might be *true*. It approaches those claims in an open-minded, interested, empathetic, and imaginative fashion, employing a negative capability that corresponds to the religious agnosticism I described in Chapter Three. The constitutional agnostic may not be able to fully occupy the worldview of the religious believer, but he can try. He can attempt to give genuine weight to the possibility that a religious claim is true, and try to imagine the centrality and importance of the practices that follow from the idea that God wills some tradition or course of conduct.

It is true that, at some point, even the constitutional agnostic will not be able to supply a complete justification for his decisions in particular cases.[196] But critics of constitutional agnosticism should not overstate this burden. The question,

---

196. See Chapter Eight for further discussion of this point.

after all, is not whether this approach to the Free Exercise Clause is perfect, but whether it is preferable to alternative approaches. I have argued that constitutional agnosticism succeeds better than these alternative accounts of religious freedom. Although it raises some important and difficult questions, it is more coherent and consistent than standard liberal approaches to the Free Exercise Clause, which give too little weight to the importance of religious claims and betray their own promise to avoid weighing the truth or falsity of religious claims.

That is true even in cases where the constitutional agnostic would reach the same outcome as the conventional approach, as in Abraham's case. In those cases, the liberal approach will either assert the interests of the state over the interests of the believer by effectively denying the truth of the religious claim, or lack a coherent account of why it reached that outcome. The constitutional agnostic may reach the same result, and may also lack a complete answer to the question of why the balancing of interests involved in such cases should favor the state over the religious believer, especially if matters of life and death are weighed against ultimate consequences such as damnation. But at least he will be open to, and candid and humble about, the tragic choices involved in those cases. His candor about these tragic choices will lead him to accommodate the religious believer as much as he can, and speak sympathetically to the believer in those cases in which accommodation proves impossible, thus preventing an unnecessary fracture in our pluralistic community.

Still, not every case is a hard or tragic case. In many instances, the constitutional agnostic, from within his empathetic and imaginative perspective, will fully appreciate the possible truth of a religious claim, and will favor religious exercise to a greater extent than current doctrine would allow. In a variety of cases, beginning with the pivotal decision in *Employment Division v. Smith*, the constitutional agnostic will redraw the balance, favoring religious exercise over relatively trivial or hypothetical state interests.

This permissive approach may not avoid controversy. Someone will always be ready to invoke Justice Scalia's specter of lawlessness and anarchy. But, by fully appreciating the potential for religious truth and its overwhelming importance, the constitutional agnostic is more likely to reach results that give proper weight to the potential for religious truth, whether he is a judge considering a free exercise claim to an exemption from generally applicable laws, or a citizen or legislator who is considering whether to create statutory exemptions in the first place. This approach is sounder and more responsive to the nature of our pluralistic society in our agnostic age.

7. CONSTITUTIONAL AGNOSTICISM AND THE ESTABLISHMENT CLAUSE
One Nation Under ___?

INTRODUCTION

In an important sense, the Establishment Clause of the First Amendment—"Congress shall make no law respecting an establishment of religion"[1]—is the subject of an overwhelming consensus among lawyers, legal scholars, judges, and citizens. Debates about the Free Exercise Clause can be polarizing because there is no simple agreement over whether current doctrine is right or wrong, whether it should be modified slightly or revamped completely. Happily, there are no such debates about the shape of current Establishment Clause doctrine. In this area of constitutional law, if in no other, everyone can clasp hands in a spirit of togetherness. Everyone agrees that it is awful.

The problem is more one of reasons than results. The Supreme Court has labored mightily to thread together a coherent set of rules and reasons that might help us to understand and apply the Establishment Clause—and failed. There is no single coherent account of the purpose and meaning of the Establishment Clause—none, at least, that commands general consensus, on the courts or elsewhere. That might be forgivable. If we cannot agree on a single account of the Establishment Clause, we might still agree on a relatively stable set of rules for applying it, even in the absence of agreement on *why* we have converged on those particular rules.[2] But we don't even have that. The Establishment Clause, as interpreted by the Supreme Court, is a farrago of unstable rules, tests, standards, principles, and exceptions. It leaves constitutional law scholars reminiscing wistfully about the elegance and simplicity of the Uniform Commercial Code or the Rule Against Perpetuities.[3]

When it comes to the broad principles, or even the basic doctrinal rules, that should guide Establishment Clause interpretation, no one agrees—not the courts themselves, and certainly not the scholars. They argue over whether the "wall of

---

1. U.S. Const., amend. I.

2. *See, e.g.,* Cass R. Sunstein, *Incompletely Theorized Agreements in Constitutional Law,* 74 Social Research 1 (2007); Cass R. Sunstein, *Incompletely Theorized Agreements,* 108 Harv. L. Rev. 1733 (1995).

3. This may be something of an inside joke. Suffice it to say that constitutional law scholars got into their field precisely to avoid this kind of thing.

separation" between church and state described separately by Roger Williams[4] and Thomas Jefferson[5] is a sound rule or a misguided metaphor,[6] although they agree that in practice the wall of separation has been "serpentine" at best,[7] and at worst "all but useless as a guide to sound constitutional adjudication."[8] They disagree about what should replace it: a regime of neutrality (whether formal or substantive), one of equality, or something else entirely.[9] They argue over whether there can be "a simple formula" of the Establishment Clause at all, or whether it is best understood "by focusing on concrete issues in context."[10] They even argue about some of the most fundamental questions of its scope and application. For example, does it apply to the states as well as the federal government, as most individual rights do,[11] or is it simply a "jurisdictional" rule that leaves the federal government out of it but permits states to erect religious establishments of their own?[12] And just what *is* an "establishment of religion" anyway?

---

4. Roger Williams, *Mr. Cotton's Letter Examined and Answered* (1644), reprinted in *The Complete Writings of Roger Williams*, at 313, 319 (Reuben Aldridge Guild & James Hammond Trumbull, eds., 1963).

5. Letter from Thomas Jefferson to Messrs. Nehemiah Dodge and Others, a Committee of the Danbury Baptist Association (Jan. 1, 1802), in *Thomas Jefferson: Writings* 510 (Merrill D. Peterson ed., 1984).

6. *See, e.g.*, Daniel L. Dreisbach, *Thomas Jefferson and the Wall of Separation Between Church and State* (2002).

7. *See, e.g.*, John Witte, Jr., *That Serpentine Wall of Separation*, 101 Mich. L. Rev. 1869 (2003); A.E. Dick Howard, *The Supreme Court and the Serpentine Wall*, in *The Virginia Statute for Religious Freedom: Its Evolution and Consequences in American History* 313 (Merrill D. Peterson & Robert C. Vaughan eds., 1988); *McCollum v. Bd. of Educ.*, 333 U.S. 203, 238 (1948) (Jackson, J., concurring) (warning that the Supreme Court's decisions in this area were "likely to make the 'legal wall of separation of church and state' as winding as the famous serpentine wall designed by Mr. Jefferson for the University he founded").

8. *Wallace v. Jaffree*, 472 U.S. 38, 107 (1985) (Rehnquist, J., dissenting).

9. *See, e.g.*, Thomas C. Berg, *Can Religious Liberty Be Protected as Equality?*, 85 Tex. L. Rev. 1185, 1186 (2007).

10. 2 Kent Greenawalt, *Religion and the Constitution: Establishment and Fairness* 433, 543 (2008); *see also Van Orden v. Perry*, 545 U.S. 677, 700 (2005) (Breyer, J., concurring in the judgment) (arguing that there is no "test-related substitute for the exercise of legal judgment" in Establishment Clause cases).

11. Through the incorporation of those rights against state and local governments via the Due Process Clause of the Fourteenth Amendment. The Establishment Clause was incorporated as a matter of legal doctrine in *Everson v. Board of Education*, 330 U.S. 1 (1947).

12. *See, e.g.*, Steven D. Smith, *The Jurisdictional Establishment Clause: A Reappraisal*, 81 Notre Dame L. Rev. 1843 (2006); *Elk Grove Unified Sch. Dist. v. Newdow*, 542 U.S. 1, 49–50 (2004) (Thomas, J., concurring in the judgment); Akhil Reed Amar, *The Bill of Rights: Creation and Reconstruction* 33–35 (1998); Carl H. Esbeck, *The Establishment Clause as a Structural Restraint on Governmental Power*, 84 Iowa L. Rev. 1 (1998).

This chapter offers the constitutional agnostic's take on the Establishment Clause. Despite the state of disagreement over Establishment Clause first principles, it will be simpler than our discussion of the Free Exercise Clause, for several reasons. First, although the disagreements in this area are significant, they are in some ways less heated. Not as a popular or political matter; public disagreements over the Establishment Clause are probably more vitriolic than disputes about the Free Exercise Clause.[13] But intellectually, the arguments here, in some respects, raise fewer deep questions than the arguments over the Free Exercise Clause. Second, although there may be plenty of disagreement over how to interpret the Establishment Clause, the nature of that clause lends itself to less interest-balancing than we have under free exercise doctrine. The thorny questions for the Establishment Clause come at the outset; if we can come up with basic rules for its interpretation, we are likely to see fewer ongoing disagreements over its application.

Finally, there is simply less excavation and reconstruction work to be done here. I do not seek to demolish the outcomes that apply under current Establishment Clause doctrine, particularly as it has developed in the past three decades or so, but to offer a more persuasive and coherent justification of those outcomes. A constitutionally agnostic approach to the Establishment Clause will, in fact, yield many of the same outcomes that currently exist in this area. With some work and a little luck, however, constitutional agnosticism will place these results on a far sounder footing. That is not to say *no* results will change under the constitutional agnostic approach to the Establishment Clause, or that none of them might prove controversial. But this chapter aims to preserve more than it destroys.

RECURRING AND COMPETING THEMES IN CURRENT ESTABLISHMENT CLAUSE DOCTRINE

Interpretation of the Establishment Clause, on and off the courts, tends to take one of three approaches: separationism, accommodationism, or a neutrality- or equality-oriented approach.[14] These general approaches have in turn given rise to

---

13. Kent Greenawalt observes that "Establishment Clause issues have been among the most controversial decided by the Supreme Court in the last half century." 2 Greenawalt, *supra* note 10, at 2.

14. A fourth approach to the Establishment Clause focuses not on principle as such, but on the original understanding of the clause. To the extent that this approach focuses only on historical meaning and not underlying principles, I will put it to one side, for the reasons I discussed in Chapter Five. In any event, things are rarely so cut-and-dried. Many writers who focus on the historical meaning of the Establishment Clause do so partly in the service of particular underlying principles; others rely primarily on the original

a variety of tests by which courts determine whether there has been an Establishment Clause violation. A brief introduction to these principles and tests will help lay the ground for a consideration of how the constitutional agnostic would approach the field.

Separationism was the principle that prevailed on the courts roughly between the Second World War and the 1980s or 1990s.[15] Although it has faded rapidly from prominence since then, it retains a strong hold on the public imagination. No public controversy over church–state relations in the United States is complete until someone has angrily invoked the "wall of separation" between church and state.[16]

Although its roots lie in Jefferson's famous use of the term in his letter to the Danbury Baptist Association, and Roger Williams's earlier similar reference,[17] separationism came to modern prominence with Justice Hugo Black's opinion for the Supreme Court in *Everson v. Board of Education*.[18] In that case, the Court faced the question whether a local government could subsidize public transportation to and from private parochial schools as well as public schools. Justice Black summed up the separationist approach as follows:

The "establishment of religion" clause of the First Amendment means at least this: Neither a state nor the Federal Government can set up a church. Neither can pass laws which aid one religion, aid all religions, or prefer one religion over another. Neither can force or influence a person to go to or remain away from church against his will or force him to profess a belief or disbelief in any religion. No person can be punished for entertaining or professing religious beliefs or disbeliefs, for church attendance or non-attendance. No tax in any amount, large or small, can be levied to support any religious activities or institutions, whatever they may be called, or whatever form they may adopt to teach or practice religion. Neither a state nor the

---

understanding of the text, but bring in those underlying principles to help interpret the original understanding in difficult cases.

15. For a history of the rise and fall of separationism as an Establishment Clause doctrine, see Ira C. Lupu, *The Lingering Death of Separationism*, 62 Geo. Wash. L. Rev. 230 (1993).

16. *See, e.g.*, Christopher L. Eisgruber & Lawrence G. Sager, *Religious Freedom and the Constitution* 6 (2007) ("Though the word 'separation' appears nowhere in the Constitution's religion clauses, most Americans seem to accept 'separation of church and state' as shorthand for the appropriate constitutional treatment of religion, and that phrase is almost certainly known to more Americans than is the constitutional text itself.").

17. For arguments about how Williams's use of the metaphor differs from the contemporary understanding of the "wall of separation," see, *e.g.*, Martha C. Nussbaum, *Liberty of Conscience: In Defense of America's Tradition of Religious Equality* (2008); Mark DeWolfe Howe, *The Garden and the Wilderness: Religion and Government in American Constitutional History* (1965).

18. 330 U.S. 1 (1947).

Federal Government can, openly or secretly, participate in the affairs of any religious organizations or groups and vice versa. In the words of Jefferson, the clause against establishment of religion by law was intended to erect "a wall of separation between church and State."[19]

The approach Black advocated, and which others on and off the bench championed for decades, was a strict one. "The First Amendment has erected a wall between church and state," he wrote. "That wall must be kept high and impregnable. We could not approve the slightest breach."[20] Its most ardent devotees argued that separationism "requires a wholly secular government," and that anything short of this would inevitably descend into theocracy.[21]

Separationism had several features. First, it suggested that "religion should be private rather than public."[22] Second, it meant that any law that lacked a secular purpose was inconsistent with the Establishment Clause.[23] Third, read broadly it prohibited a broad variety of common government actions that appeared to teach or endorse religion in general or particular religious beliefs. This conclusion led to the Court's decisions striking down various school prayer practices, from prayer itself[24] to the practice of requiring a moment of silence at the beginning of the school day for "prayer or meditation."[25] Fourth, hearkening back to James Madison's argument in his *Memorial and Remonstrance Against Religious Assessments* that not so much as "three pence" could be levied by the government "for the support of any one [religious] establishment,"[26] separationists argued that "[n]o tax in any amount, large or small," could be used to support religion.

Although the "wall of separation" metaphor is still ubiquitous in public dialogue, its use has declined precipitously on the courts.[27] Part of the reason for this is that the separation principle could not bear the weight that was placed on it.

---

19. *Id.* at 15–16 (quoting *Reynolds v. United States*, 98 U.S. 145, 164 (1878)).

20. *Id.* at 19.

21. Steven G. Gey, *Reconciling the Supreme Court's Four Establishment Clauses*, 8 U. Pa. J. Const. L. 725, 784 (2006).

22. Lupu, *supra* note 15, at 230–31.

23. *See, e.g., Lemon v. Kurtzman*, 403 U.S. 602, 612–13 (1971). *See generally* Andrew Koppelman, *Secular Purpose*, 88 Va. L. Rev. 87 (2002).

24. *See Sch. Dist. of Abington Twp. v. Schempp*, 374 U.S. 203 (1963); *Engel v. Vitale*, 370 U.S. 421 (1962).

25. *See Wallace v. Jaffree*, 472 U.S. 38 (1985). The statute was held to be constitutionally deficient not because it allowed for prayer as such, but because the amendment of the state statute, which already allowed for a moment of silence, to single out prayer had no clearly secular purpose.

26. James Madison, *Memorial and Remonstrance Against Religious Assessments*, reprinted in 5 *The Founders' Constitution* 82, 82 (Philip B. Kurland & Ralph Lerner eds., 1987).

27. *See, e.g.,* Lupu, *supra* note 15; Steven D, Smith, *Separation and the Fanatic*, 85 Va. L. Rev. 213, 213–15 (1999).

This was true from the beginning. In *Everson* itself, the Court *upheld* the subsidization of transportation for parochial school students. Despite its bold assertion that the Constitution could not support the "slightest breach" of the "impregnable" wall between church and state, the Court's very next sentence stated that the state "ha[d] not breached" the wall in the case, despite the law's obvious subsidy of religious practices.[28] In truth, given the pervasive presence of state regulation and public funds in modern society, complete separation between church and state is impossible.[29] As the saying goes (more or less), you can't be a little bit impregnable. That fact has always presented problems for separationism. Beyond that, however, separation lost support on the courts as the cultural currents of both modern society and constitutional jurisprudence shifted away from it. In its place, we have seen the emergence of two major competitors.

The first is accommodationism: the principle that the Religion Clauses, including the Establishment Clause, should provide the greatest possible degree of religious liberty.[30] Accommodationists argue that the Establishment Clause is not violated by laws that attempt to make room for religious beliefs and observances that many people hold dear.[31] An early example of accommodation is the Supreme Court's decision in *Zorach v. Clauson*,[32] which upheld a "released time" program under which public schools set aside time during which students could attend parochial schools for religious instruction. Broadly read, accommodation could sweep much further. Clergy-led prayer at a public school graduation ceremony, for example, could be understood as an accommodation of parents' desire to solemnize an important event in their lives.[33]

---

28. *Everson*, 330 U.S. at 16; *see also id.* at 19 (Jackson, J., dissenting) ("[T]he undertones of the opinion, advocating complete and uncompromising separation of Church from State, seem utterly discordant with its conclusion yielding support to their commingling in educational matters. The case which irresistibly comes to mind as the most fitting precedent is that of Julia who, according to Byron's reports, 'whispering "I will ne'er consent,"—consented.'").

29. *See, e.g.,* Eisgruber & Sager, *supra* note 16, at 6–7.

30. *See, e.g.,* Michael W. McConnell, *Accommodation of Religion,* 1985 Sup. Ct. Rev. 1; Michael W. McConnell, *Accommodation of Religion: An Update and a Response to the Critics,* 60 Geo. Wash. L. Rev. 685 (1992).

31. *See, e.g., County of Allegheny v. ACLU,* 492 U.S. 573, 657 (1989) (Kennedy, J., concurring in the judgment in part and dissenting in part) (arguing that the Establishment Clause should be understood in light of the "[g]overnment policies of accommodation, acknowledgment, and support for religion [that] are an accepted part of our political and cultural heritage").

32. 343 U.S. 306 (1952).

33. *See, e.g., Lee v. Weisman,* 505 U.S. 577, 631 (1992) (Scalia, J., dissenting) (citing Justice Kennedy's statement in *County of Allegheny,* 492 U.S. at 657, in support of the argument that a program of clergy-led non-sectarian prayer at a school graduation ceremony did not violate the Establishment Clause).

In part because of the difficulty of defining what constitutes a permissible accommodation of religion, and in part because of broader cultural tensions on the Court and elsewhere, the accommodation principle has always been subject to criticism and disagreement.[34] That brings us to the third competing Establishment Clause principle, one that has been increasingly influential on the courts in the past two decades or so: equality or neutrality.[35] Under this approach, religion need not be subject to the restrictions that separationism imposes, but neither is it necessarily entitled to official accommodation. Rather, laws that benefit or burden religion will not violate the Establishment Clause if they are at least neutral toward religion, treating the religious group or individual the same way the law treats non-religious groups or individuals.

The shift to neutrality or equality was a major change in Establishment Clause jurisprudence. Its significance has been most obvious in cases involving government funding for religious programs, especially those involving schools. The Supreme Court's decision in 1997 in *Agostini v. Felton*,[36] overruling an earlier decision that fell within the separationist tradition,[37] held that the Establishment Clause was not violated by a program that allowed public school teachers to teach remedial subjects to students in underperforming schools in low-income areas, whether those schools were religious or secular. In 2000, in *Mitchell v. Helms*,[38] the Court upheld a federal program that provided financial support for the loan of educational materials to schools in low-income areas, regardless of whether the schools were sectarian or secular. And in 2002, the Court gave its blessing to a system of financial "vouchers" for education, whether public or private, religious or secular, holding that such a program is constitutional as long as it is a "program[ ] of true private choice, in which government aid reaches religious

---

34. *See, e.g.*, Ira C. Lupu, *The Trouble With Accommodation*, 60 Geo. Wash. L. Rev. 743 (1992); Steven G. Gey, *Why is Religion Special?: Reconsidering the Accommodation of Religion Under the Religion Clauses of the First Amendment*, 52 U. Pitt. L. Rev. 75 (1990).

35. *See, e.g.*, Douglas Laycock, *Substantive Neutrality Revisited*, 110 W. Va. L. Rev. 51 (2007); Douglas Laycock, *Theology Scholarships, the Pledge of Allegiance, and Religious Liberty: Avoiding the Extremes But Missing the Liberty*, 118 Harv. L. Rev. 155 (2004); Frank S. Ravitch, *A Funny Thing Happened on the Way to Neutrality: Broad Principles, Formalism, and the Establishment Clause*, 38 Ga. L. Rev. 489 (2004); Noah Feldman, *From Liberty to Equality: The Transformation of the Establishment Clause*, 90 Cal. L. Rev. 673 (2002); Daniel O. Conkle, *The Path of American Religious Liberty: From the Original Theology to Formal Neutrality and an Uncertain Future*, 75 Ind. L.J. 1 (2000); Dhananjai Shivakumar, *Neutrality and the Religion Clauses*, 33 Harv. C.R.-C.L. L. Rev. 505 (1998); Ira C. Lupu, *To Control Faction and Protect Liberty: A General Theory of the Religion Clauses*, 7 J. Contemp. Legal Issues 357 (1996); Douglas Laycock, *Formal, Substantive, and Disaggregated Neutrality Toward Religion*, 39 DePaul L. Rev. 993 (1990). These principles could be viewed as distinct, but for our purposes we can consider them together.

36. 521 U.S. 203 (1997).

37. The overruled decision was *Aguilar v. Felton*, 473 U.S. 402 (1985).

38. 530 U.S. 793 (2000).

schools only as a result of the genuine and independent choices of private individuals."[39] In other words, as long as parents can choose to direct the government funds to religious or secular schools, and those schools are treated equally, there is no Establishment Clause violation.

In contrast to the separationist approach, with its bar against government funding for religion, the neutrality approach concludes that as long as the funding vehicle is neutral, "the amount of government aid channeled to religious institutions . . . [is] not relevant to the constitutional inquiry."[40] The Court has reached similar conclusions in the area of religious speech in public settings, holding that religious individuals are entitled to engage in speech in those settings on an equal basis with other individuals, so long as the decision to do so is not directed or influenced by the government itself.[41]

Alongside these competing principles, a huge array of different tests purports to provide some guidance for courts applying the Establishment Clause.[42] If for no other reason, the very profusion of these tests renders them unhelpful. To call Establishment Clause jurisprudence a morass is a grave insult to the average swamp.

The primary Establishment Clause test is the so-called "*Lemon* test," named after the Supreme Court's decision in *Lemon v. Kurtzman*.[43] There, the Court said that a law violates the Establishment Clause if: (1) it lacks a secular purpose, (2) it has the primary effect of advancing or inhibiting religion, or (3) it fosters excessive government entanglement with religion.[44] Usually, the inquiry turns on the second factor, whether the law has the primary effect of advancing or inhibiting religion.[45] The first prong, which asks whether the law has a valid secular purpose, rarely determines the outcome of the case.[46] The third prong, which asks whether there has been excessive government entanglement with religion, appears to have dropped out altogether in recent years.[47] The *Lemon* test

---

39. *Zelman v. Simmons-Harris*, 536 U.S. 639, 649 (2002).

40. *Id.* at 651.

41. *See, e.g., Good News Club v. Milford Cent. Sch.*, 533 U.S. 98 (2001); *Rosenberger v. Rector*, 515 U.S. 819 (1995); *Lamb's Chapel v. Center Moriches Union Free Sch. Dist.*, 508 U.S. 384 (1993).

42. For a general overview, see, *e.g.*, 2 Greenawalt, *supra* note 10, ch. 10; Kent Greenawalt, *Quo Vadis: The Status and Prospect of "Tests" Under the Religion Clauses*, 1995 Sup. Ct. Rev. 323.

43. 403 U.S. 602 (1971).

44. *See id.* at 612–13.

45. *See, e.g.,* 2 Greenawalt, *supra* note 10, at 158.

46. Andrew Koppelman has suggested that "[a] growing faction of the Court . . . may be ready to scrap the secular purpose requirement" altogether. Koppelman, *supra* note 23, at 88.

47. *See, e.g.,* 2 Greenawalt, *supra* note 10, at 158; *see Agostini v. Felton*, 521 U.S. 203, 232–33 (1997) (suggesting that excessive entanglement should be treated as evidence of an impermissible religious effect rather than as a separate and independent inquiry).

has been widely criticized by both judges and scholars, because the test is vague and there is no consensus about how to apply it. Nevertheless, *Lemon* continues to hang on by its fingernails, perhaps because the Court cannot agree on an alternative.[48] But it is now used sparsely and half-heartedly by the Supreme Court, and its days are probably numbered.

Instead, the Supreme Court has turned to a variety of alternative tests in recent cases. Two frequently used tests are the endorsement and coercion tests. The endorsement test, which was introduced by Justice Sandra Day O'Connor, asks whether a particular measure could be viewed as endorsing religion—as "send[ing] a message to nonadherents that they are outsiders, not full members of the political community, and an accompanying message to adherents that they are insiders, favored members of the political community."[49] The message of endorsement is to be evaluated from the perspective of a "reasonable" observer, a hypothetical person who is reasonably well informed about the circumstances of the law and its history.[50] Although the reasonable observer aspect of the endorsement test was supposed to lend some objectivity and uniformity to the inquiry, it leaves much room for debate.[51] For this reason, many seasoned Supreme Court watchers during the heyday of the endorsement test believed that the answer to the question of what a reasonable observer would make of a law was, "Go ask Justice O'Connor."[52] Now that she has left the Court, the future of the endorsement test is uncertain.

---

48. *Lemon* was cited, for example, in the Supreme Court's decisions on governmental display of the Ten Commandments, *McCreary Cty. v. ACLU of Ky.*, 545 U.S. 844 (2005), and *Van Orden v. Perry*, 545 U.S. 677 (2005), although the Court's citation was something less than whole-hearted. In *Lamb's Chapel v. Center Moriches Union Free School District*, 508 U.S. 384 (1993), Justice Scalia was moved to observe, with somewhat ponderous hilarity: "Like some ghoul in a late-night horror movie that repeatedly sits up in its grave and shuffles abroad, after being repeatedly killed and buried, *Lemon* stalks our Establishment Clause jurisprudence once again, frightening the little children and school attorneys of Center Moriches Union Free School District." *Id.* at 398 (Scalia, J., concurring in the judgment).

49. *Lynch v. Donnelly*, 465 U.S. 668, 694 (1984) (O'Connor, J., concurring).

50. *See, e.g., County of Allegheny v. ACLU*, 492 U.S. 573, 620 (1989); *id.* at 635–36 (O'Connor, J., concurring).

51. Thus, *Lynch* itself, which upheld the state-supported display of a Christmas crèche, along with various garish add-ons to signify the holiday season, was widely derided as introducing to Establishment Clause a "two plastic reindeer" rule, because a given number of plastic reindeer, clowns, and other secular symbols was treated as precluding the reasonable observer from concluding that the crèche display constituted an impermissible endorsement of religion. *See, e.g.,* George M. Janocsko, *Beyond the "Plastic Reindeer Rule": The Curious Case of County of Allegheny v. American Civil Liberties Union*, 28 Duq. L. Rev. 445 (1990); Lawrence Gene Sager, *Foreword: State Courts and the Strategic Space Between the Norms and Rules of Constitutional Law*, 63 Tex. L. Rev. 959, 969 (1985).

52. *See, e.g.,* B. Jessie Hill, *Putting Religious Symbolism in Context: A Linguistic Critique of the Endorsement Test*, 104 Mich. L. Rev. 491 (2005); Steven D. Smith, *Symbols, Perceptions,*

The coercion test takes a somewhat narrower, although still capacious, approach to the Establishment Clause. It states that "government may not coerce anyone to support or participate in religion or its exercise, or otherwise act in a way which establishes a state religion or religious faith, or tends to do so."[53] As with all the tests employed by the Supreme Court in the Establishment Clause arena, the coercion test is intuitively attractive. It captures something of the concerns that the Establishment Clause was meant to address. But it also leaves much to the discretion of judges. That might not be the case if coercion were read narrowly. But it is not. The Court has treated even "subtle coercive pressures" applied by the government as violations of the Establishment Clause.[54] Thus, in *Lee v. Weisman*, a case involving a clergy-led invocation at a school graduation ceremony, students were not required to do more than stand silently and inattentively while the school-selected rabbi delivered a non-sectarian prayer. That was enough to violate the Constitution, in the Court's view. "[T]he act of standing or remaining silent" could be taken as "an expression of participation in the rabbi's prayer," and the peer pressure attending such an act, although "subtle and indirect," could be "as real as any overt compulsion."[55] This conclusion leaves a good deal to the judge's discretion. For this reason, Justice Scalia derided this version of the coercion test as making the Establishment Clause turn on the "boundless, and boundlessly manipulable, test of psychological coercion,"[56] and would have required more serious and tangible coercion, although perhaps falling short of actual physical torture. (With Justice Scalia, one can never be quite sure.)

An outside contender among the ranks of Establishment Clause tests is *nonpreferentialism*, which argues that the clause "should be read no more broadly than to prevent the establishment of a national religion or the governmental preference of one religious sect over another."[57] Among other things, this approach would allow government to prefer religion over irreligion, and would permit government measures falling short of a fairly narrow definition of establishment. The nonpreferentialism test has been subjected to withering criticism for being historically inaccurate.[58] In any event, few members of the current Court have subscribed to this crabbed reading of the Establishment Clause.

---

and Doctrinal Illusions: Establishment Neutrality and the "No Endorsement" Test, 86 Mich. L. Rev. 266 (1987).

53. *Lee v. Weisman*, 505 U.S. 577, 587 (1992).

54. *Id.* at 588.

55. *Id.* at 593.

56. *Id.* at 632, 640 (Scalia, J., dissenting).

57. *Wallace v. Jaffree*, 472 U.S. 38, 100 (1985) (Rehnquist, J., dissenting).

58. *See, e.g.*, Douglas Laycock, *"Nonpreferential" Aid to Religion: A False Claim About Original Intent*, 27 Wm. & Mary L. Rev. 875 (1986). *But see* Patrick M. Garry, *Religious*

That leaves one last major contender in the Establishment Clause field, albeit one that is limited in scope. We might call it the constitutional or historical easement test, or the "What would George Washington do?" test. Kent Greenawalt describes it less pettishly as the test of "consistency with historical practice or understanding."[59] But what it amounts to is a historical easement over the Establishment Clause: a willingness to uphold government actions, like offering prayers before legislative sessions, that would otherwise contravene the courts' Establishment Clause rulings, so long as those government practices have a long pedigree. We might think of the constitutional easement less as a general test for Establishment Clause violations than as a sort of safety valve. It is a way of using history so the courts can avoid being drawn into the institutionally dangerous move of disallowing widely popular government actions that implicate the establishment of religion.

The most prominent example of a constitutional easement is the Supreme Court's decision in *Marsh v. Chambers*,[60] in which the Court upheld a practice of opening state legislative proceedings with a prayer led by a government-paid chaplain. The Court upheld the practice because "[t]he opening of sessions of legislative and other deliberative public bodies with prayer is deeply embedded in the history and tradition of this country."[61] The Court conceded that "historical patterns cannot justify contemporary violations of constitutional guarantees," but argued that the practice's venerable history—legislative chaplains were established by the very first Congress—provided strong evidence that the framers of the Establishment Clause meant to allow it.[62] Similarly, you know you're in the presence of a constitutional easement argument when a judge invokes President George Washington and his practice of issuing religious proclamations on Thanksgiving.[63]

Some busybody will invariably point out that President Thomas Jefferson "refused to issue Thanksgiving Proclamations because he believed that they violated the Constitution,"[64] and that James Madison, who did issue such

---

Freedom Deserves More Than Neutrality: The Constitutional Argument for Nonpreferential Favoritism of Religion, 57 Fla. L. Rev. 1 (2005) (defending the approach).

59. 2 Greenawalt, *supra* note 10, at 157.

60. 463 U.S. 783 (1983).

61. *Id.* at 786.

62. *Id.* at 790; *see also* Christopher C. Lund, *The Congressional Chaplaincies*, 17 Wm. & Mary Bill Rts. J. 1171 (2009).

63. *See, e.g., McCreary County*, 545 U.S. at 886–87 (Scalia, J., dissenting) (noting that Washington, at the First Congress's behest, began a "tradition of offering gratitude to God that continues today"); *Wallace v. Jaffree*, 472 U.S. 38, 100–03 (1985) (Rehnquist, J., dissenting).

64. *McCreary County*, 545 U.S. at 878.

proclamations, later regretted doing so.[65] Nevertheless, the constitutional easement remains popular among some members of the Court, who either sincerely
believe the Establishment Clause allows certain government invocations of
religion, or for strategic or prudential reasons want to avoid risking the Court's
institutional capital by overturning such widely popular practices. This tendency
is evident in the Court's abortive decision concerning the constitutionality of
requiring schoolchildren to say the Pledge of Allegiance, with its invocation of
"one nation under God."[66] There, the Court found a procedural means of getting
rid of the case, thus avoiding a direct confrontation between the Establishment
Clause and public opinion.[67] But several justices would have upheld the policy,
arguing that history showed that "our national culture allows public recognition
of our Nation's religious history and character."[68]

Arguments for constitutional easements are often accompanied by assurances that the practice in question is not an endorsement of religion as such, but
a mere "recognition" of our nation's undeniable religious heritage. At their worst
(or best, depending on your viewpoint), these arguments tend to treat such practices as a form of "ceremonial deism," under which particular state practices are
"protected from Establishment Clause scrutiny chiefly because they have lost
through rote repetition any significant religious content."[69] Preserving a government invocation of religion by asserting that the invocation has lost any religious
content has been aptly called a Pyrrhic victory, because it preserves the invocation only by denying the very religious meaning that both its supporters and
opponents see in it.[70] Supporters of constitutional easements see this as a virtue.[71] But the ceremonial deism argument for constitutional easements over the
Establishment Clause is best seen as having more to do with avoiding potentially
bruising controversies than with any genuine constitutional principle.

---

65. *See id.* at 879 n.25.

66. *See Elk Grove Unified Sch. Dist. v. Newdow*, 542 U.S. 1 (2004).

67. The Ninth Circuit decision striking down the practice, *Newdow v. U.S. Congress*,
328 F.3d 466 (9th Cir. 2003), received widespread condemnation. *See, e.g.*, William Trunk,
Note, *The Scourge of Contextualism: Ceremonial Deism and the Establishment Clause*, 49 B.C.
L. Rev. 571, 572 (2008).

68. *Newdow* 542 U.S. at 30 (Rehnquist, C.J., concurring in the judgment); *see also id.* at
37 (O'Connor, J., concurring on the judgment) (applying the endorsement test, but arguing that its application should be influenced by the "[h]istory and [u]biquity" of a particular
practice).

69. *Lynch*, 465 U.S. at 716 (Brennan, J., dissenting).

70. *See, e.g., id.* at 727 (Blackmun, J., dissenting). For scholarly criticism of ceremonial
deism, see, *e.g.*, B. Jessie Hill, *of Christmas Trees and Corpus Christi: Ceremonial Deism and
Change in Meaning Over Time*, 59 Duke L.J. 705 (2010); Steven B. Epstein, *Rethinking the
Constitutionality of Ceremonial Deism*, 96 Colum. L. Rev. 2083 (1996).

71. *See, e.g., Newdow*, 542 U.S. at 37–44 (O'Connor, J., concurring in the judgment).

RELIGIOUS TRUTH AND THE ESTABLISHMENT CLAUSE

What most, if not all, of this confusing array of Establishment Clause principles and tests has in common is the same thing we have seen in examining the Religion Clauses in general: an allergy to questions of religious truth.

This is not inevitable. One could believe that even if God wants us to profess a particular religious truth as *individuals,* the state itself should do nothing of the kind. That is especially true in pluralistic societies, in which one may favor non-establishment because not everyone is likely to agree on *which* truth-claim the government should endorse, making it more sensible for the state to avoid making religious truth-claims altogether.[72]

But it is the question of religious truth that gives the Establishment Clause its bite, that makes it so unpalatable to some religious believers, and that ties the leading Establishment Clause theories into knots. For religious individuals, religious truth demands public acknowledgment. For those individuals, to wipe religious expression from the public square is tantamount to a *denial* of religious truth. It unfairly deprives them of the opportunity to enlist the government's endorsement on issues they care about deeply—something that any other group is fully entitled to seek, as when the government actively champions the fight against smoking. To go further and argue that the government is forbidden from giving so much as "three pence" to any religious activity, that religious schools may not share in the nation's financial bounty while secular schools are free to do so, is taken as evidence that the government has actively chosen sides in favor of one view of religious truth. On this view, when it purports to remain "neutral" about religion, the government effectively denies that any such truth exists, or treats it as inconsequential.

That does not mean there are no arguments for non-establishment. From a religious point of view, the non-establishment rule can be viewed as *protective* of religion. It ensures that the affairs of the next world are not corrupted by the concerns of this one. By preventing government from supporting or endorsing religion or particular religious beliefs or practices, it guarantees that religious groups and individuals will not be subverted by the state.[73] From the secular perspective, non-establishment is necessary to ensure that the *state* is not corrupted by *religion*—that we do not see a resurgence of theocracy, with potentially divisive consequences.[74]

---

72. *See* Andrew Koppelman, *Is It Fair to Give Religion Special Treatment?*, 2006 U. Ill. L. Rev. 571, 591.

73. *See, e.g.,* Andrew Koppelman, *Corruption of Religion and the Establishment Clause,* 50 Wm. & Mary L. Rev. 1831 (2009).

74. *See, e.g.,* Steven G. Gey, *Vestiges of the Establishment Clause,* 5 First Amend. L. Rev. 1 (2006); Noah Feldman, *Divided By God: America's Church-State Problem—and What We Should Do About It* 8 (2005) (describing the traditional position of "legal secularists").

But these arguments tend either to be based on a partisan view of religious truth, or to attempt unsuccessfully to avoid the question of religious truth altogether. In the former case, one may hold a *religious* view that favors non-establishment. One may believe in non-establishment because of concerns that churches will be corrupted by their association with the state, because one believes that each person must be free to work out issues of conscience and belief for himself without the influence of the state, because one is afraid that the state will support the wrong religion, and so on. But all of these positions begin with truth-claims about religion. Conversely, from an atheist or secularist perspective, one may believe that non-establishment is the best rule for a secular democracy, or at least the best option short of a more rigorously atheist or secularist society. But this view, too, depends on religious truth-claims—in this case, the denial that there *is* a religious truth, or (for the secularist) that religious truth should influence what government does.

In the latter case, one may assiduously avoid drawing any conclusions about religious truth, and argue that non-establishment is the best way of avoiding having to draw those conclusions. But it is difficult to sustain this position in a thorough-going way without running up against questions of religious truth. If there *is* a religious truth, and that truth requires state support for religious belief, then it will be difficult to explain why non-establishment should act as a trump.[75] If there is a religious truth that *supports* non-establishment, and one relies on that truth in arguing for non-establishment, then the question has not been avoided. One might take the position that it is possible to support non-establishment in a spirit of indifference to whether or not there is a religious truth. But it will be difficult to maintain such a position without either addressing or denying the question of religious truth, explicitly or implicitly. As we saw in Part One, any attempt to justify such a position on the basis of purely neutral grounds, without addressing religious truth at all, will end up without a strong foundation. The person who attempts to justify such a stance on the basis of pluralism, or keeping the civil peace, or some other ground, will be hard pressed to support this position without smuggling in some substantive position about religious truth.

That does not mean that the agnostic strain in current Establishment Clause doctrine—the oft-stated position that "the government may not declare religious truth"[76]—is wrong. To the contrary, it provides an important starting point for justifying a good deal of the work that the Court has done in the Establishment Clause field. But in order for this argument to succeed, it must be properly

---

75. *See, e.g.,* Michael J. Sandel, *Political Liberalism,* 107 Harv. L. Rev. 1765, 1777 (1994).

76. Koppelman, *supra* note 23, at 89; *see also* Richard W. Garnett, *Assimilation, Toleration, and the State's Interest in the Development of Religious Doctrine,* 51 UCLA L. Rev. 1645, 1658 (2004) (calling this an "almost universally accepted rule" that "appear[s] over and again in a wide variety of the Court's Religion Clause decisions").

understood as a position *about* religious truth: one that squarely confronts it rather than attempting to avoid it.

That is, of course, the position of constitutional agnosticism. Constitutional agnosticism *begins* with the question of religious truth. It imagines, first and foremost, the possibility that there *is* a religious truth, a fact of the matter—whatever that fact might be. It is "agnostic about religion," but in "an interested and sympathetic" way.[77] It is emphatically not indifferent to the question of religious truth, and does not pretend otherwise.

But constitutional agnosticism, like the new agnosticism we examined in Chapter Three, is provisional and uncommitted on the question of religious truth. It imagines that there is a fact of the matter, but it does not presume to know what it is. Although it tries to envision all the possible answers to this question, it cannot or does not settle on a single answer. It remains in a state of suspension of ontological commitment. In this position, we may find the answers we seek to the puzzle of the Establishment Clause.

WHAT THE CONSTITUTIONALLY AGNOSTIC ESTABLISHMENT CLAUSE IS NOT

First, however, it is necessary to consider a competing account of what agnosticism might entail for the Establishment Clause. That account comes from Steven D. Smith, one of the most thoughtful modern theorists of law and religion. In an article titled *Our Agnostic Constitution*, Smith makes a number of interesting arguments about what the striking absence of God from the constitutional text might mean for the Religion Clauses, especially the Establishment Clause.[78]

---

77. Koppelman, *supra* note 73, at 1907.

78. Steven D. Smith, *Our Agnostic Constitution*, 83 N.Y.U. L. Rev. 120 (2008). Seth Barrett Tillman has argued that the Constitution is not quite as barren of references to God as the popular understanding suggests. He points to the use of the phrase "the Year of our Lord" in the Attestation Clause, U.S. Const., art. VII, cl. 2; the fact that the Oath and Affirmation Clause allows both *oaths* and affirmations, *see id.*, art. VI, cl. 3; the prohibition in the same article of religious tests for public office, *see id.*; and the Sundays Excepted Clause of article I of the Constitution, which excludes Sundays from the ten days allotted to the President to sign or veto a bill passed by Congress before it automatically becomes law, *see id.*, art. I, § 7, cl. 2. *See* Seth Barrett Tillman, *Blushing Our Way Past Historical Fact and Fiction: A Response to Professor Geoffrey R. Stone's Melville B. Nimmer Memorial Lecture and Essay*, 114 Penn. St. L. Rev. 391, 393–98 (2009); *see also id.* at 396 n.12 (citing articles making some of the same observations). Tillman is clear that he draws no strong conclusions from these textual references. *See id.* at 398. He is right to be cautious. Of these examples, the last three could all be read as accommodations to existing religious belief rather than as a statement of belief about religion stemming from the Constitution itself; and both the Oath and Affirmation Clause and the Religious Test Clause explicitly suggest

Smith argues that the Constitution's "discreet silence on the subject of God," which is all the more remarkable for having occurred in a relatively religious age, can best be treated as a form of agnosticism, rather than, as some would have it, a more stringent brand of godlessness.[79] The Constitution "does not affirm theism, but neither does it say anything that could be construed as an affirmation of atheism."[80] "On epistemological grounds, or perhaps for more pragmatic reasons," the Constitution takes the agnostic position that "the preferred course is to suspend judgment—to take no position one way or the other on the existence of God."[81]

Smith emphasizes the "layered" nature of agnosticism: the notion that "the agnostic's mental life is complex, operating on more than one level."[82] The agnostic can live as if God exists, or as if God does not exist; or, as with our empathetic brand of agnosticism, she can cycle imaginatively through a series of beliefs, all the while suspending any final judgment on those questions. But Smith takes an important step beyond the individual picture of agnosticism as layered belief, arguing that "a layering response may be as valuable for communities as it is for individuals."[83] He argues that "the Constitution seems almost ideally designed to facilitate such a strategy."[84]

How so? Smith's argument proceeds both negatively and positively. Negatively, he rejects the idea that the best response to the layered beliefs of communities is "simply to forgo public reliance on or expression of the controversial [religious] beliefs" that some members of a community might share, in favor of other, more widely shared interests—democracy, the rule of law, and so on—that could provide common ground for the community.[85] This approach is insufficient, both because those other values will be too thin or too unsettled to "support a secure and robust community,"[86] and because insisting that communities give up any

---

that one may honor the Constitution without having a particular belief or disbelief in God. As for the reference to "the Year of Our Lord" in the Attestation Clause, even if it is more than just a use of the "conventional dating method of the era," Smith, *supra* note 78, at 125 n.19, it is still rather a slender reed on which to hang any arguments about the godly nature of the Constitution. For our purposes, little turns on whether God is *completely* absent from the constitutional text, or only *mostly* absent.

79. Smith, supra note 78, at 128; *compare* Isaac Kramnick & R. Laurence Moore, *The Godless Constitution: A Moral Defense of the Secular State* (2005).

80. Smith, *supra* note 78, at 129.

81. *Id.* at 128–29.

82. *Id.* at 134.

83. *Id.* at 140.

84. *Id.* at 141.

85. *Id.* at 144.

86. *Id.; see also id.* at 149 ("tenets such as democracy, equality, and so forth are too few and too thin . . . to actually allow the community to act on the myriad concrete issues that confront it").

official acknowledgement of what the Founders called the "blessings of liberty"[87] might "affirmatively alienate them and forfeit their full loyalty."[88] Positively, he argues that "[t]he doubly layered nature of our political community suggests the possibility of a complex institutional response to the challenge of accommodating diverse beliefs."[89]

That response, for Smith, lies in the Constitution's creation of multiple levels of government—both vertically, as in the existence of national, state, and local political communities, and horizontally, because action at any one level of government may actually involve a variety of actions by different officials: legislative actions, executive actions, judicial rulings, and so on. This allows different communities, through different kinds of government action, to declare different religious beliefs. In this way, "a belief may be said both to be and not to be the belief 'of the community.'"[90]

According to Smith, the Constitution's agnosticism facilitates this approach. It "does not affirm theistic beliefs . . . but neither does it prescribe that governments must be atheistic or secular. By maintaining an agnostic posture, the Constitution does not require governments operating under its auspices to take any particular stance."[91] On this view, and in sharp contradiction to current Establishment Clause doctrine, state and local governments may express religious views. At the same time, the Constitution's overall agnosticism ensures that "expressions of belief by governments can never be regarded as ultimately constitutive of the political community."[92] "There is always something beyond those [local] governments and their affirmations that is more fundamentally constitutive of the community and that remains steadfastly agnostic: the Constitution" itself.[93] In addition, the broad guarantee of the freedom of speech will ensure "the freedom to dissent publicly from whatever beliefs the various levels of government may affirm."[94]

Thus, for Smith, the important thing to keep in mind is that "[i]t is the Constitution that is agnostic, . . . not politics or government."[95] This fact "permits governments, at different levels and in different ways, to sponsor the sorts of religious expression that American governments have traditionally engaged in,

---

87. U.S. Const., preamble.

88. Smith, *supra* note 78, at 146; *see also id.* at 147 ("'the very fact of enforced [religious] neutrality will oppress those who do not share that conception of the state's role'") (quoting Richard C. Schragger, *The Role of the Local in the Doctrine and Discourse of Religious Liberty*, 117 Harv. L. Rev. 1810, 1890 (2004)).

89. *Id.* at 152.

90. *Id.*

91. *Id.* at 157–58.

92. *Id.* at 158.

93. *Id.*

94. *Id.* at 159.

95. *Id.* at 164.

and that may well be important in securing the loyalty of citizens, while not making such affirmation constitutive of the political community."[96] This strategy is "all the more apt" given "the fact of pluralism," Smith writes.[97] It "allows for a more complex—but also more honest, responsible, and flexible—approach to the challenge of maintaining the unum in the pluribus of a diversely believing political community."[98]

Smith offers an important and provocative perspective on what the agnostic character of the Constitution might mean for the Establishment Clause. He successfully sweeps away arguments that the Constitution itself is a robustly secularist document, and he brings out the ways in which a rule of non-establishment can alienate the very individuals and communities whose loyalty we ought to treasure. But I draw different conclusions about what constitutional agnosticism requires for the Establishment Clause. Let us consider those differences.

First, Smith eloquently sets out a dilemma that his own approach cannot quite escape. As he notes, other common ties besides religion, such as "democracy, liberty, equality, or the rule of law," may be "too frail to support a secure and robust community."[99] Yet he argues in support of his layered position that "[t]here is always something beyond [individual] governments and their [religious] affirmations that is more fundamentally constitutive of the community and that remains steadfastly agnostic: the Constitution."[100] There is an obvious tension here. How can the agnostic Constitution be "fundamentally constitutive of the community" if it rests on a thin set of non-religious values that Smith asserts elsewhere cannot sustain a "secure and robust community?"

Smith might respond that his approach is still preferable as a second-best theory, given the agnostic nature of the constitutional text and the fact of religious pluralism.[101] But that conclusion depends on additional arguments that Smith does not make. He does not demonstrate that his layered approach to the Establishment Clause is better than its alternatives—that it maximizes public satisfaction and minimizes the exclusion of communities of citizens. To do so would be a tall order, of course, and perhaps Smith and I can be forgiven

---

96. *Id.*

97. *Id.* at 163.

98. *Id.* at 166.

99. *Id.* at 144, 145.

100. *Id.* at 158.

101. *See, e.g.,* Adrian Vermeule, *Foreword: System Effects and the Constitution,* 123 Harv. L. Rev. 4, 17–23 (2009) (discussing the relationship between constitutional theory and the theory of the second best); Lawrence B. Solum, *Constitutional Possibilities,* 83 Ind. L.J. 307, 311–12, 327–28 (2008) (same); Richard H. Fallon, Jr., *Foreword: Implementing the Constitution,* 111 Harv. L. Rev. 54, 117 (1997) ("[C]onstitutional law needs a theory of the second-best"). *See generally* Jon Elster, *Explaining Social Behavior* 439–42 (2007) (discussing the theory of the second best); R.G. Lipsey & R.K. Lancaster, *The General Theory of Second Best,* 24 Rev. Econ. Stud. 11 (1956).

for simply making competing assertions about the ideal approach to the Establishment Clause under an agnostic Constitution. Absent a stronger argument for why his approach would be the best one, however, his position cannot win by default.

And, as Smith demonstrates, *any* state of affairs is likely to cause dissatisfaction. Religious communities themselves might find Smith's "layered" approach insufficient, because they believe the *entire* political community must be able to acknowledge God without reservation. Atheists and agnostics, as well as members of minority faiths or those whose faith requires strict non-establishment, will be just as unhappy to find themselves living in communities whose majority insists upon the official recognition of some particular God, whether or not something "beyond" those communities remains agnostic on the question. Indeed, given the actual nature of religious pluralism in the United States, which is not uniformly distributed but rather lumpy, with some political communities distinguished by overwhelming religious homogeneity,[102] minority dissatisfaction is all but guaranteed.

In a kind of jiu-jitsu move, Smith tries to use the prospect of widespread dissatisfaction with his recommended approach as an argument in his favor. He makes a sort of Goldilocks argument: If the porridge is too hot for some and too cold for others, it must be just right. Those who don't like it can always exercise their right to dissent. That is too sanguine an argument. It is all very well to say that members of the minority within a particular community can dissent. But when that dissent comes with serious costs, like teachers ordering non-praying students to put on headphones to shut out the prayers said by the rest of the class, or parents receiving death threats from members of the majority,[103] we ought to be able to recognize the dangers of associating even a local government with a particular vision of religion. Indeed, it may be *especially* important that local governments, in small communities, avoid endorsing particular religious truths.

To be sure, the vast number of members of the majority community will not behave so crudely, and this kind of harassment should not be laid at the feet of religion itself. But in a nation teeming with overwhelmingly religiously homogeneous communities, we should not be blind to the possibility that these problems will be inevitable under the regime Smith advocates. Nor is it enough to argue that dissenters can always exit that community and move to another one. Voting with your feet can be expensive and difficult, and despite the strong interest that religious communities may have in government acknowledgment of their beliefs, it is not clear why the burden should be borne primarily by the

---

102. *See* Paul Horwitz, *Demographics and Distrust: The Eleventh Circuit on Graduation Prayer in* Adler v. Duval County, 63 U. Miami L. Rev. 835 (2009).

103. For examples, *see id.* at 887–88; *see also* Frank S. Ravitch, *School Prayer and Discrimination: The Civil Rights of Religious Minorities and Dissenters* (1999).

minority.[104] For this reason, we might turn Smith's argument on its head, and conclude that the agnostic Constitution is best served by having looser non-establishment rules at the *national* level, where the religious pluralism of our "extended republic"[105] will enhance the likelihood of compromise among contending religious and secular factions, and stricter non-establishment rules at the *local* level, which is more at risk of capture by particular groups and potentially violent spillover effects.[106] I am not arguing strongly for this approach, although in effect it may be the regime we already have.[107] But it may well make more sense than Smith's approach, which relaxes the constraining effect of the Establishment Clause precisely where those constraints ought to be strongest.

Moreover, Smith's approach demands too radical a shift from current jurisprudence. In essence, Smith is arguing for a revival of the approach to the Establishment Clause that existed before its incorporation against state and local governments through the Fourteenth Amendment, under which federal establishments of religion were forbidden but state establishments were permitted. We might say that the very fact that the states themselves have long had their own non-establishment clauses, often stricter than the federal version,[108] suggests that there is a strong consensus against the regime Smith recommends. That's an inadequate response, because states could always reverse course, amending their own constitutions to permit more official religious endorsements. Beyond that, however, the application of the Constitution's Establishment Clause to state and local governments is so well entrenched that it would render a wholesale revision like the one Smith contemplates too unlikely or too costly.

There is one last reason to reject Smith's approach, and it requires an important admission. There *are* costs to a rule of non-establishment, whether local or national, and those costs increase the more broadly we read the strictures of the Establishment Clause. *Some* religious communities may feel offended or excluded by a rule that says we cannot proclaim, say, the "Christian State of

---

104. *See* Horwitz, *supra* note 102, at 890–91; Douglas Laycock, *Voting With Your Feet is No Substitute for Constitutional Rights*, 32 Harv. J.L. & Pub. Pol'y 29 (2009); Richard A. Epstein, *Exit Rights Under Federalism*, 55 L. & Contemp. Probs., Winter 1992, at 147, 150 ("[T]he institution of federalism, without the rigorous enforcement of substantive individual rights, will not be equal to the formidable task before it.").

105. *See The Federalist No. 10* (James Madison (Jacob E. Cooke ed., 1961).

106. *See* Horwitz, *supra* note 102, at 881–92 (arguing that the modern Establishment Clause might be better read in a "counter-jurisdictional" fashion than in the jurisdictional fashion that Smith and others have championed).

107. *See id.* at 889 n.341; *see also* William P. Marshall, *The Limits of Secularism: Public Religious Expression in Moments of National Crisis and Tragedy*, 78 Notre Dame L. Rev. 11 (2002).

108. *See, e.g.,* Linda S. Wendtland, Note, *Beyond the Establishment Clause: Enforcing Separation of Church and State Through State Constitutional Provisions*, 71 Va. L. Rev. 625, 631–34 (1985).

New Jersey." Many people who would accept such a rule will be offended if we go a step further and say that New Jersey cannot even permit non-sectarian prayer at school graduations. Religious individuals and groups want to feel fully a part of their political community, and may feel that this requires an official acknowledgment of their beliefs. To exclude the possibility of these kinds of public acknowledgments can be destructive of the very sense of belonging to a political community that we ought to value. "The civic community, emptied of what many members believe to be significant moral content, [may come] to be seen as an irrelevant entity."[109]

It's not enough to respond to this complaint with secularist nostrums about civil strife or public reason. After all, the religious individual might respond, you cannot *ease* civil strife just by telling one side, "You lose; go away."[110] "If it is alienating to have one's views rejected by government," Smith rightly observes, "It is surely even more galling to have those views rejected by an ostensibly inclusive and neutral regime with the explanation that one's views do not satisfy even the minimal requirement of reasonableness."[111] Supporters of secularism or separationism wax rhapsodic about the psychic harms wreaked upon the minority by public religious observance, even when that observance amounts to nothing more than the obligation to stand silently for a short and milquetoast invocation of a non-specific God. But they dismiss with a wave of the hand the alienating effects of telling the religious majority that it can have *nothing*. That won't do. We should be honest about the costs of non-establishment, even if we conclude that they are outweighed by its benefits.

That having been said, we should not be too quick to conclude that a strong sense of community, or of inclusion in the political community, will collapse without *official* invocations of God, particularly the non-sectarian, non-specific kinds of invocations that comprise the politically acceptable lowest common denominator in this area. For one thing, as Smith acknowledges (somewhat inconsistently), it is at least possible that civic but secular values, such as equality, liberty, and love of country, can still sustain a community while embracing both religious and non-religious individuals. For another, it is not obvious that we ought to expect *more* than this from political community. Perhaps, in the face of ideological and religious pluralism, all we can reasonably hope for from our political community is a relatively "thin" set of values and interests.[112]

---

109. Schragger, *supra* note 88, at 1891.

110. *See generally* Richard W. Garnett, *Religion, Division, and the Constitution*, 94 Geo. L.J. 1666 (2006).

111. Smith, *supra* note 78, at 150.

112. *See, e.g.,* Glen O. Robinson, *Communities*, 83 Va. L. Rev. 269, 345, 346 (1997) (arguing that while "one should not expect too much of minimalist morality or minimalist sociability," "there is nothing shallow about the idea of a minimalist conception of morality, justice, or social solidarity. The minimal bases on which persons in different cultures,

Finally, there is an important and easily elided distinction between a political community as such, and the official expressions of that community. Just as we can be too quick to assume that the "public sphere" necessarily requires expressions by official organs of government, so we can jump too readily from the idea that political community is important to the idea that it must be embodied in official statements by government. Even if our political communities, local and national, are constrained by a rule of non-establishment, it is still possible for all kinds of genuinely *public* actions, individual and communal but not official, to form the basis of a vigorous, stable, and inclusive civic sphere. A community that cannot enlist government in its efforts to worship can still worship, not only privately but publicly; a community that cannot vote for the state to endorse a particular religious truth can still make a full-throated argument for that religious truth, not just at home but on the street. To say that the state cannot endorse or commit to a particular community consensus on religious matters is not the same thing as saying that no consensus exists, or that the members of the community cannot give voice to that consensus. Just as Smith argues that dissenters are free to raise their voices, so the majority is free to speak as well. We need not give up on the idea of community, including a genuinely religious community, just because we conclude that government itself is barred from entering the lists in favor of one version of religious truth or another.

In short, although I find much to agree and sympathize with in Smith's account of agnosticism and the agnostic Constitution, I am not convinced that his is the only version of what it entails, or the best. In the pages that follow, I return to my own brand of constitutional agnosticism and what it counsels for our interpretation of the Establishment Clause.

CONSTITUTIONAL AGNOSTICISM AND THE ESTABLISHMENT CLAUSE

Recall that the basic approach of constitutional agnosticism is to begin with the unavoidable questions of religious truth rather than trying fruitlessly to evade them. That means proceeding from a perspective that imagines that there is a truth of the matter, that there is such a thing as religious truth, positive or negative; and it means attempting to inhabit as fully as possible the perspective of a wide range of worldviews concerning religious truth, while remaining in a state of suspension of ontological commitment with respect to all of them. In the case of the Free Exercise Clause, that approach led us to adopt a broadly permissive regime, one that strains to permit the widest range of religious practices and to

---

different communities, or different societies are likely to find common ground are likely to reflect deeply human values.").

avoid weighing state interests too heavily, without abandoning altogether our concern for state interests.[113]

The implications of constitutional agnosticism are different with respect to the Establishment Clause. Here, the suspension of ontological commitments is the most important piece of the puzzle. Where the Free Exercise Clause is concerned, the suspension of any final answer to the question of religious truth, combined with the very possibility of religious truth, leads to a reluctance to allow secular state interests to burden religious practices that may indeed be compelled as a matter of fact. Our unwillingness as constitutionally agnostic decision makers to weigh in definitively on one side of a religious truth-claim or the other, combined with our acknowledgment of the possibility that a religious claim *could* be true, ultimately pushes us in the direction of robust religious liberty. Where the Establishment Clause is concerned, the same calculus leads us in the direction of a disabled state. It leads to a state that is forbidden from taking actions or making statements that amount to official conclusions about religious truth.

Consider school prayer. Constitutional agnostics believe individuals and groups should generally be able to pray as they wish. But the situation is different when government itself leads the prayer. There, the problem is not so much that the state may influence or "coerce" the decisions of individuals about whether or not to pray, to whom, and how[114]—although that *is* a problem. The problem is that the state is taking a position *at all*.

From the constitutional agnostic's perspective, the state must embody, as best as it can, the suspension of ontological commitments. It cannot do so if its voice is lent to one side of the debate or another. If the state's voice is used to lead a robustly sectarian prayer, it can reasonably be viewed as having said something about the *truth* of that prayer. Even if the prayer is mild—if it follows President Eisenhower's dictum that "[o]ur form of government makes no sense unless it is founded on a deeply felt religious faith[,] and I don't care what it is"[115]—the state has still said *something* important about religious truth. If nothing else, it has placed its imprimatur on the notion that there *is* a God, albeit a watered-down God. In the unlikely event that the state makes a strongly *secular* statement— suppose it opens a graduation ceremony by announcing, "We will now hear from some typical godless college professor, who will lead us in thanking the

---

113. *See* Chapter Six.

114. In that sense, the constitutional agnostic's approach may be contrasted with that of the Supreme Court in *Lee v. Weisman*, 505 U.S. 577 (1992), which struck down a clergy-led non-sectarian prayer policy involving public school graduations—not because the statement itself was impermissible as such, but because it impermissibly influenced and coerced religious choices made by individual audience members, especially children.

115. Gary Scott Smith, *Faith and the Presidency: From George Washington to George W. Bush* 254 (2006).

random, meaningless play of statistics that led to our being here for this occasion"—the conclusion is the same; again, the state will have weighed in improperly on one side of the controversy.

In all of these matters, the state's position should be that of Ludwig Wittgenstein: "Whereof one cannot speak, thereof one must be silent."[116] Individual speakers, such as a high school valedictorian selected because of her grades, not her views, should be free to offer religious or anti-religious views.[117] But the government itself, or its officials, should say nothing about such questions.

The result is different if we move from questions of government-led or government-endorsed religious speech or symbolism to questions of government funding for religious groups. Here, again, the state should not take sides on questions of religious truth; it should remain agnostic on those questions. But that leads it away from a position of absolute disability and toward a position of simple equality of treatment. If the state opens its coffers to secular organizations but refuses to do so for religious organizations, and vice versa, it takes sides, or appears to take sides, on underlying questions of religious truth. The best approach for the constitutionally agnostic state is not to do something or nothing, but to do the *same* thing, regardless of whose hand is outstretched. The guiding metaphor here should not be that of a wall of separation, which forbids even "three pence" from passing between government and religion, but that of Lady Justice, with her scales balanced and her eyes blindfolded.

I said at the beginning of this chapter that I would be more preservative than destructive. So it should come as no surprise that much of the Supreme Court's Establishment Clause jurisprudence in the past two or three decades has followed something like this path. A decade ago, Ira Lupu observed an "emerging trend" on the Court "away from government concerns over transfers of wealth to religious institutions, and toward interdiction of religiously partisan government speech."[118] Lupu was prescient. What he said then still rings true: "[W]ith religious pluralism and doctrines of equality at the center of the American ethos, and with the government more and more in the business of administering to persons in ways formerly undertaken by religious communities, nonestablishment concerns have shifted considerably."[119] Government subsidy of religion was once at the heart of Establishment Clause controversy, with religious symbolism cases mostly limited to cases involving outright coercion. Now, the balance

---

116. Ludwig Wittgenstein, *Tractatus Logico-Philosophicus* § 7, at 189 (C.K. Ogden ed. & trans., 1922).

117. *See, e.g., Doe v. Madison Sch. Dist. No. 321*, 147 F.3d 832, 835 (9th Cir. 1998); Horwitz, *supra* note 102, at 874–77.

118. Ira C. Lupu, *Government Messages and Government Money: Santa Fe, Mitchell v. Helms, and the Arc of the Establishment Clause*, 42 Wm. & Mary L. Rev. 771, 771 (2001).

119. *Id.* at 816.

has shifted. Evenhanded funding is acceptable to a wider range of people, and "classical separationist" objections to this kind of funding have lost much of their appeal.[120] By contrast, the Court has taken a more stringent line on cases involving government messages endorsing religion, treating more and more of these messages as beyond the pale.[121]

The distinction between Establishment Clause cases involving funding and those involving symbolism has been widely recognized. Various attempts have been made to reconcile and justify the seemingly divergent approaches taken by the Court in these two areas. Lupu, for instance, links the divergence to a broad current of "social and political changes" between the founding era and our own.[122] Douglas Laycock, whose substantive neutrality theory of religious liberty we examined in Chapter Two, argues that "[t]he speech and funding cases are . . . united by a principled commitment to government neutrality and individual choice in religious matters."[123] Conversely, others have argued, in the spirit of the movie *Ghostbusters*, that we should "cross the streams," allowing government-sponsored religious speech while rebuilding a high wall of separation with respect to government funding of religious activity.[124] (Crossing the streams, cinema fans might recall, is generally not recommended, because "[i]t would be bad."[125])

---

120. *Id.* at 774.

121. *See also* Laycock, *supra* note 35, at 157 (noting the increasing divergence on the Court between religious "speech cases" and religious "funding cases"); John C. Jeffries, Jr., & James E. Ryan, *A Political History of the Establishment Clause*, 100 Mich. L. Rev. 279, 366–68 (2001) (same). Jessie Hill has identified this trend with a broader current of "expressivist" jurisprudence, which focuses on the message sent by particular laws and takes the position that "government-sponsored religious messages are more constitutionally problematic than [evenhanded] material aid to religious entities." Hill, *supra* note 52, at 510 (citing David Cole, *Faith and Funding: Toward an Expressivist Model of the Establishment Clause*, 75 S. Cal. L. Rev. 559, 585–86 (2002)).

122. Lupu, *supra* note 118, at 775.

123. Laycock, *supra* note 35, at 158.

124. *See* Feldman, *supra* note 74, at 9.

125. *Ghostbusters* (Columbia Pictures 1984). To be more specific, "Try to imagine all life as you know it stopping spontaneously and every molecule in your body exploding at the speed of light." *Id.* Feldman's proposal is unlikely to be adopted by the Supreme Court any time soon, so we may never learn whether it would achieve equally apocalyptic results in practice. *See, e.g.,* Lupu, *supra* note 118, at 775 (arguing, also with a certain Ghostbusteresque touch, that the trajectories of the symbolism and funding cases under the Establishment Clause are "unlikely to recross in the foreseeable future"). My own view is that things would not be quite *that* bad—but not by much. For a more thoughtful critique, *see, e.g.,* Perry Dane, *Separation Anxiety*, 22 J. L. & Religion 545, 559 (2006–2007) (arguing that "even if the courts adopted something like Feldman's proposal, one might expect both sides in the current debate over religion and state both to continue to fight for

Constitutional agnosticism offers a stronger and more stable justification for this trend. The Court's heightened concern for government-sponsored religious *messages*, and its diminished concern for evenhandedly distributed *funding* for religion, are both correct as a matter of Establishment Clause doctrine. And both, rather than being fueled by a desire to avoid the question of religious truth altogether, can be viewed as reflecting a proper, and properly agnostic, attempt to address the questions of religious truth that arise in a pluralistic society. Constitutional agnosticism suggests that developments in the Court's Establishment Clause jurisprudence in the past few decades have moved in the right direction. It also reveals more starkly the areas—especially what I have called constitutional easements over the Establishment Clause—in which the Court's understandable but regrettable refusal to follow these principles leaves it floundering. Let us take up each of these areas in turn.

Money

For much of the Establishment Clause's history, money has been at the root of the hottest church–state controversies in the United States. It was, among other things, the subject of the most famous early church–state dispute, one that both predated and prefigured the Establishment Clause itself: the proposed Virginia "Bill Establishing a Provision for Teachers of the Christian Religion,"[126] which occasioned Madison's powerful and influential *Memorial and Remonstrance.*[127] Religious sentiment and language was pervasive in eighteenth-century America.[128] That rendered controversies over religious speech by government practically "unimaginable."[129] But "[w]hat the Virginians and others did fight about, and what became the primary focus in our legacy of nonestablishment, was . . . government money."[130] In particular, in an era that was beginning to define itself in contrast to the mother country's establishment of the Church of England, the idea that taxes could be levied from the people to support a preferred sect provoked fierce resistance and debate.[131]

Money remained at the heart of political struggles over church–state relations through the nineteenth century, and formed the focus of the Court's Establishment Clause rulings once the incorporation of that provision against state and local government expanded the field of conflict. The strict rulings of that era drew in

---

larger victories and, at the same time, to further nurture their identity as persecuted, aggrieved, minorities").

126. The language of the bill is set out in *Everson*, 330 U.S. at 72–74.

127. *See* Chapter One.

128. *See, e.g.*, Steven D. Smith, *The Rise and Fall of Religious Freedom in Constitutional Discourse*, 140 U. Pa. L. Rev. 149, 153–66 (1991).

129. Lupu, *supra* note 118, at 777.

130. *Id.*

131. *See id.* at 778.

part on a "broad coalition of separationist opinion" that was part and parcel of an attitude of "pervasive secularism that came to dominate American public life, especially among educated elites."[132] But they also drew on a distinct "hostility to Roman Catholics," whose schools were generally the ones at issue, "and the challenge they posed to the Protestant hegemony, which prevailed throughout the nineteenth and early twentieth centuries."[133] That anti-Catholic spirit influenced some of the most separationist justices on the Supreme Court during that era, including Hugo Black and William O. Douglas.[134]

The cultural, political, and jurisprudential landscape has changed since then. Culturally, we are no longer in an era of consensus about secularism, or the liberal values that undergird it.[135] We are instead living in what has been variously called a secular (but not secularist),[136] post-secular,[137] or agnostic age. Thus, simply invoking secularism as a justification for a strict rule of separation is less convincing than it may have been a half century ago. Politically, the old coalitions have shifted. Religious groups, including evangelical Protestants and Catholics, have made common cause.[138] With the growth of interest in private religious education among some Protestant groups, "fundamentalists and evangelicals

132. Jeffries & Ryan, *supra* note 121, at 281; *see also* Michael J. Klarman, *Rethinking the Civil Rights and Civil Liberties Revolutions*, 82 Va. L. Rev. 1, 15, 46–62 (1996) (discussing "the dramatic disestablishment of Protestantism as America's unofficial religion in the middle decades of the twentieth century").

133. Jeffries & Ryan, *supra* note 121, at 282; *see generally* Philip Hamburger, *Separation of Church and State* (2002).

134. *See, e.g., Lemon v. Kurtzman*, 403 U.S. 602, 635 n.20 (1971) (Douglas, J., concurring) (quoting with approval an anti-Catholic tract describing Catholic education as shot through with "propaganda"); *Board of Educ. v. Allen*, 392 U.S. 236, 241 (1968) (Black, J., dissenting) (using the same word to describe Catholic schools); *see also* John T. McGreevy, *Catholics and American Freedom: A History* 184–85, 264 (2003); Kyle Duncan, *Secularism's Laws: State Blaine Amendments and Religious Persecution*, 72 Fordham L. Rev. 493 (2003); Lucas A. Powe, Jr., *The Warren Court and American Politics* 365–69 (2000); Thomas C. Berg, *Anti-Catholicism and Modern Church-State Relations*, 33 Loy. U. Chi. L.J. 121 (2001).

135. *See* Chapter Three.

136. *See* Charles Taylor, *A Secular Age* (2007). I discuss Taylor's views at length in Chapter Three.

137. *See, e.g.,* Jürgen Habermas et al., *An Awareness of What is Missing: Faith and Reason in a Post-secular Age* (2010); Adam B. Seligman, *Living Together Differently*, 30 Cardozo L. Rev. 2881 (2009); Jürgen Habermas, *Between Naturalism and Religion: Philosophical Essays* (2008); *Political Theologies: Public Religions in a Post-Secular World* (Hent de Vries ed., 2006). For a discussion of the differences between Taylor's "secular age" and the "post-secular age," see Michael Warner, Jonathan VanAntwerpen, and Craig Calhoun, *Editors' Introduction, in Varieties of Secularism in a Secular Age* 1, 21–22 (Michael Warner, Jonathan VanAntwerpen, and Craig Calhoun, eds., 2010).

138. *See, e.g.,* Feldman, *supra* note 74, at 7–8 (lumping these and other groups together under the umbrella of "values evangelicals").

have moved from the most uncompromising opponents of aid to parochial schools to its most unlikely allies."[139] Jurisprudentially, whether independently or as a result of these broader trends, the Court's emphasis has shifted from one of separationism to a wider emphasis on equality as an underlying constitutional value, in the Establishment Clause and elsewhere.

All of these factors have contributed to the "collapse[ ]" of "[f]ederal constitutional restrictions on funding religion."[140] For roughly the last quarter-century, the Court has "progressively elevated the nondiscrimination principle" in religious funding cases, and "subordinated the no-aid principle."[141] This is evident in the Court's admission, in *Agostini v. Felton*, that it had "departed from the rule relied on in [earlier cases] that all government aid that directly assists the educational function of religious schools is invalid," and its shift in focus from the question of *who* can receive government aid to the question *how* that aid is distributed.[142] Provided that aid is "made available generally," regardless of who receives it, and provided that "any decision to avail oneself of government funding constitutes a genuinely independent and private [individual] choice[ ]," the Court said, there will be no Establishment Clause violation.[143]

The shift is even more apparent in the Court's decisions in *Mitchell v. Helms* and *Zelman v. Simmons-Harris*. *Mitchell* overruled *two* prior precedents of the Court in upholding the distribution of government aid for the loan of educational materials to schools in low-income areas, regardless of whether the schools were sectarian or secular.[144] Although he failed to capture a simple majority, Justice Thomas's plurality opinion for the Court would have gone even further. As Justice O'Connor, who concurred in the judgment but refused to sign on to Justice Thomas's opinion, suggested, Thomas proposed "a rule of unprecedented breadth for the evaluation of Establishment Clause challenges to government school aid programs," one that would place no limits on government aid to religious schools, even if that aid was diverted to religious uses, "so long as the aid is offered on a neutral basis and the aid is secular in content."[145] In *Zelman*, the Court approved the use of school vouchers, even if they overwhelmingly favor religious rather than secular schools in a particular jurisdiction, provided that decisions about how to use the voucher are the product of "true private choice."[146]

---

139. Jeffries & Ryan, *supra* note 121, at 282.

140. Laycock, *supra* note 35, at 156.

141. *Id.* at 166.

142. *Agostini*, 521 U.S. at 225.

143. *Id.* at 225–26 (quotations and citations omitted). *See also Witters v. Washington Dept. of Servs. For Blind*, 474 U.S. 481 (1986); *Zobrest v. Catalina Foothills Sch. Dist.*, 509 U.S. 1 (1993); *Rosenberger v. Rector*, 515 U.S. 819 (1995).

144. *Mitchell*, 530 U.S. at 835 (overruling *Meek v. Pittenger*, 421 U.S. 349 (1975), and *Wolman v. Walter*, 433 U.S. 229 (1977)).

145. *Id.* at 837 (O'Connor, J., concurring in the judgment).

146. *Zelman v. Simmons-Harris*, 536 U.S. 639, 649 (2002).

"[T]he amount of government aid channeled to religious institutions," the Court said, is simply "not relevant to the constitutional inquiry."[147] As Justice O'Connor had said in *Mitchell*, the Court's approach verged on assigning the value of neutrality, or equality, "singular importance in the future adjudication of Establishment Clause challenges to government school aid programs."[148] The dissenters (one of whom, Justice David Souter, has since been replaced by Justice Samuel Alito, who hardly shares his views) were left sputtering that Madison's objection to so much as "three pence" being spent on government support of religion had "simply been lost in the majority's formalism."[149]

For constitutional agnostics, this shift from a regime of separationism in funding cases to one of even-handedness and neutrality is largely justified. As we saw in Chapter Two, it is not justified because neutrality or equality are such pellucid and self-evidently correct terms that they need no explanation. To the contrary, they settle nothing. They have little or no independent or self-evident content. They depend on a baseline for what constitutes neutrality or equality that is itself highly contestable. The dissenters in these cases are right to see in these blunt invocations of equality or neutrality the specter of empty "verbal formalism."[150]

Rather, the Court's shift is justified because, whether it knows it or not, it is moving toward a sound approach to religious truth in a pluralistic age. As long as government wants to survive amidst the diversity of religious beliefs, including beliefs about the nonexistence of God, that characterize modern society, its best approach toward religion is one of sympathetic agnosticism—one that acknowledges the possibility of religious truth but remains suspended on the answer to religious questions. Its role with respect to religious truth-claims should be one of respect toward all and allegiance to none.

A separationist might respond that this is precisely the position that separationism offers. And on some versions of separationism, this might be true.[151] If separation is understood in a stricter and quite common sense, however, it is not genuinely agnostic. The usual brand of separationism, which sees the Establishment Clause as decisively enlisting the state in the cause of secularism,[152] privileges "secular supremacy and religious subordination."[153] It says that a

---

147. *Id.* at 651.

148. *Mitchell*, 530 U.S. at 837 (O'Connor, J., concurring in the judgment).

149. *Zelman*, 536 U.S. at 711 (Souter, J., dissenting).

150. *Id.* at 689 (Souter, J., dissenting).

151. *See, e.g.,* Douglas Laycock, *The Underlying Unity of Separation and Neutrality*, 46 Emory L.J. 43 (1997).

152. *See, e.g.,* Suzanna Sherry, *Enlightening the Religion Clauses*, 7 J. Contemp. Legal Issues 473 (1996); Kathleen M. Sullivan, *Religion and Liberal Democracy*, 59 U. Chi. L. Rev. 195 (1992).

153. Laycock, *supra* note 151, at 47.

government-funded school computer, or government funding for an alcoholism rehabilitation program, is entirely acceptable if it is used by secular recipients, but wholly unacceptable when its recipient is religious. There is nothing agnostic, or neutral, about such a position.

That is not to say we need have no concerns about where government funds end up. We might, for instance, worry about the corrupting effects on religion of a government handout, or about whether the aid represents a stealthy effort to advance a particular view of religious truth. But the former question, at least, cannot be resolved without drawing the very conclusions about religious truth that a constitutionally agnostic decision maker should be striving to avoid. How can a judge say whether religion has been "corrupted" by government aid without making a statement about what "uncorrupted" religion looks like?[154] Even the latter question may be problematic, if it leads to the conclusion that it is acceptable for government to advance only secular projects but not similarly situated religious ones, a position that again seems to take sides in the kinds of conflicts government ought to avoid.

The preferable approach is for government to aid all or none. It should open or shut the public purse to all comers, making no judgments about any of them beyond whether they serve the interest of the government-funded program in question. This ensures that government is not enlisted in the service of a particular religious truth, and leaves the question of religious corruption where it belongs—with the religious group itself. That does not mean religion may not enjoy an outsized benefit in particular cases. It seems fairly clear, for example, that the school voucher program upheld by the Court in *Zelman* gave a great advantage to private religious schools, which were more numerous than private secular schools in the area served by the voucher program. But it does mean that the state's decision to offer financial aid will not turn on the patently non-evenhanded question of whether some recipient is religious or not.

The proper approach for a constitutional agnostic in funding cases, therefore, is to disclaim any interest in who receives government aid, and focus instead on whether money is distributed in an evenhanded fashion. It should recognize that legitimate government interests can be served by a variety of groups and approaches, including religious ones, in a diverse and pluralistic society. Not every government interest will be legitimate, to be sure. A government program that distributes money for the worship of the God of one's choice, for instance, constitutes the kind of one-sided position on questions of religious truth that the government should not take. But if the question is how to improve educational outcomes, or how to ensure the rehabilitation of addicts, a constitutionally

---

154. *See, e.g.,* Koppelman, *supra* note 73, at 1932–33; Kevin Pybas, *Does the Establishment Clause Require Religion to be Confined to the Private Sphere?*, 40 Val. U. L. Rev. 71, 101–02 (2005).

agnostic decision maker should be free to provide equal access to a variety of religious and secular groups in attempting to achieve this goal.

This approach raises several subsidiary questions. First, should there be any distinction between government *subsidies* and government *tax exemptions?*[155] Here, despite some uncertainties of application, the Court seems to have hit on the right rule. As long as government is not tailoring a tax exemption in order to favor particular religious truth-claims, it should offer tax exemptions to religious groups on the same basis that it does to secular groups.[156] It may not gerryman-der the exemption in a way that suggests that one religious group is preferable to another,[157] or use the tax exemption to favor religious groups over secular groups (or vice versa).[158] It may even choose to grant such exemptions to no one at all, religious or secular.[159] The rule here should be one of evenhandedness. Provided that rule is met, religious groups should be no more or less entitled to the benefits of tax exemptions than any other group.

Second, one might ask whether government may, consistently with the Religion Clauses, subject religion to additional disabilities with respect to gov-ernment subsidies. The constitutional agnostic's position is that religions cannot be treated differently on this basis. In its 2004 decision in *Locke v. Davey*,[160] how-ever, the Court held otherwise. The state of Washington provided Promise Scholarships to students who attended college in the state, but barred students from using their scholarships to pursue a "degree in theology," defined as a degree that is "devotional in nature or designed to induce religious faith."[161] The state argued that this restriction was necessary because of a provision of the state constitution that blocked any public funds from being used for "any religious worship, exercise or instruction, or the support of any religious establishment."[162] Davey, a student who wished to use scholarship money for a theology degree, sued, alleging a violation of his free exercise rights.

---

155. *See, e.g.,* 2 Greenawalt, *supra* note 10, ch. 15.

156. *See, e.g., Walz v. Tax Comm'n of City of New York,* 397 U.S. 664, 672–73 (1970); *see id.* at 689 (Brennan, J., concurring) ("Government may properly include religious organi-zations among the variety of private, nonprofit groups that receive tax exemptions, for each group contributes to the diversity of association, viewpoint, and enterprise essential to a vigorous, pluralistic society.").

157. *See, e.g., Minneapolis Star & Tribune Co. v. Minnesota Commissioner of Revenue,* 460 U.S. 575 (1983).

158. *See, e.g., Texas Monthly, Inc. v. Bullock,* 489 U.S. 1 (1989).

159. *See, e.g., Jimmy Swaggart Ministries v. Bd. of Equalization,* 493 U.S. 378 (1990).

160. 540 U.S. 712 (2004).

161. *Id.* at 716.

162. Wash. Const., Art. I, § 11. This provision was akin to, although the Court distin-guished it from, the so-called Blaine Amendments in the state constitutions, relics of an anti-Catholic movement in the nineteenth century that sought to prevent Catholics from receiving any aid for parochial schools.

In a fairly unhelpful opinion, Chief Justice William Rehnquist concluded that the restriction was an acceptable part of the "play in the joints" between the Establishment Clause and the Free Exercise Clause.[163] The state *could* have chosen to fund theology training along with other scholarly pursuits, but was not *obliged* to do so. The case turned largely on the nature of theology studies as the Court narrowly defined it, calling it "an essentially religious endeavor" involving training for the ministry, one that could be treated as distinct from "training for secular professions" such as law or medicine.[164]

From the constitutional agnostic's point of view, the Court reached the wrong result in *Locke v. Davey*. Its decision leaves states that fund private education free to "fund religious and secular education alike, to fund secular education only, or to fund some forms of religious education and not other forms."[165] This is "the worst of all worlds."[166] It is one thing to say that the "play in the joints" left by the Religion Clauses allows government to fund everyone or no one; it is quite another to say that government is free to single out secular programs, or a limited set of secular and religious programs, for state subsidy, but is not obliged to fund both of them on equal terms once it decides to fund either one. *Locke* is a relatively narrow decision, which relies heavily on the devotional character of the educational program in question. But that very distinction leaves legislatures and courts in the untenable position of having to say what is merely the study *of* religion, and what is genuinely "devotional" study. That is not the kind of determination a decision maker can reach without running into questions of religious truth.

The final question is whether government can attach strings to religious recipients of state funds: whether it can condition their receipt of aid on their compliance with particular requirements. Typical examples include the distribution of government aid to religious groups on the condition that they refrain from proselytizing, or that they refrain from discriminating on the basis of religion when hiring employees to staff these programs.[167] Many of these questions have arisen in the course of debates over so-called Charitable Choice programs—programs that allow government funds for charitable groups to flow to religious

---

163. *Locke*, 540 U.S. at 718 (quotation and citation omitted).
164. *Id.* at 721.
165. Laycock, *supra* note 35, at 196.
166. *Id.*
167. *See, e.g.,* 2 Greenawalt, *supra* note 10, ch. 18; David Saperstein, *Public Accountability and Faith-Based Organizations: A Problem Best Avoided*, 116 Harv. L. Rev. 1353 (2003); Kathleen M. Sullivan, *The New Religion and the Constitution*, 116 Harv. L. Rev. 1397 (2003); Ira C. Lupu & Robert Tuttle, *Sites of Redemption: A Wide Angle Look at Government Vouchers and Sectarian Service Providers*, 18 J. L. & Pol. 537 (2002); Carl N. Esbeck, *A Constitutional Case for Governmental Cooperation with Faith-Based Social Service Providers*, 46 Emory L.J. 1 (1997); Stephen W. Monsma, *When Sacred and Secular Mix: Religious Nonprofit Organizations and Public Money* (1996).

organizations. These programs have sparked disputes over whether government aid can be tied to restrictions on discrimination by the recipients of that aid.[168] Similar questions have arisen with respect to government policies that deny tax-exempt status to religious educational institutions, like Bob Jones University, that desire for religious reasons to engage in discriminatory behavior, such as forbidding interracial dating.[169] (The university has long since abandoned this rule.)

These cases raise complex questions, and I cannot give a full account of them here. Suffice it to say that the constitutional agnostic must attempt to honor the principle of evenhanded distribution of aid while seeking to avoid making judgments about the accuracy of some religious organizations' assertions that their religions require them to discriminate. On this view, government may attach strings to its programs that are aimed at the efficacy of the program and closely tied to the government purpose behind aiding such programs. The closer the conditions are to the achievement of a legitimate government interest, the sounder the restrictions will be, so long as they are applied on an evenhanded basis. The more attenuated those restrictions are, however, the more problematic they will be.

Much also turns on what "discrimination" means in this context. Suppose that two groups receive government money to administer a drug rehabilitation program. One believes that its staffers should all share the belief that the best path to rehabilitation is through strict abstinence from drug use, and refuses to hire employees who advocate prescribing methadone. Another believes that prayer and confession are the best route to sobriety, and insists that its employees agree. So long as aid recipients are free to choose between these programs, the fact that the religious program involves a form of "discrimination" to achieve the legitimate end of effective drug rehabilitation should not preclude the availability of aid to that program. Government's main decision should be whether to fund this general category of programs at all, or whether to simply do the job itself. In order to avoid making determinations that touch on religious truth, and out of respect for the possibility that a variety of religious and non-religious programs may help it achieve its legitimate goals, it should minimize any downstream conditions.

In sum, the constitutional agnostic's approach to government funding of religion is permissive in some respects and restrictive in others, but it is not separationist. It does not insist on the erection of a high and impregnable wall between government and religion where money is concerned, not least because that wall

---

168. *See, e.g.,* Ira C. Lupu & Robert W. Tuttle, *The Faith-Based Initiative and the Constitution,* 55 DePaul L. Rev. 1 (2005); Michelle E. Gilman, *"Charitable Choice" and the Accountability Challenge: Reconciling the Need for Regulation with the First Amendment Religion Clauses,* 55 Vand. L. Rev. 799 (2002).

169. *See Bob Jones Univ. v. United States,* 461 U.S. 574 (1983).

has never been as high or as level as its advocates insisted. Instead, its approach allows and probably obliges government to fund religious groups on an equal basis with secular groups, whether the aid comes in the form of subsidies or tax exemptions. But the end being sought here is not accommodation as such; it does not believe that religious organizations ought to be the *special* subjects of government largesse. Neither does this approach value neutrality, that captious, capacious, and capricious value, as an end in itself.

Rather, the constitutional agnostic's approach permits or requires equal funding because this is the best way to respect both the possibility of religious truth and the pluralistic nature of our society. It is the approach that least involves the government in making loaded choices about religious truth. Our focus should be on *how* aid is distributed, not *where* it is distributed. When it comes to government funding questions, the constitutional agnostic is a long way from Madison's insistence that not even "three pence" may be distributed from state to church.

Symbols
Constitutional agnosticism's singular focus on recognizing the deep importance of the possibility of religious truth, while remaining in a state of suspension of ontological commitment with respect to what that truth is, yields a different set of conclusions with respect to cases involving symbolic support of religious messages by government. As with the funding cases, its conclusions are consistent with the Court's own approach, but better justified and more suited to our own agnostic age.

Here, again, the central point is not that government must be resolutely *secular* in its views, but that it must be resolutely *agnostic* on the question of religious truth. It must not make statements, either directly or indirectly, that embrace particular positions concerning religious truth, such as whether there is a God and what God demands.

This conclusion is compelled partly by epistemic and institutional concerns: concerns about the relative lack of knowledge and competence on these issues on the part of public officials.[170] Not everyone will agree, of course, that government is any less capable of making judgments on these questions than individuals are. Moreover, some people believe that the truth about religion is obvious—although no one seems to agree about what that truth *is*. But both those who believe that the truth of the matter is obvious and those who believe it is unknowable can still agree that special difficulties are raised when government is involved. The problem here is both jurisprudential and practical. Jurisprudentially, one may believe that the Religion Clauses, especially the Establishment Clause, take this question out of the government's hands.[171]

---

170. *See, e.g.,* Koppelman, *supra* note 72, at 590–91.

171. *See, e.g.,* Douglas Laycock, *Equal Access and Moments of Silence: The Equal Status of Religious Speech by Private Speakers,* 81 Nw. U. L. Rev. 1, 7–8 (1986).

Practically, committed believers (whether theists or atheists) and agnostics alike may agree that whether the truth is knowable or not, government cannot function appropriately and fairly in a pluralistic society unless it refuses to be enlisted in these battles.

The result in either case is the same: "The Establishment Clause forbids the state from declaring religious truth."[172] Whether through its own statements, or through efforts to encourage statements by others, it cannot weigh in on the question of religious truth at all. This is not secularism: The government is equally prohibited from making a statement that privileges secular views, if that statement is intended to champion the *truth* of a particular secular worldview. It is, instead, a matter of abstention or disability. That does not mean government cannot *value* religion; as we saw in the last chapter, constitutional agnosticism requires us to give significant accommodations to individuals' religious beliefs and practices.[173] But the same approach compels the conclusion that although government can and must recognize the importance to individuals of questions of religious truth, it cannot itself "endors[e] any diagnosis of or prescription for the universal human problem" of religious truth.[174]

This position supports the approach taken by the courts on a variety of issues involving government-sponsored religious speech. The clearest example is school prayer.[175] As the Court declared early on, "[I]t is no part of the business of government to compose official prayers for any group of the American people to recite as part of a religious program carried on by the government."[176] Things get a little more complicated, but not much more, when government attempts to advance a religious message but tries to cover its tracks. In *Santa Fe Independent School District v. Doe*,[177] for example, a school district sought to get around the restrictions placed on clergy-led prayer at school events[178] by establishing a system under which students voted on whether to give an invocation before football games, then voted again on which single student would deliver that invocation for the entire season.[179] Everyone acquainted with the facts of the case, and with the prior practices of the school district, understood that the goal of the policy was not simply to leave the decision up to the students. Rather, the district

---

172. Koppelman, *supra* note 72, at 590.

173. *See* Chapter Six.

174. Koppelman, *supra* note 72, at 592.

175. For an extended treatment of these and related issues, see Kent Greenawalt, *Does God Belong in Public Schools?* (2005).

176. *Engel v. Vitale*, 370 U.S. 421, 425 (1962).

177. 530 U.S. 290 (2000).

178. *See Lee v. Weisman*, 505 U.S. 577 (1992).

179. *Santa Fe*, 530 U.S. at 296–97.

wanted to leverage the voting power of the religious student majority to ensure that a religious message was delivered.[180]

A few things must be said about these cases and the results they require. Religious statements by government should not be viewed as problematic strictly because of tests like endorsement, coercion, and the like, any more than they should be viewed as problematic because the state ought to be secular in its orientation. Those labels are just symptoms, not the disease itself. Whether government messages taking a stand on matters of religious truth are permissible or impermissible should not turn on what the mythical "reasonable believer" thinks, although the reasonable observer test may help us evaluate the substance of the government message. Nor should it turn on questions about psychological coercion, such as whether graduating students will be impelled, lemming-like, to either religious conversion or psychological harm if they are required to stand silently for an invocation. Rather, the focus should be on the disability of government itself: on the inappropriateness of government delivering a message that endorses a particular view of religious truth, whatever the effect on its audience may be.

Two qualifications are important here. First, nothing about this rule prevents citizens from speaking as *they* wish to in the public square. Most serious people understand this. Even the most ardent separationists generally support the right of religious individuals to make strongly religious statements in public, although some argue that this rule somehow shouldn't apply when those public statements involve public policy. But a few separationists argue that these statements *can* be restricted, even if they are made by private citizens, in certain special contexts such as the public schools.[181] They are wrong. The conclusion drawn by both legislatures and the courts is the right one: Any disabilities that bar *government* from endorsing a particular view of religious truth must be accompanied by an equally strong liberty for *citizens* who wish to publicly advance their own views of religious truth.[182] If schoolchildren are allowed, for example, to select a

---

180. *See id.* at 305–15. I discuss *Santa Fe* in Horwitz, *supra* note 102, and in Paul Horwitz, *Of Football, "Footnote One," and the Counter-Jurisdictional Establishment Clause: The Story of* Santa Fe Independent School District v. Doe, in *First Amendment Stories* (Rick Garnett & Andrew Koppelman, eds., forthcoming).

181. Although he does not support such a rule with respect to *every* instance of private religious speech, Steven Gey has argued that "the Establishment Clause of the First Amendment requires the government to restrict private religious speech in some government-related contexts in which the Free Speech Clause requires the government to permit unrestricted nonreligious speech." Steven G. Gey, *The No Religion Zone: Constitutional Limitations on Religious Association in the Public Sphere*, 85 Minn. L. Rev. 1885, 1896–97 (2001).

182. *See, e.g.*, Equal Access Act, 20 U.S.C. §§ 4071–74 (2000); *Good News Club v. Milford Cent. Sch.*, 533 U.S. 98 (2001); *Rosenberger v. Rector*, 515 U.S. 819 (1995); *Lamb's Chapel v.*

story from their favorite book to read to their classmates, nothing should prevent them from choosing a Bible story instead of Beatrix Potter or Jean Genet.[183]

Second, not all speech by government *officials* should be characterized as *official government speech*.[184] Some government speech is delivered by particular individuals in their official capacity, and counts as an official communication from government to the public. Other speech by government officials is properly understood as a communication of that official's *own* views, and does not carry the imprimatur of the government itself; a government official can speak while making clear, explicitly or implicitly, that his views are his own and not necessarily those of the government. Still other speech by government officials is delivered horizontally, not vertically. It is a conversation between one official and another, not an official statement of the views of the government as such. Two senators can debate each other on the Senate floor without either view being attributable to the Senate as a whole. Religious speech by individual government officials should not violate the strict rule against *official* government speech that takes sides on questions of religious truth.

Consider three examples. The first is the venerable practice of presidents issuing official proclamations on the occasion of Thanksgiving, proclamations that often seek God's blessing on the United States. The second is the controversy sparked by then-Texas governor and future presidential candidate George W. Bush's public acknowledgment of his belief that only Christians can win admission into Heaven, and that, by implication, Americans who are not saved are condemned to eternal perdition.[185] The third is the speech that aroused Susan Jacoby's ire: President Bush's openly religious, although non-sectarian, speech at the Washington National Cathedral shortly after the September 11 attacks.[186]

Center Moriches Union Free Sch. Dist., 508 U.S. 384 (1993); *Bd. of Educ. v. Mergens*, 496 U.S. 226 (1990); *Widmar v. Vincent*, 454 U.S. 263 (1981).

183. *See, e.g.*, Richard W. Garnett, *"Modest Expectations"?: Civic Unity, Religious Pluralism, and Conscience*, 23 Const. Comment. 241, 254 (2006) (citing Kevin Seamus Hasson, *The Right to Be Wrong: Ending the Culture War Over Religion in America* 126 (2005)).

184. For treatments of this difficult issue, see, *e.g.*, Andy G. Olree, *Identifying Government Speech*, 42 Conn. L. Rev. 365 (2009); Helen Norton, *The Measure of Government Speech: Identifying Expression's Source*, 88 B.U. L. Rev. 587 (2008); Caroline Mala Corbin, *Mixed Speech: When Speech is Both Private and Governmental*, 83 N.Y.U. L. Rev. 605 (2008); Nelson Tebbe, *Excluding Religion*, 156 U. Pa. L. Rev. 1263 (2008); Randall P. Bezanson & William G. Buss, *The Many Faces of Government Speech*, 86 Iowa L. Rev. 1377 (2001); Mark G. Yudof, *When Government Speaks: Politics, Law, and Government Expression in America* (1983); Steven Shiffrin, *Government Speech*, 27 UCLA L. Rev. 565 (1983).

185. *See, e.g.*, Ken Herman, *Bush Trip Steeped in History*, Austin American-Statesman, Dec. 1, 1998, at A1.

186. *See* Susan Jacoby, *Freethinkers: A History of American Secularism* 3 (2004).

These are all instances of speech by government officials, and some people who are inclined to take offense over such things might find the second and third examples more objectionable than the first. After all, the fact that a potential leader of our country believes millions of us will be Satan's sport in the hereafter is a pretty strong statement, and is likely to be widely disseminated, as Bush's statement was. By contrast, a Thanksgiving proclamation is about as watered-down a religious statement as you can get. In any event, it is not all that well publicized. Few of us turn eagerly to the latest issue of *Public Papers of the Presidents of the United States* at the breakfast table each day.

Nevertheless, from a constitutional agnostic's standpoint, the first example is constitutionally objectionable, while the second and third examples are not. Bush's statements about damnation, and his speech at Washington National Cathedral, represent one official's views at one particular time. They need not represent government's *official* view. Unless we want to prohibit public officials from making *individual* statements on questions of religious truth in the same way that any other citizen can, we can simply accept those views or ignore them as we see fit. The Thanksgiving proclamation, on the other hand, mild as it is, in an important sense represents a conclusion about questions of religious truth by *the government* as an official body. It represents the government's own *official* conclusion that there is something to be thankful for, and Someone to whom we should be thankful. Individual government officials have opinions on questions of religious truth, just as they do on other matters. Indeed, they often campaign for office on the basis of those very views. Although they can be expected to *serve* all of us as public officials, they cannot possibly *represent* all of our views in all of their individual utterances. Government as an official body, on the other hand, *can* be expected not to take sides on questions of religious truth.

That is where the distinction should lie. Government officials should not be required to refrain from sharing their deeply held beliefs. As I said in Chapter Five, to be a *constitutional* agnostic does not require anyone, including public officials, to be a *religious* agnostic, let alone to remain mute. The way to address the conflicts that religious statements may provoke in a pluralistic society is not to insist on a rigorously scrubbed secular public square. It is to insist that these views cannot become the official orthodoxy of government *itself*—that, whatever views individual officials may hold, they cannot become the official view of the government itself.

The general rule for constitutional agnosticism where symbolic religious statements by government are concerned, then, is a narrow but strict one. Private individuals and groups, and public officials themselves, are free to take sides in our endless debates about whether there is a religious truth and what it is. But government itself is subject to a permanent disability on this subject. It can make no declarations about religious truth, no matter how mild those declarations are. In the words of Justice Robert Jackson, "If there is any fixed star in our constitutional constellation, it is that no official, high or petty, can prescribe what shall be orthodox in politics, nationalism, religion, or other matters of opinion or force citizens to confess by word or act their faith therein."[187]

Like any such broad statement, Jackson's pronouncement is subject to qualifications and criticisms. Steven Smith, for example, argues that "government ultimately cannot avoid making judgments about theological issues."[188] In a sense, that may be true. Behind every statement there is a belief. But this criticism is overbroad. For one thing, as I have argued, the prohibition against government taking stands on questions of religious truth should not be read to prohibit individual government officials from sharing their views on these questions; so the rule I have advocated is not so strict as to be unsustainable. For another, the rule is limited to official "action that explicitly *endorses* a religious view."[189] It does not prohibit government from teaching *about* religion, for example.[190] Nor does it prohibit the state from teaching the theory of evolution,[191] or from teaching that the theory of evolution is subject to criticism. But it *does* forbid the state from saying that the theory of evolution proves the nonexistence of God,[192] or that evolutionary theory's flaws prove conclusively that God *does* exist.

More difficult questions may arise where government's official pronouncements, even if they carefully avoid taking a stand on questions of religious truth, seem so comprehensive and pervasive that some individuals feel excluded. These individuals may argue that the government's views in these circumstances implicitly endorse a particular perspective—usually a secular one—or that the state's very refusal to make a statement about religious truth *is* a statement about religious truth, one that values pluralism and tolerance for their own sake, to the exclusion of worldviews that reject those values. These objections are most likely to arise in the public school context, in which educators often and probably unavoidably teach lessons or values, such as tolerance and cooperation, that conflict with some religious worldviews.[193]

---

187. *West Va. Bd. of Educ. v. Barnette*, 319 U.S. 624, 642 (1943).

188. Steven D. Smith, *Discourse in the Dusk: The Twilight of Religious Freedom?* 122 Harv. L. Rev. 1869, 1902 n.141 (2009); *see also* Steven D. Smith, *Barnettte's Big Blunder*, 78 Chi.-Kent L. Rev. 625, 653–58 (2003).

189. Andrew Koppelman, *No Expressly Religious Orthodoxy: A Response to Steven D. Smith*, 78 Chi.-Kent L. Rev. 729, 732 (2003) (emphasis added).

190. *See Sch. Dist. of Abington Twp. v. Schempp*, 374 U.S. 203, 225 (1963); *see generally* Marc O. DeGirolami, *The Problem of Religious Learning*, 49 B.C. L. Rev. 1213 (2008).

191. *See Epperson v. Arkansas*, 393 U.S. 97 (1968); *Edwards v. Aguillard*, 482 U.S. 578 (1986).

192. *See* Koppelman, *supra* note 189, at 733.

193. *See, e.g., Brown v. Hot, Sexy & Safer Prods., Inc.*, 68 F.3d 525 (1st Cir. 1995) (rejecting a request by parents to have their children exempted from a racy student assembly); *Mozert v. Hawkins County Bd. of Educ.*, 827 F.2d 1058 (6th Cir. 1987); *see generally* Nomi

On a deep level, these objections are difficult to answer.[194] On a practical level, however, they are less troublesome. Government cannot stop speaking altogether; as long as it does, *someone* will inevitably be unhappy. As you read these words, some parent somewhere is preparing to argue that a public school math class violates the Establishment Clause, because the statement that two plus one equals three is an insult to the mysteries of the Trinity, or because the study of mathematics itself improperly teaches a reductionist and mechanical view of the universe. All that government can *reasonably* do is to avoid as best as it can placing its official imprimatur on statements of religious truth.

The Constitutional Easement Mess

So far, I have argued that the Supreme Court's trend over the past several decades has been fairly clear and consistent: greater freedom for government to fund religious programs, provided that the aid is even-handedly distributed, and greater rigor in enforcing the bar against official government or government-sponsored religious speech. The best way to justify both of these lines of decisions, at least in our own age, is through constitutional agnosticism, which embraces rather than avoids the question of religious truth, but suspends final judgment on the truth of the matter.

But there is a significant exception to this trend. Consider a number of practices engaged in by government with great frequency and relatively little controversy. The list should be familiar to everyone; it is part of the standard set of talking points in the public debate over church–state relations. Our national motto, "In God We Trust," is engraved on our coins. Schoolchildren say the Pledge of Allegiance, with its words "One nation under God," every morning. Congress declares certain religious days as national holidays, and both Congress and the President issue proclamations on those occasions. Indeed, at the President's direction, Congress has set aside a National Day of Prayer.[195] The Ten Commandments and other religious displays festoon our public grounds. The Supreme Court itself, whose main chamber features a frieze portraying Moses with the Ten Commandments, opens its sessions with the phrase, "God save this honorable Court." Congress and the state legislatures have long employed chaplains, and government meetings across the country open with

---

Maya Stolzenberg, *"He Drew a Circle That Shut Me Out": Assimilation, Indoctrination, and the Paradox of a Liberal Education*, 106 Harv. L. Rev. 581 (1993).

194. *See* Chapter Eight.

195. In an apparent attempt to refute my argument that these practices draw relatively little controversy, while this book was in draft a federal district court ruled that the statute creating the National Day of Prayer violates the Establishment Clause. *See Freedom From Religion Foundation, Inc. v. Obama*, 2010 WL 1499451 (W. D. Wis. April 15, 2010). The chances that this decision will be upheld by the appellate courts are negligible.

prayer.[196] Justice William O. Douglas once proclaimed: "We are a religious people whose institutions presuppose a Supreme Being."[197] Given this long list of religious or quasi-religious pronouncements by government, it might be fairer to say that our institutions don't *presuppose* a Supreme Being; if anything, they can't seem to shut up about Him.

I have called the cases permitting such conduct constitutional or historical easements over the Establishment Clause. It has been said that hypocrisy is vice's way of paying tribute to virtue. Similarly, the constitutional easement cases can be thought of as the nation's stubborn but embarrassed admission that it cannot possibly live up to the strictures of the Establishment Clause. They are a reminder that "the Court consistently has declined to take a rigid, absolutist view of the Establishment Clause."[198]

Not all of these cases have deployed the constitutional easement argument. In many cases, courts have struggled to shoehorn their rulings into the primary framework of Establishment Clause jurisprudence. Religious displays on government property during the Christmas season, for example, have been upheld on the grounds that they simply "take[ ] note of a significant historical religious event long celebrated in the Western World," without actually proclaiming the truth or meaning of the events that occasioned the celebration.[199] Similarly, Ten Commandments displays have been struck down when the courts conclude that the display has no purpose other than the invocation of religious principles,[200] and upheld when they are viewed as simply "recogniz[ing] the role the Decalogue plays in America's heritage."[201] It helps when the religious nature of the display is covered by some fig leaf: plastic reindeer and teddy bears next to a crèche,[202] or a statue of the "Heroes of the Alamo" next to the Ten Commandments.[203]

Often, though, the courts do invoke something like a historical easement argument to uphold these instances of government-sponsored religious expression. Sometimes they follow the "What would George Washington do?" rule, concluding that a practice is so longstanding that it is too late in the day to object.[204] Sometimes they argue that these practices are simply instances of "ceremonial

---

196. For these and other examples, see, *e.g.*, *Lynch v. Donnelly*, 465 U.S. 668, 674–78 (1984).

197. *Zorach v. Clauson*, 343 U.S. 306, 313 (1952).

198. *Lynch*, 465 U.S. at 678.

199. *Id.* at 680.

200. See *Stone v. Graham*, 449 U.S. 39 (1980); *Glassroth v. Moore*, 335 F.3d 1282 (11th Cir. 2003).

201. *Van Orden v. Perry*, 545 U.S. 677, 689 (2005).

202. *See, e.g., Lynch*, 465 U.S. at 671.

203. *See, e.g., Van Orden*, 545 U.S. at 681 n.1. To the "two plastic reindeer" rule for Christmas displays, we might thus add the "Davy Crockett" rule in the Ten Commandments context.

204. *See, e.g., Marsh v. Chambers*, 463 U.S. 783 (1983).

deism," drained of most religious or sectarian content.[205] An intrepid few argue that such displays are permissible as long as they involve only invocations of Judeo-Christian monotheism.[206]

Sometimes one can detect in these opinions a note of exhaustion or frustration. Although the courts declare that "[t]here are no *de minimis* violations of the Constitution—no constitutional harms so slight that the courts are obliged to ignore them," they add in the same breath that "government can, in a discrete category of cases, acknowledge or refer to the divine without offending the Constitution."[207] The implicit message is, "Let sleeping dogs lie."[208]

How should we think about these practices? One possibility is to treat them as harmless, and any objections to them as trivial.[209] Another is to argue that, although these practices are unconstitutional, the cure would be worse than the disease. Given the public backlash that would result if the Court faithfully applied the Establishment Clause and struck down these practices, integrity must give way to pragmatism; the courts should not be "required to render decisions that

---

205. *See, e.g., Elk Grove Unified Sch. Dist. v. Newdow*, 542 U.S. 1, 37–43 (2004) (O'Connor, J., concurring in the judgment).

206. *See McCreary County v. ACLU of Ky.*, 545 U.S. 844, 893–94 (2005) (Scalia, J., dissenting). For criticism, see, *e.g.*, Frederick Mark Gedicks & Roger Hendrix, *Uncivil Religion: Judeo-Christianity and the Ten Commandments*, 110 W. Va. L. Rev. 275 (2007); Thomas B. Colby, *A Constitutional Hierarchy of Religions? Justice Scalia, the Ten Commandments, and the Future of the Establishment Clause*, 100 Nw. U. L. Rev. 1097 (2006). For a defense of this approach that is framed largely in constitutional easement terms, see Kyle Duncan, *Bringing Scalia's Decalogue Dissent Down From the Mountain*, 2007 Utah L. Rev. 287, 288 (arguing that Scalia's dissent is not an instance of "monotheistic activism," but rather is a restrained position recognizing "government's persistent acknowledgment of a generalized monotheism").

207. *Newdow* 542 U.S. at 36–37 (O'Connor, J., concurring in the judgment); *see also Walz v. Tax Comm'n of New York*, 397 U.S. 664, 678 (1970) ("It is obviously correct that no one acquires a vested or protected right in violation of the Constitution by long use, even when that span of time covers our entire national existence and indeed predates it. Yet an unbroken [government] practice [involving religion] . . . is not something to be lightly cast aside."). For a more candid, but constitutionally mistaken, view, see *Newdow v. United States Congress*, 292 F.3d 597, 615 n.9 (9th Cir. 2002) (Fernandez, J., concurring in part and dissenting in part) ("the de minimis tendency of the Pledge [of Allegiance] to establish a religion or to interfere with its free exercise is no constitutional violation at all").

208. *See, e.g., Van Orden*, 545 U.S. at 702–03 (Breyer, J., concurring in the judgment) (arguing that the display of the Ten Commandments on the grounds of the Texas Capitol should be permitted in part because some four decades had passed without any legal challenge to the monument).

209. *See generally* Steven G. Gey, *"Under God," the Pledge of Allegiance, and Other Constitutional Trivia*, 81 N.C. L. Rev. 1865 (2003) (canvassing triviality arguments under the Establishment Clause and concluding that the practices objected to are not trivial).

threaten to undermine critical constitutional values and institutions."[210] Similarly, some have argued that it would might be best not to inquire too deeply into these practices lest we end up with no loaf at all rather than half a loaf. In other words, if we don't let these practices skate by, the courts may end up loosening the rules of the Establishment Clause across the board, or we may get a disastrous constitutional amendment that does even more harm to religious freedom.[211]

For constitutional agnostics, these kinds of practices—legislative prayers, Ten Commandments displays and other religious monuments, religious mottos on coins, and so on—cannot be justified in principle. They rest on an unsound foundation. The Establishment Clause makes no room for historical easements. It blinks reality to say that these actions are a "mere" acknowledgment of our religious heritage. Not only has our nation become increasingly religiously pluralistic over the past century; in many cases, these practices are a somewhat hostile *response* to that pluralism, a way of drawing a line in the sand and saying that this is still a "Christian nation."[212] As we saw in the Introduction, the recent profusion of these practices is less a statement of social consensus about religion than it is proof that, in an age in which religion has become more contestable, different groups will urge government to make religious statements as part of a strategy of asserting themselves and trying to enlist the government in the public debate over religious issues.

Moreover, these practices violate the principle that both constitutional agnosticism and the mainstream of Establishment Clause doctrine take to be axiomatic: "The Establishment Clause forbids the state from declaring religious truth."[213] Government's official statement that we are "one nation under God," or that "in God we trust," is glaringly inconsistent with this axiom. The inconsistency can be addressed only by disingenuousness: by requiring Davy Crockett, coonskin cap perched firmly on his head, to stand guard over a public display of the Ten Commandments, for example, or by arguing, in the teeth of the evident intent of these practices, that they are nothing more than an acknowledgment of our nation's heritage. In short, they can only be salvaged by taking the religious truth out of religious displays. This will not placate those who see these displays as freighted with religious meaning, for good or for ill.

The problem with these practices is not that they are coercive, or that they violate the withered principle of separationism. The problem is that they enlist the government in the service of religious truth-claims that the government has

---

210. Steven H. Shiffrin, *The Pluralistic Foundations of the Religion Clauses*, 90 Cornell L. Rev. 9, 74 (2004) (exploring the role and limits of a pragmatic approach in this area).

211. *See* Laura S. Underkuffler, *Through a Glass Darkly*: Van Orden, McCreary, *and the Dangers of Transparency in Establishment Clause Jurisprudence*, 5 First Amend. L. Rev. 59 (2006).

212. *Church of the Holy Trinity v. United States*, 143 U.S. 457, 471 (1892).

213. Koppelman, *supra* note 72, at 590.

neither the wherewithal nor the right to make. If we place religious truth at the heart of the Religion Clauses, we lay bare the unprincipled and intellectually incoherent nature of the constitutional easement argument for particular religious statements by government, however "trivial" they may seem. In a constitutionally agnostic system in a pluralistic society, the public square may bristle with religious messages. But none of them should come with a government stamp.

It is not clear that anything much will follow from this conclusion. Any judges who have been kind enough to read this far (or have their law clerks do so for them) are unlikely to slam down this book and shout, "Holy cow—Horwitz is right!" They know it already. But they believe it is best for the long-term health of the Religion Clauses, and for the civil peace, to leave well enough alone. They think accepting "In God We Trust" on our coins is a small price to pay for a sustainable Establishment Clause. They may be right.

But some good can still come from pressing the point. In order for hypocrisy to serve as vice's tribute to virtue, vice must at least admit that it *is* vice. If constitutional easements are the price we pay to allow the Establishment Clause to escape with minimal damage to its core values, we can still recognize that these exceptions *are* inconsistent with those values. This is especially important for constitutional decision makers other than judges, such as legislators and citizens. Without sacrificing their own religious beliefs, they might acknowledge that the official public recognition of those beliefs is in serious tension with the axiom that government has no business declaring religious truth. They might even be honest enough to admit that they *want* a government declaration of religious truth—not the plastic reindeers or the "acknowledgment" of the Christmas "holiday," but the infant Christ nestled in a crèche. In some cases, this might lead constitutional decision makers either to be more explicit about their aims, or to reconsider whether they really want to enlist government in this fashion. Either outcome—more open defiance by legislators of the core Establishment Clause rule against official declarations of religious truth, or a greater willingness to forego those declarations—might give additional cover to the courts, offering them greater public support when they police the boundaries of the Establishment Clause. We might at least have a more candid discussion about the questions raised by these kinds of public displays, and acknowledge the inescapable questions of religious truth that lie at their heart.

The Role of Religion in Public Deliberation and Debate

One last question remains to be discussed in our treatment of constitutional agnosticism and the Establishment Clause. This is the question of whether religion must somehow be removed from public deliberation and discussion: whether religious reasons must be treated as illegitimate or insufficient in public debate over legislation and other questions of public policy. That question has occasioned some of the richest and most important debates in the field of law and religion, and more broadly in the discussion of the relationship between religion and liberal democracy.[214] It is important to say something about how constitutional agnosticism views these questions.

It used to be common for legal scholars to make sharp arguments that religion has no place in public or political discourse. Suzanna Sherry, for instance, argued that "government may not make decisions that are themselves based on contested religious beliefs that cannot be rationally supported."[215] Kathleen Sullivan described American society under the Constitution as a "secular public moral order" in which "no faith" may be "translated into public policy."[216] The legal philosopher Ronald Dworkin once asserted that any law restricting abortions prior to fetal viability—the point at which a fetus can survive outside the mother's body—must be religious in nature, because no secular reasons could possibly support such a rule. In Dworkin's view, any such regulations therefore violate the Establishment Clause.[217] This was an era of "de facto disestablishment."[218]

---

214. A long but still incomplete list of some of the most important contributions to this debate would include Robert Audi & Nicholas Wolterstorff, *Religion in the Public Square: The Place of Convictions in Political Debate* (1996); Robert Audi, *Religious Commitment and Secular Reason* (2000); Christopher J. Eberle, *Religious Conviction in Liberal Politics* (2002); Kent Greenawalt, *Private Consciences and Public Reasons* (1995); Kent Greenawalt, *Religious Convictions and Political Choice* (1988); Michael W. McConnell, *Secular Reason and the Misguided Attempt to Exclude Religious Argument From Democratic Deliberation*, 1 J.L. Phil. & Culture 79 (2007); Michael W. McConnell, *Five Reasons to Reject the Claim That Religious Arguments Should Be Excluded From Democratic Deliberation*, 1999 Utah L. Rev. 639; Michael J. Perry, *Under God? Religious Faith and Liberal Democracy* (2003); Michael J. Perry, *Love and Power: The Role of Religion and Morality in American Politics* (1991); John Rawls, *Political Liberalism* (1996); Symposium, *Religion and Morality in the Public Square*, 22 St. John's J. Legal Comment. 417 (2007); Symposium, *The Role of Religion in Public Debate in a Liberal Society*, 30 San Diego L. Rev. 643 (1993); and Sanford Levinson, *Religious Language and the Public Square*, 105 Harv. L. Rev. 2061 (1992). My own, more modest contributions to this debate can be found in Paul Horwitz, *Religion and American Politics: Three Views of the Cathedral*, 39 U. Mem. L. Rev. 973 (2009), and *Religious Tests in the Mirror: The Constitutional Law and Constitutional Etiquette of Religion in Judicial Nominations*, 15 Wm. & Mary Bill Rts. J. 75 (2006).

215. Sherry, *supra* note 152, at 492.

216. Sullivan, *supra* note 152, at 198.

217. Ronald Dworkin, *Life's Dominion* (1993). This position was once shared by Laurence Tribe. *See* Laurence H. Tribe, *Foreword: Toward a Model of Roles in the Due Process of Life and Law*, 87 Harv. L. Rev. 1, 23 (1973). Tribe has long since disclaimed this position. *See, e.g.*, Laurence H. Tribe, *American Constitutional Law* § 15–10, at 1349–50 (2d ed. 1988). It also made a cameo appearance on the Supreme Court, in an opinion by Justice John Paul Stevens arguing that it would violate the Establishment Clause for a law to state in its preamble that life begins at conception. *See Webster v. Reproductive Health Servs.*, 492 U.S. 490, 566–72 (1989) (Stevens, J., concurring in part and dissenting in part).

218. Steven D. Smith, *Legal Discourse and the De Facto Disestablishment*, 81 Marq. L. Rev. 203 (1998).

Those arguments have largely faded from fashion.[219] Few legal academics writing about law and religion today take a strongly separationist position on the role of religion in public and political discourse.[220] If there is a de facto disestablishment in the legal academy, its ranks include few specialists in law and religion.[221] In truth, it was never a terribly accurate description of political debate in the United States, which for all its statist orientation was never devoid of religious language.[222] As befits our age of religious contestability, one still hears the occasional argument that religion has "no place in the heart of politics,"[223] but those voices are fewer and farther between than they used to be. Those who insist that religion has been driven out of the public square[224] may not be completely wrong, but they are mostly grasping at straws.

From the standpoint of constitutional agnosticism, not only is there no bar to religious participation in public debate, including the use of explicitly religious

---

219. This decline may be traced, among other things, to widespread academic criticism of the Supreme Court's decision in *Employment Division v. Smith*, 494 U.S. 872 (1990), which I discuss at length in Chapter Six. It seems to have peaked by the time Stephen L. Carter published his popular book *The Culture of Disbelief: How American Law and Politics Trivialize Religious Devotion* (1993). It helped that Carter's book was championed by President Bill Clinton, who for both sincere and strategic reasons was eager to reclaim a role for religion in democratic (and Democratic) politics. *See, e.g.,* Peter Steinfels, *Beliefs*, N.Y. Times, Sept. 4, 1993, at 8.

220. *But see, e.g.,* Edward L. Rubin, *Sex, Politics, and Morality*, 47 Wm. & Mary L. Rev. 1, 4 (2005) (arguing that "opposition to gay marriage, abortion, birth control, sex education, and stem cell research is based on Christian doctrine, more specifically, on one contestable interpretation of Christian doctrine. It follows that legislation effectuating such opposition should be invalidated under the Establishment Clause of the First Amendment.").

221. Sometimes, perhaps, to our loss. Although I disagree with the strict separationists, they can contribute an important note of sober second thought to the discussion, reminding those of us who broadly advocate religious liberty of what William Marshall has called "the other side of religion." William P. Marshall, *The Other Side of Religion*, 44 Hastings L.J. 843 (1993). In the legal academy as elsewhere, too much harmony can be a bad thing.

222. *See, e.g.,* Marci A. Hamilton, *Religion and the Law in the Clinton Era: An Anti-Madisonian Legacy*, 63 L. & Contemp. Probs. 359 (2000); William P. Marshall, *The Culture of Belief and the Politics of Religion*, 63 L. & Contemp. Probs. 453 (2000); Kathleen M. Sullivan, *God as a Lobby*, 61 U. Chi. L. Rev. 1655 (1994). For broader historical overviews, see, *e.g.,* Frank Lambert, *Religion in American Politics: A Short History* (2008); *Religion and American Politics: From the Colonial Period to the Present* (Mark A. Noll & Luke E. Harlow eds., 2d ed. 2007).

223. Norman Lear, *Calling All Born-Again Americans*, Wash. Post, May 19, 2009.

224. *See, e.g.,* M.G. "Pat" Robertson, *Squeezing Religion Out of the Public Square–The Supreme Court, Lemon, and the Myth of the Secular Society*, 4 Wm. & Mary Bill Rts. J. 223 (1995).

arguments by citizens and lawmakers alike, but there *can be* no such bar.[225] To rule an argument out of bounds on the grounds that it is religious is, ultimately, to make a truth-claim about religion. It is to argue that there is something uniquely disabling about religious argument, that we can identify what that something is, and that the state ought to decisively settle the matter in favor of one side. This it cannot do consistently with constitutional agnosticism. The state cannot deprive "democratic deliberation . . . of certain categories of argument on the basis of controversial epistemological judgments."[226]

Nor, for a number of reasons, can this argument be made on the basis that certain (secular) arguments are publicly accessible and other (religious) arguments are not. First, at least for the agnostic, who is committed to attempting to enter and appreciate the worldviews of others, religious arguments *may* be accessible, however imperfectly. Second, with the breakdown of the liberal consensus, it is no longer clear that the kinds of liberal arguments that were once viewed as generally accessible *are* all that accessible. Third, inaccessibility is a common and inevitable feature of political debate, even when that debate is shorn of religious language. Political debates, even when they involve no expressly religious statements, quickly run out of common ground, and end up turning on conflicts over values that cannot be discussed in meaningful shared terms.[227] Not all political debates have that quality. One might argue about precisely how many troops are on the ground in Iraq, Afghanistan, or some other conflict zone. But once we debate whether the troops should be there *at all*, the discussion will quickly become a debate over fundamental and irreconcilable values. The disputants may not even agree on how to *define* those values.[228] In short, "[i]naccessible arguments are common in democratic discourse."[229]

The constitutional agnostic therefore concludes that religion cannot be excluded from public debate.[230] This certainly holds true for the arguments made by citizens. Perhaps more controversially, it is equally true for the arguments of public officials. If there is no clear standard by which we can conclude that a particular set of arguments is out of bounds for citizens, the same conclusion must hold true for arguments made by public officials. In official political debate, as in the wider public debate, anything goes.

---

225. I have made similar arguments on other grounds elsewhere. *See* Horwitz, *supra* note 102; Horwitz, *supra* note 214.

226. McConnell, *supra* note 214, at 652.

227. *See, e.g.,* Jeffrey Stout, *Democracy and Tradition* 87 (2004) ("Everyone holds some beliefs on nonreligious topics without claiming to know that they are true.").

228. *See, e.g.,* Danny Priel, *In Search of Argument,* 86 Tex. L. Rev. 141, 150–51 (2007).

229. McConnell, *supra* note 214, at 652.

230. For a similar conclusion, from an avowedly secularist perspective, see Austin Dacey, *The Secular Conscience: Why Belief Belongs in Public Life* (2008).

That is not to say there are no limits at all. In particular, three potential restraints may alleviate some of the risks posed by the prospect of uninhibited religious debate on public issues. First, for the same truth-centered reasons that constitutional agnosticism permits religious *reasons* in public debate, there are important restrictions on particular *outcomes*. As we have seen in this chapter, government must treat recipients of government funds evenhandedly regardless of their beliefs on questions of religious truth, and it may not make official statements that take sides on questions of religious truth. Politicians and citizens are free to argue as they will, on whatever grounds they will, but they cannot secure absolutely any result they wish, and they cannot enlist government to endorse their views. The limitation on outcomes is the most important guarantee that unrestricted political debate, whether on secular or religious grounds, will not devolve into an absolute rule of either secularism or theocracy.

Second, although there is no constitutional rule disabling religious individuals from making religious arguments in public debate, as a practical matter we can still think about the best *ways* for people to engage in public debate.[231] Citizens and public officials should not argue that particular kinds of reasons, such as religious reasons, are simply and absolutely out of bounds in public discussion. But they remain free to argue that particular kinds of reasons are likely to be less *persuasive* in public discussion. One may even hope that citizens and public officials who have adopted the agnostic habit will, without abandoning their own conclusions on questions of religious truth, attempt to inhabit and appreciate the views of others. If they do, their respect for this diversity of views will encourage them to offer a variety of arguments, some of which will appeal to citizens from diverse religious and non-religious backgrounds.

Finally, pluralism, the same condition that makes constitutional agnosticism the best, or even the only, option in our contemporary social order, is likely to limit the prospect that citizens or public officials will make choose to make arguments in a single-mindedly religious (or secular) fashion. Pluralism and constitutional agnosticism make it impossible for us to rule particular arguments, including religious ones, out of bounds altogether in public debate. At the same time, the condition of pluralism also serves as a built-in restraint on single-minded arguments. In a pluralistic society, one that is politically, religiously, and socially diverse, politicians who want to win the day will have to form coalitions. They will have to persuade broad groups of individuals who hold a variety of views and operate from a diverse range of premises. If they want to command majorities in a highly fragmented society, they will have to understand and argue on the basis of a variety of different positions, both secular and religious. In a pluralistic society, that is the only way to get *unum* out of *pluribus*.

---

231. I offer some suggestions in both of the articles cited at note 214.

So the constitutional agnostic believes that nothing in the Establishment Clause forbids either citizens or public officials from making arguments on religious grounds (or secular grounds, for that matter). To the contrary, he believes that the state's suspension of ontological commitments requires that *all* arguments be welcome in public and political debate. For the same reason, he believes that certain official *outcomes* are foreclosed by the Establishment Clause. Taken together, the result will be one of neither secular nor religious dominance, but pluralism. Our pluralism ensures that a broad variety of views, proceeding from a broad variety of positions on the ultimate question of religious truth, will be heard. But pluralism also helps ensure that no one position will command a majority all by itself, and encourages both citizens and public officials to attempt to understand the views of others, and to frame arguments that will respond and appeal to a variety of perspectives on these fundamental questions.

CONCLUSION

The constitutionally agnostic position on the Establishment Clause is consistent with its position on the Free Exercise Clause, although that position leads to different results in each instance. In both cases, it is motivated by the same important belief: that questions of religious truth cannot simply be evaded, and that any attempt to do so will lead judges and other constitutional decision makers down a path of incoherence and inconsistency. In a pluralistic and agnostic age, the most appropriate approach is to acknowledge and face squarely the question of religious truth, albeit without drawing strong conclusions on one side or the other of that question. It does not require individuals to abandon their own religious beliefs. But it recommends that they understand and try to appreciate the sheer fact of pluralism itself, and make some effort to inhabit the welter of worldviews that we confront every day.

In the case of the Free Exercise Clause, constitutional agnosticism leads to a broad view of religious liberty and religious accommodation.[232] In the case of the Establishment Clause, it leads to a more complex but still consistent set of results. On the one hand, government's suspension of ontological commitments, and its appreciation for religious pluralism, counsel against the strict separationist view that once prevailed on the Supreme Court and in public discourse. Madison was wrong: we should not balk at the provision of even "three pence" by government to religious groups. Neither, however, should we prefer one group or one position over another in the distribution of government funds. Our concern should be with whether government treats all recipients the same, giving money to all or none without regard to questions of religious truth.

232. *See* Chapter Six.

In a pluralistic society, it seems likely that government's objectives can best be achieved by harnessing the power of a variety of perspectives and groups, religious and otherwise; so I would emphasize "all" rather than "none." Regardless, the rule should be one of evenhandedness.

On the other hand, the suspension of ontological commitments on the part of the government also serves as a constraint on government *symbols* and *messages*. Individual citizens and individual government officials must remain free to invoke God's will, and to take what they see as his side in arguments about public policy—although they may find it easier to win a majority if they attempt to understand and convince those who hold very different worldviews. But government itself, through its official actions, has no business staking a claim on questions of religious truth. It must remain agnostic on these questions. The wrong lies in taking the position itself. Questions such as whether a particular government statement is coercive, or would be seen by a reasonable objective observer as an endorsement of a particular religious truth-claim, are helpful but not essential. These inquiries may help guide us to a conclusion about whether the government has in fact taken a position that it is forbidden to take, but they are not ends in themselves. Government is simply and broadly disabled from taking positions on matters of religious truth, whether directly or indirectly.

Both of these positions are consistent with current trends in Establishment Clause jurisprudence, although constitutional agnosticism better unites and justifies what the courts have done in this area. The single, glaring exception to this is what I have labeled the constitutional easement cases, in which the courts, for a variety of reasons but ultimately out of a sense of institutional self-preservation, have upheld certain government practices involving the invocation of God. Constitutional agnosticism suggests that these practices are unconstitutional. Whether it is worth doing something about these cases is another matter. But we can at least say something about the patent inconsistency of these practices with the Establishment Clause, properly understood. We may even hope that citizens and legislators who have adopted the habit of constitutional agnosticism, whether out of appreciation for our conditions of modern pluralism or for other reasons, will revisit some of these practices.

PART FOUR

CONSTITUTIONAL AGNOSTICISM, RELIGION, AND LIBERAL DEMOCRACY

Church–state tensions take place on several levels, and our examination of constitutional agnosticism has moved back and forth between them. The first takes place at a fairly abstract level. It is the level at which we see debates about liberalism, religion, and the pluralistic nature of our society, and challenges to the conventional liberal consensus that once ruled our society. Those philosophical debates are played out on a smaller scale in the realm of law and religion theory. A number of theories about what religious liberty requires have been proposed. Many of these theories have been undermined by subsequent cultural and philosophical developments. Theoretically, the collapse of the liberal consensus calls into question the meaning and coherence of many of the prevailing values—liberty, equality, and so on—that have been put forward to justify religious liberty. Culturally, religious pluralism calls into question the practical prospects of more coherent but one-sided approaches to religious liberty, including openly religious and openly secularist theories of religious freedom. These questions were canvassed in Part One.

Church–state conflicts also operate at a more concrete level, although even this level has theoretical and cultural aspects. These conflicts involve the question of what we believe, how we know we believe it, and what position the state ought to take with respect to these questions of belief. Many people hold strong beliefs about the nature of the universe. Those beliefs may be theistic or atheistic, and the heated nature of our public debates over religion often takes on the same either/or quality. The paper war between the New Atheists and the New Anti-Atheists is a prime example. These debates over religious truth invariably spill over into questions about the role of the state. Should the state eschew tolerance for those who hold ostensibly irrational beliefs, as some New Atheists claim? Or, as some religious groups and individuals assert, should the United States reassert itself as a Christian nation?

These discussions have been heated but rarely helpful. They involve clashes of diametrically opposed worldviews. These conflicts cannot simply be settled by the imposition of a liberal consensus, for two reasons. First, liberalism considers itself disabled from commenting on questions of religious truth. Second, at a practical level the weakened force of the liberal consensus undermines its ability to impose order in this conflict, other than by brute force.

These conflicts between polar opposites are all the more unhelpful because the ground beneath them has shifted. We live in what Charles Taylor calls a "secular age,"[1] and what I call an agnostic age. That is true not in the sense that we are all secularists or agnostics, but in the sense that we live in a strongly *pluralistic* age. Friends, neighbors, and family members differ on foundational premises—on the fundamental answers to questions of religious truth. Belief in God, in all its varieties, is now importantly seen by many as an *option*—not a trivial option, but one that is always potentially in play. Our sense of what we know and how we know it is increasingly up for grabs. In this environment, the culture war between the New Atheists and the New Anti-Atheists, as much as it may captivate the public, can increasingly be seen as leaving out a vast excluded middle.

This conflict, and one possible response to it, was the subject of Part Two of this book. Its recommendation is that we might productively look toward agnosticism, or at least one brand of it. The purpose of this agnostic turn is to find a way of acknowledging and confronting the questions of religious truth that remain firmly embedded in our church–state conflicts and that, despite heroic efforts, can no longer simply be evaded, avoided, or ignored—if they ever really could. The agnostic turn provides a way of responding to questions of religious truth without staking a strong claim in favor of one version of religious truth or another. It does so by acting in an imaginative, open, and empathetic fashion, in which the religiously or constitutionally agnostic actor attempts to understand and inhabit the welter of potential views that exist on questions of religious truth, in a spirit of humility and negative capability.

For several reasons, that approach is both important and available—certainly more available than either secularists or religionists may assume. First, it is responsive to the *pluralistic* nature of our age, one in which a remarkable diversity of religious and other viewpoints share space and jostle for attention. Second, it is responsive to the *agnostic* nature of our age, one in which individuals may hold strong beliefs on questions of religious truth but are aware that other individuals hold very different good-faith views on the same questions and that our own views may change. Third, it is responsive to the *layered* nature of belief in our age. It responds to our capacity both to hold strong religious views *and* to hold second-order beliefs about our own beliefs and about how to coexist with others.[2] Constitutional agnosticism does not demand that we abandon our own strongly held conclusions on questions of religious truth. It only demands that, as citizens, we make some effort to understand and inhabit the views of others in our relations with them, particularly those relations that take on the official and potentially coercive character of state action.

Finally, it is consistent with deeply engrained habits of mind, habits that stem less from academic philosophy than from a commonplace activity: the

---

1. Charles Taylor, *A Secular Age* (2007).
2. *See* Steven D. Smith, *Our Agnostic Constitution*, 83 N.Y.U. L. Rev. 120, 124 (2008).

appreciation of art in a post-Romantic age. In the experience of art, most of us—sometimes without being aware that we are doing so—draw on our cultural inheritance of negative capability, in which we (partially) efface our own identities and appreciate radically different worldviews and characters. This common experience has given most of us the resources to be constitutional agnostics, perhaps more than we may realize.

In Part Three, we examined what a constitutionally agnostic perspective might require with respect to the Religion Clauses of the First Amendment. Constitutional agnosticism requires a major shift in our conventional way of thinking about church–state conflict: that we abandon the effort to simply avoid the question of religious truth altogether. Quixotic hopes may be fine for Cubs fans, but not here. The illusory belief that we can apply the Religion Clauses without confronting questions of religious truth has ended up tying this area of constitutional doctrine into knots. Constitutional agnosticism argues that we are better served by openly acknowledging questions of religious truth. In doing so, it provides the foundation for an approach to law and religion that may be stronger, sounder, and longer lasting than an approach that is grounded on—and founders on—liberal assumptions that no longer work as effectively or uncontroversially as they once did.

The result, we saw, is a revision of our understanding of the Religion Clauses. It is a revision, not a revolution, although some aspects of that revision may also be revolutionary. For the Free Exercise Clause, constitutional agnosticism counsels a shift of the pendulum away from the restrictive approach to religious freedom that currently prevails under the Supreme Court's decision in *Employment Division v. Smith*,[3] which denies free exercise protection to religious believers whose practices are burdened by general laws that are not aimed specifically at religion. Instead, it requires a broader approach to religious freedom, one that resembles the rule that ostensibly reigned prior to *Smith*. Under that rule, religious individuals and groups can challenge even neutral and generally applicable rules that significantly burden religious exercise.[4] Constitutional agnosticism would turn back the clock from our current era, in which the Free Exercise Clause is interpreted under a rule of non-discrimination, to the Court's earlier and more explicitly liberty-based treatment of religious freedom.

Constitutional agnosticism recommends this approach not because it seeks to *avoid* religious truth, but because it seeks to recognize and respect it. In a pluralistic society that genuinely acknowledges the possibility of religious truth, but suspends any commitment to a particular truth, the state should accord significant weight to the possibility that some religious claimant's understanding of the truth is *right*—that the truth he perceives *is* the truth. The constitutional

---

3. 494 U.S. 872 (1990).

4. *See, e.g., Sherbert v. Verner*, 374 U.S. 398 (1963); *Wisconsin v. Yoder*, 406 U.S. 205 (1972).

agnostic does his best to understand religious truth from the perspective of the believer, acting under the assumption that the believer sees the world and its mysteries clearly and accurately.

From this perspective, it will not do to adopt the statist perspective that is so apparent in the *Smith* regime. A truly constitutionally agnostic state, one that is seized by the importance and possibility of religious truth, will not allow statist concerns, important though they may be, to overwhelm a religious believer whose God actually compels or counsels particular religious practices. Nor can we settle these conflicts by appealing to some vision of the public good—often a decidedly secular and statist one. Our very understanding of what the "public good" requires is itself a deeply contestable question, particularly in an agnostic and pluralistic age. For the "public good" to mean anything in our own age, it must incorporate the possibility and importance of religious truth.[5]

The constitutional agnostic does not deny that state interests must be weighed against the interest of religious individuals engaging in particular religious practices. Sometimes those interests *will* outweigh the interest in religious freedom, no matter how seriously we take the possibility of religious truth. For every Abraham, there is an Isaac. Although the agnostic cannot say with absolute certainty whether it would be better for Isaac to live or die, we can still conclude that the Constitution is no more a murder pact than it is a suicide pact.[6]

But the constitutional agnostic can face this fact with a candor, a sense of imagination and humility, and, bluntly put, a moral integrity and maturity that is too often absent from the mechanical and somewhat secular-leaning balancing of interests that the courts today engage in under the Free Exercise Clause. By keeping the question of religious truth in the forefront of her thoughts, the agnostic can resist the urge to water down religious truth by converting it into a mere shadow, or a matter of personal "conscience" that is viewed as having less to do with the truth than with a feeling in someone's head. That way lies statism: the decision maker will, too often, treat that kind of claim of conscience as a good thing, all things considered, but one that quickly yields to more tangible worldly concerns. We will fail to honor what is most important about these claims: that they represent a statement about the fact of the matter, about God's actual existence and all that follows from it—one that, if true, should be insuperable.

Because the constitutional agnostic is alive to the possible truth of these claims, she will place a thumb heavily on the scale in favor of religious liberty.

---

5. *Cf.* Angela C. Carmella, *RLUIPA: Linking Religion, Land Use, Ownership and the Common Good*, 2 Alb. Gov't L. Rev. 485 (2009); Angela C. Carmella, *Responsible Freedom Under the Religion Clauses: Exemptions, Legal Pluralism, and the Common Good*, 110 W. Va. L. Rev. 403 (2007).

6. *See Terminiello v. Chicago*, 337 U.S. 1, 37 (1949) (Jackson, J., dissenting) ("There is danger that if the Court does not temper its doctrinaire logic with a little practical wisdom, it will convert the constitutional Bill of Rights into a suicide pact.").

She will be less likely to allow the exigencies of the moment, or such factors as efficiency, administrability, or convenience, to outweigh the profound interests asserted by the religious claimant. That does not mean she will impose no limits on permissible religious practice. But it does mean she will be fully aware of just how incommensurable the interests at stake really are. She will appreciate how profound and difficult the conflict really is between the needs of religious belief and practice and the needs of the state. She will be deeply aware of the tragic choices that such decisions require when we take religion seriously.

That awareness matters for all kinds of constitutional decision makers—not just judges, but citizens and public officials as well. Before a case ever reaches a judge, it must first pass through the formation of public policy by citizens and by those charged with making and executing the law. If these citizens and officials adopt the agnostic habit, they may be more willing to second-guess what would otherwise be a reflexive invocation of state interests, and less willing to invoke the specter of "anarchy."[7] Citizens and public officials alike may be more willing to consider the costs for religious believers of compliance with particular laws if they begin by imagining the possible truth of different religious beliefs and practices. They may be more willing to accommodate those practices when drafting their laws. Although courts would still have a role as final arbiters, the pressure on them would be lessened significantly if other actors fully appreciated the stakes of the conflict between the needs of the state and those of religious believers and sought to make room for those believers in the law. Constitutional agnosticism is a strategy for addressing questions of religious truth and social pluralism that applies to everyone, not judges alone.

With respect to the Establishment Clause, constitutional agnosticism largely tracks the distinction in current Establishment Clause jurisprudence between cases involving government *funding* for religion and cases involving government *speech* about religion. That distinction conceals a common bond. In both cases, the animating concern is with *confronting* religious truth, not *avoiding* it. That concern ultimately unifies and justifies the courts' Establishment Clause decisions better than the courts themselves have managed. Our respect for the possibility and intractability of questions of religious truth, and our awareness of the value of pluralism, should lead us to reject a separationist approach that would deny so much as "three pence" going from government to religion. Instead, our concern should be that aid is distributed to all or none in an evenhanded way.

Conversely, but consistently with the broader aims of constitutional agnosticism, government should be disabled from declaring religious truth. That does not mean government *officials*, or citizens engaged in public debate, must forgo religiously grounded arguments, whether those arguments run in favor of a particular vision of God or against the existence of God altogether. Nothing in

---

7. *Smith*, 494 U.S. at 888.

constitutional agnosticism requires either the cleansing of religion from the public square or that individuals, whether in their private or public capacity, abandon their own religious beliefs and arguments. Constitutional agnosticism is a lens through which we can better appreciate and incorporate the diverse range of religious views that are present in our pluralistic and agnostic age; it is not a set of blinders. It does not prevent religion from taking its rightful place among the myriad motivations and arguments that guide us in our debates over public policy.

What it does mean is that government's official statements must be thoroughly agnostic—not secular, not religious, but agnostic.[8] In the robust system of religious freedom and accommodation that constitutional agnosticism demands, the central limitation—the rule that makes all else possible—is that government cannot itself take a stand on questions of religious truth. That position undergirds many of the decisions that have become part of our commonplace understanding of government's limitations in this area: that it cannot, for example, force prayer on schoolchildren, whether directly or indirectly, by fair means or foul. But it also lays bare the inconsistency and incoherence of the courts' effort to preserve, through what I have called "constitutional easements," government practices invoking God in a wide variety of contexts—on our coins, in the Pledge of Allegiance that children say in school every day, in the practice of legislative prayer, in the mundane holiday proclamations issued by governments, and so on.

This is perhaps the most radical conclusion made by constitutional agnosticism. But it is radical only in some senses. One hardly needs to be a constitutional expert to be aware that these practices present grave constitutional difficulties. By the same token, it does not take a political scientist to see why these practices are so entrenched, why their frequency has increased in an era in which religion itself has become increasingly contestable, and why any challenge to them provokes such heated resistance. These practices may therefore be inevitable. But that does not make them right, and it does not make them any less unprincipled. At the very least, we can hope that, in a pluralistic society, citizens and officials might hesitate before adopting any new practices along these lines. They might be more candid about what they are doing, rather than relying on weak arguments based on a "tradition" of government practices that have always been controversial,[9] or on a concept—"ceremonial deism"—that is "unconvincing both

---

8. To be clear, I do not mean by this that government's statements should openly *advocate* religious agnosticism; only that government's statements should remain in a suspension of ontological commitments, refusing to declare a position on fundamental questions of religious truth.

9. *See, e.g., McCreary County v. ACLU of Ky.*, 545 U.S. 844, 878–881 (2005); *Marsh v. Chambers*, 463 U.S. 783, 806–08 (1983) (Brennan, J., dissenting).

to serious nonbelievers and to serious believers."[10] We cannot have a meaningful debate about these practices if it is not an honest debate.

ADVANTAGES AND POSSIBILITIES

All of these conclusions are underwritten by the same basic insight. Strategies of avoidance of questions of religious truth, if they were ever truly successful, no longer are. At best, they rest on a foundation—the conventional liberal consensus—that is no longer a genuine consensus, and that is especially fragile in a world of deep and abiding pluralism. At worst, they rest on no foundation at all.

Questions of religious truth, in short, can't be avoided. What can't be avoided ought to be confronted—as openly, honestly, and humbly as we can manage. The constitutional agnostic may suspend any final judgment on questions of religious truth, but he refuses to pretend those questions don't exist, or that they can be wished away by invoking controversial "shared" liberal premises.

This move is necessary in our age. Whatever theory of religious freedom we come up with must be capable of negotiating a path between the religious and the secular that respects both, but does not award a final victory to either. We must explore and incorporate a variety of views, both secular and religious, if religious liberty is to be either intellectually or practically sustainable.

As Mark Modak-Truran has observed, neither a "unitary religious" nor a unitary "secular" vision of law or society is likely to succeed alone.[11] A secular or liberal vision is unsustainable: It is fundamentally in tension with its own premises, and no longer commands the deep allegiance of a wide enough spectrum of society. Today, the secularist liberal order can succeed only by fiat, only by proclaiming itself the victor and suppressing its competitors.[12] That might be what the New Atheists hope for. But if the resurgence of religious belief in the public square in the past few decades, its "deprivatization," [13] whether in mild or violent forms, has shown us anything, it is that secularism cannot hope to win even by force.

10. Douglas Laycock, *Theology Scholarships, the Pledge of Allegiance, and Religious Liberty: Avoiding the Extremes but Missing the Liberty*, 118 Harv. L. Rev. 155, 235 (2004); *see also* Steven H. Shiffrin, *The Pluralistic Foundations of the Religion Clauses*, 90 Cornell L. Rev. 9, 71 (2004) (pretending that obviously religious statements "are not religious is simply insulting").

11. Mark C. Modak-Truran, *Beyond Theocracy and Secularism (Part I): Toward a New Paradigm for Law and Religion*, 27 Miss. Coll. L. Rev. 159, 231 (2007–2008).

12. For thoughtful discussion of these issues, *see* Robert M. Cover, *Foreword:* Nomos *and Narrative*, 97 Harv. L. Rev. 4 (1983).

13. *See generally* José Casanova, *Public Religions in the Modern World* (1994).

Nor can a unitary religious vision succeed. For one thing, there *is* no "unitary" religious vision anymore—not in our society, at least. Religious belief is too varied in a pluralist age for a single religious vision to hold sway. Even generic terms like "monotheist" conceal more differences than they describe. And, of course, this is not the only option; there are many other ways of believing. Many religious individuals would prefer pluralism and freedom of religious choice to the dominance of their own faith. But even those who do want their own faith to prevail over all the others are unlikely to succeed in a pluralist age.

Both the religious and the secular approaches, in short, "fail[ ] to take religious pluralism seriously."[14] In an age of "contestation, in which every position is rendered uneasy and questionable because it can be challenged from many angles,"[15] monistic solutions are doomed. It is not necessary to show that this will be true everywhere, in all times and places. What is important is that monism, whether secular or religious, is likely to fail *here and now*, in *our* time. No single set of values or principles is likely to offer a viable approach to religious freedom in our pluralistic society. Religious freedom today must stand or fall on its capacity to recognize and confront the question of religious truth, particularly under conditions of extraordinary pluralism.

That is what constitutional agnosticism offers. It is important to note one last time that although constitutional agnosticism is partly inspired by the new agnosticism, and certainly draws on many of the same social currents that led to the new agnosticism, it is not a religious worldview of its own. Constitutional agnosticism does *not* require those who subscribe to it to abandon their own religious views. It does not require a single atheist to abandon her faith in the nonexistence of God, or a single theist to forswear his equally fervent certainty in the existence of God.

Some readers may find the vision of religious agnosticism offered in these pages attractive. Some may conclude that the empathetic new agnosticism I have described captures their own views and become enthusiastic converts. Some may reaffirm their own religious beliefs or unbeliefs but discover to their surprise that doubt, or agnosis, is equally at home within both religious and secular worldviews.[16] Others may not become converts to the new agnosticism as such, but may conclude it still has something to offer in our public conversation: a neglected perspective in the pitched battle between the New Atheists and the New Anti-Atheists, and a way of reaching a cooling-off point in the religious culture wars.[17] If this book makes any converts to the new agnosticism, however, that will be a wholly incidental and unlooked-for effect. I would be overjoyed if

---

14. Modak-Truran, *supra* note 11, at 231.

15. Charles Taylor, *Afterword*, in *Varieties of Secularism in a Secular Age* 300, 306 (Michael Warner, Jonathan VanAntwerpen, & Craig Calhoun eds., 2010).

16. *See* Stephen White, *A Space for Unknowing: The Place of Agnosis in Faith* (2007).

17. *See* Chapter Four.

we could reclaim the debate over religious truth from the sterile impasse between the New Commissars of Enlightenment, and find new ways of incorporating the voice of doubt into that debate. But I will be just as content if readers with strong convictions about religious truth, whether they believe in God's existence or nonexistence, disclaim any interest in *religious* agnosticism but focus instead on the virtues of *constitutional* agnosticism. In many respects, these strong believers are the readers I most hope to reach.

What is constitutional agnosticism, if it is not a belief system or a worldview? It is a strategy, an attitude, a response. It addresses the simple fact of pluralism and the withering away of the liberal consensus. It is a way of responding to the enormous diversity of religious beliefs in our pluralistic age: to the fact that this diversity is apparent and salient to all of us, and that the very question of religious truth is finally unavoidable.

It is not an attempt to *answer* the question of religious truth, whether with a yes, a no, or even a maybe. If there is a cardinal sin for the constitutional agnostic, it is not belief or unbelief. It is indifference: indifference to the fact of religious pluralism and diversity, and to the pressing need to find an approach to religious liberty and social coexistence that encompasses that diversity of belief. It is unalterably opposed to the kind of indifference that believes we can deal with the question of religious truth by privatizing it, by shunting it off to the side, or by pretending it doesn't exist or is unimportant. Constitutional agnosticism honors Pontius Pilate's question—"What is truth?"—but condemns Pilate's shrug.

Instead, constitutional agnosticism demands that we take on, at least provisionally, a "layered" sense of the existence of multiple beliefs in our social world. It requires us to recognize the importance of attempting to understand and empathize with the worldviews and truth-claims of others, and to give full weight to those views when we shape the legal rules that apply to all of us. It does not require us to pit our own religious beliefs, or those of others, against the "public good." Instead, it requires us to form our view of the public good with an appreciation of others' diverse perspectives in mind.

The result is an approach to religious freedom that offers some hope of negotiating and responding to the present conditions of our age. It does so not by hazarding an answer to the question of religious truth, but by acknowledging the possibility of religious truth and the sheer fact of religious diversity, while provisionally suspending any specific commitments about what that religious truth is. In this way, it seeks to bring everyone into the conversation. It rejects the idea that questions of religious truth are or can be purely private. It suggests that our conclusions about what religious truth is, and what it compels, matter to us, both individually and as a larger society. It argues that the best way for the state to respond to this fact is with an "interested and sympathetic agnosticism."[18]

---

18. Andrew Koppelman, *Corruption of Religion and the Establishment Clause*, 50 Wm. & Mary L. Rev. 1831, 1907 (2009).

The possibility offered by this approach is that, if they adopt the agnostic habit, citizens, lawmakers, and judges alike can find an approach to religious liberty that will be more coherent, consistent, and justified than the competing accounts of religious liberty that have been offered so far. Because these individuals can maintain their own religious beliefs, it will be a second-order strategy. It will be only one layer in our understanding of the world. But that layer marks an important, perhaps even an essential, step forward in the story of religious liberty. It means that our approach to religious liberty will be underwritten by a respect for the possibility of religious truth rather than a futile attempt to avoid it altogether. It will not depend on an increasingly fragile liberal consensus. Instead, it will rely on a meaningful acknowledgment of and response to pluralism.

The result, as we have seen in the preceding pages, is a regime of religious liberty that is characterized by both a broadly permissive approach to religious practice and a deeply constrained state. The approach of decision makers—whether judges, lawmakers, or citizens—to questions of religious belief and practice will be empathetic and imaginative. It will avoid the statism that so often characterizes the Free Exercise Clause today, in which judges and others cannot quite bring themselves to take seriously the *truth* of religious truth-claims when weighing them against the needs of the state. At the same time, government itself will be constrained when it comes to questions arising under the Establishment Clause. It will be disabled from imposing an absolute rule of separationism, and instead will be required to treat all requests for government aid equally. But it will also be disabled from making official statements in favor of or against one view of religious truth or another. In both cases, the rule that applies will be underwritten by the same concerns: a genuine respect for the possibility of religious truth, and a meaningful response to conditions of religious pluralism.

We cannot predict the future. The notion that secularization is inevitable, that religion will gradually fade away, seems to have been refuted, given the resurgence of religious belief and its increasing emergence from the private sphere to which liberalism consigned it.[19] Still, things change. Perhaps, fifty or a hundred years from now, the withering away of religious belief that many thought was just around the corner will finally arrive. Or it may be that secularism and secularization themselves will be the losers. We may become, as the Pledge of Allegiance says, "one nation under God"—whichever God that turns out to be.

But that is not our concern. As the Gospel of Matthew says, "Sufficient unto the day is the evil thereof."[20] All we can say for now is that the existing theories

---

19. *See, e.g.,* Peter Berger & Anton Zijderveld, *In Praise of Doubt: How to Have Convictions Without Becoming a Fanatic* 4 (2009); Casanova, *supra* note 13.

20. Matt. 6:34.

of religious freedom, however far along they may have brought us, can no longer keep the peace or deliver what they promised. They can no longer keep pace with the conditions of our own age—call it a secular age, a post-secular age, an agnostic age, or what you will. Constitutional agnosticism hopes to succeed where its competitors have failed.

QUESTIONS AND PROBLEMS

Some of what I say in this book has had a rhapsodic quality. Although I have no interest in proselytizing for religious agnosticism as such—although, indeed, I have attempted to say nothing about my own religious beliefs—I have tried to make the best possible case for a particular brand of "new" agnosticism, if only because that voice is so often missing from the debates over religious truth that embroil our society. If I do not seek to make converts to *religious* agnosticism, however, I certainly wish to put *constitutional* agnosticism in the best possible light. Although my argument for constitutional agnosticism is not perfectionist—that is, I do not pretend it is capable of solving every problem, of tying church–state relations together with a neat and tidy bow—I have certainly argued that it is the strongest basis for a sound theory of religious liberty.

No account of religious freedom can attain perfection, however. Every attempt to resolve church–state conflicts will have its problems; every regime will have its dissenters. Constitutional agnosticism tries to answer these questions in the best possible way. But it is no panacea.

Let us take a close look at some of the possible objections and problems that confront constitutional agnosticism. I will not suggest that these objections are capable of absolute refutation. To the contrary, although I think some of them are weaker than they may appear at first blush, they raise deep and lasting questions about the sufficiency of this or any other theory of religious freedom, and they are worth considering, fully and in a proper spirit of humility. Call them the liberalism objection, the religious objection, and the incommensurability objection.

What is striking about the first two objections is that they attack constitutional agnosticism from diametrically opposed positions. The liberalism objection argues that constitutional agnosticism is possible but unnecessary, while the religious objection argues that it may be necessary but is impossible. I will argue that both objections, although important, are mistaken. The incommensurability objection, by contrast, is deeper and more troubling, but it is too broad. The problem of incommensurability afflicts every approach to church-state relations. Like the other approaches, constitutional agnosticism cannot defeat it. But it may be able to acknowledge it more candidly and address it with greater success than its competitors do.

THE LIBERALISM OBJECTION

The liberalism objection consists of two overlapping arguments. The first is that constitutional agnosticism gives short shrift to both the variety and the depth of liberal ideas, reducing liberalism unfairly to a straw man. A second and related objection is that by caricaturing liberalism, constitutional agnosticism fails to see that at least some forms of liberalism are in fact wholly compatible with it. Constitutional agnosticism, on this view, is not an adversary of liberalism; if anything, it is just liberalism under a different label. Let us set out each of these objections in greater depth before responding.

The first part of the argument is that liberalism deserves better than the skeptical and sometimes dismissive treatment it has been given in this book. Much of liberalism's virtue is its adaptability, its capacity to respond to changing circumstances and mediate among a variety of competing interests and worldviews. Its own longevity is a testament to its success at absorbing its critics' blows and responding to changes in the social environment. In particular, liberalism need not be viewed as antagonistic toward pluralism. To the contrary, under some forms of "thick or comprehensive liberalism, tolerance, pluralism, and mutual respect are not merely the background conditions for social cooperation; they are affirmative goods in themselves."[21] On this view, "liberal democracy is, among other things, a kind of strategy for addressing the challenge of pluralism that characterizes the modern Western world."[22] In fact, pluralism "provides a rational and ethical foundation for liberalism: if pluralism is true it gives us a set of reasons to support a liberal form of politics."[23]

The second part of the objection, which is related to the first, argues that by reducing liberalism to something of a caricature, constitutional agnosticism misses the fact that it does exactly what liberalism does. Just as constitutional agnosticism is intended to be compatible with a broad range of religious beliefs, including nonbelief, so some forms of liberalism are consistent with a broad range of beliefs and nonbeliefs.

This approach is said to be the hallmark of what John Rawls called "political liberalism."[24] Political liberalism takes as a given that a "modern democratic society is characterized . . . by a pluralism of comprehensive religious, philosophical, and moral doctrines."[25] In the face of this pluralism, it seeks an

---

21. Michael C. Dorf, *God and Man in the Yale Dormitories*, 84 Va. L. Rev. 843, 846 (1998).

22. Steven D. Smith, *Educating for Liberalism*, 42 U.C. Davis L. Rev. 1039, 1042 (2009) (referring to what he calls "detachment liberalism").

23. George Crowder, *Pluralism, Liberalism, and Distributive Justice*, 46 San Diego L. Rev. 773, 776 (2009).

24. John Rawls, *Political Liberalism* (1993).

25. *Id.* at xvi.

approach to basic questions of political justice that can win support among a variety of individuals who hold different comprehensive views.[26]

Its answer to this dilemma is to propose a political philosophy, political liberalism, that is "impartial ... between the points of view of reasonable comprehensive doctrines."[27] "Which moral judgments are true, all things considered, is not a matter for political liberalism," Rawls writes.[28] Instead, political liberalism proceeds by setting out a basic set of rules for a just state that can command "an overlapping consensus of reasonable comprehensive doctrines," and by requiring public discussion on "constitutional essentials and questions of basic justice" to take place in terms of "public reason"—that is, in terms that are compatible with "society's conception of political justice" and broadly accessible to people holding a variety of comprehensive views.[29] In terms that sound somewhat similar to constitutional agnosticism, political liberalism is meant to be what Rawls calls "a module, an essential constituent part, that in different ways fits into and can be supported by various reasonable comprehensive doctrines that endure in the society regulated by it."[30]

In short, the argument goes, political liberalism is really just a form of constitutional agnosticism. More to the point, constitutional agnosticism is just political liberalism relabeled. Anywhere constitutional agnosticism goes, it will find political liberalism's flag already planted there. Broad protection for religious practice? We've got that. Distribution of government aid on an evenhanded basis? No problem. Restrictions on government statements about religious truth? You bet—check Aisle Four. And if we haven't got it—say, the right to sacrifice your son—you probably don't want it anyway.

There are a variety of more or less stringent responses to the liberalism objection. The first is to clarify the ground on which constitutional agnosticism proceeds. Its main focus is not liberalism in all its senses—and there are many senses, many definitions of liberalism,[31] so many that liberalism has been called an "essentially contested concept" for which no generally agreed upon definition is possible.[32] Its focus is not liberalism as it has been described and defended at the most sophisticated and rarefied levels, but liberalism at its most basic and

---

26. Rawls's famous statement of this dilemma is as follows: "How is it possible that there may exist over time a stable and just society of free and equal citizens profoundly divided by reasonable though incompatible religious, philosophical, and moral doctrines?" *Id.* at xviii.

27. *Id.* at xix.

28. *Id.* at xx.

29. *Id.* at 44, 213.

30. *Id.* at 144–45.

31. *See id.* at 223 ("there are many liberalisms").

32. *See* Larry Alexander, *Liberalism, Religion, and the Unity of Epistemology*, 30 San Diego L. Rev. 763, 765 (1993). On essentially contested concepts, see W.B. Gallie, *Essentially Contested Concepts*, 56 Proc. of the Aristotelian Soc. 167, 169 (1956) (defining essentially

widely understood level. It is liberalism not as an *ideal* overlapping consensus, but as an *actual* social consensus, a public philosophy[33] that everyone accepts (more or less) as a reasonable compromise, not because it comports absolutely with their own comprehensive views.

Hence the metaphor of the liberal consensus as treaty. Like a treaty, the liberal consensus as popularly understood is what Rawls calls "a mere modus vivendi," a provisional agreement between different sides whose "aims and interests put them at odds" and who might reject the treaty if conditions changed to give one party the advantage.[34] Rawls has grander ambitions for political liberalism than that, although some of his critics have asked whether a modus vivendi is so bad and whether we can really expect anything better.[35] But our project here is more practical. It is not to ask whether liberalism as a philosophy is capable of being perfected in some intellectual laboratory, but whether the liberal consensus we actually have is consistent, coherent, and in good health.

On that score, few if any liberal philosophers are willing to let the perfect be the ally of the bad, so to speak. They acknowledge that liberalism as it is generally, if crudely, understood suffers from a number of inconsistencies—that it is incapable of being resolutely neutral, that it forswears any reliance on a particular conception of the good but smuggles in a host of substantive values, that in its non-ideal form it is unable to avoid questions of religious truth, and so on. And those who descend to a worldly level from the empyrean heights are willing to concede that the liberal consensus, in its non-ideal form, runs into a host of practical difficulties as a result: that even if the cracks in its basic structure were not apparent, an increasing number of groups and individuals in an age in which both liberalism and secularism have faded in popularity are likely to reject the terms of that treaty, or accept them only in a lukewarm fashion. Indeed, that is one reason that Rawls the theoretician rejects any approach to liberal politics that constitutes a "mere" modus vivendi. He recognizes that it is too fragile to persist indefinitely.[36] But the liberal consensus, as it is actually understood and practiced, *is* a modus vivendi; and although Rawls may overstate the instability of such a working arrangement, he is right to be skeptical about its prospects. To the extent that this book expresses some skepticism about the coherence and

---

contested concepts as concepts "the proper use of which inevitably involves endless disputes about their proper uses on the part of their users").

33. *See, e.g.,* Mark Tushnet, *A Public Philosophy for the Professional-Managerial Class,* 106 Yale L.J. 1571 (1997).

34. Rawls, *supra* note 24, at 147.

35. *See, e.g.,* Nelson Tebbe, *Witchcraft and Statecraft: Liberal Democracy in Africa,* 96 Geo. L.J. 183, 210 n.174 (2007) (collecting examples); Eduardo M. Peñalver, *Is Public Reason Counterproductive?,* 110 W. Va. L. Rev. 515, 543 (2007); John Gray, *Two Faces of Liberalism* (2001); Douglas G. Smith, *The Illiberalism of Liberalism: Religious Discourse in the Public Square,* 34 San Diego L. Rev. 1571, 1619–20 (1997).

36. *See* Rawls, *supra* note 24, at 147–48.

long-term viability of the liberal consensus as it is generally understood, then, liberals should agree with it rather than treat it as a cause for criticism.

Suppose, however, that we accept the existence of more sophisticated forms of liberalism than the popular form of the liberal consensus. What does constitutional agnosticism have to say to *those* forms of liberalism? The answer is that it depends on the form of liberalism we are talking about. Following the usual custom, we can divide liberalism into two forms: comprehensive and political liberalism. Comprehensive liberalism "affirms liberal political arrangements in the name of certain moral ideals, such as autonomy or individuality or self-reliance."[37] It "favor[s] some conceptions of the good life over others."[38] In partial contrast to the kind of procedural liberalism that writers like Stanley Fish, Steven Smith, and Larry Alexander argue hides the ball, comprehensive liberalism is up-front about asserting a particular set of values.

There are three major problems with this approach. First, it conflicts with what the standard understanding of liberalism asserts—namely, that liberalism is neutral as to its conception of the good. This could, of course, simply mean that the comprehensive liberals are right, and that the popular and crude conception of liberalism as neutral on these questions is wrong. But since we live under the popular conception of liberalism, or at least purport to live under it, that is an important point. It suggests just what I argued in Chapter One: that the current liberal consensus suffers from serious inconsistencies. Second, it reinforces the other point made in that chapter: that liberalism, at least as it is generally and popularly understood, cannot escape the need to reach a conclusion on questions of religious truth. To say that autonomy, individuality, self-reliance, or any other value is *the* value, the lodestar around which our society *must* be constructed, is to "take sides in the moral and religious controversies that arise from comprehensive doctrines."[39] Again, this cannot be consistent with the liberal consensus as generally understood, which is supposed to be a way of remaining neutral between the different conceptions of religious truth that were responsible for social discord in the first place. This is the very struggle that the liberal consensus was supposed to quell, and by its own lights it cannot do so by simply taking sides and enforcing a particular understanding of religious truth against its adversaries.[40]

This leads to the third and, for practical purposes, the most important point. The point is simple: the comprehensive approach cannot succeed, except perhaps by force of arms. It was problematic enough to imagine that it would prevail even under conditions in which religious beliefs were relatively tame and private

---

37. Michael J. Sandel, *Political Liberalism*, 107 Harv. L. Rev. 1765, 1771 (1994).

38. Steven H. Shiffrin, *The Religious Left and Church-State Relations* 216 n.45 (2009). Shiffrin refers to these sorts of comprehensive liberals as "perfectionist liberals."

39. Sandel, *supra* note 37, at 1771.

40. This is what Rawls calls "the fact of oppression." Rawls, *supra* note 24, at 37.

and most people were glad to sign on to the liberal treaty. In the present age, however, under present conditions of religious vitality and pluralism, as well as internal disagreements within liberalism itself about *which* value is the "right" comprehensive value around which liberal thought should orient itself, that hope seems even more forlorn. Any form of liberalism that asserts that it has not only the right answer as to how we should govern ourselves, but also the right answer to the question what we should believe and value, is bound to produce conflict, not consensus.[41] And so it does, at an increasing rate. This is not to say that any particular comprehensive liberalism is *wrong*. Naturally, I remain agnostic on that question. It's simply to say—and it's saying plenty—that comprehensive liberalism, in whatever form, cannot simply win over by argument those who hold alternative understandings of religious truth or the nature of the good.[42] In an "agnostic age" of significant religious pluralism, comprehensive liberalism is unlikely to be able to stem the tide of disagreement.

The other form of liberalism, political liberalism, brings us back to Rawls. Political liberalism, as we have seen, asserts that it *does* remain neutral as to various conceptions of the good and various religious and other comprehensive doctrines, or at least those comprehensive doctrines that are "reasonable." It insists that it does *not* take sides in favor of or against any reasonable comprehensive doctrine. Instead, it arrives at a set of basic rules and structures that allow the greatest number of reasonable people to arrive at an overlapping consensus, without having to sacrifice their own deeply held beliefs about questions of religious truth.

Rawls, and political liberalism, have had their fair share of critics, despite the undeniable influence Rawls has had on modern liberal thought. Some of those criticisms are highly relevant to this book and what it has to say about the ineluctability of questions of religious truth. Many critics, for example, argue that political liberalism doesn't exist: that it inevitably takes sides of its own, and thus collapses into a form of comprehensive liberalism, with all the problems of dissent and rejection that any such approach must face in a society like ours.[43]

---

41. *See* Ronald C. Den Otter, *Can a Liberal Take His Own Side in an Argument? The Case for John Rawls's Idea of Political Liberalism*, 49 St. Louis U. L.J. 319, 337–38 (2005).

42. *See id.* at 338 (arguing that comprehensive liberalism "seems to be dismissive of the way in which those who have nonliberal conceptions understand the value of their own lives," and that it is unlikely to convince them to agree to it).

43. *See, e.g.,* Jeff Spinner-Halev, *Liberalism and Religion: Against Congruence*, 9 Theoretical Inquiries L. 553 (2008); Ruth Abbey, *Back Towards a Comprehensive Liberalism?*, 35 Pol. Theory 5 (2007); Abner S. Greene, *Government of the Good*, 53 Vand. L. Rev. 1 (2000); Eamon Callan, *Creating Citizens: Political and Liberal Democracy* (1997); Robert Justin Lipkin, *In Defense of Outlaws: Liberalism and the Role of Reasonableness, Public Reason, and Tolerance in Multicultural Constitutionalism*, 45 DePaul L. Rev. 263 (1996); Stephen Macedo, *Liberal Civic Education and Religious Fundamentalism: The Case of God v. John Rawls*, 105 Ethics 468 (1995); Harry Brighouse, *Is There Any Such Thing as Political*

Similarly, many critics argue that by stipulating a concern only with "reasonable" comprehensive doctrines, defined in such a way as to rule out of bounds those who "insist, when fundamental political questions are at stake, . . . that their beliefs alone are true,"[44] political liberalism ends up excluding "a much larger and more important group of comprehensive views than Rawls believes."[45] These two criticisms converge around a third criticism, one that goes to the heart of this book: Where questions of ultimate *truth* are concerned, "it is not always reasonable to bracket, or set aside for political purposes, claims arising from within comprehensive moral and religious doctrines. Where grave moral questions are concerned, whether it is reasonable to bracket moral and religious controversies for the sake of political agreement *partly depends on which of the contending moral or religious doctrines is true.*"[46] In some cases, it just might be that the truth of such a doctrine ought to be enough to "burst the brackets . . . and morally outweigh" liberal political values such as toleration and fairness.[47]

I find these criticisms of political liberalism, and others,[48] deeply compelling, but I am far from confident in my own power to demonstrate the validity of my misgivings. My response to political liberalism here will be more in the nature of a confession and avoidance. To the extent that political liberalism, whether Rawls's version or some other, *is* consistent with constitutional agnosticism, I see no reason to shrink from the label. Although I have had critical things to say about the popular understanding of liberalism represented by the liberal consensus or treaty, this book is not a brief against liberalism as such—at least if liberalism is defined as a bona fide approach to coexistence in a pluralist society that directly confronts questions of religious truth rather than attempting to avoid them altogether. Since that is the very goal of constitutional agnosticism, it would seem churlish at least to reject prospective allies just because they insist on attaching a different name to the project. I think few self-described political liberals would in fact agree with this definition; they would more likely insist that the goal remains one of avoiding questions of religious truth, not confronting them. But if I am mistaken, I welcome their company, no matter what banner they march under. I think political liberals of this stripe can still learn a great deal from constitutional agnosticism: namely, how we might address questions

---

Liberalism?, 75 Pac. Phil. Q. 318 (1994); Abner S. Greene, *Uncommon Ground*, 62 Geo. Wash. L. Rev. 646 (1994).

44. Rawls, *supra* note 24, at 61.

45. Miriam A. Galston, *Rawlsian Dualism and the Autonomy of Political Thought*, 94 Colum. L. Rev. 1842, 1844 (1994)

46. Sandel, *supra* note 37, at 1776 (emphasis added).

47. *Id.* at 1777.

48. For a useful list, one that describes only the "first wave" of criticism of Rawls's *Political Liberalism*, see Heidi M. Hurd, *The Levitation of Liberalism*, 105 Yale L.J. 795, 803–05 (1995).

of church-state conflict in an empathetic way that acknowledges and confronts questions of religious truth rather than simply asserting or concealing some comprehensive conclusion of its own. Nor, I hope, will religious believers of a non-liberal stripe who are inclined to accept constitutional agnosticism reject such allies, at least if those allies are sincere about acknowledging and confronting questions of religious truth rather than bracketing them.

That said, there are still three good practical reasons to think in terms of constitutional agnosticism, whether as an adjunct to liberalism, political or otherwise, or as a replacement. The first has to do with attention to detail. Constitutional agnosticism offers a number of specific conclusions about how we ought to address church-state conflicts under both of the Religion Clauses. It is possible that some or many of those conclusions could be arrived at through a liberal position, or through the conventional positions currently taken by the courts (which is saying much the same thing). At the "abstract plane" of "high moral theory" at which philosophical liberalism dwells, however, there are few concrete answers to specific problems.[49]

Constitutional agnosticism, which dwells closer to the earth, attempts to provide clearer answers to the actual church-state conflicts that confront us than liberalism does. Liberalism is fully consistent in theory with, for example, the lamentably restrictive version of free exercise rights in *Employment Division v. Smith*, which fails the test of constitutional agnosticism. If anything, liberalism has to contort itself in order to accommodate religious exercise in the way that cases like *Sherbert v. Verner* or *Wisconsin v. Yoder* did. Those who are sympathetic to some form of "political liberalism" that recognizes rather than obscures questions of religious truth, and who want to explore what such an approach might mean in practical terms, may find some of the concrete answers they seek in constitutional agnosticism. Where they do not find definite answers, as in the case of Abraham and Isaac, they may at least find humility and candor—candor about the inability of *any* theory to bridge the tragic choices that confront us in this area, rather than a Gatsbyesque assertion that if we could just theorize a little harder, we could reach a final and perfect resolution of these questions.[50]

The second reason that constitutional agnosticism is worth pursuing, despite the arguments that it is just liberalism relabeled, is that there *is* an important difference between them. The primary goal of constitutional agnosticism is not to get to the right results, but to offer the best *justification* for those results. That means the justification that is the most internally consistent, and the most consistent with the conditions of modern pluralism in our agnostic age. That is the task at which most versions of liberalism arguably fail, for both theoretical and practical reasons, although the practical reasons are of more concern to us here.

---

49. Richard A. Posner, *The Problematics of Moral and Legal Theory* 47, 59 (1999).

50. *See* F. Scott Fitzgerald, *The Great Gatsby* 144 (Ruth Prigozy ed., Oxford Univ. Press 1998) (1925).

We have covered the theoretical problem already. The popular liberal consensus purports to remain neutral on questions of religious truth but, because it ultimately smuggles in a host of substantive values and positions touching on these questions, it cannot. (As we have seen, some critics argue that the same is true of more sophisticated forms of political liberalism as well.)

But we need not resolve that theoretical problem to see that there is a deeper practical problem, one that afflicts all forms of liberalism and makes constitutional agnosticism all the more urgent. At a practical level, too many people are unwilling to sign on to any liberal theory of religious freedom that proceeds from contested values like equality, neutrality, or justice, however much they might like the results those theories offer. Rightly or wrongly, they see all forms of liberalism as failing to give proper respect to the possibility of religious truth. They believe that liberalism either ignores that possibility altogether (the liberal consensus), or asserts a primary value other than religious truth (comprehensive liberalism), or respects religion only in a limited fashion, excluding a variety of beliefs and arguments that liberalism insists are "unreasonable" (political liberalism). If we are to retain the loyalty and commitment of those individuals, what is needed is an approach that *starts* from religious truth rather than seeking to avoid it. Even if constitutional agnosticism ends up suspending an ultimate commitment to any particular religious truth, it is still likely to command wider agreement in an agnostic age than an approach that treats religious truth-claims as irrelevant or private, as just one more set of beliefs to be factored into the overlapping consensus, or as potentially "unreasonable."

None of this is to say that any of these forms of liberalism is necessarily wrong at the level of theory. But at a practical level, these approaches are unlikely to command widespread consensus in an agnostic age, one in which a variety of religious views are at large in society and refuse to simply retreat to the private sphere. It may be true that liberalism, in whatever form, has largely succeeded in keeping the peace so far, and some may argue that it is still getting the job done.[51] But, for the reasons we canvassed in Chapters One and Three and that are captured in José Casanova's description of the "deprivatization" of religion,[52] we can no longer rest assured that this state of affairs will continue. Claims that "[n]o one of any consequence outside the academy worries about the foundations of liberal democracy, or whether it has any," are no longer true.[53] Increasing numbers of religious individuals and groups inside and outside the liberal sphere, and increasing numbers of liberals themselves, question some or all

---

51. *See* Posner, *supra* note 49, at 59 (arguing that "[l]iberal democracy is not under attack from people who have any political heft," and that "[t]he only worriers are academics, and they worry at a level of abstraction that has no political significance").

52. Casanova, *supra* note 13, at 65–66.

53. Posner, *supra* note 49, at 59.

forms of liberal justifications for our church-state settlement that avoid rather than confront questions of religious truth, and seek a justification that does justice to their concern. However imperfectly, constitutional agnosticism seeks to address those concerns. In an agnostic age, it may capture more consensus than the alternatives can.

This leads to the final practical reason to defend constitutional agnosticism against the liberal objection, a reason that has to do with language and dialogue. We have already seen that the liberal consensus, as generally understood—the version of liberalism that has the widest popular understanding—is flawed by its inability to keep its own promise to refrain from asserting a particular religious truth or conception of the good. But even if liberalism can be salvaged at the level of high theory, it is not clear how productive that enterprise can be. The debate at that level can be "increasingly hermetic and esoteric."[54] "Most liberal theorists," Robert Justin Lipkin writes, "spend their energies defending various forms of liberalism against attack from other liberals."[55] Jeffrey Stout adds: "We might even come to think of 'liberalism' as the name for a particular kind of obsolete ideology whose critics and defenders thought there was something worth calling *the* liberal project and who therefore engaged in fruitless debates over whether it was a good or a bad thing."[56]

One gets a sense that these debates over liberalism have reached a point of exhaustion, or at least of diminishing returns. "The very term [liberalism]," Stout writes, "may at this point be blocking the path of inquiry."[57] Whatever the fate of the liberal debate in rarefied circles may be, in our own age we may need other language, other modes of thinking, to succeed in capturing consensus at a practical level. Recall Keats's words, which we encountered in Chapter Three: "What shocks the virtuous philosopher delights the [chameleon] poet."[58] In our own agnostic age, we may have more need of chameleon poets than virtuous philosophers.

There is something to be said, then, not for defending or attacking liberalism, in whatever form, but for finding new language that may yet hope to resonate and persuade in an agnostic age—in an age of resurgent and varied religious beliefs and nonbeliefs. In such an age, the model we need is one of respectful but unbracketed conversation informed by negative capability. It is one, says Jeffrey Stout, in which our model of conversation should be twofold. Each of us is entitled to state our own views and reasons, even if they involve religious or other comprehensive truth-claims; where those claims conflict, each of us should attempt to engage in "fair-minded, nonmanipulative, sincere immanent

54. *Id.*
55. Lipkin, *supra* note 43, at 333.
56. Jeffrey Stout, *Democracy and Tradition* 130 (2004).
57. *Id.*
58. Walter Jackson Bate, *Negative Capability: The Intuitive Approach in Keats* 31 (1976).

criticism against one's opponent's reasons."[59] In other words, we must acknowledge questions of religious truth and bring them out into the open, both voicing our own truth-claims and attempting to understand and answer, from an *internal* perspective, the truth-claims of others. To succeed in this model of conversation, we will need the Keatsian poet's skill at humility and empathy: humility about our own point of view and its ability to persuade those who do not share it, and empathy in trying to occupy and understand the points of views of others.[60]

That is what constitutional agnosticism offers. It is a way of thinking about dialogue in an agnostic age, a dialogue that respectfully and empathetically confronts the religious truth-claims that surround us and cannot be bracketed or ignored; and it is a way of thinking about what this dialogic model says about the constitutional resolution of church-state conflicts. Whether we conclude that it is consistent or inconsistent with one or another form of liberalism is less important than the possibility that it may move the dialogue *forward*. It is more likely to command the allegiance of a wider group of people in an agnostic age, in which the vocabulary of liberalism itself may serve as a stumbling block than a rallying point. It may be imperfect, but it is worth trying.

So my responses to the liberalism objection are varied—appropriately so, given that there are "many liberalisms"[61]—but they lead to roughly the same place. To the extent that we focus on the liberal consensus as broadly understood, few liberals would disagree that this consensus *does* face serious internal inconsistencies and practical difficulties. To the extent that we focus on comprehensive liberalisms, there is reason to doubt that those approaches can satisfy their many objectors, at least in a pluralistic age. *If* political liberalism succeeds where the other two brands of liberalism fail, *if* it is capable of respecting *and confronting* questions of religious truth, then it may well be consistent with constitutional agnosticism. But there may yet be reasons why constitutional agnosticism is worth pursuing: a desire for additional guidance and concrete details on how to resolve actual church-state conflicts, a desire to capture consensus in an age in which the liberal verities no longer command as much allegiance as they once did, and, not least, a sense of exhaustion in the very terms of the liberal debate and the need for a more empathetic model of dialogue.

---

59. Stout, *supra* note 56, at 85. Stout defines immanent criticism as one in which the critic "tr[ies] to show that their opponents' religious views are incoherent, or . . . to argue positively from their opponents' religious premises to the conclusion that the proposal [under debate] is acceptable [to the opponent]." What the interlocutor does *"not* do is argue from a purportedly common basis of reasons in Rawls's sense." *Id.* at 69 (emphasis added).

60. *See id.* at 73 ("Real respect for others takes seriously the distinctive point of view *each* other occupies.") (emphasis added).

61. Rawls, *supra* note 24, at 223.

THE RELIGIOUS OBJECTION

In my experience, the liberal objectors to constitutional agnosticism may think it is unnecessary, but they rarely question one of its fundamental premises: that it is both possible and important to attempt to imagine and understand the world-view of those who hold deep religious convictions. They do not doubt that it is possible to appreciate the perspective of religious individuals on questions of religious truth. Liberal efforts toward that end, as we have seen, can sometimes seem indifferent or half-hearted. It is easy enough for them to accord some religious belief a minimal level of respect as a claim of "conscience" without treating it as a matter of religious truth, or to profess an appreciation of that belief so long as the belief is "reasonable," or so long as it is understood that a secular set of state interests will still hold the upper hand. Nevertheless, none of these liberal objectors believe that an empathetic approach to questions of religious truth is impossible.

That is precisely what the religious objection contends. Religious objectors to constitutional agnosticism argue that it is ultimately impossible to make the imaginative leap into another person's religious perspective. Religious belief is too powerful and too comprehensive to be the subject of a moment's sport or a well-meaning fancy that we can hop in and out of that perspective.

That is particularly true for those who insist that a full appreciation of religious truth—of *the* religious truth, whatever it may be—requires not only adherence to a set of propositions about the world, but a complete surrender, a leap of faith or a moment of salvation or revelation. "Except a man be born again, he cannot see the kingdom of God," the New Testament tells us.[62] To *imagine* the truth without fully accepting and believing it will, at best, offer only a counterfeit of religious experience; at worst, it will be like asking someone who has been blind from birth to describe Van Gogh's *Starry Night*. For others, including those whose religious beliefs and practices are rooted in, say, an experience of community rather than strict faith or revelation, a religious life may be too all-encompassing a set of practices and traditions to be understood by outsiders. This objection may also be shared by atheists, who believe firmly that the ultimate religious truth is that there is no God. For them, asking a religious person to understand a thoroughly secular or atheist worldview is like asking the village idiot to explain the theory of relativity. For all of these objectors, the task that the constitutional agnostic sets himself is impossible at best, and sheer arrogance at worst. It's a form of religious tourism. We all know that no one likes a tourist.

All agnostics, whether religious or constitutional, must be deeply sensitive to this criticism. If they are sincere in their suspension of ontological commitments, they cannot know that they have *not* been badly misled by their

---

62. John 3:3.

imaginative exercise. They believe it is important to consider the possibility that a religious truth is out there. But they cannot say with certainty that, when they try to imagine another person's perspective on that truth, they are getting any-where close to occupying that person's perspective. They may be altogether wrong. Even if they are not, they may still have conjured up only a simulacrum of the truth, like the prisoners in Plato's cave who see only shadows and think they are seeing the real world.[63]

So the religious objection must be met in a spirit of deep humility and an acknowledgment of the possibility of failure. But although this objection is pow-erful, it is not unanswerable. There are three responses to the religious objec-tion. The first is the one I have made repeatedly throughout this book. *Constitutional* agnosticism does not require *religious* agnosticism. It requires only that we attempt to understand others' perspectives and try to appreciate what those perspectives might mean for our shaping of legal rules. It does not require us to share or even understand those perspectives completely. To the extent that a religious objector worries that constitutional agnosticism is a stalk-ing horse for religious agnosticism, that its covert goal is to win converts for the new agnosticism, that fear should be laid to rest.

Second, the constitutional agnostic would respond that although the religious objector *may* be right, he of all people should still appreciate the value of consti-tutional agnosticism, if only as a second-best strategy. Perhaps the religious objector believes the best outcome would be for everyone to adopt his own view of the religious truth, and for the law to reflect that view alone.[64] That is not the only possibility: A religious individual may believe that each person must be allowed to find his *own* religious truth, even at the risk of choosing a false belief.[65] But *some* religious individuals—and, as we have seen with the New Atheists, some nonbelievers—may indeed prefer victory to toleration.

In a deeply divided, diverse, and pluralist society, however, there is no guar-antee that one's own view will prevail. As a strategy or a modus vivendi, then, constitutional agnosticism may be the best that the religious objector can hope for. He does not agree with the premises that underlie liberalism—that there is such a thing as "liberal" neutrality or equality, or at least that these values can

---

63. Plato, *The Republic* 220–23 (G.R.F. Ferrari, ed., Tom Griffith trans., 2000).

64. *See, e.g.,* Larry Alexander, *Good God, Garvey! The Inevitability and Impossibility of a Religious Justification of Free Exercise Exemptions,* 47 Drake L. Rev. 35, 43 (1998) ("[T]here is no general religious point of view that sees compliance with imagined religious duties as good. Rather, there are particular religious points of view, each of which sees compliance with its own list of duties as good.").

65. *See, e.g.,* Vatican Council II, *Declaration on Religious Freedom, Dignitatis Humanae* (Dec. 7, 1965), available at http://www.ewtn.com/library/councils/v2relfre.htm. *See also* Kevin Seamus Hasson, *The Right to be Wrong: Ending the Culture War Over Religion in America* (2005).

exist independently of conclusions about fundamental questions of religious truth. So he will be reluctant to sign on to the liberal approach. But neither will he want to sign on to an approach that privileges some *other* view of religious truth over his own. His best bet, then, is to retain his own religious beliefs but look for an approach to religious freedom that takes *all* conceptions of religious truth seriously, including his own. Short of his own final victory, he ought to prefer a system, like constitutional agnosticism, that grants no one the final victory but is respectful to all versions of religious truth.

In fact, he may not even *want* a final victory. After all, constitutional agnosticism is not a theory of religious truth as such. Rather, it is a strategy of *coexistence* under conditions of pluralism. As we have seen, the denizens of an agnostic age retain their own religious beliefs, but are aware of the potential plasticity of religious belief, of the capacity for change in their own religious beliefs or in those of others. Even one who is absolutely convinced of the truth and immutability of his own religious beliefs, and the falsity of other beliefs, still recognizes that his friends and neighbors, with whom he has to live on a daily basis, hold differing views on these fundamental questions. In those circumstances, the religious objector might believe that constitutional agnosticism is the best way to respect and acknowledge his own beliefs, while creating ways to appreciate and coexist with others.[66] For a variety of reasons, then, the religious objector may conclude that constitutional agnosticism is the best way to respect both his own religious beliefs and those of others, even *if* he thinks that this approach is overconfident in asserting that one can really inhabit someone else's religious perspective.

Finally, and perhaps more controversially, the religious objector may not be as right as he thinks he is about the impossibility of empathetically inhabiting religious beliefs. He may not even be as right as he thinks about his *own* inability to adopt the agnostic habit. The ability to make this imaginative leap comes from two different but common activities. First, the religious individual, no matter how strongly he holds his own beliefs, has friends and neighbors who hold beliefs quite different from his own. Unless he has shut himself off completely in an enclave of like-minded individuals, he is likely to regularly encounter those others, usually quite amicably. Pluralism is not just a demographic fact. It is a habit of mind that may be far more ingrained in our own daily activities than the religious objector recognizes.

Second, the religious objector, like most of us, is likely to experience something of the imaginative spirit demanded by the agnostic habit when he interacts

---

66. Indeed, as we have seen, some religious individuals may hold this view not only for practical reasons, but for religious reasons as well. They may believe in respecting the religious views of others, even if those views are false, on *religious* grounds. In addition to the sources cited in the previous note, see, *e.g.*, John H. Garvey, *An Anti-Liberal Argument for Religious Freedom*, 7 J. Contemp. Legal Issues 275 (1996); Steven D. Smith, *The Rise and Fall of Religious Freedom in Constitutional Discourse*, 140 U. Pa. L. Rev. 149, 154 (1991).

with art. Acts of imagination, including the kind of negative capability that requires the temporary and partial effacement of our own identities, are common in our experience of art in an age built on more than two centuries of Romanticism. *Dumbo* and *Titanic* may not be great art, and to the religious objector they may certainly not approach the fullness of a genuinely religious experience. But in experiencing these and other art forms, the individual still makes an imaginative leap into the perspective of other characters—even flying elephants; even Billy Zane, for that matter.[67] This experience is so commonplace today that the religious objector may not appreciate its full force, or what it says about our capacity to make the kind of imaginative leap demanded by the agnostic habit. But it is there just the same.

Two caveats might be added to this argument. The religious objector might respond that, however much he appreciates art or attempts to understand the religious perspective of others, he always does so from a partial, or "encumbered," perspective.[68] Furthermore, art is not religion. However much we may appreciate art, it is far less possible to inhabit *religious* truth unless we make a total commitment to it.

He may be right, or he may be wrong. The constitutional agnostic resists making a final pronouncement on this question. The important thing is for the religious objector to recognize just how deep-seated this imaginative habit is, both in our dealings with others and in our experience of art. However imperfect it may be, it is far more common than he may have acknowledged, even to himself. More than he may recognize, we all already possess the cultural and imaginative tools to be constitutional agnostics.

Second, we must admit that some individuals and groups *do* live in comprehensive enclaves of religious belief.[69] This idea has been brought home forcefully, if often in a caricatured fashion, in the post-9/11 environment, in which the war on terror has been cast as a "clash of civilizations" between the liberal

---

67. Some readers may share my view that it is probably easier to inhabit the perspective of Dumbo than of Billy Zane. Of course, opinions may differ.

68. *See, e.g.*, Michael J. Sandel, *Democracy's Discontent: America in Search of a Public Philosophy* 14 (1996).

69. Some popular examples include the Satmar Hasidim, whose struggles with the broader society are described in *Board of Education of Kiryas Joel Village School District v. Grumet*, 512 U.S. 687 (1994), and the Rajneesh community, "who believed that the practice of their religion required that they live separately from others in a homogeneous society." Mark D. Rosen, *Multiple Authoritative Interpreters of Quasi-Constitutional Federal Law: Of Tribal Courts and the Indian Civil Rights Act*, 69 Fordham L. Rev. 479, 579 n.541 (2000). *See, e.g.*, Mark D. Rosen, *Searching for the Peaceable Kingdom*, 20 Const. Comment. 611 (2003–2004); Mark D. Rosen, *The Radical Possibility of Limited Community-Based Interpretation of the Constitution*, 43 Wm. & Mary L. Rev. 927 (2002); Nomi Maya Stolzenberg, *The Return of the Repressed: Illiberal Groups in a Liberal State*, 12 J. Contemp. Legal Issues 897 (2002).

West and the illiberal and totalizing culture of global Islamism.[70] However over-drawn and cartoonish this depiction might be, it is true that some groups, both in the global environment and in the United States itself, resist any act of imagi-nation of the kind contemplated by constitutional agnosticism. They see this sort of imaginative leap as inimical to their own worldview.[71]

Again, we must be sensitive and humble toward this possibility, and I will have more to say about its deeper implications below. But if this possibility speaks to a broader dilemma, it should not be so strongly emphasized that it blinks the larger reality. That reality is that such groups are relatively few and far between, at least in our own pluralist culture. The constitutional agnostic may at least attempt to understand *them*, whether that understanding is reciprocated or not.[72] Some of these groups may be unreachable by *any* strategy. Others may be more reachable than we assume. At the least, attempting to understand and acknowledge their own views of religious truth, and to speak to them in some-thing approximating their own language, may draw them into the conversation more than competing strategies would, even in cases in which the conclusion is that the state's needs must overrule their own obligations.

In sum, constitutional agnosticism is deeply sensitive to the criticisms raised by the religious objection. But those criticisms do not raise insuperable obsta-cles. It may be impossible to fully occupy the religious worldview of others. But it is more possible than some may realize, and the habits of constitutional agnos-ticism are more ingrained in our culture than some may admit. In any event, constitutional agnosticism may still be preferable for the religious objector than any approach that either denies the importance of religious truth altogether, or simply declares victory for an opposing religious viewpoint, whether in the name of liberal or secular values or in the name of a contrary version of religious truth.

THE INCOMMENSURABILITY OBJECTION

The final objection to constitutional agnosticism is the incommensurability objection. In many respects, this is the most powerful attack on constitutional

---

70. *See, e.g.,* Fareed Zakaria, *The Future of Freedom: Illiberal Democracy at Home and Abroad* (2003); Samuel P. Huntington, *The Clash of Civilizations and the Remaking of World Order* (1996).

71. *See, e.g., Mozert v. Hawkins County Bd. of Educ.,* 827 F.2d 1058 (6th Cir. 1987); *see also* Nomi Maya Stolzenberg, *"He Drew a Circle That Shut Me Out": Assimilation, Indoctrination, and the Paradox of a Liberal Education,* 106 Harv. L. Rev. 581 (1993).

72. *See* Jeff Spinner-Halev, *Surviving Diversity: Religion and Democratic Citizenship* (2000) (discussing the tension between illiberal religious groups and liberal democracy, and arguing that the liberal state should attempt to reach out to those groups).

agnosticism. This argument says that any approach to religious freedom, including constitutional agnosticism, that attempts to balance religious beliefs and obligations against state interests will find itself weighing things that cannot be measured or compared.[73]

This is a compelling criticism. As the case of Abraham and Isaac shows, there is no uncontroversial way to weigh religious obligations against state interests. Religious obligations are often absolute. Even where they do not take the form of divine commands, the fact (or the possibility) that they are *true*, that they represent the genuine will of God, makes them potential trumps in any argument against state interests. They are "conversation-stoppers," in Richard Rorty's words.[74] A constitutional agnostic who absolutely inhabits the worldview of a religious believer, and who does so from a perspective of religious truth, might believe that he ought to be compelled to permit *any* religious practice, no matter how harmful. But he does not, and cannot. He *does* find cases in which state interests must trump religious obligations.

Few people will object to the fact that the constitutional agnostic is willing to set limits on religious license. To the contrary, they will *applaud* the constitutional agnostic's willingness to draw a line. But the religious agnostic still lacks a deep account of when and why he will allow state interests to trump religious obligations. Although he must balance the needs of religious believers against the needs of the state, he cannot supply a formula that tells us when one is outweighed by the other. Isaac must live, despite God's command that he die; but the constitutional agnostic cannot tell us why. He is caught in a dilemma.

There are some partial responses to this dilemma. One is that old standby, the second-best argument. It is true that constitutional agnosticism confronts the dilemma of incommensurability and cannot resolve it. But its own effort to wrestle with this problem is better, all things considered, than other approaches. It is more sensitive to both sides of the interest-balancing equation than its competitors.

Moreover, constitutional agnosticism at least *recognizes* the dilemma. It does not sweep it under the rug, or declare a preemptive victory for one side or the other. Any approach to religious freedom that fails even to take seriously the possibility of religious truth will fail to see that there is an issue there at all, or to give proper weight to the religious side of the equation. This is what often happens when we convert religious claims, which rest on a fundamental view of religious truth, into claims of "conscience." That approach tends to water down these claims and leave them relatively defenseless against invocations of tangible and compelling state interests. And any approach that simply declares one version of religious truth to be *the* truth, or privileges religion absolutely against state interests, will fail to satisfy those who do not share those religious beliefs, and fail to

---

73. *See also* Chapter Six.

74. Richard Rorty, *Religion as Conversation-Stopper*, in *Philosophy and Social Hope* 168 (1999).

fully appreciate the force of the competing state interests. Constitutional agnosticism cannot fully resolve the dilemma of incommensurability, but at least it doesn't pretend it's not there.

Furthermore, constitutional agnosticism approaches this problem in a proper spirit of candor and humility. It is deeply aware of the difficulty of balancing incommensurable goods. It is alive to the tragic choices that are presented by any effort to balance these goods. It understands, as some approaches do not, that what we often label easy cases are in fact exquisitely hard ones, once we fully appreciate the interests at stake on both sides. If it cannot answer these questions to its own satisfaction or to anyone else's, it can at least acknowledge the difficulty of these cases, attempt to reduce the magnitude of the conflict through accommodation, speak to the losers in something like their own language, and acknowledge the moral remainder that is left over.

Finally, it must be said that the dilemma of incommensurability is hardly unique to constitutional agnosticism. Rather, it is a problem that *any* theory of religious freedom must confront. Simply denying that the problem exists, by privileging one side over the other, doesn't make the problem go away.

Nor does an approach that deals with the problem by setting an absolute rule, rejecting the idea of interest-balancing altogether, and warning that any approach other than sheer formalism courts anarchy.[75] For one thing, this approach is just another form of denial. It denies what is conspicuously true, that there are important interests at stake for both the state and the religious believer. For another, it is simply false. Every rule, whether it is honeycombed with exceptions and accommodations or not, contains within it an implicit weighing of interests.[76] If judges don't do the weighing of interests, then legislators will. Where that task is concerned, legislatures may be more democratically legitimate than courts, but they are no more competent. The problem of incommensurability runs deep, and it is not resolved by asking lawmakers to weigh religious needs against interests and come up with some mechanical or generally applicable rule. Legislators are no more able than judges, or anyone else, to tell us "whether a particular line is longer than a particular rock is heavy."[77]

So the incommensurability objection is a serious one. But it is one that may be raised against *any* approach to religious freedom. The hope—and perhaps it

---

75. *See Smith,* 494 U.S. at 888.

76. *See, e.g.,* Daniel A. Crane, *Rules Versus Standards in Antitrust Adjudication,* 64 Wash. & Lee L. Rev. 49, 71–72 (2007) (noting the compelling nature of this argument without fully subscribing to it); Frederick Schauer, *The Tyranny of Choice and the Rulification of Standards,* 14 J. Contemp. Legal Issues 803, 803 (2005) (observing that rules involve the making of "substantive choices . . . at the time of the drafting" of that rule).

77. *Bendix Autolite Corp. v. Midwesco Enterprises, Inc.,* 486 U.S. 888, 897 (1988) (Scalia, J., concurring in the judgment).

is a slim one—is that constitutional agnosticism can at least recognize the problem and deal with it more openly and sensitively than its competitors.

DILEMMAS: OF RELIGION AND LIBERAL DEMOCRACY

To say that the incommensurability objection is not a fatal objection to constitutional agnosticism, or that it applies equally to any theory of religious freedom, is not to say that the objection is unfounded. It is, in fact, a deeply important objection. It raises profound questions about the unsettled relationship between religion and liberal democracy, and the ultimate fragility of *any* theory of religious freedom.

This is a both a very old problem and a current and pressing one. Much of Western thought has been an effort to arrive at just terms for accommodating both religious belief and civil order.[78] Liberalism itself, in all its changing forms, is ultimately just a recipe for the resolution of church–state conflict. Liberal democracy is so well settled a feature of our landscape that we may take it for granted. Today, we may see it as an established regime, almost a natural one, for which religion happens to pose difficult problems. It would be just as accurate, in fact, to say that *religion* is our default, and that liberal democracy is just something we came up with after the fact to deal with it. At this point in our history, it is truer still to say that religion and liberal democracy are an interlocked pair, Siamese twins in the grip of an eternal struggle over who will be master.[79]

Benjamin Berger has written that we must abandon the idea that religion is a problem for which law, or liberal democracy, can offer a solution. Rather, "the meeting of law and religion is not a juridical or a technical problem but . . . an instance of cross-cultural encounter."[80] They are not, to be sure, two solitudes. Over the course of their long relationship, each has acted upon the other. Religion has changed as a result of its encounter with liberalism and liberal democracy, and liberal democracy would likely not exist without its encounter with religion. Most of us, believers and nonbelievers alike, are actually dual citizens in the realms of religion and liberal democracy. But Berger's description still captures something important about the relationship between what he rightly calls these two cultures. Long connected, they have also been long divided.

---

78. *See* Chapter One.

79. Or, if you prefer a more culturally sophisticated analogy, *see Star Trek: Let That Be Your Last Battlefield* (NBC television broadcast, Jan. 10, 1969). In this episode from the original series, two aliens, each of whom is black and white on opposite sides of his body, are locked in a battle that has lasted for eons. It's better than it sounds.

80. Benjamin L. Berger, *The Cultural Limits of Legal Tolerance*, 21 Can. J.L. & Juris. 245, 246 (2008).

It would be simplistic and misleading to describe the relationship between religion and liberal democracy as antagonistic. Most religious individuals would argue vehemently that there is no conflict between their status as religious believers and their status as liberal democrats. Some would go further and point out that their own religious beliefs require some degree of tolerance and liberal democracy; others would contend that liberal democracy in fact *depends* on religious belief.[81] Conversely, those who see themselves first and foremost as liberal democrats, but who also hold religious beliefs, would argue just as strongly that liberal democracy is no barrier to religious belief—that it is, if anything, the primary guarantor of freedom of religious belief.

Both are right, and both are wrong. Religion and liberal democracy can and do coexist. What divides them is not a question of what to do about any particular example of church–state conflict. Indeed, it is just as likely that there will be *internal* debates about how to resolve particular church–state conflicts, within both the religious and the liberal democratic communities, as that there will be debates *between* the two realms.

What divides them, finally and intractably, is religious truth. What is it? How much does it matter? What is to be done about it? Liberalism's strategy has been to avoid the matter as much as possible: to render it a private concern, to disclaim any views on the question of religious truth or the nature of the good, and to seek to move the discussion to "neutral" ground. Religion's strategy has been more divided, in part as a result of its encounter with liberal democracy. Many faith traditions have embraced liberal democracy and religious toleration, bringing them within the fold of their own beliefs; this is, for example, a central theme in contemporary Catholic thought.[82] Other faith traditions have reacted against and repelled liberal democracy's overtures. Although this is emphatically an exaggerated picture of Islam, it is an important element in the rise of radical Islamism that captured the attention of the post-9/11 world. But this reaction is not unique to Islam alone, by any means.

Regardless of the particular approach taken, what divides these two realms is their fundamentally different reaction to the question of religious truth. Its primacy is central to religious belief; its avoidance is central to liberal democracy. Even those religious faiths that have adopted the tenets of liberal democracy and religious tolerance do so as a matter of *religious truth*, not prudence or political philosophy. If God were to repudiate tolerance and liberal democracy tomorrow, their views would have to change. In short, a world of difference lies between

---

81. *See, e.g.*, Michael J. Perry, *Toward a Theory of Human Rights: Religion, Law, Courts* (2008).

82. *See, e.g.*, Vatican II, *Declaration on Religious Freedom: On the Right of the Person and of Communities to Social and Civil Freedom in Matters Religious*, in *The Documents of Vatican II* 675 (Walter M. Abbott ed., 1966).

them. We might say that much of Western history is just one long footnote to Pontius Pilate's shrug.

This is why the incommensurability objection looms so large as a dilemma, not just for constitutional agnosticism but for *any* theory of religious liberty. It is why Stanley Fish somewhat gleefully pronounces the effort to arrive at a firm foundation for church–state relations a "mission impossible,"[83] and why Steven Smith calls the search for a sound theory of religious liberty a "foreordained failure."[84] Religious claims about the world are claims about the *truth*: about what the fact of the matter is and what it means for human affairs. Liberal democracy cannot avoid those claims either. Either it denies their importance, at the cost of its own incoherence, or it stakes its own claim to the truth and enforces it under penalty of law. There can be accommodation and coexistence. Much of the history of Western civilization is a story about how to accomplish this, and it has succeeded beyond the wildest hopes of its many authors. But there cannot be two truths—and, in the end, there cannot be two masters.[85]

In the end, despite the many genuine compromises and accommodations between them, religious truth and the liberal democratic state remain what they always have been: an irresistible force meeting an immovable object. The story of the conflict between them is still the story of Abraham and Isaac. Either God has spoken, or he has not. If he has, our only options are obedience or rebellion. Although rebellion can be an attractive option (or at least it has been ever since Milton gave Satan all the best lines in *Paradise Lost*), most religious people would argue that true belief requires compliance with God's will.[86] But the state has needs of its own, needs that most of us share most of the time. If forced to, it will respond by asserting itself, with or without the truth at its side. In that sense, the needs of the liberal democratic state *are* its truth.

Each can give some ground to the other—up to a point. At that point, the needs of the two must be balanced. But no scale can hold these two very different conceptions of the good, and no measure can tell us which is weightier. Either the truth matters, absolutely, or it does not. But it can't be weighed.

This book thus ends where our own culture begins: with the deep and lasting tension between religion and liberal democracy. In many ways, liberal democracy is a response to a dilemma it cannot openly name, an answer to a problem it cannot finally solve. That does not make the attempt to reach a solution any

---

83. Stanley Fish, *Mission Impossible: Settling the Just Bounds Between Church and State*, 97 Colum. L. Rev. 2255 (1997).

84. Steven D. Smith, *Foreordained Failure: The Quest for a Constitutional Principle of Religious Freedom* (1995).

85. Or, again with reference to high culture, "There can be only one." *Highlander* (Thorn EMI Screen Entertainment 1986).

86. At the least, they may remember that things did not go well for Satan and his band of rebel angels.

less vital, especially under our own conditions of startling diversity and plural-ism. But, as the philosophers never tire of reminding us, ought does not imply can. The tensions between religion and liberal democracy are encoded into the very DNA of our society; they are an unalterable fact of its genetic heritage. They admit no final resolution short of absolute victory for one side or another. As poor and clichéd as the idea of a clash of civilizations is, as much as it ignores the fact that religion and liberal democracy are uneasy partners within the *same* civi-lization, it remains true that the problem of religion's relationship to liberal democracy can only be solved by remaking society itself—if it can be solved at all. One of constitutional agnosticism's most important contributions to our under-standing of the relationship between church and state is its candor about its central problem—a problem that constitutional agnosticism shares with every other approach to church-state relations, whether they admit it or not. That is, it recognizes that our world is filled with unbridgeable conflicts and tragic choices.

CONCLUSION: CONSTITUTIONAL AGNOSTICISM, CONVERSATIONS, AND HOPE

There is no hope that we can resolve the deep tensions that exist between reli-gion and liberal democracy. There is no hope that we can find a final answer to the unavoidable questions of religious truth in a pluralistic society, especially in an age in which religious belief has become both diverse and contestable. There is no hope that we can find a perfect scale on which to balance the needs of religious believers with the needs of the liberal democratic state itself.

But that doesn't mean there is no hope at all. Constitutional agnosticism does not offer a way out of the dilemma of religion and liberal democracy, because there *is* no way out of the dilemma. Instead, it offers a tentative way forward.

Constitutional actors, Philip Bobbitt wrote in another context, have to make tragic choices.[87] There is no way out of them, not on this side of Heaven (if there *is* a Heaven). That is just as true of law and religion as it is of any other issue. Indeed, it is *especially* true of law and religion. Isaac lives or dies; a child receives or forgoes lifesaving medical treatment; religion obtains government aid or it does not; the state speaks on questions of religious truth or is silent. Some of these are momentous choices, some less so. But all are choices, all must be made, and all of them leave a measure of tragedy in their wake: a residue of moral remainder that cannot be avoided and should not be ignored or forgotten. In making these tragic choices, there are no "mechanics by which such choices

---

87. Philip Bobbitt, Youngstown: *Pages From the Book of Disquietude*, 19 Const. Comment. 3 (2002).

can best be made"[88] in any ultimate sense—certainly not one that will either avoid the question of religious truth or wipe out the moral remainder.

Our hope, then, does not lie in the possibility of perfection. Nor does it lie in the indifference of Pilate's shrug. Instead, our hope, such as it is, lies in candor, conversation, and humility. It is found in an approach to law and religion, and more broadly to the relationship between religion and liberal democracy, that begins with the question of religious truth rather than hoping to avoid it altogether. It lies in the recognition that ours is an agnostic age. We are the inhabitants of a time in which religious beliefs are not dead, dying, or privatized, but multiplying and breaking through the public–private divide into the public realm. We are a pluralist society, one that embraces a vast number of beliefs for and against religion, and for and against even the most seemingly uncontroversial values. And we are an unsettled people, who are strongly aware that God, in his, her, their, or its many forms, is one option among many.

Our best hope is to acknowledge these facts and form our response around them. If we do not understand the conditions of our age, we cannot address them. We know that the old liberal treaty, the lasting but imperfect compromise between religion and liberal democracy, has collapsed under its own weight, and no longer captures the loyalty of our age. We know, too, or most of us do, that any single religious answer is equally unresponsive to our conditions of pluralism, and equally unlikely to succeed. Few us today would wish otherwise. We must start, then, by recognizing the conditions of our age, and by confronting directly rather than avoiding the fundamental question that divides and perplexes us: the question of religious truth.

Constitutional agnosticism is one way of acknowledging these self-evident truths, and of finding a way forward. It does not require us to abandon our own beliefs or non-beliefs. But it does call on us to recognize them as just one among many views in an unsettled and plural society, in an agnostic age. It asks us to consider constitutional agnosticism as one of the layers of our belief system—as a way of approaching and respecting the views of others without disparaging our own. It calls on us to adopt the agnostic habit, as citizens, lawmakers, and judges. It asks the state to consider as much as possible the needs of religious believers, treating those needs not just as a matter of individual conscience, but potentially as a matter of absolute truth. It asks us to treat all religious claims seriously and all religious groups equally. And it also asks us to give favor to none, and for the state to refrain from telling us what the final religious truth is.

Constitutional agnosticism knows that the state has its needs, and that sometimes it must win. Even if Abraham is telling the truth, Isaac must still live. And it knows that when it comes time to strike the balance, it—along with every other theory of religious freedom—will be faced with an impossible, imponderable,

---

88. *Id.* at 35.

tragic choice. It hopes that by approaching these questions openly and empathetically, by doing our best to make an imaginative leap into the perspective of the other, by using all the tools of negative capability that our culture has bequeathed to us, we can make these choices as wisely, as sensitively, and as painlessly as possible, giving as much leeway to the possibility of religious truth as we can. It does not deny or shy away from the inevitable moral remainder that will still be left behind by every such choice. But it hopes that by hearing the voices of others, by appreciating their perspectives, and by trying to speak to them as much as possible in their own language, it will open the lines of communication, accommodation, and acceptance in a way that the old liberal formulas no longer can.

It seems fitting to end this book where, in many respects, it began: with the magisterial work of Charles Taylor, whose description of our "secular age," or what I call our agnostic age, has opened so many important conversations and brought a richer perspective to the tiresome war between the New Atheists and the New Anti-Atheists.[89] In a subsequent response to his critics, Taylor has offered these powerful words:

> [W]hat we badly need is a conversation between a host of different positions, religious, nonreligious, antireligious, humanistic, antihumanistic, and so on, in which we eschew mutual caricature and try to understand what "fullness" means for the other. . . . [I]t's possible to build friendship across these boundaries based on a real mutual sense, a powerful sense, of what moves the other person. . . . We're in the business of friendship, which incorporates the kind of understanding where each can come to be moved by what moves the other.[90]

That is constitutional agnosticism's purpose, and its hope. Church–state conflict in a pluralist age is not just a dilemma. It is also an opportunity: a chance to achieve genuine mutual understanding and appreciation. It offers us the hope of a more meaningful and respectful conversation than the one we have had in recent years—or centuries.

That we cannot finally resolve the tortured relationship between religion and liberal democracy is a certainty. That we can improve upon it, and work to rebuild it in our own language, in ways that speak to our own condition, is a genuine possibility, and one we must seize. Perhaps, two millennia later, we can begin, in our own agnostic way, to answer Pilate's shrug.

---

89. *See* Taylor, *supra* note 1.

90. Taylor, *supra* note 15, at 318–20. *See also* Josef Schmidt, S.J., *A Dialogue in Which There Can Only Be Winners*, in Jürgen Habermas et al., *An Awareness of What is Missing: Faith and Reason in a Post-secular Age* 59 (2010); David Tracy, *Plurality and Ambiguity* 20 (1987).

INDEX